00014767

Donizetti and his Operas

To
FLORENCE
and to
All the Lucys

Donizetti
and his Operas

WILLIAM ASHBROOK

CAMBRIDGE UNIVERSITY PRESS

Cambridge
London   New York   New Rochelle
Melbourne   Sydney

Published by the Press Syndicate of the University of Cambridge
The Pitt Building, Trumpington Street, Cambridge CB2 1RP
32 East 57th Street, New York, NY 10022, USA
296 Beaconsfield Parade, Middle Park, Melbourne 3206, Australia

First published 1982

Printed in the United States of America

Library of Congress catalogue card number 81-12235

British Library Cataloguing in publication data
Ashbrook, William
Donizetti and his operas.
1. Donizetti, Gaetano
I. Title
782.1'092'4   ML410.D7
ISBN 0 521 23526 X

Contents

Preface

Donizetti instinctively dramatized his involvement with his life and work. Many of his most jovial letters fall into the form of imaginary dialogues. To adapt his technique for a moment:

What? *Another* book on Donizetti??... *Sissignore*... But, isn't that subject a little – ?... Not at all, believe me!!... But not too long ago didn't you yourself?... I did, but you see, as his operas are more and more known, there's an irresistible temptation to find out more, to look a little closer...

When I first started off on the traces of Donizetti nearly twenty years ago, I was embarking on an area that then was rather generally regarded as almost disreputable but with an abiding feeling that if it only could be seen in a fair perspective its true value would be more generally appreciated. This is not to imply that the Donizettian trail had not begun to be blazed usefully even then. But in the intervening years, thanks to the continuing efforts of scholars, conductors, singers, enthusiasts, the figure of Donizetti has come to assume something approaching his just place in the history of nineteenth-century opera.

My earlier book on Donizetti has been out of print for a number of years, and some time ago I was approached about a reprint of it. Knowing that it contained some errors and covered too much ground too broadly, I decided to revise it, concentrating only on Donizetti's operatic output. The final form of this book owes much to the very helpful and encouraging suggestions made by Julian Budden. The first part deals with Donizetti's career as an operatic composer, and is not intended to be a full-length biographical portrait. The second part begins by setting off Donizetti against his principal contemporaries who wrote for the Italian stage; throughout Part II, but particularly here, special attention is paid to Donizetti's position in relation both to Bellini, his chief rival in the years 1827–35, and to Verdi, whose development as a composer can scarcely be grasped without some notion of the influence of Donizetti upon him. After a preliminary overview of the formal conventions within which Donizetti worked, there follows a descriptive discussion of the completed operas in chronological order. The result is a book that has been almost entirely rewritten. Hopefully it will prove more useful than its predecessor.

There is still much work to be done on Donizetti. There is a great need for scholarly editions of his major scores, and work is already afoot to fill that need. There are corners of his life, details concerning his use of sources, his compositional processes, his non-operatic works, a wealth of topics that need further study. This volume is an attempt to fulfill two perhaps not entirely reconcilable functions: first, to give the general reader a good deal of information about the composer and his operas; second, to serve as a point of departure for further, more detailed studies.

The more one works on a subject, especially in these helpful days of international conferences devoted to the work of a single composer, like the stimulating one held on Donizetti in Bergamo in 1975, the more keenly one is aware that scholarship is a corporate effort. My indebtedness for information, ideas and encouragement run deep and some of them are of such a long-standing character that it is difficult to find adequate words to express my gratitude. Without these people, this book would never have come about: John Allitt, Rudolph Angermüller, the late Joseph Ashbrook, Leo Balk, John Black, Claire Brook, Tito Capobianco, John Carter, Kent Christensen, Carlo Clausetti, H. Robert Cohen, Marcello Conati, Jeremy Commons, Francesco Degrada, Max de Schauensee, Rosemary Dooley, Patricia Falk Feely, Philip Gossett, Clemens Höslinger, Tom Kaufman, Jan Kryzwicki, Walter Lippincott, Luisa Mismetti, Maria Teresa Muraro, John Nadas, Sergio Paganelli, Luciana Pestalozzi, Andrew Porter, Michael Recchuiti, Gabriela Roepke, David Rosen, Valeriano Sacchiero, Patric Schmid, Wolfgang Suppan, the late Raffaele Tenaglia, Sir William Trethowan, John Watts, William Weaver, the late Herbert Weinstock, Don White and Richard Woitach. I wish specially to mention the many helpful suggestions made by Julian Budden, who has read this work at many stages and to whom I am indebted for its final form. But my greatest gratitude is to my long-suffering wife. Further, I have received valuable assistance from these institutions: the Museo Donizettiano, Bergamo; Casa Ricordi, Milan; the Bibliothèque Nationale, Paris; the library at the Conservatorio di San Pietro a Majella, Naples; the Fondazione Cini, Venice; the Library of Congress, Washington D.C.; and the Library of the University of Pennsylvania, Philadelphia. The editorial help of Rosemary Roberts on the text and of Desmond Ratcliffe on the musical examples has placed me permanently in their debt.

WILLIAM ASHBROOK

Strafford, Pennsylvania,
23 July 1980

PART I

6

1

1797–1821
The beginnings

Gaetano Donizetti was born in Bergamo in the province of Lombardy on 29 November 1797. His baptismal certificate, dated 3 December 1797, is to be found among the parish records of Santa Grata inter Vites, the church that stands not a stone's throw from the house in which he was born. The notice reads:

Dominicus Cajetanus Maria filius Andreae Donizetti et Domenicae Nava Legitimum Iujalium natura die 29 9mbris in hoc suburbio, hodie baptizzatus a me Antonio Mauro Bonzi Praeposito – Patrino Dominico Iraina ex Zanica.

At the time of Gaetano's birth his parents had been living for about eleven years in the basement apartment at Borgo Canale, no. 10 (now renumbered 14), a street that slants down the north-west shoulder of the hill occupied by the old town of Bergamo Alta. Today the house is marked by a plaque and has been designated a national museum. The dark, cramped quarters eloquently testify to the poverty in which the family lived. Donizetti never forgot the place. He described it a few years before his death in a letter to his teacher and benefactor Simon Mayr: 'I was born underground in Borgo Canale. You went down cellar steps, where no glimmer of light ever penetrated. And like an owl I took flight . . . never encouraged by my poor father, who was always telling me: it is impossible that you will compose, that you will go to Naples, that you will go to Vienna.'[1]

For many years local tradition identified the wrong house in Borgo Canale as Donizetti's birthplace. Not until Ciro Caversazzi made his exhaustive study of census reports and parish records (published in 1924) was the correct site identified.[2] The confusion is not surprising because many Donizettis lived in Borgo Canale: Gaetano's paternal grandfather Ambrogio had lived next door but one; his father's brother Giovanni had rooms in the same house and raised his family there; his father's half-sister, married to a musician named Giacomo Corini, lived next door.

3

About 1786 Andrea Donizetti married Domenica Nava and moved into the basement at Borgo Canale, no. 10. Here his six children were born. The eldest, Giuseppe (6 November 1788 – 12 February 1856), became a musician. The musical instruction he received from his uncle Corini and from Mayr equipped him to embark on a career as a military bandsman. After service with the French and Sardinian forces, he moved in 1828 to Constantinople, where he accepted an appointment as Chief of Music to the Ottoman Armies, first under Sultan Mahmud II and then under Sultan Abdul Medjid, by whom he was made a pasha. The second child was a daughter, Maria Rosalinda (1 May 1790 – 8 February 1811), of whom little is known save that she is supposed to have died of apoplexy.[3] Next came Francesco (7 February 1792 – 20 December 1848), who grew up deficient in intelligence and initiative; his musical prowess encompassed no more than playing the cymbals in the civic band of Bergamo. After Andrea's death in December 1835, Francesco, through the intervention of Gaetano and Giuseppe, succeeded his father as porter at the town pawnshop, but he was to remain dependent upon the allowance his brothers gave him. Maria Antonia (20 September 1795 – 5 March 1823) married a local fellow named Tironi; after her death, from what was said to be tuberculosis, her infant daughter Beppina was taken in by her grandparents, later keeping house for them until their deaths. Fifth of these children was Domenico Gaetano, the subject of this study. Last came another daughter, Maria Rachele, who was born in March 1800 and lived barely a month.

It is not known for sure exactly how Andrea supported his family during the early years of his marriage. At the end of the eighteenth century many families who lived in Borgo Canale were engaged in the trade of weaving, and perhaps for a time Andrea may have worked at it. Caversazzi suggests that he may have been at one time a tailor or even a musician.[4] The latter possibility seems unlikely considering that his son Giuseppe received his first musical training from his uncle Corini rather than from his father. Further, Andrea's notorious lack of enthusiasm for Gaetano's career, his repeated urging that his son check his ambition and seek regular employment as a village organist or music-master, indicates Andrea's failure to appreciate his unusual talent. In 1808 Andrea assumed the humble duties of janitor and later of porter at the civic pawnshop, the Monte di Pietà. Since this post entitled him to an apartment on the premises, he moved his family into it.

From these undistinguished roots Donizetti sprang.[5]

The influences that his hometown of Bergamo exercised upon the growing boy were a stimulating antidote to the drabness of his home. Chief among these influences was the church of Santa Maria Maggiore; architecturally a striking example of Lombard Romanesque style, the church could boast musical traditions that extended back to the fourteenth century. Here Donizetti made his earliest contact with serious music; here his beloved teacher Mayr was *maestro di cappella*; here he sang in the choir, first as a contralto and later as a bass.

During Donizetti's youth Johann Simon Mayr (1763–1845) was the most influential musician in Bergamo. Born in Bavaria, Mayr had launched his career in Venice, and then in 1802 had moved to Bergamo upon his appointment at Santa Maria Maggiore. A born teacher and convinced of the need for well-founded musical instruction, Mayr persuaded the local authorities to subsidize a free music school under his personal supervision, to be known as the Lezioni Caritatevoli. This school still exists, but now it is named, after its most famous student, Istituto Musicale Gaetano Donizetti.

Although there had been musical instruction in Bergamo from at least the early sixteenth century, the suppression of the religious orders at the close of the eighteenth century by the French had disrupted the old traditions. The primary purpose behind Mayr's proposal to found the school was to provide trained choristers and instrumentalists for the services at Santa Maria Maggiore. The first students at the Lezioni Caritatevoli were enrolled on 6 May 1806, and the third name on the list is that of eight-year-old Domenico Gaetano Donizetti, admitted on a three-month probation as a student of voice and *clavicembalo*[6] to the classes, which were held in Mayr's house.

It would be difficult to overestimate the importance of Mayr's influence upon Donizetti. In Mayr he found a teacher, a benefactor and a friend, who offered assistance and encouragement unstintingly as long as he lived.[7] Mayr's satisfaction in his pupil's success was never corrupted by jealousy, nor was Donizetti's loyalty to Mayr. So deeply did Mayr care about Donizetti's development that he refrained from addressing him by the often glibly used title 'Maestro' until he felt that his former pupil had truly proved himself a 'master composer' – with *Anna Bolena* (1830); and although he had already written more than thirty operas, Donizetti so valued Mayr's good opinion that this compliment, so long delayed, was more significant to him than many another more easily won.

Mayr was one of the first in Italy to make a thorough study of the works of Haydn, Mozart and Beethoven, and he was eager to promote performances of their works. In his memorial urging the establishment of a music school, he pointed out that Haydn's oratorios and Mozart's Requiem had not yet been performed publicly in Italy because of the lack of adequate choral groups. In Bergamo in 1809 Mayr directed the first performance in Italy of Haydn's *Creation*. This performance, in which Donizetti almost certainly took part, was given for the founding of another project dear to Mayr's heart, the Pio Istituto Musicale, designed to aid indigent musicians and their widows and children. Through Mayr, Donizetti had further and more extensive opportunities to become familiar with the music of the Viennese masters, as he often accompanied his teacher to the home of Alessandro Bertoli, where, from 1814, a group met regularly to play the chamber music of Haydn, Mozart, Beethoven, Reicha and Mayseder. As a proficient viola-player, Mayr was a devoted participant in these evenings of chamber music, which made such an impression upon Donizetti that he was moved to compose fifteen string quartets between 1817 and 1821. These experiences, coming to Donizetti at a most impressionable age, were then scarcely to be duplicated in Italy.

Clearly, it was Donizetti's amazing good fortune to come early into the hands of such a man as Mayr, whom wit and a warm heart saved from pedantry. His wide interest in other music than his own prompted him to the taxing labor of copying whole scores so that he could extend his own and his pupils' knowledge. Most important for Donizetti's future, Mayr was a composer of operas,[8] a man with extensive practical knowledge of the theater and of the world of opera as it was then constituted in Italy. Throughout Donizetti's close association with Mayr, the older man was engaged in writing operas, sometimes turning out as many as five a year. Such productivity was not unusual then, and if at times Donizetti's operas were to tumble on each other's heels with astonishing rapidity, a persuasive example was close at hand. To a remarkable extent Mayr had the uncommon humility to recognize his own limitations. When he had taught his star pupil Donizetti all he could, he made all the arrangements to send him to study counterpoint and fugue with the famous Padre Mattei at Bologna, the man who had been Rossini's principal teacher. Mayr enlisted patrons to help defray the cost of this further education, even contributing what he could himself. From such a man as Mayr, generous with his learning, his experience, and his resources such as they were, an eager and talented youngster could

not fail to profit. Small wonder that Donizetti loved Mayr as a second
father.

Like any self-respecting Italian center of that period, Bergamo was
addicted to opera. By the time Donizetti was ten, the town could
boast two permanent theaters. The older, which opened in 1784 with
a performance of Sarti's *Medonte,* was situated in the lower city and
was called the Teatro Riccardi[9] (it was renamed Teatro Donizetti on
the centennial of the composer's birth in 1897). In 1807 a group of
dilettanti in the upper city organized the Teatro della Società (or
Sociale).[10] To the rest of Italy at that time Bergamo's musical fame
resided chiefly in a remarkable series of tenors who hailed from that
region. (At the beginning of the nineteenth century principal male
roles in serious operas were assigned to tenors, while basses – the
term was then applied indiscriminately to baritones and basses –
were used sparingly and secondarily.)[11] This famous constellation of
Bergamasc tenors (the father and son Giacomo and Giovanni
David,[12] Domenico Viganoni,[13] Andrea Nozzari,[14] Marco Bordogni,[15] Domenico Donzelli[16] and last, but scarcely least, Giovanni
Battista Rubini)[17] could not help but exert a powerful influence on
the young Donizetti. Not only were they living proof of the prestige
and material rewards that could be reaped in the opera house, but
they were paragons of highly developed vocal art, a discipline that
Donizetti could scarcely neglect as an Italian composer. The aura of
success and fame associated with these tenors reinforced, if only
indirectly, Donizetti's natural gravitation – once his marked aptitude
for musical composition had manifested itself – toward the opera
house as his chief arena of activity. In his day the musical stage was
the principal road open to an Italian composer who wanted to establish his independence, and Mayr's influence was not the only force
in Donizetti's environment that propelled him toward the theater.

Domenico[18] Gaetano Donizetti came to the Palazzo della Misericor-
dia in Bergamo on 20 April 1806 to be tested for his musical aptitude. The judgment of the examiners was that 'he has a good ear,
his voice is not outstanding, and he should be admitted for a three-
month probation'.[19] This report is signed by the faculty of four at the
Lezioni Caritatevoli: Mayr, Francesco Salari, Antonio Capuzzi and
Antonio Gonzales. Salari (1751–1823), a Bergamasc by birth, had
studied at Naples with Piccinni, and, after a lengthy stint as a
singing-master in Venice, had returned to Bergamo as second *maestro di cappella* at Santa Maria Maggiore. Capuzzi (1755–1818), a

violinist from nearby Brescia, had been a pupil of Tartini. Gonzales (1764–1830) was the organist at Santa Maria Maggiore.

When Donizetti started attending classes in May 1806, the rules of the institution limited the number of free pupils to twelve: eight to study voice and clavicembalo, four to study violin and cello. Donizetti's studies included lessons in singing and declamation with Salari, in piano with Gonzales (the first of his masters to recognize his unusual aptitude), and in the elements of music theory with Mayr. The first report of the faculty to the funding Congregazione, dated 13 September 1806, praises Donizetti's diligence and attentiveness, but notes that 'his voice is defective and throaty'. Seven months later Mayr claimed that Donizetti had progressed further than any of the other students.

Donizetti's vocal shortcomings were to jeopardize his continuing to attend Mayr's school. In September 1808, when Salari reported that in spite of Donizetti's perseverance 'it has not been possible to correct his defective voice', the Congregazione demanded his dismissal. Unwilling to lose such a promising pupil, Mayr contrived to keep him at the school; he even assigned him a small singing part in his oratorio *Sisara*. In March 1809 Donizetti was again threatened with suspension, but this time Mayr arranged to have the regulations amended to permit boys whose voices were changing to continue their keyboard studies. Later that year Mayr reaffirmed his confidence in Donizetti by assigning him a small role in the farce *Alcide al bivio* (really a pasticcio with spoken dialogue), which he had put together for the concert to mark the end of the term.

At one point Donizetti's hopes of completing his musical education reached such a low ebb that he applied to the local art school, the Accademia Carrara, for admission among the *dilettanti* to study design and figure.[20] On 15 November 1810 he was informed that he had been admitted to the Accademia Carrara, but how often or for how long he attended classes has not been ascertained. All his life he showed a facility in sketching, but whether this resulted from training or from natural aptitude would be difficult to determine.

The clearest evidence of Mayr's determination to direct Donizetti toward a musical career turns up in the libretto he wrote for the pasticcio–farsa *Il piccolo compositore di musica*, performed on 13 September 1811 at the final concert of the academic year.[21] The hero of this farce, 'the little composer' of the title, is Donizetti himself, and the other characters are his fellow students (Giuseppe Manghenoni, Giuseppe Pontiroli, Antonio Tavecchi and Antonio Dolci), all of them appearing under their own names in the list of characters. Of these, Antonio Dolci (1798–1869) played a significant role in Donizetti's life: remaining in Bergamo, he taught at the music school from 1831 to 1866, and, with Mayr, he remained Donizetti's closest tie to his native town. The plot of *Il piccolo compositore* is, in sum, nothing less than Mayr's argument that Donizetti be allowed to continue his musical studies.

Beneath its humorous exaggerations, *Il piccolo compositore* gives some realistic details of life at the school. Donizetti, the first character to appear, has come to the school, even though it is vacation, to work in peace on an aria. Soon he is interrupted by his fellows, who chide him for his pretensions. Donizetti's reply is anything but modest, but his words have the force of prophecy:

> Vasta ho la mente, rapido l'ingegno,
> Pronta la fantasia, e nel comporre
> Un fulmine son io.

(Huge is my mind, speedy my talent, ready my imagination, and at composition I am like lightning.)

Claiming that it has taken him only seven weeks to compose a little waltz, Donizetti goes to the piano and plays it. A note in the libretto affirms that the waltz was 'expressly composed' by Donizetti.

The plot alternates pranks with opportunities for the five students to exhibit their musical accomplishments,[22] and culminates in Donizetti's arrival, edict in hand: 'Whoever is bold enough to discourage another's talent deserves rigorous punishment!' When he urges his schoolmates to join him in diligent study, they promptly second his sentiment. Obviously Mayr aimed this moralizing conclusion not only at his pupils but at the ears of the Congregazione.

From *Il piccolo compositore* one might assume that Donizetti's career at Mayr's school would progress smoothly, but problems lay ahead. On the positive side, he was nominated the outstanding piano student and allowed special classes in harmony; his voice settled to 'una sufficiente voce di basso', which allowed him to fill a second buffo role at the Teatro della Società and to sing an occasional solo at Santa Maria Maggiore. By 1814, however, the school reports mention his 'not too regular conduct outside school'. At sixteen Donizetti found certain aspects of his schoolwork oppressive: the newly instituted classes in mathematics, geography and languages, taught by a recent addition to the faculty, Abate Baizini, who seems to have been a pedantic authoritarian, Donizetti avoided like the plague; nor was he charmed by his lately acquired responsibility of teaching fundamentals to entering students. Soon the reports speak of his 'negligence in all the responsibilities placed upon him' as 'verified', complain of his 'irregular life', and request that the Congregazione 'suggest and specify some means of correction'.

The threatened punishment was never imposed; instead Donizetti was awarded a prize of 18 *lire milanesi*, though at the same time he was 'to be seriously rebuked'. Considering Donizetti's high spirits and his abiding interest in the female sex, his restlessness at sixteen is not surprising. Contributing to his impatience was the atmosphere at home: his gloomy father had little sympathy with or understanding of Mayr's hopes for his youngest son. Andrea was principally interested in his boys as potential contributors to his support; Giuseppe had briefly returned from army service but had soon gone off again to join Napoleon's forces on Elba, and Francesco was soon to be called up. Gaetano's loyalty to his parents ran deep, but he had no illusions for he had to bear the brunt of their anxieties and fears. It was Mayr, whatever his feelings about his prize pupil's 'irregular life' might have been, who provided a means of escape from these frustrations and who furthered his progress.

In the month of October 1815 Mayr brought to fruition his scheme of sending Donizetti off to Bologna to study with the famous Padre Mattei; but not before he had overcome considerable opposition. Andrea had to be persuaded that the long-term gains from such an opportunity outweighed the desirability of his youngest son's promptly finding a modest post near home. Then there was the bad impression the Congregazione had received of Donizetti in the past year or so. To offset this there was the undeniable promise the boy had publicly demonstrated and the enthusiastic support of most of his teachers, especially Mayr. On 28 October 1815 Mayr addressed a warm-hearted appeal to the Congregazione di Carità of Bergamo, enlisting their support to help finance for two years Donizetti's acquiring 'the most solid and valuable instruction that Italy can boast today'.[23]

On the same day that Mayr wrote this appeal, which must have made official some prior understanding, Donizetti, a month before his eighteenth birthday, set out by diligence for Bologna. Besides giving him money for the journey out of his own pocket, Mayr sent him on his way with two letters. The first recommended him to the publisher Giovanni Ricordi of Milan;[24] the second, to Marchese Francesco Sampieri of Bologna, asked assistance in finding the lad a cheap, comfortable lodging.

When Donizetti arrived in Bologna he found a room on the third floor of the house that is now Via Pepoli, no. 1. Occupying an apartment at the same address was Tommaso Marchesi, one of the teachers at the Liceo Musicale. The principal attraction of that school was the course in counterpoint and fugue conducted by Padre Stanislao Mattei (1750–1825). Mattei had been the favored pupil of the famous Padre Martini (1706–84), the most learned musician of his time and Mattei's predecessor as *maestro di cappella* at San Petronio. When the monasteries were suppressed in 1798, Mattei, who was a minorite, returned to the world; he lived with his elderly mother and continued to teach his pupils.

Of Mattei's methods as a teacher we gain some glimpses from Rossini, who had studied with him between 1806 and 1810. 'Mattei with a pen in his hand', Rossini told Hiller, 'had few equals, but for the rest he was terribly taciturn. Every word of explanation had to be dragged from his mouth by force'. Rossini reported to Fétis that any questions he put to Mattei about the reason behind a correction would invariably be answered, 'It is the custom to write it that way.' Donizetti's reactions to Mattei's teaching are unrecorded. Significantly, in the hundreds of Donizetti's letters written after he left Bologna in 1817 there is none to Mattei and no mention of his name; this is particularly striking when compared to the correspondence with and frequent affectionate allusions to Mayr. In the notebooks of Donizetti's counterpoint classes, preserved in the Museo Donizettiano, Bergamo, there is a weekly succession of exercises, forty-nine examples of increasing complexity. These notebooks demonstrate his diligence and prove that he worked hard to justify Mayr's faith in him. From the marginalia in them we learn that Mayr visited his former student in Bologna in mid-September 1816.

We catch only fleeting glimpses of Donizetti in these days at Bologna. Alborghetti and Galli,[25] without naming their source, tell how on the day of his lessons Donizetti would wait until Mattei had finished with Vespers at San Petronio and follow him home, whereupon Mattei would go over his latest exercise, and then Donizetti would play *briscola* with Mattei's aged mother. Others, such as the composer Carlo Coccia, who knew Donizetti during this time, testify to Mattei's good opinion of his Bergamasc pupil. Francesco Giorgi,[26] in a brief and not very informative essay about Donizetti's student days in Bologna, tells that he was awarded a prize at the end of his course of study there. A rather different view is suggested by Corrado Ricci, who, after mentioning the stories of Donizetti's waiting at the church and playing cards with Mamma Mattei, continues:

That this, and only this, should be the life of Donizetti between the ages of eighteen and twenty, especially in a city like Bologna, where the carefree atmosphere suggested diversions of every sort, is difficult to believe. At

Bologna, he certainly studied, but there he would have amused himself as well with companions, with university students, with . . .[27]

One of Gaetano's companions in these days was Piero Maroncelli (1795–1846), then studying at both the university and the Liceo Musicale. When Maroncelli first came to Bologna he already belonged to a secret political society, La Colonna Armonica, and later he joined the Carbonari. In 1820 he was arrested and condemned to death, but his sentence was commuted to twenty years in the infamous Austrian fortress of Spielberg, where he and his friend Silvio Pellico, author of *Le miei prigioni*, were both tortured. After his release Maroncelli drifted to Paris and married a singer[28] with whom he went to New York, where he led a precarious existence as chorus-master to various opera troupes and taught singing and Italian; he died there, blind and mad. In 1843 he wrote to Donizetti, referring nostalgically to those distant days in Bologna: 'You will not have forgotten the beautiful youthful years we spent together at Bologna. You at the Liceo Musicale, and I there and at the university, and furthermore the dear conversations in the house of the degli Antonj.'[29] Music must have loomed large in those 'dear conversations' (for evidence there is a *Laudamus* composed by Maroncelli that Donizetti thought enough of to copy out for himself), but that liberal or revolutionary politics played a part there is no indication other than the record of Maroncelli's life.

It is considerably easier to argue that a man in Donizetti's position throughout his later career would avoid compromising political activity than to demonstrate that he actually did avoid it; his engagements at various theaters under royal patronage and his freedom to travel to them depended upon his staying in favor with those repressive powers whom the liberals despised: the Bourbons and the Habsburgs. But his extensive correspondence, where he might be expected to air his views freely, contains almost no references to political matters. While this might show simple discretion in a period of stringent censorship, in a time of spies and counterspies, Donizetti's silence is so consistent that it suggests lack of interest more than discretion. Unless additional evidence comes to light, the best course is to regard Donizetti as apolitical.

On the other hand, there is in Italy an oral tradition that Donizetti was politically active. This may be a case of wishful thinking, for I have found no documentary evidence to support it. In fact, he had close friends on both sides of the fence: Giovanni Ruffini, with whom he was associated in Paris, was a *mazziniano* (an adherent of

Mazzini's Young Italy movement) and a fugitive from an Italian prison, living in exile; Michele Accursi, Donizetti's personal agent in Paris, was a counterspy in the pay of the Vatican. If there is any corroborative evidence that Donizetti engaged in political intrigue, it might be found to relate to those years in Bologna, 1815–17, when he and Maroncelli held their 'dear conversations'.

Demonstrably, Donizetti's chief concern in Bologna was with music, both his studies and his continuing efforts at composition. At this time he wrote his first opera. The autograph score of *Il Pigmalione*,[30] a one-act comedy, bears this note: 'begun on 15 September and finished 1 October [1816] at almost two in the morning'.[31] While the score of *Il Pigmalione* is complete, there are problems relating to two other operas traditionally ascribed to the following year, 1817. Only one duet from *Olimpiade* and parts of *L'ira d'Achille* (Act 1 and a duet from Act 2 scene v) are known to have been composed. Jeremy Commons has suggested that the *Olimpiade* duet is probably an isolated piece, a setting of a highpoint from one of Metastasio's most famous librettos, rather than a stray survivor from a completed score now lost.[32] The 1970 catalogue of the Museo Donizettiano lists this duet and a bass aria with chorus from *L'ira d'Achille* in a copyist's full score.[33] That separate orchestral and vocal parts were copied suggests that these pieces were performed in Bologna during the fall of 1817, either at the Liceo or at an *accademia* (concert) put on by local amateurs.

Donizetti may well have put *L'ira d'Achille* aside unfinished, because he realized that the vogue for operas on classical subjects was all but over in Italy.[34] (The long list of his later operas contains none on a mythological subject.) It is perfectly possible, then, that the surviving parts of *L'ira d'Achille* are all he composed. He did, however, complete a number of non-operatic compositions, both vocal and instrumental, before he left Bologna; the most significant of them was a *sinfonia concertata*, performed at the annual exercises of the Bologna Liceo on 9 June 1817, and later published by Carish.

During the summer of 1817 Gaetano returned to Bergamo for a visit of several weeks. As his formal education was drawing to a close, he was naturally eager to begin his career, and he had consulted Mayr about the possibility of finding an engagement to compose for some theater. But he returned empty-handed to Bologna early in August to remain there until December. The latter part of this period he spent negotiating with a group of aristocratic families in Ancona who were looking for a resident music-master whom they would pay 10 *scudi* a month. Donizetti ultimately refused this modest proposal because he wished to leave himself free to accept engagements during the Carnival season. This refusal confirms his intention to pursue a career as an opera composer, because Carnival was then the major season in most opera houses and the contracts of those days specified that a composer had to be present in the theater for the rehearsals and the first three performances of a new opera. After renouncing the Ancona post Donizetti returned to Bergamo. While he had as yet no source of income, he was in possession of the best musical training available in Italy.

Home again, Donizetti celebrated Santo Stefano (26 December), the traditional day for the opening of the Carnival opera season, not by writing an opera but by composing a string quartet in four movements; it was to be the first of sixteen, all written before the end of 1821. This burst of activity was due to the presence in Bergamo of the amateur quartet, in which Mayr played the viola. Marco Bonesi (1796–1874), who had been a fellow student of Donizetti at Mayr's school, played second violin in the group; he has left a revealing account of how Donizetti composed his quartets:

I was surprised when he produced quartets written *alla* Haydn, *alla* Beethoven, etc. . . . Writing them he never approached the keyboard, not even for an instant. He evolved his compositions at his desk in his room, as though he wrote a note to a friend . . . [He could compose] in the midst of confusion, [but] if he heard anyone playing or singing, he would quickly break off his work, saying he could not continue.[35]

Donizetti's facility and his power of concentration, here described by Bonesi, were precisely the traits stressed by Mayr's training (as the libretto of *Il piccolo compositore di musica* makes clear); and they explain his later productivity, and the rapidity with which he could sometimes compose without allowing carelessness or ill-considered whims to mar his craftsmanship. Although no opera house had yet opened its doors to him, his chamber music and other compositions, religious and secular, afforded him a means of participating in the musical life of Bergamo.

Bonesi's 'Note biografiche' are also the source of a familiar anecdote showing Donizetti's early knack for musical portraiture. One night at a party given by the tenor Viganoni, Donizetti improvised so vivid a musical caricature of a decrepit string-player that the guests recognized the way the old man pronounced his words in his raucous voice and his limping with his cane, and applauded the young performer heartily. But Bonesi is less than reliable when he speaks of Donizetti's first commission to write for the stage. As Bonesi tells it,[36] Donizetti became friendly with the singer Ronzi and her husband de Begnis when they appeared at the Teatro della Società during the Carnival season of 1817–18;[37] he followed them to Verona in the hopes of writing an opera for them, but nothing came of it. Bonesi notwithstanding, it has lately been shown that something indeed did come of that trip to Verona.

A letter written by Bartolomeo Merelli to Mayr from Venice and dated 18 April 1818 states that 'Donizetti by now will have received from the impresario the contract for September which has been delivered to Verona.'[38] The impresario in question was the Sicilian Paolo Zancla, who had been active in northern Italy at least since 1810, when he held leases on theaters in Bergamo, Lodi and Cremona. It was Zancla who had engaged Giuseppina Ronzi and her husband for the Teatro della Società in the Carnival season of 1817–18, but they chose to part company with him following their engagement in Verona during April 1818. The contract between Zancla and Donizetti has not yet been found, but that it specified a two-act opera to be given at the Teatro San Luca[39] in Venice during September 1818 is confirmed by a second contract, this one between Zancla as impresario and Merelli as librettist, the latter obligating himself to write for Donizetti a libretto based on a play by Kotzebue.[40]

A Bergamasc, Merelli (1794–1879) had received private music lessons from Mayr while Donizetti had been a student at the Lezioni Caritatevoli. His later fame (or notoriety, depending on one's point of view) derives from his activities as one of the most prominent (and irresponsible) impresarios of his time. He seems to have begun his career as an impresario, following activities as a theatrical agent, when he assumed the lease of the theater at Varese in 1830.[41] He was in charge of La Scala from 1836 to 1850 and 1861 to 1863, and was co-director (with Carln Balocchino) of the Kärntnertortheater in Vienna from 1836 to 1848. As a librettist Merelli worked with Donizetti from 1818[42] through 1821; he left his own account of their association in a little pamphlet written long after the events, *Cenni biografici di Donizetti e Mayr raccolti dalle memorie di un vecchio ottagenario dilettante di musica* (one of the more interesting byproducts of the festivities of 1875 held to mark the reinterment of the bodies of Mayr and Donizetti near their monuments in Santa Maria Maggiore). When Donizetti and Merelli came across each other again in the mid-1830s their relationship was strictly on a business footing; a decade later when Donizetti was in Vienna he was on more than one occasion outraged by Merelli's flagrant misrepresentations of the merits of some of the singers he sent to appear at the Kärntner-tortheater.

In October 1818 Zancla's company was back in Verona, rehearsing for the season due to begin the following month in Venice. Donizetti arrived there with his completed score of *Enrico di Borgogna* to find that, instead of the mezzo-soprano Costanza Petralia whom he had expected to fill the important role of Elisa, Zancla had engaged Adelaide (also known as Adelina) Catalani,[43] who had never yet set foot upon an operatic stage. In a letter written on 13 October 1818 Donizetti informs Mayr of this change of cast and optimistically hopes for 'the happiest outcome', claiming that he has only 'to rewrite a few things for this soprano'.[44]

The first performance of *Enrico di Borgogna*, marking Donizetti's debut as an opera composer, took place at the Teatro San Luca in Venice on 14 November 1818, the delay from the September date specified in Merelli's contract having been caused by the redecoration of the theater. Until Luigi Pilon uncovered a circumstantial account of this performance in the *Nuovo osservatore veneziano* (17 November 1818), writers on Donizetti (myself included) had assumed that the terse review in the *Gazzetta privilegiata di Venezia* (19 November 1818), which says nothing of the composer beyond a condescending acknowledgment of his 'talent', told the whole story. The critic from the *Gazzetta* must have attended one of the later performances, for the *prima* was blemished by the inexperienced Catalani's fainting from stage fright at the end of Act 1, a debacle that necessitated omitting some of her music from Act 2 and her replacement by another singer in the finale.

The lengthy review in the *Nuovo osservatore veneziano* is worth citing as it is one of the earliest judgments of Donizetti's music. After mentioning that the overture was applauded, the critic continues:

What ought I to say? Ought I to acknowledge the warfare between orchestra and singers? Ought I to commiserate with this young composer for exposing himself as a debutant to a public which, according to its whim, now demands too much and again tolerates too much? The young composer had the bad luck to see his work violated both in the singing and in the action. Should he perhaps accuse himself of imprudence? The spectators, however, knew well how to distinguish the merits of the composition from those of the performance. A terzetto in Act 1, a duet in Act 2, the aria of Verni[45] in Act 1 were applauded. And in Act 2 there would have been more applause were it not for the unexpected indisposition of Adelaide Catalani . . . If it is possible now to judge tranquilly after such disagreeable circumstances the merit of the music, one cannot but recognize a regular handling and expressive quality in his style. For these the public wanted to salute Signor Donizetti on stage at the end of the opera.[46]

Adelaide Catalani recovered sufficiently to appear in the two succeeding performances, on 15 and 16 November. On the second, less
distracting evening Donizetti's score was held to be 'well considered
and appropriately lively and spirited'.[47]

From Donizetti's point of view the most important result of *Enrico
di Borgogna* was a commission to compose again for the same
troupe. In less than a month Merelli concocted a text for a one-act
farsa, *Una follia*, and Donizetti composed the score. (Merelli, in the
Cenni biografici, refers to this work as *Il ritratto parlante*, but he
clearly means the same work that Donizetti, for his part, spoke of as
Una follia, and it is under this title that the critic of the *Nuovo
osservatore veneziano* reviewed the performance in the issue of 24
December 1818.) Donizetti rehearsed the company for the *prima*,
which occurred on 17 December 1818 and not two days earlier as has
been traditionally reported. In the *Cenni biografici* Merelli claims
that *Una follia* had a favorable reception, but the critic of the *Nuovo
osservatore* was less enthusiastic: 'the vocal writing was not outstanding. The young maestro has done what he has done shrewdly.
This time necessity can serve him as an excuse. The applause his
works have aroused here may encourage him in the pursuit of his
career, but let it not delude him.'[48]

Una follia closed Zancla's fall season at the San Luca and he
moved his company on to Mantua. Donizetti returned to Bergamo
with no further contracts, arriving there at the end of the year. It has
been claimed that *Enrico di Borgogna* was given in Bergamo at the
Teatro della Società during Carnival 1818–19. Two operas were
staged there that season: Rossini's *Aureliano in Palmira* and Mayr's
Lodoiska. If Donizetti's work had been given there then, one would
expect the first professional production by a local composer in his
hometown to leave some trace, but there is none. It is conceivable
that Donizetti approached the management of the Teatro della
Società and asked them to put on *Enrico*, but without success. More
likely, the second production of *Enrico*, if it took place at all, occurred at Mantua with Zancla's company, who already knew the
work and had the orchestral parts and the singers suited to it.

Somewhat at a loose end for at least the first half of 1819, Donizetti
turned out some sacred and instrumental music, attended musical
parties and engaged in flirtation. Evidence of this last activity survives in the form of a one-sided dialogue carried on in Italian and
French, with even a phrase in English, addressed to a Giuditta Paga-
nini and written down on the autograph of one of the string quartets
he composed that spring.[49] More importantly for his future,

Donizetti had not lost sight of his determination to write for the stage. Clearly he had composed at least a part of *Le nozze in villa* by the end of the summer of 1819, as a scena and aria with chorus[50] from that score were included in the pasticcio–farsa *I piccioli virtuosi ambulanti*, assembled by Mayr for the end-of-term concert at his school in 1819. *Le nozze in villa*, to a libretto by Merelli that drew on another Kotzebue play, *Die deutschen Kleinstädter*, was probably composed for a commission that either did not materialize as expected or had to be postponed; it was not staged for almost eighteen months, finally being sung at the Teatro Vecchio, Mantua, during Carnival 1820–1. The scena and aria with chorus from *Le nozze in villa* was not Donizetti's only contribution to *I piccioli virtuosi ambulanti*: he also composed the opening episode or *introduzione*. In the past *I piccioli virtuosi ambulanti* has been erroneously included in the list of Donizetti's completed operas; it is an occasional piece, like Mayr's *Il piccolo compositore di musica* of 1811, drawing on music from a number of composers. It should, more accurately, be attributed to Mayr, Donizetti and others.[51]

As 1819 drew to a close, Donizetti threw himself into the composition of yet another opera, *Il falegname di Livonia, ossia Pietro il grande, Tsar delle Russie*, which had its first performance on 26 December 1819 at the Teatro San Samuele in Venice. The libretto, based upon Duval's comedy *Le menuisier de Livonie*, was written by the Marchese Gherardo Bevilacqua-Aldobrandini.[52] Although *Il falegname* was not greeted with particular enthusiasm at its first production, the score was to prove the hardiest that Donizetti had composed to date. Its second production opened the Carnival season of 1823–4 at Bologna; it was the first of his operas to be given there. Subsequent productions were mounted at Verona (1825),[53] Padua (1826), Venice (Teatro San Benedetto, 1827) and Spoleto (1829).

Again Donizetti returned to Bergamo, to while away his time until *Le nozze in villa* was brought out in Mantua during the Carnival season of 1820–1 (the precise date is still undetermined). Merelli, in his *Cenni biografici*, reports that *Le nozze in villa* was a failure because, 'in spite of many successful numbers, it could not maintain itself on account of the caprices and ill will of several of the singers, especially the prima donna'. The prima donna in question was Fanny Eckerlin, who as a *musico*[54] had taken the title role in *Enrico di Borgogna*. At the time of *Le nozze in villa* she was still only eighteen years old and on the threshold of a career that was to take her to Vienna with Barbaja's company in 1822 and later found her singing Arsace at the Théâtre-Italien on the night Giulia Grisi made her Paris debut in *Semiramide* in 1832. It is possible that her ill humor derived more from chafing at her contract, which still kept her tied to Zancla, than any particular dissatisfaction with Donizetti's score. In any event, the at best lukewarm reception meted out to *Le nozze in villa* at Mantua did not prevent its being put on at Genoa during the spring of 1822, where it was given as *I provinciali, ossia Le nozze in villa*.

The whereabouts of the autographs of *Enrico di Borgogna, Una follia* and *Le nozze in villa* are unknown.[55] According to Merelli's *Cenni biografici*, Zancla, who bought these scores outright, took them home to Sicily where he died not long afterward; certainly a good deal more needs to be known about Zancla and about the disposition of his property.

Donizetti's annual pattern of a retreat to Bergamo repeated itself after the initial discouragement of *Le nozze in villa*. That this was a time of re-evaluation and self-examination for the frustrated composer, as he sought to find the road to an unequivocal success that would launch a notable career, is indicated by Bonesi:

I participated in his first vicissitudes and at the same time shared with him my frank opinion of his music . . . Appreciating his talent more than anyone, I wanted to see him emerge with glory . . . Straightforwardly he told me that he had to cultivate the Rossinian style, according to the taste of the day. If once he made his own way a little, nothing would prevent him from developing his own style. He had many ideas how to reform the predictable situations, the sequences of introduction, cavatina, duet, trio, finale, always fashioned the same way. 'But', he added sadly, 'what to do with the blessed theatrical conventions? Impresarios, singers, and the public as well, would hurl me into the farthest pit at least, and – *addio per sempre*.'[56]

The significance of Bonesi's account, although written long after the reported conversation, can scarcely be overstressed. About 1820 the modern concept of repertory in the opera house could scarcely be said to have existed. Then the public craved not merely novelty, but immediately accessible novelty (much like the mass television audience of today). An Italian composer of Donizetti's generation, to gain a hearing, had to arouse the enthusiasm of his first audiences or his opera would disappear without much trace. To make a name the writer of operas had to adopt, but not too slavishly, the idiom most appealing to the public, and in 1821 Rossini's music was the public's yardstick when they were assessing new scores. That Donizetti did in fact adapt the Rossinian manner can be seen in the score of his next opera, *Zoraida di Granata*, where vocal melodies are introduced and embellished in typically Rossinian ways. Yet Donizetti's eclecticism should not blind us to those passages in his operas of the 1820s where the training he had received from Mayr and his own predilection assert themselves, as in his fluent handling of ensembles in slow tempos for instance. Donizetti only became a *rossiniano* for a while and up to a point, and that not without reluctance. As Bonesi put it: 'If once he made his own way a little, nothing would prevent him from developing his own style.'

While Donizetti was fretting about how to unlock the door to his future, an event threatened to postpone or even to cut off his musical career. In December 1820 the Austrian governor of Milan called up to military duty the five classes born between 1795 and 1800, the conscripts being ordered to report between 15 and 24 December. At this point both Donizetti's brothers were under arms: Francesco was in the Austrian service; Giuseppe was a bandsman with the *piemontesi*, and in 1821 those troops were to fight against the Austrians.

Contrary to the unfounded and mindlessly repeated story that Donizetti was in uniform as early as 1818 and that his early operas won him a discharge from the army, he was able to avoid conscription completely. On 15 December 1820 he wrote to Mayr, then in Milan rehearsing his *Fedra* for its *prima*, informing him that a friend had been called up and adding, 'but the hectic ones will be exempted, I believe'.[57] By 'the hectic ones' he meant himself and his friend Dolci. Nearly twenty years later Donizetti referred to this matter in a letter to Dolci, reminding him of 'the worthy woman' who did 'a favor for you and me in the matter of the conscription when we needed money'.[58] This woman was Marianna Pezzoli-Grattaroli, who believed in the promise of these young musicians to the extent of buying their exemptions from military service.[59]

Not long after the vexatious problem of his military service was settled, Donizetti embarked upon the project that was to raise him from obscurity. Some things about this project are explained by three letters[60] Donizetti wrote to Giovanni Paterni,[61] impresario of the Teatro Argentina in Rome, but they contain no clear account of how or why Paterni entered into these negotiations. The most plausible hypothesis is that Paterni originally approached Mayr, but Mayr, nearing sixty and soon to give up composing for the stage, suggested that Paterni accept his prize pupil in his place. Unless contradictory evidence is discovered, this explanation satisfies, as it is consistent with what we know of Mayr's generosity and his abiding concern for Donizetti's career.[62]

From the first of these letters to Paterni it appears that by 17 June

1821 Donizetti had received the contract from the impressario and had only to sign it himself, and that he had already spoken to Merelli about writing a libretto for him. The subject had not yet been chosen, for Donizetti wants to know whether the singers are suited to serious or comic works. By 7 August he knows that his opera will not open the season but be put on second, and he worries that it may be staged skimpily, this concern perhaps reflecting his experiences with Zancla. He complains of Merelli's laziness, but on 9 August he is confident that soon some sections of the libretto will be in his hands.

It is clear from these indications that the bulk of *Zoraida di Granata* was composed between about the middle of August and 1 October 1821, the date of Donizetti's departure from Bergamo for Rome. It was not in final form because, while he would have wanted to avail himself of Mayr's counsel, he was prepared to adjust the vocal parts to the capacities and strengths of his singers once he had had a chance to hear them in Rome. On 1 October 1821 Mayr gave Donizetti a letter of introduction to the Roman librettist Jacopo Ferretti in which he praises his pupil's outstanding talent and genius, and his frank and ingenuous character, specifying 'his fertile imagination, his rich fount of invention and his ease at extending his musical ideas', and modestly gives all the credit for his musical education to Padre Mattei, without mentioning that he had studied with Mayr himself.[63] With this letter, his score of *Zoraida di Granata* and his passport, Donizetti set out for Rome. In those days of a divided Italy one needed a passport to travel from the Austrian province of Lombardy to the Papal States. His passport describes Donizetti as twenty-three years and eleven months old; hair, chestnut; eyes, blue; coloring, fair; height, tall; physique, slender; purpose of travel, to produce an opera at the Teatro Argentina.

Thus Donizetti left Bergamo, a place he would see again infrequently, and 'like an owl [he] took flight' on the journey that was to bring him not only fame and wealth, but also humiliation and tragedy.

2

1822–1830
Zoraida di Granata to *Imelda de' Lambertazzi*

Soon after his arrival in Rome, Donizetti delivered Mayr's letter of introduction to Jacopo Ferretti.[1] Ferretti's apartment was a gathering-place for people interested in literature and music. Mayr could not have made a wiser choice of a man to befriend Donizetti on his first visit to Rome. Not only was Ferretti familiar with the cross-currents of the Roman opera stages, but he had a wide acquaintance among people whose support would prove valuable. To someone like Donizetti, whose experience as a composer had been confined to Bergamo and to the smaller theaters of Venice, it must have seemed that he had come into the mainstream of the operatic world. For if at that time Rome had no single theater with the special prestige of Milan's La Scala or of Naples's San Carlo, it could boast three important opera houses: the Argentina, the Valle, and the Apollo,[2] the last of which had a tradition that extended back to 1671.

For the Carnival season of 1821–2 only two of these three Roman opera houses were open: the Valle was closed for remodeling. The buffa company that usually played at the Valle had moved into the Apollo, and opera seria held the stage at the Argentina; both companies were under the management of Giovanni Paterni, and both opened their seasons on the traditional date of 26 December (Santo Stefano). The Apollo mounted a new opera by Carafa,[3] *La capricciosa e il soldato;*[4] the libretto was by Ferretti, but he refused to put his name to it because the censors had altered it extensively. The season at the Argentina began with the *prima* of Giovanni Pacini's[5] *Cesare in Egitto*, performed by the company that would soon appear in *Zoraida di Granata*. These new works by Carafa and Pacini were favorably received and ran for about a month.

The performances of *Cesare in Egitto*, however, were cut short by a tragedy that precipitated a crisis for Donizetti. One night during the second-act quintet, the second tenor, Americo Sbigoli, attempting to imitate the powerful tones of the first tenor Domenico Donzelli in a climactic phrase first sung by Donzelli and later repeated by Sbigoli, had the misfortune of bursting a blood vessel in his throat. Within a few days Sbigoli was dead (leaving a pregnant wife and four young sons).[6] Sbigoli's death created a serious problem for Donizetti, as he had written the important role of Abenamet in *Zoraida* for a second tenor and there was no available replacement for Sbigoli, whose death occurred about the middle of January 1822. Donizetti found himself unexpectedly confronted with the problem of revising the music of Abenamet as a *musico* role for a contralto named Mazzanti.[7] These revisions were forced upon Donizetti so shortly before the scheduled first performance that he had to eliminate three numbers from his score. One can imagine his trepidation, his music abbreviated and a last-minute replacement in an important role, knowing that his future hung upon the outcome of his first encounter with the public at a major theater.

The hastily recast *Zoraida di Granata* was first given at the Teatro Argentina on 28 January 1822, with two important singers of the day in leading roles: Maria Ester Mombelli[8] (Zoraida) and Donzelli (Almuzir). The evening's entertainment included two ballets: *Le amazzoni di Boemia* and *L'avaro*. Although the ballets failed to please, *Zoraida* aroused real enthusiasm and fervor – the sort of reception that Donizetti had dreamed of but had not dared expect.

Luck was with him. Not only did the ballets fail at the Argentina, but at the Apollo Vincenzo Puccita's[9] *La festa in villaggio* had been received in stony silence, circumstances that enhanced the success of Donizetti's work. The general knowledge of the hardship the new composer had suffered because of Sbigoli's inopportune death may have influenced the audience in his favor. And he was fortunate to have Donzelli, then at the height of his impressive powers as singer and actor, for the popular tenor seems to have exerted himself on Donizetti's behalf. These circumstances no doubt predisposed the audience to concentrate on the solid merits of Donizetti's score; they applauded his thorough training, his gift for fluent melody, and his sure handling of concerted pieces. The *prima* of *Zoraida di Granata* had all the unique aura of a first success.

The sense of a special occasion illumines the review of *Zoraida* that Abate Celli wrote for the Roman weekly, *Notizie del giorno*.[10] After greeting Donizetti as a 'new hope' for Italian opera, Celli mentions the applause that greeted every piece, believing it would have been still warmer had the public heard the three numbers that had had to be omitted. He praises the cast warmly, and concludes: 'All thoughts, however, revolved round the young composer, tacitly urging him not to desist from his chosen path and not to deviate from the beautiful style that does him honor.' The seal was set on Donizetti's success when, following the third performance (30 January), he and Donzelli were serenaded by a military band and marched with torches to a banquet. Earlier that day Donizetti had sent word to Mayr about *Zoraida:* 'I limit myself to saying the outcome was *felicissimo.*'[11]

The good fortune that attended the *prima* of *Zoraida di Granata* made Donizetti's name known from Naples to Milan, and before the year was out he would have new operas produced in both cities. This visit to Rome was not only a landmark in Donizetti's professional career, it opened a new phase of his domestic life as well. At some point during the four-month stay he was introduced to the household of Luigi Vasselli,[12] who was to become his father-in-law.

Gaetano's chief contact with the Vasselli family at first was with the eldest son, Antonio or Toto,[13] three years older than himself, and a member of the Ferretti circle;[14] at that time he was a surgeon assigned to the papal troops, but later he would follow the family profession of the law and serve as agent in Rome for the Milanese music-publisher Ricordi. The only daughter of the family,[15] Virginia, was then only thirteen, and had just returned from school at the convent of the Monastero delle Vergini. All the Vassellis were interested in music, and Virginia had already demonstrated some aptitude as a pianist and singer. Although Gaetano's first friendship was with Toto, and their loyal attachment would continue until Gaetano's death, he became increasingly aware of the dark beauty and gentle disposition of young Virginia.

Besides his in-laws-to-be, Donizetti formed a friendship with another prominent Roman family of *dilettanti,* having been given by Saverio Mercadante[16] a letter of introduction to the Carnevalis. Dr Paolo Carnevali, his wife Anna, and their daughters Tina (Clementina) and Giggia (Edvige) were prominent members of a circle of talented amateurs; Tina also belonged to the Accademia di Santa Cecilia for many years. Donizetti offered proof of his friendship and esteem for this family by composing music for them.[17]

Donizetti remained in Rome as long as *Zoraida* held the stage, and then left for Naples, where he had been engaged to write an opera. There he found he missed his Roman friends, as he wrote to Ferretti: 'Naples does not please me, Rome very much; therefore I live at Naples for Rome.'[18]

Donizetti had left Rome during the latter half of February 1822, arriving at Naples just at the end of one of its most brilliant periods of operatic history. Before the middle of March Rossini and the prima donna he was shortly to marry, Isabella Colbran, were to leave the city where they had been idolized, never to return.[19] One of Rossini's last functions before abandoning Naples was to conduct a Lenten performance of Mayr's oratorio *Atalia*. Donizetti, who was present at these rehearsals, sent Mayr a revealing picture of Rossini's last days in Naples:

I have come to Naples before the end of this month [February] as specified by my contract; therefore I am able to help your cause with the oratorio, but I see it will be entirely useless . . . Rossini complains jesuitically to the singers that they have not performed well, and then at the orchestral rehearsal he was standing there gossiping with the prima donnas instead of conducting. This should suffice, but as though that were not enough, [they have cut] the first aria . . . some recitatives and some choruses, [and] the little finale of the second act . . . They are like so many dogs and they deserve to be kicked for not performing this music. This is Colbran's gratitude, after having been such a favorite.[20] As for me, I stay out of sight, and so this morning they asked for me.[21]

Angry, and jealous of his teacher's reputation, Donizetti had no patience with Rossini's cynical behavior. Donizetti's concern for the integrity of the work to be performed is a trait that emerges frequently in his later correspondence, and, as here, it was as genuinely exercised over others' compositions as over his own.

At Naples Donizetti's contract with the impresario Barbaja[22] involved not only composing new operas but also the preparation for performance of operas by other composers, when they were being introduced to Naples after having had their *prime* elsewhere.[23] One of his first assignments was to rehearse Carafa's *La capricciosa e il soldato*, which he knew from its recent *prima* at the Teatro Apollo in Rome. As Ferretti's libretto had been badly mauled by the Roman censor, Monsignor Piatti, Donizetti wrote to Ferretti for a copy of the uncensored text. In this same letter, of 26 March 1822, he speaks of his own plans: 'I write as speedily as possible [*precipitevolis-simevolmente*] to speed the staging of my opera, which will take place after the novena of San Gennaro,[24] toward the middle of May.'[25]

Before the opera, another composition by Donizetti, a cantata to celebrate the birth of the Prince of Salerno's daughter (who would later become a pupil of the composer) was performed. The opera, *La zingara*, was given at the Teatro Nuovo on 12 May 1822.[26] In spite of a crude libretto[27] by Andrea Leone Tottola,[28] one of the more prolific if one of the least gifted theater poets then active in Naples, *La zingara* delighted the public.

The critic of the *Giornale del Regno delle Due Sicilie*,[29] speaks of Donizetti as 'crowned with success', and goes on to say that 'the public called him out many times, according him animated applause'.[30] Two days after the first performance, on 14 May, Donizetti sent his own account of the opera's reception to Anna Carnevali, giving more space to the singers than to himself. But he does report:

> The lucky Donizetti appeared on stage on Sunday with *La zingara*, and the public was certainly not stingy with compliments. I could almost say they lavished them, all the nicer since in Naples they applaud very little . . . Yesterday at the second performance the audience did not neglect some pieces that had slipped by the first evening. I was called out again to collect applause which perhaps the singers deserved more than I. This evening for the first time the king will come.[31]

La zingara marked an auspicious beginning to Donizetti's Neapolitan career, for it ran for twenty-eight consecutive nights, and then in July it was put on again for twenty more.[32] A striking instance of the favorable reception of *La zingara* is cited by Florimo,[33] who describes the composer Carlo Conti's telling some students at the Conservatory, among them Bellini and Florimo himself, to be sure to hear *La zingara* as it contained a septet that only a pupil of Mayr could write.

A little more than six weeks after the *prima* of *La zingara* Donizetti produced another opera: on 29 June 1822 *La lettera anonima*, a one-act farsa, had its first performance at the Teatro del Fondo. The libretto, by a former monk Giulio Genoino, who was also one of the three-man board of Neapolitan censors,[34] is both pallid and padded. On 22 July Donizetti wrote to Mayr about his latest work, saying that 'even though half ruined by a novice singer,[35] it did not have the most unhappy reception'. And he continues: 'I am sending you the article from the paper' (almost certainly the review of *La lettera anonima* that had appeared in the *Giornale del Regno delle Due Sicilie* on 1 July 1822), 'not to draw attention to the praise, but rather to show you how much I seek not to stray from a sound style'. The article in the *Giornale* singles out the quartet ('Stelle! che intesi!') because it 'made fresh again the old-time procedure of our so-called concerted pieces without those cabalettas, and [further] without that symmetrical repetition of motifs which obliges all the actors to repeat the same musical phrases no matter what very different emotions may agitate them'.[36] Donizetti concludes his report to Mayr with unassuming modesty: 'Although I do not have the ability to restore music to its former glory, at least I do not have the notoriety of being one of its corrupters [*depravatori*].'³⁷

This review and Donizetti's reaction to it are significant because they make clear that his concern with the dramatic essence of opera rather than the mechanical working out of musical formulas was, even at this early stage, already present and active. The characterization of Donizetti's early career, up to the time of his great success with *Anna Bolena* (1830), as *anni di galera* (years spent turning out an embarrassing profusion of journeyman's work) is as misleading in its way as is the application of that pejorative term to the first decade of Verdi's output. There is hardly a score of Donizetti's from the 1820s that does not have some pages that anticipate his future achievements. *La lettera anonima*, in spite of the contretemps that marred its *prima*, managed to achieve a run of twenty performances.

In the letter to Mayr quoted above, Donizetti mentions that he is leaving for Milan 'on Friday', which would have been 26 July 1822. By 3 August he was there, for on that date he and the librettist Felice Romani signed a contract to write the third opera for that autumn season at La Scala.³⁸ Felice Romani (1788–1865) was even then known as the most literate librettist in Italy, but he had the frustrating habit of accepting more commissions than he could reasonably fulfill and agreeing to deadlines that he had no intention of meeting. Such was the case in the fall of 1822, for Romani was also writing the text for the opera scheduled to precede Donizetti's, *Adele ed Emerico* by Mercadante. 20 September, the date specified for the submission of Romani's text for Donizetti, came and went without a sign of the libretto. Eight days later Donizetti was still without a text, and Mayr wrote to Bonesi, giving him a picture of Donizetti during this nerve-racking period: 'Our Donizetti is in Milan, saying he feels an unusual fear of the theater, but I would like to hope this is only because his friend Mercadante was not (it is said) as fortunate there this year as last.'³⁹ Not until 3 October did Romani hand in to the overseer at La Scala just the first act of *Chiara e Serafina, ossia I pirati*. The same day the censor returned the first act with but one slight change. Only on 3 October, then, could Donizetti start to set the text, and yet by 15 October *Chiara e Serafina* was ready to go into rehearsal⁴⁰ and the *prima* took place on the 26th. October 1822 was a frantic month for Donizetti!

Aware of the importance of making a good impression with his first opera at La Scala, since the Milanese were notoriously disdainful of reputations made elsewhere, Donizetti was understandably anxious. Given short shrift by Romani, hampered by the routine of a theater in which the members of his cast performed another opera while they were rehearsing his, tormented by the unfavorable position he found himself occupying, he let all his worries boil over in a letter to Mayr, written on 16 October:

and I must inform you that unfortunately the *prima* will be on the 26th, as only yesterday the first piano run-through [*piccola prova*] took place. I hope, however, I will have the pleasure of seeing you if not at the first performance at least at the third. I suggest you bring a Requiem, for I shall be slaughtered, and thus the funeral rites will be taken care of.[41]

Another clue to Donizetti's state of mind is found in the few words he scrawled on the final page of the autograph of *Chiara e Serafina*:[42] 'Così finirà l'opera: o bene o male.' (Thus will the opera end: either well or badly.)

For a time even the date of the *prima* was in doubt, when Isabella Fabbrica[43] caught cold and missed several rehearsals; but she appeared on the appointed date, even though not yet completely recovered. Two repertory ballets were part of the evening's bill: *Gabriella di Vergy*,[44] danced between the acts of *Chiara e Serafina*, and, after the opera, *Il merciaiolo in angustie*. *Chiara e Serafina* was reviewed by Francesco Pezzi in the *Gazzetta di Milano*.[45] He began with a diatribe against the repetitiousness common to operas based on French plays (Romani's libretto was derived from de Pixérécourt's *La cisterne*), an observation reflecting the censors' official distrust of French thought and attitudes. Finally Pezzi condescended to mention Donizetti's opera:

the new score might have been able to sustain itself discreetly if, along with the prolongations and repetitions alluded to, the poet and the composer had not exposed themselves too openly, for which it is no slight matter that the public maintained a certain constraint that it has not shown on other similar occasions . . . To sum things up, I will say that after sparse applause for the diligence of la Morandi[46] and la Fabbrica and after some sign of discontent at the weakness of the music, the audience watched the final curtain descend with faces of bronze.

Pezzi's review seems too severe in the face of the actuality, since *Chiara e Serafina* was performed twelve[47] times before it was put aside. Verzino reports that La Scala was just then under close surveillance by the Austrians, as a major treason trial was in progress, and the theater was attracting sparse audiences.[48] If Donizetti had counted on some sympathy from the *milanesi* for the adverse conditions surrounding the composition of his opera (conditions he could little control), or if he had relied on some tolerance from his fellow Lombards, he was sadly disappointed. Even more disappointing was the decision of La Scala not to offer him a contract for a new opera, as would have been done automatically if *Chiara e Serafina* had enjoyed even a modest success. Nearly ten years were to elapse before Donizetti won unconditional acceptance from a Milanese audience.

When Donizetti left Milan is uncertain, nor is it known whether he made a detour to Bergamo before making his way back to the south; but he was in Rome on 19 December 1822, for on that day he composed and dated a soprano–bass duet for Tina Carnevali and Nicola Cartoni.[49] Although the music of this duet is unexceptional, the dramatic situation is significant, dealing as it does with a dying woman protesting her innocence to a disbelieving man,[50] for here for the first time Donizetti confronted a dramatic motif that occurs frequently in Romantic opera plots. His most important business in Rome was to sign a contract with Paterni for a *rifacimento*[51] of *Zoraida di Granata* (Ferretti being assigned the task of patching up Merelli's original libretto and adding some new material) and a new opera buffa, the libretto to be by Ferretti, for the Teatro Valle. For both assignments Donizetti was to receive 500 *scudi*.

By the end of March 1823 Donizetti was back in Naples faced with a heavy schedule: a cantata for the San Carlo in May, an opera seria for the same theater, and an opera buffa for the Nuovo – all this in addition to the work he had contracted to do for Paterni in Rome. Donizetti's days as a 'workhorse' composer had begun.

The cantata, *Aristea*, employed an old-fashioned pastoral libretto by one of the resident Neapolitan poetasters, Giovanni Schmidt.[52] To Mayr Donizetti sums up Schmidt's contribution in one contemptuous word: 'neve' (snow), and complains that the audience on 30 May 1823 (the king's name-day) was excessively noisy.[53] To Ferretti he had already epitomized Schmidt's plot as 'shepherds (bitchery [*cagnara*], in brief)'.[54]

Donizetti's first opera to be performed at the Teatro San Carlo, *Alfredo il grande*,[55] was given on 2 July 1823, with the English prima donna Elisabetta Ferron,[56] and the Bergamasc tenor Andrea Nozzari in the title role. Donizetti had written frankly to Mayr about the work: 'I speak sincerely: it will be as it will, but I do not know how to do more.'[57] On the same subject the critic of the *Giornale del Regno delle Due Sicilie* commented tersely: 'in this work one could not recognize the composer of *La zingara*'. *Alfredo il grande* achieved only one performance. Donizetti's last work for the Neapolitan theaters that year was *Il fortunato inganno*, a two-act farsa, given at the Teatro Nuovo on 3 September 1823.[58] Its total of performances was three.

After some uncertainty owing to the death of Pope Pius VII (the

Roman theaters were closed during a papal election),[59] Donizetti arrived in Rome to carry out his obligations to Paterni about the middle of October 1823. The little success of his most recent operas in Naples did not deter him from approaching his Roman projects with enthusiasm. He was taken aback, though, by the extensiveness of Ferretti's changes in the libretto for Zoraida.

Five pieces?... We will go on forever with this stuff... This awful Ferretti [Ferrettaccio] comes merrily along with a choral cavatina, choral aria, choral duet, choral introduzione and choral chorus, and besides we have choruses. Does it not mean, however, that Zoraida, instead of being a fine thing, will be a great bitchery because everything is done over again? As far as the cavatina and aria of Pisaroni[60] I was in agreement, but then a duet, a final rondò with all those people on stage who have to sing! Ah, by God, this business is getting out of hand... Yet I understand everything is for the good of the opera, and if everything goes as swimmingly as I hope, since I am not sparing any labor, I hope for reciprocal friendliness from [Paterni]... I must work like a stevedore and I get 500 scudi, while Mercadante gets 700 for a single opera.[61]

Work on the revised Zoraida occupied Donizetti at least until 10 November, for on that date he sent to Pisaroni for her approval the final rondò, an aria with bravura variations, along with an obsequious letter that contains such phrases as 'only my scarcity of talent has hindered my will to do better'.[62] Beneath the conventional courtliness of this letter one glimpses both Donizetti's genuine modesty and his awareness of the relative importance of composers vis-à-vis star singers in those days, a distinction reinforced by the relative sizes of the fees they received.

Zoraida di Granata in its revised form was given at the Argentina on 7 January 1824.[63] In spite of a stronger cast[64] than that of two years previously and in spite of the new pieces, it evoked nothing like the enthusiasm the original version had aroused. Only one number, the new duet for Pisaroni and Donzelli, received extended applause, and it elicited from the critic of the Notizie del giorno the comment that it would ensure Donizetti 'the most glittering crown among composers of opera seria'.[65]

A more jaundiced account of the revised Zoraida comes from Stendhal.

Donizetti, over whom the Romans went mad two years ago, and whom they followed home the night of the first [it was the third] performance of Zoraida di Granata with shouts of admiration, has bored us fatally the 7th of this month with this same Zoraida, strengthened by new pieces. La Pisaroni, who plays the lover's role, is admirable in it; the tenor Donzelli very fine. His voice, however does not please me at all; it is veiled and, in the upper notes, resembles a yell[66]... Donizetti is a tall, handsome young man, but cold and without a shred of talent; it seems to me that they applauded him two years ago to give affront to the Princess Pauline,[67] who protected the young Pacini.[68]

In spite of its disappointing reception, the revised *Zoraida* continued at the Argentina until 7 February;[69] but before that run petered out Donizetti had enjoyed a substantial success at the Valle, where on 4 February 1824 his opera buffa, *L'ajo nell'imbarazzo*, was first given. For most of his professional life he was able to regard the mixed fortunes of his career objectively; after one opera had been launched he could let it go its way as he immersed himself in composing and preparing the next.

L'ajo nell'imbarazzo has one of Ferretti's best librettos. It is based upon a comedy of the same name by Giovanni Giraud (Rome, 1807), and the entertaining plot deals with a father who, with the help of the tutor of the title, tries, in vain needless to say, to raise his two sons in ignorance of women. The opera, strongly cast,[70] held the stage at the Valle for the remainder of the season, gaining in popularity at every repetition. This is the first of Donizetti's works to reveal his great natural flair for operatic comedy. The reviews of the first performance were enthusiastic, praising the score for its spontaneity and inventiveness, and for the clarity and originality of its ideas.[71] Donizetti's bent for enriching his comedies with moments of pathos is clearly represented in *L'ajo nell'imbarazzo*. Such was the work's success that Donizetti promptly signed a contract with Francesco Tortoli[72] to adapt it to the special requirements of the Teatro Nuovo – spoken dialogue instead of recitatives and the buffo role translated into the Neapolitan dialect. In addition this contract called for a new opera, and for both tasks Donizetti was to receive 300 ducats.

The Neapolitan version of *L'ajo*, rechristened *Don Gregorio*, was not performed until 1826, but the new opera, *Emilia di Liverpool*, had its *prima* at the Nuovo on 28 July 1824. The libretto, which would later be revised by Giuseppe Checcherini, was based upon an earlier opera text[73] and contains that mixture of melodramatic and buffo elements which forms the genre known as 'semiseria'. *Emilia* is a significant work in the Donizetti canon because of its incipient Romanticism; it includes, besides a hapless heroine, a storm scene and an episode in an underground tomb. If today the melodrama seems puerile and the buffo episodes seem progressively to subvert the dramatic conviction essential to the spirit of Romanticism, this is the fault of the old semiseria genre, in which the comic interludes fail to form a coherent extension of the serious scenes. The Romantic aura of works like *Emilia* found little favor with the official arbiters of taste in Naples, but the kinds of plot to which the critic of the *Giornale del Regno delle Due Sicilie* (9 October 1824) is objecting were to carry the day in the 1830s:

Not finding a hint of passion in the midst of the sea of impassioned words in these wretched dramas, composers are forced to utilize strong or surprising situations in the poet's work and to capitalize on the contrast of characters and coincidence, permitting themselves some effects of light and shade in order to obtain some variety in the composition. That is the condition of Donizetti, for example, who recently wrote the pretty music of *Emilia di Liverpool*.

In *Emilia* one can discern something of the beginnings of the shift in emphasis that would bear fruit for Donizetti in his Romantic melodramas of the 1830s; but first he had to find a way to break away from the tradition, sternly guarded by the censors, of the happy ending, and he had to develop a musical rhetoric that would lend conviction to Romantic sentiments.

Emilia attained only seven performances before it was allowed to lapse, but Donizetti's subsequent attentions to this score show that he regarded it as somehow salvageable. On 18 August 1824 he wrote to Mercadante, who was in Vienna with Barbaja for a season of Italian operas, one of which was planned to be *Emilia*. This letter is instructive as it reveals Donizetti's pragmatic approach to his works when he could not be present to superintend their production personally:

in the second act there are some new pieces[74] and I therefore recommend them to you. But not only these. I recommend the whole opera to your care. You are familiar with my manner of composing, and you understand well where sometimes an alteration of tempo is needed. See to it, then, for I entrust everything to you. The role [Claudio] of Lablache, which Fioravanti[75] sang, I know will be a little uncomfortable for him. I have made *puntature*[76] for some things, but in most cases the composer is the worst one to do this, because he lives with his original ideas. Between you two you can adjust everything.[77]

Although this letter shows that Donizetti prepared a new version of *Emilia di Liverpool* in the summer of 1824 for Vienna, there are no Viennese records to confirm that *Emilia* was actually performed there then.

Much more extensive were the revisions Donizetti made to *Emilia* in 1828.[78] He added four numbers to the original score, while removing eight and part of a ninth. Giuseppe Checcherini modified the libretto in 1828, renaming some of the characters and adjusting the text, much reducing the spoken dialogue. For all the work it entailed, the 1828 *Emilia* fared no better than the original version.[79] (In

June 1957 the 1828 revision was dusted off and given at Liverpool; the following September it was broadcast by the BBC with Joan Sutherland as Emilia, a spoken commentary being substituted for the spoken dialogue.)

Details of Donizetti's activities during the latter half of 1824 and early 1825 are not plentiful. He hoped that Paterni might engage him to write a new opera for the fall season of 1824 in Rome, but that expectation remained unfulfilled. Apparently he remained in Naples with little to occupy him as the theaters there were not prospering under Joseph Glossop's management.

As 1825 was a Holy Year the Roman theaters remained closed for the entire year, so there was no hope of employment there. In Naples, too, the theaters were closed for an extended period of mourning when King Ferdinando I died on 3 January.[80] With these sources of potential income shut off, and with no engagements forthcoming from Milan, where his reputation was still insufficiently established to offset the unfortunate memory of *Chiara e Serafina*, Donizetti, whose livelihood depended upon writing for the stage, was faced with a bleak prospect.

Relief arrived from an unexpected quarter, but it brought about what was to be one of the most trying years of Donizetti's life. He was engaged from 15 March 1825 to 15 March 1826 as *maestro di cappella* at the Teatro Carolino[81] in Palermo, for which he was also to write a new opera. For his services he was to receive 45 ducats a month, and some sense of the relative values of those days will be appreciated when we set his salary against that of the prima donna, Elisabetta Ferron, who received 517½ ducats a month. In addition, Donizetti was to be granted the full receipts of one benefit evening and was allowed one month's vacation.[82]

Donizetti arrived in Palermo on 6 April 1825, but as the company, which included Ferron, the tenor Berardo Winter,[83] and Tamburini[84] and his wife, was slow in assembling, the opening of the season had to be postponed from 21 April to 4 May. The catastrophic playing of the orchestra on the opening night produced such complaints that Donizetti, who was responsible for the musical preparation, was called before the Superintendent of Public Spectacles.[85] The arrival of the prima donna Ferron was much delayed as she was recovering slowly from the difficult birth of a son; in her absence Rossini's *L'italiana in Algeri* and *Il barbiere di Siviglia* were performed, but Tamburini was the only member of these casts to find favor with the public. Ferron finally arrived, and appeared in Mayr's *Il trionfo del-*

la musica[86] without creating any particular enthusiasm. As the season limped on, morale grew shaky. The impresario Morabito was arrested on some complaint near the end of August and spent a day in jail. Then the second bass, Antonio de Rosa, with whom Donizetti lost patience one day at rehearsal, made a scene, and when he refused to apologize for insulting Donizetti he too was taken off to jail for a day.

The one cheering note in the gathering gloom was the successful staging of *L'ajo nell'imbarazzo* on 5 September 1825. Two members of the original cast, Tamburini and Tacci, were on hand, and the second tenor role of Pipetto was taken by Salvatore Patti (the father of Adelina). For this production, which he prepared himself, Donizetti made a number of changes in the score, including an arrangement of the tenor aria 'Nel primo fior degli anni' for soprano. Such was the success of *L'ajo* that the critic of one of the Palermitan papers[87] felt that only with this opera had the season finally got under way. But one fortunate production could not stem the problems inherent in hasty management and insufficient funding. The impresario Morabito had naively thought that all he had to do to put together a company of dancers was to apply to the royal ballet school at Naples, and he was startled to learn at the last moment that the students were not free to come to pirouette in Palermo, as they were on permanent call at the San Carlo. When a few dancers were finally engaged, Donizetti resented their being paid extravagantly while his own salary was in arrears. The financial problems reached such proportions that by early December 1825 the singers were threatening not to perform, but some money must have been found because the season continued to struggle on.

About the middle of December Donizetti started rehearsals of the new opera he had contracted to write for the Carolino. The preparation of a new opera was always a period that took a severe toll of Donizetti's nerves, but the trying situation that season he found nearly intolerable. His frustrations boiled over in a letter to Mayr, written on 21 December 1825, which begins with a German quotation that Donizetti must have learned from his old teacher: 'Die Vergebung ist die beste Rache' (Forgiveness is the best revenge). He assures Mayr that he understands this maxim and puts it into practise. He continues:

I know the good Mayr loves me. I have seen it on thousands of occasions. To receive one of your letters from time to time always relieves me of agitation, and it was high time you sent me one . . . I am entirely convinced we will leave here with broken heads, that is to say with several months' salary owing. For me, it is certain, but, patience, this worries me less. My real displeasure is to see myself forgotten by everyone and to come to the close of an engagement without hopes of getting another ... I do not go around flattering people behind their backs but here that is [anyway] not worth the trouble. They look on people of the theater as infamous, and consequently they pay us no attention, while we care nothing for them. The trade of the poor writer of operas I have understood from the beginning to be most unhappy, and it is only necessity that keeps me bound to it, but I assure you, dear Maestro, that I suffer much from the type of beasts we have need of for the execution of our labors ... Only you and I in all the summer have drawn audiences, with your *Che originali!* and with *L'ajo nell'imbarazzo* ... I was to have given my new opera by now, but because of Ferron's illness I will go on stage toward the first of the year. I am more than a little apprehensive ... They do not want to hear Ferron; the wife of Tamburini (the daughter of Gioia)[88] is a dog, the tenor Winter, etc., etc. And in the midst of all this I have had to play with music that requires some intelligence.[89]

Postponed by Ferron's indisposition, *Alahor in Granata* was finally staged at the Carolino on 7 January 1826. The critic of *La Cerere*, in the issue of 9 January 1826, wrote that the indifference of the public had been checked since the true merit of the new work had to be applauded. He praises Donizetti, who 'has the prudence to hold a middle road between the beauty of the old school and the energy of the new'. The score of *Alahor* was long thought to be lost, but first a copy of the revised version used by Andrea Monteleone for the 1830 revival at the Carolino came to light in Boston,[90] and more recently the autograph was discovered in Palermo. James Freeman has shed considerable light upon what was heretofore one of the more obscure items in the Donizetti list. The libretto of *Alahor* is signed with the mysterious initials 'M.A.', but it is an adaptation of Romani's libretto for Meyerbeer's *L'esule di Granata*.[91] More of us have heard music originally belonging to *Alahor* than we had realized, for it is the source of the march accompanying Belcore's entrance in Act 1 of *L'elisir d'amore*.

Obscurity still surrounds a composition Donizetti is supposed to have written for this season at the Carolino – *Il castello degli invalidi*. Although no trace of the score nor any record of its performance has yet been found, this title crops up in a letter Gaetano wrote to his brother-in-law Toto Vasselli on 24 October 1841. The letter starts: 'To the list of operas add: La *Pia, Maria Padilla, Il duca d'Alba*;[92] to the *farse, Il castello degli invalidi* and *Rita*; the first at Palermo, the second very soon at the Teatro Nuovo.'[93] Apart from the mysterious *Il castello degli invalidi*, the oldest work mentioned is *Pia de' Tolomei* (of 1837), and it is significant that Donizetti mentions no date when *Il castello degli invalidi* was given 'at Palermo'.

Thus there is no obligation to assume, as Zavadini does,[94] that it was performed during 1825–6 when he served as *maestro di cappella* at the Carolino. For that engagement his contract called for only one new opera, a condition satisfied by *Alahor in Granata*. The broadest spread of time during which *Il castello degli invalidi* might have been given is between March 1822, when Donizetti first came to Naples, and October 1841, when he wrote the letter to Vasselli quoted above.

I believe it is more likely that *Il castello degli invalidi* was composed after 1826 than before. If the farsa was publicly performed in a theater, it was almost certainly not the Carolino, as Tiby has demonstrated.[95] It is, of course, perfectly possible that *Il castello degli invalidi* was not originally designed for public performance but was written out with piano accompaniment to be performed privately by *dilettanti*, as seems to have been the case with *La bella prigioniera*.[96]

The chief evidence against *Il castello degli invalidi*'s having been composed during Donizetti's tenure at the Carolino is to be found in a scherzo for violin and piano built on themes all but one of which are from Donizetti's compositions. The themes are catalogued and numbered, with a corresponding enumeration throughout the music, in Donizetti's hand; he dedicated the piece to Virginia Vasselli, and in effect he was dedicating his total output so far to the girl he intended to marry. Since this scherzo is little known, I give here the list as Donizetti wrote it:

1. Ajo nell'Imbarazzo. Opera. in Roma Teatro Valle
2. Ideale
3. Il fortunato inganno. Opera. In Napoli Teatro nuovo
4. Cantata per la partenza del Luogotenente general di Sicilia. In Palermo. Teatro Carolina.
5. Cantata per la Nascita del Rè di Napoli Francesco primo. In Palermo. Idem.
6. Lettera Anonima. Farsa. Teatro del Fondo. Napoli.
7. Alahor in Granata. Opera. Teatro Carolina. Palermo.
8. Ideale
9. Alfredo il Grande. Opera. S.ᵗ Carlo Napoli.
10. Chiara e Serafina. Opera. Teatro La Scala. Milano.
11. Cantata come al .5.
12. Ajo nell'Imbarazzo
13. Alahor in Granata Sinfonia.
14. Emilia di Liverpool. Opera. Teatro Nuovo Napoli
15. La Zingara. Opera. Teatro Nuovo idem.
16. Enrico di Borgogna. Opera. S. Luca. Venezia.
17. La Bella prigioniera. Farsa. Non rappresentata.
18. Falegname di Livonia. Opera. S. Samuele Venezia
19. Il voto de' Sudditi. Cantata. Per la prima volta che il Rè Francesco I. di Napoli onorò il Teatro di S. Carlo.

20. Aristea. Opera d'un atto. S. Carlo Napoli
21. Ajo nell'Imbarazzo. Idem.
22. Zoraida di Granata. Opera. Roma
23. Idem.
24. Una follia. Farsa. S. Luca Venezia
25. Le Nozze in villa. Opera. Mantova.
26. Alhaor [sic] come al 7.
27. Classica, celebre, unica monferrina eh – eh – eh – eh[97]

The last item on this list, the only one not by Donizetti, is a traditional Piedmontese dance,[98] and his entry captures its lighthearted feeling. The most recent work on his list is *Alahor in Granata*, unless we take the 'Idem' in no. 21 to refer to the Neapolitan production of *L'ajo*, which took place in June 1826. The presence of the two cantatas he had written in July 1825 in Palermo (nos. 4 and 5), fugitive compositions, suggests that Donizetti compiled this scherzo while his Palermitan adventure was still quite fresh in his memory. The absence of *Il castello degli invalidi* suggests that it had not been composed yet, since the list even includes the 'unperformed' *La bella prigioniera*, as well as every one of his operas from *Enrico di Borgogna* to *Alahor*. A further indication of the probable date of *Il castello degli invalidi* is supplied by Tiby,[99] who mentions a list of Donizetti's operas compiled in 1835 by the Palermitan journalist Vincenzo Linares,[100] which does not include that title. It seems, then, that *Il castello* is most likely to have been composed between 1835 and 1841. If a copy of the long-lost *Alahor* could be rediscovered in a Boston attic, there is perhaps hope that a final resolution to the nagging question of *Il castello degli invalidi* may yet materialize.

To return to the known facts about Donizetti's stay in Palermo: the performances of *Alahor in Granata* were terminated on 25 January 1826 by the departure of Ferron the following day. Donizetti himself left Palermo on 14 February, even though the season would struggle on until 18 February, when it ended because the pope had decreed that the Jubilee of 1825 would be extended through Lent of 1826.

Back in Naples Donizetti had no commitment until June, when *Don Gregorio*, as the Neapolitan version of *L'ajo nell'imbarazzo* was called, went on stage. His year in Palermo marked the lowest point of his career as an operatic composer. His sense of the precariousness of his situation – theaters that closed for reasons he could not control, theaters that were mismanaged when they were open, an apathetic public, indisposed and ill-disposed singers – produced a sense of frustration that was somewhat mollified by news from Mayr that he had been honored by the Unione Filarmonica in Bergamo. He responded to this news in a letter to Mayr on 30 May: 'I have heard of things from another world...How the world lives by illusions! There they celebrate and honor one who has no other merit than to have been away from home for a few years.'[101]

Earlier in the same letter he had reported on Bellini's coming debut at the San Carlo: 'Due to be performed this evening is *Bianca e Gernando* (Fernando, no, because it is naughty)[102] by our Bellini, his first work.[103] Beautiful, beautiful, beautiful, especially since it is the first time he writes. It is unfortunately beautiful, as I give *Don Gregorio* in two weeks' time.'[104] *Don Gregorio* made its bow at the Teatro Nuovo on 11 June 1826, and was received with delight. *L'ajo nell'imbarazzo*, with the score frequently modified as was the custom in that adaptive age, was the first of Donizetti's scores to be widely produced, and almost everywhere successfully – one notable exception being the production at Bergamo in 1830, prepared by Mayr himself, which was a solemn fiasco.

The weeks after the Neapolitan *prima* of *Don Gregorio* were hectic ones for Donizetti, but he always thrived on activity. The Neapolitan *prima* of *Alahor in Granata* was scheduled for 21 June at the San Carlo, but the rehearsals were suspended so that the tenor Berardo Winter, who had created the role of Alamor[105] in Palermo the previous January, could come on from Milan to make his local debut. In the meantime another opera by Donizetti on a similar subject, the warfare between the Spaniards and the Moors, had its *prima* at the San Carlo on 6 July 1826, the birthday of the queen-mother. *Elvida* is, unusually, a one-act opera seria, for the libretto of which Giovanni Schmidt used the same kind of material that had yielded the subjects for *Alahor* and the earlier *Zoraida*. Donizetti tried to disguise the staleness of this overworked vein by writing exceptionally florid music for the agile voices of Henriette (known in Italy as Enrichetta) Méric-Lalande and Rubini, crowned by a bravura duet for the final *rondò*. There were even practicable catapults on stage to divert the audience. Although the first performance of *Elvida* was a royal gala and the work was applauded, it soon disappeared. And then hard on the heels of *Elvida* came *Alahor in Granata*, on 19 July; but the two operas so similar in subject seemed to have canceled each other out.

Donizetti had no illusions about them. Of *Elvida* he had written to Mayr: 'It is no great thing to tell the truth, but if I catch their fancy with Rubini's cavatina and the quartet, that will be enough for me.'[106] Of *Alahor* he reported to his father: 'It did not make a great impression. All that pleased was the overture, the cavatina of the prima donna, the tenor's aria and the final *rondò*,[107] but for Naples that is not enough – here they want everything excellent. Suffice it then: whistles, no; applause, yes.'[108]

Besides all his activity in the theaters at this time, Donizetti was composing still another opera. As he reported to Mayr: 'for my diversion I am writing the *Gabriella* of Carafa; I know the music is beautiful . . . I was seized by the desire and now I am satisfying myself.'[109] That Donizetti should compose an opera for which he had neither signed a contract nor made any plans for a production is striking indeed.[110] He adopted the libretto Tottola had written some ten years before, a text that is derived from de Belloy's play of the same name (Paris, 1777)[111] because he felt compelled to attempt a drama dealing with violent situations that came to a tragic conclusion. It is not surprising that while he was having to cope with the over-exploited dramatic conventions that lie at the heart of *Elvida* and *Alahor* he should have felt the impulse to try his hand at stronger stuff.

It is not overstating the case to maintain that the 1826 *Gabriella* was for Donizetti the first clear step in his effort to free Italian opera from conventional restraints and to push it ahead into the world of Romantic melodrama. He was preparing himself for what was to be a long, largely undercover, struggle with the Neapolitan censors, a struggle that was finally to drive him from that city in disgust. The Neapolitan censors of the 1820s and 1830s were concerned with more than changing the name of Fernando to Gernando to protect royal sensibilities and more than suppressing plots dealing with conspiracies or religious characters. They sincerely believed that plots should be morally uplifting, and that the depiction of violence on stage was detrimental to the public welfare. The Neapolitan censors retained a marked preference, more insistent after 1832, for happy endings, as they believed they affirmed the status quo and upheld the principle that benevolent intervention could reconcile differences.

That *Gabriella di Vergy* was something more than a means of channeling Donizetti's excess creative energy in 1826 has recently been demonstrated by the discovery of his 1838 version – a thorough revision – of that score.[112] That he returned to this work at the height of his powers, when the transitional period that first attracted him to the plot was long past, indicates that its tragic violence appealed to something fundamental in Donizetti's dramatic vision. He made the significant shift of changing the role of Raoul from a *musico* part into one for a leading tenor, demonstrating that he had left behind the outmoded concept of *travesti* vocal types. A third version of the opera, entitled simply *Gabriella,* was sung at the San Carlo in 1869, twenty-one years after Donizetti's death; this was a *rifacimento* compiled by Giuseppe Puzone and Paolo Serrao, then co-directors of that theater, who utilized parts of both the 1826 and 1838 versions as well as music from some of Donizetti's cantatas and from some of his by then forgotten operas.

After all this strenuous activity in June and July of 1826, Donizetti fell ill, but whether this sickness had any connection with his future medical history is unclear. On 11 August 1826 he writes that he has been stricken by 'a most tiresome fever that only today seems to have left me'.[113] This fever appears to have put him in low spirits, for in the surviving fragment of a letter to Toto Vasselli he says: 'I shall certainly not complete half my career . . . I feel that very strongly.'[114] On the last day of August 1826 he left Naples for Rome, where he signed a contract with Aniceto Pistoni for an opera buffa to be given at the Teatro Valle during the coming Carnival season.

There is some possibility that Donizetti had made a quick trip to Rome earlier in 1826, possibly during Lent when the theaters were still closed owing to the extension of the Jubilee of the year before. One reason for thinking so is that the scherzo on themes from his works, which he dedicated to Virginia Vasselli, includes nothing later than *Alahor,* which was first performed in January 1826. Considering the comprehensive coverage of his works represented by the scherzo, it seems reasonable to suppose that, since it contains no quotation from *Elvida,* it was composed before that opera was far advanced, and certainly before its *prima* on 6 July 1826. The dedication of the scherzo, which is undated, reads: 'alla Sig.ra Virginia Vasselli', then, after a considerable space, 'Roma'; the last word probably refers to Donizetti's whereabouts at the time of writing, though it might simply indicate Virginia's home. However, since Gaetano obviously regarded the scherzo as a symbol of his offering to Virginia all he had so far written, it is difficult to believe that he would not personally have placed it in her hands. The possibility that Gaetano visited Rome early in 1826 is also suggested by a letter that Toto wrote to him in 1837 shortly after Virginia's death, which contains the sentence: 'Remember that July evening in 1826 in Piazza Colonna when I promised you Virginia?'[115] It seems almost certain that Toto misremembered the month, for during July Gaetano was deeply involved at the San Carlo with both *Elvida* and *Alahor.* While it could, of course, be a mistake for a later month, it could as well have been one earlier than July. (When in 1826 Toto, as he says, 'promised' Virginia to Gaetano, he was not yet head of the family: his father did not die until 1832. What he probably promised was his all-important support to Gaetano's formal request for Virginia's hand.)

When Donizetti went to Rome in early September 1826 he began a five-month sojourn. During this stay he composed a new opera for the Teatro Valle, *Olivo e Pasquale*, to a libretto by Ferretti. By 30 September he could report to Mayr that he had sketched his score (that is, without completing the orchestration) as far as the middle of Act 2. The rest of his time in Rome seems to have been devoted to his courtship of Virginia. Besides the earlier scherzo for violin and piano he also composed and dedicated to her a duet for two sopranos,[116] three days after her eighteenth birthday and one day after his own twenty-ninth.

The actual date of Gaetano's formal proposal for Virginia's hand cannot now be identified, but it surely belongs to this stay in Rome, for by the following May the terms of her dowry were well under discussion. To secure his financial position and to make his marriage feasible he had signed in Naples a demanding contract with Barbaja calling for four operas a year for the next three years; for these works he would receive a monthly stipend of 200 ducats. In addition he would be paid 50 *scudi* a month as musical director of the Teatro Nuovo, in charge of musical preparation of the repertory and responsible to the management if problems arose. Since 1822 Naples had been the primary scene of Donizetti's labors and this new contract would tie him even more closely to that city.

Before he left Rome to assume his new duties, he brought out *Olivo e Pasquale* at the Teatro Valle on 7 January 1827.[117] This first production of *Olivo* was rather coolly received because of the inaptitude of the prima donna Emilia Bonini; moreover the text of the opera was not satisfactory, Ferretti having created a rather loosely constructed libretto based principally on one play by Sografi, but with the insertion of a single episode from another. However, the opera was at least a succès d'estime, for it managed to hold the stage until 5 February. It enjoyed fairly frequent productions for about a decade and continued to be staged until about 1869; nor were its performances confined to Italy: it was given in Spain, Portugal, Germany, Austria and England. (At the time of writing, it has never, apparently, been performed in the United States; it received its first modern performance at Barga during summer 1980 in a version by Bruno Rigacci.) An opera dealing with contrasts of character, *Olivo e*

Pasquale contains a fine quartet for tenor and three basses at the close of Act 1 part i, and a charming duet in Act 2 where the wealthy and kind-hearted suitor Le Bross realizes that Isabella genuinely loves another and agrees to help her attain her heart's desire. One of the causes of the tepid reception of the first production – the use of a mezzo-soprano for the part of Camillo, the young merchant Isabella loves – was corrected by Donizetti when the opera was given at the Teatro Nuovo from 1 September 1827; for this performance he recast the role for the tenor Regoli and also made other changes in the score.

Donizetti left Rome for Naples before the middle of January 1827 to undertake his new responsibilities for Barbaja. The first of the operas required by his new contract, *Otto mesi in due ore*, had its *prima* at the Teatro Nuovo on 13 May 1827. (This work was sometimes given under the alternate title of *Gli esiliati in Siberia*, as at La Scala in September 1831 – when it achieved a run of seventeen performances.) A significant result of Donizetti's new official connection with the Nuovo was the elaborate staging accorded *Otto mesi*. The day after the *prima* he wrote to his colleague Andrea Monteleone in Palermo about his new work, and the first thing he mentions is the excellence of the stage machinery, the scenery and the costumes. When he suggests that *Otto mesi* is a work that Monteleone might want to recommend for the Teatro Carolino, he cautions: 'large-scale effects are needed, that is, a flood, illuminations and a stage band, etc.'.[118] The ingredient of spectacle, however naive, in *Otto mesi* is indicative of Donizetti's continuing efforts during these years to expand his technical control of a wide variety of theatrical situations and effects. Donizetti was a composer of the theater in a sense that neither Rossini nor Bellini was; that is, he tried always to bring music and drama into a closer, more direct conjunction than his great contemporaries. *Otto mesi in due ore* is a clear case of his search to do this; it is a direct adaptation of a play by Luigi Marchionni,[119] *La figlia dell'esiliato, ossia Otto mesi in due ore*,[120] that had been a hit at the Teatro dei Fiorentini not long before.

Otto mesi brought Donizetti into collaboration with a new librettist, Domenico Gilardoni,[121] who would supply him with ten further librettos in the next four years; for a while Gilardoni became, in effect, Donizetti's official Neapolitan librettist, a function that, from the time of *Lucia*, was assumed by Salvatore Cammarano. *Otto mesi* proved to be the most successful of his Neapolitan operas up to this point, attaining a run of fifty performances. (In 1833 he was to revise it, but in this version it seems not to have equaled its initial effectiveness.)[122] Outside Naples, too, *Otto mesi* enjoyed considerable vitality for a couple of decades, being given in various Italian cities and in Spain, Portugal, Germany and Austria; (it has never been performed in France,[123] England or the United States). It earned a special reclame at Modena in 1831, when, during a local uprising, the public, in the absence of an official anthem for their cause, took over the tune of the Act 3 march from Donizetti's score.

On 25 May 1827 Donizetti wrote a letter to his father which shows how his marriage plans were progressing.

I hope to find you less displeased now that you know the name of the young lady that perhaps I will marry, because I certainly could not have found a better one as to character; I will not say beauty because that lasts only a little while. Now I want you to know that they give me 2000 *colonati* payable in three years; that is, for three years yet one only receives six percent interest. Afterward I am master of the full amount to place it where I please; earlier no, because the contract her father made with the bankers was for six years and only three have passed. There is another 1000 worth of household goods and silverware for her; therefore it seems to me that a man who does not have a penny could afford to marry her. And last, what more would other girls have? And then, who knows, but I might come and settle with you and the family? The young lady does what I want, so...?[124]

This letter demonstrates Donizetti's knack for diplomacy. At some earlier time Andrea must have responded with objections to the news that Gaetano planned to marry, afraid that his son, whom he had not seen for years, would establish his home at Naples or some other distant point and would soon become less inclined to give financial support to his parents. To ease his father's anxieties Donizetti spells out the terms of the marriage settlement and, to the same end, throws out the suggestion that he might settle in Bergamo again. For all the genuine love Donizetti retained for his birthplace, there is no confirmation that he ever seriously, or for very long, considered such a move. After Virginia married him she never went to Bergamo nor met her husband's family. From this it would seem that he was not particularly anxious to bring them together or to have his wife see the humble circumstances in which he had been born and in which his family still lived. On the only occasion when a proposal was made for such a meeting, an invitation was issued to Andrea, and to none of the others, to come to Naples.

There were reasons for Andrea's worry at this period over his sons and their ability to help him out financially from time to time. Giuseppe was married and the father of a son, Andrea;[125] he was then living in Sardinia but was soon to move on to Constantinople, much to his father's consternation. The other brother, Francesco, was living at home without any particular employment, a drain on the family rather than an asset to it. It was to Gaetano that his father looked first for financial help. Many of Donizetti's letters deal with this ongoing problem. On 21 July 1826 he responds to one of his father's frequent requests for money, first by telling him the exact sums he has received for his recent works, and then by assuring him that 'in every case I will try to help you as best I can'.[126] And again: 'I am sorry you are in such critical circumstances', followed by two lines heavily crossed out, and going on: 'I believe that in the account I sent the 20 ducats should equal precisely 100 *svantziche*.[127] After Genoa I hope to send you something more.'[128] Although his father could be selfish and stubborn, and must have been difficult to love, Donizetti treated him with almost unvarying patience and generosity; he never wavered in his filial duty and the old man's death in 1835 distressed him deeply.

At his post in Naples, Donizetti continued to turn out operas to satisfy the terms of his contract. At the Teatro del Fondo on 19 August 1827 *Il borgomastro di Saardam* appeared. The libretto, by Gilardoni, deals with the same plot as that of Lortzing's *Zar und Zimmermann* (Leipzig, 1837) and derives from a French melodrama of 1818, *Le bourgmestre de Sardam*. For the *prima* the role of Marietta was entrusted to one of the leading prima donnas of the day, whom Barbaja had recently brought to Italy – Carolina Ungher.[129] *Il borgomastro* was well received in Naples and ran for more than thirty-five nights. The Neapolitan public was undeniably well disposed toward Donizetti, and they had the advantage of seeing his opera produced under his supervision and sung by casts that been rehearsed by him. How great a difference these circumstances made is shown by the fact that at La Scala, with Ungher repeating her role of Marietta for her debut there, surrounded by a mediocre cast, *Il borgomastro* was an utter failure, receiving only a single performance. Bellini, who was in Milan at the time and was a popular figure there following the great success of his *Il pirata* at La Scala the previous October, wrote to his friend Florimo about the dress rehearsal of *Il borgomastro*: 'in the first act there is nothing, in the second a duet that might please, but as a whole the work will be a fiasco'.[130] In contrast to the high Romanticism of *Il pirata*, the gentle charm and the generalized buffa formulas of Donizetti's opera must have seemed old-fashioned.

(The opera continued to be performed until about 1840; it then dropped from sight until 1973, when, unexpectedly, it became a candidate for resuscitation in the current revival of Donizetti's operas. Burdened with a clumsy libretto, the score is uneven but shows frequent signs of careful workmanship. The opera made its twentieth-century debut, appropriately enough, at Zaandam (formerly Saardam) in Holland.)

If with *Il borgomastro* Donizetti had not yet found the way to imprint his own personality fully upon the tradition of opera buffa, with his next work, a farsa, he was to do just that. He refers to his new project in a letter to his father: 'I am engaged in writing a farsa for my benefit evening that I shall give in November, and all this is to attract the public.'[131] The farsa was to be *Le convenienze teatrali*, and it proved a significant advance for Donizetti as a composer of operatic comedy. For it, Donizetti turned his hand to libretto-writing, fashioning his text from a comedy by Sografi. The plot concerns the vagaries of temperament and the manifold vicissitudes that can beset a rehearsal of an opera seria in a provincial theater. Opera satirizing itself was scarcely a novel subject in 1827 (indeed the opening episode of *Il fortunato inganno* of 1823 can be seen as a preparatory sketch for *Le convenienze*), but by now Donizetti had accrued enough firsthand experience to throw himself into his farsa with great vivacity. His libretto is full of verbal felicity, testifying to his genuine flair for versifying and to his high spirits in the months preceding his marriage. His letter to his father shows his concern for raising money at his benefit evening, and it is quite possible he was tempted to turn librettist not just to provide himself with the satire he wanted but to earn a double fee. Whatever his motives, the quality of this libretto and of those he was later to write for *Il campanello* and *Betly* make one wish he had made more frequent use of his ready talent for verse. If one takes a larger view, however, *Le convenienze* can be appreciated as a milestone in Donizetti's efforts to free himself from the conservatism that held back the development of Italian opera, at least in Naples, during the 1820s. In this farsa he not only satirizes the foibles and pretensions of the personnel of the theater but, at the moment when the cast assembles for the run-through of the opera seria, he exposes the weakness and pomposity of that exhausted genre.

Le convenienze enjoyed a fine success. It had its *prima* at the Teatro Nuovo on 21 November 1827, with Gennaro Luzio[132] *en travesti* as Mamm'Agata,[133] the irrepressible mother of Luigia, the Seconda Donna, enjoying one of the greatest successes of his distinguished career. In 1831 *Le convenienze* was still playing in Naples, but now at the Fondo, where Berlioz heard it. 'At the Fondo opera buffa is played with such fire, spirit and *brio* as to raise it above almost every theater of its class. While I was at Naples they were performing a most amusing farsa by Donizetti, *Le convenienze teatrali.*'[134] Donizetti later expanded this work into two acts, drawing on a companion play by Sografi, and made substantial changes in the plot and characters and retitled it *Le convenienze ed inconvenienze teatrali*. A non-autograph manuscript in the Conservatorio di Musica, Milan, shows the revisions made for a production at the Teatro Canobbiana, where from 20 April 1831 it ran for twenty-two nights. Yet when it was put on at the Kärntnertor in 1840 and at La Scala in 1842 it survived for only one performance on both occasions, suggesting that by the 1840s the satire had come to seem less relevant. Donizetti's continuing affection for the work is shown by his considering a further revision of it, but this was in 1845, at a time when the deterioration of his health prevented his carrying out his intention. (In recent years, however, *Le convenienze*, under a wide range of titles, has enjoyed a vigorous new lease on life.)[135]

A month and a half after the *prima* of *Le convenienze*, Donizetti won one of the greatest successes of this period of his career with *L'esule di Roma*, to a libretto by Gilardoni, based on an adaptation by Marchionni of a French play; the censors insisted on the addition of *Il proscritto* ('The outlaw') to the title, for although the action was set in the time of Tiberius, political exiles from Rome and elsewhere in Italy were common enough in the 1820s and 1830s for the censors to be nervous about any possible allusion to them. The new opera, given at the San Carlo on 1 January 1828, was greeted with enthusiasm, particularly the trio at the end of Act 1. Rossini is supposed to have said that it alone would suffice to make a composer's reputation. Donizetti saw the use of a trio, even a fairly conventional one, instead of the customary concertato to end the first act of a two-act opera seria[136] as a step in extricating himself from long-established tradition. He wrote to Mayr with contagious exhilaration:

Next year I will finish a first act with a quartet and the second act with a death, according to my intention. I want to shake off the yoke of the finales . . . but for now to finish with a trio, never again, since everybody tells me that were I to die and to return to the womb of Signora Domenica and be born again, I could not equal it . . . I am encouraged and feel myself capable of better things.[137]

When Donizetti writes of finishing a second act with a death, it recalls his *Gabriella di Vergy* project of two years before, and communicates his eagerness to expand the range of subject matter and to escape from the inadequate motivation all too common in the happy endings which were then the order of the day. That it took Donizetti until 1830 – with *Anna Bolena*, significantly an opera composed for Milan not Naples – to demonstrate conclusively that he had embarked upon a new path makes it seem that he took an unconscionably long time to find himself; but it seems less excessive when the strangling conservatism of the theaters, the censors and the public are taken into account. Increasing familiarity with the operas Donizetti wrote before *Anna Bolena* reveals that achievement in a new perspective as the logical culmination of tendencies present in his work from the beginning, and not as a sudden, scarcely anticipated step from mediocrity into greatness, not as the sudden throwing-off of a consciously adopted *rossinianismo* from which he emerged abruptly as his own man. *L'esule di Roma* is an important landmark along this road: it shows signs of Donizetti's awareness of the need to loosen the conservative vise, and of his growing desire to choose genuinely affecting and gripping subjects with tragic conclusions.

At first glance *L'esule di Roma* seems to be almost a compendium of the structural formulas then in vogue, the trio at the end of Act 1 aside; but the score repays a closer, more sympathetic look. It is one of the two Donizetti operas (the other is *Fausta*) to be set in ancient Rome, and there are indications, as in a chorus that starts off bravely as a canon, that he deliberately tried to give the work a neo-classic flavor. The bass role of Murena, tailored to the vocal and histrionic talents of Lablache, deserves attention as Donizetti's first full-length portrait of a disordered mind. If the happy ending of the work today seems chillingly contrived, it must be remembered that the affirmation of justice prevailing was the note insisted upon then at gala evenings at the San Carlo.

L'esule di Roma received its second production at La Scala[138] in July 1828, after the censor Monsignor Rolla had made numerous changes in the text. Francesco Pezzi, the critic of the *Gazzetta di Milano* (15 July 1828), judged the opera with characteristic grimness.

In a trio, a duet, and in the *largo* of an aria one recognizes an inspired pupil of Mayr; in the rest there is more reminiscence than inspiration. If rumor does not lie, *L'esule di Roma* made a furore on the stage at Naples. This reception justifies its choice for our theater. Donizetti's opera received applause from us as well.

If this applause was not a furore, it will be perhaps the fault of the air, less volcanic along the Olona than the Sebeto.[139]

In Naples on 16 January 1828 Donizetti signed a further contract with Barbaja for two new operas, each of them to bring him 500 ducats, a clear acknowledgment that the success of *L'esule* had furthered the composer's career. On the same day that this contract was signed, Bellini in Milan, still buoyed up by his success with *Il pirata* and still gloating over the fiasco of *Il borgomastro* at La Scala two weeks before, wrote to Florimo: 'I believe Donizetti has been forced to take two bottles of Le Roy to make his anger pass.'[140] Bellini's spite was aroused, as it was to be on several future occasions, by the prospect of competing directly with Donizetti when they were both presenting new operas in the same season at the same theater. In May of 1828 they would both be in Genoa for the inauguration of the new Teatro Carlo Felice. For his part, Donizetti was on the crest of the wave. Exhilarated by the Neapolitan reception of *L'esule* and eager to stop off in Rome to see Virginia on his way to Genoa, he needed no physic.

At Genoa, for the opening of the new opera house, a gala season had been planned, featuring works by Rossini, Bellini, Donizetti and Morlacchi.[141] Of this group, Bellini was the only southern Italian and the only one of the four who had not studied with Padre Mattei at Bologna. Rossini did not go to Genoa from Paris, but the three others were present to stage their operas, two of which were *prime*: Morlacchi's work in praise of Genoa's most prominent son, *Colombo*, and Donizetti's *Alina, regina di Golconda*. Donizetti's new opera was to have a libretto by Felice Romani, whose recent text for *Il pirata* had set him unchallenged at the head of the librettists of the day. Donizetti had worked with him before, on the ill-fated *Chiara e Serafina* of 1822, and had learned by painful experience that punctuality was not Romani's long suit; in fact Donizetti was not to receive the libretto of *Alina* until after he arrived in Genoa at the end of February 1828. Writing from Rome on 2 February, Donizetti tells Mayr of his frustration: 'That Romani, who promises everything, keeps his word about nothing! [*che tutto promette, nulla mantiene!*] I have written to him; he does not answer. He chose the subject, and it does not please me too much.'[142] Then he goes on to give Mayr a sketch of Virginia:

The one chosen to be my companion in life is more than worthy of me. She is the daughter of excellent parents, educated as a lady, one who without making an issue of it knows how to adapt herself to every situation, one who has never got herself talked about, one who respects me and loves me when I am both far and near.[143]

After his happy days in Rome near Virginia, Gaetano arrived in Genoa on the morning of 28 February 1828. That evening he wrote to his father, feeling both exhausted from his trip and upset because his brother Giuseppe, whom he had hoped to see, had already sailed for Turkey. Genoa seemed to him a less hospitable place than Naples:

Here they do not have too good an opinion of me because of the fiasco of the opera [Il borgomastro] in Milan that had pleased so much in Naples. Perhaps it is better. The libretto, however, is truly a great pastiche, and tell M[aestr]o. Mayr that Romani has served me in his fashion.

I expect, nonetheless, something agreeable to come of it, and I hope it will prove so. In April[144] I put on my opera and afterward leave at once for Naples, where I feel better than excellent. If I am able to make three *soldi* a day, I will prefer it to traveling and writing for the theater.[145]

Donizetti's mention of leaving 'at once for Naples' after he had seen his new opera through its first three performances is an intentional falsehood. He hoped to put his father off the scent about his approaching marriage and had decided to notify him of it after the event.

The season opened on 7 April 1828 (Easter Monday) with a gala. The first music heard in the Teatro Carlo Felice was Donizetti's 'melodious and well-sung' hymn for the occasion,[146] a compliment to the royal house of Savoy, which was present in force. The evening continued with a performance of Bellini's *Bianca e Fernando*;[147] but the greatest applause went not to the singers but to the ballerina Elisa Vaque-Moulin, who appeared in a ballet between the acts of the opera.[148]

Bellini's letters of this period reveal his suspicions concerning Donizetti. The prima donna Adelaide Tosi[149] was not particularly happy with her final cavatina in *Bianca*, and she showed it to Donizetti, who, being familiar with her voice from Naples, made some suggestions, all of which Bellini took amiss, seeing it as a plot against him.[150] 'It is completely impossible to have friendships in the same profession':[151] that is Bellini's summary of his feelings toward his rivals. For his part, Donizetti shared nothing of Bellini's neurasthenic malice, and his attitude toward his fellow operatic composers was, on the whole, generous and supportive. He fully understood the many contingencies that could compromise a success in the theater, and he hoped to see his profession gain in prestige. He was not a man to bear grudges, even against those who maligned him or treated him unfairly.

The Genoese season of 1828 did not enjoy unalloyed success. The singers formed two overlapping companies, one for serious operas and one for opera buffa. As *Alina* was a comedy, Donizetti was, as Bellini gleefully reported to Florimo, 'extremely agitated'[152] by the weakness of the second troupe, and he managed to have the prima donna Letizia Cortesi, who was ill suited to opera buffa, replaced before his new work went into rehearsal. Feeling confident that *Alina* would fail, Bellini left Genoa before the opera had its first performance; it was given on 12 May 1828 with Serafina Rubini[153] in the title role, and it survived a total of thirteen performances.

Three days after the *prima*, Donizetti sent Mayr a picture of recent events:

In just seven days I was obliged to prepare my opera because the gentlemen directors had told His Majesty that it would be put on on Monday, and they were performing an opera every evening. *Basta!* When heaven wants to grant protection one can go on even without rehearsals, and my *Alina* received a most happy reception. His Majesty had the complacency to applaud . . . I could have been better pleased. The tenor [Verger][154] was sick, the prima donna was – *basta*. Even with all this the singers were called out twice and the composer twice. I swear to you that the disorder at the general rehearsal, held the same morning as the first performance and lasting until three, made me believe that I would be clubbed to death.[155]

While this letter explains the unpropitious circumstances that endangered the opening run of *Alina*, the gaiety and charm that frequently enliven the score kept it on the stage through most of the nineteenth century, until 1891.[156] *Alina* was revised by Donizetti for its Roman *prima*, at the Teatro Valle on 10 October 1829 – a production he supervised personally – and it is in this form that the opera made its way. (*Alina* seems never to have been given in either the United States or England. That this, the best of Donizetti's comedies between *L'ajo nell'imbarazzo* and *L'elisir d'amore*, has not yet attracted the attention of the Donizetti revivalists is surprising indeed.)

Before he left Genoa on 19 May, Donizetti composed a a cabaletta for the Pamira–Maometto duet to go into Act 2 of Rossini's *L'assedio di Corinto*.[157] This cabaletta, 'Pietoso all'amor mio', was much applauded at its first performance by Tosi and Tamburini, and it was included in a number of later performances of Rossini's score in Italy.

In the same letter in which Donizetti told Mayr about the *prima* of *Alina*, another passage stands out, particularly in view of Gaetano's plan to leave Genoa and go directly to Rome and marry Virginia.

I wanted to leave Saturday, but the courier is delayed and therefore it will be Monday. The disappointment of not being able to see you is greater for me, dear Maestro, particularly as I had set great store by it. But what can I do? On 16 August I must put on an opera [in Naples], and the subject is not even decided yet. I do not live for profit, but honor, and I assure you that could I write a *Medea*,[158] I would be content to die afterward. I am making you a little souvenir of my music, including *L'esule* and various other pieces that have pleased me in Naples. Among them there is the *Ugolino*[159] of Dante. It has received some indulgence, but I want yours . . . I hope to give you my news from Naples soon.[160]

Donizetti's decision not to mention his approaching marriage to the man he called his 'second father' is consistent with his determination to wait until after it had taken place to mention it to his 'first' father. Donizetti had no desire to argue with Andrea in Bergamo just then, nor did he want to postpone his arrival in Rome.

Gaetano Donizetti married Virginia Vasselli on Sunday, 1 June 1828 in the church of Santa Maria in Via, with Antonio Vasselli and Giovanni Battista Zampi as witnesses.[161] In a few days the newly married couple left for Naples with their household goods, including a piano, and moved into an apartment on the third floor of Vico Nardones, no. 6. The only extant letter from Donizetti to his father that deals with his marriage was written on 19 July 1828, seven weeks after the event. In it he tries to make peace with the offended old man.

I do not thank you for the letter you have written me . . . I understand that you might have been offended not to have been present at the wedding, but I believed that I would spare you the expense and send you with a single letter news of both your children,[162] but my consideration was not understood. You say further that you know more about politeness than I do (and this may be so, too), but I have shared news of this blessed marriage with you for a long time now; therefore I think I have not failed in any great measure.

If for now I cannot send you a portrait of my wife, I do send you her handwriting,[163] for she wants to write to you, so be patient for now. Whether you see her or not is up to you, since you would be welcome both here and at Rome, and I will arrange to pay your way home. Therefore make an effort. At the first of October, her papa and her brother will look for you, you will see Rome, you will come here and leave together. After all, we are not *in finibus terrae*. Take courage. To come to Rome requires only a few *bajocchi*. When you are there, I assure you, you will not need one penny more. Apply for a leave of three months, and everything is arranged. Now we will see if you are a man of your word . . . I beg you to keep this invitation to yourself and not to extend it to Francesco, for then the affair changes aspect.[164]

To this letter Virginia adds a few formal lines of greeting to

Gaetano's parents and expresses her hope that Andrea will indeed make the effort. Apparently Andrea did not undertake the proposed trip, because on 21 October Donizetti acknowledges his father's complaints that he is lazy about writing and assures him that no news is good.[165]

His first operatic activity upon his return to Naples was the production of another new work, *Gianni di Calais*, first staged at the Teatro del Fondo on 2 August 1828. With Rubini in the title role and Tamburini, who was much admired for his singing of the barcarolle in Act 1, the opera kept the stage for some time. Its luck held when it was produced at the Carcano in Milan exactly a week after the triumphant *prima* of *Anna Bolena*, with Rubini repeating his Neapolitan success as Gianni. But despite the famous tenor's fondness for this role, the work failed to produce an impression in Paris, when, in 1833, he persuaded the management of the Théâtre-Italien to put it on for him.[166] (After a few years *Gianni di Calais* disappeared from view into the obscurity that remains undisturbed until now, but the experience of the last two decades prevents one from assuming that any score of Donizetti's is immune to revival.)

At some point during the fall of 1828 Barbaja offered Donizetti the post of musical director of the royal theaters of Naples, a promotion from his duties at the Nuovo. Donizetti sent his father in Bergamo his reactions to this offer.

Next year Barbaja wants me to become musical director of the royal theaters, but here after Rossini no one has discharged those duties well; that is, he routed his enemies with his operas, while on the other hand Mercadante and Pacini only added to their enemies. Therefore the public says that the director sends into confusion all the operas written by others in order to bring himself alone into prominence. I do not know if I will accept.[167]

In 1829 Donizetti did assume that post and held it until his departure from Naples in 1838.

The exact date of the first performance of the one-act farsa, *Il giovedì grasso*, which is traditionally listed as Donizetti's next opera, was until recently unknown. In a letter of 21 October, referring to his current project, Donizetti tells his father: 'I am composing but I do not know for when, perhaps for the end of December, awaiting Lablache from Milan.'[168] Lablache was singing in almost every performance at La Scala that autumn, an engagement that could not have terminated before 1 December at the earliest.[169] He was, at all events, in Naples in time to learn and rehearse his role in *Il paria*, given in January; it was not until six weeks later that *Il giovedì grasso* came to the stage – at the Fondo, probably on 26 February 1829.[170]

Il giovedì grasso is set to a libretto by Gilardoni, derived from a comedy by Scribe and Delestre-Poirson, *Le nouveau Pourceaugnac* (Paris, 1817). It is one of that group of *farse* that have spoken dialogue and a buffo role in Neapolitan dialect; but what sets it off from the others of this genre in the Donizetti oeuvre is the beguiling charm of its characters. (During the nineteenth century it had few performances outside Naples and those it had were confined to the decade following its first appearance. The neglect of this ingratiating work was reversed when Bruno Rigacci brought it out at the Teatro de' Rinnovati, Siena, in 1959. Since then a concert version has been broadcast by Radio Monteceneri (in 1962), and it has been staged at Bergamo, Bologna and Wexford. In February 1971 it entered the repertory of the Piccola Scala.)

Donizetti's depressed state of mind at the end of 1828 darkens the letter he addressed to his father on 30 December.

Also this year is over, thank God, without disasters . . . I learned from your letter of your troubles, and especially the illness of mamma, and of the death of the good Maestro's mother-in-law.[171] These things I have been feeling very much . . . It displeased me that little Andrea does not show talent for music,[172] after all the praise I have heard from Giuseppe. Remember that he should change his occupation at once, so that he will not remain among the mediocrities as I do . . . I will go on stage with my new opera at the Teatro San Carlo on the 12th, title: *Il paria*.[173]

Donizetti's view of himself as 'among the mediocrities' is more than an ironical reflection upon his nephew Andrea's incapacity for music.[174] Donizetti's innate buoyancy was temporarily sapped by poor health, but, even more, he felt galled that the enthusiasm he could arouse in Naples still eluded him in Milan. The previous May he had exposed his bitterness on this subject to Mayr: 'Though I die of hunger I will not compose even one appoggiatura for Milan. I have said it, I have said it and I have taken a deep breath.'[175]

The Neapolitan response to *Il paria* when it had its *prima* at the San Carlo on 12 January 1829 was respectful rather than genuinely enthusiastic, although it is the most carefully worked out of all Donizetti's scores up to this time. Strongly cast, with Tosi, Rubini and Lablache in leading roles, the opera failed to meet the expectations Donizetti had for it. *Il paria* is set in India, Gilardoni's uncommonly expressive libretto being drawn from Casimir Delavigne's dreary tragedy, *Le paria* (Paris, 1821).[176] The score contains nothing one would identify as local color, but it reveals the composer's attention to expressive detail, as in the effectively asymmetrical phrases of Neala's entrance aria and the genuine ardor of the tenor's phrase 'La mano tua, deh vedi or che concedi' in the Act 2 love duet.

Donizetti's judgment of *Il paria* to his father is frank: 'I have given the opera and I was called out to acknowledge the applause. I declare, however, that I have miscalculated in several places, and I will make it good by adjusting the score.'[177] His 'adjustments' did not take the form one would naturally assume. Once *Il paria*'s original run of six performances was over, he withdrew the opera from circulation and used it as a mine for music to go into several of his later operas. Almost ten years later he refers in a somewhat exaggerated way to something of what he had done to *Il paria* in a letter dated 15 July 1838 to his brother-in-law Toto. The casual reader of Zavadini can easily miss the point, since Zavadini mistranscribed the title of the opera, causing the passage to read: 'Quanto al Patria in Poliuto'. What Donizetti says, denying a rumor that his newest opera was largely borrowed from his earlier score, is this:

As to *Paria* in *Poliuto*, go screw yourself. I am not the man to do such things! Anyway half of that score is in *Anna Bolena* and the other half is in *Tasso*, and I repeat I am not the man to do such things. *Poliuto* is completely, completely, or almost completely, new, except for the *adagio* of the first finale [borrowed from *Maria de Rudenz*]. The rest is absolutely new, and they have heard too much of my stuff at Naples, nor am I capable of such monkey-business [*scimear*].[178]

The whole question of Donizetti's self-borrowings, raised here by *Il paria*, is an exceedingly complex matter, requiring a whole book to do it full justice. Something of its complexity may be grasped from this example: the music accompanying Neala's Act 1 entrance in *Il paria* recurs in *Anna Bolena* at Anna's entrance for her duet with Percy, but in the later score it is much amplified and more fully developed; between these scores Donizetti had used a very similar idea in his overture to *Il diluvio universale*. And one never knows when further familiarity with Donizetti's many scores will yield other instances of this basic musical idea.

A few points about self-borrowing as it was then practised can put this matter in perspective. The composers of Donizetti's generation did not regard self-borrowing as a bad thing per se; to them an opera score was not a fixed entity, but rather a concatenation of interchangeable parts. With such a view, self-borrowing served a very pragmatic purpose, as long as it was done discreetly. Discretion lay in adherence to a few obvious rules of thumb. If a work had failed or had had only a brief run and seemed unlikely to be given again, then effective parts of it could be safely salvaged; or if familiarity with a work was restricted to a single place, then parts of it could be re-used in scores intended for other cities. By and large, but not always, Donizetti followed these principles, and his borrowing was not limited to putting pieces from one opera into another; sometimes he would adapt music from cantatas or songs for use in his opera scores. In his letter to his father of 19 January 1829 Donizetti sends a different sort of news: 'I believe we are going to increase our family . . . we shall see!'[179] Then, in the spring of 1829, while he was composing his next opera, *Elisabetta al castello di Kenilworth*,[180] he fell seriously ill. By 7 May 1829 he had recovered sufficiently to report to his father:

I write to you after the storm. I have been severely sick with convulsions, bilious attacks and, even worse, internal hemorrhoids, and as a result: bleedings, baths, purges, a regimen, and afterwards – I fell sick again. Now, however, the cure is making me well, and I am on my way to recovery. I was to have written for the San Carlo for 30 May, but my illness has made me postpone it to 6 July, the queen's gala.[181]

Beneath Gaetano's letter Virginia adds a note of her own, expressing her grave concern over his health and her hope that 'soon he will be completely recovered'. In the light of future events, this illness was more ominous than they knew.

Gaetano and Virginia remained in Naples for the launching of *Elisabetta al castello di Kenilworth*, which duly appeared at the San Carlo on 6 July 1829. Tottola's ungainly libretto has a devious provenance: its immediate source seems to be Gaetano Barbieri's play *Elisabetta al castello di Kenilworth*, itself an adaptation of Scribe's libretto for Auber's opera, *Leicester ou Le château de Kenilworth*, performed without success at the Opéra-Comique on 25 January 1823; and behind them all stands Walter Scott's novel.[182] On 24 July Donizetti reported to Mayr on the reception of his newest opera.

The fate of theatrical spectacles is always bizarre. I went on stage with *Castello di Kenilworth* the 6th of this month, at the gala for Her Majesty the Queen. And this opera that had been applauded so much at every piece during the dress rehearsal was almost rejected at its first performance. I suffered very much because of it, all the more for having seen the rehearsal of what should have been an excellent first performance. Or perhaps it was the court etiquette, because they do not applaud on such evenings . . . The opera ended up neither very well performed nor very well heeded by the audience. Then la Tosi fell sick, and only on the 12th was it given again . . . It was Sunday, a beautiful day, the theater packed, the singers in good spirits . . . I alone was uneasy. The King and Queen of Piedmont came and applauded. Prince Leopoldo came and did likewise. The King and

Queen of Naples came and did likewise. Thus the singers were full of animation, the public could express themselves, and the result of all this was continuous applause! We were all called on stage, and the evening was most brilliant . . . Between us, I would not give one piece of *Il paria* for all of *Il castello de Kenilworth* . . . but meanwhile: fate is bizarre.[183]

For all the success of the second evening, reported by Donizetti, the opera did not long hold the stage. After its initial run at the San Carlo it returned the following season, Donizetti having revised the score, but without making a deeper impression upon the public. (A solitary production at Madrid in 1835 sums up the nineteenth-century performance history of this work; a revival was performed in March 1977 by Opera Rara of London.) Donizetti's judgment that one piece of *Il paria* is worth the whole of *Il castello di Kenilworth* seems much too harsh: disregarding the dramatically ludicrous *Alfredo il grande* of 1823, this opera marks Donizetti's first major attempt at dealing with English history, an area that would prove particularly fruitful to him in the future.

Before the end of July 1829 Gaetano took Virginia to Rome so that she might be delivered of their baby in her family home. For this purpose Barbaja had granted Donizetti a six-week leave of absence. According to the birth certificate,[184] the baby was born on 29 July 'at the second hour of the night' and was christened Filippo Francesco Achille Cristino. On 11 August the infant died, after only thirteen days of life. That sad day Donizetti wrote to Barbaja asking for an extension of his leave of absence. His grief and agitation are manifest:

the blow you have dealt me asking me to return, dear Barbaja, is too cruel. You have granted me a month and a half, and it is only two weeks since I arrived. My wife you know needs at least forty days, and much more now, since tonight my son died. If truly you should need me I should want to help you out, but now for the 19th you have Guglielmi[185] and on 4 October there is Pacini. Gilardoni is working for him and cannot do anything for me. Why make me travel to Naples? *I have barely delivered and already you want me to get pregnant?*[186]

The clearest description of the melancholy events of these days is to be found in Donizetti's graphic letter to his father, written on 20 August.

Your congratulations have been most welcome to me, although they came too late. I say late since the baby after the twelfth day went up to heaven. The uncertainty of the pregnancy and the visit paid her by the best doctors of Naples, who denied the danger of miscarriage, caused her to follow the remedies prescribed by these beasts, and in spite of all this the baby was born at seven months. But he had a very broad vein on the top of his head that ran from one ear to the other across the top of his skull. The facts are that after seven days of life he went into convulsions, he twisted up his eyes, he did not eat any more, and after so short a life, barely prolonged by feeding him spoonsful of milk, he remained two days with his mouth closed and died. Better so than to have a boy devastated by illness. For they say had he recovered, at the least he would have remained crippled. Let us not say anything further about it.[187]

Any discussion of medical history a century and a half after the events must remain conjectural.[188] The consensus of the medical opinions I have consulted posits this diagnosis: at some point, probably not very long before his marriage, Donizetti contracted syphilis; the symptoms of his illness in the spring of 1829, in particular the convulsions, strongly suggest the primary invasion of his nervous system by syphilis. From this a regrettable conclusion seems unavoidable: that Gaetano infected Virginia, as her difficult pregnancy and the premature birth of the deformed child who lived not two weeks would seem to bear out. Tragic as these consequences were, it is only fair to observe that because Donizetti suffered from syphilis he was not necessarily any more of a libertine than a man of his time, his disposition, his profession, his opportunities, might be expected to be.

Barbaja apparently took the requested pity on Donizetti and extended his leave of absence from Naples so that Virginia could regain her strength and adjust to her loss with her family to comfort her. Donizetti remained in Rome until at least 10 October 1829, for on that date the revised *Alina*, a production he supervised personally, was first given at the Teatro Valle. Also, he contributed the final terzetto to a cantata, *Il genio dell'armonia*,[189] honoring the accession of Pope Pius VIII; the work was sung by the Accademia Filarmonica Romana on 20 December, but this was most likely after the Donizettis had made their melancholy return to Naples.

From Naples Donizetti reported to his father that he had been reading extensively the poetry of Lord 'Bayron', among other things, as background to his projected work about Noah and the flood, to be called *Il diluvio universale*. 'This time I want to show myself as inventor of the plan of the drama as well as the music.'[190] This is another of the many demonstrations of the very active role Donizetti customarily took in the preparation of the texts he set. The generic term then in common use for works like *Il diluvio universale* was 'azione tragica-sacra' rather than 'opera'; the same cumbersome term had been applied to Rossini's *Mosè in Egitto*, first given at the San Carlo during Lent 1818, which suggested this direction to Donizetti.

And as Rossini's opera had ended with the parting of the Red Sea, so Donizetti planned to end his with the spectacle of the ark floating on the flood.

His intention to create a monumental biblical drama did not succeed as Donizetti had hoped. The opening night, on 28 February, did not go well: Luigia Boccabadati,[191] singing the part of Sela, almost wrecked the first-act finale by coming in twenty bars too soon, although the conductor Nicola Festa[192] and Lablache, the Noè of the piece, succeeded in averting a complete collapse; most discouraging of all, the final tableau caused the audience to whistle in derision at the inadequate staging. Il diluvio had won enough favor with part of the public for it to hold the stage through the rest of Lent, but the San Carlo was never tempted to revive it. In winter 1833–4, Donizetti revised the work extensively for a production at the Carlo Felice in Genoa, stressing the operatic and dramatic aspects of the work and toning down its oratorio-like original form; and in this guise the work held the stage for thirteen performances before disappearing from the footlights forever.[193] That Donizetti was tempted to undertake such a work in the first place is evidence of his ambition to prove his versatility; that he was not tempted to repeat the experiment shows that he shrewdly understood that the vogue for Lenten azioni tragiche-sacre had passed.

A better demonstration of his versatility is that almost concurrently with Il diluvio he brought out at the San Carlo, for his benefit evening on 6 February 1830,[194] a one-act farsa entitled I pazzi per progetto. He composed this farsa for the unusual combination of two sopranos and five basses,[195] with no tenor. The text by Gilardoni was an adaptation of a play of the same name by Giovanni Carlo di Cosenza, which in turn stemmed from a French farce, Une visite à Bedlam. Donizetti informed his father that his farsa had been much applauded, adding: 'indeed this time I would rather have had less applause and more money, but because the Russian Minister gave a ball the same evening as my benefit the theater was half full'.[196] I pazzi per progetto held the stage for several seasons in Naples and in Palermo before it lapsed. (It, too, has shared in the recent Donizetti revival, being dusted off by Bruno Rigacci for a production at Barga in 1977.)

Besides reporting the public's response to I pazzi per progetto, Donizetti reacts in the same letter to the news that L'ajo nell'imbarazzo, even though Mayr himself had prepared the opera, had been a fiasco at Bergamo.

Bravo! Bravo, bravo! I really take a crazy relish that *L'ajo* has been a fiasco. Only the labor spent by the good, rather the excellent, Mayr displeases me, but for the rest I laugh at it. From there they whistle, and here I receive applause... *I pazzi per progetto* succeeded most brilliantly; that will be because I am well thought of here, but here everything I do goes well. And you others in Lombardy should never do my work, never, never. The newspapers have discredited me too much and you allow that to go on. I see for example that Ricci[197] made at Rome an indescribable fiasco with *Il sonnambulo* and now with *Fernando Cortes* a second fiasco. And yet if you consult the papers!

I gave *Alina*; all the papers cried fiasco. And yet one should speak the truth in the face of what everyone says, meanwhile my pieces are heard everywhere in society, all the singers insert them into other operas, even now in *Corradino* [Rossini's *Matilde di Shabran*], and in the same cities and in the same theater. And yet they say fiasco... Very well... I laugh at it myself.[198]

Again it is clear that Donizetti smarted under what he felt was the unfair treatment he received from north Italian critics. His determination to succeed would, before the year was out, bring him a sweet revenge.

It had been raining in Naples almost continuously since the previous October; in his letter to Mayr Donizetti says: 'Everyone tells me that since I started to compose *Il diluvio* I have brought down a veritable scourge upon Naples.' If in choice of subject matter *Il diluvio* had seemed somewhat a backward step, his next opera found him closer to the vein he would explore in his serious operas for the rest of his career. Late in May 1830 he was already at work on *Imelda de' Lambertazzi*, but his work was hampered by poor health. The unfavorable reception of the first performance of *Il diluvio* had so upset him that he was seized with convulsions and had to be escorted home, where he lay sick for a week with fever. He had not fully recovered by the end of June, for he wrote to his father: 'Here it is very hot and working as I do I suffer very much between pains in my head and hemorrhoids in my...'[199]

Imelda de' Lambertazzi had its *prima* at the San Carlo on 5 September 1830.[200] Its libretto was the last example that Donizetti used of the work of the feeble Tottola. The plot is a Romeo and Juliet affair,[201] set in Bologna and dealing with a family feud that ends in the deaths of the young lovers, who are children of the opposing factions. This subject, along with *Gabriella di Vergy*, marks a significant step in Donizetti's transition toward the Romantic emphasis on tragic love and suffering so characteristic of his later serious works. Romanticism was regarded as a subversive influence by the Neapolitan censors, and it is not surprising to discover that they dealt harshly with Tottola's libretto. The uncensored text appears in the autograph score,[202] while the alterations made by the censors are printed in the official text sold in the theater.

Imelda is one of the more obscure titles in the Donizetti list. The opera seems to have been relatively unsuccessful, owing to a weak prima donna and the obscurity of the censored text, and it seems rarely to have been given elsewhere.[203] Yet *Imelda*, in terms of the direction that Donizetti was to make his own, is a significant straw in the wind, and the composer thought well enough of some of the music to introduce it into contexts where it has become more familiar.[204] Not the least interesting feature of *Imelda* is that the role of the male lover was assigned to the baritone Tamburini, while the two tenor characters, Imelda's father and her murdering brother Lamberto, are conceived as antagonists. Donizetti's interest in developing the expressive range of his baritone parts would bear significant fruit in *Il furioso* and *Torquato Tasso*.

Probably the chief reason that *Imelda de' Lambertazzi* seems such a shadowy work today is that it was eclipsed by the great success of Donizetti's next opera, *Anna Bolena*, which brought him at last the Milanese triumph he had long hoped for, and which made him, at a single stroke, a leading figure in the world of Italian opera. Lest the importance of *Anna Bolena* as a watershed in his career be exaggerated, it is helpful to remember that the score contains a good deal of music written during the years when only Naples fully recognized his potential, and one melody that even dates back to his beginnings with *Enrico di Borgogna*.

The relative insignificance that seems to afflict *Imelda* is largely the fault of past critics who have tended to dismiss the serious operas preceding *Anna Bolena* as of small account. A representative example of this bias can be found in Verzino's *Le opere di Donizetti*: 'All these operas were quite soon forgotten – and not altogether undeservedly, since they were written almost entirely without true individuality and after the Rossinian pattern.'[205] Looking at these works today, with the experience of more than two decades of the Donizetti revival, it is not so easy either to generalize or to reject. Uneven as they are, there is not one of them that does not give some insight into Donizetti's development as a musical dramatist. To see their true import one has only to think of the portrait of the unhinged Murena in *L'esule*, the romantic ecstasy of Idamore as he declares his love in *Il paria*, the emotional surge as Amelia confronts her would-be poisoner in *Il castello di Kenilworth,* and the onstage deaths of the lovers in *Imelda de' Lambertazzi.*

The frequently made charge that these operas as a group are imitations 'after the Rossinian pattern' is not very enlightening, as it depends upon what one means by 'Rossinian'. If this is taken to describe the structure, the general layout of individual numbers, then it is true that one can find plenty of Rossinian prototypes or analogies. But when this term is applied to patterns of vocal melody and to the writing for the voice generally, then the accusation of Rossinian imitation becomes obscurantist, for it is precisely in this area, particularly in the operas following *Elvida,* that Donizetti's struggle to find his own expressive idiom can be observed with increasing frequency. His growing sensitivity to verbal values becomes marked.

No group of operas in Donizetti's large output has been less deservedly ignored. The comic operas from this period that have been revived since World War II reveal many pages of grace and wit, an honesty of sentiment that is one of Donizetti's most engaging traits. Of the serious works, only *Il castello di Kenilworth* has so far attracted the attention of the modern revivalists. But no group of operas by Donizetti is more deserving of serious study, since these works have much to tell us about Donizetti's struggle to find himself as he felt an increasing opposition to conservative values upheld in Naples.

3

1830–1835
Anna Bolena to *Marin Faliero*

While *Imelda de' Lambertazzi* was in rehearsal, Donizetti signed a contract for the Teatro Carcano in Milan; a group of disgruntled *dilettanti*, angered by the way that La Scala was being run, were determined to teach the management of that theatre a lesson by putting on an outstanding season at the Carcano. Although he had vowed to write not even one appoggiatura for Milan, considering the shabby treatment he had received from the *milanesi*, Donizetti saw at once that here was a chance to produce an impression that could not be ignored. The contract contained a number of attractive clauses: it offered him the opening night of the Carnival season (26 December, Santo Stefano) for his new opera, the position of honor; the company would be headed by Giuditta Pasta[1] and Rubini; the librettist would be Felice Romani and the text was to be ready by the end of September; and he would be paid 650 *scudi*.

Early in September Gaetano and Virginia set out for Rome, where after several weeks he left her with her family and set out by the overland route for Milan. From Bologna he wrote to his father on 5 October:

Sunday the 10th I will be at Bergamo, and I urge you not to come to Milan to meet me, for fear we should miss one another on the road. I leave here tomorrow. I will find lodgings in Milan, leave my things there and come straight off in the express coach ... Do not get upset should I be delayed, because who knows how long I shall have to negotiate with the poet in Milan, but I hope no delay will occur. I am alone, and you will not be able to see my wife, who is staying in Rome. If she did not, my earnings[2] would suffer.[3]

On Sunday, 10 October 1830, for the first time in nine years Donizetti returned to Bergamo.[4] His visit was certainly brief because he still had work to do on the new score, but he stayed long enough to see his parents and relations and to have a reunion with Mayr and Dolci and other old friends.

Romani's libretto for *Anna Bolena* was in Donizetti's hands complete on 10 November. To compose his opera he went to Como to stay in the villa belonging to Pasta, and it is certain that she with her international experience and her interpretative genius could offer him helpful advice. It is even more certain that Pasta, whose fee was many times larger than Donizetti's, would promptly inform him about anything in her music that did not please her or suit her voice. By 10 December he was back in Milan, his score complete enough to begin rehearsals of *Anna Bolena*.

Virginia wrote from Rome to her father-in-law in Bergamo, begging him to tell her truthfully how *Anna Bolena* went at its *prima*. 'You can imagine in what agitation I am living, especially since I am familiar with the sensitivity of his character.'[5] She had not forgotten how the problems that afflicted the first performance of *Il diluvio universale* had driven him into convulsions. When word of the outcome of the *prima* reached Virginia, it came not from Andrea but from her happy husband.

My respected and most beloved Lady:
I am pleased to announce to you[6] that the new opera by your beloved and famous husband has had a reception that could not possibly be improved upon.

Success, triumph, delirium; it seemed that the public had gone mad. Everyone says that they cannot remember ever having been present at such a triumph.

I was so happy that I started to weep, just think! And my heart turned toward you, and I thought of your joy had you been present, but you know that I do not want to expose you to such strong emotions, because needless to say there are emotions that seem like dying when one is still uncertain of the outcome.

Even though I had faith in a favorable reception because everyone – singers, orchestra and even the impresarios – spoke well of the opera, I was suspended between heaven and hell during the first quarter hour . . . Now I am in heaven, and I cannot express my happiness to you. I lack only a kiss from my Virginia, which I shall come to collect at the first opportunity. I beg you therefore – *deh t'en priego,* as Romani would say[7] – to prepare the reception merited by a great maestro who returns home full of ardor wanting first thing to embrace his wife.[8]

Anna Bolena had its memorable first performance at the Carcano on 26 December 1830. Besides Pasta as Anna and Rubini as Percy, the impressive cast included Filippo Galli[9] (Enrico VIII) and Elisa Orlandi[10] (Giovanna Seymour). Francesco Pezzi's review of the *prima* in the *Gazzetta di Milano* does not match the excitement of Donizetti's own account, but at the same time his notice contains little of the acerbity he had previously applied to Donizetti's music.

The cabaletta of an aria sung by Rubini . . . the animated idea in the finale:
here is the essence of what truly pleased in the music of the first act. The
other applause that was heard was due only to the singers.

But in the second act the affair changed aspect, and the talent of the
maestro demonstrated itself with uncommon strength. A duet, a trio, and
three arias are of beautiful and grandiose structure. As for the performers
one has to have heard Pasta and Rubini in their two arias of differing type
and pattern to form an idea to what point the power of declaimed song and
the enchantment of perfect sounds may attain. In the trio Pasta, Rubini and
Galli showed themselves not only at their best, but truly masters in the
perfection of their ensemble. This is all the more notable to the extent that in
this trio, rendered very complex by its beautiful harmonies, Donizetti has
revealed himself a worthy and favorite pupil of Mayr.[11]

If in his review Pezzi achieves a certain impartiality, the critic of
L'eco, another Milanese periodical of the time, certainly did not. On
3 January L'eco reported that the audience remained 'somewhat
cold, except for the applause accorded the singers'. On 4 February
L'eco again turned its attention to Anna: 'This opera has been corrected in some places by M[aestr]o. Donizetti. In the first performances (after an interruption) we will hear changes in it which we
hope will bring greater glory to the composer.' The give-away word
in that quotation is 'corrected' as it implies that Donizetti had been
wanting in knowledge of his craft; an unbiased critic would have
said 'revised'. Since there had been a general feeling among the
public that the first act of Anna Bolena was not up to the same high
level as the second, Donizetti had made a number of changes in the
score:[12] these included a major change in the introduzione (opening
episode), the replacement of the earlier Anna–Percy duet with a
much more traditional duet[13] in three sections (the third coming
practically unchanged from Imelda), and alterations in the Act 2
trio.

After these changes had been made, some three weeks having
passed, L'eco once again reverted to the subject of Anna Bolena on
25 February. It 'has been heard coldly for a month or more, and in a
theater I will not call empty but which was certainly not entirely
full.' The coolness demonstrated by L'eco toward Donizetti is in
marked contrast to its enthusiasm for Bellini. 'Indeed', reported the
critic of L'eco on 7 March, the day following the prima of La sonnambula, 'we, who make a profession of not allowing ourselves to be
seduced easily, could not help joining in the general enthusiasm.'[14]
It is not difficult to tell which camp L'eco belonged to.

The opera Bellini had originally intended to write for that season
at the Carcano was Ernani, to a libretto by Romani; but Romani

abandoned the project when he learned that the Austrian censors in Milan would drastically modify Victor Hugo's plot. Romani's conservative nature and his fondness for being on the side of authority – he would be the editor of the *Gazzetta ufficiale piemontese* from 1834 until blindness forced him to relinquish the post – explain his willingness to drop this particular hot potato. If at the start of that Carnival season in Milan *Anna Bolena* produced a stronger impression than Bellini's *I Capuleti e i Montecchi*, given its local *prima* on the opening night of the rival season at La Scala,[15] the score was evened when *La sonnambula* with Pasta, Rubini and Luciano Mariani (as Rodolfo) made history at the Carcano on the night of 6 March 1831. It would be difficult to find a parallel instance of one opera house in a single three-month season introducing two operas of such high merit as *Anna Bolena* and *La sonnambula*. From this season on, the names of Donizetti and Bellini, as long as the latter lived, would be linked as the two outstanding Italian composers of opera (Rossini having retired). They had competed at the Teatro Carlo Felice, Genoa, in the inaugural season of 1828, and now at the Carcano, Milan, during Carnival 1830–1. They would compete again at La Scala in 1831–2 and at the Théâtre-Italien in Paris in 1835. For all the excitement it generated at the time, it is clear today that this sort of competition is essentially irrelevant. Each composer has his own special qualities, and while there are interesting similarities in the musical vocabulary and syntax they employed, the dissimilarities in the subjects they treated and in their dramatic ideals are more revealing.

Anna Bolena, externally at least, marks the great turning-point in Donizetti's career. Internally it marks the culmination of growing tendencies that can be observed in his operas of the previous decade, and the sizable amount of self-borrowing it contains affirms that. What is significant about *Anna Bolena* in this regard is that the borrowed materials are usually reworked, and are often given stronger and more expressive treatment. An illustration of this is the difference between the relatively brief entrance music of Neala in Act 1 of *Il paria* and the fuller, more dramatic handling of the same material when Anna hurries on before her scene with Percy (*Anna Bolena*, Act 1 scene iii).[16]

The success of *Anna Bolena* was crucially important to Donizetti's later development because it opened for him the doors of important opera houses, first in northern Italy and then abroad; for these centers, which, if they could scarcely be called liberal were at least less conservative than Naples, he could write works that indulged and developed his taste for tragic Romantic melodrama. A certain faction of the north Italian press, *L'eco* for instance, was hostile to Donizetti, and some Neapolitan journals, *Omnibus* for example, were anything but supportive of him. Bellini and his partisans, and those of Mercadante and Pacini on more than one occasion, feared Donizetti as a rival, feeling threatened by his sound musical education, by his facility and productivity, and by the sincere affection that the Neapolitan public had for him. As long as the view could be sustained, in Milan for instance, that Donizetti's popularity in Naples represented nothing more than an aberration on the part of a volatile public (as Pezzi concluded in his review of *L'esule di Roma*, quoted on p. 47 above) there was less for the others to fear; but after *Anna Bolena* that view could no longer be sustained.

With *Anna Bolena* Donizetti for the first time had an exceptionally good libretto to set[17] and a plot that contains a real Romantic catharsis: it portrays the lovers' preparation for death,[18] their yearning for heaven and their release from their sufferings. At last he could compose upon a subject that contained the dramatic emphasis he had long been seeking, and that subject released in Donizetti a vein of Romantic pathos that was to become his particular trademark.

Anna Bolena was the first of Donizetti's operas to be performed in London (8 July 1831) and Paris (1 September 1831). Chorley describes its initial reception in London in these terms:

Anna Bolena, brought hither under the protection of Madame Pasta's royal robes, was permitted rather than admitted, though in this historical English opera might be discerned something of Donizetti's own; and though three of the characters – those of the Queen (Pasta) and Percy (Rubini) and Henry VIII (Lablache), were played and sung to perfection. Donizetti, however, was not an utter stranger here. A duet of his, introduced into a pasticcio opera by Bochsa,[19] *I messicani*, had, a season or two earlier, excited attention. But he was credited with small individuality by those who then ruled public opinion. So it is curious to recollect how Bellini's second opera, introduced here (also by Madame Pasta), *La somnambula* [*sic*], was treated on its introduction with contempt . . . It may have been that truth in expression was not then much cared for by those who frequented our Italian opera. The time of Donizetti and Bellini, though at hand, was still to come.[20]

First with Pasta and Rubini and later with their replacements Giulia Grisi and Mario, *Anna Bolena* held a prominent place in the repertory in London and Paris for more than a quarter of a century. It was first performed in the United States at New Orleans in 1839 (in a French translation; it was also given in the original Italian). (By the close of the nineteenth century the vogue for *Anna Bolena* had passed. The first revival in the present century took place at Bergamo in 1956. The revival at La Scala the following year – directed by Visconti, with scenery and costumes by Benois, conducted by Gavazzeni, and with Maria Callas in the title role – gave the work such impetus that it has re-established itself as one of the hardiest products of the Donizetti revival, having been performed in more than a dozen operatic centers.)

Before leaving Milan, where *Anna Bolena* had gained him influential friends, Donizetti composed on 24 January 1831 a cantata for the marriage of the Austrian Archduke Ferdinand to Anna, the daughter of Vittorio Emanuele I; the couple were to become his patrons in Vienna in 1842.[21] Donizetti set out for Rome on 31 January. In the wake of the July Revolution in Paris in 1830 the Papal States had flared into revolt, and he arrived in Rome to find the city and its environs in turmoil. On 15 February 1831 he sent word to his father: 'I am writing to you so that you will not think I am lying dead among those who have been shot. I am a man whom few things disturb, or rather only one: that is, if my opera goes badly. For the rest, I do not care.'[22] This letter contains one of Donizetti's allusions to the political events of the time, and he was probably sincere when he wrote to his father: 'For the rest, I do not care.' What nettled him most about the troubles in Rome was that they caused the closing of the local theaters. Donizetti's desire for reform ran along aesthetic rather than political lines.

Though politics had apparently little appeal for Donizetti, a politician would before long try to make political capital out of his music. Giuseppe Mazzini, writing in 1836, hailed *Anna Bolena* as 'approaching epic poetry in music', and claimed that in his portrait of Enrico VIII Donizetti had exposed the tyrant sui generis.[23] Mazzini hoped to make Donizetti's operas a focus for feelings of national identity, but in retrospect they seem only incidentally and occasionally to have served this non-musical function. Issues that were beginning to emerge in the early 1830s became rallying-points a decade later, when the operas of Verdi directly and deliberately appealed to nationalistic aspirations.

On 19 February 1831, as soon as sufficient order had been restored to make the road to Naples safe for travel, Gaetano and Virginia set out to return to their home.[24] Once there, he threw himself again into composition and into his duties at the theaters, but it is clear that now, with the incontrovertible success of *Anna Bolena* behind him, he wanted to press his advantage and compose more for theaters beyond Naples, even for important ones outside Italy.

One symptom of Donizetti's ambition to obtain a hearing in France is *Gianni di Parigi,* an opera he wrote for Rubini some time during 1831. Since the autograph bears no date and the composer's correspondence with the tenor has yet to be found, it is not absolutely certain when it was written, but it is clearly a product predicated upon Rubini's participation in *Anna Bolena* and his subsequent departure from Italy to appear in that work in France and England, which would henceforth be his chief arenas of activity. Donizetti composed *Gianni di Parigi* as a vehicle for the tenor, making him a present of it and reserving for himself only the rights for the reduced scores. He counted on the tenor's good graces, which he hoped to win by this gesture, to obtain for him another first performance abroad. His plans in this direction were frustrated, chiefly because his choice of an old libretto by Romani[25] was not a happy one, since its source, Boieldieu's *Jean de Paris* (Paris, 1812), still held an honored place in the repertory of the Opéra-Comique. Donizetti was convinced that Rubini did not make any effort to press the case of *Gianni di Parigi.* Two years later his disappointment at the tenor's neglect of this score spills over in a letter to Mayr:

All the tenors from my hometown have shown me the tiniest fraction of the friendship that I have received from those from elsewhere. Rubini, in particular, to whom I gave *Gianni di Parigi,* written expressly for him, so that he might give it in Paris or in London for his benefit evening . . . [He] said he received it . . . [but] I have not even had an acknowledgement.[26]

Gianni di Parigi finally had its *prima* at La Scala in 1839, but without Rubini, and even without Donizetti's permission.

Two one-act works, *Francesca di Foix,* a semiseria, and *La romanziera e l'uomo nero,* an opera buffa with spoken dialogue, were Donizetti's next operas to be publicly performed. The first at the Teatro San Carlo on 30 May 1831 (a gala on the king's name-day), and the second at the Teatro del Fondo on 18 June 1831.[27] Certainly these slim works were not the expected sequel to *Anna Bolena.* Both had librettos by Gilardoni, and, undeniably, both seem to express Donizetti's desire to wind up this phase of his Neapolitan career with the minimum exertion. *Francesca di Foix* apparently has no subsequent performance history after its first run in Naples; *La romanziera* was restaged once, in Palermo, before lapsing into obscurity.[28] One clue to Donizetti's attitude toward these two one-acters is his failure to mention them in his few surviving letters of this period, for it was his custom to refer to work in hand and to forward reports of the reception obtained by his most recent opera.

A less negative clue to his attitude at this time occurs in a letter to Gaetano Melzi of Milan. 'Tomorrow I hope to break my contract with Barbaja, since I am not free to choose whom I want in my new opera. So be it, for I desire it very much. Thus I will stop shouting and complaining. Already we are both free verbally, and tomorrow I bring the matter to a formal conclusion.'[29] By breaking his wearisome contract with Barbaja, Donizetti hoped to gain greater freedom to accept engagements away from Naples and to earn higher fees, the success of *Anna Bolena* having made his music a more valuable commodity. In this instance, as in many others, his thoroughgoing professionalism is striking. Without being particularly vain he was well aware of his value as an artist, and he was dedicated in his desire not only to advance his own position but to raise the standing of composers generally in that jungle of a world that the Italian opera house all too often appeared to be.

The new opera that Donizetti refers to in his letter to Melzi was to be *Fausta*. The opera was far enough advanced by 26 September 1831 for him to be able to send further news of it to Melzi: 'I am in the final stages of my *Fausta* for [performance on] 12 January 1832.'[30] On many occasions Donizetti was still completing his orchestration as rehearsals of a new score got under way; that *Fausta* was ready some three months before its *prima* is exceptional. Clearly, he intended *Fausta* to be the worthy successor to *Anna Bolena*. The subject is the strongest yet chosen by Donizetti, dealing with an empress who, like Phaedra, lusts for her stepson, accuses him of improper advances to avoid being compromised herself, and finally takes poison. The plot attracted unfavorable attention, not on political or religious grounds but for its 'immorality'. Jeremy Commons has unearthed a letter, dated 13 December 1831, from the Minister of Police[31] to King Ferdinando II himself, in which the minister gives a scandalized résumé of the plot of *Fausta* and urges that it is a highly inappropriate[32] spectacle for the gala on the king's birthday (12 January) at the San Carlo. It can only be interpreted as a tribute to the high opinion of Donizetti held in Naples at this time that *Fausta* was duly performed at the royal gala. Behind this tolerant gesture was a forebearance that would erode away in the future.

Zavadini reprints two letters purportedly by Donizetti and supposed to have been written from Milan at this time, one on 27 December 1831, the other on 31 December 1831.[33] These two letters, both of which give a highly enthusiastic reaction to the first performance of Bellini's *Norma*, which took place on 26 December 1831, strike me as being of dubious authenticity, but not because of their praise for *Norma*. With his own *Fausta* in rehearsal at Naples and with the Minister of Police suggesting that that performance be postponed or even prevented, it is not likely that Donizetti would dash off to Milan, no easy journey in those days, at just this time. Until the original autographs of these letters are found and can be proved to be by Donizetti (and no one to my knowledge has ever seen them), I believe they should be regarded as nothing more than propaganda, manufactured or adapted by Bellini's idolaters to show Donizetti voluntarily putting himself in a secondary position to their hero.[34] 'As for me, I would have been most happy to have composed it', Donizetti is supposed to have said in one; while in the other he allegedly adds parenthetically to his praise of a duet, 'Verdi thinks so too.' How probable is it that Donizetti would have consulted a boy of eighteen who did not even apply for admission to the Milan Conservatory until six months after this judgment is supposed to have been given! In the context of December 1831 what would the name Verdi mean, what weight would it carry?

Fausta, with Ronzi in the title role (instead of Luigia Boccabadati, whom Barbaja wanted him to use but whom Donizetti had not forgiven for her part in the *prima* of *Il diluvio*), was a major success at the San Carlo and had a second series of performances there before the year was out. Gilardoni was the librettist, but he died before the text was completed; according to Zavadini, it was finished by Donizetti himself.[35]

Several points about *Fausta* are significant. Seeking to advance from the triumph of *Anna Bolena*, Donizetti turned once more for his subject to Roman history,[36] as though he were making good part of the plan he had outlined to Mayr after the successful *prima* of *L'esule di Roma*: 'I will finish . . . the second act with a death.'[37] With Romani's superior text to *Anna Bolena*, Donizetti came to a full realization of the importance of a powerfully motivated and clearly articulated libretto, which led inevitably to a tragic conclusion rather than avoiding it at the last minute to arrive at a happy ending. With *Fausta* he had a plot that was at once tragic, powerful and even shocking for its time, and he persevered with it, even in the face of ominous rumblings from the authorities. He worked on a larger scale than he had attempted before: the chorus is given great prominence, the extensive *introduzione* brings most of the principals on at once, and the first finale is unusually massive.[38] The heroic tone and a certain striving to be grandiose make parts of the score of *Fausta* seem rather cold and monotonous, but in the great final scene of Fausta's suicide Donizetti communicates real pathos and tragic immediacy, testifying in the aria 'Tu che volli' and its cabaletta, 'No, qui morir degg'io', to his innate understanding of the nuances of human suffering. Marianna Barbieri-Nini (1820–87), Verdi's first Lady Macbeth, regarded the final episode of *Fausta* as a touchstone of its kind.[39]

Its initial success in Naples provided *Fausta* with an auspicious start, but in the long run it proved to lack the stamina that kept *Anna Bolena* before the public.[40] It opened the Carnival season of 1832–3 at La Scala – the first time Donizetti was accorded that honor. Although he wrote a full-length overture for the occasion[41] and although the opera achieved a run of thirty-one performances, there were signs that all was not well with *Fausta*. Adelaide Tosi, singing the title role, substituted an aria from *Il castello di Kenilworth*[42] for her first-act aria, while the tenor Francesco Pedrazzi also changed his aria but, instead of turning to an earlier score by Donizetti, he inserted one composed by Cesare Pugni.[43] When *Fausta* was put on at Venice the following year, with Pasta and Donzelli, it did not arouse the expected enthusiasm, even though Donizetti supplied a new opening scene and a new soprano–tenor duet. Its last performance, apparently, was at La Scala on 26 December 1859, when it opened the season and was immediately dropped.

After *Fausta* was well launched in Naples, Donizetti set off on 27 January 1832 for Rome; whether Virginia had gone on ahead, her father having died on 2 January, is now not clear. Nor is it clear how long Donizetti stayed in Rome before he went off to Milan, leaving Virginia as usual with her family. Verzino claims[44] that Romani had already sent the libretto for *Ugo, conte di Parigi* to Naples, where Donizetti composed most of the score.[45] Upon his arrival in Milan he discovered that the Milanese censors had taken such drastic objection to the text, cutting some sections and insisting on substantial revision of others, that Romani disowned the libretto. These changes produced confusion for the unhappy singers, who had to learn new music and words,[46] all the while participating in a strenuous season of nightly performances.[47]

In its botched, semi-anonymous form *Ugo, conte di Parigi* had its *prima* at La Scala on 13 March 1832, with a strong, if distracted cast, headed by Pasta, Giulia Grisi[48] and Donzelli. The critic Pezzi reviewed *Ugo* more kindly than he had done Donizetti's music in the days before *Anna Bolena:*

The composer of the music was pressed for time. The singing-actors barely had the opportunity to study their parts passably. Each of them was visibly tired, and the strain . . . was manifest in each of them to a most numerous public the first evening of the opera. Yet, we say it again, the outcome was very favorable.[49]

In spite of Pezzi's generally favorable review, *Ugo* did not catch the fancy of the public. After four performances at La Scala it had only a handful of scattered productions until 1846.[50]

The score of *Ugo* is noteworthy for its great preponderance of concerted numbers over solo arias. It contains several duets, a trio and a quartet, while the first-act finale is a quintet. It is a score full of passionate encounters and brimming with intensity. Although the characters are not always clearly individualized, nor their motivation always convincingly established, the score attests to Donizetti's increasing skill in dramatic rhetoric and his easy effectiveness at composing ensembles that often have clearly contrasted part-writing.

Donizetti's dissatisfaction with the reception of *Ugo*, manhandled as it had been by the censors, was not echoed in his feeling for the score, for, like *Il paria*, *Ugo* was to become a mine for music to go into later works.[51] Regarding *Ugo* as irretrievable, he was anxious to move quickly ahead with a success to make people forget the apparent failure. He was still in Milan when he was approached by the impresario Alessandro Lanari,[52] who then held the lease on the Teatro Canobbiana, to compose an opera buffa for the spring season. While it has long been a tradition that Donizetti composed *L'elisir d'amore* in two weeks, it is possible, since he had been in Milan at least since the beginning of March, that Lanari's proposal could have been made as much as ten weeks before the first performance of *L'elisir.*

For his librettist Donizetti again had the services of Romani, who adapted his text from Scribe's book for Auber's *Le philtre.*[53] Romani followed Scribe's plot, but made many significant modifications in it. He changed the names of the characters,[54] and he played down the coquetry of the French version by stressing the element of pathos. Further, there are no counterparts in Scribe's text for some of the most familiar passages in Donizetti's score: Nemorino's plea, 'Adina, credimi', which leads off the *larghetto* of the first-act finale, Adina's 'Prendi, per me sei libero' from Act 2, and the opera's most celebrated moment, Nemorino's 'Una furtiva lagrima'. It is precisely these three passages that add a balance of human poignancy to the comic spirit of the rest of the work. To help him in his adaptation, Romani had at hand an authority on *Le philtre*, Henri-Bernard Dabadie,[55] who had been Auber's first Jolicoeur and would be Donizetti's first Belcore.

There are gaps in Donizetti's correspondence for the early months of 1832 that prevent a clear understanding of how and exactly when the project of *L'elisir* was initiated. By 24 April a good deal of the music had been composed, as he informs his father:

I am here, very much here, as in the coming week I will start rehearsals, even though I may not have finished (though I am lacking only a little). Romani was obliged to finish quickly, and now he is adjusting certain things for the stage. Yesterday was the first performance of the season,[56] and the only tenor is passable, the donna[57] has a pretty voice, the buffo[58] is a bit hammy.[59]

The general rehearsal of *L'elisir d'amore* was held on 11 May, with the censors in attendance; when they raised no objections to the opera, its first performance could be scheduled for the following day – Saturday, 12 May 1832. The success of *L'elisir* was instantaneous.[60] (Since that time *L'elisir* has never really been out of the active repertory, making it the earliest of Donizetti's operas to which the word 'revival' cannot be relevantly applied.)

Within a week of the opening of *L'elisir* in Milan, Gaetano was on his way to Rome and Virginia, without having taken time to visit Bergamo. In Rome on 21 May 1832 he signed a second contract with Lanari, this one for an opera for the Teatro della Pergola in Florence, the hub of Lanari's operation. This opera was *Parisina*, but its *prima* would be delayed until the following March by Romani's slowness in completing a libretto. On 14 June 1832 Donizetti signed yet another contract in Rome, this one with Paterni for an opera that was to reach the stage before *Parisina*. The contract with Paterni committed him to an opera to a libretto by Ferretti for the Teatro Valle. For this work, *Il furioso all'isola di San Domingo*, Donizetti was to receive 570 *scudi*.[61]

Gaetano returned to Naples shortly after the middle of June 1832, accompanied by Virginia. There his first occupation was to rehearse *Anna Bolena* for its Neapolitan *prima*, given on Queen Maria Isabella's birthday, 6 July 1832.[62] Although the evening was a royal gala, the opera was enthusiastically applauded. This was the start of a typically busy period for Donizetti in Naples. Early in August he received the first installment of Ferretti's libretto for *Il furioso*. He began to compose, but soon saw that he needed modifications in

Ferretti's text. That same month of August he prepared a revival of *Fausta* at the San Carlo, with the bass Lablache taking over the role of Costantino, but the censors apparently forbade the actual performances. Donizetti had to make *puntature* for Lablache, and he added a new duet for him.[63] Besides these activities, he had signed a contract to compose a new opera for the San Carlo to be ready in October. Again Donizetti hoped to have a libretto by Romani for this work, but Romani balked at the Neapolitan assignment, claiming, much to Donizetti's exasperation, that the 500 francs he was offered for it would be insufficient. In the middle of August Donizetti still lacked both librettist and subject for the opera due in October.

But by 18 September that uncertainty had been unresolved, for on that date he informed Ferretti: 'I am roaring and writing my newborn, which will consist of seven numbers in all. *Sancia di Castiglia* – poisoned children – death of the mamma.'[64] He had turned in desperation to a new librettist, Pietro Salatino, of whom little is known save that he came from Palermo and became a lawyer. *Sancia di Castiglia* was duly completed, rehearsed, and produced at the San Carlo on 4 November 1832, with Ronzi in the title role. Two days after the *prima* Donizetti reported to Ferretti:

My *Sancia di Castiglia* was performed marvelously, and the applause was sufficient to call forth the singers and the maestro with them, amid shouts of joy! . . . May things go as well in Rome . . . How Ronzi sang and Lablache and Basadonna[65] . . . Oh, what happiness for me! Today is the second performance. Friday [the 9th] is the third, and goodbye [to Naples], and I will see you soon.[66]

In spite of the warmth of its first reception, *Sancia* soon disappeared from the stage. (It has yet to be given anywhere in the twentieth century.)

The day following the third performance of *Sancia* Gaetano and Virginia duly started for Rome, arriving at the Vasselli apartment in the Via della Muratte on 12 November 1832. Donizetti had been occupied with *Il furioso* since the previous August, and he brought the completed first act and part of the second with him. Although the subject originally stemmed from *Don Quixote*,[67] Ferretti had worked from a five-act play entitled *Il furioso* that had been given at the Teatro Valle in 1820. Donizetti and Ferretti had agreed upon the subject the previous June, before the composer returned to Naples. Their separation meant that their exchange of ideas concerning adaptations to the poem to suit Donizetti's requirements had to be carried on by correspondence.[68] Since Donizetti almost always worked with a librettist at hand and discussed changes orally,[69] his letters about Il furioso are among the comparatively few that shed much light upon this phase of creating an opera. His proposals to Ferretti for changes in the text reveal his practical professionalism in action. For instance, he is worried that in the storm scene in Act 1 the thunder will reduce the audibility of the words. But his chief concern is brevity. He coins a maxim for Ferretti's benefit: 'The good consists in making things small and beautiful, and not in singing a lot and being boring.'[70]

In a later letter to Ferretti Donizetti refers to the dramatic power of the singer who was to create the role of the mad Cardenio in Il furioso. 'This Ronconi makes me tremble as though I were at the cembalo for an opening night.'[71] The object of this accolade was the baritone Giorgio Ronconi,[72] then not yet twenty-three, who had already attracted attention as a singing-actor of uncommon ability. In contrast to Tamburini, a singer of great technical finish but only an adequate actor, Ronconi, although he developed vocal difficulties early on, could create theatrical magic in a career that lasted almost forty years. It is Ronconi, rather than Tamburini, who stands as the prototype of the dramatically intense and vocally powerful Verdi baritone, and a little more than ten years after creating Cardenio, Ronconi would become the first Nabucco. In Il furioso Donizetti for the first time wrote a role for a baritone hero.[73]

The prima of Il furioso at the Teatro Valle on 2 January 1833 was a prompt and resounding success, with particular praise being lavished on young Ronconi. The following day Donizetti sent the good news to his Milanese publisher Giovanni Ricordi: 'Last night the opera was performed . . . In Il furioso Ronconi bears himself very well, and la Orlandi likewise, and the buffo, the tenor and the seconda donna also. And more than anything else the public bears itself well and shouts and calls us out.'[74] Il furioso continued its successful run at the Valle throughout the Carnival season, being performed even during the run of the next opera (Il disertatore svizzero by Donizetti's protégé Lauro Rossi) – a sure sign of popularity in those days – and it was revived at the Valle that fall for a further series of performances with Ronconi. In October 1833 it was introduced at La Scala, where it was given thirty-six times before the end of the year. Within a space of six years Il furioso was staged at more than seventy different theaters. Its nineteenth-century vogue lasted as long as Ronconi (who continued to sing Cardenio into the 1860s) and other baritones of his type flourished.

(The not always happy twentieth-century performance history of

Il furioso begins with its revival at the Accademia Chigiana in Siena in 1958. The work attracted attention when it was given at the Spoleto Festival of 1967, a production that was subsequently recorded, which gained wide dissemination for this travesty of a noble and deeply felt, if naive, work: the orchestration was reduced, the score was badly cut and illogically rearranged, and the buffo elements of this semiseria work were pulled out of proportion, disguising one of the truly remarkable aspects of *Il furioso* – the way in which the comedy relates to and reinforces the serious plot. This misrepresentation of one of Donizetti's most original operas has been repeated at Charleston, South Carolina, and elsewhere. *Il furioso* is in need of a full and accurate contemporary production, and it is an opera that will repay handsomely such an effort.)

Two problems that arose at the time of the successful launching of *Il furioso* are worth mentioning here because they illuminate some of the occupational hazards that beset a composer of Donizetti's generation. On the same night that *Il furioso* began its fortunate career, the Teatro Apollo in Rome opened its season with a disastrous production of *Anna Bolena,* which caused Donizetti to complain: 'This *Anna* was not mine, and it was given without my supervision and I was excluded from the theater.'[75] When an opera made a success in those days, unscrupulous impresarios would try to avoid paying the rental of the full score and parts from the impresario or publisher who owned the performing rights by engaging someone to orchestrate the work from a piano score. This form of musical piracy not only defrauded the owner but compromised the composer, whose work was presented to the public in an incorrect and often wretchedly botched form.[76] Donizetti attempted to vindicate *Anna Bolena* by conducting a special concert performance of the authentic score on 6 January 1833 at the Accademia Filarmonica Romana.

The second matter was related to *Il furioso* itself, which was then the property of the impresario Paterni. After the Carnival season of 1833 at the Valle was over, Paterni discovered that Elisa Orlandi was introducing the final *rondò* from *Il furioso* into other scores, but not in its original form as she employed an orchestration to the aria contrived by Giacomo Panizza.[77] Paterni promptly protested against this misuse of the aria by placing notices in several papers denouncing it as 'contrary to the intentions of the composer and contrary to the sacred rights of property'.[78]

His contractual obligations for *Il furioso* satisfied and the reputation of *Anna Bolena* rescued, Donizetti left Rome on 10 January 1833 to go to Florence to compose his opera for Lanari. He arrived there to find that Romani still had not forwarded the libretto for his new work. On 13 January he wrote to his father:

Here I am at Florence, *without the libretto,* and I am supposed to give the opera the second Sunday in Lent [3 March]. As usual Romani has failed me, but Donizetti has not failed to protest at the specified time, and so here I am being paid without working.

Since I understand the fault is not that of the poor impresario, I offered therefore to make an accommodation rather than to start a legal action. This would be: to stage *Fausta,* which is very well suited to these singers, and to write several new pieces for it . . . The impresario is not here, however, but at Venice, and his agent supports my position fully; now I am awaiting Lanari's yes or no.[79]

While he waited for Romani's libretto to materialize or for Lanari to agree to some alternative plan, Donizetti had an affair with a contralto named Giuseppina Merola. That this affair occurred is substantiated by a letter Lanari wrote to Romani on 1 August 1833: 'If you should need a *musichetto,* I could give you Merola, who has an excellent figure, is handsome and competent, and with her Donizetti gave me horns; using her you would do Donizetti a service.'[80] In all Donizetti's correspondence there is only one mention of her name; he asks Lanari to give his greetings 'to the couple Duprez, to Cosselli, to Merola, and to everyone'.[81] This casual reference would argue against serious involvement; it is worth mentioning only because it is one of the few pieces of evidence for an extra-marital relationship between Donizetti and one of his singers.

It is not known exactly how long Donizetti had to wait for Romani's complete libretto for *Parisina,* but he must have had it by the middle of February at the latest. It is possible he had parts of the text earlier, for he wrote to Lanari on 6 August 1833, 'I finished the opera for you in a very few days.'[82] Donizetti directed the rehearsals, and the first performance of *Parisina* took place at the Teatro della Pergola, Florence, on 17 March 1833, only two weeks after the date originally projected for the *prima.* The first cast of *Parisina* included Carolina Ungher in the title role, the French tenor Gilbert Duprez as Ugo, and the baritone Domenico Cosselli[83] as Azzo. The opera, which Donizetti described as his own favorite among his operas, was enthusiastically received, especially the dramatic scene in Act 2 between Parisina and her husband, which according to the review in the *Commercio* for 19 March 'could not help but move the hardest heart'. As Lanari's season at the Pergola ran only through Lent, the initial run of *Parisina* was limited to nine performances, but Lanari's touring companies played it frequently, and the opera was soon put on in many theaters.

(When *Parisina* was sung at the St Charles Theater in New Orleans on 4 June 1837, it became the first opera by Donizetti to be performed in the United States. By 1850 it had been performed in London, Paris and Vienna, and even Rio de Janeiro had seen it, but its vogue had already passed. In the twentieth century it has been sung at Siena in 1964, and there have been further performances at Bologna, Parma and Bergamo. In 1974 it was sung in New York in concert form with Montserrat Caballé as Parisina.)

Parisina has a powerful and tragic plot, derived from Byron's poem of the same name,[84] but the exposition is somewhat awkward. The plot contains strong elements of Romanticism and two of the characters, Parisina and Azzo, are vividly realized. In many express-ive details *Parisina* foreshadows *Lucia*.

As soon as *Parisina* was under way, Donizetti returned to Rome. Here he and Ferretti embarked harmoniously on a project that he had long considered, an opera honoring the poet Tasso, who had strong associations with Bergamo. Ferretti drew on a number of sources, particularly Rosini, Goethe, Goldoni, and Byron's *The Lament of Tasso*, but also on the works of Tasso himself. Originally Donizetti had conceived of *Tasso* as a potential vehicle for Rubini, but when Rubini ignored the present of *Gianni di Parigi* Donizetti began to think of Ronconi as the famous poet – a prospect that proved more and more appealing to him. In the space of less than a year Donizetti was to write a second opera with a baritone hero. In contrast to the frustration and haste that attended the launching of *Parisina*, the preparation and composition of *Torquato Tasso* proceeded with rel-ative calm and deliberation.[85]

Work on *Tasso* had begun even before the contract with Paterni for it was signed. The impresario had originally offered Donizetti 600 *scudi* (a slight raise over the 570 for *Il furioso*), but he held out for 650. When Paterni acceded to that demand, the contract for *Tasso* was signed on 10 June 1833. One month later the censors approved the libretto. Rehearsals started on 22 August and the *prima* of *Tasso* occurred at the Teatro Valle on 9 September 1833. Ronconi sang the title role, and the mezzo-soprano Adelina Spech was Eleonora d'Este.[86] The opera was so well received that the sing-ers, the composer and, exceptionally, the librettist were all called out to acknowledge the applause.

Tasso continued to be performed at the Valle throughout Sep-tember, but without ever quite recapturing the enthusiasm aroused by the first performance. The Roman critics were generally com-plimentary, particularly about the scene in which Tasso reads his verses to Eleonora, and about the two concerted finales. *Tasso*, more than *Il furioso*, suffers from the discrepancies in tone that afflict most semiseria works, and Donizetti recognized this problem as he later seriously considered recasting the work as an opera seria.[87] (In spite of this generic defect *Tasso* held the stage for a generation not only in Italy, for it was given with considerable success at various theaters in Germany and Austria, though it had scant fortune when it was put on in London. *Tasso* has not, so far, been performed either in Paris or in the United States. One unusual feature of its performance history is that the short third act, for baritone and chorus, was frequently performed apart from the rest of the score. Battistini sang Act 3 of *Tasso* as recently as 1925, but that performance must be regarded as a postscript to the nineteenth-century career of the work. *Tasso* has participated in the contemporary Donizetti revival, having been performed in 1974 and again in 1975 by Opera Rara at the Camden Theatre, London.)

During the summer of 1833 Donizetti, in spite of his growing success, found himself frustrated. Besides the increase of inauthentic versions of his works circulated by the pirates (one measure of his success), he was at loggerheads with Lanari, trying to arrange the timing of his next new work for the impresario so that he might be free to accept an engagement in Paris. That summer Édouard Robert and Carlo Severini, the co-directors of the Théâtre-Italien, were making one of their annual trips to Italy to engage singers and to acquire new works for their repertory. Among the singers they signed was Carolina Ungher, who was eager to make her debut at the Théâtre-Italien in *Parisina*; but Lanari, who owned the score or at least the rights to it relevant to this transaction, demanded such a large fee that Robert and Severini refused to consider it. Lanari's avarice only added fuel to Donizetti's frustration. He lamented to Ricordi: 'The success of *Parisina* has not managed to ease the road to Paris for me with the impresarios, who say: Since we have Rossini,[88] why do we need works by anyone else? (almost as though that colossus might be jealous of the insects). My misfortune.'[89] Near the end of June 1833 Donizetti managed to talk in Rome with Robert and Severini, who told him that on their return from Naples they would discuss the possibility of a new opera for Paris for the following year. But when they got back to Rome they refused to meet Donizetti, who tried to approach them in the theater and left messages for them at their hotel. What Donizetti did not know was that Robert and Severini had been ignominiously arrested as conspirators at Naples and banished from its territories,[90] and they, knowing of Donizetti's close ties with Naples, had decided that they should do him, and possibly themselves, the favor of avoiding him. This mysterious contretemps left Donizetti deeply discouraged. The importance of the incident is that it shows, even more clearly than his making a gift to Rubini of *Gianni di Parigi,* how eager was Donizetti to get to Paris one way or another.

By the middle of September 1833 he was in Milan, where his first task was to prepare *Il furioso* at La Scala, adding three 'new' pieces and amplifying the orchestration.[91] For this effort he received 120 *scudi. Il furioso* made a successful debut at La Scala on 1 October 1833 and achieved a run of thirty-six performances. Then on 10 October Donizetti signed a contract with Duke Carlo Visconti di Modrone, who had recently assumed the directorship of La Scala, for two operas, one to open the coming Carnival season and one for the following year. For each of these operas Donizetti would be paid 6500 Austrian lire. The first of these was to be *Lucrezia Borgia.*

The situation in Milan just then was confusing. Visconti had cashiered his agent, Teodoro Gottardi, who had proven himself incompetent at handling the affairs of La Scala. Gottardi had already contracted Mercadante to compose an opera to open the coming Carnival season. Mercadante wanted to compose a *Saffo* and had put Romani, the house librettist at La Scala, to work to write him a libretto on that subject before he learned that the prima donna engaged for that season, Henriette Méric-Lalande,[92] declined to appear in such a part. To appease the prima donna, whose fee for that season was nine times larger than that a composer would receive for writing an opera, Visconti diplomatically persuaded Mercadante to postpone his contract until a later season, a withdrawal that left Donizetti the field.[93]

Donizetti urged the subject of *Lucrezia Borgia* upon Romani, who approached the task of reducing the prose of Victor Hugo's five-act play with considerable misgivings. Fastidiously aware of the censor's dislike of offensive subjects, Romani did his best to treat with caution a plot that deals with a pope's daughter who poisons her own son. When Romani had completed his distasteful task, he sent his text to Visconti on 26 November, saying: 'I could not treat this subject better, nor go more carefully in view of the censorship.'[94] Romani had finished the prologue by the end of October and had sent the rest of his text piecemeal to Donizetti, who as usual started to compose as soon as he had any of the verses before him. Significantly, Romani never worked directly with Donizetti again. He shortly afterwards took up a full-time career in journalism at Turin, but this was undoubtedly not the only reason why he refused subsequent proposals for their collaboration.[95] *Lucrezia Borgia* left the essentially conservative librettist soured: he was put off by the subject Donizetti was so enthusiastic about; he was irked by the composer's insistence on changes in his text; and he was horrified when the censors made a great fuss about the opera and insisted on many modifications. Indeed, there was a period early in December 1833 when it seemed that *Lucrezia Borgia* would not be approved in any form. Nor was this the last time the score was to encounter such problems.

The rehearsals of *Lucrezia* began at La Scala on 3 December 1833. Almost at once Lalande started to cause difficulties. She was distressed by the stage direction that she should make her first entrance masked; rather than risk not being recognized and welcomed by appropriate applause, she elected to enter mask in hand. More crucial was her outrage at the proposed ending of the opera, with its emphasis upon the tenor's death. A proper opera, according to Lalande's rigid view, should end with a brilliant aria for the prima donna. In vain did Donizetti try to argue that such an aria would be offensive,[96] that the spectacle of a grief-stricken mother indulging herself in torrents of coloratura as she stands over the body of her son, dead through her treachery, would be repellent. Lalande insisted on her prerogatives, and rather than risk a disaffected prima donna Donizetti acceded.

The *prima* of *Lucrezia Borgia* took place on the appointed date of 26 December. Besides Lalande, the principal singers included Marietta Brambilla[97] (Maffio Orsini), the tenor Francesco Pedrazzi[98] (Gennaro) and Luciano Mariani[99] (Alfonso). The new opera was applauded that first night, but the reception it was given was not such as to suggest that it would become one of Donizetti's most popular operas and remain so throughout the nineteenth century. Pezzi reviewed it in the *Gazzetta di Milano* of 28 December, claiming that he found little novelty or inspiration in the score, although he praised the orchestral writing and the elaboration of the musical designs. He ventured the prediction that the score would gain in favor with the public.[100] Later performances that season went better, and *Lucrezia* received a total of thirty-three performances in its first production, which had all the aura of a succès de scandale.

Significantly, *Lucrezia Borgia* did not have a second production anywhere for almost three years; it was then brought out at the Teatro della Pergola in Florence, disguised under the title of *Eustor-*

gia da Romano. The subject matter in its original form was clearly offensive to legitimist sensibilities, and for a number of years it was performed more frequently under such aliases as *Alfonso, duca di Ferrara, Giovanna I di Napoli* and *Nizza di Grenade* than under its original title. Ironically, it became *La rinnegata* at Paris on 14 January 1845 and the scene was moved to Turkey because Hugo threatened legal action over the use of his plot, even though, under its original title, *Lucrezia* had been in the repertory of the Théâtre-Italien since 1840! It was not until after the unification of Italy, when stage censorship became more lenient, that *Lucrezia Borgia* could dispense with its aliases. (For at least forty years the opera retained a dominant position in the international repertory, and then it began to lose ground. Unlike most of Donizetti's other serious operas (except *Lucia* and *La favorite*), *Lucrezia* did not entirely disappear in the earlier twentieth century. For instance, it was sung at the Metropolitan in 1905, at La Scala in 1917, at Florence in 1933. But since 1946 it has taken on a hardy new lease on life. There have been more than thirty productions, and two complete recordings.)

1833, the year that saw the first performances of *Il furioso, Parisina, Tasso* and *Lucrezia,* marked a new level of more consistent achievement for Donizetti. While these operas are not without unevenness, they show his increasing ability to sustain dramatic expressiveness beyond the compass of single numbers. Each of these scores rises more than once to a pitch of genuine eloquence. The dramatic vision in *Lucrezia Borgia* rarely dims, and unforgettable are such moments as the unmasking of Lucrezia in the prologue, the superbly contrasted emotions of the trio 'Guai se ti sfugge un moto', the gallows humor of the little duet for Astolfo and Rustighello,[101] the chilling contrast of the rollicking brindisi with the offstage chorus chanting for the dead, and Lucrezia's intensity as she pleads with Gennaro to drink the antidote. The dramatic imagination and rhetorical incisiveness of these moments offer a well-made preview of the world Verdi was to explore. Verdi was a twenty-year-old music student in Milan at the time of the *prima* of *Lucrezia Borgia;* there is no doubt that Donizetti's score became a point of reference for the younger composer, then at an impressionable time in his development.

At the end of 1833 Donizetti paid a visit to Genoa. He went there partly to visit his difficult nephew Andrea, then fifteen and a student in Genoa while his parents were in Constantinople. Another motive for his Genoese trip was the forthcoming production of the revised *Il diluvio universale* at the Teatro Carlo Felice, with the baritone Cosselli as Noè.[102] He revised his score, adjusting it for the new cast, eliminating some passages he had borrowed for other operas, and adding some new music, particularly in the mezzo-soprano role of Ada. During the first two weeks of January 1834, he also went to Turin to supervise the rehearsals of *Fausta* at the Teatro Regio. Donizetti had been uneasy about this production because he knew that the prima donna, Amalia Schütz-Oldosi,[103] was a past master (*arciprofessoressa* is Donizetti's word for her) at altering her music to suit her whim, but he must have succeeded in restraining her, for he pronounced himself satisfied with the success of *Fausta* at Turin.[104] The performances of *Il diluvio* at Genoa (from 17 January 1834) did not begin until after Donizetti's departure, but it proved the hit of that season, being given thirteen times.

The day Donizetti left Genoa he wrote to Visconti at La Scala about the seating of the orchestra in that theater. During the rehearsals of *Lucrezia Borgia* he had changed the former arrangement so that the leaders of each of the string sections sat close to the conductor, a change he explained as conforming to the practise in other theaters. Apparently there had been some complaints in Milan about the reseating, for Donizetti justified the change in such a diplomatic way that Visconti found himself taking responsibility for it.[105]

From Genoa he traveled to Florence, via Livorno, to fulfill his latest contract with Lanari. The new opera was to be *Rosmonda d'Inghilterra* to a libretto by Romani, but not a new one – it had already been set by Carlo Coccia (Venice, 1829). The choice of subject had been agreed upon in Milan the previous November, and Romani had adjusted his old text before he decided not to work again with Donizetti. Donizetti could well have brought with him to Florence some, if not all, of the music already composed. One of his tasks after his arrival would be to try out his music with his principal singers and adjust it to their particular vocal capacities.

Rosmonda d'Inghilterra had its first performance at the Teatro della Pergola on 27 February 1834. The title role was sung by Fanny Tacchinardi-Persiani,[106] who had then been singing in public for only two years, and who the following year would win a permanent place in operatic history as the first Lucia. Others in the *prima* of *Rosmonda* were Anna del Sere (Eleonora), the obliging Merola (Arturo),[107] and the tenor Duprez (Enrico II). The plot of the opera is derived from the story of 'Fair' Rosamond Clifford, whose love for Henry II of England aroused the wrath of Queen Eleanor. Romani's immediate source for this plot has not yet been identified. After the opera's initial run, which Donizetti described to Ricordi as 'having pleased increasingly',[108] *Rosmonda* fell into neglect: in 1837 Donizetti revised the score, but the new version seems not to have been performed, and the only nineteenth-century revival of the original version, apparently, was a production at Livorno in 1846. (*Rosmonda* was revived by Opera Rara in London and Belfast in 1975.) And yet, in accordance with the accommodating habits of the time, at least one scena from *Rosmonda* survived for quite a while, because the cavatina and cabaletta at Rosmonda's first entrance were frequently substituted for Lucia's arias in Act 1 scene ii of *Lucia di Lammermoor*. When Donizetti made his French version of the latter in 1838 he officially replaced Lucia's entrance arias with those from *Rosmonda*.[109]

After *Rosmonda* had had its third performance, Donizetti went from Florence south to Rome, collected his wife, and returned to Naples for the first time in seventeen months. In his absence he had been appointed professor of composition at the Naples Conservatory, and music-master to the daughter of the Prince of Salerno, the king's uncle. But the best news of all had reached him in Florence not long before his departure. Rossini had written to him inviting him to compose an opera for the Théâtre-Italien for the winter of 1834–5. Thrilled by this prospect, Donizetti accepted, begging only that he be allowed to compose for later on in the season, as he was already obligated to write for the Carnival season at La Scala, which opened on 26 December.[110] For his Paris opera Donizetti hoped to have a libretto by Romani, and was even ready to pay him double his usual fee for it; he also wanted Romani to write the text of his new opera for the San Carlo, for which he had signed a contract on 12 April 1834, not long after his return to Naples. When Donizetti heard nothing from Romani, for this was the season of Romani's discontent and changing of jobs, Donizetti turned to a seventeen-year-old law student, Giuseppe Bardari, for a libretto.

At first Donizetti believed his new opera for Naples would be ready in time for the royal gala on 6 July,[111] but the time consumed in finding a substitute for Romani caused the date to be set back. The subject chosen by Donizetti was *Maria Stuarda*, derived from Schiller's play, which he had seen in Milan acted in Andrea Maffei's translation. Bardari's text was completed by 19 July 1834, for on that date the director of the theater submitted it to be passed by the censors, requesting prompt attention as 'it is urgent this opera be staged as soon as possible'.[112] Although no definitive reply to this request was given, Donizetti went ahead and completed his score, which went into rehearsal in the last days of August. The director ordered the scenery to be constructed and the costumes sewn. The normal course of events was interrupted when, on the morning of 4 September, Bardari was summoned by the censor Francesco Ruffa and ordered to make substantial changes in his text – changes 'which were promptly passed on to Maestro Donizetti so that he might adapt his music, which he immediately did'.[113]

This summons of 4 September could well have been caused by a famous row that took place at the first orchestral rehearsal of *Maria Stuarda*. When Ronzi, playing the role of Maria, turned on Anna del Sere, the Elisabetta, she had these pointed lines to deliver:

> Figlia impura di Bolena,
> Parli tu di disonore?
> Meretrice – indegna, oscena,
> In te cada il mio rossore.
> Profanato è il soglio inglese
> Vil bastarda, dal tuo piè!

(Impure daughter of Boleyn, do you speak of dishonor? Obscene and unworthy prostitute, may my blush fall on you. Profaned is the English throne, vile bastard, by your foot!)

Ronzi delivered these sentiments with such conviction that del Sere took them personally and set upon her rival, seizing her hair, pommeling her with her fists and, some swore, even biting her. Not surprisingly Ronzi lost her footing under this onslaught and fell, but she regained her feet and returned the attack. Ronzi so outweighed[114] her adversary that del Sere fainted and had to be carried home. A month later, after worse problems had beset *Maria Stuarda*, Donizetti wrote to Ferretti about a sequel to this skirmish.

You know about the battle between the women, and I do not know if you are aware that Ronzi spoke against me, believing me out of earshot. She said, 'Donizetti protects that whore of a del Sere.' And, to her surprise, I answered: 'I do not protect any of you, but those two queens were whores, and you two are whores.' She was convinced; either she was ashamed or decided to keep quiet. She spoke no more, the rehearsal went on, and then the opera was not performed.[115]

That the opera was not performed was due to the king's personal prohibition, though the ban did not arrive until after a successful dress rehearsal had been given before an enthusiastic audience. The reason why the king forbade the performance of the opera is not known since, as an absolute monarch, he did not need to account for his actions to his subjects. A story used to be current[116] that *Maria Stuarda* was banned because Queen Maria Cristina attended the dress rehearsal and fainted at the moment when the Queen of Scots was led away to be beheaded; but it is highly improbable that the Queen of Naples would have done such an unconventional thing as attend a public rehearsal, particularly a queen who had wanted to become a nun and one who did not approve of theaters on principle. It is possible that a member of the court had attended the dress rehearsal and had given the queen such an upsetting account of it that she prevailed upon the king to forbid its performance. Maria Cristina was, after all, a twelfth-generation descendant of Mary Stuart, and Mary was generally revered in Italy as a martyr to her faith.[117] Conjecture aside, it is a fact that *Maria Stuarda* had never been officially approved when word of the king's ban reached the San Carlo.

To place these events in a larger context: there had been an increasing disfavor on the part of the censors, the same ones who had temporarily approved *Fausta* for performance two years earlier,[118] toward bloody and violent subjects as disruptive of public morale and tranquillity. It is not unlikely that the censors came to associate Donizetti in particular with a tendency they wanted to discourage, for one of the librettos submitted with that of *Maria Stuarda* on 19 July had been Romani's text for *Lucrezia Borgia,* an opera that had already upset the Milanese authorities and which would not be passed for performance in Naples until 1848. *Maria Stuarda* would be given in its original form elsewhere, but in Naples compromises had to be made.

The theaters in Naples were suffering under the inept management of the royal commission,[119] headed by Prince di Torella, which had undertaken to run them when Barbaja had resigned in protest at the interference he was encountering. To attract audiences the commission felt they needed an opera by Donizetti, a proven favorite in Naples, and they needed it promptly as the composer would soon be leaving for Milan. It was agreed between Donizetti and the commission that the best solution would be to adapt the music of *Maria Stuarda* to a new subject.[120] The first proposal was the subject of Lady Jane Grey, which although it had the merit of utilizing the Tudor sets and costumes already prepared for *Maria Stuarda* had the greater demerit of dealing with a quasi-royal beheading. When permission for Lady Jane Grey was denied, the subject of the strife between the Guelphs and the Ghibellines at Florence was suggested, and was found sufficiently unsubversive to be passed by the censors. The text for *Buondelmonte*[121] was the work of Pietro Salatino, who had written the libretto to *Sancia di Castiglia* in 1832; the musical modifications were made by Donizetti himself, for 'if the revision was not made by me, it would have been done by somebody else after my departure so that the management could have given a new opera by Donizetti'.[122] For this revision he was paid an extra 600 ducats, in addition to the 1400 he had received for *Maria Stuarda*. *Buondelmonte* went into rehearsal on 7 October 1834 and had its first performance at the San Carlo on 18 October, with Ronzi (now as Bianca) and del Sere (now as Irene) heading a cast of ten, where there had been only six characters in *Maria Stuarda*. The performance history of *Buondelmonte* is limited to this single production, as Donizetti was determined to salvage *Maria Stuarda* in a more hospitable climate.

The prohibition of *Maria Stuarda* raises the whole question of Donizetti's attitude toward censorship and royal interference with the plots of his operas. In 1838, at the time of the prohibition of *Poliuto* in Naples, he clarified his position in a letter to his lawyer and close friend, Aniello Benevento. But when he writes: 'if I can still maintain not to have been involved at all in the choice of subject and not to have given my decision whether it pleases me or not until I see the text completed and approved',[123] he is describing his legal posture, not what we know of his actual practise. He chose subjects such as *Lucrezia Borgia* and *Maria Stuarda*, knowing that they contained details and relationships that would antagonize the censors, but recognizing in them the sort of powerful, passionate situations that stirred his creative impulses. The latter consideration mattered more to Donizetti than the former. Elsewhere in the same letter to the lawyer Benevento, he writes: 'I am here for the music and not to guarantee the poetic text to the authorities.'[124] What Donizetti regarded as his function was not to reinforce the status quo to please the censors, but to offer to his audiences a true dramatic experience that probed deep.

During the Italian phase of his career, Donizetti was frustrated again and again by conservatively oriented censorship. In the face of cumulative evidence it is difficult not to conclude that he exerted what pressure he safely could against the stifling atmosphere. When he found its restrictiveness unbearable, he adopted the only course open to him – he left Naples and Italy for good and, by way of a parting shot, made clear exactly why he felt he had to leave.

While Donizetti's problems with *Maria Stuarda* were coming to a head, he was hard at work on another project, one that seemed particularly important to his future career – his first opera for Paris. The previous February he had joyfully accepted Rossini's invitation to compose for the Théâtre-Italien. At first he had hoped, as usual, for a libretto by Romani, but when no text was forthcoming,[125] he addressed a letter[126] to Severini, the director of the Théâtre-Italien, to announce that he had chosen a subject based on a tragedy, *Marino Faliero*, by Casimir Delavigne. He justifies his choice by pointing out that since the play was well known in Paris it would offer small difficulty to the public when it was presented in a language not theirs.[127] In the same letter Donizetti passes on the information that he already has a libretto for it, by Emanuele Bidèra, a man of mixed Italian–Greek extraction. By 7 October he had composed (that is, sketched) all his score, with the exception of one duet. Since 7 October 1834 was the day that rehearsals started for *Buondelmonte* and since the previous weeks had seen Donizetti wholly engrossed in converting *Maria Stuarda* into *Buondelmonte*, it is justifiable to assume that he must have begun work on *Marin Faliero* some time before, probably in early summer. Certainly he had completed his sketches before he began to compose his next opera for La Scala, a work designed to open the Carnival season of 1834–5 and one which would be performed before *Faliero*.

This next opera for La Scala was to be *Gemma di Vergy*. By late September 1834 Donizetti had not even definitely decided upon a subject. He had been toying with the idea of a work about Giovanna I of Naples. Something of Donizetti's sensitivity to the censors at this time is revealed by his letter of 27 September 1834 to Visconti[128] mentioning this subject, for he has already secured an official confirmation from the Neapolitan police that Giovanna I was in no way related to any member of the royal family currently reigning in Naples. On 14 October he informs Visconti that he has decided on the subject of Gemma di Vergy rather than Giovanna, and again he shows that he is still keenly aware of the hornet's nest he has stirred up with *Maria Stuarda*, for he informs Visconti that in *Gemma* there will be 'nothing . . . to interfere with its production, since it is free of any matter that could be prohibited'.[129] Since Romani was still technically the official poet of La Scala, and since he declined to cooperate with Donizetti, the composer turned again to Emanuele Bidèra, who had already written the libretto for *Marin Faliero*. Because it was then the rule that a libretto should be written by a poet resident in the same town as the theater, so that he could be held accountable by the local censors, Donizetti had to receive a special dispensation to use his Neapolitan libretto.

Donizetti left Naples on 13 November 1834 to travel to Milan via Genoa. On 4 December the Milanese censors passed his libretto without any changes and the rehearsals began. His manipulations to insure that his opera would open the season had been successful, and *Gemma di Vergy* was duly given at La Scala on 26 December 1834, with Ronzi (Gemma), the tenor Domenico Reina[130] (Tamas) and the baritone Cartagenova[131] (Il Conte di Vergy). The plot of *Gemma* is derived from a tragedy by Dumas, *Charles VII chez les grands vassaux* (1831).[132] *Gemma* was successful enough in this production to achieve a run of twenty-six performances, Ronzi being acclaimed in her very demanding role. For a while *Gemma* enjoyed a great vogue in Italy, but elsewhere it seems not to have made a comparable impression. During the exciting days before the risings of 1848, it touched off a turbulent scene in Palermo, causing the audience to break into slogans of the Risorgimento and prompting the prima donna, Parodi,[133] to appear with the tricolor.[134] Such scenes were repeated at other productions of *Gemma*, assuring the opera a particular place in patriotic Italian hearts. (By 1880 its popularity was in decline, and the performance at Empoli in 1901 seemed likely to be the last. Yet *Gemma di Vergy* proved a moving experience when it was revived for Montserrat Caballé at the San Carlo in December 1975. Later she repeated the role on stage in Barcelona and in concert at New York in March 1976.)

On 31 December 1834 Donizetti hurried away from Milan for Genoa, where he embarked for Marseilles, and from there traveled on to Paris. The attraction of Paris for Italian opera composers had begun in the days of Lully and had continued through every succeeding generation. To Donizetti none of his predecessors was more symbolically important than Rossini. Few contested that in the mid-1830s Paris was the artistic capital of Europe, and a resounding success upon that city's stages set a special seal upon a composer's reputation. The Paris of Louis Philippe was more cosmopolitan and sophisticated than the conservative courts and provincial capitals that Donizetti had so far known. Paris offered a heady intellectual freedom, vastly different from the confining and censor-ridden atmosphere in which he had labored up to now. Paris meant fatter fees and greater protection from the musical pirates. Paris was a city where artists were regarded as something resembling an aristocracy, and not as the hirelings of princes or the obsequious attendants of prima donnas. This was the city that Donizetti aspired to conquer, hoping that a solid success at the Théâtre-Italien would gain him access to the lucrative possibilities of the Opéra and the other state theaters.[135]

Donizetti was already in Paris when Bellini's *I puritani* had its *prima* at the Théâtre-Italien on 24 January 1835, with Giulia Grisi, Rubini, Tamburini and Lablache, the same quartet that would appear in *Marin Faliero*.[136] Few of Donizetti's letters from this Paris visit of 1835 have survived, but a number of long letters from Bellini exist and their tone toward Donizetti might fairly be called paranoid.[137] This final chapter of their rivalry – and the hostility was very one-sided – had its antecedents in their confrontations at the Teatro Carlo Felice in 1828, at the Carcano in 1830–1 and at La Scala in 1831–2. It is only fair to remember that at this time Bellini's health, never robust, was declining, and that he would die the following September at the regrettably early age of thirty-three.

Bellini had been in Paris since August 1833, but it was not until the following February that Rossini offered him a contract to compose for the Théâtre-Italien, at about the same time that Donizetti, then in Florence for *Rosmonda*, received a similar offer. Bellini's initial reaction on discovering that his chief rival would again be competing against him was anger mixed with fear. Bellini suspected that Rossini favored Donizetti and was somehow working against him. And to counteract this imagined prejudice against him, Bellini paid court to Rossini and sought his advice. As he reported to Florimo on 4 October 1834:

You should know I have begged Rossini (to flatter him and also because I believe he can give me golden advice) to be kind enough to give me his counsel . . . Up to now he has only spoken badly, very badly, of me, saying that the one with the most talent in Italy is Pacini[138] and for the working out of pieces the best is Donizetti.[139]

Responding to Bellini's flattery, Rossini helped to revise and strengthen the score of *I puritani*. Yet even this support did not calm Bellini's apprehensions, for he feared Donizetti's greater productivity.[140] He tried to soothe himself with the thought of *Buondelmonte*, which Florimo had praised 'at the first performance, but [which] at the end of its run . . . was being whistled at'.[141] The frenzy that *I puritani* aroused lifted Bellini to the apex of happiness.

According to Bellini, Donizetti too had recourse to Rossini's advice for his new opera. Bellini informed Florimo: 'I know that Rossini had him revise the introduction, the finale, and many other pieces.'[142] In another context Donizetti reported to Ricordi that in Paris he wrote many new pieces for *Marin Faliero* and had the libretto revised,[143] all of which substantiates the revision of *Faliero* before its *prima*.

The rehearsals of the opera began on 5 February 1835 but, since the rehearsal schedule in Paris was more leisurely than in the opera houses of Italy, the dress rehearsal did not take place until 4 March. As the *prima* occurred more than a week later, on 12 March 1835, it seems probable that the indisposition of one or other of the singers caused the delay. The principal quartet of the Théâtre-Italien appeared in *Marin Faliero*: Giulia Grisi (Elena), Rubini (Fernando), Tamburini (Israele Bertucci) and Lablache (Doge Marin Faliero), and to them was added the tenor Ivanoff[144] in the brief but effective role of the Gondolier.[145] *Marin Faliero* enjoyed a respectable success, but, having a more tragic plot and a less showy role for the prima donna, it did not arouse the same furore as *I puritani*. The day after the *prima* of *Faliero*, the fire marshals insisted that the preventive measures installed in the Théâtre-Italien be tested, with the result that the theater was flooded and the stage machinery was put out of commission. Consequently the first scheduled repetition of *Faliero* was canceled. This, together with the fact that Donizetti's opera had come out so late in the season, meant that it managed to achieve only five performances before the company moved on to London. That Donizetti was generally satisfied with the results appears in his letter to Dolci of 16 March 1835:

I had planned to send you just the article from the *Messager*, but now I am sending you two further words about the second and third performances, which were very brilliant. Rubini has sung as I have never heard him, and because of this I have had to repeat the cavatina and aria every evening two or three times. Bellini's reception with *I puritani* made me tremble more than a little, but as our works are of contrasting genres[146] we have both therefore obtained a fine success without displeasing the public.[147]

As a recognition of their accomplishments at the Théâtre-Italien that season, both Bellini and Donizetti were made Chevaliers of the Légion d'Honneur.[148]

On 14 May 1835 the same company that had sung the first *Marin Faliero* in Paris introduced that work to London. Chorley's account of the production explains in part why *Faliero* made less impression at the outset than *I puritani*.

In spite of the grandeur of Lablache as the Doge of Venice, in spite of the beauty of the duet of the two basses in the first act of *Marino*, in spite of the second act containing a beautiful moonlight scene with a barcarolle, sung to perfection by Ivanoff, and one of Rubini's most incomparable and superb vocal displays, *Marino Faliero* languished, in part from the want of interest in the female character – a fatal fault to an opera's popularity.[149]

The following season it was given again in Paris; in 1841 it was revived again in London.[150] *Marin Faliero* was first given in Italy at the Teatro Alfieri, Florence, in April 1836, with Ungher, Moriani and

Cosselli, in a lavish production by Lanari; it aroused great enthusiasm.[151] During the next thirty years it was performed extensively throughout Italy and elsewhere in Europe, being translated into French, German, and Hungarian. It was introduced to the United States at New Orleans in 1842 and New York heard it in December 1843. (Its share in the current Donizetti revival has been limited to a handful of performances at Bergamo in 1966 and a hearing in London the following year. *Marin Faliero* is an opera with many eloquent moments and a fine role for a star bass; unfortunately the Donizetti revival of the second half of this century has been so oriented toward the prima donna that works whose chief interest lies in other directions are too easily ignored. This opera, which contains many powerful anticipations of Verdi,[152] deserves a first-class production, strongly cast.)

Marin Faliero is a somber work, full of dramatic insight, particularly in the great baritone–bass duet and in the final scene.[153] Although the tenor role of Fernando is tailored to Rubini's vocal type and abounds with difficulties, his music won the most applause at the early performances. Chorley speaks of *Faliero* as 'a fine specimen'[154] of Donizetti's art, preferring it to *Lucrezia Borgia*. Even though, when it first appeared in competition with *I puritani* at the Théâtre-Italien, it did not arouse equal enthusiasm, it is too facile a judgment to dismiss *Marin Faliero* as the opera that came off second best; for it is now clear that *I puritani* was a more old-fashioned work for its period than was *Faliero*, which looked toward the 1840s and beyond.

Donizetti left Paris on 25 March 1835, thirteen days after the *prima* of *Marin Faliero*. Although he had seen a great deal and had been entertained incessantly, he resented the lack of tranquillity. Some of the people he got to know would play a strange part in his later years in Paris: Michele Accursi, who acted as his *homme d'affaires*,[155] and the banker August de Coussy and his wife Zélie. He met musicians of all persuasions. He went to the theater, and he saw Halévy's *La juive*, the latest novelty, at the Opéra;[156] he found the realism of the acting harrowing and the staging daring and lavish, but the music left him cold. He almost certainly also saw Adam's *Le chalet*, which had received its first performance at the Opéra-Comique the previous September, for the following year he was to adapt its plot for the libretto he wrote for *Betly*.

Donizetti left Paris almost a month after his leave of absence from his duties in Naples had expired. He traveled south to Marseilles and then by ship to Livorno as he had to pick up Virginia in Rome, where she had waited for him since the previous November. He returned to Naples about the middle of April 1835 to fulfill the terms of a contract he had signed on 9 November 1834 for three operas, the first of which was supposed to be ready by July 1835. When he returned to Naples he had not yet decided upon a subject for this opera, but by the end of May 1835 he knew that it would be *Lucia di Lammermoor*.

4

1835–1838
Lucia di Lammermoor to *Poliuto*

On Donizetti's return to Naples in April 1835 he and Virginia packed up their belongings and on 3 May they moved into new quarters on an upper floor at Via Corsea, no. 65, over the Aquila Nera inn.[1] The turmoil of changing apartments, however, was nothing compared to the confusion resulting from the mismanagement of the Neapolitan opera houses by the royal commission. Signs of trouble had been clear the previous year, at the time of the prohibition of *Maria Stuarda*, when the censors' interference, as well as the king's own *non fiat*, had resulted in works being abandoned after they had been rehearsed, others dropped from the repertory to which they had earlier been admitted, and still others, although they had been successfully produced elsewhere, regarded as unfit for the Neapolitan stage. It is obvious, too, that at this time there was insufficient discipline in the conduct of performances.

A letter of 3 January 1835 from the Neapolitan music-publisher Guillaume Cottrau[2] to his sister in Paris gives a vivid picture of the careless way things were being done.

The opera *Amelia* by Lauro Rossi, upon which great expectations were founded, could scarcely meet them, although the music was sufficiently spontaneous and singable. The move of giving an opera buffa at the San Carlo ... ran up against the Neapolitans' regard for an auditorium they regarded as consecrated exclusively to grand opera. They have protested at this sacrilege, in part because of the lack of dramatic effectiveness in *Amelia*, in part because of Malibran, who was badly supported in it by Pedrazzi and Frezzolini and a crowd of *dogs* of the second and third class, and in part because the work was horribly mounted with sets that were frayed and falling apart, to say nothing of the costumes, completely disparate, anachronistic, like some impromptu charade. Add an unfortunate mazurka, a crazy idea suggested by Malibran, who wanted to dance in Act 2 all alone with the dancer Mattis ... You can imagine how this scandalized the more conservative members of the audience.[3]

The following May things were no better, as Donizetti reports to Ricordi:

Oh what a cage of madmen! Today there was a big general meeting about the affairs of the theaters, but up to now I know nothing officially about it; this evening the papers will spread the word. Meanwhile after eighteen days of novena, they will reopen the San Carlo with the same *Gemma* that has already been unfavorably received here. Poor singers that evening! And that is truly their only decision after having passed eighteen days debating the choice of a subject and not having found it . . . They say that many people want to call Barbaja back to act as director for the royal commission. Then the fat would be in the fire. Lanari[4] would get angry. Barbaja would not want him as director, and the whole affair would end in a brawl.[5]

When Donizetti writes of 'eighteen days debating the choice of a subject', he is obliquely referring to his own next opera, for which he had signed a contract the previous November and which was to have been ready for staging in July 1835. The seventh article of that contract states that the royal commission is obligated to give Donizetti 'the libretto approved by the authorities at least four months prior to the first performance'.[6] After his problems with *Maria Stuarda* in 1834, Donizetti obviously wanted to take no chances with another last-minute prohibition and insisted that the subject be approved before he started to compose. A major cause of the delay and its resulting frustration was the failure of the commission to approve a librettist to work with Donizetti.

This problem had moved somewhat closer to a solution by 18 May 1835; on that day Donizetti apologizes in a letter to his friend Count Luigi Spadaro del Bosch of Messina that he cannot visit him there in August because of 'the delay in preparing my libretto for the San Carlo, which will be based on *The Bride of Lammermoor* by Walter Scott'.[7] Since Donizetti refers to the title of the novel rather than to that of the libretto, it seems likely that his librettist, Salvatore Cammarano,[8] was still working on the dramatic synopsis of the plot.[9] The synopsis, including the breakdown of the scenes and the number of characters, was completed by 25 May 1835.

The incompetent commission, plagued by financial problems and a disenchanted public, could not bring themselves to approve the project until Donizetti took matters into his own hands. Writing to the commission on 29 May, he exposes the whole exasperating situation:

After having developed for you as clearly as possible in my letter of the 25th of this month, the reasons that induce me to compose *Lucia di Lammermoor*, I cannot understand how you can attribute the delay in staging the opera scheduled for July to my long indecision over the choice of a subject. Permit me to inform you with my customary frankness: you have among the articles of the contract one that states that you should have given me the text approved by all the authorities as early as the beginning of March 1835, while only a few days ago have you placed at my disposition, and only as a result of my repeated urgings, the poet Sig.[nor] Cammarano, with whom I have quickly agreed upon the subject mentioned above. You should remember that when I myself delivered the scenario into your hands a few days ago, with the performers indicated therein, you not only did not disapprove the choice, but you personally forwarded it to the censors for the scenic aspect to be approved, a formality you could have well dispensed with, considering how many times the claim of urgency has got us out of some difficulty. The delay therefore does not at all come from my part, seeing that I would even be within my rights to have protested on several occasions, did I not trust in your loyalty.

Time is pressing. And I assure you that I cannot remain longer in such uncertainty, since I have other obligations. Therefore either be pleased to authorize the poet Sig. Cammarano to busy himself without delay on the scenario of *Lucia Lammermoor* [sic], already presented to and approved by the censors, and in this case I believe I can promise to have the work completely finished by the beginning of August, without having to insist on the four-month interval specified in the contract. Otherwise permit me to put myself in a completely legal position, adhering to my rights as specified in the articles of the contract and annulling every accommodation offered in my earlier letter of 25 May and in this letter.[10]

This important letter shows what an active part Donizetti played in the negotiations with the indecisive commission. He urged the acceptance of Cammarano, whom he had quickly judged to be a collaborator he could work with. He had a tragic subject that pleased him, one that contained nothing to offend the censors. It is through just such a letter as this that Donizetti's skill and decisiveness at coping constructively with the frustrations of the opera house are revealed. Moreover, the letter produced the results he desired.

Even though he had offered at the end of May to finish *Lucia di Lammermoor* only by the beginning of August, he exceeded his estimate, for the final page of the autograph full score is dated 6 July 1835.[11] It is likely that in his eagerness to get on with *Lucia* he had actually started working with Cammarano earlier than his letter of 29 May would indicate. Between the time of the agreement on a subject and that of the score's being completed not more than six weeks elapsed. By the middle of July he expected that *Lucia* would be on the stage by August, for he wrote to a friend in Paris: 'Now they will give an old opera by Persiani, *Danao*, at the San Carlo, then my *Lucia di Lammermoor* which is already finished. The crisis is at hand. The public is fed up. The commission is about to be dissolved.

Vesuvius is smoking and the eruption is near.'[12] The crisis that Donizetti foresaw took the form of the royal commission's attempt to declare itself bankrupt. On 24 July, the name-day of Queen Maria Cristina and as usual the occasion for a royal gala at the San Carlo, all the commission could manage to put on was a ballet, without an opera to complete the evening's entertainment. The commission's threat of bankruptcy meant that they were trying to avoid producing *Lucia*, but Donizetti must have protested, for he informs Salatino, 'His Majesty said the commission had signed an agreement with me, and they or I acting for them will have *Lucia* performed.'[13] Donizetti was successful in getting the production of *Lucia* under way, but during the rehearsal period the commission pronounced itself unable to pay the singers, who refused to continue to work. Donizetti reports this crisis to Ricordi in a letter on 5 September 1835: 'Here the commission is going bankrupt! Not being paid, la Persiani refuses to rehearse, and tomorrow I will protest . . . God knows if I will be paid. And yes, my music deserves it, because by God it is not disgraceful.'[14] Whatever the uncertainties of the finances of the commission and whatever other problems plagued Donizetti at this time, the opera was finally ready for performance at the end of September. On the day of the *prima* Donizetti wrote to Innocenzo Giampieri:

Dear Friend:
Better late than never. (Dante Canto 8690)
Yes sir, I am living! Yes sir, I am writing! And of my living I give you the proof of this tardy but affectionate reply. And of the writing I will give you a detailed account from the newspaper *Sicule Sicilie*. Today the 28th, this very day, or this evening, will be performed at the royal theater of San Carlo for the first time, *Lucia di Lammermoor*, text by Sig.r Salvatore Cammarano, music by M[aestr]o. Donizetti! . . . Rehearsals, very good! Performance, up to now a mystery!
   That which is no longer a mystery are two facts: that is, the cholera, and that I am going to Turin and Venice in Carnival. For Turin *Gli illinesi*, for Venice *Belisario*.[15]

Although Donizetti quite specifically mentions the date of the 28th (September) in this letter, he was mistaken (and anyone who has dealt with Donizetti's letters knows all too well how hazy he could be about dates); there is no doubt that the *prima* of *Lucia* took place on the customarily assigned date of 26 September 1835. For one thing that date was the traditional one for the reopening of the San Carlo after the novena of San Gennaro, an occasion when more often than not a new opera was introduced. The Neapolitan papers of that period announced the scheduling of the first three performances of *Lucia* for 26, 27 and 29 September. Further confirmation is provided by the autograph of the opera where, in the same hand that wrote 'Proprietà di Girard e Cia', there appears the inscription 'rappresentata 26/9/1835'.[16] The first performance, sung by Fanny Tacchinardi-Persiani (Lucia), Gilbert Duprez[17] (Edgardo), Domenico Cosselli (Enrico) and Carlo Porto[18] (Bide-the-Bent), was a triumph. On 29 September Donizetti sent a glowing report to Ricordi:

Lucia di Lammermoor has been performed, and kindly permit me to shame myself and tell you the truth. It has pleased and pleased very much, if I can believe in the applause and the compliments I have received. I was called out many times, and a great many times the singers, too. The king's brother Leopoldo, who was present and applauded, paid me the most flattering compliments. The second evening I saw a thing most uncommon in Naples: namely, at the finale after the great cheers for the *adagio* [the sextet], Duprez in the curse caused himself to be applauded to the heights before the stretta. Every number was listened to in religious silence and spontaneously hailed with shouts of *Evviva!* ... You will know that I have already dissolved my contract with Turin; therefore I could come to Milan to adjust *Maria Stuarda* if it should be needed or to stage it ... La Tacchinardi, Duprez, Cosselli and Porto have carried themselves very well, especially the first two, who are marvelous.[19]

In a postscript Donizetti explains that he wants Ricordi to spread word of *Lucia*'s success because 'now it is finally forbidden that any of the newspapers here speaks of the theaters after certain disagreements'. In spite of this rumor, a review of *Lucia* did appear in *Omnibus* on 3 October 1835. In a season when the San Carlo was troubled by dissension and dissatisfaction, *Lucia* proved a splendid exception.

In Donizetti's letter to Ricordi, quoted above, he refers to the dissolution of his engagement at Turin. Although this project came to nothing, it sheds light on Donizetti's career because, in his correspondence with the Torinese impresario Giuseppe Consul, he makes some illuminating comments on the qualities he seeks in a libretto. The suggestion that Donizetti make his opera *Gli illinesi*[20] for Turin came from Consul, and it involved the use of an old libretto by Romani, already set by Francesco Basili (Milan, 1819) and by Feliciano Strepponi (Trieste, 1829). Romani had offered to revise his libretto, but only to the extent of rewriting three sections, and the proposed revision specifically did not include changing the happy ending.[21] Donizetti felt these proposed revisions would be inadequate; in a letter written while he was completing *Lucia*, the work that contributed much to establishing Romantic tragedy as the preferred form of Italian opera for years to come, he says:

I have the old libretto, and for today's taste it does not please me very much, unless Romani, who could do everything for it, would revise more than three sections . . . If Romani wanted to, he could do it; and if so far he has not wanted to do anything for me, I can see that for you in Turin at least he might do something[22] . . . And now that I have reread the libretto, I tell you that only the finale of Act 1 seems up-to-date, and only there does one see the Romani who tried to improve [the standards of libretto-writing]. If the rest was revised by him . . . it seems to me it could become worthy of the author of *Il pirata, Norma, Anna, Parisina* . . .[23]

Donizetti's objections to *Gli illinesi* were not confined to the old-fashioned libretto. In addition, he did not like the proposed distribution of roles to the singers Consul had engaged. He thought the tenor Donzelli was too old to play the romantic hero.[24] He suggested that role should be given to the mezzo-soprano Giuditta Grisi, 'as she is long accustomed to playing the *musico*'.[25] Today it seems strange that, while Donizetti could object to a libretto as old-fashioned, he could at the same time propose the outdated convention of the contralto hero. But in 1835, while a composer might hope to persuade a librettist to revise his text, it would not cross his mind to suggest that an impresario might hire additional singers or engage others better suited to a particular work. In those days Italian impresarios, in all but the largest theaters, often engaged a single cast to populate a season's repertory. The hardships this limitation caused the composers can easily be imagined;[26] under the circumstances it is amazing that the system worked as well as it sometimes did.

Although Donizetti gave the proposed *Gli illinesi* careful consideration, his correspondence with Consul leaves no doubt that he did not really expect to write the opera. He informs Consul that he will give up the whole project, and will even sue for his release from their agreement, if he does not have the fully-revised libretto in his hands by the first days of September. He doubts that Romani will exert himself on his behalf. 'Remember that I am to have a new libretto and not an adjusted one, and that if I am not in complete sympathy with it I shall send it back. I want love, violent love, without which these subjects are cold.'[27] In this sentence Donizetti expresses his understanding of what Romantic opera is really about. Having just completed *Lucia*, and being, at the time of this letter, engaged in the struggle with the faltering commission to get it on the stage, Donizetti's faith in himself had stiffened. In the future he was to show a decisiveness that had not always characterized his earlier professional dealings.

On 24 September 1835, not having received the first line of Romani's revision of Gli illinesi, Donizetti protested to Consul, asking to be released from his engagement at Turin. This letter of Donizetti's is not known, but Consul's friendly and understanding reply, specifically acknowledging Donizetti's letter of 24 September 1835, is at Naples.[28] Consul assures Donizetti that he has done his utmost to send the libretto by the specified date, but adds that 'from that benedetto [damned] Romani one can never obtain anything'. He further informs Donizetti that Gli illinesi will be composed instead by Pier Antonio Coppola (1793–1877).[29] Significantly, Coppola's opera was performed with the roles distributed as Consul wanted them: Giuditta Grisi as the heroine and Donzelli as the young lover.

Freed from his obligation at Turin, Donizetti now found himself at liberty for the opening of the Carnival season. His thoughts turned, not unnaturally, to Milan and La Scala, where the past three Carnival seasons had opened with his operas,[30] and he promptly notified Ricordi that he was available to help with Maria Stuarda, planned for Malibran.[31] In December 1834 Cottrau had written to his mother in Paris that Malibran, 'having only seen the score' of the work, 'has fallen in love with it [s'est amourachée] to the point of absolutely wanting to put it on at Milan as Maria Stuarda'.[32] Malibran had a keen appreciation of the sensational, and Cottrau's letter makes it clear that she was the motivating force behind the performances of Maria Stuarda at La Scala. Donizetti could scarcely have been unaware of Malibran's intentions, since Cottrau, a close friend, had known of them for months.

Before the question of his participation in the La Scala production of Maria Stuarda was settled, Donizetti busied himself with a bout of non-operatic composition. Early in October 1835 word reached Naples of Bellini's untimely death at Puteaux, outside Paris, on 23 September. Donizetti was sincerely shocked and saddened by this news, for Bellini was four years younger than he; (he was not, of course, directly aware of the spiteful things Bellini had written about him to various correspondents). From Ricordi came a proposal that Donizetti write a cantata in memory of Bellini to verses by Andrea Maffei, and this suggestion he accepted with alacrity: 'I have much work in hand, but an affirmation of my friendship for Bellini takes precedence over everything else.'[33] This work, Lamento per la morte di Bellini, a song with piano accompaniment, was dedicated to Malibran. More important is the Messa di Requiem in Bellini's memory which he began in October 1835.[34] This work was left incomplete (it lacks the Sanctus, Benedictus and Agnus Dei) for reasons that can be deduced from Donizetti's letter to Ricordi of 20 October 1835:

Already I had offered to do something here because the Filarmonica wanted to affirm the general sorrow. The departure of one of the instigators of the project left the thing up in the air. I was to have conducted a mass at the conservatory and I had already begun to compose it, but the performance being scheduled for December prevents me from directing it and that grieves me. All that I was preparing has been nullified by the fate that has obligated me to go to Milan.[35]

Composed less than a month after the *prima* of *Lucia*, the Requiem[36] affords fascinating evidence of Donizetti's conscious mixture of sacred and theatrical styles and of the sharp memories he retained of Mayr's compositions for Santa Maria Maggiore.

Donizetti was anxious not to have his active participation in the Milan production of *Maria Stuarda* become common knowledge in Naples until after the event. He had learned of Malibran's eagerness to appear in that work shortly after his return from Paris in April 1835. On 3 May he had written to Ricordi offering to compose an overture expressly for *Maria Stuarda*,[37] adding that 'Malibran will be performing' in it; but he did not offer to participate actively in the preparation of the opera until 29 September, less than a week after he had extricated himself from *Gli illinesi*. In none of Donizetti's letters of this period, except in those addressed to Ricordi, does he refer to the Milan production of *Maria Stuarda*. His formal request for a leave of absence from Naples, addressed to the Minister of the Interior on 30 October 1835, says nothing of his going to Milan; he merely says he will travel to Venice to put on a new opera, *Belisario*. By this tactful omission he avoided reminding the Neapolitan authorities of King Ferdinando's displeasure with *Maria Stuarda* the year before.

He left Naples near the end of November, and after a rough voyage to Genoa, arrived at Milan on 3 December 1835. Malibran was already there, having sung forty performances at La Scala that autumn. The Milanese censors had already approved the libretto of *Maria Stuarda*, without demanding any changes. To judge from the printed libretto of this La Scala production, the version passed by the censors used language less strong than that in the original, 'vil bastarda' being replaced by 'donna vile'.[38]

The rehearsals of the work, which according to his contract[39] Donizetti was obligated to supervise, began shortly after his arrival in Milan. Rehearsals always caused Donizetti acute nervous ten-

sion. A few months earlier he had written to Spadaro: 'Sleep agreeably and quietly, and not like me, who leap up convulsed by
dreams of eternally getting a work ready for the stage.'[40] This rehearsal period proved to be one of the most emotionally devastating times he ever experienced. His morbidly sensitive nature
was stricken by the news of his father's death on 9 December 1835
to the extent that he could not bring himself to go to Bergamo,
only thirty miles from Milan, for the funeral. His letters at this time
to Dolci,[41] who took charge of the arrangements for him, reveal that
he was sincerely affected by his loss. The situation he found confronting him in the rehearsal rooms of La Scala could scarcely have
added to his peace of mind. As late as 16 December two roles were
still unassigned.[42] Sofia dall'Oca-Schoberlechner had refused the
part of Elisabetta as too insignificant, and her last-minute replacement would be Giacinta Puzzi-Toso. The *comprimaria* role of Anna
was coveted by Rafaella Vernier, a contralto without appreciable
talent, whose mother actively campaigned for her daughter's engagement (shades of *Le convenienze!*), but eventually that part went
to Teresa Moja. An even more unsettling prospect was opened up by
Malibran's determination to sing the original text, 'vil bastarda' and
all, rather than the bowdlerized version approved by the censors.
Specific evidence is lacking as to when Donizetti became aware of
the irrepressible Malibran's intention; he might have learned of it
from Cottrau before he came to Milan, but in any event, once rehearsals were under way he could not have remained long in the dark
about her plan to flout the censors. And then, to add a final element
of uncertainty to the preparations, Malibran fell ill and missed rehearsals, causing the first performance to be delayed.

Instead of opening with *Maria Stuarda,* that Carnival season at La
Scala began with one of the two simultaneous Italian *prime* of Bellini's *I puritani,*[43] with Schoberlechner as Elvira. It says a great deal
for Malibran's determination to appear in Donizetti's opera that she
passed up this opportunity to pay posthumous homage to Bellini,
who shortly before he died had even prepared a special version of
his opera for her.[44] What must have attracted Malibran to *Maria
Stuarda* was the dramatic intensity of the unexpurgated version of
the original text, and she must have counted upon her huge popularity with the Milanese public to carry her through her audacious plan
of disobeying the censors. To some extent Donizetti must have entered into her scheme, and it is not difficult to believe that he hoped
her audacity would be successful.[45] If his opera made an irresistible
hit it might somehow contribute to a relaxation of the censorship.

Whatever hopes Donizetti had for *Maria Stuarda* were doomed to disappointment. At the last moment, and then only to obtain her fee of 3000 francs, Malibran sang in *Maria Stuarda* on 30 December 1835, even though she had obviously not recovered from her indisposition. The audience at La Scala that night was antagonized by her bravado in appearing in poor vocal condition, as Donizetti reports to Dolci:

I have not seen you up to now and perhaps it is better, for not the second nor the third evening but the opening night of *Stuarda* would have made you suffer from start to finish. Madama Malibran would have lost 3000 francs had she not sung that evening; therefore . . . [though] without voice . . . the diva wrote to the governor that she personally guaranteed her fitness to appear . . . But the public clearly saw her error, and after having made her understand they did, they applauded her at the second and third performances. A sad recompense for me who was suffering for everybody. I do not go near the theater any more. My brother writes that Mamma's arm now seems afflicted by a stroke. Everything is in order![46]

Then Donizetti informs Dolci that he is leaving Milan the following day (4 January) to go directly to Venice, where he will put on *Belisario*.

When Donizetti left Milan the problems with *Maria Stuarda* at La Scala were far from over. The first three performances, which the composer was contractually obligated to attend, had been given on three successive days: 30 and 31 December 1835 and 1 January 1836. After a day's interval, on 3 January, a fourth performance took place, consisting of just Act 1 of *Maria Stuarda*, to which was appended Acts 2 and 3 of Rossini's *Otello*. No wonder Donizetti had written Dolci on that day: 'I do not go near the theater any more.' There are two plausible explanations for this mixed bill: either Malibran suffered a recurrence of her earlier illness and, therefore, the only act of *Maria Stuarda* in which she did not appear was given; or, perhaps, the authorities had temporarily forbidden those acts of Donizetti's opera in which things they disapproved of were sung or acted. The later course of events suggests that the latter is the more likely. A week passed and then the fifth performance of *Maria Stuarda* occurred on 10 January, followed by a sixth two days later. After that the authorities forbade all future presentations.

The librettist and one-time friend of Donizetti, Pietro Cominazzi, contributed to the pages of *La fama*, more than forty years after the event, a firsthand account of the Milanese *prima* of *Maria Stuarda*. He mentions 'the imposing finale, in which the audience grew pale and trembled at the terrible *bastarda*'. He goes on to say that after two performances certain noble persons turned to Count Hartig, the [Austrian] governor of Lombardy, to cause him to have other words substituted for the profanity. The count agreed, but his goodwill ran up against the reef of the artist [Malibran], who sharply refused and at the next performance repeated the outrage. Then the governor, to avoid worse problems, and seeing that he would not win by arguing, forbade that further performances of that opera be given.[47]

Early in March 1836 Donizetti explained in a letter to Bardari, the youthful librettist of *Maria Stuarda*, what had happened:

Here I am back home [in Naples] as of yesterday! La *Stuarda* was forbidden in Milan after six performances, and just at the moment when it was going very well indeed! They did not want *bastarda!*; they did not want the Order of the Golden Fleece worn around her neck; they did not want her to kneel for her confession to Talbot. Malibran said: 'I do not trust myself to think about such things' . . . therefore, *forbidden*.[48]

It was rare indeed in those days for an opera to be prohibited outright once it had begun its series of performances, as this would indicate an oversight on the part of the censors. Undoubtedly the banning of *Maria Stuarda* had direct repercussions upon Donizetti's career in Milan. For the previous three seasons he had been assigned the position of honor at the opening of the Carnival season at La Scala, but now six years would elapse before another Donizetti *prima* (that of *Maria Padilla* in 1841) would be given on the important night of Santo Stefano.[49] At that point Donizetti was a prospect for the position of *Hofkapellmeister* to the Habsburg court at Vienna, a position that carried considerable weight in Milan, which was then just a provincial capital in the Austrian Empire.

The banning of *Maria Stuarda* at La Scala by no means signalled the end for that opera in Italy during the nineteenth century.[50] Donizetti, giving up hope that, under existing conditions, the work would be allowed to produce its intended effect, came to take a laissez-faire attitude toward it. His resignation shows clearly in a letter he wrote to Raffaele Mazzetti about a proposed production with Carolina Ungher for Reggio Emilia and Modena in 1837; he suggests that arias which did not go well might be reduced to recitatives, and he even advocates the tenor's introducing an aria of his own choosing.[51] In bowdlerized form *Maria Stuarda* was staged in more than a dozen theaters in Italy, Spain and Portugal up to 1866. In 1865 it was finally given at the San Carlo in something approaching its original form, the Bourbons who had banned it in the first place being by then permanently off stage themselves. Several of these Neapolitan performances were marked by the placing of ceremonial wreaths on Donizetti's statue. (After a single disastrous performance at the San Carlo in 1866, *Maria Stuarda* was heard no more until it was revived at Bergamo on 16 October 1958. Since that evening, this opera has come to be performed with such frequency that it now rivals those of his operas which have held the stage uninterruptedly over the years.)

When Donizetti left Milan on 4 January 1836 to go to Venice, he was returning to the city where he had begun his professional career, and a place he had not visited since 1819. Something of his feelings about revisiting his past appear in a letter he had earlier written to Ferretti: 'I will do *Belisario* at Venice, and I am really going there like a blind man because I don't remember the way, and I don't know who the tenor will be.'[52]

The contract for *Belisario* is dated 26 July 1835 and is signed by the composer and by the impresario Natale Fabbrici. Fabbrici had first suggested a subject set in Venice, but Donizetti was uneasy at such a prospect, fearing that a plot dealing with the days of the doges might easily offend the Austrian censors. The subject of *Belisario* was not agreed upon until 20 October 1835, when Donizetti wrote to Fabbrici:

I am most amenable and I shall compose *Belisario*, as that subject pleases you more. I urge you that the costumes of that period not be used in the preceding operas, and that is for your good as well as mine. La Ungher, la Vial, Salvatori and the tenor (whose identity I soon hope to know) will be the principals. But we will need an excellent second bass,[53] two other secondary male singers and a *comprimaria*.[54]

Barely had Donizetti written this letter when he received one from Fabbrici that temporarily cast doubt upon the choice of *Belisario*. The impresario suggested that he use a text by the Venetian librettist Pietro Beltrame.[55] On 24 October 1835 Donizetti replied, trying to escape tactfully from Fabbrici's proposal, and his letter makes an illuminating statement of his views about a composer's relationship with his librettist and about fitting roles to particular singers.

Your proposal would be difficult to agree to for two reasons. The first is that Signor Cammarano has already begun to write,[56] and not knowing moreover who will come to Naples to sing next year ... I cannot tell [Beltrame] whether his text might be adapted by me on a later occasion or not. The second reason is that, not having the fortune to be acquainted with any verses whatever by Signor Beltrame, it seems imprudent to me to have the poet situated so far away from the composer, when one is not familiar with the style of the other. I might fall out with him, or perhaps I might fall into the bad graces of Signor Beltrame with all those infinite conversations I would need prior to weaving together a libretto. The singers have certain shortcomings, and it is always a good thing not to discuss them in writing. I have already communicated them to Cammarano; I could not discuss them with Signor Beltrame in Venice, for I would arrive there too late to change the characters in a plot. The singers have their sympathies for one role, none for another. One needs to know these things, to be familiar with them . . . If not, the structure falls.[57]

Fabbrici must have found Donizetti's arguments convincing because, for a while at least, nothing more seems to have been said about a libretto by Beltrame.

The composer's concern over the singers engaged to appear in the *prime* of his operas did not stop with their dramatic abilities; he was, of course, even more anxious to know their vocal strengths and defects. In his letter of 24 October to Fabbrici, he voices his anxiety at still not knowing who will be the leading tenor for *Belisario*. He has heard that it might be either Ignazio Pasini or Antonio Poggi,[58] but until he knows for sure, he says, 'I cannot compose duets, finales, trios'. In this context, he mentions ensembles rather than arias because he knows that he can easily adjust solo passages during the rehearsal period.

Donizetti began to compose *Belisario* in Naples late in October 1835. His score was substantially complete when he arrived in Venice on 6 January 1836, expecting rehearsals to begin almost at once. He discovered that the Carnival season at the Fenice had not even started, owing to the threat of an outbreak of Asiatic cholera. The season finally opened on 10 January,[59] and on the 12th there was a performance of Rossini's *L'assedio di Corinto,* which interested Donizetti because the cast included three of his singers for *Belisario*. Two days later he sends an account of them to Ricordi: '*L'assedio* did not please, rather la Vial did not please at all. Only Salvatori[60] was applauded a great deal, and Pasini avoided disaster. It is to be taken off Saturday after two performances . . . What will I do now with this Vial, who is both a bastard soprano and a veiled contralto?'[61] During the rehearsal period for *Belisario,* which began on 13 January, Donizetti adjusted the sympathetic role of Irene to suit the vocal limitations of Antonietta Vial to such good effect that when the opera was given on 4 February 1836, she was applauded and her second-act duet with Salvatori reduced the audience to tears.[62]

Belisario was well received, particularly the contributions of Ungher (Antonina) and Salvatori (Belisario), but the evening began with some show of hostility toward Donizetti by partisans of other composers and by those who resented his being paid a fee of 8000 francs, a high figure in Italy at that time.[63] He reported to Ricordi his sanguine expectations: 'There was some opposition, but you know how opening nights go ... it will go better and better.'[64] He included in this letter a detailed account of how the individual numbers were received, knowing his publisher would be interested in the future sale of excerpts as well as of the complete score.

Here is the news. The truth above all and without self-esteem, as far as a papa can report it. Prelude, so-so. Vial's cavatina, applause. Ungher's cavatina, shouts and turmoil so she could not begin the reprise of the cabaletta. The duet for Pasini and Salvatori, equal applause. The chorus, so-so. Finale, applause and repeated curtain calls for everyone. Act 2: Pasini's aria, three curtain calls. The duet for Vial and Salvatori, many shouts of *bravi*, but at the end (so they say) the situation is so moving that they were weeping. The terzetto, applauded. Final scene: Ungher, much applauded and called out, both alone and with the others, and with me.[65]

Belisario went so well after the *prima* that following the third performance Donizetti was escorted to his lodgings by a shouting crowd carrying torches and accompanied by a band. Before that season ended *Belisario* had achieved a run of twenty-eight consecutive performances.[66] (The work was revived at the Fenice in spring 1969, at Bergamo on 7 October 1970, and in Naples on 25 January 1973.)

Donizetti left Venice on 8 February 1836, exhilarated by the enthusiastic reception of *Belisario*. He journeyed to Milan by a vehicle that he dubbed a 'negligenza' (instead of *diligenza*) because, being overloaded, it took nearly four days to complete the journey. On 15 February he went to Genoa and embarked on what proved a stormy voyage to Civitavecchia. This return passage became even more trying for him when he received the news that in Naples Virginia had had a miscarriage, terminating a pregnancy at seven and a half months.[67] Furthermore, he was forced to spend a two-week quarantine period in Rome, required of those traveling from the north where there had been a recent outbreak of cholera. Impatient to get back to Naples to see Virginia and concerned because his leave from his post with the Neapolitan theaters had expired at the end of January 1836, he stayed with the Vassellis.

Donizetti was still in Rome when, on 4 March, he was handed a letter that been held back from him because it contained bad news. His brother Francesco had written from Bergamo to Naples, and Virginia had forwarded the letter to Rome, to tell him that his mother Domenica had died in Bergamo of a stroke on 10 February, just at the time when he had been en route from Venice to Milan and passing near Bergamo. Donizetti's state of shock is obvious from the letter he wrote to Dolci the following day.

Then all is over? If I did not have such a strong constitution that I amaze myself at it, I too would join the others, and forever. Only three months away, and in three months I have lost father, mother and infant daughter ... I had some little momentum to keep going because of the outcome of *Belisario* and because of the Légion d'Honneur, but having learned only yesterday of the loss of Mamma too, I am in such a state of dejection that time alone will be able to pull me through ... I had Francesco's letter, sent on to me from Naples (since I am here in quarantine and leave the day after tomorrow).[68]

When Donizetti finally got back to Naples about 9 March 1836, he discovered that the commission had allowed the royal theaters to deteriorate further. Both the San Carlo and the Fondo were closed, only the Nuovo[69] continued to limp along. On 30 March he described the situation to Ricordi in these terms: 'Here the theaters are closed, and no one has offered yet to take them on – therefore desolation and poverty.'[70] Apparently not until the end of May did Barbaja come to the rescue, taking over the operatic reins in Naples for the next four years.[71]

With no activity in the theaters to keep him busy, Donizetti again took up his classes in counterpoint and composition at the Conservatory. He also reverted to a type of composition that had not occupied him for many years: he wrote a string quartet, his eighteenth, of which he was later to adapt the opening movement, in E minor, as the main section of the overture to *Linda di Chamounix*. His spirits did not begin to improve until he found himself again involved in writing for the stage. During May and June of 1836 he was engaged in lengthy negotiations with the impresario Lanari, who had secured the lease of the Fenice for the Carnival season of 1836–7, over a new opera, which would be *Pia de' Tolomei*. In much less time than it took him to come to final arrangements over *Pia*, Donizetti had written a libretto, set it to music, and rehearsed and produced one of his minor masterpieces, *Il campanello di notte*.

According to Cottrau,[72] Julius Benedict, who had earlier been on the musical staff of the San Carlo, had sent him from Paris a vaudeville entitled *La sonnette de la nuit*, which Cottrau in turn proposed as a subject to Donizetti. The idea appealed to him, and the one-act farce was completed in a matter of days. Since there are no references to the composition of *Il campanello* in Donizetti's known correspondence, it is not possible to be sure exactly when he wrote it. But Adolphe Adam's often repeated anecdote about the origins of *Il campanello* is certainly misleading.[73] Adam tells of the manager of a little Neapolitan theater who applied to Donizetti to help him out of financial difficulties and of how one week later he submitted the completed score of *Il campanello*. But Cottrau makes clear it was he who suggested the subject of the farsa, and that it was not dashed off at the last minute is demonstrated by Cottrau's having already printed parts of the score within a few days of the first performance.[74] It is most probable that Donizetti composed *Il campanello* during the first half of May 1836, for the work had its first performance at the Teatro Nuovo on 1 June 1836,[75] with Giorgio Ronconi in the bravura role of Enrico.[76]

Pleased with himself at the eager reception of *Il campanello*, a bright spot in that gloomy summer for opera in Naples, Donizetti sent a copy of the libretto, which he had written himself, to his old friend the librettist Ferretti in Rome. Ferretti acknowledged the composer's verses in a tone of humorous despair, inspiring Donizetti to reply: 'And the sweetest thing was your complaining over *Il campanello*. That my Ferretti believed me to be a semi-poet has made me proud, and now I hope to accumulate verses.'[77] What he had in mind when he spoke of accumulating verses is explained in a letter he wrote to Dolci on 6 August 1836: 'Within days I will come out with another opera at the Teatro Nuovo (*Betly*), words and music mine, as it was with the very fortunate *Il campanello*.'[78]

Donizetti obviously regarded *Betly* as a pendant to *Il campanello*. For both works he doubled as librettist and composer, as he had done earlier with *Le convenienze*; both works were drawn from French sources, for in the case of *Betly* he adapted the text by Scribe and Mélesville for Adam's *Le chalet*.[79] Both works were in one act.[80] But where *Il campanello* is a farsa, with recitatives rather than spoken dialogue, *Betly* is an *opera giocosa*. During his Parisian visit of the previous year Donizetti had presumably heard *Le chalet* at the Opéra-Comique and had been attracted to its engaging plot. When *Betly* was first given at the Teatro Nuovo on 21 August 1836,[81] with Adelaide Toldi in the title role and Giuseppe Fioravanti as her brother Max, it did not make a strong impression because Fioravanti's abilities as a singer were no longer equal to his prowess as an actor. (Fioravanti, a baritone, had sung in *La zingara*, the opera that introduced Donizetti to Naples in 1822.) After the second performance Donizetti substituted a new cavatina for Fioravanti,[82] and the comedy became such a success that a week later the royal court attended the Nuovo, and 'half of Naples rushes to hear it', as Donizetti reported to Dolci.[83]

In the second half of Donizetti's career, operatic comedies make up only a small proportion of his works, although among them are such hardy examples as *La fille du régiment* and *Don Pasquale*, while in the years leading up to *Anna Bolena* approximately one third of his output had been buffe and *farse*. The composition of two comedies in 1836 marks a striking divergence from a path that, after *L'elisir* in 1832, led him almost undeviatingly through the landscapes of Romantic melodrama. In a year when opera in Naples had been crippled by mismanagement, in a period when the frequent threat of cholera terrified and depressed the population, at a point when Donizetti was trying to regain his emotional equilibrium after his recent triple bereavement, *Il campanello* and *Betly* testify to his still potent recuperative powers, affirming the innate buoyancy of his creative drive.

With the return of Barbaja as impresario in Naples, Donizetti embarked on one of his most ambitious projects for the San Carlo. Although *L'assedio di Calais* has not yet proved itself capable of living up to Donizetti's high expectations for it, it is a work that marks an important stage in his continuing struggle to expand his range as an operatic composer. The subject was a familiar one – that of the burghers of Calais.[84] Cammarano prepared a scenario for the libretto during the early summer of 1836, and, after consultation with Donizetti, he wrote out a draft of his text.[85] This draft, with the composer's annotations and some sketches of musical ideas, provides evidence of the care that went into the preparation of what Donizetti was soon to describe as his 'most carefully worked-out score'.[86] Significant, too, in judging the importance that Donizetti would place upon this project is that he had it in hand at least five months before the first performance, scheduled for November. The myth, fostered by Donizetti himself, that he always worked rapidly and at the last minute is by no means invariably true.

   The earliest reference to *L'assedio di Calais* in Donizetti's correspondence occurs in a jocular letter to Ferretti,[87] in which he responds to Ferretti's observations upon his libretto to *Il campanello*. He casts his remarks in the form of a half-humorous dialogue. 'I am working on *L'assedio di Calais* with appropriate dances. Eustacchio [*sic*] di Saint-Pierre will be Barroilhet.[88] With Manzocchi[89] in a *musico* role and (God) la Franceschini.[90] You're joking? . . . Really la Franceschini? I still don't believe you! . . . She, indeed . . . Ah, the San Carlo has never been reduced to such a level.'[91] Two things are striking about Donizetti's comments to Ferretti. First, he was planning an opera with an extended ballet divertissement[92] of the sort then obligatory at the Paris Opéra, a clear indication that he had set his sights on following Rossini's example by gaining admission to the stage of what was then regarded as the ne plus ultra of opera houses. Donizetti's idea of including a considerable amount of dancing in his opera may have been suggested by the full-length ballet, also called *L'assedio di Calais*, choreographed by Luigi Henry and mounted at the San Carlo in 1828.[93] The second striking comment Donizetti made to Ferretti concerned his intended use of a *musico* or contralto hero, in the outworn tradition of eighteenth-century opera seria, rather than a tenor. This decision stemmed from the lack of an adequate tenor for *L'assedio* and not from Donizetti's abiding fondness for an already old-fashioned vocal type.[94] Early in September 1836 Donizetti unburdened himself to Dolci about this problem, telling him that he had been trying in vain to find a satisfactory leading tenor. Giovanni David's agent had not replied to Barbaja's inquiries, perhaps, as Donizetti seemed to think, because that tenor's vocal decline was already far advanced. Giovanni Basadonna, a tenor then in his prime, was not free to begin his Neapolitan engagement until the end of November, too late to participate in the *prima* of *L'assedio*, which was set for 19 November, the gala honoring the name-day of the queen-mother, Maria Isabella. To Dolci, Donizetti described the three tenors currently available in Naples as 'almost useless'; therefore he had decided to give his opera '*without a tenor*'.[95] At that stage Barbaja would not consent to a change in subject to one better adapted to the uneven company at the San Carlo, nor, I suspect, would Donizetti have wanted it.

Donizetti's true intentions for *L'assedio di Calais* emerge in a letter he wrote the following year to the tenor Duprez, who had left Italy to return to Paris (where he made a wildly successful debut at the Opéra on 17 April 1837).

Years ago we spoke, if you have not forgotten, about how I could produce a sure impression at the Opéra along with you. Perhaps now that you are there, you recognize that it would not be advisable, and I respect your goodwill and your opinion, but if you should find a way to bring it about [*il buco di ficcargliela*] it would be a great thing.

The management would spend hardly anything ... I would write them as many *ballabili* as they want. I would change or lengthen what you wanted ... I believe that the work that I would most like to give at the Grand Opéra would be *L'assedio di Calais*, which is the most erudite of my operas, the most congruent to the French taste, and, as such, believed by everyone to have been composed for Paris. In it there are dances, effective choruses, adequate orchestration (to the extent that I am capable), and if that could come about I would be your particular debtor for life.

You see that after having been first given in November, *L'assedio* is still being performed. It is scheduled now for 6 July.[96] Don't think it is a father's love that makes me speak out; you know that I am father to various children, but I swear to you that you would not regret this. I would compose new numbers for you (who must do the part I wrote for la Manzocchi as *musico*).

And, by God, if it does not produce an effect, I would give you leave to castrate me.[97]

Donizetti's plan to employ *L'assedio di Calais* as his weapon to breach the defenses of the Opéra is obvious in this letter to Duprez, as is his willingness to revise the *musico* role as a leading tenor part. Yet *L'assedio* was not to be produced at Paris, nor anywhere else, apparently, outside Naples.[98] Donizetti did not, however, insist absolutely on *L'assedio* for Paris. In his letter to Duprez, he goes on to say: 'I leave a free choice up to you, although I lean toward *L'assedio*. In any case, if *Lucia* is not given at the Italiens I urge you to say a word from time to time, as you know my intentions.'[99]

The path toward the Neapolitan *prima* of *L'assedio di Calais* was cleared in the usual way. On 5 October 1836 Barbaja sent a letter to Prince di Ruffano, the Superintendent of the Royal Theaters and Spectacles, submitting the libretto for approval and asking for prompt action since the first performance was scheduled for 19 November.[100] The musical preparations began shortly, and the stage rehearsals were already under way when the Minister of the Interior, Marchese Niccola Santangelo, on 9 November sent the approval for the performance, adding 'observe, however, the corrections that are found herein'. One of these changes is highly indicative of the concerns of the censors in those days. The autograph score in the Conservatorio di San Pietro a Majella in Naples shows that in Act 3, when the English queen pleads with Edoardo III to spare the lives of the hostages, she asks a pointed question: 'È di Dio più grande un Re?' (Is a king more powerful than God?), while in the printed libretto her line is toned down to a declaration of orthodoxy: 'È di Dio l'immago un Re.' (A king is the image of God.) With the uncertainties of the censorship and all the other problems that could arise in the theater, Donizetti found these preparations devastating to his nerves. On 19 October he had written to his friend Spadaro in Messina: 'The rages are beginning for me, and along with them the frenzies, the heartaches and the terrors.'[101]

The *prima* of *L'assedio* occurred at the Teatro San Carlo on the appointed date of 19 November 1836. On the 22nd, two days after the second performance, Donizetti sent the details to Ricordi.

L'assedio di Calais went well. I was called out six times (the evening after the gala).[102] The third act is the least felicitous (see my sincerity). Who knows but I might retouch it? God knows who is reducing the pieces for you, it's all a mystery to me. It is my most carefully worked-out score. Barroilhet, la Manzocchi, la Barili, Gianni, everyone applauded. But the cholera keeps everyone in the country. I am leaving [for Venice] the first of next month. If you print all of *L'assedio,* wait until I can check it over at Milan. And place on the first page of the complete score: 'Dedicated to Her Majesty the Queen, etc.'

The king sent a chamberlain to congratulate me, and tomorrow I go to thank him. But the cholera depresses everybody, and the theater will be deserted just the same. Farewell.[103]

The opera had scored an honest success, but it had aroused nothing approaching that pitch of enthusiasm generated by *Lucia* the preceding year. Donizetti's comments about the weakness of the third act of the opera are confirmed by the revival of 6 July 1837, when only the first two acts were performed, the evening being rounded out with another composer's ballet. Some of the blame for the ineffectiveness of the third act during *L'assedio*'s first run of performances must be laid at the feet of Federico Lablache, the son of the great Luigi, whose inadequacy in the important role of Edoardo III proved embarrassing.

A document in the Archivio di Stato, Naples, relates to the time of the early performances of *L'assedio di Calais* and sheds light on a common, if reprehensible, practise of that period. A recurring motif in many of Donizetti's letters is his dismay over the musical pirates who illegally copied and circulated scores, which were frequently full of errors, to unscrupulous impresarios glad to avoid paying royalties. For all the complaints of Donizetti and his fellow composers, only rarely does independent evidence of these surreptitious activities come to light. The document in question is a letter from Barbaja to Prince di Ruffano, dated 28 November 1836. In it he asserts that on Saturday, 26 November (the evening of the fifth performance of *L'assedio*) one of the members of the orchestra, Pietro Paolo Rispoli, was caught copying a first violin part in pencil; and on the following evening (the sixth of *L'assedio*) another musician, Giovanni Battista Bonica, was surprised with pen and inkwell copying on twenty-four-stave paper the full score of *L'assedio* that had been prepared for Nicola Festa, who conducted the San Carlo orchestra. Barbaja requests that Rispoli be suspended from the orchestra for a month and that Bonica be suspended for three, 'although he deserves to be fired'. The Archives show that Ruffano ordered an investigation of the matter, but they do not reveal its ultimate disposition.[104]

(*L'assedio di Calais* was given sixteen times during the winter of 1836–7; it was revived in July of both 1837 and 1838, achieving a grand total of thirty-eight performances, the last taking place on 4

February 1840. This eloquent and frequently powerful score has only a few pages that are not among Donizetti's best, and it does not deserve the neglect that has been its lot for 140 years. It is welcome news that Opera Rara plans to record it.)

The composition of Donizetti's next opera, *Pia de' Tolomei*, overlapped the writing of *L'assedio di Calais*. The trail of *Pia* begins in May 1836, before the subject had been decided upon, with a correspondence between Lanari,[105] who had obtained the lease of the Fenice in Venice for the Carnival season of 1836–7, and Donizetti. The composer refused Lanari's initial offer of 8000 francs and finally won his grudging acceptance of a fee of 10,000, which Donizetti insisted be paid in 20-franc *napoléons d'or*. His insistence on this form of payment was part of a plan, decided upon the year before, to invest his earnings, as far as was practicable, with the Parisian banker August de Coussy, whom he had met at the time of *Marin Faliero*. This question settled, Donizetti signed the contract on 31 May, and in his covering letter he refers for the first time to the subject he has selected: 'I propose *Pia* to you as a subject well adapted to the company.'[106] Lanari had already told Donizetti that his prima donna would be Fanny Persiani and the tenor Antonio Poggi.

Cammarano was to be the librettist. Lanari had assumed from the start that Donizetti would prefer to work with Cammarano, but Count Berti, the president of the committee that administered the Fenice, accepted this choice only reluctantly; he, like Fabbrici the year before, urged the merits of Pietro Beltrame, but Donizetti again avoided the problem of collaborating with a poet whose work was an unknown quantity. In seeking an appropriate vehicle for Persiani, both the composer and librettist hoped to duplicate the success of *Lucia*; they cast about for a heroine of similar traits – one who was gentle, beset by forces she could not oppose, and one whose death evokes genuine pathos. They found the figure they sought in Bartolomeo Sestini's novella *Pia de' Tolomei*.[107] About seven weeks before Donizetti proposed the subject to Lanari, a play entitled *Pia de' Tolomei* by Giacinto Bianco was given at the Teatro dei Fiorentini at Naples. While engaged with his libretto Cammarano seems to have consulted both this and Marenco's verse play of the same title, though the latter was not given its first performance until after the libretto for Donizetti was under way; there were obvious advantages to working with a plot already adapted to the stage, and of the two dramas Cammarano found Bianco's the more useful.

If Count Berti of the Fenice did not succeed in forcing Donizetti to accept Beltrame's services, he managed to interfere in artistic decisions by helping to add to the cast of *Pia* a practically unknown singer, Rosina Mazzarelli. It is more likely that the pushing forward of Mazzarelli started with Lanari rather than with Count Berti, for in May 1836 the singer had yet to make a debut and was only a promising vocal student of Pietro Romani,[108] the conductor at the Teatro della Pergola in Florence. On 10 May, Berti still did not know much about Mazzarelli, for on that date he asked for Donizetti's opinion of her talent; the composer replied guardedly that he had heard her sing only once and advised waiting for the outcome of her debut. Donizetti saw no reason to concern himself with her as the plot of his opera involved, besides the title role, only the insignificant character of Pia's confidante, Bice. But once Mazzarelli had achieved a creditable debut early in June, as Adalgisa in *Norma* at the Teatro Alfieri in Florence, the pressures on Donizetti from both Lanari and Berti increased. Lanari assured him that the young singer's merits surpassed his expectations and predicted a major career for her, while Berti would not accept her exclusion from the cast and insisted upon an opera for two prima donnas. Rather than consider a change of subject, because he thought *Pia* particularly suited to the strengths of Persiani, Donizetti offered Lanari a compromise on 28 June: 'She will do the part of Pia's brother.[109] She will have a cavatina, not much in the finale, as he must escape, and a big scene with chorus in the second act. An understudy's role and nothing more.'[110] Without having originally intended to, Donizetti found himself once more forced to adopt the old *musico* tradition. In the same letter to Lanari he announces: 'I am already working on Poggi's music in the opening scene', thereby giving us 28 June 1836 as an approximate starting date for the composition of *Pia*.

By 11 October Donizetti could inform his friend Agostino Perotti, the *maestro di cappella* at San Marco in Venice, that he was composing the second piece of Act 2 of *Pia* and that he would have time to rework his score before he orchestrated it.[111] Since this letter was written at about the time that *L'assedio di Calais* went into rehearsal, it is clear that Act 1 and the beginning of Act 2 of *Pia* were composed concurrently with *L'assedio*. Since there are few references to the progress of *Pia* in Donizetti's correspondence, its development can only be traced from other evidence. Not until 11 July did Lanari inform Donizetti that the baritone (who would take the part of Pia's husband Nello) would be either Celestino Salvatori or Giorgio Ronconi[112] and that he had initiated a lawsuit to assure himself of Ronconi's services. Nor is it probable that the project had advanced very far by 19 August 1836, for on that date Lanari wrote to the composer asking for a scenario of *Pia* and an indication of the number of sets and types of costumes that would be needed. On these grounds, and taking into account as well that this was the time at which *Betly* was being prepared and first performed, it seems safe to assume that more intensive work was done on the first act of *Pia* in September and early October 1836 than in July or August.

When Gaetano set out for Venice from Naples on 6 December 1836 he left Virginia behind in Naples as she was some months into her third pregnancy. In addition to the normal hazards of winter traveling, that year there were added the lengthy quarantines due to the fear of Asiatic cholera. On 8 December Donizetti arrived at Genoa, where he had to spend almost three weeks in a *lazzaretto* (quarantine station). There he received from Venice the unsettling news that the Teatro La Fenice had been totally destroyed by fire on the night of 12 December, that the season would be transferred to the Teatro Apollo but would be delayed in starting, and that he was requested to take a cut of a quarter of his fee, a sacrifice already accepted by the others in Lanari's company. Donizetti replied that under the circumstances he could only renounce 1000 francs (one-tenth of his fee) and no more, since he himself had to meet the expenses of his travel and of his quarantine. Unsure whether his counterproposal would be accepted, he asked for definite word to be sent to him in Milan, where he arrived not long after Christmas.

At Milan he accomplished for Ricordi his promised corrections of the piano-vocal score of *L'assedio di Calais,* but, finding no word of acceptance or refusal from Lanari, he pushed on to Venice in a state of considerable uncertainty. The season at the Apollo opened with Persiani as *Lucia,* a choice of opera with which Donizetti was none too happy;[113] in fact it ran successfully for twenty-three performances. Donizetti's hopes that *Pia* would soon start rehearsal were dashed when Salvatori, who had been assigned the role of Nello, fell ill and had to be replaced. His substitute was Giorgio Ronconi, who had to be brought from Florence and had to learn a lengthy role. At this point Donizetti grew anxious that the delay of the *prima* would force him to overstay his two months' leave from the Neapolitan theaters; he was also concerned that, with the *prima* coming near the close of the season (which had to end before Lent), the opera could not have much of a run, even if it were very successful. But with Ronconi he was particularly pleased because the baritone's extraordinary dramatic powers were shown to advantage in the role of the jealous Nello.

At long last on 18 February 1837 *Pia de' Tolomei* received its first performance, to a mixed reaction from the audience. While the tenor and soprano cavatinas in Act 1 were applauded, the tenor–baritone duet was the only music in the opera to arouse real enthusiasm. The first-act finale evoked whistles and disapproving comments. Things improved in Act 2, where Mazzarelli's scena, the soprano–tenor duet, and, particularly, the tenor's moving death scene were warmly applauded. Pia's final aria, which Donizetti regarded as the crown of his score, had only a discreet reception. The second performance went rather better than the first, but still the work had only a succès d'estime.[114]

The composer's own account of the first performance was confined to a single sentence he wrote to Dolci: 'All of *Pia* pleased, except for the finale to Act 1.'[115] Rumors appeared in the Venetian press that Donizetti would change the 'unfortunate' finale to Act 1 even before he left Venice,[116] but this word was premature, for he promised, as a gesture of goodwill toward Lanari, to revise it only for the performances that the impresario planned to give at the Adriatic resort of Sinigaglia that summer. On 22 May 1837 Donizetti sent the new text[117] and music to Lanari; as well as revising the offending first-act finale he abbreviated the *musico* role of Rodrigo, causing that character to appear only in the new finale.[118] The revised version of *Pia* was first performed at Sinigaglia on 31 July 1837, with Eugenia Tadolini[119] (Pia), Letizia Suddetti (Rodrigo), Napoleone Moriani[120] (Ghino) and Ronconi (again as Nello).[121] Donizetti was not present at this production. In May 1838 Giuseppina Strepponi[122] sang *Pia* at the Teatro Argentina in Rome, with Moriani and Ronconi, but in this case it was the accomplishment of the 23-year-old prima donna that excited the audience rather than Donizetti's score. Four months later in Naples, in the wake of the prohibited *Poliuto*, *Pia* was brought out at the San Carlo, this time with Ronzi as the hapless heroine. The censors insisted on several alterations to the plot, including a new denouement in which Pia survives and is reconciled with Nello, but in spite of these distortions, the work managed to maintain itself in Naples for two seasons before disappearing from the repertory.

Even though *Pia* had more than a dozen different nineteenth-century productions, the work was dropped by 1860. The fundamental reason for its failure to capture the public lies in its peculiar dislocation of emphasis. The tenor villain Ghino has the best and most moving music in the score, while the heroine is rarely more than a pallid wraith though the work is constructed to place the major emphasis upon her. (After more than a century of neglect, *Pia* was revived at Siena in 1967, in a version that was not notably faithful to Donizetti's intentions. A more authentic version was used to introduce the score to England on 26 February 1978 in a concert performance at the Queen Elizabeth Hall, London, conducted by Leslie Head. The reviews of this performance were largely favorable, raising hopes that this score, which contains one of Donizetti's great tenor roles, will get the wider attention it deserves.)

After the third performance of *Pia de' Tolomei* Donizetti hurried back to Naples, arriving there on 20 February 1837, two weeks after the expiry of his leave of absence. After his return, or possibly before, he fulfilled an assignment to write a *sinfonia*[123] for a cantata in memory of Maria Malibran. The famous singer had died 23 September 1836, aged twenty-eight, supposedly as the result of a fall from a horse the preceding April. The other contributors to this cantata were Pacini, Mercadante, Vaccai and Pier Antonio Coppola. Given only once, at La Scala by the full forces of the company on 17 March 1837, the cantata was judged thoroughly bad.[124]

At the end of April 1837 Gaetano wrote to his brother-in-law Toto Vasselli in Rome: 'I am cursing trying to find the subject of my new opera.'[125] From that brief statement one cannot be sure which he meant of the two operas he was then under contract to compose. He was obligated to have a score ready for Barbaja at the San Carlo that fall (this was to be *Roberto Devereux*), and on 20 February 1837, just before he left Venice, he had signed with Lanari a contract to compose a work (*Maria de Rudenz*) to open the rebuilt Teatro La Fenice, a *prima* scheduled for 26 December. His other news to Toto in this letter was that on 5 May he would be moving Virginia into a larger apartment at Strada Nardones, no. 14, close to the San Carlo. He also bought a horse and carriage, but as it turned out they were never used.

If the new apartment and the carriage were signs of prosperity and appropriate to Donizetti's rising status as a highly successful and active composer, another event of this period seemed to hold out further improvement of his professional position. On 5 May Niccolò Zingarelli,[126] the director of the Naples Conservatory since 1813, died. Donizetti, who was already professor of composition there, was named pro-director and, according to Florimo,[127] assured that it would be simply a matter of time until the king confirmed his full appointment as director. Without any doubt, Donizetti sincerely wanted to have the position offered to him because it meant much in terms of security and prestige, and he still regarded Naples as his musical base. Zingarelli, who was eighty-five at the time of his death, was Neapolitan by birth, a contemporary of Cimarosa, a conservative and deeply religious man, dedicated to the perpetuation of the traditions of the old Neapolitan school.[128] Bellini had studied with him, and of his many former pupils then active in Naples, Florimo and Mercadante could exercise considerable influence, particularly since both of them were subjects of the Kingdom of the Two Sicilies. To them Donizetti was scarcely a happy choice as Zingarelli's successor, as he was an Austrian citizen (being a Lombard) and had been educated in the north at Bergamo and Bologna. Even though he had resided principally in Naples for the past fifteen years, he was still regarded as a *forestiere* (outsider), and the local opposition to his appointment is not surprising. Donizetti's general attitude throughout his career was to place himself above prejudice and petty criticism, and on this occasion he made the diplomatic gesture of composing in three days a Requiem Mass in Zingarelli's memory.[129]

One clear sign of an opposing faction can be found in the pages of *Omnibus*, a literary and artistic weekly published in Naples. In the issues of 26 October and 2 November 1833 there appeared a two-part article, reprinted from the Milanese journal *Il Barbiere di Siviglia*; it was an unfavorable, even malicious, review of *Il furioso* at La Scala, implying that the opera was a grotesque failure. Yet the records of La Scala prove that this production was judged 'buonissimo'[130] and enjoyed a run of thirty-six performances. (A contemporary perspective may be gained from the fact that the *prima* of *Norma*, nine months earlier, was also judged 'buonissimo' and ran for thirty-four performances.) Not only did *Omnibus* take the space to reprint, in two parts, an adverse and inaccurate report of *Il furioso*, but it failed to make any mention at all of the successful *prima* of *Lucrezia Borgia* on the opening night of the Carnival season two months later. The attitude adopted by this weekly can only be construed as evidence of local bias, in some quarters at least, against Donizetti.

On 8 June 1837 Donizetti concludes a letter to Lanari: 'As for *Pia* [at Sinigaglia] I am waiting for news; as for *Rosmonda* I am working on it.'[131] Lanari had suggested, at least as early as the preceding June, the possibility of Donizetti's revising *Rosmonda d'Inghilterra*, in the hope that Barbaja would produce it at the San Carlo in 1838. Lanari had a particular fondness for operas with equal but contrasting roles for two prima donnas, and so enthusiastically endorsed this revision to the extent of offering to pay Donizetti 500 francs for it. Lanari bent the truth when he wrote to Donizetti in a letter of 31 May 1837, 'Note well that *Rosmonda* under the name of *Eleonora di Gujenna* can pass with Barbaja as a completely new opera.'[132] For whatever combination of reasons, *Eleonora di Gujenna* seems never to have been produced at the San Carlo;[133] all that seems to have come of the project was the publication of ten numbers under that title, nine of which had formed part of *Rosmonda*.[134] When Donizetti departed from Naples in October 1838 he was still trying to collect his 500 francs for *Eleonora* from Lanari.[135]

The events of the next six weeks did not allow Donizetti sufficient composure to think very much about *Rosmonda*. On 13 June 1837, just five days after he had notified Lanari that he was working hard on this revision, Virginia gave birth at four in the afternoon to a son, who lived barely an hour. According to the child's death certificate, the tiny body was carried the following day at six to the registry of the San Ferdinando district by two of Donizetti's closest Neapolitan friends, Aniello Benevento, 'a lawyer, 30 years old', and Tommaso Persico, 'a businessman, aged 31'. After the delivery Virginia's health remained precarious. Something of Donizetti's morbid sensitivity during these days is revealed in a letter he wrote to Mayr on 21 June:

How are you? How is your wife's health? And your daughter? And her husband? And their children, past and future? I wish them all well now and forever . . . Dear Maestro, I am not indolent by nature, and 57 operas prove it.
    In three days I wrote a Requiem Mass for poor Zingarelli . . . But if it is performed perhaps it will not make an evil effect. I remembered one of your imitations . . . I included it. How, after so many years? Yes sir, after so many years. The beautiful remains engraved inerasable like the word of God. I could tell you many sad things, but what good would that do?[136]

What some of these 'sad things' were is evident from other letters Donizetti wrote at this time. He informs Spadaro in Messina of the cholera epidemic that had engulfed Naples. One day there had been more than 500 cases, and on many occasions more than 300 deaths a day. One of the queen-mother's ladies-in-waiting had died of the disease, surrounded by doctors, just an hour before the royal family set out for Manfredonia to escape the epidemic. He mentions other prominent people who had died of it, and continues: 'My Conservatory too has been attacked by it . . . long may we live. I cannot go into the country because of the forty days of Donna Virginia; therefore I stay to see if it attacks me.'[137] A few days later he gives Cottrau more specific details of his wife's condition: 'I am writing jokingly but my soul is serious because Donna Virginia has been very ill indeed, but now things are going better. Diarrhea, her milk almost completely disappeared! She coughs. We hope for the best.'[138] In the middle of all this public horror and private distress Donizetti was struggling to complete *Roberto Devereux,* which was scheduled for the San Carlo in a few months. And at some point during these unhappy days he wrote a cantata, entitled *La preghiera di un popolo,* for the birthday of the king's second wife;[139] it was performed at the San Carlo on 31 July 1837.

The day before this performance Virginia died at four o'clock in the morning, at the age of twenty-eight. Because of the conditions in Naples, she was buried the same day. Later a memorial service was held at Santa Maria delle Grazie on the Via Toledo. The causes of Virginia's death have aroused much speculation. From the symptoms of her condition that Donizetti reported to Cottrau at the end of June, it appears that after her delivery she had a bout of puerperal fever. Then she grew gravely sick and died. Donizetti seems to have believed that she had somehow been exposed to measles[140] and that in her weakened condition this disease proved fatal. Yet adults did not usually, even then, die of this complaint. Distasteful as the suggestion may seem, it is difficult to rule out the possibility, in the face of what evidence survives, that instead of measles she succumbed to a severe syphilitic infection.[141]

Gaetano was devastated by the death of his beloved wife. His friends, not wanting to leave him alone for fear of what he might do in his grief-stricken condition, moved him to the home of Persico. There he remained for several days in bed, unable to get up. Gradually he steeled himself to pick up his work again, but he kept his grief always locked in his heart. He did not want anyone to mention to him that he was a widower. He could never bring himself to utter or to write Virginia's name again. He closed the door to her bedroom and never reopened it. Only to her brother Toto could he express the sorrow that kept welling up.[142]

On 5 August 1837, six days after Virginia's death, Gaetano made his first tentative moves toward resuming his old life. On that day he wrote the first of his letters to Toto about recent events. He could not face writing to Lanari about some pressing business, but he dictated to Cottrau what had to be said, and the letter is written on Cottrau's business stationery. A few of the phrases reveal Gaetano's struggle:

Moriani (whom you will greet) wrote to me about *Pia* and just today I am doing what he wants about the duet. He is wrong to complain about having too little to sing in the *adagio* of the finale; at the end of the act everyone has to sing something.

If you want *Pia* given here, send it at once to Cottrau. Don't think of asking me to change anything else in it because the misfortunes I have suffered make any such request useless.

At the bottom of this letter he added a few words in his own, unsteady, hand:

I am a widower. Nothing more. Pray for her. Farewell.

Donizetti.[143]

There is another significant document, also dated 5 August 1837, which affords further insight into Donizetti's sensibilities at this time. This is a draft of a letter asking that he be released from his position as musical director of the royal theaters of Naples[144] because he believed the post was 'totally useless'. He demonstrated that it was so by citing instances in which all sorts of musical decisions had been made both at the Fondo and at the San Carlo without his being notified or even consulted. That there was another point of dissatisfaction that rankled shows in this ironical passage:

and I thank the management for the extreme courtesy accorded me the evening of the cantata,[145] that is, for taking away the box assigned me so that others could use it for their diversion; and for not having given me the text of the said cantata [in time] when I was composing it for the benefit of the management gratis.[146]

Donizetti was deeply affronted that his box had not been left empty as a sign of respect for his very recent bereavement. There was, of course, no question of his having attended the performance, since he was at Persico's house, confined to his bed. In time Donizetti's rancor subsided and the authorities ignored his request to give up the title of director of music of the royal theaters, but he retained few illusions about official regard for him in Naples.

Donizetti needed to pull himself together as he expected *Roberto Devereux* to go into rehearsal about the end of August; the *prima* was scheduled to follow the reopening of the San Carlo (26 September) after the novena of San Gennaro. During the closure of the theaters for the novena the company concentrated on the preparation of works new to the repertory. On 4 September 1837 he told Toto: 'In a few days I begin rehearsals. For me this will be the opera of my emotions, but I have no eagerness to begin the exertions when at every page . . .'[147] Donizetti left that sentence unfinished, clearly implying his dread of preparing for performance the music he had composed during Virginia's final illness.

On 12 September he wrote to Toto: 'The beginning of my rehearsals is postponed; therefore I, with either a clear or muddled head, must finally think about the opera for Venice in January. The poet still has to decide on a subject, and I have to deliver it complete in December.'[148] As days went by without any word as to what was delaying the official approval of *Roberto Devereux*, Donizetti's apprehension increased. On 23 September he unburdened himself again to Toto:

Still there is no word about rehearsing my opera, and I am afraid to guess the reason: it could really be an ugly thing for me . . . Toto! If the management should fail? That would be a buggery. We'll see! That the world is a stage and the stage a lesson is an old story. But oh! if only we could show many other truths there, truths that are not permitted in Italy, how much more would be learned, without betraying Christianity or our loyalty as subjects![149]

That the management was in difficulties is not surprising, as the cholera, even though by then it had markedly subsided, still kept many people away from the theater. Donizetti understood that Neapolitan censorship had become increasingly sensitive to situations in plots that could, by even the most far-fetched reasoning, be construed as 'dangerous', and he was fearful lest the execution of Essex, an important factor in the action of *Devereux*, had disturbed the censors in some way. This letter of 23 September makes clear Donizetti's deep desire for a more enlightened censorship. The only relief he found from these preoccupations was the preparation of *Betly*, now expanded into two acts, for a revival, probably at the Fondo on 29 September 1837. Finally on 4 October, the long-awaited approval for *Roberto Devereux* was sent down, and this allowed the manuscript to be sent to the copyists, clearing the way for rehearsals, which started at long last on 9 October.

The *prima* of *Roberto Devereux* took place at the Teatro San Carlo on 28 October 1837,[150] with Ronzi (Elisabetta), Almerinda Granchi (Sara), Basadonna (Roberto) and Barroilhet (Nottingham). Donizetti wrote to Tito Ricordi on 31 October: 'The day before yesterday I gave my opera at the San Carlo; it is not up to me to tell you how it went, for I am more modest than a whore, and therefore I would blush. But it went very, very well indeed.'[151] If *Pia de' Tolomei* had somehow failed to match Donizetti's expectations, *Roberto Devereux* surpassed them. Although its initial run in Naples had to be interrupted when Barroilhet fell ill and had to stay in bed for two weeks, the public's interest in the new opera continued unabated. (For more than forty years, it continued to be performed widely, reaching New York in 1849, and appearing in Rome during six different seasons and at the San Carlo during eight. By 1882 it had pretty well run the course of its nineteenth-century life. It was revived in Naples in 1964 for Leyla Gencer, and then Montserrat Caballé took it up. When Beverly Sills first sang it at the New York State Theater on 15 October 1970, *Roberto Devereux* became for a time the 'hottest ticket on Broadway'.)

Donizetti had signed the contract for the opera that was to be *Maria de Rudenz* on 20 February 1837 at Venice. The chief specifications were that the opera should be ready to open the season at the rebuilt Teatro La Fenice, that he would be paid 10,000 francs for it, and that the librettist would be Cammarano. A touching indication of Donizetti's steadfast loyalty to Cammarano may be found in a letter he wrote to Innocenzo Giampieri about two weeks before the *prima* of *Maria de Rudenz*, evading an offer to work with a different librettist, by asserting: 'And then in Naples I would not have the heart to deprive the worthy Cammarano of bread, for he is the father of five children, and he has no other livelihood than this, and he is such a good and worthy gentleman.'[152] Several months passed after the signing of the contract before Donizetti found either the time or the necessary serenity to tackle this new opera; he did not start to think about it until the middle of September 1837.

If Donizetti was unable to concern himself much with the new project during that spring and summer, it was very much on Lanari's mind, as more than a dozen of his letters to Donizetti, written between February and October 1837, demonstrate. Reporting that Carolina Ungher would be his prima donna that season, he mentioned that he would like to use the services of Eugenia Tadolini for this new work, and suggested that Donizetti direct his attention toward a subject with two important female roles. Then Lanari, obviously upset, sent word that Count Berti, the administrative head of the Fenice who always liked to have his opinions count, was promoting an engagement for Pasta instead of Ungher. If Lanari's lack of enthusiasm at this time for the great Pasta seems strange, it should be remembered that her voice, particularly in matters of pitch, was no longer what it had been. Speaking of her appearances in London during the summer of 1837, Chorley, who was a sincere admirer of Pasta's genius, concedes that 'her voice was steadily out of tune ... painful to the ear'.[153] Lanari clearly doubted that Pasta could content the public of the Fenice for even half a season as a prima donna, and he was keenly aware that as Pasta's vocal powers had declined her capacity for raising all sorts of difficulties had proportionately increased. On 12 July Lanari informed Donizetti that he was finding Berti so intransigent that he had offered to surrender his lease on the theater. By the end of August Lanari had visited Venice and discovered that Berti was suffering from cancer of the cheek; making allowances for the Count's stubbornness, he agreed to stay on as impresario, even though he was discouraged to learn that Berti's obstinacy had divided the Venetian public into two factions, which he describes as: 'the *Ungheresi* (all the public) and the *Pastisti* (only a few nobleman, but influential), and that is how it is'.[154] Next, he compromised with Berti by agreeing that Pasta share the season with Ungher; but all was finally settled, happily from La-nari's point of view, when Pasta declined the engagement. When Donizetti discovered that he could not get leave of absence from Naples early enough to stage his new opera on Santo Stefano, Lanari reassured him that this was not insoluble, for Giuseppe Lillo (1814–63) would have his new opera ready by 26 December. While all these matters were under discussion, a constant theme of Lanari's letters, raised with increasing impatience, was his insistence on knowing just what subject Donizetti and Cammarano had decided upon.

The subject of *Maria de Rudenz* was arrived at after several false starts. On 19 September Gaetano replies to a suggestion from Toto Vasselli:

Your subject for the opera at Venice would be beautiful and appropriate in another situation. Did you find Ronconi adapted to it? Ungher? Moriani? I have chosen *Un duel sous le cardinal Richelieu*. It is an effective drama, and especially I see in it comic and tragic aspects, something that matters very much to me for Ronconi and for Ungher.[155]

A week later in another letter to Toto, he was still enthusiastic about Lockroy's and Badon's *Un duel sous le Cardinal de Richelieu*. He mentions as one of its attractions that Bellini had once considered it,[156] before going on; 'Moreover it is adapted for three personalities: Ungher, Ronconi and Moriani. It contains spectacle, the court of Louis XIII. It is original and luxurious.'[157] A few days later *Un duel* was discarded as a possible subject, as Donizetti informs Vasselli on 30 September in a letter that clearly reveals his nervous agitation:

[Cammarano] is finding the subject for Venice difficult and yesterday he told me so.[158] And today I must write [to Venice] that I will do another subject, but I do not know which, and still (it is now three o'clock) I have not seen the poet to find out what to write.

I suffer the pains of purgatory in my body from such uncertainties. Yesterday I read all day, but only things filled with gore! God knows when Cammarano is coming and what I will have to write.[159]

The upshot of the conference between Donizetti and Cammarano on 30 September 1837 was the choice of a subject derived from a gothic

French play, *La nonne sanglante*,[160] which may well have been one of those 'things filled with gore' that Gaetano had mentioned to Toto. A week later he reported to Toto: 'You can imagine how I feel, not having yet one comma of the book for Venice and being obligated to turn over the score in December!'[161] This letter was written just before the rehearsals for *Roberto Devereux* started.

Although on 7 October Donizetti had not yet seen 'one comma' of the text, the project was soon under way, for on the 13th Lanari wrote that he had read the scenario and felt that 'too much blood is shed';[162] in the original draft Maria kills Matilde, Enrico and Corrado before committing suicide. Count Berti was so repelled by the subject that he refused it, describing it as one of those 'that are the shame of the Italian theater'.[163] As an example of what would appeal to the refined Venetian taste, he included with his letter to Donizetti a libretto, entitled *Gismonda di Mendrizio*, by his favored poet Beltrame. But once Donizetti had made up his mind he persevered with *Maria de Rudenz*, even though Lanari urged that one of the victims be allowed to survive 'because without that Berti would never approve it'.[164] The plot was accordingly modified sufficiently to win Count Berti's reluctant consent.

The process of composition proceded slowly because of Gaetano's frequent periods of depression. He pours out his heart to Toto:

I keep asking: For whom do I work? Why? I am alone on earth. Can I live? And such thoughts make me drop my arms, dear Toto!

It matters little to me any more if I have or if I don't have what I ask for. I am apathetic. So many beautiful things planned for October, and here with the month already begun I am tied down with work, and for whom? For no one.[165]

Although he complained to Toto on 7 November that *Maria de Rudenz* was going ahead slowly and that he was enraged by his own irresolution, yet he was able to report just nine days later that the opera was half finished. From this it would seem that his periods of apathy were succeeded by bouts of highly concentrated work. When he left Naples to go to Venice on the evening of 3 December 1837 he carried the completed score with him.

From Naples he traveled first to Rome in the coach of the tenor Basadonna, and then, after two days with the Vassellis, continued his journey via Florence and Ferrara, reaching Venice by 20 December. That day he wrote to Mayr, telling him among other things: 'Here I am working . . . and oh! music has great power over me. I would be dead [without it]. I am still weeping as though it were the first day.'[166] In this frame of mind Donizetti prepared *Maria de*

Rudenz. The opera was given its prima on 30 January 1838 at the rebuilt Fenice, with the appointed triad of Ungher, Moriani and Ronconi. Although some of the music was applauded, the opera as a whole so antagonized the Venetian public[167] that it was taken off after the second performance, and Parisina was hastily substituted for it. Later Donizetti sent his friend Spadaro a one-sentence account of the opera's reception: 'Maria de Rudenz was half successful – the first half, yes, the second, no.'[168]

In spite of the hostility it initially encountered, Maria de Rudenz managed to maintain a foothold on Italian stages for nearly thirty years.[169] Giuseppina Strepponi, to whom the vocal score is dedicated, won a personal success as Maria in 1841, and in 1843 Teresa Brambilla in one of Lanari's lavish productions earned popular acclaim for the opera at the Teatro Apollo in Rome. When Donizetti heard of its later favorable reception, he wrote to his friend Perotti in Venice that he was happy for it, 'but I still bleed for the severity with which I was judged in Venice'.[170] (Its last nineteenth-century performance seems to have been at Sinigaglia in 1867, when Benedetta Colleoni-Corti sang Maria. Rudenz is one of the scores that has been a beneficiary of the current Donizetti renascence, having been revived on 27 October 1974 by Opera Rara of London in a concert performance.[171] More recently it was revived at the Fenice (from 21 December 1980), where it was given eight well-received performances – a happier encounter with the Venetian public than at the time of its prima.)

All this time the question of Donizetti's confirmation as permanent director of the Naples Conservatory had been hanging fire. In the months that followed Zingarelli's death in May 1837, Donizetti's doubts about the appointment increased as he could not get a definite answer from either King Ferdinando or Marchese Niccola Santangelo, the Minister of the Interior. And as his doubts increased so did his uncertainty and frustration about his future.

On 9 August 1837 he wrote to Spadaro at Messina: 'If His Majesty does not grant me the directorate of the Conservatory, I shall leave in order to return when – I don't know.' And then he makes an oblique reference to the cholera riots that had broken out in Sicily the month before: 'But if you don't calm yourselves down there, I can't find out the king's wishes, for now it would be an indiscretion.'[172] On 17 August he broaches the subject to Toto, alluding to the desolation he feels after Virginia's death three weeks previously. 'Come in October, because perhaps by then it will be decided whether I must die here for the sake of the Conservatory or if I shall be able to escape at least for a little from these scenes, from this furniture, from these stairs.'[173] On 26 August, he mentions the problem again to Spadaro:

I am bored staying here, I am sad. I want to get away because already I see that even at the Conservatory there is opposition to me for the position of director. Everything for the best. It saddens me because I love those students who want to study and who lack encouragement, but, for the loss I have suffered, I am unable to remain here.[174]

On 4 September Donizetti had an audience with the king, who told him that his request for an answer would be granted as soon as possible. Then, on Monday, 18 September, there was a meeting of the royal council, at which Santangelo had promised him that without fail the matter would be discussed and brought to a definite decision. A new motive for Donizetti's eagerness for a prompt and decisive resolution to his uncertainty appears in his letter to Toto of 16 September, where he writes that he has been engaged in negotiations with theaters outside Italy.[175] Here he is referring to his efforts, through his agent Accursi in Paris and through singers he trusted, like Duprez and Lablache (but not Rubini), to come to satisfactory terms with Charles Duponchel at the Opéra and with Robert at the Théâtre-Italien. The whole of October passed without any word from the royal palace. In November he had another audience with the king to present his request for leave of absence to go to Venice to put on *Maria de Rudenz*. On 14 November he saw the king again to thank him for his leave of absence and to tell him that it would be difficult for him to return; whereupon the king replied: 'Come back soon and then it will be decided.' In describing this scene to Toto, Donizetti adds: 'Under these circumstances I am finally leaving; yet because of this uncertainty, if I find an engagement while I'm away, I'll accept it. As for coming back, I have to for the opera.'[176] He refers here to his contract with Barbaja which committed him to compose an opera for the San Carlo to be ready in May 1838.

All through the fall of 1837 Donizetti wrote about his problem over the directorship only to Toto and Spadaro, and to them he spoke of it discreetly, in terms of his own reactions, never indulging in an explicit criticism of the king or of Santangelo. When he left for Venice on 3 December, the whole question was still unsettled. When he returned to Naples the following February, his self-esteem jolted by the rough handling both he and his *Maria de Rudenz* had received from the Venetian public, his references to his appointment become increasingly ironical. He gives Toto this pointed description of his interview with the king on 6 March 1838:

Yesterday I was with the king. He said to me, smiling: 'Addio, cavaliere'. I, seeing him in a joking mood, followed along and said that if he did not believe me worthy of that post (gently, however, you know) I would have accepted Paris, and therefore I begged him to give me an answer soon. He laughed, took the paper, shook me by the hand affectionately, and said: 'Va bene, addio, cavaliere'. I laughed, he laughed, and I shall see now what this laughter brings about.[177]

A month later there had still been no word. Donizetti had wanted the honor of being offered the directorship, but since nearly a year had passed with no clear offer, whatever honor might have been attached to the position had become distinctly tarnished in Donizetti's view. On 11 April 1838 he advises Spadaro of his resolution: 'After I go on stage here, in September at the latest, I am going to Paris at liberty and to work . . . Here they keep too long a silence about my future. And I respect it and I am leaving.'[178] From this statement it is clear that Donizetti had already definitely decided to escape the frustrations and unhappy associations of Naples, even before he experienced difficulties over the staging of *Poliuto*.

A further amplification of Donizetti's position vis-à-vis the Naples Conservatory appears in the reply he wrote on 5 May 1838 to a letter from his Milanese friend Count Gaetano Melzi, who had suggested that he apply for the vacant position of director (*censore*) of the Milan Conservatory:

As to the Conservatory of Milan I cannot deny that I would have accepted with pleasure the honorable position of *censore*, but I could not have asked for it without appearing an ingrate to the King of Naples. Offered, it would have been another matter . . . I have every prospect of writing for the Paris Grand Opéra, and if letters do not lie Scribe is sending me a libretto. I am in close negotiations with the Théâtre-Italien. As for the Naples Conservatory, it is in disorder. It seems that people have worked to convince the king that a director is a useless personage.[179]

For several months at least Donizetti had been aware that there was a cabal opposed to him within the Conservatory, determined to prevent his becoming confirmed as permanent director and hoping to ease him out entirely. The lengths to which they would go are revealed by Gaetano's admission to Toto on 12 June 1838 that his salary from the Conservatory was five months in arrears.[180]

Florimo[181] offers an apocryphal report, complete with dialogue, written almost fifty years after the events described, in which King

Ferdinando dismisses Donizetti by telling him that he wishes he had a double directorship to offer him and Mercadante, but since it is a single post it must go to Mercadante as a subject.[182] And then Donizetti, who is supposed to have recounted the king's speech to Florimo, allegedly added: 'I who had gone there to complain did not know what to reply, as the king's answer had struck me dumb.' Florimo's account falls apart on a number of grounds. First, he was no supporter of Donizetti's candidature for the post, and cannot be trusted to have given an impartial view of the events. Then, Donizetti was neither dismissed from his post, nor directly refused that of permanent director; rather, he offered his resignation and never received definite word as to whether it had been accepted or not. Further, Mercadante was not offered the directorship of the Naples Conservatory until 1840, a year and a half after Donizetti had gone to Paris. One detail of Florimo's tale is probably not misleading, and that is his claim that the principal argument against Donizetti's being offered the post was that he was not a citizen of the Kingdom of the Two Sicilies. Yet one should remember that many Italian composers, Zingarelli among them, had held positions in various Italian states other than those in which they had been born.

Late in June 1838 Donizetti submitted his resignation from the Conservatory to King Ferdinando, but it was neither accepted nor rejected. In reporting this to Toto, he comments: 'I have my back against the wall.'[183] Having made up his mind to go to Paris, he feared that his passport might be revoked. In September 1838 King Ferdinando, accompanied by a large retinue, among them the Marchese Santangelo, went on a three-month state visit to Sicily, creating a hiatus in which no moves, honorific or punitive, toward Donizetti could in effect be taken. Certainly Ferdinando had many other problems to occupy his attention besides his Royal Conservatory, and experience had taught him that if certain kinds of problems were left dangling long enough they would eventually go away.

Before Donizetti could go away, he still had to fulfill his contract for a new opera at the San Carlo. An important person in his plans for that new opera was an acquaintance he had made in Venice at the time of *Maria de Rudenz*. This new friend was the famous French tenor, Adolphe Nourrit (1802–39), a pupil of Garcia and Talma, who had made his debut at the Opéra in 1821 and remained a major figure there until he abruptly announced his departure on 1 April 1837. At that theater he played a pivotal role in the successful premieres of *La muette de Portici* (Auber), *Guillaume Tell*, *Robert le diable*, *La juive*, and *Les Huguenots*. Nourrit was a man of unusual culture: he suggested stage effects adopted by Halévy and Meyerbeer; he was the first to sing Schubert lieder in Paris; he wrote the scenarios for a number of ballets, including *La sylphide* (Schneitzhoeffer, choreographed by Salvatore Taglioni) and *Le diable boiteux* (Casimir Gide, choreographed by Jean Coralli); he was an intimate of Liszt and of others in the vanguard of the Romantic movement in Paris. Nourrit was, of course, an incomparable source of detailed information about the French capital, particularly its musical traditions and factions. Since the tenor had arrived in Italy without an engagement, Donizetti urged him to betake himself to Naples. Here a contract with Barbaja was soon devised, and one of its provisions was that Nourrit would make his Neapolitan debut at the San Carlo in Donizetti's new opera.

It is usually assumed that this work was from the start intended to be *Poliuto*. There are good reasons, however, to believe that at first another subject was undertaken and was then put aside: Filippo Cicconetti's 1864 biography of Donizetti (a work notably lacking in dates and documentation, and not particularly reliable) provides a confused clue as to what probably occurred. Briefly recounting the story of the prohibition of *Poliuto*, he tells how Barbaja came to Donizetti determined to have his contract fulfilled:

Donizetti, who had previously chosen increasingly arduous labors . . . made up his mind to satisfy the impresario, and took up again *Gabriella di Vergy*, an opera he had written in 1827 [actually, in 1826], which remained abandoned among his papers, and undoubtedly set himself to revise it. He had only arrived at the fifth number when there came to him lucrative offers from Paris, whereupon thinking that he might be able to make use of *Poliuto*, he summoned the impresario and satisfied him with 300 ducats, and at once set out for that city.[184]

A quarter of a century separated Cicconetti's written account from the time when he had known Donizetti in Rome, and therefore it is not surprising that he was somewhat confused over the sequence of events. For instance, the prohibition of *Poliuto* was announced on 12 August 1838, but Donizetti had received his contract from Paris in the middle of May; therefore, if the arrival of that contract caused the suspension of work on *Gabriella*, this cannot have occurred after *Poliuto* was banned. Is it not altogether more probable that the Parisian contract suggested to Donizetti that it would be advisable to write an opera for the San Carlo that could later be adapted to the particular requirements of the Opéra? *Gabriella di Vergy* would be a far less appropriate work to do such double duty than *Poliuto*, which is based on one of the great French classics, Corneille's *Polyeucte*. In fact, Donizetti had just begun to compose *Poliuto* on 15 May, for on that date Nourrit wrote to his wife: 'Our opera is going well. Donizetti has already written the introduction and had me rehearse the prayer, which I am to sing at the moment when I become a Christian.'[185] This prayer, 'D'un alma troppo fervida', occurs early in Act 1 of *Poliuto*. That Nourrit speaks of 'our' opera indicates that he had participated in the choice of subject, so different in scope and emphasis from those Donizetti had dealt with so far, and suggests that he was actively working with Cammarano on the treatment of the libretto.

Although Cicconetti confused the chronology of *Gabriella* and *Poliuto*, he was not entirely mistaken, for Donizetti did not abandon *Gabriella* in 1838 after just five numbers; this was proven when Don White and Patric Schmid identified a complete manuscript score of *Gabriella* at the Sterling Library of the University of London, as being this 1838 revision of *Gabriella*.[186] A slight rearrangement of Cicconetti's timetable can reconcile the facts. When Donizetti and Nourrit arrived in Naples, about 1 March 1838, Donizetti expected his new opera to be given in May. He wanted a French subject for Nourrit and, still in the mood for a work like *Maria de Rudenz*, characterized by overwrought Romanticism, he remembered the abandoned *Gabriella*. He began work upon it, just at the time when his negotiations with Paris were reaching their climax. After the fifth number, he put *Gabriella* aside and turned to *Poliuto*, a subject not only better adapted for subsequent use in Paris but more sympathetic to Nourrit, who was a notable actor as well as a singer. By 11 July, *Poliuto* was 'almost completed',[187] but Donizetti already had discouraging premonitions that the subject, dealing with the conversion and martyrdom of a saint, would have difficulties with the censors. When the news came on 12 August that the king himself had forbidden *Poliuto*, Donizetti turned back to *Gabriella*, completing it in haste by adapting a considerable amount of music he had composed for other contexts.[188] (Donizetti's optimism is almost inexplicable in the light of his past experience if he thought that the censors would accept the grisly and tragic plot of *Gabriella*.) Cicconetti, then, is most likely correct in stating that Donizetti took up *Gabriella* after *Poliuto*, but it was to complete the score he had started to revise back in March and had then put aside.

The first mention in Donizetti's correspondence of *Poliuto* occurs in a letter to Toto, dated 8 May 1838. 'Here I am writing for September for la Ronzi, Nourrit and Barroilhet.' He does not identify the subject, unfortunately, but he reverts to his opera near the end of this letter. 'Only Cammarano is taciturn as usual and walks up and down San Francesco seeking verses.'[189] The work progressed steadily, but signs of approaching trouble began to appear. Toto was duly informed of them:

Do you know that His Majesty has dismissed all the superintendents and the theater censors over the ballet given on 30 [May]? (*Faust* by Goethe.)[190] Do you know that perhaps my *Poliuto* will be prohibited now, because he is a saint? And I have written half of it. Imagine with what a will I go on writing.[191]

Preparations had begun for a first performance scheduled for 26 September when the king, a sincerely religious man, absolutely forbade the production. By an ironical twist that recalled the events of the previous year, Donizetti had written a cantata to celebrate the safe delivery of Queen Maria Theresa's first child, a son; it had been performed at the San Carlo only a few days before Ferdinando forbade *Poliuto*.

The prohibition of this opera precipitated a crisis for Donizetti that had political, artistic and legal ramifications. The political aspects arose from Donizetti's uncertainty as to whether this clear indication of royal displeasure would compromise his freedom to get away to Paris, where by now he had contracts in force. The artistic problems were intertwined with the legal. His contract with Barbaja for a new opera was still unfulfilled, and there were three options available to him: quickly to cobble together a substitute work – but *Gabriella*, which he intended as such, could not get past the censors either; to patch a new and inoffensive libretto to the music of *Poliuto*, the solution that he had adopted in 1834 when similar circumstances obliged him to convert *Maria Stuarda* into *Buondelmonte*; or to bend the contract to permit the performance of one of his scores that was new to Naples but had already been given elsewhere – an alternative that would involve either some reduction of fee or the payment of a fine. The patching of a new libretto to the music of *Poliuto* was considered, briefly, as is shown by a letter to Ricordi of 18 August 1838, where he speaks of '*Poliuto* (if not forbidden) or *I Guebbri* (expedient title)'.[192] This reference indicates that Donizetti had not yet abandoned hopes that somehow *Poliuto* might be approved, and for this purpose an alternative libretto, which would convert the Christians of Corneille into Zoroastrians and would transfer the action from Armenia to India, was proposed. For one reason or another, this possibility was soon discarded.

The alternative of presenting one of Donizetti's operas that would

be new to Naples, *Pia de' Tolomei*, was accepted. For this produc-
tion the Neapolitan censors forced changes upon the opera that
Donizetti found both exasperating and ludicrous, as he reported to
Giacomo Pedroni, who was in charge of the preparation of scores at
Ricordi:

Here we go from *good* to *worse*. Finally it is decided that I should give *Pia*
with some alterations in place of the forbidden *Poliuto*. The said Pia must
not die (but Dante . . .). Don't let's screw ourselves up with Dante. Pietro
Pettinaro, a historical monk, in the novel is a *hermit*, but we want him to be
called an elderly philosopher, tutor to Pia (yes, sir). And the other hermits?
Shepherds. Very good. Never mention the name of God – yes, sir. If you
should have a dangerous line of verse, we will dilute it into prose, and it
matters little whether it can or can't be sung: meaning that the music stops,
the diluted line is spoken, then the music starts up again.[193]

This is one of Donizetti's clearest statements of his attitude toward
the censors' meddling and the kind of aesthetic damage it caused;
behind his irony and outrage, his disgust with the censors' suggestions and his helplessness against them is strikingly evident. This
modified *Pia* was duly rehearsed by Donizetti and unveiled at the
San Carlo on 30 September 1838 with Ronzi, the tenor Basadonna[194]
and Barroilhet. For failing to provide a brand new score Donizetti
had to pay a fine of 300 ducats. *Poliuto*, in its original form, was not
put on at the San Carlo until 30 November 1848, some seven months
after the composer's death; this occurred during the currency of the
short-lived constitution, which temporarily brought about a more
liberal political climate and made any remonstrance from
Ferdinando II unadvisable.

Some light on the legal questions raised by censorial interference
in the wake of the prohibition of *Poliuto* is shed by a memorandum
that Donizetti wrote to his lawyer friend Aniello Benevento on 25
August 1838.[195] That day Donizetti had received Barbaja's formal
complaint about the non-maintenance of their contract, and he wrote
to his lawyer instead of answering Barbaja directly because he was
afraid of answering 'imprudently'. His argument turns on the point
that it was the libretto and not the music that provoked Ferdinando's
interdiction. He wants to know if he can obligate Barbaja to procure
him a new libretto 'tomorrow', either from Cammarano or from
another librettist satisfactory to the authorities. He wonders whether
it will be possible for him to maintain legally that he has nothing to
do with the choice of a new subject, reserving his judgment on
whether it is satisfactory until after it has passed the censors. He
knows that he might hear the old argument that he has chosen his

subject along with the poet. He continues: 'It is true, but what of it? Is it perhaps my responsibility to have the libretto approved? ... I am here for the music and not to guarantee the text to the authorities.'[196] It is undeniably true that here Donizetti was trying to extricate himself from a tight spot, and always in the back of his mind was the fear that a lengthy suit might interfere with his departure for Paris, planned to take place as soon as his obligation to Barbaja was fulfilled. This memorandum is important evidence of the position he had come to take in the face of the censors' increasing exigence.[197] Not least among the attractions of Paris for Donizetti was that there the censors had no scruples about permitting saints' lives, royal assassinations, conspiracies, or any of the many forms death can take in operatic plots to be exhibited on stage.

5

(1838–1843)
Les martyrs to Dom Sébastien

The more lenient French censorship was not, of course, the only attraction beckoning Donizetti to Paris. Principally he was drawn there by the prestige that a Parisian success could add as a crowning touch to a composer's career. And from a purely practical point of view he did not scorn the fatter fees paid there, nor the prospects of more favorable terms with publishers. Neither was he immune to the thought that there musical properties enjoyed better protection than they did in Italy, where for more than a decade he had been complaining about both the loss of income and the distortion of his music at the hands of the pirates.

The steps leading to Donizetti's going to Paris had been carefully planned for at least three years. At the time of *Marin Faliero,* in the early months of 1835, he had engaged an agent to represent his interests in Paris – the loquacious and improvident Michele Accursi – and he had acquired a Paris banker in the person of August de Coussy, whose wife Zélie would alternately fawn over and tyrannize Donizetti. He was at pains to cultivate his contacts in Paris, particularly those with people active in the musical life of the city. In May 1837 his campaign to move to Paris accelerated as his letter of the 21st to Duprez shows; he urged the tenor to consider the possibility of a production of *L'assedio di Calais* or one of his other scores at the Opéra, for which Donizetti himself, following Rossini's example, would make a revision to accord with local taste and tradition. The person above all that Donizetti had to convince of his eligibility for such an opportunity was Charles Duponchel,[1] the director of the Opéra. Donizetti discusses him with Duprez, describing him as one 'who does not esteem me, I know it. I have made a thousand proposals to him and two thousand times he has refused me.'[2] The directorship of the Opéra at that period was, among other things, about the most modish form of speculation that an ambitious man could indulge in, and Duponchel's views were colored more by this aspect of his position than by purely aesthetic considerations. He would only be interested in a composer who could set a French libretto with enough panache to divert an exigent French audience, but he could only be enthusiastic about one whose work would prove highly profitable. In May 1837 Duponchel could scarcely be blamed if he failed to discern through his monocle any particular evidence that Donizetti could satisfactorily meet either of these requirements.

At that time Donizetti was not exactly an unknown quantity in Paris, but the view of him that obtained there was scarcely what it was in Italy. Four of his operas, *Anna Bolena*, *L'ajo*, *Gianni di Calais* and *Marin Faliero*, had been produced at the Théâtre-Italien, the last having its *prima* there. *Faliero* had had only eight performances in two seasons before it was dropped from the repertory, being eclipsed by *I puritani*, whose vogue had been enhanced by its composer's early demise. The careers of *L'ajo* and *Gianni di Calais* had been even briefer. Only *Anna Bolena*, the first of his works to be played at the Théâtre-Italien, had proven itself genuinely durable; on the basis of this limited exposure Donizetti could be regarded in Paris as a 'one-opera' composer.[3] Some of his songs and excerpts from his operas were performed in concert and interpolated into scores by other composers, but none of his Italian successes since *Anna* had as yet been staged in Paris. From Italy there came rumors of Donizetti's astonishing productivity and his remarkable speed of composition, but to the Parisians such stories were only the occasion for jokes and bons mots, and they provided the foundation for a persistent view that Donizetti was not really to be taken seriously. To some extent he continued to be confronted by that opinion throughout his years in Paris.

From Italy Donizetti tried to bring to bear all the pressure he could to induce a serious offer from the French capital, enlisting the help of the singers he knew, his agent Accursi and his banker de Coussy, all of whom stood to gain both in commissions and prestige from a Paris success for Donizetti. But the decisive influence in obtaining for Donizetti a contract on his own terms was his music itself. For when *Lucia* was first produced at the Théâtre-Italien on 12 December 1837, with Persiani making her Paris debut and Rubini in one of his celebrated roles, the enthusiasm it evoked bordered on hysteria. From the start it was clear that here was a triumph not only for extraordinary singers but for a composer whose music touched contemporary sensibilities to their depths. After *Lucia*, the road to Paris lay open to Donizetti.[4]

In a letter to Accursi Donizetti set out the terms he was prepared to consider. He wanted 10,000 francs for each opera. He wanted the entire rights for Europe for any reductions made of his scores and half of any rental fees. The rehearsal period and first performance must be scheduled for a time convenient to him. He would bring his libretto with him, though the subject could be suggested by the Parisian impresario, and he would pay the librettist himself. Since the singers should be selected for their appropriateness to the subject, he wanted to choose them himself. For necessary adjustments of his setting of the French text, he professed himself ready to participate in as many discussions as were necessary.[5]

Three months later serious negotiations were in progress. On 12 May 1838 he reported their current state to Duprez:

> To you (with the understanding that you do not show anyone my letter) I speak frankly. If Duponchel wants to have me, I am eager to compose for you.
>
> I know from one of my intimate friends that M. Scribe has already sent the libretto, *Le comte Julien*. But I, without reading the text, have already written back that I do not want such a subject, that I myself refused it from Romani, who had already given me the first act of it in the first year of the Società d'Industria e Belle Arti.[6] A traitor to his country and love treated almost as an episode displease me.
>
> You see that I am writing without having read the libretto, and therefore that cannot offend M. Scribe. Then, I would like to bore the pants off the public [*vorrei seccare i . . .*], like all the others, with an opera in five acts. I would want them quite short, as in *La muette de Portici*, but I want five of them, and I want besides a drama of character with two or three interesting and moving situations that would differ from those that have been done a thousand times in Italy.[7]

Next he discusses singers. Apparently, Duponchel was eager to have Donizetti compose an opera to serve as Mario's[8] debut, but Donizetti was uneasy at the thought of an inexperienced singer, no matter how enthusiastic the advance reports; he would rather write for Duprez, with whom he was familiar and more than content. He wanted very much to avail himself of the services of the famous bass Levasseur;[9] Accursi had warned him that Cornélie Falcon,[10] although eager to appear in whatever opera Donizetti might write, was no longer vocally reliable.

Less than two weeks after this effusion to Duprez, Donizetti, at long last, received two copies of his contract with Duponchel. On 25 May 1838 he replies in formal French: 'and it is with joy that I receive and accept the proposition that you have been good enough to make me', from which it is clear the the terms and conditions were at least a satisfactory approximation of those he had insisted upon to

Accursi the previous February. He goes on to make a dignified request to be treated with all the same consideration accorded to the
regular composers for that stage. 'And I want the same support,
otherwise the struggle would be too unequal, and it would be rashness in me to expose myself there.' He begs to be informed when the
two operas he is contracting for will be scheduled, 'particularly the
first (for which I ask for three months of rehearsals of three hours'
duration a day)'.[11] He hopes to have a new libretto so that he may
begin work on it as soon as possible.[12] Significantly, nothing yet has
been mentioned about the possibility of an opera derived from Corneille's *Polyeucte*, although Donizetti was at the time of this letter
actively engaged in composing an Italian opera on that subject.

At about this time the Italian newspapers published the announcement of Donizetti's engagement to compose two new operas
for the Académie Royale de Musique, as the Opéra was then officially known. During the succeeding months, while he was em-
broiled in finding a way of fulfilling his contract with Barbaja after
the prohibition of *Poliuto*, he learned that he would have further
employment in Paris. Accursi had negotiated for him the welcome
task of preparing *Roberto Devereux* and *L'elisir d'amore* for their
first performances in Paris, at the Théâtre-Italien. As soon as the
third performance of *Pia* at the San Carlo was safely behind him,
Donizetti took ship for Marseilles.

Donizetti arrived in Paris on 21 October 1838 and found an apartment at 5 rue Louvois, the house where the composer Adam was
living. Soon he was working at the Théâtre-Italien rehearsing
Roberto Devereux. Even more important, he promptly came to an
agreement with Duponchel that his first work for the Opéra would be
a French version, expanded, of *Poliuto*. Scribe would undertake the
French revision of Cammarano's Italian text, enlarging it into four
acts and altering the motivation of the plot to conform more closely
to Corneille's drama. Donizetti informs Dolci of these activities in a
rather homesick letter written less than a month after his arrival in
Paris, and goes on to make what turned out to be not very accurate
predictions of his future movements.

Just as soon as *Poliuto* is given at the Opéra, however, I am coming back to
Italy to breathe a little, since the courtesies, the dinners, the portraits, the
busts in plaster, etc., all these, however much they flatter my self-esteem,
nevertheless are boring to a poor artist such as I. Here I clearly see there are
ways to profit from a thousand opportunities, but I, accustomed to little,
desiring little, cannot even adapt myself to earning money. I am not Rossini

and I do not have his fortune, but when a man has enough to live on and enough to amuse himself, I think he should retire and be happy . . . I love Italy because to her, after my debt to Mayr, I owe my existence and my reputation . . . My leave [from Naples] expires in December, and I have already written asking for another three months. Either the king accepts my resignation or he grants me leave. In March I am coming back to Italy for a while, then I return to Paris for three months, and after that *I leave France forever.* I do not want the theater to leave me, rather I want to leave it . . . Oh, if you could see how flattering it is to travel through France and Italy and be recognized, how at every turn you find kindness. That does not last you know. And certainly I am not becoming proud because of it.[13]

Donizetti regarded being asked to compose for the Opéra as the apex of his career, and once his contract was satisfied he hoped to retire. A number of circumstances, external and internal, prevented the fulfillment of that hope. Nor did he see Italy as soon as he hoped, because his work on *Les martyrs* (as the French expansion of *Poliuto* was called) dragged on for eighteen wearying months, keeping him in Paris, where he worked so hard at a number of projects that he induced something bordering on panic in his French rivals, who were accustomed to pursuing their careers with more deliberation. Not the least significant thing about this letter to Dolci is that it shows Donizetti achieving a level of detached self-evaluation that would elude him in the future. It also helps to explain Dolci's determination to bring his old schoolmate back to Italy after his tragic collapse in 1846. Such sentences as 'I love Italy because to her, after my debt to Mayr, I owe my existence and reputation' must long have reverberated in Dolci's mind. On the other hand, this letter gives no inkling of Donizetti's future obsessiveness about his career, of his hopes that behind each success would lurk the possibility of another and greater one.

In preparing *Roberto Devereux* for its French premiere at the Théâtre-Italien, Donizetti added an overture, featuring the tune of *God save the Queen*, modified the cabaletta of one duet and composed a new tenor double aria for the tower scene, of which the cabaletta reflected the second theme of the new overture. *Roberto Devereux* was first sung at the Théâtre-Italien on 27 December 1838, by Giulia Grisi (Elisabetta), Rubini (Roberto) and Tamburini (Nottingham); it won little more than a succès d'estime, in part because the public expected vocal pyrotechnics of the sort to be found in *Lucia.* Two weeks later Donizetti sent Dolci his perceptive explanation of the public's coolness:

Last month I gave my *Roberto* with encouraging success, the later performances are still better received; since here the habitués of the theater do not understand the Italian language too well, and as I seek to bring out the nuances of the text, it often happens that they do not understand the dramatic situation.[14]

On the other hand, the success that met *L'elisir d'amore* when it was first performed at the Théâtre-Italien on 17 January 1839 bordered on the ecstatic. Persiani, Ivanoff, Tamburini and Lablache, were all resoundingly praised for their singing and acting. For the first performance at this theater Donizetti, as he usually did under these circumstances, added some new music to his score: an aria for Persiani and a duet for her and Tamburini. Later, at Tamburini's request, he wrote a new cavatina for him. The difference in the audience's response to these two operas is revealed by the number of performances the company gave of them: *Roberto Devereux* was performed five times in two seasons; *L'elisir* sixty-one times in eighteen seasons.

His duties at the Théâtre-Italien over for the time being, Donizetti began to think seriously about *Les martyrs*. Wanting enough time to do himself justice, he sent a petition to the composer Halévy on 14 January 1839: 'not wanting my work to follow directly after that of M. Auber [*Le lac des fées*], which is in rehearsal, I beg you to be willing to take my turn with your *Le drapier*'.[15] Meanwhile Scribe had translated and expanded Cammarano's text of *Poliuto*, and not least of his concerns had been to adapt French text to the considerable amount of music Donizetti planned to retain from his original Italian score. By early April 1839 Donizetti was hard at work on *Les martyrs*, and he sent to Mayr an illuminating description of the difference between composing for the French stage and the Italian.

I will give my *Poliuto*, forbidden in Naples because it was too holy, at the Opéra enlarged into four acts instead of the original three, and translated and adjusted to the French stage by Scribe. Because of this I have had to rewrite all the recitatives, make a new finale to Act 1, add arias, trios, [and] dances related to the action, as is the custom here, all so that the public won't complain that the texture is Italian, and about that they won't be wrong. French music and librettos have a cachet all their own, to which every composer must conform, both in the recitatives and in the sung pieces. For example, banished are the *crescendi*, etc. etc., banished are the usual cadences, *felicità, felicità, felicità;*[16] then between one verse of the cabaletta and the other you should always have lines that heighten the emotion, without the usual repetition of lines which our poets customarily use. This *Poliuto* changed into *Les martyrs* will be given within the year.

I am obliged under penalty of 30,000 francs to turn over the score on 1 September. On 1 January 1840 I am obligated to consign the finished score of my second grand opera,[17] also in four acts and which I have started, with the same penalty. In the midst of these occupations I find and will find time to finish my three mates [*conjugi*], the other being the opera that I will give at the Italiens here for their opening when they return from London.[18] I hope that suffices ... Perhaps you will ask where do I find the time? I find it and I also go out for walks half the day, and while walking I work even more. I love art and I love it with passion.[19]

Within the space of a little more than six months in Paris, Donizetti had prepared two of his older works for the stage of the Théâtre-Italien; he was well advanced with a major reconstruction of another work which would be performed in a language other than his native tongue; he had begun, from scratch, a second grand opera,[20] Le duc d'Albe; and he was planning yet another project for the Théâtre-Italien. Even though nothing came of this last plan, Donizetti had done a formidable amount of work.

He was composing at an exhausting rate. On 15 May 1839 he writes again to Mayr to tell him that Les martyrs is finished and Le duc d'Albe 'already begun'. The strain caused by his overworking appears obvious in the opening of this letter:

Oh, how gladly I saw your handwriting, how delighted I am to know you are always in good spirits. You don't feel your age then. And I who am sad already feel mine very much. I am gray and tired of working ... The world believes me to be what I am not, but I care little for the world ... I have a hundred thousand francs in capital; should they not be enough to live on discreetly?[21]

Further on, he tries to make a joke about how thin he has become: 'I am afraid I shall pass on to the next life from galloping consumption, something that will never happen to our Dolci.'[22] He still talks of retiring from the theater, but now his farewell will be 'bitter', and he will say it 'from the heart in order to escape so much suffering'. Some deterioration in Donizetti's health had taken the edge off his spirits of the previous month, but his pace scarcely faltered.

His next new venture upon the stages of Paris was at neither the Opéra nor the Théâtre-Italien, but with a company called the Théâtre de la Renaissance, then giving performances in the Salle Ventadour. This was not one of the state-supported theaters,[23] but a private venture headed by Anténor Joly, who earlier had managed the Porte-Saint-Antoine theater, and on 8 November 1838, with the backing of Dumas père and Hugo, had opened his newest venture with the premiere of Hugo's Ruy Blas. Joly himself is described as being 'tall, thin and deaf as a bowl',[24] but the loss of hearing did not prevent him from assembling a company of singers as well as actors. For them Donizetti prepared a special version of Lucia di Lammermoor to a French text by Alphonse Royer and Gustave Vaëz.[25] When it was first given on 6 August 1839, and in spite of a cast the composer described to Persico as being made up of 'beginners and dogs', it equaled the success of the Italian *Lucia* at the Théâtre-Italien the previous December. In the same letter to Persico he recounts what happened following the opening night of the French *Lucia*:

I was in bed with a headache. After the opera I was obliged to get up, as the singers, chorus and orchestra came with torches to repeat the choruses of *Lucia* under my windows, and from above (like royalty) I thanked them amid shouts. Last evening the second performance, theater packed. I had made a loan of 5000 francs to this company which had barely managed to survive and now the impresario has returned my money because he does not need it any longer, being able to raise funds in various quarters to pay his old debts.

In this form this opera will make the tour of France, and from time to time I will have some francs from the provinces, too.[26]

Nor was *Lucie* confined only to French provincial theaters: on 20 February 1846 it was received into the repertory of the Opéra itself, sung by Maria Dolores Nau and Duprez (the original Edgardo). Donizetti did not underestimate the vogue for *Lucie* in its adopted country, where it soon came to be regarded as part of the native culture.[27]

Early in September 1839 Donizetti got wind of the intention of the impresario of La Scala, Bartolomeo Merelli (who twenty years earlier had written librettos for him), to stage *Gianni di Parigi*. Donizetti had composed this score in 1831 as a present for Rubini – a gesture that was an expression both of the euphoria of the days following the *prima* of *Anna Bolena* and of Donizetti's having already set his sights on Paris – for the tenor to produce on one of his benefit evenings at the Théâtre-Italien. Rubini had never sung the work, had never even acknowledged it, and that now, after so many years, the score should have found its way into the none too scrupulous hands of Merelli infuriated the composer. On 6 September 1839 he wrote a stiff letter[28] to the committee in charge of La Scala, asking them to use all their authority to oppose this production and charging that the score had been obtained fraudulently. At just about the time that this letter would have reached Milan, *Gianni di Parigi*, on 10 September 1839, was given a belated *prima* at La Scala, with Lorenzo Salvi in the title role and Antonietta Rainieri-Marini as the Princess of Navarre. The production was judged mediocre,[29] but it managed to eke out twelve performances before it disappeared from the stage. As a result of this illicit production, Donizetti filed a lawsuit against the publisher Ricordi, but the action was settled amicably in May of 1841.

In Paris Donizetti's commitments continued without letup. A letter to Persico of 9 October 1839 gives a glimpse of his unrelenting activity:

In the coming week I begin rehearsing *Poliuto* at the Opéra. Meanwhile I have written, orchestrated and delivered a little opera for the Opéra-Comique [*La fille du régiment*], which will be given in a month or forty days to serve for the debut of la Bourgeois.[30] You will see from the announcement I am sending you with Leopoldo[31] that I have two operas promised at the Renaissance, where *La fiancée du Tyrol* will be *Il furioso* enlarged, *L'ange de Nisida* will be new. And thus I will pass my winter in three theaters, except the Opéra, where now I must turn over [*Le duc d'Albe*] at the beginning of next year. You will understand that when one has so much to do there is no time to play the rooster, either with old women or with young ones. In any event, I am bored and I divert myself.[32]

Once again Donizetti's prophecies were invalidated by the dilatory habits of French operatic life. *Les martyrs* (*Poliuto*) did not begin rehearsals, although it was ready to do so, because it was blocked behind Halévy's *Le drapier*, which was repeatedly delayed as the irresolute composer kept tinkering with his score. Of the two projects for the Théâtre de la Renaissance, the *rifacimento* of *Il furioso* is heard of no more, but *L'ange de Nisida* he did complete, dating the final page 27 December 1839. As of 9 October 1839, at least, *Le duc d'Albe* still seemed a viable undertaking, but it was put in abeyance in favor of other projects and because of the pileup at the Opéra that was delaying *Les martyrs*. The most surprising feature of this letter to Persico is the almost casual notice that *La fille du régiment*, to which there is no earlier reference in Donizetti's known correspondence, had been composed, orchestrated and turned over to Crosnier, manager of the Opéra-Comique; but Donizetti's estimate that it would be given within a month or so was, in the event, three months wide of the truth. As for his claim that 'there is no time to play the rooster', he was undoubtedly trying to calm Persico, who, back in Naples, had heard persistent rumors of Donizetti's unrestrained sexual activity and had sent his brother Leopoldo to Paris to check them out. This gossip was to continue and increase, and undoubtedly there was foundation for it. The excitation of his nerves that found one outlet in intensive bouts of composition would demand, as his disease continued its inroads, another.

In early December 1839 Donizetti wrote to Persico to report on the progress of *Les martyrs*.[33] He had recently written a new aria for Duprez and he tells Persico that the tenor 'is enthusiastic about it'.[34] He had also finally received word that rehearsals of the opera would begin, but when he arrived at the theater he discovered that Habeneck,[35] the leader of the orchestra at the Opéra, wanted to interweave the first rehearsals of Donizetti's score with the final ones of Halévy's *Le drapier*.[36] Discovering this situation and suspecting the motives behind it, Donizetti 'coldly' retrieved his score and carried it home; he did not restore it until he had written assurances from Scribe[37] and Halévy that *Le drapier* would be given before the end of December (it was actually performed on 6 January 1840), thereby leaving January free for rehearsals of *Les martyrs*. Taking away his score of *Les martyrs* symbolized Donizetti's insistence that he be treated with the same respect as his French colleagues; but at the same time he was reducing the pressures on himself, as during December he was attending the rehearsals of *La fille du régiment* at the Opéra-Comique, while at home he was finishing the composition of *L'ange de Nisida*.

Although the final page of *L'ange* is dated 27 December 1839, it was not until the following 5 January that Donizetti signed a contract for the opera with Joly and his librettists Royer and Vaëz. This contract[38] specifies that *L'ange de Nisida* would go into rehearsal on 1 February 1840, a date that tells us that Donizetti had no compunction about interweaving rehearsals of three of his works in different theaters: by then *Les martyrs* was well into its preparation and *La fille du régiment* was still eleven days away from its premiere, although on 5 January he might well have expected that that event would take place before the month was out. Joly's company at the Théâtre de la Renaissance had no outside subsidies and survived in a hand-to-mouth fashion, as is confirmed by Donizetti's tale of lending Joly 5000 francs before the premiere of *Lucie*. During January 1840 Joly was forced to disband his opera company, but in February he tried to mend his fortunes by forming a ballet troupe, headed by Carlotta Grisi (a cousin of the singing sisters Giuditta and Giulia Grisi) and featuring her in *Le zingaro*, in which she not only danced but sang. Carlotta's popularity could not save the tottering company, and in May 1840 it ceased performing altogether. On 9 May Donizetti broke the news to Persico: 'The Renaissance is closed and I lose *L'ange de Nisida*, an opera in three acts,[39] good only for that company. *Auff!* The impresario was very much an ass; he threw money away in every direction.'[40] He not only lost the chance of having *L'ange* performed by Joly's company, but because of the impresario's bankruptcy he also lost the 20,000 francs the impresario was contracted to pay for failure to produce that opera.[41] What Donizetti did not lose was possession of his score, and before 1840 was out he would find a way to make excellent use of it.

The first of Donizetti's French operas to be produced in Paris was

La fille du régiment; it was given at the Opéra-Comique on 11 February 1840,[42] and the cast included Juliette Bourgeois (Marie), Mécène Marié de l'Isle[43] (Tonio), Henri (Sulpice) and Marie-Julie Boulanger[44] (the Marquise). The opening night was a barely averted disaster, as Duprez confirms: 'Donizetti often swore to me how his self-esteem as a composer had suffered in Paris. He was never treated there according to his merits. I myself saw the unsuccess, almost the collapse, of *La fille du régiment*.'[45] Although this comedy soon established itself as a great popular favorite, it was initially given a hostile reception, organized, undoubtedly, by Donizetti's French rivals and their journalist friends in the hope of pruning the proliferation of his works in so many of the Parisian theaters.

A sneering review by Berlioz in the *Journal des débats* of 16 February 1840 supports this view. He chides Donizetti for detracting from the interest aroused by the forthcoming *Les martyrs*, which was being mounted 'at great expense' at the Opéra, by putting on a trifling work at the Opéra-Comique. He falsely accuses Donizetti of incorporating into *La fille* music which is 'at least in great part . . . imitated or translated from *Le chalet* of M. Adam'. Although he claims the score is one that neither the composer nor the public can take seriously, yet he concedes it is not utterly without merit:

The best parts, to my mind, are the pieces that M. Donizetti added to his Italian score to make it viable at the Opéra-Comique. The little waltz that serves as an entr'acte and the trio *dialogué* . . . lack neither vivacity nor freshness.

A little later the true cause of his harshness appears:

What, two major scores for the Opéra, *Les martyrs* and *Le duc d'Albe*, two others at the Renaissance, *Lucie de Lammermoor* and *L'ange de Nisida*, two at the Opéra-Comique, *La fille du régiment* and another whose title is still unknown, and yet another for the Théâtre-Italien, will have been written or transcribed in one year by the same composer! M. Donizetti seems to treat us like a conquered country; it is a veritable invasion. One can no longer speak of the opera houses of Paris, but only of the opera houses of M. Donizetti.

After imagining what would happen if Adolphe Adam were to have made a comparable 'invasion' of Italy, Berlioz returns to his topic of Donizetti as a threat to French musicians. To resist him is a patriotic duty:

And since our government, which subsidizes at great expense our Conservatoire and supports our theaters, takes no care for either the present or future welfare of its artists, for whose education it has paid, to whom it has distributed prizes . . . and it abandons them thereafter, then these artists must acquire an awareness of their strength and must cherish their ambition.

It is up to them to form ranks and to defend themselves energetically and with complete loyalty.[46]

On the same day that Berlioz's diatribe appeared, Donizetti wrote a dignified letter of protest that was published in *Le moniteur universel* of 18 February 1840.

The author of the feuilleton is not afraid to claim that my score has already been heard in Italy, at least in great part, and that it is a little opera imitated or translated from *Le chalet* by M. Adam. If M. Berlioz, who rightly places conscience among the prime duties of an artist, had taken the trouble to open the score of my *Betly*, which has been engraved and published in Paris by M. Launer, and of which the poem is indeed a translation of *Le chalet*, he would have assured himself that the two operas he cites do not have any pieces in common. Let it be permitted me in fairness to affirm that the pieces which comprise *La fille du régiment* were all composed expressly for the Opéra-Comique and that not one of them has figured in any of my previous scores whatever.

I must limit myself ... to pointing out this fundamental error, upon, which, nonetheless, the entire article by M. Berlioz rests.[47]

Donizetti had felt the sting of Berlioz's prose but, as we learn from a letter he wrote to Giampieri on 20 April 1840, he did not feel rancor.

Have you read the *Débats?* Berlioz? Poor man ... he wrote an opera, it was whistled at, he is writing symphonies and they are whistled at, he writes articles ... they are laughed at ... and everyone is laughing and everyone is whistling. I alone feel compassion for him ... he is right ... he has to avenge himself.[48]

In spite of the efforts to discredit it at its premiere, *La fille* was performed fifty-five times through 1841 at the Opéra-Comique. Revived there in 1848, it became such a popular success that 'Salut à la France' took on the status of a patriotic song; it remained in that repertory until 1916, being performed more than a thousand times. The first Italian performance[49] was prepared by Donizetti in Milan during August 1840, but he was called back by work to Paris before it was produced at La Scala on 3 October 1840.[50] In Italy *La figlia del reggimento* never caught and held the popular imagination as *La fille* did in France, perhaps because Maria seemed an insipid figure compared to a real-life *garibaldina*. (In England and the United States during the nineteenth century the opera, most often sung in Italian or English, continued to be performed with some regularity until about 1875. By 1854 it had been staged as far afield as Buenos Aires, San Francisco, St Petersburg and Sydney. For some time a mixture of the French and Italian versions, often with interpolated material,[51] was revived sporadically in New York, but not until the

Sutherland–Bonynge revivals at Covent Garden and later at the Metropolitan was the integrity of the original score re-established. A recent television performance with Beverly Sills was probably seen by more people than the opera's total audience up to that time.)

Following the *demi-succès* of *Le drapier* on 6 January and while *La fille* was being rehearsed at the Opéra-Comique, Donizetti began the painful three-month preparation period for *Les martyrs*. What this time was like is described in a letter he addressed to Persico on 7 April 1840:

You believe *Les martyrs* has already been given and repeated, eh? Not yet, and yesterday for the fourth time the dress rehearsal was scheduled and then postponed because of indispositions. All the singers, everyone except me, have fallen sick, and still today one of them is sick. You can imagine if I am not bursting, if I am not still dying. You know well what the agitation of a dress rehearsal is like. Four times in this condition up until one hour before beginning, and then everything postponed.

You can imagine what I feel like now, that I am suffering horribly from nerves. Oh! if you knew what one suffers here to stage an opera! You have no idea, enough to tell you that they even bothered Rossini . . . The intrigues, the hostility, the journalism, the direction of the theater, *auff!* But, by God, I will bring it out. Today I am obstinate and I would like to give the opera after Easter,[52] as we are in Lent. But such is the eagerness that I do not know if I can hold out. Or must I let it be sung with the role of Félix performed by an understudy. Now Félix is for a first bass, the part is long, but such and so many are the contrarinesses that I cannot do any more.[53]

Up to the last minute Donizetti was still making final adjustments to his score, adding some music to accommodate the movement of the host made up of the chorus, dancers and supernumeraries, seeing to details of orchestration and altering tempos. There has survived a hasty note from Donizetti to Pillet, undated but clearly from late in the rehearsal period of *Les martyrs*: 'You must tell M. Habeneck that the *adagio* of the overture is *maestoso* and not *larghetto*, I was mistaken about the tempo. There is still a little music needed before the march in Act 2, I will give it to you.'[54] On 10 April 1840 *Les martyrs* received its delayed premiere at the Opéra, with Julie Dorus-Gras[55] (Pauline), Duprez, still hoarse from a recent cold (Polyeucte), Jean-Étienne Massol[56] (Sévère) and Prosper Dérivis[57] with his arm in a sling (Félix). *Les martyrs* was applauded, but the only part of the score that aroused enthusiasm was the finale of Act 3, which was encored.[58]

Donizetti's letters contain few details of the first performance of *Les martyrs* as, instead of describing it, he sent journals with reviews to his close friends in Italy so that they could arrange to have them translated and reprinted. Berlioz wrote sternly about *Les martyrs* in the *Journal des débats* of 12 April 1840. He takes Donizetti to task for not providing music sufficiently original and appropriate to the plot, which he dismissed as 'a Credo in 4 acts', but he praises Donizetti's skill as an orchestrator. Théophile Gautier's review is full of descriptive detail, and he writes about the spectacle in the second scene of Act 2 with a connoisseur's appreciation. Spectacle was the cornerstone of grand opera as Duponchel understood it.

The decoration of Act 2, which represents the great square of Mélitène, is of rare beauty. A triumphal arch, an example of elegant and noble architecture, occupies much of the stage. The curtain at the back represents structures of all sorts: temples, arenas, colonnades, obelisks and porticos. An immense crowd covers the square, and the painted people harmonize very happily with the live ones; this difficult transition from painting to reality is managed with much art. For brightness of light, ardor of tone, powerful effect of relief it is difficult to go further. The antique style is well understood, and all the architectural details are of that perfect exactitude that MM. Feuchères, Sécham, Diéterle and Despléchin have accustomed us to. It is across this magnificent decoration that the triumphal procession of Sévère defiles: here are the velites [light infantry] with their bows, the hoplites or heavily armed soldiers, the golden vases and trophies taken from the enemy; there are the musicians with their gigantic horns and their crooked trumpets, the gladiators with the bronze half-boots on their left legs, the dancers, the singers, the pages and the Asiatic children; then the triumphant one himself in his starry chariot drawn by four horses: all this train made one remember Delacroix's beautiful painting *La justice de Trajan.*[59]

Gautier found Scribe's libretto to be 'without rhythm, without rhyme, without caesura, without number, in a word the most antimusical versification imaginable, all of which explains why the furnishing of libretti is exclusively confided to him'. Of the music, he had particular praise for the overture, singling out the famous passage for four bassoons, and the choral hymn. Pauline's Act 1 prayer to Proserpine he felt could just as well have been one to Venus, and found it lacking in 'antique severity'. But he was most of all impressed by the finale to Act 3:

M. Donizetti has understood in a superior way all the beauties this situation should contain, and he has known how to express the emotions of the crowds and the feelings of the principal characters with great variety and incontestable talent. The hymn to Jupiter, performed by the priests and the people, is *fatale* . . . The profession of faith by Polyeucte roused the listeners and decided the success of the work.[60]

The success of *Les martyrs* was, however, of discouragingly short duration: Donizetti's work disappeared from the stage of the Opéra after just twenty performances. Even those who did not share Berlioz's blanket resentment of the Donizettian invasion greeted *Les martyrs* with respect tempered by reservations, rather than with sustained enthusiasm. The causes of its ultimate rejection are various. Part of the blame lies in the choice of that subject for the Opéra: to an audience that relished the titillations of the ballet of the spirits of the unchaste Nuns in *Robert le diable* and the bathing scene in *Les Huguenots*, the conflict between pagan authority and early Christian piety was not so much moving as puzzling, for the sophisticated Parisians had difficulty in divorcing religion from politics. Then, too, the Italian origins of much of the score showed beneath the recently acquired French veneer. But the major share of the blame must be ascribed to backstage politics at the Opéra. To get the directorial reins securely into his own hands, Léon Pillet strove to make Donizetti's opera appear to be a very expensive error of Duponchel's judgment. Another reason for Pillet's coolness toward *Les martyrs* was the unsuitability of the role of Pauline to the vocal and dramatic strengths of his mistress, the mezzo-soprano Rosine Stolz;[61] operas in which she could not shine were not given much attention by the management of the Opéra. Significantly, when *Les martyrs* was discarded there had not been a marked falling off at the box office; some perseverance in continuing to give it would, at least, have helped to pay off the large investment the Opéra had made in scenery and hundreds of costumes.[62]

In Italy the Italian translation, either as *I martiri* or as *Poliuto e Paolina*, of the four-act French score was soon overtaken in popularity by the original three-act *Poliuto*,[63] which was frequently performed in Italy right through the nineteenth century, the title role being favored by dramatic tenors such as Enrico Tamberlik and Francesco Tamagno.[64] (More recently *Poliuto* has served to open the season at La Scala in December 1940 (with Gigli) and again in December 1960 (with Corelli) and in 1977 it served a similar function at the San Carlo. One result of the recent re-examination of Donizetti's scores has been the re-emergence of *Les martyrs* in French. A concert performance in London was followed by another at the Donizetti conference at Bergamo in 1975; then in 1978 it returned to the stage, being revived at the Fenice.)

The premiere of *Les martyrs* behind him, Donizetti found new sources of frustration. Its run had first been interrupted by a recurrence of Duprez's illness and then terminated on 23 May by the start of Dorus-Gras's leave of absence. Although there was talk of putting it on again in the fall, Donizetti rightly foresaw that obstacles would prevent it. A further aggravation was the behavior of Juliette Bourgeois, whose appearance as Marie in *La fille* ceased when her contract with the Opéra-Comique expired at the end of April; Donizetti wanted her to resume her role of Marie in some other theater, but she demanded too much money. Her lack of co-operation frustrated another plan he had been considering – giving her the leading role in *L'ange de Nisida;* the obstinacy of the 'rotten' Bourgeois left him in a quandary over *L'ange*, since, as he confessed to Persico, 'it is an opera that I cannot give in Italy because of the plot'.[65]

Donizetti wrote about all these irritations to Persico, his closest friend in Naples, as a prelude to the most galling exasperation of all. He had just learned that the Neapolitan papers had refused to print any announcement about the premiere of *Les martyrs*. Writing with unaccustomed harshness, he borders on the incoherent:

At this point I received your letter of 9 May. It robs me of every illusion. Sgregli,[66] too, prevents the publication of an article? Oh, clowns, clowns. Well then, since Maestro Giarretelli and Maestro Florimo are the factotums of the Conservatory, I do not at all intend to be subject to anyone whatever. With my name one does not serve under such gentlemen, one commands them. Excuse this outburst of self-esteem or Gallic rage. Now you see that I am more eager than ever to come and resolved to sell everything,[67] maybe without even moving from here. It is certainly not the Conservatory that attracted me,[68] but when I see my name in newspapers here and Italy placed too high, and then from the Neapolitan papers placed too low, then I laugh, eat, drink, and I will do what my heart and friendship suggest. The two attached clippings will show you whether my opera merited the reproduction of an article or not. I don't give a ... *Bonjour.* You see, I myself do not know what I will do. Good, good. Long life to us, to our friends, to the relatives. Greet your whole household. If you see me, you see me, if I will be there, you will see me. Whatever is broken or worn out in my house sell it or burn it. *A rivederci*, I am hungry.

Your Gaetano.[69]

Usually Donizetti was above backbiting and petty finagling, adopting the attitude, which stemmed from sincere conviction, that his work spoke for itself. Indeed, he emerges from the cumulative evidence of his time as an admirable person, in some ways even noble, and in all ways intensely human. But the thought of this ingratitude from Naples, where he had worked hard for sixteen years to make some contribution to the city's musical life, now made him ready to break his last and most sacred tie to it – the deserted apartment with the bedroom door he had never opened since the day of Virginia's death. The news that there was still a group in Naples actively opposing his candidacy for a post he had renounced, even to the extent of suppressing word that one of his works had been respectably received at the Opéra, robbed him of 'every illusion' because he thought he had brought honor to Italian music, while Florimo and his cohorts feared that any favorable reports of Donizetti's accomplishment might somehow jeopardize the chances of their candidate for the directorship, Mercadante.[70]

About the middle of June 1840 Donizetti left Paris to return to Italy for the first time since October 1838. He traveled overland by way of Switzerland, spending some time there,[71] then coming on to Milan, where he put up at the Albergo Passarella. From Milan he entered into a friendly agreement to return to Bergamo to supervise a production of L'esule di Roma at the Teatro Riccardi. His previous reluctance to return to Bergamo was overcome by a combination of factors: he was genuinely eager for a reunion with the 77-year-old Mayr and with Dolci; he was assured that there was an equal eagerness on the part of his native town to do him honor; and he was confident that the recent appointment of his old schoolmate Marco Bonesi as director of the orchestra at the Riccardi meant congenial working conditions.[72] Swallowing whatever feelings he might have had that this recognition was coming belatedly, he spent almost two weeks in Bergamo and thoroughly enjoyed himself. He touched up L'esule, writing a new tenor aria for Donzelli.[73] The first night of this production evoked real enthusiasm, the lion's share going to the composer. The singers Eugenia Tadolini[74] and Ignazio Marini, along with Donzelli, were well received. The warm reception by his fellow citizens changed Donizetti's diffident attitude toward Bergamo, erasing all the painful memories. His sensibilities, which had been chafed by the shabby treatment he had been accorded in Naples, were soothed.

From Bergamo he returned to Milan to resume the preparations for the Italian prima of La fille du régiment, but this activity was cut short by a summons from Pillet to return to Paris to put on the second of the works he was under contract for at the Opéra. Replying to Pillet, Donizetti was frank: 'Doubtless you remember all the difficulties, all the obstacles, all the injustices, all the delays I encountered with Les martyrs. I hope there are no more of them and that you give me credit for the sacrifice I make in seeking to break a contract at a place where I would encounter none of the difficulties I experienced in Paris.'[75] The contract he speaks of breaking was with the impresario Vincenzo Jacovacci, lessee of the Teatro Apollo, Rome. This contract, for Adelia, was not in fact broken, for Donizetti arranged to have the *prima* postponed until later in the Carnival season of 1840–1.

Within a week he was back on the road to Paris, to some extent relieved that he had avoided the painful associations of his projected visit to Naples. He arrived in the French capital at the beginning of September and moved into 1 rue Marivaux, where Accursi lived with his sister. The month of September was a busy one for him, but, before he could start putting notes to paper, a number of decisions had to be made promptly. Donizetti had already begun composing *Le duc d'Albe* the previous year, intending it for his second work at the Opéra; he had put it by, expecting to complete it relatively quickly, but he had learned even before he left Milan that it would be indefinitely postponed: 'Do you know that I must return to Paris at once instead of going to Rome? A grand opera *L'ange de Nisida* will be given instead of *Le duc d'Albe,* this last for later on, thus there will be three in the same theater.'[76]

The voice that determined that the half-completed *Le duc d'Albe* be dropped and a transmogrified *L'ange* substituted was that of the imperious Rosine Stolz. The unfriendly comments of Duprez help to explain her ability so to influence events:

With the direction of Léon Pillet began the domination or rather the reign of Madame Stolz at the Opéra, an absolute and despotic reign if ever there was one . . . Not content with her share of the public favor, Madame Stolz could no longer endure that anyone but herself should arouse enthusiasm, and she used her influence, which day to day grew stronger with the new director, to diminish the success of those males and females whose talent or beauty offended her . . . Among those who resented 'la favorite', as we came to call to her, was Barroilhet, who was as scandalized as I to hear Pillet say: 'Madame Stolz is a Malibran, but without her shortcomings.'[77]

In the summer of 1840 Stolz had her heart set on a new opera in which she would be the central, the title character. It was Donizetti's 'turn' in the cycle of composers, Meyerbeer having ceded his place by once again postponing *Le prophète* (only one in a series of postponements of this score, which would not be performed until the end of the decade), and, since Stolz decided that *Le duc d'Albe* would not afford her the desired prominence, it was shelved in favor of the reworked *L'ange* which she found more promising. (Stolz may also have rejected *Le duc d'Albe* because the role of the heroine had been composed for her arch rival Julie Dorus-Gras.)

Donizetti's contract required the premiere to take place on 1 December 1840, a deadline that allowed precious little time for a work on the grand scale appropriate to the Opéra. One can only admire his rashness in considering this proposal seriously, particularly when one thinks of the almost glacial torpor with which such undertakings customarily moved. Since there was scarcely leeway to compose and make ready an entirely new score, it was as well that Donizetti's suggested revision and expansion of the existing *L'ange de Nisida* met with Stolz's approval. The original libretto of *L'ange de Nisida* had been the handiwork of Royer and Vaëz; now Scribe was brought in to supervise the remodeling of that text under its new and, considering the status of Stolz vis-à-vis Pillet, ironical title of *La favorite*.[78]

An autograph copy of the neglected libretto of *L'ange de Nisida* is in the Archives Nationales, Paris; without it, it is impossible to gain a clear picture of the evolution of *La favorite*.[79] The characters in *L'ange* were altered in *La favorite* as follows:

L'ange de Nisida	*La favorite*
Don Fernand d'Aragon, King of Naples	Alphonse XI of Castille
Don Gaspar, chamberlain of the King	Don Gaspar[80]
Leone de Casaldi, a soldier	Fernand, a novice and son of
A Monk (called 'Le supérieur' in the final scene	Balthasar, Superior of the monastery of Santiago de Compostela
Countess Sylvia de Linares	Léonor
	Inès, confidante to Léonor

The action of *L'ange* takes place on the island of Nisida and at Naples in 1470, that of *La favorite* at Compostella and Castille before 1350. But the similarity between the names of characters in the two versions is some indication of the close association of the plots: the same conflict is retained with only a few important alterations. Most of the changes were made to the first half of *L'ange*, only occasional echoes of which remain in *La favorite*;[81] from the marriage scene to the tragic conclusion the two operas are substantially the same.[82] By comparison with the plot of *L'ange*, that of *La favorite* is altogether tighter, somewhat more plausibly motivated and more symmetrical.

Several others points emerge from the relationship between these two works. An old tale that Donizetti composed the last act of *La favorite* in a few hours one evening is, like other similar claims, patently untrue. Both the libretto of *L'ange* and the composite autograph score of *L'ange–La favorite* prove that what became substantially Act 4 of *La favorite* was completed months before September

1840, when Donizetti returned to Paris to prepare his second work for the Opéra: the final page of *La favorite*, previously that of *L'ange*, is dated 27 December 1839. Further, the transferral of the action from Naples to Castille and the renaming of certain characters in the revision were intended to prove some help in getting the work performed in Italy[83] – an important financial consideration for Donizetti; although, in view of his treatment by Ferdinando II, he may have relished writing a work in which a King Fernand of Naples is thoroughly compromised, he was well aware, as he had written to Persico in May 1839, that *L'ange* could not be given in Italy 'because of the libretto'. And finally, the source of *La favorite* has often been identified as Baculard d'Arnaud's play, *Les amans malheureux, ou Le comte de Comminge* (1790),[84] but that drama is the source only of the final scene at the monastery.[85] It bears no resemblance at all to anything else in either *L'ange de Nisida* or *La favorite*. The true source, or sources, of both plots are yet to be identified.

The work of adapting *L'ange* into *La favorite* and of composing some new music for it[86] was substantially complete by 1 October 1840. On that date Gaetano reported to Toto: 'I am being murdered by the rehearsals. At this moment I am finishing my opera in four acts and rehearsing every day, which is a thing to die of. I have the compensation that the artists are very well known, except the secondary singers (as usual), but no one is absent, *et voilà tout*.'[87] And while the rehearsals for *La favorite* occupied the Opéra, Donizetti, who at this time seems to have been constitutionally incapable of concentrating on a single production, was busily preparing *Lucrezia Borgia* for its introduction at the Théâtre-Italien on 31 October 1840.[88] This production with Giulia Grisi,[89] Mario and Tamburini was well received, but after twenty performances its successful run was brought to a halt[90] by Victor Hugo, who filed a lawsuit claiming that Étienne Monnier's translation of Romani's libretto, as it appeared in the *livrets* sold at the Théâtre-Italien and elsewhere, amounted to a plagiarism. But once Donizetti had his retouched *Lucrezia* apparently safely launched he could concentrate on the chores confronting him at the Opéra. In contrast to the three months' rehearsal period required for *Les martyrs*, *La favorite* was completely prepared in two.

On 2 December 1840 *La favorite* received its premiere at the Opéra, the principal roles being entrusted to Stolz, Duprez, Barroilhet in his Opéra debut, and Levasseur. Considering that this work was for the next sixty years to be a staple of the French repertory,[91] the initial response to it was surprisingly cool. Gautier's review in *La presse* (7 December 1840) is scarcely enthusiastic:

This opera, where one finds the virtues and the faults (above all the faults) of M. Donizetti, has succeeded without great enthusiasm, or, one should say, without opposition. It contains facility, happily conceived melodies, passages well written for the voice, a certain éclat, but one also finds in it at each step shopworn melodies and threadbare, trivial phrases; a hasty negligence which one forgives in Italy, but which is inappropriate to the more serious habits of our lyric theaters. The poem is rapid, well shaped, and offers two or three fine situations.[92]

In contrast to his active discouragement of *Les martyrs*, Pillet supported Donizetti's newest opera because of the great opportunities it allowed Stolz both as singer and actress. Before long, the final duet of the opera won a loyal and sentimental following as representing a touchstone of Romantic escapism.[93] *La favorite* gained steadily in favor, but it became a true hit overnight on 12 February 1841, when the irresistible Carlotta Grisi made her Opéra debut, dancing in the Act 2 divertissement. *La favorite*, *Lucrezia* and *Lucia* formed a triad of Donizetti's serious operas that for the rest of the century managed to hold their own – and not just in France and Italy – against later Italian and German works that pre-empted space in the repertory. (Today *La favorite* continues to be revived regularly in Italy, and it has since 1960 been performed in half a dozen cities in the United States,[94] but in France it has fallen into almost total neglect.)

On 14 December 1840 Donizetti left Paris for Rome, setting out to oversee the production of his most recent opera, *Adelia*; he had composed and assembled this, borrowing some pages from the 1838 *Gabriella di Vergy* among other works, during the rehearsal period of *La favorite*. The origins of his contract go back to the previous June, when he was in Milan. The Roman impresario Vincenzo Jacovacci, who held the lease of the Teatro Apollo, wrote to inquire whether Donizetti was free to write the opera to open the Carnival season of 1840–1. On 7 June Donizetti replied in terms that reveal a good deal about the working conditions for operatic composers at that period:

We can arrange a contract for the coming Carnival if little things do not interfere. Who will be the singers? Who will do the libretto? Will it be the first opera or the last? I am asking all this to know if the singers are worthy of Rome, because sometimes agents exalt to the skies those who do not much deserve it. As to the ownership of the score, I do not customarily ask for the entire property, but only for the rights to the piano-vocal reduction, which would not at all detract from your right to have the opera performed or to sell

it in order to have it performed anywhere at all. And if this does not please
you or if you believe you would lose a lot, I will yield half the price that I
would expect to receive in Italy. And thus I myself will supervise the translation [into French] and reserve to myself the property rights for France,
where you, even if you wanted to, could not intervene, since once it is
printed in Italy, it can be reprinted here by anyone.[95]

There was no difficulty over either Donizetti's terms or the company
of singers, which included Giuseppina Strepponi,[96] the tenor Salvi
and the bass Ignazio Marini.[97]

About the libretto, however, there would be problems. Donizetti
left the final choice of subject to Jacovacci, giving him the responsibility of having it approved by the exigent Roman censors, but he
had a preliminary suggestion to make. He had heard from Naples
that a recent opera by Giuseppe Lillo, *Il conte di Chalais* (6
November 1839),[98] had failed because the music did not please. This
subject appealed to him because he had already discussed it with
Cammarano. By mid-August Donizetti had learned that the Roman
censors refused to pass this subject because it was too tragic; to take
its place Jacovacci promptly decided in favor of an old libretto by
Romani that Carafa had first set back in 1817 as *Adele di Lusignano*.[99] In 1834 the libretto, with a new last act (ending with the
heroine's suicide) by another poet, had been set by Carlo Coccia,[100]
but since a tragic ending was to be avoided in Rome, Jacovacci
would have to commission another new last act from another librettist. For this purpose Donizetti recommended either Ferretti or
Girolamo Marini,[101] 'both of them Romans' and therefore readily
available. 'I believe', he continues, 'that Marini has already prepared
a libretto. If this is true as they tell me and if it should be appropriate
to the singers, it would be an excellent thing.'[102]

Before he left Milan in August 1840 to return to Paris Donizetti
sold the right to print the piano-vocal reduction of *Adelia* to the
publisher Lucca. Back in Paris in early September 1840 he started to
complain about the libretto and toward the end of the month he
appealed to Romani himself, asking him to search for the original
last act of the old libretto in the hope that it could be used as a way
out of the problem raised by the censors. About this time Donizetti
seems to have resumed cordial relations with Romani, after they had
become strained at the time of *Lucrezia Borgia*. In the course of his
letter Donizetti says:

I believe the original French play caused Adelia to throw herself from her
balcony. Then goodbye *rondò*, goodbye prima donna who would have broken her neck. If you have lines to give me relating to these situations or if

you believe the drama might this time be presented as would please you (subject to revision by the censors), tell me your every intention and I will redo anything you want. *Un mot* (if you have time).[103]

Not until 1 October did the composer receive Marini's third act for *Adelia* and he was appalled by it: 'Such verses, such a scenic effect ... I cannot even tell you what the changes will be because I would use a whole letter explaining them to you.'[104] By now there was no time left for anything but to go ahead, alternating periods of composition with the rehearsals of *La favorite* in Paris. The first two acts of *Adelia* completed, he sent them off to Jacovacci, but, as he confessed to Toto on 3 December 1840, 'I fear for *Adelia*, and I am completing now the third act, except for a few verses that will have to be written for me at Rome.'[105]

Donizetti's fears for *Adelia* found confirmation in a number of omens. A rumor that the pope had died, an event that would have closed the Roman theaters for a period of mourning, caused him to delay his departure until he heard that it had been a false alarm. He sailed from Marseilles in the teeth of a fierce storm that after five furious days landed him, not at Civitavecchia but Toulon, where he spent Christmas; the following day he took ship again for Livorno, reaching Rome on 28 December 1840 without further problems. He stayed with the Vasselli family and when he was not occupied at the Apollo he enjoyed an active social life.

The season at the Apollo opened two days before Donizetti's arrival. Strepponi was to have sung the opening performance of *Marin Faliero*, but she had contracted German measles and had to be replaced by the Bergamasc soprano Benedetta Colleoni-Corti.[106] The Roman public was unenthusiastic over *Marin Faliero*, caring little for the cast or the plot, which the censors had mangled. When the recovered Strepponi sang Elena on 31 December, she had a personal success, but the public remained cool toward Donizetti's score. The second opera of that season was the Paris version of Rossini's *Mosè*, given as *Mosè e Faraone*, and it pleased very much. When *Adelia* finally had its first performance on 11 February 1841 it provoked a near riot. The eager impresario had oversold the theater, and the throng that could not be admitted to the already packed auditorium raised such a fuss that at one point the performance had to be halted. Before the evening was over Jacovacci was arrested and kept overnight in custody. All this turmoil compromised the first performance of the work, even though it elicited some applause. By the end of the season, on 23 February, *Adelia* had been given a total of nine times.

The only town that really took to *Adelia* was Naples, where it was introduced at the San Carlo on 4 October 1841 with Antonietta Rainieri-Marini, Basadonna and Colini; it remained in the repertory until 1848 and was revived in 1852–3 and again in 1856–7. Fanny Persiani sang it in London on 11 March 1843 but produced no impression. (*Adelia* has never been given at La Scala, nor has it ever been performed in France or in the United States. As of this writing it has yet to be proposed as a work to share in the current Donizetti revival.)[107]

Leaving Rome just after the middle of February 1841, Donizetti traveled to Civitavecchia, where he heard the local Accademia perform *L'esule di Roma* in his honor and was greeted by the vociferous applause of the local *dilettanti*. From there he made a smooth crossing to Marseilles, arriving back in Paris on 2 March; shortly afterward he moved into an apartment in the Hôtel Manchester, 1 rue Grammont. If Donizetti had expected to settle down at once to a new round of activity in the Parisian theaters, things did not turn out quite as he anticipated; he wrote some concert songs and adjusted his score of *Parisina* to mesh with Hippolyte Lucas's French translation of Romani's libretto, but otherwise he had no engagements. Before he left Rome he had written to Dolci that he was returning to Paris 'for an opera buffa',[108] but this plan must have fallen through since no new operas by him were given in Paris in 1841. He refused most of the offers that came his way, apparently having learned from frequent ribbing in the French journals that being too prolific could be construed as a liability; or perhaps the urge that had driven him so unmercifully for the past two years had temporarily subsided, leaving him drained.

Among the offers Donizetti entertained, the most pressing came in one way or another from the Opéra. Pillet was so delighted with the increasing success of *La favorite* and Stolz's popularity as Léonor that he was anxious to have a prompt successor. Donizetti had been back in Paris only a few days when Scribe showed him a libretto, which he did not find to his taste. Later, as he reported to Ricordi, he was rather mysteriously approached by Marquis Aguado[109] himself, who was the true power at the Opéra; Aguado 'wanted an opera in four acts for the Académie, other than my *Le duc d'Albe*. Let it be as though I had not written that, since I rely only on contracts and not on verbal agreements.' Near the end of this letter he reverts to the same subject: 'For now do not speak to anyone about the opera that Marquis Aguado wants, since perhaps there is a secret connected with it.'[110] Two weeks later, on 8 June 1841, he mentions Aguado's

proposal in a letter to Toto, but in terms that suggest he had no great
expectations of it: 'I will leave [Paris] when I want to, all the more so
because the opera that Aguado asked for is not, it seems to me, a
thing to do right away.'[111] Donizetti's correspondence affords no
further clue to Aguado's request or to the secret connected with it. It
came to nothing, it resulted in no contract. Nor was the Opéra the
only theater eager to stage new works by Donizetti. The Opéra-
Comique offered him two subjects, but what they were cannot now
be established; he refused them both.

The only contract that he had in force at this time was one to
compose the opera to open the approaching Carnival season at La
Scala. While he awaited with increasing impatience the arrival of the
libretto for this work from Milan, Donizetti happened to meet Gustave Vaëz on the street one day and begged him for a one-act subject,
simply to keep himself occupied. Vaëz was happy to oblige. The
upshot of this chance encounter was Rita, a one-act work consisting
of eight numbers connected by spoken dialogue. Within a week the
score was complete, even to the orchestration. Since apparently
Crosnier,[112] the director of the Opéra-Comique, rejected it, Donizetti
started arrangements to have it translated into Italian so that it might
be produced at the Fondo in Naples, but the death of Barbaja in
October 1841 apparently put an end to that scheme. The still unperformed score of Rita was among Donizetti's effects when he died,
but it had to wait a dozen years before it was finally produced;
appropriately, its premiere took place at the theater it had been originally designed for – the Opéra-Comique – on 7 May 1860.[113] (During the nineteenth century Rita enjoyed only a desultory life, but in
the wake of a successful revival in Rome in September 1955, Rita
became a hit at the Piccola Scala in 1965, and now, on the merits of
its well-crafted score, its genuinely amusing plot and its relatively
modest vocal demands, it has become one of the most frequently
performed of all of Donizetti's operas.)[114]

In contrast to Rita, written for fun as an escape from boredom, Maria
Padilla was from the start an arduous and troublesome work.
Donizetti had not had a new opera put on at La Scala since the
problematic Maria Stuarda in December 1835, and although the
circumstances of its prohibition may have compromised Donizetti
with the local authorities for a while, the passage of time and his
continuing success might well have mitigated any lingering reluctance. A major stumbling block in the path of Donizetti's understandable ambition to open another Carnival season at La Scala was

Bartolomeo Merelli, who had provided him with some of his earliest librettos. By 1836 Merelli had established himself as a powerful figure, and notoriously not an overly scrupulous one, on the Italian operatic scene. From his beginnings as a librettist, Merelli had progressed to theatrical agent, occasional impresario in minor theaters, and right-hand man to Duke Carlo Visconti at La Scala; by the autumn season of 1836 he held the reins as impresario at La Scala as Visconti's successor.[115] Nor was Milan his only arena of activity, for in April 1836 he, with Carlo Balocchino, had acquired the lease to the Kärntnertortheater in Vienna. Here Balocchino was in residence as general supervisor, while Merelli was principally involved from Milan in putting together the three-month Italian season that the Kärntnertor held each spring.

That Merelli should wait until the fifth year of his tenure at La Scala before putting on a new Donizetti opera is a striking omission. After the universal success of *Lucia*, whose *prima* had taken place only a few days after Bellini's death, Donizetti was clearly the most important Italian operatic composer then active. Yet for five years Merelli ignored Donizetti, in that time inviting sixteen other composers to write for his stage,[116] of whom five were asked to provide a second opera between 1836 and 1841.[117] The conclusion seems unavoidable that Merelli would rather have anyone other than Donizetti, even though he regularly mounted Donizetti's older works.

Donizetti's relationship with Merelli can be traced to some extent in his letters, which reveal his desire to compose for the impresario's theaters. For example, in 1830 Donizetti asks Mayr to recommend a tenor to Merelli, explaining that he does not do it himself because 'on my behalf Merelli would do nothing'.[118] In 1837 Donizetti is still approaching Merelli indirectly, but this time he wants the recommendation for himself. He writes to Ricordi: 'Tell Pedroni that since I have a desire to see Vienna he should mention it to Merelli, because there is no use in my doing it myself.'[119] In 1838 he explains his current feelings about writing for La Scala to Count Melzi: 'As for Milan, from the artistic point of view, I sing a Requiem for it, since Merelli does not want to and (almost) cannot pay. I will come there just the same and I want to.'[120] On 27 April 1840 he writes to Dolci from Paris, explaining why he has not been composing for Milan: 'When will we see one another again, dear friend? Since Merelli has been impresario at Milan I have not had even the tiniest offer. Perhaps I could not have accepted it, but at least I would have discovered who still remembered me.'[121] Six weeks later he gives an

ironical account of his situation in regard to the impresario in a letter
to the Milanese journalist Pietro Cominazzi:

Pray heaven that the great Merelli will give me an engagement one day,
because since he has been impresario he has never addressed two lines to
me. And having made proposals to him, through the offices of Mlle Ungher,
to make sacrifices on my part to come to Vienna, he answered that he would
not engage me because my music was not liked at Vienna. If that is true, I am
sorry for it and I am also sorry for him, since either through the wishes of the
singers or through his own foolishness I see that every year my operas are
put on, and therefore that must be at his loss.[122]

Obviously Donizetti's eagerness to write for La Scala and the
Kärntnertor outweighed his distrust of Merelli. One can only guess
at the reasons behind Merelli's reluctance; clearly Donizetti suspected a personal resentment. All the evidence about Merelli
suggests that his sense of his own self-importance was immense and
that he was unreliable about financial dealings.

The long-delayed rapprochement between Donizetti and Merelli
began during Donizetti's brief visit to Milan in August 1840. They
discussed inconclusively some proposals initiated by Donizetti who,
with his Parisian success behind him, was now ready to appear
again before an Italian public. A month after his return to France he
finally received from Merelli an offer to write for both Milan and
Vienna. Anxious not to have to deal directly with Merelli any more
than he could help, Donizetti informed his Milanese friend Paolo
Branca[123] that he found Merelli's offer insufficient. He was accustomed to receive 10,000 francs for a new opera, but under the circumstances he would make the concession of accepting 10,000 Austrian francs, which were then worth 15 percent less than French
ones, if Merelli would pay for his lodging in Vienna. He explains in
the ribald tone common in his later letters:

Two rooms are enough. This should not cause Merelli to miscarry since he is
accustomed to granting lodging to many singers, and besides it relieves me
of the embarrassment of searching a foreign city and getting castrated, as
people usually say. Just as long as the apartment is decent. I live like an
artist. I do not think that will be difficult to agree to. For Milan, also, I will
make the same sacrifice of Austrian francs.[124]

Merelli not only commissioned two operas from Donizetti, he also
asked him to serve as musical director for the Italian season in
Vienna, over which they soon came to an agreement as to terms and
dates. Since Donizetti was, at the time of this exchange, obligated in
Paris for *La favorite* and Rome for *Adelia*, it was settled that the new
opera for La Scala would open the Carnival season of 1841–2 and
that the score for Vienna would be ready the following April.

Donizetti's choice of a librettist for his opera for La Scala first fell upon Cammarano, but, since the departure of his colleague from Naples, Cammarano had begun writing texts for other composers and had to turn him down. Donizetti found his subject himself in François Ancelot's *Maria Padilla*, a play that had been brought out in Paris in 1838. Donizetti drew up a scenario from the play, sending it to Merelli in April 1841, asking him to see to getting it approved by the censors. When Merelli had not replied in a month, Donizetti wrote to Ricordi to find out if Merelli had been away from Milan, wondering whether his scenario was lost or forgotten: 'You can imagine that I await his reply with the liveliest impatience.'[125]

After Cammarano's refusal, the choice of librettist was left to Merelli, who selected Gaetano Rossi,[126] then the doyen of Italian librettists. Donizetti's circumspection in submitting the scenario to Merelli for the censors' approval before he started composing and in leaving even the choice of librettist to the impresario shows him putting into practise the principles of which he had written to Aniello Benevento back in August 1838,[127] and his care in these matters may be interpreted as a first glimmer of his Viennese ambitions. He had to wait in Paris until the end of July 1841 before he received some installments of Rossi's text, which pleased and stimulated him. On 17 August he sent Rossi a long letter about the libretto, and one passage shows his dramatic imagination vividly at work: 'For the big duet in Act 3, I leave everything to you. It seems best to me, however, that Maria should begin the story of her life since she has become the King's mistress and that her father should listen to her distractedly.' At this point in the action, Maria's father, Don Ruiz, has become irrational owing to his daughter's dishonor.

Afterwards, by his few broken words unrelated to what she has said, Maria perceives his madness; but it is necessary that the first time, that is, in the middle of Maria's narrative, he should give an answer that she can believe relevant to what she has been saying so that she continues. Then finally he (if it is wanted), instead of answering his daughter, can begin an *adagio* in tearful phrases, reproving her behavior without seeing her, without looking at her, etc., and stopping suddenly in the middle of the last phrase, he sees at his feet his daughter (or a woman) and goes into a rage, etc., but it should finish with both of them still weeping.[128]

A month later Gaetano described his current work in a letter to Toto, adding 'the text is by Rossi and Donizetti',[129] indicating that since he had arrived in Milan early in September he had been actively collaborating in the writing of the libretto; Rossi was a librettist of the old school and Donizetti felt that he needed help in making the emotional impact of the text sufficiently vivid and specific.

Although Rossi alone is usually credited with the libretto of *Maria Padilla,* it would be more accurate to list Donizetti too – as co-librettist. In the same letter to Toto, he continues: 'I do not know about Vienna yet. For Milan I have la Löwe[130] (a German), la Abbadia[131] (both of them good), Donzelli and Ronconi.' He had earlier hoped to have as his prima donna Erminia Frezzolini, whose great success at La Scala in the revised *Lucrezia* of 1840 had endeared her to him, but she had recently married the tenor Poggi and her pregnancy would prevent her from singing in public in December and January. He had begun composing *Maria Padilla* with Frezzolini in mind, but when he learned that the energetic Löwe would be his heroine he revised the embellishments of the part.

Shortly before *Maria Padilla* went into rehearsal at La Scala on 10 December 1841, Donizetti was furious to learn that the censors wanted the opera's denouement changed; they insisted that suicide was not an edifying spectacle and that the heroine 'die of joy'. He was disgusted not only because he found joy, as a terminal complaint on the stage, dramatically weak, but because this solution seriously compromised the motivation of his final scene.[132] The general rehearsal was held on Christmas eve and the invited audience had mixed reactions, while Donizetti was upset by Ronconi's first-act costume, which he intended to have changed, and by the 'horrid' set for Act 2. The whole rehearsal period he described to Dolci as a 'flagellation'.[133]

The first performance, on the traditional date of 26 December, did not kindle the enthusiasm Donizetti had hoped for, but he was called out several times by the audience.[134] The reception was more enthusiastic at the second performance, when he had to take a dozen curtain calls. On 31 December he reported to Accursi in Paris the audience's later reaction:

Third performance. (I was sick: headache.) At the duet between the women the announcement had to be made that the Maestro was not present in the theater, but every number had a warm reception.

Fourth performance. Applause for the singers, male and female. I too was called out, and at the end twice alone and twice with the cast. La fama,[135] which was reserved and picky about the first night, yesterday declared itself in a general confession to have been mistaken and now puts itself on the side of the public – of the public that has called me out so very many times.[136]

Donizetti included the article from *La fama* so that Accursi could help spread the word of *Maria Padilla*'s success in Paris.[137] On the other hand, remembering how the censors had maltreated the conclusion of his opera, Gaetano found ironical delight in informing

Toto that the *Gazzetta di Milano* pronounced the finale to Act 3 to be 'the *truly great* piece'[138] in the whole score.

During its first (and only) run at La Scala, *Maria Padilla* held the interest of the public through twenty-four performances. Its next production was during the Lent season at Trieste, where Eugenia Tadolini sang Maria; for her Donizetti reinstated the final cabaletta, which he had been forbidden to use in Milan, and now he caused the opera to end happily with Maria alive.[139] He further retouched the score for the opera's first production at the San Carlo; it was first given there, with Tadolini, on 28 July 1842 and maintained itself in the repertory for the next four years. *Maria Padilla* held the stage until about 1858, receiving performances in Vienna (again with Tadolini), Lisbon and Barcelona, as well as almost a dozen Italian cities. (So far, its only twentieth-century revival has been the opera's English premiere: a concert performance at the Queen Elizabeth Hall, London, under the auspices of Opera Rara on 8 April 1973, the 125th anniversary of Donizetti's death.)

Donizetti decided to remain in Milan to compose his opera for Vienna, which was to be *Linda di Chamounix*. On 2 January 1842 he explained to Accursi why he would not be returning to Paris just then:

La Löwe is the prima donna who would satisfy me there for *Le duc d'Albe*. La Stolz, no, because that would mean going back to the beginning.[140] She causes me so many worries and M. Pillet has broken his word to me so many times that I am in no haste whatever to return to Paris. In March I am leaving for Vienna. Afterwards, God knows what I will do, I do not even know myself.[141]

He had positive reasons for staying on in Milan: Rossi, his librettist for *Linda,* was accessible, he had a circle of friends there, and he could make the round trip to Bergamo in six hours.[142]

As with *Maria Padilla,* Donizetti himself suggested his next subject to Rossi, remembering a French play, *La grâce de Dieu* by d'Ennery and Lemoine, that he had seen in Paris earlier in 1841.[143] Rossi worked on the libretto late in 1841, and Donizetti began composing his opera on the last day of that year. Ten days later he could report to Accursi: 'I am at the end of Act 1 of *La grâce de Dieu*. Tomorrow I hope to begin Act 2.'[144] He was still in Milan on 4 March 1842, when he reported to Toto: 'My opera for Vienna is finished, orchestrated, retouched, etc., and today it leaves for Vienna, where they will make the necessary copies.'[145]

In the early months of 1842, while he was engaged on *Linda,*

Donizetti was half expecting that he might have another opera to compose. About the middle of the previous November he had received a visit from the manager of the Italian season in London, Benjamin Lumley,[146] who brought a letter of introduction from Romani and an offer to commission an opera for 12,000 francs; the text would be by Romani, and the first performance would be given in May 1842. As a result of this visit from Lumley, Donizetti wrote a letter full of practical advice to Romani:

I hear that you have promised to write a libretto for the Italian company at London, to which I would write the music.
Is [Lumley] correct in saying you gave your word? Excuse me if I am dubious, but you have put me many times in an embarrassing situation. Truly the wrong is not completely mine if I ask you whether it is true. I spoke with Signor Lummlay [sic] . . . he departed for Modena and left me the charge of asking you if this libretto would be ready by the middle of January at the latest . . . You choose the subject: but remember that, having to contend with a public that scarcely understands Italian, it would not be a bad idea to let the choice fall on some familiar subject by Sakespearre, Bayron, Valter Scott or Bulwer [sic] . . . If you could write me a libretto in just two short acts, that would be divine. In London after the theater people go out in society[147] . . . Do not try fantastic subjects because there the stage machinery is abysmal. Speak to the heart as you know how to do . . . I await your reply. Remember that I must give my opera [Linda] in April and that if you cannot give me the libretto by the middle of January, as Lummlay says, we are cooked [siamo fritti].[148]

On 23 November Romani replied, agreeing with Donizetti's sensible suggestions and adding that brevity and clarity are not easily obtained. Then he turns to his personal relationship with Donizetti.

As to the reproachful recollections [reminiscenze] with which you honor me, I believed oblivion had obliterated them. Nonetheless, if I remember well there has always been room for many recriminations; and there always will be, since composers will never be persuaded that the amount of time they require to write well is equally necessary to poets, and perhaps more so. I speak of the good poets, not those who produce the smudged sheets that now flourish like rank weeds to the great misfortune of Italy. But of all this we will talk better face to face, and I will surely persuade you that I have nothing, or at least very little, to reproach myself with in this matter.
Farewell. Love me as I love you, because I am always the same and full of affection and esteem for you.[149]

When the middle of January 1842 arrived and no first act of the libretto had reached Donizetti, he made allowances, for he was just starting the second act of Linda di Chamounix and Romani was a 53-year-old bridegroom[150] on his honeymoon. Donizetti decided to wait exactly one month and not one day more. When the middle of

February arrived and still not one verse from Romani had reached him, Donizetti was angry. On 16 February he expresses his outrage to Toto:

I have lost a big opportunity because of Romani. He promised me the first act of a libretto for London yesterday, and he broke his word. I have to keep things straight and write: *he broke his word.* But if he was a man of honor,[151] *I would have earned in two months 12,000 francs* from London. Damn those men who after making a contract do not keep their word! *Pazienza!*[152]

On other occasions when Romani had failed to provide a text by a stipulated date Donizetti had been able to find a substitute librettist so that he could maintain his contract,[153] but there was now no time to find another poet, and consequently he lost the largest fee he had ever been offered.[154] There was no time for the London project at this point because he had to leave for Vienna in a month, and on his way there he had to stop off at Bologna to conduct, at the composer's urging, the first Italian performances of Rossini's *Stabat mater.*[155]

Before he received Rossini's invitation, late in February 1842, Donizetti had intended to travel in the company of some of the singers Merelli had engaged for Vienna; but he could accept Rossini's flattering offer if he left earlier for Bologna and then caught up with them at Vicenza. He explains it all in a letter to Toto, where his high spirits find their outlet in the form of imaginary dialogue, an epistolary style that Donizetti found irresistible when he was in a good humor and which speaks of his instinct for drama even in daily life:

I am leaving next Tuesday.[156] For where? For Bologna. Ah, you are joking with me. But, I don't believe it . . . Do you know why I am doing this? Because Rossini had scarcely heard of my trip [to Vienna] when he wrote me that he absolutely entrusted to me the direction of his *Stabat,* and he is placing at my disposition *his life and all his goods.* You see that one does not refuse such an invitation. Already I don't feel like conducting because I would tremble in front of him. But I want to show my gratitude.[157]

The preparation of the *Stabat mater* had already begun when Donizetti arrived in Bologna, but he conducted the orchestral rehearsals and, on 18, 19 and 20 March 1842, the three public performances,[158] the proceeds of which were to go to a retired musicians' home that Rossini was sponsoring. The Italian *prima* of a major new work by the man who was generally regarded as the greatest living composer attracted extraordinary attention, especially since Rossini was then residing in Bologna. Rossini's ill health[159] and overwrought nerves prevented his actually attending the performances, but he listened to the last one from an adjoining room. When the closing section of the work had been encored, Rossini appeared before the audience and publicly embraced Donizetti. Since these performances were charity benefits, Donizetti received no fee, but Rossini presented him with four diamond studs that Donizetti always treasured because of the donor.

Rossini, typically, had an ulterior motive in asking Donizetti to conduct the *Stabat mater*. While Donizetti was in Bologna, Rossini 'besieged' him and 'tried to seduce'[160] him to accept the joint position of director of the Liceo Musicale at Bologna and *maestro di cappella* at San Petronio, thinking that as Donizetti, like himself, had studied there, he would be ultimately persuadable. Donizetti had already turned down these positions the previous October, not only because they had been previously refused by both Mercadante and Pacini, which scarcely added to their attractiveness, but also because he disliked the restriction Bologna might impose upon his pursuit of his career; moreover, he had received some indirect assurances that he could be a candidate for a far more imposing position in Vienna, a prospect that his amour propre preferred. In March 1842 Rossini was hoping to pressure Donizetti into reconsidering his earlier refusal, reminding him of his student days there, telling him of his own efforts to improve the Liceo, reminding him how high he stood just now in the esteem of the *bolognesi*. Considerably embarrassed by Rossini's entreaties and unable to allude to his Viennese expectations, Donizetti managed to escape by making a counterproposal, asking a fee and conditions that he knew would be unacceptable. There the matter was allowed to drop.

Elated by the success of the *Stabat mater*, Donizetti left Bologna and traveled to Vicenza, where he met the baritone Varesi and three other singers bound for Vienna. Even though their coach broke down four times on their journey, the high spirits of the group were unaffected by such inconveniences. On 27 March 1842 Donizetti and his companions arrived in Vienna by train. At first he was enthusiastic about the imperial capital, finding it beautiful, more grandiose than Paris and more expensive. The preparations for the Italian season at the Kärntnertortheater began almost at once, and much of Donizetti's time was taken up with them.

The Italian singers made their first appearances that year on 2 April 1842 in Mercadante's *La vestale*, which was new to Vienna, and was positively disliked, particularly its hapless prima donna, Antonietta Rainieri-Marini.[161] As the season progressed with more downs than ups, Donizetti came to count more and more heavily on *Linda di Chamounix* to turn the tide of public favor. The rehearsals of his opera were delayed until 26 April because the copyist was slow in preparing the individual parts. Once the rehearsals were under way Donizetti learned that his public expected a full-length overture to precede his opera. Being well aware of the musical traditions of Vienna, and the taste that prevailed there for substantial musical forms, he adapted the first movement of his 1836 string quartet and set it in front of his otherwise complete score.[162] On 10 May he held the first orchestral run-through, but to his dismay he found it took four full hours just to get through the first act because the instrumental parts were full of errors. These corrections and the uncertainty over the tenor Moriani's health[163] delayed the *prima* until 19 May 1842.

On that night Donizetti conducted the first performance of *Linda*, sung by Tadolini, Marietta Brambilla, Moriani, Felice Varesi,[164] Dérivis and Agostino Rovere,[165] before a crowded house that grew so enthusiastic that by the time the evening was over Donizetti had been called before the curtain seventeen times, alone and with the singers. At the third performance of *Linda* the imperial family attended and remained to the end and applauded cordially. A few days later Donizetti sent to Ricordi, who had acquired the rights for *Linda*, a graphic account of the opera's fervent reception, of which the most interesting part is the description of Tadolini in the title role.

All the singers compete in zeal, all know how to win applause, but la Tadolini revealed herself in a surprising manner. She is a singer, she is an actress, she is everything, and imagine that she is applauded just at her appearance in Act 3. I believe if you see *Linda* with Tadolini, you will see madness represented in a new way. She has been so obedient to me, weeping, laughing, remaining stupefied when she has to, that I myself say that this scene (performed in this manner) stands above all the other mad scenes I have written.[166]

The fourth performance of *Linda* was conducted by Heinrich Proch,[167] yet Donizetti had to be summoned to acknowledge the applause. At the tenth performance (13 June), he resumed the baton at the request of the Archduchess Sophie, and again the court was present, demanding encores of their favorite numbers. The Italian season closed on 30 June 1842 with the seventeenth performance of *Linda*. Donizetti dedicated the score to the Empress Anna.

The Viennese critics were on the whole well-disposed, some of them enthusiastic. Heinrich Adami, writing in the *Allgemeine Theaterzeitung* described it as 'such a decisive and brilliant success that I recollect nothing similar to it in this theater for many years'.[168]

Many of the critics commented on the music in detail, praising the *pianissimo* ensemble statement in the Act 1 duet, 'A consolarmi affrettisi', and the muted violins that accompany Carlo's aria in Act 2. The return of melodies for dramatic effect, those of the Act 1 love duet and Pierotto's ballata, was generally noted. Perhaps the most frequently recurring theme in these criticisms is praise for Donizetti's attention to musical detail, his lack of affectation, as though he had to some welcome extent 'Germanized' his talent.

After its auspicious launching in Vienna, *Linda* went on to become one of Donizetti's hardiest scores throughout the nineteenth century. Its second most important production, also prepared by Donizetti, was in Paris at the Théâtre-Italien, where it was first given on 17 November 1842; both the work and cast (Persiani, Mario, Tamburini and Lablache) were well received, Gautier hailing *Linda* 'as an almost irreproachable work'. For Persiani, Donizetti added the best-known aria in the score, 'O luce di quest'anima', to a text that he wrote himself. In June of the following year the same cast introduced the opera to London, where the musical quality of the score was better received than the awkwardly constructed drama, especially in Act 2. *Linda* reached New York in 1847 and maintained itself as a favored vehicle for a number of sopranos[169] until about 1890. It was first given in Italy in 1842, the year of its *prima,* and quickly established a lasting popularity; after some slackening in the number of performances in the early part of this century, *Linda* has enjoyed a number of revivals there in the years since World War II.

The Kärntnertor was not the only scene of Donizetti's activities during his first visit to Vienna. His well-publicized participation in the Italian *prima* of Rossini's *Stabat mater* led to insistence that he conduct the first Viennese performance of that score. On 4 May 1842 he conducted a private performance at court, at which the orchestral parts were played in a two-piano reduction and the vocal parts, six soloists and chorus, were taken by singers from the Kärntnertor. This was a preview of the first public performances held in the Redoutensaal on 31 May and 7 June, this time with full orchestra, Donizetti again conducting. These were a great success and marked the apex of his popularity in Vienna. The person in charge of arranging the public hearing of the *Stabat mater* was Baron Eduard von Lannoy,[170] whose staunch friendship would prove invaluable to Donizetti in 1847. Donizetti composed for the emperor a five-voice *Ave Maria* with string accompaniment, which he presented in person to Ferdinand on 20 May 1842. On the 28th he was invited to become an honorary member of the Gesellschaft der Musikfreunde. He was lionized by high society; on 31 May he was invited to a *musicale* at Prince Metternich's[171] to enjoy one of Vienna's vocal treats, the singing of Countess Rossi.[172]

In the many letters Donizetti wrote during May 1842 a dominant motif is his uncertainty about his future, uncertainty undoubtedly heightened by impatience. Numerous offers came to him from many quarters, but he held back, hoping that the rumors and hints he had heard that he was to be offered the post of *Hofkapellmeister* would at last materialize in some acceptable form. The etiquette of the Habsburg court was complicated, and Donizetti sent word on 4 June to Peppina Appiani,[173] who had been his landlady in Milan the previous winter, that the first indirect contact concerning this matter had been made.

I don't know if you are familiar with Figaro's aria in *Il barbiere* by Rossini – 'tutti mi chiedono, tutti mi vogliono', etc. Here is a case in point. Paris: *come at once*. No! Naples: *make haste*. No! Bologna: *establish yourself here*, here are *your terms*. No. Do you want to accept (here comes the *adagio*) the post in V...i...en...na[174] of *maestro* at court [*Hofkapellmeister*]? If you say yes, then Maestro [?Ministero] Kolowrat will make you an offer of it. But what will I have to do? What salary will I have? I will tell you about it later. *Hofkapellmeister* sounds well, it seems to me, if the conditions are ample. The title is decorous. It should not entail too much work.[175]

He cautions her to keep the news of this negotiation to herself, since as yet there had not even been an official inquiry as to whether he would accept it. Yet, as Donizetti's barely contained elation shows, he knew that such an inquiry was imminent.

Less than two weeks later the next steps had been taken. Donizetti, after enjoining the strictest secrecy, details them to Dolci:

I was called to court to discover if I wanted to accept the post that Krommer, Mozart and Kotzeluch [*sic*] formerly held,[176] that is: *Hofkapellmeister* to His Majesty the Emperor, receiving orders only from him through the Grand Chamberlain. There would be the obligation of directing concerts in the royal apartments only two or three or times a year, separate payment for every cantata that might be commissioned, every year five or six months' leave of absence, and attached to the post is an honorarium of 3000 florins a year. I said that if His Majesty wanted it, I would serve for nothing, but if His Majesty wanted to put a limit on his benevolence I would have accepted such conditions for 4000 florins, making him understand that I have taken in the same amount in two months with one opera.

My remark was not found unjust, I was told to put that in writing and I did so and gave it to him so that it could be presented, and perhaps today His Majesty will see it.[177]

By the end of June he learned informally that the post was his and that his annual salary would be 12,000 Austrian francs, which would be paid in monthly installments to his Viennese agents, Carlo and Pietro Mechetti, music-publishers and dealers. The official notification of his appointment reached Donizetti on 13 July 1842.

On 1 July Donizetti had already left Vienna to go to Milan. There he remained a month, taking a few days to go to Bergamo for a reunion with Mayr, now almost totally blind, and with Dolci and other friends. Those who saw him at Bergamo at this time thought he was out of sorts, but he explained that he suffered from almost continual headaches, and the uncommonly hot weather disagreed with him. Something else bothered him too, for he discovered that his friends did not share his exhilaration over his post in Vienna. The most disapproving was the one Gaetano thought would have been the most understanding, Toto in Rome. It is clear his brother-in-law was worried by the thought of Gaetano far away and without any close friends to keep an eye on him. From Toto's point of view the offer of the joint post at Bologna was infinitely more desirable. The old rumors of Donizetti's dissolute ways had increased rather than abated, as is clear from a letter he wrote to Toto from Civitavecchia on 3 August 1842, in which he seeks to justify himself: 'What? You speak to me of other women? Oh, laugh freely and believe that I weep [for Virginia] as if it were the first day. Oh, if I could distract myself! Believe it, I seek to stupefy myself. Enough!'[178]

Early in August 1842 Donizetti returned to Naples for the first time since had moved to Paris nearly four years earlier. Except for the inevitable pain of seeing places closely associated with his dead wife, this visit was as agreeable as his health would permit. He describes to Dolci the reception he found there:

In the twenty-five days I have been here I have been twice in bed with fever. I am leaving in about five or six days. It has pleased me so much to see Naples and to find all my friends the same as ever and to see a large crowd that had assembled almost spontaneously at the theater to greet me again. Condemned to my bed by fever, I had almost to be forced by the police to get up and go there to make an appearance.[179]
This reception proves that my conduct here for fifteen years has always been honorable, and I find myself surrounded by the same pupils, by the same friends, as if four whole years had not elapsed.[180]

It was not just to see old friends that Donizetti returned to Naples; he also had business to conduct. He still maintained his old apartment there, with a caretaker to look after it, and although he had spoken of selling it and its contents he discovered that when he was confronted with the actual step he drew back. He decided to postpone his decision until the following year, when he expected to return to Naples to produce an opera at the San Carlo for which he had signed a contract in May 1842. Shortly after signing this contract, he had accepted the appointment as *Hofkapellmeister*, which tied him to Vienna for the first six months of the year. To arrange a mutually agreeable time for the new opera at the San Carlo he conferred with Edoardo Guillaume, who was Barbaja's successor as impresario in Naples. After negotiations, the date was settled as July or August 1843, but no final decision was reached about either a subject or a librettist.

Donizetti left Naples on 6 September 1842, taking nearly three weeks to reach Paris, where he settled in once more at the Hôtel Manchester. At the time he left Naples, he imagined that perhaps the turn of *Le duc d'Albe* would come round at last.[181] For some time he had been reconsidering it as a suitable vehicle for Rosine Stolz. In January 1842 he had set out his ideas on this development to Accursi, expecting, of course, that Accursi would spread them around Paris.

I, too, am of the opinion that there are some changes to make in *Le duc d'Albe:* the conspiracy less dominant, the love interest warmer. All told I expect it would be very effective. Above all, I have cherished the role of the heroine, it is possibly a new role in the theater, an active role, where almost always the heroine is passive. Here she is young, enthusiastic, loving, a Joan of Arc. And I think Mme Stolz would be admirable for it, because there are many, many situations that seem to have inspired me.[182]

But as had happened twice before, *Le duc d'Albe* was postponed, now until 1845. While Pillet was planning to bring Scribe and Donizetti together to hatch a new five-act grand opera, Donizetti was hoping to persuade Pillet to revive *Les martyrs*, which was still doing well in the provinces. Pillet was unmoved by his hopes; he had scored against Duponchel by discarding *Les martyrs* in the fall of 1840, and he had no desire to have it appear that his judgment had been mistaken. Besides, there was no suitable role for Stolz in *Les martyrs*.

On his way back to Paris, Donizetti had written a discouraged letter to Dolci, one colored with thoughts of his own mortality, and his uncertainty about the future: 'I am going to Paris for the translation of *Padilla* and *Linda*, God knows what else I will do there.'[183] In fact he found a great deal else to do, for he entered upon one of the most strenuous and concentrated periods of working of his whole prolific career. In the space of three months he revised[184] and rehearsed *Linda* for the Théâtre-Italien; he wrote half of one opera for Vienna and put it by when Balocchino informed him that another opera on the same subject was being given that winter at the Kärntnertor;[185] he composed and rehearsed *Don Pasquale* at the Théâtre-Italien; and he made a complete compositional sketch of another three-act opera for Vienna to take the place of the one he had set aside.[186] Not only is this a staggering amount of work, but much of it is of very fine quality indeed.

Of the new operas, the first to reach the stage was *Don Pasquale*, for which Donizetti signed a contract on 27 September 1842, almost immediately upon his return to Paris from Naples. Needing a pliant librettist, close at hand, he turned to Giovanni Ruffini (1807–81), a follower of Mazzini then living as an émigré in Paris, and offered him 500 francs to assist in adapting and updating a libretto written in 1810 by Angelo Anelli, *Ser Marc'Antonio*.[187] Not only did Donizetti himself choose this subject, but his was the idea to adapt it as a contemporary comedy to be played in what was then modern dress – a radical innovation for those days.[188] Donizetti's active participation in shaping the plot did not leave the inexperienced Ruffini much freedom, particularly since it was Donizetti's undisclosed intention to incorporate into his score a good number of pieces of music he had originally composed for other contexts.[189] The composer seemed to remain dissatisfied with multiple versions of text for the same passage which Ruffini produced on demand, and when he finally approved a piece of text it would often be one that the librettist regarded as inferior to others he had provided. Donizetti's apparent unreasonableness in this matter finally upset Ruffini to such an extent that he refused to allow his name to appear on the libretto, claiming that he could not recognize his own work when Donizetti had finished with it. In the light of this protest Donizetti should be credited as co-librettist of *Don Pasquale*, but for more than half a century after the opera entered the repertory the identity of its librettists was a matter of confusion.

Donizetti boasted that he composed *Don Pasquale* in eleven days,[190] but his claim should not be taken too literally. It is perfectly possible that he completed a compositional sketch,[191] which included at least five pre-existing numbers, in that brief space of time. Those eleven days certainly did not include the time taken to orchestrate his opera, for when he first brags to Toto on 12 November 1842 that *Don Pasquale* 'cost me more than ten days' labor', he adds a few lines further down: 'I am in the process of orchestrating my opera buffa.'[192] It would be more realistic to say that Donizetti worked on the opera for three months, from the time he began to collaborate with Ruffini up to the inevitable changes and retouchings that he carried out right through the rehearsal period. The sketches of Ernesto's 'Cercherò lontana terra' demonstrate the care and thought he put into the score of Don Pasquale.[193] The rehearsals began on 28 November, but were subsequently interrupted when both Mario and Tamburini fell ill. Donizetti had originally expected the first performance to take place in late December, but it did not occur until 3 January 1843.

The new work was immediately recognized as an outstanding example of its kind, and Lablache (Don Pasquale), Giulia Grisi (Norina), Tamburini (Dr Malatesta) and Mario (Ernesto) enjoyed an instantaneous success. The only parallel at the Théâtre-Italien in recent memory of a work that had scored a comparable triumph at its prima was the non-comic I puritani of eight years before. That three of the same singers appeared in both first casts (Rubini had been the tenor in Bellini's opera) helped to establish a sense of connection between the two events, in spite of the quite different character of the two works. Many in the audience at the prima of Don Pasquale felt that history was repeating itself. Donizetti describes that evening in these terms: 'The reception was most cheering. The adagio of the finale to Act 2 was repeated. The stretta of the duet between Lablache and Grisi was repeated. I was called out at the close of the second and third acts. There was not one piece, from the overture on, that was not more or less applauded. I am very happy.'[194] To Ricordi he reported that Lablache was the 'pivot' of the new work and that 'he revealed his talent as skillfully as possible.'[195]

The central importance of Lablache to Don Pasquale was recognized on all sides. Gautier's review of the prima vividly describes his performance:

The uncle, played by Lablache in the most fluttering manner, wearing a house coat of white dimity, nankeen trousers, and a black silk bonnet, is like all uncles everywhere, very displeased with his nephew. Following ancient and solemn precedent he seeks to disinherit him . . . Why should he be anybody's uncle? Don Pasquale, despite his sixty-eight years and his gout, finds himself a bold fellow [gaillard] still green enough to make heirs less collateral than M. Ernest. He consults with Dr Malatesta on this delicate point . . . The doctor returns with a young woman wearing a dress of the most virginal carmélite and a black lace veil that hardly lets one suspect her pretty face.

To receive this angel of youth and beauty, Don Pasquale makes a most extravagant toilette: a superb wig the color of mahogany with too many curls; a green tailcoat with engraved gold buttons, which he could never fasten because of the enormous rotundity of his figure. All of this gives him the look of a monstrous beetle that wants to open its wings to fly and cannot succeed. With the most gallant air he advances with popping eyes, his mouth heart-shaped, to take the girl's hand. She emits a cry as though she had been bitten by a viper.[196]

Chorley, too, never forgot the impression Lablache produced as Don Pasquale when the same company introduced the work at Her Majesty's Theatre on 29 June 1843.

Lablache seemed especially to court favour by presenting the farce of fatness trying to make itself seductive . . . But throughout the entire farce . . . nothing was more admirable than his entire avoidance of grossness or coarse imitation. There was, with him, that security which only belongs to persons of rare and admirable tact . . . which belongs to one who will risk nothing hazardous, but who is not afraid of daring anything extraordinary . . . and when I think of Lablache, I am tempted to feel as if I had parted company with real comic genius on the musical stage forever![197]

The following May when Donizetti prepared *Don Pasquale* for its introduction at the Kärntnertor, he added a new and more extensive recitative, with words of his own, to precede the baritone–bass duet in Act 3. The success of *Don Pasquale* caused it to be taken up with unusual rapidity all over Europe, and it was first given in the United States at New Orleans on 7 January 1845.[198] From its earliest days *Don Pasquale* was recognized as the true successor to Rossini's *Il barbiere di Siviglia*, and today it is regarded as the last great Italian opera buffa; there have been later great Italian operatic comedies, *Falstaff* and *Gianni Schicchi*, for instance, but neither of them springs directly from the glorious old buffa traditions.

On 7 January 1843 Donizetti departed from Paris for Vienna, buoyed on his fatiguing journey by the immensely favorable reception of *Don Pasquale*; he was also gratified at having been accepted as a corresponding member of the Académie Française.[199] He arrived in Vienna on 16 January 1843 to find the city gripped by subfreezing temperatures and chilling winds. Once there he took to his bed with a fever, but after three days he began to get back to work, although still not fully recovered. On 30 January he sent Toto a terse account of his projects in hand, which reveals that he was still as obsessed with work as he had been during those last months in Paris: 'At Vienna I am writing a *Duello sotto Richelieu* (a French drama); for Naples, *Ruy Blas*, its setting transposed; at Paris, for the Opéra-Comique a Flemish subject. At the Opéra, if it is my 'turn' instead of Meyerbeer's, I am writing a Portuguese subject in five acts. And all this in the course of a year.'[200]

All these projects require some explanation. *Duello sotto*

Richelieu[201] is the score that by February 1843 he had started to call Maria di Rohan; it was to be given during the coming Italian season at the Kärntnertor.[202] He had completed the musical sketch for it before leaving Paris, and now he elaborated and orchestrated it, substantially completing that task by 15 February 1843. The second work, Ruy Blas, with 'its setting transposed', was intended to satisfy his contract at the San Carlo for a work tentatively scheduled for July 1843. As yet he had not begun this opera because Cammarano was behindhand in sending him the first installment of the libretto; Cammarano's tardiness is hard to understand in view of the existence among his papers in the Lucchesi-Palli library in Naples of a scenario for this plot that had been approved by the censors on 5 September 1842.[203] Less than a week after mentioning Ruy Blas to Toto, Donizetti wrote to Persico in Naples, pleading the uncertainty of his health as grounds for either dissolving his contract with Guillaume or allowing the opera to be prepared and performed in his absence, a suggestion he had never made before.[204] The third project, the Flemish subject for the Opéra-Comique, was probably what is known as Ne m'oubliez pas, to a libretto by the Marquis de Saint-Georges.[205] Donizetti composed, and even orchestrated, seven numbers for Ne m'oubliez pas,[206] but he eventually managed to break his contract with Crosnier and the Opéra-Comique and seems to have abandoned this opera incomplete. The last of the works he mentioned, the 'Portuguese subject in five acts', was Dom Sébastien, his most time-consuming project during 1843.

Donizetti was becoming increasingly preoccupied with his declining health. Hardly a letter he wrote from Vienna during the first six months of 1843 omits some reference to the now 'usual' fever or to the recurring headaches. An ominous note appears at the very end of the letter that contains the list of projects just discussed. 'I have', he says 'a new ... illness [malanno] contracted at Paris, which has not yet gone away and for which I await your prescription.'[207] The little hesitation after 'new' (which Donizetti himself indicated by dots) suggests that he was speaking of a new venereal infection. Not surprisingly, he always referred to his disease obliquely.[208] Yet it is most unlikely that he never suspected the true nature of his condition and its possible consequences, since people suffering from advanced syphilis were no rarity in those days. Donizetti's excessive work during the last months of 1842 and all of 1843 suggests that he recognized what was wrong with him and that he wanted to compose as much as he could while he was still able.[209]

Donizetti finished orchestrating Maria di Rohan on 13 February

1843 and at once began work upon the massive five-act framework of *Dom Sébastien*. Many things were to distract his attention from it. He conducted two of his sacred compositions at the Concerts Spirituels: his *Ave Maria* was given on 2 March 1843, without a rehearsal; his *Miserere*, which he had composed the previous December for the imperial chapel, was given some time in the same month and then 'revised and retouched'[210] for its first official performance on Good Friday, 14 April. Upset by the news that both *Maria Padilla* and *Linda* had, because of ill-chosen singers, been adjudged failures at their recent introduction to the Teatro La Fenice, he was enraged to receive an offer to compose a new opera for that theater. He retaliated by demanding the preposterous sum of 30,000 francs, and, as he intended, his letter asking it was not even acknowledged. The Venetians, who had treated him so well at the time of *Belisario*, had not, since *Maria de Rudenz*, been overly sympathetic to his work. On the other hand, he was amused to receive an offer from Buda-Pest asking for an opera to a Hungarian libretto; this inquiry he declined more tactfully. Until the Italian season at the Kärntnertor opened on 1 April, he spent most of his time at his desk, composing, but even here his attention was divided. When he heard from Naples that Guillaume had refused to release him from his contract at the San Carlo, and because Cammarano seemed stuck over the draft of the work based on *Ruy Blas*, he turned back to the discarded *Caterina Cornaro*, first intended for Vienna, which would require less effort to complete than a fresh work on a completely new subject. He finished the orchestration of *Caterina Cornaro* about 25 May 1843,[211] and when time permitted he continued work on *Dom Sébastien*.

The Italian season at the Kärntnertor opened with *Linda di Chamounix*, which, with the new music[212] Donizetti had added the year before for the Théâtre-Italien, scored as resounding a success as it had in Paris. Donizetti conducted the opening performance and Alboni made her local debut as Pierotto. The second opera of the season was *Nabucco*,[213] prepared by Donizetti. This was the first production of a Verdi opera in Vienna. On 19 April Malibran's sister, Pauline Viardot, made her debut in *Il barbiere*.[214] This was the best of the four Italian seasons with which Donizetti was associated in Vienna because of the high quality of the singers and the warm public response to most of the operas.[215]

When Donizetti had finished preparing *Don Pasquale* for its Viennese debut, which took place on 14 May 1843, he began to make ready *Maria di Rohan*. The first orchestral run-through of the new work took place on 27 May, and the first performance was given on 5 June

1843, with Donizetti conducting. The following day he described its reception to Toto: 'With the utmost sorrow I must announce to you that last evening, 5 June, I have given my *Maria di Rohan* with la Tadolini, Ronconi and Guasco. All their talent was not enough to save me from a sea of – applause ... Everything went well, everything, everything.'[216] He also reports that the imperial family had made a point of coming in from the country to attend the performance. Donizetti's account of the enthusiastic reponse is seconded by the Viennese critics. Especial praise was given to the overture and the final trio; the strong dramatic elements were appreciated, particularly since they were not subordinated to purely musical considerations. Of the singers Ronconi aroused most comment, especially for his acting in the final scene. A revealing observation was made by the writer who signed himself 'A.S.' in the *Allgemeine Wiener Musikzeitung*: 'Donizetti has composed an opera for Germans, with that aura of seriousness and dignity that lies so close to the German character.'[217]

Maria di Rohan soon established itself as one of the more enduring of Donizetti's serious operas, succeeding whenever it was performed by singers who were also good actors. The composer continued to pay attention to his score, subsequently making a number of changes in it. For the Théâtre-Italien, where it was given in November 1843, he changed the *comprimario* tenor role of Gondì into a major contralto *musichetto* role for Marietta Brambilla by adding two arias for her.[218] When the work was introduced to Italy, at Parma on 1 May 1844, Donizetti changed the soprano–tenor duet in Act 2. For its return to the Kärntnertor in the spring of 1844, Donizetti incorporated all these changes, as well as adding a new section to the soprano–tenor duet at the opening of Act 3 and a new cabaletta to the succeeding aria for Maria.

Although *Maria di Rohan* was widely performed outside Italy, it received the bulk of its performances there, a popularity due in large part to the stress laid on dramatic values in the score and the composer's adroit setting of the text. Much of the initial impact was owed to Ronconi's Chevreuse, which belongs to that elite list of unforgettable characterizations that includes Pasta's Norma and Chaliapin's Boris. Throughout his long career, which lasted until 1870, Ronconi was such a powerful dramatic personality that he could overwhelm an audience, even when his voice was far from what it had been in his youth; the role most intimately associated with his name was that of Chevreuse and with it, he realized the essence of Romantic melodrama.

(By the 1890s when the enthusiasm for *verismo* works had turned the tide against the older Romantic melodramas in Italy, *Maria di Rohan* came to be performed relatively infrequently; but it still possessed one champion who perpetuated the older traditions, the baritone Battistini, who favored the showy role of Chevreuse throughout his career and continued to perform it regularly into the 1920s. More recent revivals of *Maria di Rohan* started in 1957 in Bergamo, from where much of the incentive for the current Donizetti renascence has stemmed. Since then it has been staged in Naples, Lisbon, Milan and Venice, and has been sung in concert form in New York. Hopefully, further revivals will be forthcoming, for Act 3 of *Maria di Rohan* represents Donizetti's summit of achievement as a musical dramatist.)

Although *Caterina Cornaro* was actually performed after *Dom Sébastien*, the score had been hastily completed by the end of May 1843, at a time when Donizetti had not yet begun intensive work upon his last opera for Paris. Apparently he had first encountered the story of Caterina, the Venetian lady who became Queen of Cyprus, in some now unidentifiable source he had read in Toto Vasselli's library in Rome,[219] but when he came to regard the subject seriously for an opera to be composed for the 1843 Italian season at the Kärntnertor he wanted a compression of Saint-Georges's text for Halévy's *La reine de Chypre*.[220]

When, on 5 June 1842, Donizetti signed his contract with Merelli for his second Viennese opera, he anticipated that Cammarano would be his librettist, for the contract specifies 'an opera seria to a verse libretto that will be written either by Cammarano or by another worthy librettist to be approved'.[221] The day after he signed this document, he wrote to Persico in Naples, specifying his need of a libretto: 'If I come to Naples and if there is time, I can also discuss the libretto for Vienna, but not from a distance, as it wastes too much time ... Does Cammarano think of me? ... Tell me if Salvatore [Cammarano] has thought of any subject for me. Don't answer me here, as I am leaving shortly.'[222] When he visited Naples in August 1842, he learned that Cammarano would be unavailable for this assignment, and so he appealed to Merelli, who had to approve a 'worthy' substitute. The man who took Cammarano's place was Giacomo Sacchèro, the author of the librettos of four operas performed at La Scala between 1841 and 1844.[223] By 12 August 1842 Donizetti was asking Ricordi to keep an eye on Sacchèro and his text, but the libretto was completed without much delay.

Donizetti's first stint of work on *Caterina* took place in October

1842. When he heard the news of Lachner's rival German setting, he angrily informed Ricordi:

Read the enclosed for Merelli and see in what an imbroglio it places us. I had written the first act, except for one chorus, and of Act 2 I had done the most salient parts, that is a duet and a quartet.[224] Now I learn from Vienna they they are giving Lachner's opera on the same subject. I am losing my head. For goodness sake, give it to Merelli at once, seek him out either on sea or on land, make him answer that I may learn my fate . . . My poor *Regina di Cipro*. I lavished care on it and I believed it was not going badly. It might be for La Scala if Merelli would want it.[225]

Donizetti returned to the composition of *Caterina* on 9 March 1843, for on that date he wrote a letter to Sacchèro suggesting some modifications to his text. But now the opera was destined for Naples, since Guillaume would not cancel Donizetti's contract for the San Carlo. The impresario did, however, grudgingly agree to release Donizetti from his obligation to go to Naples to supervise the musical preparation and to conduct the first performances; to be let off, Donizetti had to accept a reduction in fee and submit medical certificates attesting to his poor health. In his letter Donizetti asks Sacchèro for a new cabaletta for the dying king, Lusignano, at the end of his duet with Caterina in Act 2, 'and to make it more interesting it is necessary to say that the lover [Gerardo] is dead'.[226] By the end of May 1843 he had completed *Caterina* and sent it off to Naples.

Almost at once he seems to have been assailed by qualms over the fate of this opera, since he would not be present to guide it through its preparation. In a state almost of panic he wrote to Persico on 14 June 1843; he does not want Anna Bishop,[227] who in Vienna 'made the very stones laugh with her tremolo [like a] *tamburello* [little drum]'; and though he worries about Fanny Goldberg because he does not know her range or whether she is an animated actress, he decides he much prefers her to Bishop, 'who has a small voice'. Most of all, he wants an experienced eye to go over his score: 'I urge you to beg Mercadante to help me, if during the rehearsals something inconvenient should turn up: if a passage should not prove well orchestrated, or if it should be too weak or too powerful, to help me as if it were his own work.'[228] Two weeks later he repeated many of these points in another letter, this one to Teodoro Ghezzi, the friend who managed his Neapolitan affairs. Again he is worried about the singers and anxious that the censors should approve the Maltese cross Gerardo wears on his breast. He hopes that they will not be as hard on this text as they were on that of *Maria Padilla*: 'I have labored conscientiously, and I would not want to see, because of the caprice or malice of a few people, an interesting subject made ridiculous.'[229]

Not until shortly after the first performance of *Dom Sébastien* in November 1843 did Donizetti again voice his preoccupation with *Caterina*, whose production by now had been postponed until January 1844.[230] On 18 November 1843 Donizetti wrote again to Ghezzi, bothered about the rumors that have reached him from the San Carlo.

For the rest, it seems to me that Flauto[231] is losing his head, promising roles to whom he wants, without considering the conditions he has already agreed to with the composers. For the rest, I see well what will fly away or be driven underground by all these disagreements. My opera will be the poor, innocent victim. It does not matter, I will give it after I hear your judgment of its reception in Naples, then in Vienna, directed by me and adjusted where you tell me it did not please; there it will be reborn to a new life far from the harsh treatment[232] of this management and its quarreling ... Now on 15 December I will leave for Vienna, and from there I will learn the outcome of *Caterina* (if it is given at all).[233]

Caterina Cornaro was performed. Having gone into rehearsal on 28 December 1843, the *prima* finally occurred on 18 January 1844.[234] It was sung by Fanny Goldberg (Caterina), Gaetano Fraschini (Gerardo) and Filippo Coletti[235] (Lusignano), and conducted by Antonio Farelli.[236] The audience was hostile to the work, which survived for only six performances, the prologue being given alone on one other occasion. Ghezzi duly informed Donizetti of the outcome, and the composer sent him a noble reply on 31 January 1844.

Dear Ghezzi,

A fiasco? Then let it be a fiasco! But who says that this music is not mine, or that I wrote it sleeping, or for revenge against the management? No. I assume all the responsibility, the blow and the blame for it. Why should I have others write it? Did I not perhaps have the time? Why sleeping? Don't I work perhaps with facility? Why for revenge? Could I be so ungrateful toward a public that has endured me for so many years? No! It may be that inspiration, experience and taste have deceived me, that they may be totally lacking, but that I should descend to unworthy acts, to hidden deceptions, never!

As to the echoes of other music [*reminiscenze*]? *Eh, mon Dieu!* who does not make them? To steal (and what is worse, without wanting to), who does not steal? Note well that I do not in the least mean to justify myself. I repeat that I assume all responsibility for it. I had believed that the various pieces did not deserve all the blame that erupted, that the duets, the quartet, etc., but what use now to discuss it? I will not make the wounds shed fresh blood. If one day this score returns to my hands I will give proof to the Neapolitans that I obey their advice. It has been my error therefore to believe that this music perhaps was not unworthy of their indulgence.

I renew to Mercadante my most lively thanks. Make known to Signor Flauto all my displeasure in not being able to serve him according to his conditions, and to Signor Bochsa, and I recommend him to you, let him know that I have received his letter, which made me laugh a lot, and that I am sorry that he had not given me with equal frankness the news about *Linda* when it was put again with la Bishop. I want the Neapolitans to be compensated with interest [*ad usura*] by another composer more fortunate than I, and may it be soon so that my mistake is the sooner forgotten. My friends, whom I greet, will be afflicted by this, but what's the use? I am afflicted by it enough for everybody.

Farewell

your Donizetti[237]

Donizetti was upset by the failure of *Caterina* because he sincerely believed that his work had some merit, that it was 'not so much beneath my other operas',[238] as he confessed to Dolci. The performance Donizetti had hoped to mount in Vienna, for which city the opera had originally been conceived, did not take place, as Donizetti's flagging energy was taken up with the revised, German-language production of *Dom Sébastien;* but his faith in the work was justified when *Caterina* was sung at Parma on 2 February 1845.[239] For this production Donizetti modified the opera somewhat: his most important change was to amplify the originally neglected part of Lusignano;[240] he replaced Caterina's *rondò* with a new finale which shifts the spotlight off Caterina to the dying King, a change of focus analogous to that of the *finale nuovo* to *Lucrezia Borgia.*

(These productions in Naples and Parma are the sum total of *Caterina*'s nineteenth-century performance history. The opera lay neglected until 28 May 1972, when Rubino Profeta's idiosyncratic edition was given at the San Carlo with Leyla Gencer in the title role. Six weeks later Caballé introduced the opera to London in a concert performance, which was later reproduced in both New York and Paris. Since then the opera has been staged at Barcelona and Nice. *Caterina* is another score badly in need of a modern critical edition.)

Dom Sébastien was the last complete opera Donizetti composed, and he hoped it would be recognized as his greatest accomplishment. The third of his scores to be performed at the Opéra, it was the only one originally intended for that theater and its special requirements.[241] By 1843 and for a number of years thereafter the Paris Opéra represented the highest form of musical theater as it was then conceived,[242] and with *Dom Sébastien* Donizetti struggled to meet its peculiar aesthetic challenges. He often stressed his desire for brevity in composing an opera, and more than once he confessed that when he worked at length on music it was often not well received: 'what I have done that is good has always been done quickly, and many times the reproach of carelessness falls on that which has cost me more time'.[243] *Dom Sébastien* is his longest opera; it is the one he spent most time upon.

The history of this opera begins in early December 1842. At that time Donizetti conferred with Eugène Scribe about the libretto. On the 3rd he sent the poet a letter complaining that, though he had been waiting all week for a promised discussion, Scribe had not yet been to see him. Pointing out that he would very soon be leaving Paris for Vienna, he continues: 'You understand that it would be very difficult for me to work without having discussed the subject to its conclusion with you.'[244]

From the very beginning of this project, then, Scribe as a collaborator posed problems for Donizetti. Used to his Italian librettists with whom he could argue in his native tongue, and who understood the informal and sometimes improvisatory ways of Italian opera seasons, Donizetti found the official librettist of the Opéra difficult to approach and high-handed. For his text for *Dom Sébastien* Scribe used no acknowledged co-librettists, as he so often did, and thus Donizetti had no chance to play one off against the other; he had to deal with Scribe alone. Except for Duprez and Barroilhet, whom he had known from working with them in Italy, Donizetti had no real partisans within the Byzantine establishment of the Opéra. He was forced to work under handicaps that few of his French colleagues had to contend with in quite the same way. It says a great deal for Donizetti's courage that he refused to let any of these disadvantages deter him.

He was in Vienna during the first half of February 1843, when the first act of Scribe's libretto reached him. On the 13th he sent a letter to Accursi[245] asking him to have the poet make a single modification. And then he continues, revealing once again how from the start the individual singers of the cast figured in his conceptions: 'Recommend to him brevity, since it is distressing to cut later. And above all do not forget that Barroilhet's strong point is in *affettuoso* passages, and with that tone we will be able to make a fine contrast with Massol.'[246] By 21 March he had made such progress that he could send Accursi a packet containing the compositional sketches for the first two acts of *Dom Sébastien*, lacking only the ballet for Act 2 scene i. 'These two unorchestrated acts are full of corrections and things crossed out, etc., but in one day I can redo everything and get them ready to be copied. I keep waiting impatiently for the third act [of the libretto].'[247] It was at this point that he interrupted his work on *Dom Sébastien* to complete *Caterina Cornaro* for Naples. That spring he sold the Italian rights for *Dom Sébastien* to Ricordi.

On 18 June 1843, when his various duties at the Kärntnertor were almost over for that year, Donizetti sent Accursi his reactions to the rest of Scribe's five-act text. He is worried that the finale to Act 3 – a passage that would give trouble for months – is too long. He raises a number of perceptive questions about dramatic motivation and effectiveness:

I always find that Zaïda is badly situated in it, and it would be much better to do without her there, or at least it would be better if Camoëns has to take her off as a witness before the people, at least that would give some reason for why she is arrested, and [Scribe's] note does not explain enough about it to me. I find it reasonable that D. Juan causes her to be arrested, but she is not an interesting enough figure to the public. Therefore pay attention. Fix it at least so that there might be some sort of trio (this means that Camoëns, the King and Zaïda should be the principals in this confusion in order to prepare for the fourth act). In the fourth act I approve of Abayaldos masked, but not of Zaïda veiled in a corner, that doesn't please me. Or at least it requires that Juan says to her beforehand: 'keep yourself veiled, understand that any single word you say without being questioned will condemn you and forever', and thus it is that speaking out without being questioned she compromises herself in order to spare the King. I don't want Camoëns in this scene any longer. But he has been arrested, what to do? Save him somehow. In the fifth act the trio of Zaïda, King and Camoëns, come to save him, is good. Try to see that this act is really quite short. I beg you to do this. It is an act for the scenic designer. (Don't forget that the scene in which one sees the preparations for the stake is almost the same as in Act 3 of *Le duc d'Albe*.) My only fear is that this finale of the third act might be too long. For goodness sake, pay attention to that. The public sympathizes with Camoëns, the King, with Zaïda, one after the other; let all this be well *expressed*, well connected and quite short. The rhythm of Camoëns's lines should move the chorus. If Camoëns seeing Zaïda should show her to the crowd (no, no, that's stupid). I fear for the role of Zaïda in the third act, and I am particularly aware of it when she is arrested with Camoëns and the King. Camoëns should only appear as a witness before the Inquisition if it is absolutely necessary and disappear in the rest of the act . . . As for me, I demand only *brevity*. Let the verbal rhythms be quite clear, with the accents on the first or second syllables. That is everything.[248]

This rather cryptic letter is important because it indicates the state of flux in which this unwieldy plot remained right up to the rehearsal period. The finale to Act 3 would undergo a number of alterations, including the removal from it of Zaïda, nor would Camoëns appear before the Inquisition in Act 4. The most significant feature of the letter is perhaps the evidence it provides that Donizetti could, at least up to a point, persuade Scribe to make some alterations.

Five days later he writes to Accursi again, but now he is concerned as to whether Duprez[249] can sing his aria 'Seul sur la terre' at the prescribed pitch, and whether perhaps the whole stretta of the Act 3 finale will have to be lowered by a whole tone: 'It will lose thereby, but . . .'[250] This comment shows that Donizetti had by this time sketched most of Act 3. At the end of June, he tells Dolci that *Dom Sébastien* is going ahead slowly.

On 11 July 1843 Donizetti left Vienna, traveling in style in his own new coach, accompanied by his private student Matteo Salvi and his servant Antony. His style was not equaled by the coach's performance, since it kept breaking down and every time it rained the occupants were drenched. He abandoned it in Munich, where he interrupted his journey to see an old musical friend of Mayr's, Johann Caspar Aiblinger. On 15 June he wrote to Mayr about this visit and then went on to report on his progress with *Dom Sébastien:*

They are spending vast sums on the scenery and costumes. New painters have been engaged and are already at work. And I will work and be working because up to now I have only sketches of every act, but however they are such that I can complete the music at the rate of an act per week for four acts.[251] After my usual custom, when I reach Paris I will work from seven in the morning until four in the afternoon, and the thing will progress.[252]

Within a month after his return to Paris on about 20 July he was engaged in the rehearsals of *Dom Sébastien.*

He had not been to many rehearsals before he made the unhappy discovery that he was not really in control of them. He informed Ricordi on 22 August: 'they are changing many things that influence the reception of the opera'.[253] On 2 September he ironically described his hours in the rehearsal hall as 'enjoying myself'.[254] He was becoming increasingly upset with Scribe who, it seemed to him, kept making verbal changes and rearranging entrances and exits within scenes without regard for the music. On 15 September Donizetti addressed his librettist, explaining what problems all these changes made for both the composer and the singers, who had already memorized the text in its earlier version. The pressure of time was weighing on Donizetti, as the premiere was less than two months away, and he reminds Scribe:

Remember that I still have the ballet music to write, think of these new arrangements that still have to be made, they have to go to the copyist, they must be learned in the rehearsal room, on the stage, etc. I do not draw back before this work, but be good enough to hear for yourself what has been done, and to assist us in person for several days, for I value your advice very much.[255]

That Scribe had the power to make changes without having to attend the daily rehearsals was a problem that would continue to play upon

Donizetti's already frazzled nerves. Even under the best of circumstances he had always found the preparation of his operas a trying time.

In early October the orchestral rehearsals began. On the 5th he told Ghezzi that he was 'beyond measure fatigued by this immense opera', adding 'a few notes more and it is all complete'.[256] In spite of all the pressure and exhaustion, he was able to remain optimistic about *Dom Sébastien* because he realized that in it he had achieved a level of power and grandeur beyond anything he had heretofore accomplished. On 25 October he wrote to his friend the Viennese banker August Thomas that the premiere was twenty days off. 'Who knows? There is a bundle of music, we shall see, infinite luxury, a huge spectacle.'[257]

Ten days later the rehearsals were halted for still another rearrangement of the Inquisition scene in Act 4, and now Donizetti hoped that everything had assumed its final form. But it had not, for as he wrote to his Viennese friend Leo Herz on 9 November:

You want some news about *Dom Sébastien?* Well then, here it is, before the fact. Let all this remain just between us, and be assured that within five days you will have the critics' judgment, too, and then you will say: my friend has a great knack for knowing the public. Here is the résumé, according to me: Act 1 – it will be liked. Act 2 with the ballet, a duo, and the final *romance* above all, that will also have a success. Act 3 – a *romance* (perhaps it will be applauded), but the rest has been too swamped with continual changes, therefore *no*. Act 4, much action, the ensemble will not displease, but it will not excite enthusiasm. In Act 4 there is an effect in the middle that will go very well indeed. In Act 5 – a little cavatina (nothing much), the big duo will attract attention; the succeeding barcarolle, of which I must cut half because of the situation, will be lost. A very short trio almost unaccompanied will be received neither hot nor cold. After that, the denouement for which music can do nothing. From all that you will understand that my opera ends with a rat's tail as they say, or like wax in the sun. After the big duo in the fifth act, one can leave.

Today they are going to change the staging of the funeral march entirely (and today is Thursday, and Monday is the first performance). An *adagio* has been cut from the finale of Act 3 in order to move it to the fourth act, and this poor finale is now only *bavardage*. Thus the finale of Act 3 is lost because M. Scribe (conceitedly) said that the scene will gain from this change. There will always be sufficient pieces of music and *de luxe*, but I complain about my finale.[258]

After nearly four months of preparation the great day arrived, but even then Donizetti was not spared harassments. Before the first performance of *Dom Sébastien* Meyerbeer invited the leading journalists of Paris to a lavish dinner, a not very subtle gesture of consolation for their not yet having had the pleasure of hearing *Le prophète*.[259] Donizetti himself spent the evening of 13 November

1843 nervously walking up and down a corridor backstage while Accursi or one of his other friends brought him reports every few minutes.[260]

There was more applause than Donizetti had anticipated, particularly for the duet for Stolz and Massol at the beginning of Act 3 and for the septet in Act 4, which had to be repeated. Donizetti felt that the ballet went on too long, but he was more than pleased. The public seemed to be interested in the opera and to appreciate Donizetti's score, in spite of the ironic comments it aroused in some quarters of the press. Yet it must be confessed that *Dom Sébastien* did not sustain itself in the favor of the Paris public as Donizetti hoped it would.[261] Before it was dropped from the repertory of the Opéra in 1845, it had been played thirty-two times. Not long after its introduction in Paris, it was taken up by some of the French provincial theaters, and for them Scribe arranged a new denouement less taxing to their resources than the one played at the Opéra.

The next important production of *Dom Sébastien* was prepared by Donizetti himself when his work was sung in German at the Kärntnertor, the first performance taking place on 6 February 1845.[262] He made some cuts in the score, used a different ending (this may have been the simplified version arranged for the French provinces), and added a cabaletta to Zaïda's aria in Act 2. All these changes were designed to reduce the opera to manageable proportions for a Viennese audience, who liked to be out of the theater well before midnight. In German *Dom Sébastien* proved a great success; it was given twenty-four times in its first season, more often than any other opera in the repertory, and in the next three seasons it had forty-eight further performances. The version that was first performed at La Scala[263] on 14 August 1847 and went on to attain a total of forty-two performances, is much closer to the Viennese than the French, but it omits Zaïda's German cabaletta and reverts to the original conclusion for the score. How far Donizetti participated in making the changes that are unique to the Italian score, considering that he was already incapacitated by the time of the introduction of his last opera to Italy, is a question that needs to be examined. The Italian translation is by Giovanni Ruffini and shows that his difficulties over the libretto of *Don Pasquale* were not such as to prevent him from working again with Donizetti.

The career of *Dom Sébastien* did not accord with its merits. It was given in Turin during Carnival 1847–8 and revived there once – in 1858. It was put on at Bergamo in 1854, followed by productions in 1875 and 1909. The San Carlo put it on in 1856–7 and has never revived it. Bologna had a single exposure to it, in 1868. Other Italian theaters followed much the same pattern; after about 1870 productions became increasingly infrequent, ceasing after a Roman staging in 1911. The score was introduced to the United States in Italian at New York in 1864, and in French at New Orleans in 1875. It seems never to have been heard in England, although performances were promised in prospectuses in 1853, 1862 and 1866.

(The only production since World War II was one of the highlights of the 1955 Maggio Fiorentino, where the work was given in Italian and conducted by Carlo Maria Giulini.[264] Most of the lengthy score was performed, and, surprisingly, the Act 1 quartet from *Belisario* was grafted into the final scene, apparently in the hope of making it seem less abrupt. If the renewed interest in Donizetti that has been demonstrated in so many welcome productions of unfamiliar scores points toward one towering achievement that still requires to be revealed in something like its original form, that cloud-obscured peak is *Dom Sébastien*. For richness of invention and mastery of resources this opera deserves the trouble and expense of an adequate modern production in French.)

6

1843–1848
The last years

During the trying period of the rehearsals for *Dom Sébastien* new and grave signs of Donizetti's physical deterioration became apparent. For a long time he had worked at a strenuous pace, but all through 1843 he labored practically without respite, against time one cannot help but feel. His inexorable disease was passing out of its relatively latent phase. Sometimes he would have lapses of memory and would become acutely embarrassed when they were called to his attention. Sometimes in mid-sentence he would lose track of his thought and stare in a queer, fixed manner. His temper would explode in sudden bursts of fury that would leave him shaken and confused. The Parisian music-publisher Léon Escudier recounts an episode during the rehearsals of *Dom Sébastien* when Stolz objected to standing around with nothing to do during Camoëns's offstage barcarolle of Act 5 and the management ordered the number to be cut in half, whereupon Donizetti's furious protests brought on some sort of seizure and he had to be helped home, barely able to stand.[1] At first he seemed to recover from these alarming symptoms, but each new recurrence gravely troubled his friends.

He arrived in Vienna from Paris on 30 December 1843. Now he was taking digitalis on a doctor's prescription. His Viennese doctors prescribed baths and applications of boiling mustard to his neck. Although he tried to carry on his career, it was becoming increasingly apparent that his ability to concentrate was impaired. During this winter of 1843–4 his friends noticed an alarming change in his physical condition. He had lost some teeth, his gait had altered in a telltale way, and at times his legs would not support him. His state of depression alternated with high spirits, but his hilarity seemed excessive. Episodes of unrestrained sexual excitation gave rise to a thickening cloud of gossip that accumulated around his head.

With the close of the Italian season at the Kärntnertor at the end of June 1844, he went to Italy, traveling with his brother Giuseppe, who was on leave from his post in Constantinople. The second half of that year seems marked by a pathetic restlessness. He went to Bergamo, to Lovere on Lake Iseo, back to Bergamo, to Milan, to Genoa, to Naples, to Rome, back to Naples, to Genoa and on to Milan again, then back to Bergamo for a third visit. At the end of the year his post in Vienna claimed him for the first six months of 1845.

His complaints about his health became constant. He was increasingly sensitive to the weather; he wrote to Peppina Appiani: 'Under the influence of this climate my nerves have become so sensitive that to stay a year would kill me.'[2] Yet there were periods in which he could still work and still consider new projects. Even though his command of German was uncertain, he shepherded *Dom Sébastien* through its successful introduction to Vienna in that language, conducting at least the first performance of it. On 27 May 1845 he wrote to Ruffini in Paris about a play by Cosenza called *Onore vince amore*, which he remembered having seen in Naples. He suggested it to Ruffini as the subject for an opera for the Théâtre-Italien, with Persiani, Mario, Tamburini and Lablache. It sounds rather like a pendant to *Don Pasquale*, only this time Lablache would have the serious role, while Tamburini would be the high-spirited character.[3] This intriguing idea was no more than a flash in the pan; nothing further is heard of it. There were other offers and projects in the year and a half following *Dom Sébastien*, but most of them amounted to nothing but talk, for from this time on Donizetti was no longer capable of sufficient sustained concentration to produce more than a short song or a setting of a brief religious text. Early in 1844 there had been pressure to get him to accept another five-act Scribe libretto, *Jeanne la folle*,[4] but he disliked the somber and monotonous text, and behind his refusal of it lay his dread of confronting so soon again the frustrations and contrarinesses that he always encountered at the Opéra. In 1845 Lumley wrote to him from London, suggesting an opera buffa this time, and offering to pay him 21,000 francs for it, but by then he was incapable of considering seriously even such a lucrative offer. The German production of *Dom Sébastien*, in what turned out to be its most successful series of performances, was his last real labor in the theater.

He left Vienna for the last time on 10 July 1845, arriving back in Paris before the end of that month. Early in August, he fell on the pavement in front of the Hôtel Manchester and was carried inside, still unconscious. A meeting of three doctors took place on his name-day, 9 August. Two days later, in a pitifully disjointed letter, he attempted to tell Toto what had happened: 'I was examined by

three prominent doctors *Andral, Ricord, and . . . and . . .*'.[5] The name
of the doctor Donizetti could not remember was Mitvié. They prescribed a change of climate, the avoidance of excitement and a rest
from composition. At the time of his collapse Donizetti had been
considering a revision of *L'ajo nell'imbarazzo* for Vatel, the impresario at the Théâtre-Italien, but this project was stillborn. The doctors' insistence that he give up composing for a while alarmed
Donizetti, because he had the fixed idea that he had five pending
contracts for operas in various theaters. Although he himself could
not contemplate the idea that his career was over, that fact was
generally recognized by others. In the fall of 1845 Liszt had heard
rumors of Donizetti's condition, and he wrote to the Countess
d'Agoult in Paris, asking her to sound out the possibility of his
succeeding to the position of *Hofkapellmeister* in Vienna.

Toto was, obviously, dismayed by Gaetano's disordered letter. If
he had recognized the name of Philippe Ricord, his anxiety would
have been greater, for Ricord was noted for his demonstration that
gonorrhea and syphilis were two distinct diseases. Ricord's presence
at this the first of many medical consultations over Donizetti's case
proves that the nature of his illness was never in serious doubt. If
before his collapse there had been rumors about his relations with all
sorts of women, after it, they multiplied a hundredfold. Understandably distraught by this tide of gossip, Donizetti's friends in
Italy wrote urging him to come back to Naples, to Rome, to Bergamo,
anywhere close at hand where they could keep an eye on him. Not
only were they concerned about his physical well-being, but they
worried that unscrupulous people in Paris would exploit his condition.

In the latter part of August 1845 there was a period when Donizetti's health seemed to take a turn for the better. Rereading all those
anxious letters from Italy, he found offensive their implication that
he could no longer take care of himself. On the 21st he wrote a letter
to Dolci that could not have eased the latter's anxiety; he mentions
the doctors, their advice, and his suit with Pillet over *Le duc d'Albe*,
but his style is disjointed and cryptic: 'Farewell. Vienna is killing me
in order not to kill me [all at once?] after the *winter* then the *spring,
the same*. Here in Paris the *air* is lighter and the rain heavier. My
head is cured, that is enough for me. My nerves are irritated every
time that one writes, therefore . . . ? *Pazienza!* The tomb! It is
finished!'[6] The oblique reference to the tomb is probably a reference
to the elaborate mausoleum that he had ordered for Virginia in
Naples, as he had recently learned that it was finally completed. But
to Dolci those last words must have seemed a dread prophecy.

During October 1845 Donizetti wrote several letters to friends. Those to Leo Herz in Vienna and Count Melzi in Milan are relatively coherent and straightforward; for instance, he reports to Melzi what a disadvantage the higher pitch in Paris is to the Italian singers, and how Grisi, Ronconi and Moriani all resent it.[7] But his letters to Cottrau, Ghezzi, Persico and Dolci all reveal mental confusion. Dolci was particularly distressed because, besides his grave concern for Donizetti, he was a daily visitor to Mayr, now eighty-two and slowly dying after a stroke; Dolci could not share his grief with either. When Mayr died on 2 December 1845 Donizetti's mind was in almost total darkness.

All the friends agreed that some member of Donizetti's family should go to Paris to determine what was the true state of affairs and to decide what steps should be taken. His 27-year-old nephew Andrea, Giuseppe's only son, was elected to fill this function. He set out from Constantinople and, after a leisurely trip of forty-two days, arrived in Paris on Christmas Day 1845. His description of his uncle's condition confirmed the worst fears of Giuseppe, Dolci and Vasselli. The effort of holding up his head, even for a short period of time, was too much. Every movement was painful. His emaciated body slumped inert; his lifeless eyes caused his face to appear expressionless, even stupid. His ideas were few and confused. His disposition had radically altered; he was alternately gloomy, taciturn, angry and suspicious. He had delusions of persecution, sometimes shouting that he had been poisoned. Worst of all, he was periodically gripped by compulsive eroticism.

Finding his uncle impossible to deal with and resenting the lack of positive help from the other relatives and friends, Andrea turned to the doctors. On 28 January 1846 Drs Calmeil, Ricord and Mitvié (this last the director of a sanatorium at Ivry) held a consultation and issued a comprehensive report, which confirmed the symptoms Andrea had already described, and then went on to recommend that the patient be placed in an institution, since 'M. Donizetti is no longer capable of estimating sanely the consequences of his decisions and actions.'[8]

On the morning of 1 February 1846 a carriage drew up in front of the Hôtel Manchester. The bundled figure of Donizetti, supported by his Austrian servant and by Andrea, was helped into it. As the carriage started off, another containing Dr Ricord followed. Since their destination was a secret, word had been spread that Donizetti was leaving for a cure at Nice. Donizetti himself was led to believe that he was starting out for Vienna to fulfill the obligations of his court appointment that required him to spend the first six months of the year there. After traveling for three hours the carriage came to an abrupt halt. Donizetti was told that there had been an accident to the vehicle, which would take some time to repair, but that fortunately they had stopped near a comfortable inn where he could wait until the coach was ready to resume the journey. The unsuspecting Donizetti was shown into a suite of three rooms that opened on a garden.

He had not waited long before he realized that his servant was missing. When he tried to leave the 'inn', he was told that he could not. Convinced that he had to get to Vienna, he grew increasingly agitated as he was physically restrained from trying to leave. When the story of the damaged carriage no longer satisfied him, he was told that his servant had robbed him of some petty cash and diamonds, and therefore his trip to Vienna must be delayed while this crime was thoroughly investigated by the police. When he protested that he was an Austrian citizen and held an appointment from the emperor himself and that the French police had no jurisdiction over him, the unpleasant suggestion was made to him that the police were investigating to see whether he had not taken the things himself to make his servant seem a thief. What he did not know was that the servant Antony had been given money and, after having been sworn to secrecy, sent back to Vienna to find a new job.

Donizetti was not as unaware of events as Dr Mitvié seems to have anticipated, for he knew he was being held against his will and that he was being lied to. Days passed and he was still being detained and still being told the same threadbare untruths. On 7 February 1846 his desperation drove him to write a number of frantic notes, incoherent appeals for help. These letters were never delivered, but remained in the possession of his nephew Andrea.[9] In one of them occurs this revealing phrase: 'My health is weak, but I am not stupid.'[10] To know that Donizetti was to some extent aware of what was happening to him arouses sympathy. One of these repetitive, befuddled letters, addressed to the Countess Appony, was really intended for Zélie de Coussy to pass on to the Countess; it begins: 'Madame, come to *Ivry* . . . in an hour! I too have been arrested. My servant has stolen a second time? My nephew's grief gives me courage.' and continues: 'They have arrested my nephew and it was the *servant!* They have arrested him. I haven't seen him any more. Come! May the blood of God descend on you: cursed him who *lies:* – Come, but when you do not . . . you wish the death of a poor *friend! I have four* thousand plus *eight* – *I am innocent.* Everything has been restored! Your servant *Donizetti.*' But the letter does not stop there:

'(*Gesù et Maria*); save me . . . save me, for I lose honor and the carriage. *Peace,* I beg you. Let there be good *will. Good night* . . . Zélie, come! I weep all the time!!' And it ends: 'Fait que je sorte pour Elle, moi voler mes effets? Si le Domestique est un voleur, moi? *Non!* c'est à moi, pour la vengeance publique! – [signed] *Le pauvre Donizetti.*'[11]

For all the efforts to keep Donizetti's whereabouts a secret, word soon leaked out and tongues wagged harder than ever. The relatives and friends in Italy were distressed, but they were convinced that Donizetti must be taken back to Italy, not only for his sake but to stop the gossip that they had washed their hands of him. Ghezzi made the trip from Naples, arriving in Paris about the middle of April 1846. At the earliest opportunity Andrea took him out to Ivry, where Ghezzi found his old friend slumped in a chair. After recognizing Ghezzi briefly with a smile, he relapsed into a state of apathy. Ghezzi mentioned all sorts of things, even Virginia, but when Donizetti failed to respond even to his wife's name, Ghezzi left broken-hearted and convinced that it was hopeless even to consider moving him anywhere. Significantly, after Ghezzi's visit, the talk of bringing Donizetti to Naples began to diminish, and the campaign to get him moved to Bergamo became the dominant plan.

In Bergamo Dolci consulted with Baroness Rosa Rota-Basoni, who had been an admiring hostess to Donizetti and his warm friend for the past ten years. Rosa Basoni announced herself ready to provide Donizetti with whatever care and comfort he might require, and declared herself eager to welcome him no matter what his physical condition might prove. As soon as he learned of this proposal, Andrea, whom it relieved of a difficult responsibility, started to make the necessary arrangements for Donizetti's transfer. First he arranged a consultation with three doctors on 12 June 1846; it was their opinion that a long trip would be risky and would do nothing to improve the patient's condition. Undaunted, Andrea approached Appony, the Austrian ambassador in Paris, for the necessary passports and documents. Appony obtained a report from Dr Moreau, the resident director at Ivry, who opposed the move. Nonetheless the ambassador started, via diplomatic channels, an investigation of the proposed accommodations and medical treatment in Bergamo. From there he received a favorable report, and he was ready to issue the necessary passport.

At this point Gabriel Delessert, the prefect of the Paris police since 1836, cast his shadow over the negotiations. Whatever his motives, Delessert opposed for as long as he could all proposals to transport

Donizetti back to Italy.[12] He specifically forbade Andrea to attempt such a move, and he sent official orders to Ivry that Donizetti was under no circumstances to leave the premises. In the face of Andrea's protests, Delessert himself ordered still another medical consultation, this time between three doctors assigned to the police force. Their examination of Donizetti on 9 July 1846 found that his condition had deteriorated, and they claimed that efforts to move him would be futile and foolhardy. On the strength of this report, Delessert sent Andrea an order, dated 16 July, formally forbidding him to take any further action in his uncle's case. Refusing to give in, Andrea arranged a consultation of his own on 30 August 1846, attended by Ricord, Calmeil, Mitvié and Moreau. They issued a lengthy report, first giving a harrowing description of Donizetti's condition. They concluded that he should not be moved because of danger to his partially paralyzed neck, because his bladder might suddenly constrict, necessitating use of a catheter, and because of the danger of convulsions. 'Some other considerations of another degree, although very secondary, should be added to those opposing his transfer to Italy: M. Donizetti's fame makes it imperative to dissemble as much as possible to avoid the impressions that his present state would give rise to in those who see him; out of respect for him his last moments must be kept from the eyes of strangers.'[13]

Feeling that nothing more could be done, Andrea wrote to Dolci that he was returning to Constantinople, using the excuse that his father had ordered him home since his mother was in poor health. Andrea left Paris on 7 September 1846, but before he started home, he went out to Ivry to take leave of Donizetti. On this occasion, Donizetti wrote the last letter of his life, scrawling a few words to his brother Giuseppe: 'Gaetano Donizetti fa saluto – Andrea parte oggi – 7 settembre 1846.'[14] His nephew traveled first to Bergamo, taking with him the incomplete score of Le duc d'Albe, the completed Rita, and a box of Donizetti's jewelry, all of which he handed over to Dolci. Before he left Bergamo he told the Basoni family that under no circumstances was anyone to try to move Donizetti from Ivry, and he left with them detailed instructions for the embalming and funeral of his uncle. He also gave the Basonis the impression that he had exaggerated his uncle's condition and had abandoned him to die unattended.

For Donizetti at Ivry time passed in a blur. A few hardy visitors made the lengthy journey from Paris to see him. Royer and Vaëz went out, but he failed to recognize them, and they watched him being fed a bowl of soup, which he lapped up 'comme aurait fait un animal'.[15] Michele Accursi brought out his sister and her son on what Accursi said was 'one of [Donizetti's] good days'. Accursi wrote to Dolci that Donizetti tried to embrace the boy when he learned he was attending the Paris Conservatoire. They asked if he wanted to go back to Paris with them (an incredibly heartless question under the circumstances), and poor Donizetti tried to struggle to his feet. The tenor Duprez paid him a visit, singing to him 'Tu che a Dio spiegasti l'ali' from the final scene of *Lucia,* hoping to elicit some memory of that *prima* in Naples in happier times; Donizetti shuffled to the piano and sat down, but his knotted fingers could produce only discords, then his head slumped down on his chest and his features drained of expression.

Of all his visitors, the crucial one was Baron Eduard von Lannoy, the director of the Concerts Spirituels in Vienna, who saw him several times in late December and early January 1847. A man familiar with courts and diplomatic circles and capable of decisive action, he made a thorough investigation of the situation at Ivry. When he returned to Vienna, he wrote to Giuseppe in Constantinople a letter that was effectively an ultimatum:

He is still aware of the presence of friends, his face grows animated, he struggles to talk, he smiles and weeps. Dr Moreau says these visits are beneficial to him rather than harmful; now to go to Ivry to spend an hour with the poor invalid takes five hours, carriages are expensive. The unhappy Gaetano spends too much time alone with only his custodians.

If he were moved to Paris, he could be cared for by the same doctors, have the same custodians and the same care; furthermore physically he would be as well there as at Ivry and his morale would be a thousand times better because his friends could see him at any hour... I beg you, sir, to think deeply about these alternatives and to give me your answer. His friends are disinterested; they neither want to profit by Gaetano's misfortune nor to live at his expense. The bills will be perfectly in order and supported by a complete set of vouchers.

If neither brotherly feeling nor all the other considerations bring you to agree to Gaetano's leaving Ivry and being situated and cared for in his own house in Paris, I beg you to write to Count von Lesser. The other relatives will be forced to have recourse to the law. The French civil code expressly says: a person who is of age, who is in a state of imbecility, of dementia, or of violence *must* be interdicted even when there are moments when he is lucid.

It would be necessary in this case to direct the courts not to fail to pronounce the interdiction, to name a *trustee,* and to obtain from you, sir, what you have refused.

You have too noble a heart, sir, to permit matters to come to this extremity.

Then give your consent to the just demand of the friends of the unfortunate Gaetano . . . Excuse my frankness, but I have believed it my duty to tell you all I feel in my heart and to neglect nothing to brighten by however much it may be the last days of the life of my ill and unhappy friend.[16]

Unable to ignore Lannoy's argument, Giuseppe once again dispatched Andrea from Constantinople, and he arrived back in Paris on 23 April 1847. Andrea was charged with the duty of inserting articles into various newspapers and journals to justify the moves and intentions of the Donizetti family on Gaetano's behalf. That they felt this to be necessary speaks volumes about the criticism and innuendo that repeatedly appeared in print in the wake of Donizetti's confinement at Ivry. The morning after his arrival, Andrea went out to see Donizetti, later writing this account in his daybook: 'I went to Ivry at high noon and I saw Gaetano. Oh God! in what a condition! He keeps his eyes closed constantly! He recognized me, and his servant assured me that he had not seen him so observant of anyone for many months as he was of me. He kissed me at my request; often he looked at me.'[17]

As soon as he started to make arrangements to move Gaetano to Paris, Andrea encountered the same opposition he had met the year before. On 8 May he had an audience with Delessert, informing him of the family's determination, and letting fall several hints that he suspected a conspiracy against them. Andrea never made a direct charge, but he left little doubt that he believed de Coussy and his wife to be exerting their influence to keep Donizetti at Ivry, because, as his banker, de Coussy had charge of Donizetti's income. It was Madame de Coussy whom Andrea regarded as his bête noire, and he encountered her when he returned to Ivry on 10 May. 'She tried to make me believe that from time to time she cried. She asked me about my plans. I answered that I did not even know myself. She is dying of fury.'[18]

By pestering Delessert, Andrea was finally able to arrange for Donizetti's return to Paris, to an apartment that he had found and rented at 6 avenue Chateaubriand. He described the move in his daybook: 'Went to get Gaetano at Ivry to take him to Paris. I cannot describe my feelings this memorable day! Left Paris at six in the morning, with Gaetano by half past nine. I arrived back in Paris with my uncle at half past eleven . . . Mitvié came and found Gaetano very well, in fact he did not suffer at all during this trip.'[19]

Freed from his confinement at Ivry, where he had spent sixteen months and twenty-three days, Donizetti could now go out for drives in his carriage, which Andrea hoped would prepare him to undergo

the long journey back to Bergamo. Ricordi, who was in Paris during
the summer of 1847, went out driving on 15 July with Donizetti,
Andrea, and the servant Pourcelot; he reported that the invalid rode
along with his eyes open, looking around him and seemingly content, in marked contrast to his apathy indoors. On 3 August Andrea
summoned a photographer to the apartment in the avenue Chateaubriand. A daguerrotype was taken of Donizetti and Andrea, which
shows the composer slumped in his chair, his eyes shut, his chin
resting on his chest, his fists knotted; Andrea in a plaid jacket sits
next to him, with both his hands on his uncle's right arm, and he
stares somberly straight at the camera. A copy of this picture was
sent to Rosa Basoni in Bergamo to prepare her for the tragic alteration she would find in her long-awaited guest.

The summer was passing and with it the most favorable time to
transport the invalid back to Italy, but Delessert remained obdurate
in his refusal to permit this departure. The first move to bypass
Delessert was taken in Constantinople where, on 16 August,
Giuseppe, having been prompted by Lannoy, made a formal statement to the Austrian ambassador, explaining all the careful plans for
the journey and going on to state that the Paris police 'persist in
taking the greatest interest in the tragic position of Gaetano Donizetti
and continue to raise difficulties just as they did last year'.[20]

Meanwhile Andrea arranged what he hoped would be a decisive
consultation between six doctors who met in Donizetti's apartment
on the afternoon of 17 August. The opinion was divided: four doctors approved the journey, provided suitable precautions were taken;
two opposed. If Andrea hoped that this majority opinion would pre-
vail, Delessert soon shattered that hope by sending a police physician to examine Donizetti; the physician brusquely declared that
he was entirely opposed to any idea of moving Donizetti. When
Andrea protested, Delessert retaliated on 26 August by placing gen-
darmes in the conciergerie of 6 avenue Chateaubriand. The following morning they refused to allow Donizetti's daily drive. This interference infuriated Andrea, but to his protests Delessert blandly explained that he had taken precautions to prevent an 'illegal' departure for Italy. Andrea now took advice of a lawyer and was ready to
go to court if the police continued to intervene. Delessert was finally
forced to back down. The combination of the publicity Andrea gave
to this unwarranted opposition and the diplomatic pressure exerted
by Lannoy proved effective. Since the Paris police had no legal
grounds for detaining Donizetti, an Austrian subject and, as *Hofkapellmeister*, a member of the imperial household, Delessert had no

choice save to retreat, unless he chose to provoke an international incident.

On 19 September 1847 the long-delayed journey to Bergamo finally began. The party consisted of Donizetti, his brother Francesco,[21] Andrea, the servant Pourcelot, and Dr Rendu, especially engaged to oversee the patient on this trip. They left Paris by train for Amiens, proceeding next to Brussels, where they were forced to stay over because of a congestion of the invalid's bladder. The next phase of the journey was by boat down the Rhine to Basel, where they took a carriage over the St Gotthard Pass. On 5 October 1847 the company reached Como, where Dolci joined them, traveling with them to Bergamo, where they arrived the following evening. As the carriages drew up in front of the Palazzo Basoni in Bergamo Alta, the assembled crowd of notables and well-wishers were grieved to see the emaciated figure who had almost to be carried into the house.

This incontrovertible evidence of Donizetti's condition dispelled the hopes that somehow the reports had been exaggerated. All that could be done, realistically, was to maintain his physical functions; nevertheless, the temptation to arouse some sign of recognition from the patient, who passed his days in a specially contrived armchair with a padded board to support his head, was irresistible. Rosa Basoni's daughter Giovannina would play Donizetti's music for hours at a time on the piano he had personally selected for her in Vienna four years before, anxiously glancing across at him to see if this aria or that would elicit some change in expression. Dolci stopped by several times a day to talk of old times in Bergamasc dialect. Rubini, now living in retirement in a villa at Romano Lombardo, some twenty kilometers from Bergamo, drove over one day to sing 'Veranno a te' from *Lucia* with Giovannina, but Donizetti remained inert. When a visitor first arrived Donizetti would study the new face for a moment before his eyes closed and his head sank back on his chest. On rare occasions he would mutter some monosyllable, but no amount of straining helped a listener to grasp what he had tried to say.

His days passed in this manner until February 1848, when he passed through an alarming phase of fever and profuse sweating, and coughed so incessantly that he had difficulty eating. His doctors, Cassis and Calvetti, modified his diet and increased the number of purges. Gradually his symptoms abated and, although he had grown very thin, by the end of February he had recovered enough to be able, with help, to move from his bed to sit in his armchair for a few hours each day. This routine continued through March. He was being helped to eat his dinner at five in the afternoon on 1 April 1848 when he was seized by a convulsion that contorted his eyes and mouth and left his arms and left leg paralyzed. All night they tended him, applying mustard plasters to his feet and legs. The following morning the paralysis subsided and his teeth unlocked, allowing him to be fed a few spoonfuls of broth. Two days later he was seized again by more violent convulsions that racked him for an hour. A priest was summoned to administer the final rites.

Donizetti was still in this dangerous state on 5 April, when the Basonis impulsively decided to have his portrait painted by a local artist named Rillosi.[22] Giovannina described this episode: 'his features, which in the preceding days had been distorted by his illness, suddenly relaxed again and his eyes became expressive so that one would have thought he took an interest in what was going on around him.'[23] Giovannina also left an account of Donizetti's last hours:

During the evening of the 5th his fever increased. On the morning of the 6th he was fed nourishment fortified with egg yolk. The 7th and the 8th Signor Donizetti kept getting worse and worse.

He was in agony.

At 5.0 p.m. on the 8th, the famous invalid took his last breath, the priest being present, surrounded by my mother and me, by his intimate friend Dolci and by his affectionate servant.[24]

It is, in a way, fitting that Donizetti died when he did. His works encapsulate much of the sensibility of the era of Metternich and Louis Philippe, and he succumbed in the year that marked its end. On 11 April, the day of his funeral, Genoese and Piedmontese troops were advancing across Lombardy, but his native town staged an elaborate civic function in his honor. The ceremonies began at ten in the morning when a crowd of clergy and civic leaders, the Guardia Nazionale and four hundred torchbearers gathered. A few hours later the final scene was played out in the toolshed of the Valtesse cemetery, in a suburb to the northeast of Bergamo Bassa. Here eight doctors gathered around Donizetti's corpse, while two of them, Giovanni Locatelli and Federico Maironi, performed an autopsy.[25] At five they had completed their task, and the remains were interred in the nearby vault of the Pezzoli family.[26] They remained there until 1875, when they were transferred, along with those of Mayr, to Santa Maria Maggiore, where nearly seventy years earlier Donizetti had sung as a choirboy, and where, in 1855, an imposing monument by

the Torinese sculptor Vincenzo Vela had been erected, which bears
an epitaph by Andrea Maffei. Donizetti's body was reinterred under
the floor directly in front of his monument.

After Donizetti's death, problems over his estate were to persist for
many years. His funeral had cost 761 Austrian lire. Teodoro Ghezzi,
who had managed Donizetti's business affairs in Naples, was owed
1188 ducats when his account was settled in 1849; most of it had
gone to pay for Virginia's mausoleum and for the bi-weekly Masses
that were said for her, but there were other items too: bracelets and
pins of coral and tortoiseshell that Ghezzi had purchased and forwarded to Vienna on Donizetti's orders. Ghezzi negotiated the sale of
the still unperformed score of *Poliuto*, the original Italian version of
what became *Les martyrs*, and he tried, unsuccessfully, to do the
same with the 1838 version of *Gabriella di Vergy*. On Gaetano's
death, since there were no surviving children of his marriage to
Virginia, his estate was divided equally between his two brothers.
Virginia's dowry reverted to the Vasselli family; Antonio Vasselli
wrote to Andrea about the return of the principal, and the question
grew bitter before it was finally settled.

There were squabbles within the Donizetti family as well. When
Francesco Donizetti died eight months after Gaetano, Giuseppe, the
one surviving brother, became the sole heir. But great was his fury
and that of Andrea when they discovered that Francesco had left a
will of his own, bequeathing everything he owned to Elisabetta Santi
Pesenti, the woman who had taken care of him before he died and
who now claimed to be his common-law wife. Giuseppe, until he
died in 1856, and after him Andrea, did their best to invalidate her
claims. There is an interesting letter from Dolci to this woman, who
by then was calling herself Elisabetta Santi Donizetti. On 2 April
1861 he informs her: 'Most honored Signora: Moretti has sent me
your greeting, and I send you mine with these few lines. [Andrea]
Donizetti has become mad; this I read in the paper, *La Lombardia* of
Saturday last. I was very surprised to learn of that misfortune, but
God is just.'[27] Dolci's last words here reveal much about his judgment of Andrea and his actions. Andrea's last years were spent in
trying to realize as much as he could of Donizetti's estate and combatting claims against it. In 1858 he had married Giuseppina
Gabuzzi, who bore him two sons, Giuseppe and Gaetano. On 11 June
1861 he was admitted to the asylum at Aversa, near Naples, where he
died on 11 February 1864 of meningovascular syphilis, the same
disease that had killed his uncle. Andrea's two sons are generally

represented as having supported themselves largely by the sale, in bits and pieces, of the manuscript music and letters which constituted the Donizetti inheritance. The younger Gaetano perished in an air raid during World War II; his brother Giuseppe died about 1949.

Ultimately, it is the other inheritance that matters, the bounty Gaetano Donizetti bequeathed to the whole world. The second part of this volume takes an overview of the most important part of the patrimony he left us, his operas.

PART II

7

Donizetti's Operatic World

From the point of view of half a century ago no recent musical phenomenon would have seemed less likely than the extensive and so far unabating revival of Donizetti's operas. In spite of the unevenness of his output, works such as *Anna Bolena, Maria Stuarda* and *Roberto Devereux* have become established in the repertory and seem unlikely ever to slip back into obscurity. Donizetti was not a great originator; he found his mature voice more slowly than most of his contemporaries; he eludes the handy labels that help us to pigeonhole composers from the past. He is a central figure, much more consistent and true to himself than one might expect of a composer whose arena was the highly eclectic and adaptive world of Italian opera in the first half of the nineteenth century. At that time a composer enjoyed little status in the musical hierarchy, especially in the jungle world of the Italian opera house, where, for instance, Méric-Lalande was paid more than nine times as much for singing the Carnival season at La Scala as the composer was paid for writing *Lucrezia Borgia.*

A fair estimate of Donizetti's qualities can only be achieved by considering his music in the context of the theater within which he worked, its musical conventions, and its personnel of singers and other composers, all of whom were struggling to capture and maintain the loyalty of the public.

Donizetti began his career with a single goal in mind: to escape from obscurity by pleasing the public for his own profit and prestige. For an Italian composer of his generation the only way to accomplish this goal was to turn out operas readily and frequently. Undoubtedly he regarded his facility in composition as a strength to be exploited, and near the end of his career, when the conditions that had put a premium upon that facility had begun to change, there is a certain pathos in Donizetti's boasts, often not literally accurate, about the rapidity with which he wrote; in the same way there is something poignant in all his talk of the many simultaneous projects he had in hand, as he sought to disregard those Parisian writers and cartoonists who found his nonstop activity an irresistible target for their jibes.[1] The origins of Donizetti's drive to compose rapidly and voluminously go back to his training under Mayr, who positively reinforced these tendencies.

Mayr's attitude was an acknowledgement that about 1815 there scarcely existed any established group of repertory operas, in today's sense.[2] Before 1817, the year that saw the first production of a Donizetti opera, only a few resoundingly successful works ever received a second production at the theater where they were first performed. This point is proven by a glance through Carlo Gatti's chronology of La Scala,[3] which shows that from the inauguration of that theater in 1778 until the end of 1816 a total of 298 different works were performed. Only thirty of these were repeated in a second season, and just eight of them returned for a third staging. The only operas to better that record during those years were both by Paisiello: La molinara was repeated in four seasons, and Il barbiere di Siviglia in five. These statistics show that a composer was forced to hope, given the odds against a work's being mounted a second time in the same theater, that his opera would make a sufficient hit at its prima to attract offers of local productions from many other Italian opera houses. In those years success was counted in terms of a brief breadth of exposure rather than of longevity. Gatti's chronology confirms the Milanese appetite for operas that had succeeded elsewhere. Of the 298 works performed at La Scala between 1778 and 1817, exactly half had first been performed in other theaters.

During the years of Donizetti's active career the percentage of revivals gradually increased. Rossini's phenomenal success began this change. By the end of 1825 twenty of Rossini's operas had been staged at La Scala, fourteen of them in more than one production. In June 1827 Rossini's Il barbiere became the first opera at La Scala to reach a sixth production, and by 1848, the year of Donizetti's death, it had been performed in thirteen seasons. Bellini's career at La Scala further confirms this tendency toward more frequent revivals. Between 1827, when Il pirata introduced Bellini's music to that theater and launched his enduring popularity, and 1848, eight of his operas were performed there in thirty-one productions.[4] The first opera by Donizetti to be given in Milan, Chiara e Serafina (1822), was so unenthusiastically received that it retarded his acceptance by Milanese audiences; yet by 1835 fifteen of his operas had been mounted there, though only two, L'ajo nell'imbarazzo and Il furioso, were given in a second season. Between 1835 and 1848 seventeen more of his operas were put on at La Scala, and the number of revivals jumped from two to thirty, with *Lucrezia Borgia* and *Gemma di Vergy* both attaining to five productions.[5]

The gradual increase in revivals did not, of course, diminish the tremendous importance a composer placed upon an opera's achieving a successful run in its initial production. One consequence of this emphasis and of the absence of anything approximating a stable repertory is that it encouraged Donizetti and his contemporaries to follow the example of their predecessors in borrowing from their own less successful scores.[6] A brief glimpse at some of the principles underlying the habit of self-borrowing are germane to an understanding of the kind of world Donizetti worked in. If an opera failed irredeemably or even if it lacked the vitality to sustain itself in more than a handful of productions, a composer would have no compunction about re-using whole sections of music, sometimes with little or no modification, in a subsequent score. This widespread practise of self-borrowing may be seen as a by-product of the structural conventions then generally adhered to. Whole numbers from scores could be regarded as interchangeable, with the proviso that old music in a new context should not be performed first in the town where the original setting had been heard.

Throughout his career Donizetti borrowed music from his earlier scores, observing as far as he was able the proprieties that discretion demanded. Among many examples there is the significant one of *Maria de Rudenz*, which was such a fiasco at its Venetian *prima* in January 1838 that for a time he felt it could be dismembered and parts of it salvaged without risk of offense. As is well known, he adopted 150 measures from the *larghetto* to the finale of Act 1 of *Maria de Rudenz* to serve, only slightly altered, as the slow movement of the Act 2 finale of *Poliuto*. Less well known, until the manuscript of the 1838 revision of *Gabriella di Vergy* in the Sterling Library of the University of London was closely examined a few years ago, was the fact that he had further drawn upon *Maria de Rudenz* that same year for several sections of the revised *Gabriella*.[7] *Maria de Rudenz* went on, however, after Donizetti had left Naples for Paris, to prove itself more durable than he had at first imagined; by 1842 it had been staged in a number of Italian theaters, including La Scala. After this resurgence he no longer turned to it as a source for self-borrowing.

These examples of re-using music are from one tragic opera to another. Earlier in his career Donizetti had seen nothing amiss in adapting music from serious contexts to comic ones, a procedure that implies a surprisingly flexible attitude toward the conventional distinction between the genres. For instance, when Donizetti had to compose L'elisir d'amore in a short time during the spring of 1832 he took for the march accompanying Belcore's Act 1 entrance music that had first been used in the heroic context of Alahor in Granata; similarly the choral buildup anticipating the arrival of Dr Dulcamara had originally served to prepare for the entrance of a very different figure, Queen Elizabeth I in Il castello di Kenilworth. Another example of Donizetti's adaptation of music from one genre to another is more readily understandable. Since Le convenienze presents a satirical view of a provincial troupe rehearsing an opera seria, it is appropriate that in the 1827 one-act version he used the heroine's entrance aria from Elvida (1826) as the number that the Prima Donna runs through during the opening ensemble of the comedy.[8] Since both these operas received their prime in Naples just a year apart, one can only assume that Donizetti counted on the audience's recognizing his self-borrowing as part of the humorous effect.

Not all the borrowing that went on in those years was planned, or even sanctioned, by the composer. It often happened that singers who had won a success with a scena in one opera inserted it in another score in place of one they regarded as less well suited to their abilities. When Adelaide Tosi sang Fausta at La Scala to open the Carnival season of 1832–3, she substituted for Fausta's Act 1 aria Amelia's scena[9] from Act 3 of Il castello di Kenilworth,[10] altering the text of the cantabile[11] but retaining the original words of the cabaletta.[12] Tosi's insertion was included in Ricordi's score of Fausta printed at the time, with a note explaining the original provenance of the arias. Perhaps the best-known instance of such borrowing was Persiani's adoption of Rosmonda's entrance scena to replace Lucia's' Regnava nel silenzio' and 'Quando rapito in estasi'. This substitution became habitual with Persiani, and she maintained it when she introduced Lucia at the Theâtre-Italien in December 1837. Donizetti gave Persiani's choice his official approval, for France at least, when he included it in the printed score of the French Lucie de Lammermoor.

On occasion, however, such changes exasperated Donizetti, as we can see from a letter he wrote in December 1841, replying to the request of his brother-in-law Toto Vasselli for an aria to replace Lucia's 'Spargi d'amaro pianto' to accommodate the soprano Fanny Maray:

What? You have the courage to ask for a new cabaletta to use in *Lucia*? From the composer of *Lucia*? Ah, why am I not within reach of you, disgraceful man! And why indeed? For a woman the Romans did not want [in the first place], a woman who performs *Lucrezia* and lacks the talent to sing Lucia's rondò[13] in some fashion! Oh, tell her to go to Mass, in my name! In sum, if she wants, sacrilegiously, to do it, let her take a cabaletta from where she likes. She can have one from [*Sancia*][14] *di Castiglia*, 'Se contro lui mi parlano'; she can have the *rondò* from *Fausta*, 'No qui morir degg'io'; she can have the cavatina from *Maria Stuarda*, the cavatina from *Ugo di Parigi*, 'No, che infelice appieno'. One of these will do; if not, the one from *Roberto* – have her do a little searching.

He goes on, finding this request so outrageous that he turns to ridicule:

If not, give her Agata's aria from *Le convenienze* [an aria for a baritone to sing partly in falsetto], give her the cabaletta written for Ronzi to use in *Pia* [imposing a happy ending upon a tragic subject].[15]

Although Donizetti found absurd the idea of a prima donna who thought Lucia's *rondò* beyond her appearing at a major theater (the Apollo),[16] nevertheless he tried, until irony overcame him, to suggest alternatives that were stylistically and dramatically appropriate and from works which, except for *Roberto* and *Pia*, had not then been performed in Rome.

Only rarely would Donizetti sanction the introduction of music by other composers into performances of his operas. On one occasion he allowed Pauline Viardot to replace the *rondò* from *Alina, regina di Golconda* with one written by her brother-in-law de Bériot. This episode took place in 1843 when Viardot was appearing in the Italian season in Vienna. Donizetti was making the best of a bad situation. The part of Alina as written had a tessitura too high for Viardot's mezzo-soprano, and moreover that outspoken lady was not one to disguise her low opinion of operas like *Alina*. 'She does nothing but rail against these stupid scores, which she calls horrors.'[17]

As a general rule, Donizetti was opposed to the insertion of any music into his operas without his permission, particularly when it was done with the intention of deceiving the public. During the summer season of 1843 Merelli tinkered high-handedly with the score of *Fausta*, and for a production at Bergamo of all places; when Donizetti heard about it he was so incensed that he wrote an article denouncing the production. He refers clearly and forcibly to the whole question in a letter to his friend Count Melzi of Milan.

I believed with the letter I published that I would open the public's eyes to the direction of the theaters [i.e., the high-handed ways of the impresarios and musical directors]. I believed it would be of use to my colleagues. I hoped to draw away from our shoulders the whirlwind of whistling that oppresses us when pieces by another composer are introduced into an opera, or when they are transposed or altered. All these things are most damaging to poor composers who cannot come out on stage and say: *This is not mine, this was not originally designed like this, this does not go so slow or so fast, this is not suited to the voice of A or B.*

Drawn into error, the public and the journalists disapprove and whistle without deeply examining the question. My letter was only *a voice . . . in the wilderness. La France musicale* last Sunday published a little article on such assassins, but it will serve for France and not for where these grievous problems exist.

For the rest, Merelli has the habit of doing such things, and the proof of it would be *Fausta* at Bergamo. He said that it had just been revised by me, and in order to make it seem so he inserted into it a cavatina by M[aestr]o. Savi[18] and the finale from *Les martyrs*.[19]

In this letter Donizetti's active opposition to anyone's tampering with his scores is manifest. His position anticipates that of Verdi, whose indignation at the damage impresarios like Merelli could inflict upon his operas was boundless. During the years of Donizetti's activity, the position of the composer in the operatic hierarchy had improved perceptibly, and that Donizetti felt impelled to speak out against misrepresentation of his work undoubtedly reflects his experience in France, where the creative artist was more highly regarded than in Italy. Yet his concern for the integrity of his own and others' work was not a pose he struck only late in his career, for he sincerely felt that he and his contemporaries labored under the same disadvantages and that all of them stood to gain if abuses could be eliminated. As a youth of twenty-four, newly arrived in Naples, he had been forced to stand helplessly by and watch the blasé Rossini rehearse singers ill suited to the task at hand in an unconscionably cut version of Mayr's oratorio *Atalia*, and he had been indignant.

At the outset of Donizetti's career, the two composers who exerted the greatest influence upon him, in their different ways, were Mayr and Rossini. The earlier and in some ways more pervasive influence was Mayr's. He was Donizetti's teacher of composition at the Lezioni Caritatevoli from 1806 to 1815, and upon Donizetti's return from Bologna and his studies with Padre Mattei in late 1817 Donizetti remained in close contact with his teacher until his departure for Rome in early October 1821.[20] It stands to reason, given the warm relationship that existed between them, that Donizetti would show his old teacher whatever he was working on, and that this would include his early operas from *Enrico di Borgogna* through however much of *Zoraida di Granata* he had completed before he struck out for Rome. It is important to remember that during these years of their closest association Mayr was an active composer, producing no fewer than eighteen operas, and at the peak of his powers. Three of Mayr's most widely produced works, staged not only throughout Italy but beyond the Alps as well, were composed during this time: *Adelasia ed Aleramo* (La Scala, first given on 26 December 1806, and having fifty-four performances that Carnival), *La rosa rossa e la rosa bianca* (Genoa, Carnival 1812-13, with a libretto by Felice Romani – his first in fact), and *Medea in Corinto* (San Carlo, from 28 November 1813, and revived there in eight seasons until 1827). The advantages to Donizetti of his association with Mayr at this particular period can scarcely be overestimated.

Nor was the stimulation that Mayr provided confined to stage works. Although Mayr was primarily an operatic composer, he also wrote a large number of oratorios and solo cantatas, as well as religious music of all kinds. Significantly, Donizetti wrote most, though not all, of his non-operatic works during his years in Bergamo. And it was to provide material for the string quartet in which Mayr played viola that Donizetti produced the majority of his chamber music. Clearly, then, part of Mayr's helpful influence lay in his keeping Donizetti at work turning out music while he awaited his big chance – the engagement at the Argentina that Mayr almost certainly renounced in his favor.

Mayr exerted an influence on Donizetti not only as his teacher but also as a composer. The ease with which Donizetti moved from one genre to another finds an immediate precedent in Mayr's output, for the elder composer worked in all the genres from one-act *farse* through sentimental and heoric comedies to opera seria. Although Stendhal in his *Life of Rossini* dismissed Mayr's efforts at comedy as elephantine,[21] his dim view is simply a reflection of his pro-Rossini bias. The earliest of Mayr's works to be widely produced was a one-act farsa, *Che originali!* (Teatro San Benedetto, Venice, 18 October 1798);[22] its libretto, by Gaetano Rossi, is a satire about a passionate lover of music. Baron Febeo is such an enthusiastic *dilettante* that not only must his servants share his love of music, but also he will consider only a musician as a worthy match for his daughter Aristea, who is a singer mad about Metastasio's verse. Aristea's predilection for Metastasio indicates that *Che originali!* is somewhat backward-looking, and Febeo's penchant for trying out music by

Pergolesi and Jommelli immediately recalls Dr Bartolo's reactionary taste in music as demonstrated in the lesson scene from Rossini's *Il barbiere*. In spite of this, *Che originali!* is an attractive score, with moments of real tenderness and sentiment, and its finale in eight sections is ingenious and satisfying. Satire of musicians as an operatic subject did not begin with Mayr,[23] but *Che originali!*, in conjunction with the pasticcio – *farse* that Mayr concocted for his students at the ends of terms at his school, indicates one of the major sources of Donizetti's fondness for parody and satire of this kind. Mayr's comic characterizations of Febeo in *Che originali!* and of Carolina, the exigent Prima Donna, in *I virtuosi* (Venice, 1801) – in which, notably, the whole finale takes off an opera rehearsal – look forward directly to the vein Donizetti would exploit in *Le convenienze*.

Mayr's reputation in his day rested more securely upon his serious than his comic operas. In his approach to opera seria, he occupies a crucial and transitional place in its evolution between the eighteenth century and the beginning of the nineteenth. Mayr helped to internationalize this genre in two ways. His Germanic background and his study of his slightly older contemporaries of the Viennese school caused him to increase the importance of the orchestration, particularly the woodwind, to which he occasionally gave elaborate solo passages,[24] and to emphasize generally the expressive importance of his introductions and accompaniments. Mayr absorbed much from the example of the French school – particularly as exemplified by such non-French composers as Gluck and Cherubini – in the areas of grandiose declamation and prominent choral parts (he even wrote double choruses on occasion), and of creating compound musical numbers combining recitative and aria and chorus for the purpose of dramatic immediacy. Mayr expanded the expressive range of traditional opera seria, but not always in a very forward-looking way; for example, he wrote prominent castrato parts when the day of that vocal type was all but over. While he dispensed with secco recitative for the original Neapolitan version of *Medea in Corinto*, supplying instead effective accompanied recitatives, this change did not mean that he abandoned secco recitatives in later serious operas, and, regrettably, he supplied them for later productions of *Medea in Corinto* elsewhere in Italy, but not in Milan (though he made a number of other alterations to his score for that city). This modification in the score of *Medea* suggests that Mayr lacked the conviction to maintain the integrity of his best work; certainly this is consistent with the retiring nature that made him prefer a modest school in Bergamo to the many more prestigious appointments in larger centers that he repeatedly turned down.[25] Mayr's work was not judged strong enough by audiences after 1820 to maintain itself against the excitement and vivacious impetus of the operas of Rossini.

Mayr's concept of large-scale compound scenes was to leave an abiding impression upon Donizetti, although in the latter's operas this concept is transmogrified by the dramatic values of Romantic melodrama. A clear example is the tomb scene from *Lucia*, where Donizetti even paid Mayr the compliment of quoting one of his melodies – in the chorus 'Fur le nozze a lei funesta;'[26] in this scene Donizetti creates a structural breadth that is equivalent to Mayr's achievement in *Medea*. The accruing emotion is similarly sustained in the final scenes of *Anna Bolena* and *Roberto Devereux*. Nor is Mayr's influence, though by then thoroughly digested, unconnected with Donizetti's readiness to adapt himself to the requirements and flavor of the French stage, for his first acquaintance with the repertory of the Opéra had come from Mayr's library when he was still a schoolboy. And it is no coincidence that Donizetti's most detailed letter about his changing of *Poliuto* into *Les martyrs* should be addressed to Mayr, for no-one else he knew could appreciate these details more fully.

Rossini changed the operatic climate in Italy so drastically that he became a force for all his contemporaries to reckon with. The emphatic success and rapid succession of Rossini's operas in the years following *Tancredi* (1813) created in audiences an almost insatiable appetite for the tonal brilliance and rhythmic energy of his music, and concomitantly, a growing impatience with scores that lacked these qualities. For a composer just starting out during the years when the Rossini vogue had first caught hold, the only way to get on was to adapt himself as best he could to that dominant style. Donizetti recognized this necessity, as he admitted to Bonesi in those tentative days of trying to launch his career from Bergamo. Years later Bonesi reported what Donizetti had said:

Straightforwardly he told me that he had to cultivate the Rossinian style, according to the taste of the day. If once he made his own way a little, nothing would prevent him from developing his own style. He had many ideas how to reform the predictable situations, the sequences of introduction, cavatina, duet, trio, finale, always fashioned the same way. 'But', he added sadly, 'what to do with the blessed theatrical conventions? Impresarios, singers, and the public as well, would hurl me into the farthest pit at least, and – *addio per sempre.*'[27]

Although Bonesi supplies no precise date for these remarks, it seems plausible that Donizetti had tried to make his own mark in his own way and had been disappointed before he saw that there was no alternative to the Rossinian style. One surprising piece of evidence suggests that *Enrico di Borgogna* (1818) his first publicly performed opera, possesses a true connection with, or at least a direct anticipation of, his mature style. Most critics glibly assert that Donizetti's maturity first became strikingly evident in Anna Bolena's 'Al dolce guidami' and that in this aria he found his own equivalent to Bellinian cantilena. Yet its melody is to be found in Donizetti's distant beginnings with *Enrico di Borgogna*, where it occurs, not as a slow aria, but as the cabaletta to the contralto hero's entrance aria (Example 1).[28]

Example 1. *Enrico di Borgogna*, Act 1 scene i, cabaletta of Enrico's *aria di sortita*

Undeniably, in 1818 Donizetti lacked the skill that he had by 1830 to exploit this melody to its maximum effectiveness, yet the germ of it was there in his early score, conceived long before he had ever heard of Bellini, or Giuditta Pasta for whom he wrote 'Al dolce guidami'.[29] This unexpected example of self-borrowing suggests a core of consistency in Donizetti's music that may help to explain why he was less successful at putting on a Rossinian disguise than were two of his slightly older contemporaries.

The first *rossiniano* to capture the public's attention was Giovanni Pacini (born 1796), whose *Il barone di Dolsheim* (La Scala, 1818) and *Il falegname di Livonia* (La Scala, 1819) both enjoyed runs of forty-seven performances in their first productions. (Significantly Donizetti's choice of the *rossiniano* Pacini's subject, and his decision to have it adapted by Marchese Bevilacqua-Aldobrandini, who was a friend of Rossini, suggest that Donizetti adjusted his course to take account of the current vogue, as his remarks to Bonesi – probably from about this time –imply.). Pacini received the reward of a good *rossiniano* when he was invited by Rossini himself to contribute two numbers[30] to *Matilde di Shabran* at the time of its *prima* in Rome in 1821. But perhaps Pacini was unaware of Rossini's later ironic comment: 'Guai se sapesse la musica! Nessuno potrebbe resistergli.' (Look out if he should ever learn how to write music! No-one could stand up against him.) Rossini's low opinion of Pacini in later years is borne out by the discouraging frequency of fiascos in his list of nearly ninety operas; for instance, of the twenty-nine works by Pacini performed at the San Carlo only eight lasted into a second season. Pacini is remembered today chiefly for his *Saffo* (San Carlo, Naples, 1840), the work in which he most nearly achieved an individual style.[31] As early as 1834 Pacini took up teaching, first in Viareggio and later in Lucca, but he kept turning out operas with mechanical regularity until his death in 1867.

A more considerable composer than Pacini, Mercadante (born 1795), was the second *rossiniano* to attract wide attention. *Elisa e Claudio* (La Scala, 1821) went the rounds of Italy in record time and within a little more than two years had been performed as well in London, Paris and Vienna. At La Scala it was followed the next year by *Adele ed Emerico*, given fifty times (this being the work that so decisively eclipsed Donizetti's Milanese debut with *Chiara e Serafina*). With these two major successes, back to back as it were, one might imagine that Mercadante would continue to figure prominently on the billboards of La Scala, but such is not exactly the case. His next opera, *Amleto*, with a libretto by Romani, opened the Carnival season of 1822–3 (having fifteen performances), but then nearly four years passed before his name appeared again, when *Elisa e Claudio* returned for a third and final production on 25 September 1826. There was a brief flurry early in 1827 with two operas by Mercadante, *Didone abbandonata* and *Il montanaro*, but then more than five years passed before another work by him was performed at La Scala,[32] – *Caritea, regina di Spagna* in September 1832. This petering out of Mercadante's early vogue demonstrates that while imitations of Rossini might serve briefly to capture the public's attention they could not long retain it. Indeed Mercadante found that the popularity he enjoyed in and shortly after 1821 dwindled so fast that he spent the years between 1827 and 1829 in Spain and Portugal trying to sustain his career there.

This dwindling of Mercadante's 'first' career suggests that change was in the wind in the mid-1820s. Rossini's departure from Italy following the launching of *Semiramide* (Venice, 3 February 1823) removed the immediate pressure of his physical presence from his younger rivals, but it scarcely removed him from his dominant position in the opera houses. At La Scala during 1823 and 1824 half of the operas staged were by Rossini, and from the end of March until the middle of September 1823 out of a total of 129 performances given there his works account for 125. Clearly the *rossiniani* were no match for the great original. Once this considerable flurry receded, prompted no doubt by the news of his leaving Italy for Paris, two composers with rather opposite tendencies emerged briefly into special prominence. Giacomo Meyerbeer's *Il crociato in Egitto* (Venice, 1824) is a heroic opera with a happy ending, and while there is evidence of the composer's assimilation of Rossinian musical rhetoric, there is also a new note of amplitude and expressive detail in the orchestral writing to suggest that Meyerbeer had also been turning over the pages of Mayr's serious operas. *Il crociato* marked not merely the climax of Meyerbeer's Italian phase, which had begun in 1817, but its end, for in 1825 he, too, moved on to Paris, first to supervise the production of *Il crociato* at the Théâtre-Italien and then to absorb the French grand style, in which he demonstrated his new proficiency with his next opera, *Robert le diable* (1831).

The second composer to gain the limelight was Nicola Vaccai (1790–1848), whose *Giulietta e Romeo* (Teatro Canobbiana, Milan, 1825) gave him the single major success of a career that had begun back in 1815 and would end in a string of nine successive failures. Several aspects of *Giulietta e Romeo* account for Vaccai's brief moment of success: Romani's libretto, the effective vocal writing (not for nothing had Vaccai taught singing and composed *vocalizzi*, which are still used today), and, most important, the pathos of the subject and the tragic ending.[33] The heyday of Italian operatic tragedy was about to dawn, and Vaccai's *Giulietta* was an anticipatory glimmer.

To look at Donizetti's career against the activities of his contemporaries up to 1825 is to realize that he did not exactly shine as a *rossiniano* among *rossiniani*. His detractors accused him of being an imitation of an imitation, claiming that his success with *Zoraida di Granata* in 1822 was in part an expression of the Romans' displeasure with Pacini,[34] and that he was offered a contract at La Scala later the same year because 'he was something on the order of Mercadante' (*sul fare di Mercadante*).[35] But when *Chiara e Serafina* failed to make a positive impression, which Mercadante's *Adele ed Emerico* had just emphatically done, the management of that theater without regard to the extenuating circumstances, failed to offer Donnizetti a follow-up engagement.

Yet he made his way. The chief success of this phase of his career was *L'ajo nell'imbarazzo* which contains Rossinian echoes (for instance, in the *allegro* of the Pipetto–Gregorio duet in Act 1, the movement of the second period into the key of the mediant rather than the more obvious dominant) and Rossinian structures (the general plan of the overture with the *crescendo* in the second thematic unit, first in the key of the dominant then recapitulated in the tonic). It is possible to find some distinctive Donizettian touches, too, such as casting the *allegro* of the first finale in 3/4 and repeating rhythmic patterns that suggest dance rhythms: (♪♪♪ | ♪.♪♪♪♪ | ♪.♪♪ etc.). The final section of this finale is a 3/8 *presto* which anticipates the *allegro vivace* in the same meter that concludes the first finale of *L'elisir d'amore*.[36]

If Rossini shone like a sun among the luminaries of these years, certainly Donizetti passed through his gravitational field and his subsequent orbit was permanently modified by that exposure. The twentieth-century obsession with originality is inappropriate in this connection: there is no need to apologize for Donizetti's adoption of certain convenient features of the Rossinian syntax, which he assimilated into his own instinctive expression. The general structure of pieces was a sort of lingua franca, and quite a sophisticated one, for the composers of Donizetti's generation, yet in comparison with Rossini's vocal writing Donizetti's is generally much simpler and less highly embellished, except in the baritone roles written for a Tamburini and the prima donna's moments of parade – her entrance aria and her aria–finale.[37]

Donizetti's contemporaries noticed and applauded non-Rossinian effects in his scores. Florimo says that the Act 2 septet in *La zingara* was, in the opinion of the composer Carlo Conti (1796–1868), one 'that only a pupil of Mayr would have the capability and knowledge to create'.[38] Florimo was no partisan of Donizetti yet that he should remember the gist of Conti's remark sixty years later and take the trouble to record it suggests that this septet made a particular effect, learned (Mayrian) rather than witty (Rossinian). Its opening *andante*[39] is striking for the much greater independence of the vocal parts than was usual in scores of the early 1820s; certainly there is more independence per se than in the parts of the *Lucia* sextet, but in *La zingara* the melodic ideas lack the salient shapes and mounting tension of those in the *Lucia* ensemble (Example 2).

Example 2. *La zingara*, Act 2, septet

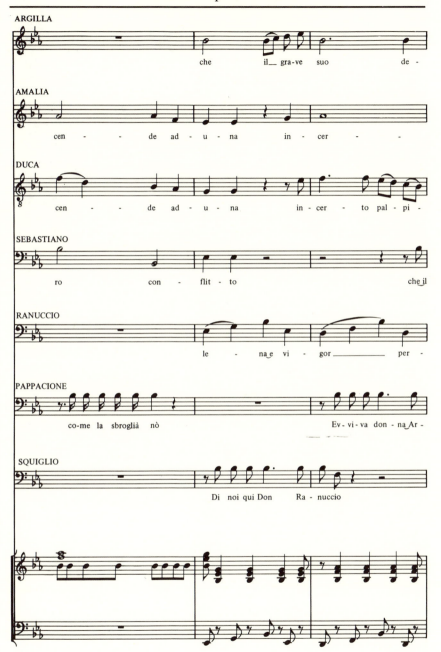

In 1825 Italian audiences found the sentimental pathos that led to the onstage death of the lovers in Vaccai's *Giulietta e Romeo* stirring. This opera was a straw in the wind because momentum was gathering for a shift away from operas that ended happily toward an emphasis on suffering (frequently helpless) victims and fatal consequences. The happy endings in opera seria most often fit one of three patterns: an oracle, a god, or a benevolent monarch (as in *Idomeneo*) intervenes; the tyrant realizes his error and turns compassionate (as in *Il castello di Kenilworth*); the hero's enterprise and timeliness foil the villain (as in *Enrico di Borgogna*). Not all opere serie came to a happy ending, but those that did not tended to follow classical decorum so that violence occurred off stage. Medea in Mayr's opera (1813) drags her children off to murder them out of sight; when she is next seen she carries the bloody dagger, hurling it at Jason. After Medea makes her exit in a chariot drawn by dragons, Jason tries to stab himself with the dagger but he is prevented from doing so. Within ten years, violence was being shown on stage, as in *Semiramide*, though here the fatal consequences are hidden: Arsace believes he is stabbing the wicked Assur, but in the darkness he stabs his mother, Semiramide, instead. But since she has murdered her husband Ninus, her death is retribution and Arsace becomes an Orestes figure, unwittingly avenging his father's murder upon his mother. Once stabbed, Semiramide, according to the stage directions, must die 'behind the tomb of Ninus', that is, out of sight.

In 1816 in Naples, however, there had appeared two operas that notably dealt with violence and involved onstage deaths. The first of these was Carafa's *Gabriella di Vergy* (Teatro del Fondo, 3 July 1816), which held the stage of the San Carlo until 1827. Fayel, believing his wife Gabriella to be guilty of infidelity with Raul, throws her into a dungeon and slays his rival in a duel. Then he brings her a casket containing the freshly excised heart of Raul, and she, beholding the contents, dies of shock and horror.[40] The plot of the second, Rossini's *Otello* (Fondo, 4 December 1816),[41] was much changed from Shakespeare's original, but Desdemona's murder at the hands of the jealous Otello formed the climax of Act 3, except in cities where the censors' insistence on the *lieto fine* made them an object of ridicule. In 1826 Donizetti set himself the task, 'for my diversion',[42] of providing music of his own to Tottola's libretto of Carafa's *Gabriella*, because of its violence and the heroine's death on stage. Up to that time he had not composed a death scene for the stage. Two years later he turned his attention to an even stronger subject in his preparation for dealing with onstage suffering when he wrote for

Lablache a setting of the Ugolino passage from Canto XXXIII of Dante's *Inferno*, but here Donizetti's music can serve as a prime example of the principle that music is a superfluous addition to great poetry.

To move from Vaccai's *Giulietta e Romeo* to Bellini's *Il pirata* (La Scala, 27 October 1827) is to observe the growing emphasis upon suffering, on violent confrontations and on implicitly tragic endings. In the second act of Bellini's opera, Ernesto the baritone villain is slain off stage in a duel by the tenor hero, who is condemned to death, causing the soprano Imogene to lose her reason and all desire to live. Although Imogene's affecting mad scene is the concluding episode of the score, Romani's libretto continues for another scene that ends in the tenor Gualtiero's onstage suicide; Bellini omitted it because Méric-Lalande, the first Imogene, insisted on her prima donna's prerogative of an aria–finale to end the opera.[43] This melodramatic plot, which goes back to an English play, Maturin's *Bertram* (London, 1816), ends without any possibility of a happy outcome, suggesting that tragedy can be measured by other means than the presence of corpses on stage, or by a Count di Luna surviving to ask 'E vivo ancor?' The opening episode, in which the pirate Gualtiero is driven ashore in a storm, looks forward to the opening of Verdi's *Otello*, but even more it looks back to the first act of Gluck's *Iphigénie en Tauride*, where tormented strangers, whose inner turmoil is symbolized by the storm, are washed up on an alien shore. The emphasis upon suffering, frustration and human frailty found an extraordinarily effective medium in Bellini's long-lined cantilena with its recurring stress on downward-resolving suspensions – melodies ideally suited to the poetic pathos that Rubini, for example, could spin out in nuanced fioriture, and quite different from the energetic, rhythmic roulades the Rossinian tenors made their specialty. The vogue for Romantic melodrama which *Il pirata* played such a significant role in establishing owed a significant measure of its success to the emotional outlet it afforded a politically repressed people; in less than twenty years Verdi and his librettists would find ways in their work to appeal directly to long-checked nationalism.

Il pirata affords an opportunity to compare Bellini's and Donizetti's uses of a typical convention of the time. After the well-articulated quintet in the first finale comes a stretta (Example 3). The characteristic convention for the stretta is the insistence upon a repeated rhythmic figure, which Bellini here confines to Imogene and continues through a passage of more than thirty measures. (A striking feature here is Bellini's use of the minor mode – the stretta

Example 3. Bellini, *Il pirata*, Act 1, stretta of the finale

ends in the parallel major; the stretta of a finale–ensemble customarily, though not invariably, begins in a major key.) In his *Gabriella di Vergy*, composed during May and June of 1826, Donizetti had applied the identical rhythm to a more obviously triadic melody in the stretta to his Act 1 quintet. Bellini did not avail himself of this convention as often as Donizetti did; he resorted to something like it in *Beatrice di Tenda* (Act 1, finale) where he introduces a melody in an insistent rhythm ($\quad$) in the *tempo d'attacco* and repeats it in the *tempo di mezzo*, first in the accompaniment and then in the voices (in unison except for the basses). He makes a more subtle use of an iterative unison figure in the *allegro vivace* of the first-act finale to *I puritani*.[44] Donizetti had a marked fondness for beginning the stretta of an ensemble in this way, and examples of it may be found in *Anna Bolena*, *Il furioso*, *Maria Stuarda*, and *Roberto Devereux*,[45] where such passages are launched by a single voice, are later reinforced by others, and build up to an emphatic statement of a second melodic idea. Vocal doubling and unison effects were frequently used to achieve an insistent sonic climax at a time when all but the major opera houses had comparatively slender forces.

Nor was Verdi immune to this convention, for it can be found in the stretta of the Act 1 finale to *Nabucco* and again in the Act 2 finale to *Il corsaro;* but it is interesting to see how relatively early Verdi underplayed the old-fashioned two-movement finale, either by retaining only the slow section, as at the end of Act 3 of *Ernani,* or by reducing the *allegro* to the status of a short coda, as in Act 3 of *I due Foscari. Aida* is the last of his operas to have an extended finale in several movements, and in this score Verdi's solution for the concluding section was to introduce a series of short melodies associated with different aspects of the dramatic conflict and then to combine them contrapuntally. Even up to the end of his active career, Donizetti found ways to utilize the device of a repeating rhythm, becoming skillful at varying its development and at adapting it for more intimate contexts than full-scale finales.[46] In Example 4, from *Poliuto,* the shifting of the rhythmic pattern in measures 6 and 7, demanded by textual emphasis, shows Donizetti growing more subtle in his manipulation of this device.

The same section from *Poliuto* shows Donizetti's use of more chromatic melodic movement in building up sequences. Near the end he brings back the opening chorus of the priests, which creates a contrapuntal effect, though the other parts have mostly short sequences and lack the melodic character of the priests' tune. Donizetti here took a first step in the direction that Verdi would pursue with the triumphal scene from *Aida.*

Where did this convention for the stretta of the finale come from? The multi-sectioned finale came into serious opera from opera buffa; the ultimate source for this repetition of a pattern therefore lies in some comic opera of about the middle of the eighteenth century. But for the purposes of the composers of Donizetti's and Bellini's generation a familiar source, which fully demonstrates the utility and effectiveness of the device, was the *vivace* of the first finale of Rossini's *Il barbiere,* where all the principals sing in unison 'Mi par d'esser colla testa' to the rhythmic pattern ♩ ♪.♪♪.♪ | ∕ | ∕ | ♩. ♪ | Donizetti had discovered the efficacy of such patterns at least as early as 1822, for in *Chiara e Serafina* he starts the stretta to the finale of Act 1 as shown in Example 5.

The success of *Il pirata* was instantaneous and widespread, making Bellini the composer of the hour, and for the next three years or so he

Example 4. Poliuto, Act 2, *allegro non troppo* of the finale

Example 5. *Chiara e Serafina*, Act 1, stretta of the finale

occupied a more prominent place in public esteem than Donizetti. *Il pirata* colored the public's expectation of what new operas should be like. Until the famous confrontation between Bellini and Donizetti in the Carnival season of 1830–1 at the Teatro Carcano in Milan, the season that saw the *prime* of *Anna Bolena* and *La sonnambula*, the two composers had pursued their careers apart, Bellini in northern Italy, and Donizetti in Naples. The only previous occasion on which they had been in direct competition was the inaugural season of the Teatro Carlo Felice in Genoa in the spring of 1828. It turned out not to be much of a confrontation, since Bellini's offering was a *rifacimento* of *Bianca e Fernando,* a serious opera with a happy ending, and Donizetti's was the opera buffa, *Alina, regina di Golconda.* Bellini's opera was better cast and opened the new theater, but in spite of its initial good reception, the music, even as revised, was soon recognized as on the whole much inferior to that of *Il pirata. Alina* got off to a less promising start, beset by generally inferior singers, but in the touched-up version that Donizetti made the following year for its first production in Rome the opera had sufficient vitality to be brought back at gala performances to celebrate both the thirtieth and fortieth anniversaries of the Carlo Felice's opening. A century and a half was to pass before *Bianca e Fernando* was revived there.

Donizetti's reaction to the success of *Il pirata* is somewhat unexpected. The five serious operas he composed between October 1827 and the fall of 1830 – his comic operas can be ignored since Bellini never essayed that genre and consequently could have exercised no influence there – far from showing Donizetti adjusting his style and tacking along a Bellinian course, reveal few signs of his trying to become a *belliniano.* The operas in question are *L'esule di Roma, Il paria, Il castello di Kenilworth, Il diluvio universale* and *Imelda de' Lambertazzi.*

In *L'esule di Roma,* a large-scale (larger than anything Donizetti had undertaken to date) evocation of Classical Rome, the influences most strongly felt are those of Mayr and the Italian composers who absorbed post-Gluckian French style, Cherubini and Spontini, with both of whom Donizetti became acquainted through Mayr's library. In *L'esule* there is a severity in the choral writing that strongly suggests the work of these predecessors, but Donizetti's score contains as well clear signs of his own future preoccupations, as in the pathos he gives to Murena's madness. On the whole, though, *L'esule di Roma,* for all its careful workmanship, was not an opera that indicated what new road Donizetti would follow, except perhaps for the hint of Romantic expression in certain details. Nor did *Il diluvio universale,* his only attempt as a biblical opera, prove a major signpost toward his future accomplishments. The Parisian influences discernible in *L'esule di Roma* are closer to hand and more specific with *Il diluvio,* for here Donizetti was measuring himself against *Moïse,* a revision of his *Mosè in Egitto* which Rossini had lately made for the Paris Opéra. Yet Donizetti evidently did not find this track especially congenial or fruitful, for when he revised *Il diluvio* for its production at Genoa early in 1834 he made the score sound more Italian and less French by inserting a number of cabalettas to round out arias that originally had none.

If Rossini's French style, which Donizetti had first encountered closely when he prepared *L'assedio di Corinto* for performance at Genoa in 1828, was a formative influence upon *Il diluvio*, it was Rossini's Neapolitan style that cast a shadow on *Il castello di Kenilworth;* with its *lieto fine* this work stands closer to Rossini's *Elisabetta, regina d'Inghilterra* than to Donizetti's later English tragedies. The brilliant rhetoric of Donizetti's Elisabetta is cut from much the same piece of cloth as that of her older prototype, as for instance in the final cabaletta, 'È' paga omai quest'alma' of *Il castello*. There are, moreover, other significant aspects to this score, for it is the earliest of Donizetti's operas to have two female figures of almost equal significance. Besides the Rossinian Elisabetta, there is the suffering figure of Amelia (Amy Robsart), whose complaints to Leicester about her treatment anticipate the accents of Lucia (Example 6).

Example 6. *Il castello di Kenilworth*, Act 2, recitative of the Amelia–
Leicester duet

AMELIA

son   di   War - ne - y   per - ché?   per -

ché?   per - ché pri - gio - nie - ra   son   di War - ne - y?

a piacere   *a tempo*   *p*

que - sta è la fè — pri - mie - ra   che un di — giu - ra - sti a me?   é

Larghetto

que - sta   Lei - ce - ster   e   que - sta   che un di giu - ras - ti a   me?

Il paria was a score that Donizetti worked hard upon and thought well of, even though it did not prove successful with the public. As he confessed to Mayr: 'I would not give one piece of *Il paria* for all of *Il castello di Kenilworth*.'[47] Donizetti's failure to revise this score and set the work on a successful course is explained by his dismembering it to use pieces from it in later scores. So much of *Il paria* became successful in new contexts that he saw nothing to be gained by revitalizing the original. That *Il paria*'s music could fit without strain into such diverse contexts as *Il diluvio, Anna Bolena, Tasso* and *Le duc d'Albe* testifies to a greater consistency in Donizetti's style than has been usually granted.

Imelda de' Lambertazzi is perhaps the most original of Donizetti's scores before *Anna Bolena*. It has a genuinely tragic subject, with deaths on stage; the hero, Bonifacio, is a baritone role, while Imelda's villainous brother is assigned the tenor range. In this score, then, occur Donizetti's first experiments with the Romantic baritone, which were to come to fruition in *Il furioso* and *Tasso*. There are persuasive melodies, as in Imelda's cavatina[48] in Act 1, 'Amarti, e nel martoro', where Donizetti delays the broad melodic idea until the second period, 'Mancar di vita insieme/Del cielo imploro ognor' (That we might die together is my constant plea to heaven). *Imelda* had, apparently, only two productions following its baptism at the San Carlo in September 1830, but Donizetti had decided, as with *Il paria*, to draw upon this score for other works.

In *Anna Bolena*, the opera that Donizetti composed to compete with Bellini for the favor of the Milanese public, and his first work for Milan since *Chiara e Serafina* in 1822, he drew extensively on his earlier scores. Besides borrowing the main melodic idea for 'Al dolce guidami' from *Enrico di Borgogna* (discussed above, see Example 1), he also drew on the 1826 *Gabriella*, and on *Il paria, Il diluvio universale* and *Imelda de' Lambertazzi*. To remember all this self-borrowing is to dispose of the erroneous idea that *Anna Bolena* represented a new start and a consequent repudiation of his earlier works. It is more helpful to look upon *Anna* as a refinement and development of tendencies that had been present in his work from the beginning.

Donizetti enjoyed some advantages during the time he composed and assembled *Anna*: for the first time he had a first-class libretto from Romani; he had the advantage of Pasta's professional advice, as much of his work on the score was carried out at her villa on Lake Como; and he had the challenge of knowing that if he could win over the Milanese public all the major theaters would open their doors to

him. The autograph of *Anna Bolena* is eloquent testimony to his
care in revising and reworking this score. If *Anna Bolena* seems at
times to approach the emotional climate of *Il pirata* more nearly
than had its predecessors, it is because Donizetti had come to a
deeper appreciation of the Romantic sensibility that was then the
dominant mode in Milan, while it was still regarded with official
distrust in Naples.

Donizetti's *Il diluvio universale* was one of the earliest Italian scores
to show the impact of Rossini's Parisian scores – more clearly so in
the original version (without cabalettas) for Naples than in the revision of four years later for Genoa. As Rossini's French scores became more widely known their influence made itself felt increasingly; evidence of this can be found in such scores as *Norma*
(Oroveso's 'Ite sul colle'), *Belisario* (the Belisario–Alamiro duet)
and *Nabucco* (the role of Zaccaria). The French operas of Rossini
were introduced into Italy quite promptly compared with most
French scores of that period, as this chart shows:

French title	Derived from	Paris premiere	First staged performance in Italy[49]
Le siège de Corinthe	Maometto II	9 October 1826	Parma, 26 January 1828
Moïse	Mosè in Egitto	26 February 1827	Perugia, 4 January 1829
Le comte Ory	Il viaggio a Reims (partly)	28 August 1828	Venice, July 1829
Guillaume Tell		3 August 1829	Lucca, 17 September 1831

These works were speedily diffused throughout Italy, but by the
end of a decade *Guillaume Tell* was the only one of them that continued to be performed with any regularity. *L'assedio di Corinto*
supplanted *Maometto II* immediately, but during the 1830s both
versions of *Mosè* were in circulation, the Italian version of the
French revision being distinguished from the original Italian work
by the title *Mosè e Faraone*, or, more familiarly, *Il nuovo Mosè*.

Perhaps the composer whose work was most affected by Rossini's
French scores was Mercadante, who in the later half of the 1830s
showed many signs of that influence. His first attack of the Rossinian

virus, at the time of *Elisa e Claudio* (1821), had proved difficult either to assimilate or to throw off; by the time of *Il pirata*, he was seeking a cure in Spain and Portugal. When he returned to Italy he launched a 'second' career with *Zaïra* (San Carlo, 31 August 1831), turning, significantly, to a libretto that Romani had originally written for Bellini.[50] Mercadante was determined to make a career as a Romantic melodramatist (like Donizetti, he had experimented with a *Gabriella di Vergy*, performed at Madrid in 1828), and his next operas, *I Normanni a Parigi*, *Il conte d'Essex*, *Emma d'Antiocha*, *Uggero il danese* and the Shakespearean *La gioventù di Enrico V*, all settings of librettos by Romani, show his consistent efforts to heighten dramatic intensity and to broaden his orchestral sound.

On the strength of these scores Mercadante was invited in 1836 by Rossini to compose for the Théâtre-Italien. In the same way that Rossini had offered advice and practical suggestions to Bellini for *I puritani* and to Donizetti for *Marin Faliero*, so he performed the same office for Mercadante with *I briganti*, and it seems indisputable that this experience formed the point of departure for Mercadante's 'reform' operas, which followed hard on the heels of *I briganti*. In *Il giuramento* (1837), *Le due illustri rivali* (1838), *Elena da Feltre* (1838), *Il bravo* (1839) and *La vestale* (1840), Mercadante largely adheres to the precepts he outlined in a letter to Florimo, in which he describes the 'revolution' he had started with *Il giuramento*. In this letter he renounces several well-worn devices: cabalettas, save when they are justifiable dramatically; the cliché of predictable *crescendi*; the insertion of solo passages in concertatos because they chill the dramatic effect and deflate the impetus of the ensemble; and the use of the stage band, that noisy and predictable effect that Rossini had inflicted upon Italian opera back in 1818 in his score for *Ricciardo e Zoraide*. The common denominator in Mercadante's reforms is to give dramatic considerations relatively more prominence than musical convention.

Unfortunately for his future reputation, Mercadante slid back from his reform position in his last works, which are uneven and lacked sufficient vitality to compete with the scores Verdi was turning out in the 1840s. By the end of that decade performances of Mercadante's works had sharply decreased in frequency. The final nineteenth-century performance at La Scala of an opera by Mercadante took place in January 1872; significantly, it was followed by the Milanese *prima* of *Aida*. Before that, no work by him had been produced there for almost ten years.[51] Even on the stage of the San Carlo, in the city with which he had had the closest professional ties, his record was little better: only one production in the last quarter of the century.[52]

The performance history of La Scala during the decade between the last two nineteenth-century productions of Mercadante operas sheds some light on the relative standings of composers then. Verdi, whose *La forza del destino* and *Don Carlos* were introduced to Milan during this period, leads with fifteen different productions; Meyerbeer, whose *L'africana* was a current novelty, follows with ten. In third place is Donizetti with nine; then Bellini with seven; and next Rossini with six. Of those other composers like Vaccai and Pacini who had seemed of such consequence nearly half a century before there is no trace.[53] Donizetti's nine productions at La Scala between 1862 and 1872 were spread among five different operas: *Lucia*, *La favorita*, *Lucrezia*, *Poliuto* and *Don Sebastiano*; Bellini was represented by only two titles (*I puritani* and *Norma*) and Rossini by three (*Il barbiere*, *Guglielmo Tell* and *Mosè e Faraone*). Donizetti's vitality, through the third quarter of the century at least, withstanding the Verdian onslaught of the 1840s and 1850s better than Mercadante, for instance, is attributable to his greater aptitude for assimilating influences into his own style: the composer of Edgardo's aria 'Tu che a Dio spiegasti l'ali' in the tomb scene of *Lucia* was also able to write the Offenbach-sharp trio in *La fille du régiment*, 'Tous les trois réunis', and the craggy septet from *Dom Sébastien*. Donizetti did not create a readily identifiable style as early as Bellini did, for instance, but there is a great consistency in his work; his operas are closely interrelated as is demonstrated by the self-borrowings that establish connections even between early and late works. He developed a breadth of manner, in both comic and tragic veins, even though he worked under conditions that were rarely advantageous; this gave him a solidity and permanence of achievement that had greater Romantic scope if not the sheer inventiveness of Rossini; it allowed him to encompass a range of experience broader if not deeper than Bellini's; and it made him the most fruitful of Verdi's antecedents.

8

Donizetti's use of operatic conventions

In the musical world that Donizetti entered as an opera composer in 1817, new works were designed to produce, hopefully, an immediate success. The ready assimilability of opera in Italy at this time was assured by the composer's general adherence to a number of conventions of musical forms and procedures; and it follows that a work's success was measured by the composer's skill, or want of it, in filling these forms with music that struck an audience as fresh and dramatically appropriate, rather than as novel or innovative. During the years of Donizetti's activity he gained greater freedom and adroitness in his treatment of these units of the basic framework, but he never came to the point of breaking away from them completely. Indeed, his fecundity, and that of some of his contemporaries, is unthinkable without this undergirding of traditional procedures. The measure of Donizetti's originality is to be taken from his adaptiveness in handling these conventions and the skillful ways he learned of modifying them.

The conventions applying to preludes and overtures afford a logical starting-point. There is no opera by Donizetti that does not start without some music, however brief, to precede the curtain's rise. Preludes and overtures are distinguishable on structural terms. A prelude is short, ranging from five measures (*Elvida*) to fifty-two (*La zingara* and *Dom Sébastien*). Preludes follow no set pattern, but they always end with a dominant pivot that leads without pause into the *introduzione*, and they are closely related harmonically to, or are even occasionally in the same key as, the *introduzione*. Overtures are longer and usually follow the basic Rossinian pattern – first movement form without development. They always end with a coda and a full set of cadential figures.

Donizetti did not always regard preludes and overtures as interchangeable options, although sometimes he did, for *L'ajo nell'imbarazzo, Le convenienze, Otto mesi, Maria Stuarda*,[1] *Marin Faliero*,

Betly and *Roberto Devereux* all began their careers with preludes which Donizetti later replaced with overtures. These substitutions took place when he revised a score or when he introduced it at an important theater. Although he sometimes replaced a shorter prelude with a longer overture, there is no instance of his reversing this procedure.[2]

Donizetti does not seem to have favored overtures over preludes at one phase of his career more than at another. The list of operas in which the *sinfonia*, to use the term he characteristically applied to his overtures, forms part of the original score covers a span from 1818 to 1843. In chronological order, these are: *Enrico di Borgogna, Una follia, Il falegname di Livonia, Zoraida di Granata, Chiara e Serafina, Alfredo il grande, Il fortunato inganno, Il borgomastro di Saardam, Alina, regina di Golconda, Il diluvio universale, Gianni di Parigi, Anna Bolena, Ugo, conte di Parigi* and *Parisina* sharing the same *sinfonia, Rosmonda d'Inghilterra, Gemma di Vergy, Poliuto* and *Les martyrs, La fille du régiment, La favorite, Adelia, Linda di Chamounix, Don Pasquale* and *Maria di Rohan*. The remaining forty-one operas in the Donizetti canon originally had preludes, of which only those in the seven works mentioned above were later replaced with overtures.

From the list in the preceding paragraph it is clear that genre was not a deciding factor with Donizetti in the choice between a prelude and an overture (nor was it with Rossini). An opera buffa, a semiseria or a tragedy may all begin with either; *L'elisir, Il furioso* and *Lucia* have preludes, while *Don Pasquale, Linda* and *La favorite* have overtures. Location undoubtedly played some part in his decision, particularly when he was writing for theaters outside Italy; then the principal consideration seems to have been the audience's expectations. Only three weeks before the prima of *Linda* did he discover that 'everybody is asking for an overture',[3] and so he revised the opening movement of his 1836 string quartet in E minor to fill that requirement. All the scores he composed for the Parisian theaters have overtures, with the exception of the very long *Dom Sébastien*. Among the operas he designed for the San Carlo, La Scala and the Fenice, for instance, there is no clear preponderance in favor of preludes or overtures. Clearly Donizetti did not regard a prelude as inferior per se to an overture. Two of his most popular operas, *Lucrezia Borgia* and *Lucia* begin with preludes, and I have seen no evidence to suggest that he ever considered changing them for something more formally elaborate.

The briefest preludes, such as those to *Elvida* and *La romanziera e l'uomo nero*, are short chordal sequences designed to warn the audience that the work was beginning (for at this period the auditorium was not darkened during a performance). Longer preludes have a further structure appended to the opening, 'audience-hushing' chords. The prelude to *L'elisir* begins with such a chordal sequence which is followed by a *larghetto* (forty measures) consisting, exceptionally,[4] of a theme and three variations; after a dominant pivot this leads directly into an orchestral statement (*allegro*) of the opening chorus. The prelude to *Tasso* begins with a brief insistence on the dominant in unharmonized octaves which is followed by thirty-three measures of *vivace* (this recurs in Act 3 when the chorus informs the poet that he is to be crowned poet laureate on the Campidoglio); the *vivace* leads directly into the *introduzione*.

Most of Donizetti's preludes, however, lie somewhere between the short chordal sequence and the extended forms encountered in *L'elisir* and *Tasso*. More usually they consist of a single tempo in which rhythmic and melodic ideas occur in balanced groupings. The rather brief prelude to *Il giovedì grasso* shows this pattern (Example 7). It suggests a miniature first section of an overture. The first idea moves from the tonic to the dominant minor; a second, more melodic, idea prolongs that tonality, and is followed by a closing sequence in the dominant major. Noteworthy here is the ambivalent (or interchangeable) use of major and minor modes that Donizetti so frequently exploits. Within the short compass of this prelude, he hints at the complication, intensification and resolution of a minuscule drama. Not all of Donizetti's preludes of the 1820s are as economically tidy as that to *Il giovedì grasso*. *Il paria* starts out with a prelude of twenty-three measures, in which, over a dominant pedal point, brief thematic ideas are put through sequential paces; its chief purpose is to build up a sort of agitated tension to contrast with the solemn and expansive *introduzione*. The prelude to *Il castello di Kenilworth*[5] creates a mood of ceremonial anticipation, having a theme in dotted rhythm set against a descending chromatic movement from the tonic (D minor) to the dominant that culminates in two *fortissimo* chords in the dominant before the *introduzione*.

In the 1830s Donizetti, responding to the increasing tide of Romanticism, turned more and more to atmospheric preludes, evoking the emotional states of his suffering characters. An early, and undeniably crude, example is supplied by *Sancia di Castiglia*: seven measures of *adagio non tanto* introduce twenty-seven of *allegro vivace*, consisting of agitated chordal sequences in which unprepared dissonances stab against a shuddering *tremolando*. Here

Example 7. *Il giovedì grasso*, prelude

Donizetti is attempting to work directly upon the nerves of his audience to depict immediately an atmosphere of strain and dread. This is more than a mere signal to the audience that a performance is beginning, nor is it the ordered presentation of a miniature drama in terms of exposition and logical working out of musical ideas.

The direction taken in *Sancia di Castiglia* finds its fulfillment in the preludes to *Lucrezia Borgia* and *Lucia*, though it is a big step from the emotional assault of the *Sancia* prelude to the succinct cohesive power of that to *Lucrezia*. Here an ominous drum roll is followed by a horn phrase, which the clarinet extends to form a dominant cadence and which becomes the principal idea of the prelude (Example 8). It recurs as a bass line (Example 8b) and in diminution

(a)

(b)

Example 8. *Lucrezia Borgia*, prelude

high in the violins over trombone chords. Then the oboe has a wailing figure which is immediately echoed two octaves lower by the trombone against harmonic shifts from dominant and subdominant to tonic; the accentuation of this oboe figure –  – is one that recurs when Lucrezia sings 'Gennaro' or 'mio figlio' at various points in the opera, and in view of Donizetti's sensitivity to verbal values it is not implausible to make that association. The thrice-repeated pairing of the oboe cry echoed by trombone catches the essence of the gothic strain in Romantic melodrama. After this the clarinet motif returns in diminution as a bass line, supporting a combination of the horn melody and the trombone chords, and a quiet echo of this idea provides a dominant pivot. To supply a transition between these thirty-three measures of *maestoso* and the jaunty homophonic *vivace* of the *introduzione*, Donizetti makes an *allegro crescendo* over a dominant pedal. The emotional atmosphere of the ensuing tragedy has been richly and economically evoked.

There are certain clear resemblances between the preludes to *Lucrezia* and *Lucia*: both are in the parallel (tonic) minor to the key of the opening chorus; and both start with a tonic timpani roll followed by a phrase for the horns. But there are far-reaching differences in form and tone between the two. In place of the (less common) *allegro* bridge that connects the prelude of *Lucrezia* to the *introduzione*, the prelude to *Lucia* ends (as is more usual) with a dominant seventh and a sententious pause, resolving straight into the opening chorus melody – *allegro giusto* 6/8. And instead of the restless thematic interplay that dominates the *Lucrezia* prelude, the prelude to *Lucia* evokes an air of solemn pathos, initiated by the dirge-like opening horn melody and broken only by the irruption of three unprepared *fortissimo* dissonances. At measure 22 there starts a funereal rythmic pattern (4/4: ♩ ♩ 𝄾 ♩♪ | ♩ ♩ 𝄾 etc.) that continues throughout the prelude; above it a solemn horn progression leads to a keening figure on flutes and clarinets in octaves. Where the prelude to *Lucrezia* prefigures the lethal plotting of that story, the prelude to *Lucia* is an elegiac anticipation of the heroine's hapless fate, set against flashing hints of the implacable forces that will destroy her. The raw energy of the *Sancia* prelude is replaced in these later works by a greater sense of power, deriving from the greater refinement and plasticity with which Donizetti worked his material. The preludes to *Lucrezia* and *Lucia* reveal his persuasiveness as a musical dramatist and demonstrate his ability to create an intense emotional atmosphere with relatively few strokes. No wonder he never thought of replacing these preludes with overtures.

Donizetti's *sinfonie* follow the general Rossinian format, but they rarely attain the note of irresistible brilliance and neatness that characterizes the overtures of his great precursor. On occasion Donizetti modifies the customary arrangement, but his modifications usually have antecedents in Rossini's practise. Donizetti's overtures open characteristically with a slow introduction; this establishes the tonic and moves on to the dominant which is often stressed by a pedal. The slow introduction is followed by a quick main section of two contrasting themes or thematic groups. The first of these is in the tonic and is usually motivic, sometimes using a rapid, infinitely extendible idea; this first theme or group ends with bare chords or cadential figures in the dominant. The second theme is apt to be more lyrical, its intrumentation usually contrasting with the orchestral color of the preceding material; given the prevailing character of this section Donizetti sometimes uses a melody that recurs later in the score, as is the case with his overtures to *Maria Stuarda* and *Roberto Devereux*. The concluding part of the second thematic group is worked up into a *crescendo*, utilizing a carefully regulated intensification of material and accretion of instruments in the Rossini manner. The quick main section (or exposition) is followed by a brief transition (instead of a development section) that leads back into the tonic for the recapitulation. At this point the usual procedure is sometimes varied. In the overture to *Anna Bolena* the transition reaches the subdominant, and the recapitulation begins in the key of the flattened leading-tone – C major in relation to the tonic D – moving into the parallel minor of the tonic in what is only a partial restatement of the opening material; the tonic is not re-established until the return of the second thematic group. Usually, however, in the recapitulation all the material reappears in the tonic, although the opening group may be condensed. At the end of the recapitulation the cadential figures that conclude the exposition are repeated, now to introduce the coda, usually at a brisker tempo. The coda normally contains new motivic material, often supported by scalar figures in the bass; it culminates in the final cadential sequence in the tonic.

Although in his overtures Donizetti rarely loses sight of the Rossinian prototype, as with his handling of other conventional devices he achieves considerable variety, but by availing himself of solutions already employed by Rossini. The overture to *L'ajo*, for example, conforms to the prototype quite closely, but even in so early a work Donizetti was experimenting, for the first thematic unit is shortened at its return in the recapitulation.[6] Least Rossinian of the early overtures is that to *Il borgomastro di Saardam*, where the main *allegro* section is all but monothematic. A useful example of Donizetti's adapting the form to his purposes in the early 1830s is provided by the overture that served for both *Ugo, conte di Parigi* and *Parisina* (its doing double duty is another Rossinian echo). The introduction, marked *cantabile*, in E minor, runs to forty measures; the first thematic group, beginning in E major, has a tendency to move to B minor, giving the impression that the second group is simultaneously in a parallel major and dominant relationship to the first. The transition to the recapitulation is built of fragments of the first group, sequentially treated; the recapitulation itself omits the second part of the first group, which recurs only in the coda (*più allegro*). Not the least of the attractions of this overture is the brief suggestion of formal ambiguity supplied by the presentation of material in positions where one would not strictly expect it.

The overture to *Adelia* is markedly asymmetrical.[7] Dispensing with a slow introduction, it opens with an *allegro giusto* in D major, establishing a rhythmic pattern (2/4: ♩ ♪♪♩ ♩) over an extended dominant pedal; upon these the first theme is superimposed. The *crescendo*, instead of dealing with material that comprises the second part of the second thematic group, is built upon the opening, giving the exposition an *a b a* pattern. Like the overture to *Anna Bolena*, also in D major, the *Adelia* overture has a transition that ends in the subdominant and a recapitulation that starts in the key of the flattened leading-tone. The recapitulation is both abridged and foreshortened, and the order of the ideas in the first group is altered. Like the *Ugo–Parisina* overture, the coda is introduced by a thematic allusion to the opening group and brings back the opening rhythmic pattern. The overture to *Adelia* is structurally one of Donizetti's most interesting because of its asymmetry enriched by a wealth of motivic cross-reference.

In the overture to *La fille du régiment*, Marie's regimental song, 'Chacun le sait', provides the melody of the second subject and the coda, creating the pattern *a b c a b d b*. In that to *Poliuto* (and *Les martyrs*), with its opening for four bassoons, the 'conversion' duet, 'Il suon dell'arpe angeliche', serves as second subject only in the exposition; in the recapitulation its place is taken by a choral passage, with a change of tempo to *larghetto*, which produces a striking and original effect. Donizetti re-uses the choral passage in Act 1 as Poliuto's baptismal hymn, and takes from it thematic material for the prelude to the final scene in Poliuto's prison cell. The only other nineteenth-century Italian opera with the same type of choral episode as part of its overture is Rossini's *Ermione*.[8] Elsewhere, the nearest approach to the same effect is to be found in the overture to Meyerbeer's *Dinorah* (also known as *Le pardon de Ploërmel*; Paris, 1859); this contains the hymn 'Sainte Marie' which recurs at the denouement of the opera to set a seal upon the final happy resolution of the plot. Less similar to Donizetti's effect is the choral participation in the overture to Gounod's *Roméo et Juliette*; here the curtain rises to show the chorus and principles who intone lines equivalent to those of the sonnet that forms the prologue to Shakespeare's play (Gounod does not re-use this material later in the work). Quite different from Donizetti's choral hymn are those in the prologues to Boito's *Mefistofele* and Mancinelli's *Ero e Leandro* (to a libretto by Boito); in both these cases the overture connects directly with a complex, multiform dramatic episode for solo voice and chorus interacting, which is played with the curtain up.

The two overtures Donizetti wrote for Vienna are among his finest achievements in this form. That to *Linda di Chamounix* is derived from the opening movement of his eighteenth string quartet and has a development section forty measures in length, prefaced by eight measures of transition. In the recapitulation the second half of the second group reappears not in the relative major as in the exposition, but in the parallel major, which is also the key of the extended coda, marked *vivace*. The second of Donizetti's Viennese overtures, that to *Maria di Rohan*, stands as his finest accomplishment in this form. No other example contains more thematic and harmonic cross-reference; the recurrence of ideas in modified form gives this overture an unusual coherence, but, more importantly, creates a forward propulsion that the sonatina pattern[9] with its predictable repetitions does not always possess. After a six-measure *allegro* of solemn trombone octaves with timpani punctuation, there are fifty-six measures of *larghetto* in ternary form (*a b a'*), concluding with a transitional passage (*a²*) over a dominant pedal. The middle section of the ternary form (in C sharp minor), while it does not directly quote a melody that recurs later, can readily be interpreted as anticipating the openings of two later arias: Maria's Act 1 'Cupa, fatal mestizia' and the tenor's Act 2 'Alma soave e cara'. The exposition opens with a coiling scalar figure, ascending in the minor but descending in the major, that recurs in the brief prelude to Act 3; here it forms a neat contrast to its attractive pendant for the woodwinds (Example 9). The transition between the two thematic groups of the exposition harks back to the introduction. The coda to this overture provides a true climax rather than an emphatic tailpiece, as is so often the coda's function. Its special nature is indicated by the introduction of a new melodic idea that recurs in Act 3 to Maria's despairing phrase 'Ah, più non avanza alcuna speranza' in her duet with Chevreuse. Then, in measures 267–9 a harmonic sequence unfolds – C⁷, F, D⁷, G, E, (a), F⁷, B flat, A – which encapsulates the cycles of fourths, thirds and half-tones that undergird much of the earlier structure. The only shortcoming of this interesting overture is Donizetti's unselective scoring of the tuttis; the resulting doublings give such passages an unattractive blatancy. But this reservation aside, the overture to *Maria di Rohan* is a significant achievement, not only for the skill with which it is formed but for its powerful foreshadowing of the tragedy that follows.

'Introduzione' is a term used in Italian operas during the first half of the nineteenth century to mean the piece or pieces that followed the

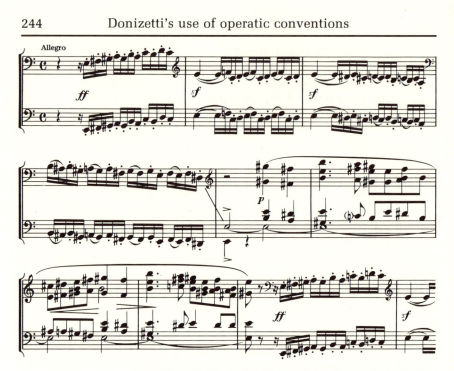

Example 9. *Maria di Rohan*, overture

rise of the curtain and launched the exposition of the plot. Musically the *introduzione* could include a wide variety of forms, but its essential dramatic function remained constant. There was a rule of thumb in those days that the *introduzione* lasted until the first passage of recitative, but there are exceptions to this principle.

Generally speaking Donizetti favored three types of *introduzione*. The simplest of these is the introductory chorus, often beginning as a dialogue between two choral groups, one questioning, the other answering, which then combine as a unit for the main choral period; in some examples a soloist is introduced. This type is clearly set off from the rest of the score by the rubric 'dopo l'introduzione' placed over the succeeding section. The second type is a compound unit made up of episodes in a variety of tempos, sometimes with changes of meter as well; it is restricted almost exclusively to the short comic works of the 1820s. It brings on stage some of the characters (as in *I pazzi per progetto*, and *Le convenienze* where all but one are involved), building up gradually; the assembling personnel function as a chamber chorus (as in *Il giovedì grasso*) or are sometimes reinforced by the chorus itself (as in *La zingara*). There is little ambiguity about the extent of these compound openings as they are characteristically followed by a burst of spoken dialogue. By the time of *L'elisir d'amore* (1832) the comic *introduzione* had come to combine a series of discrete numbers without recitative; this pattern is common in Donizetti's Italian works after 1830, though it is anticipated in *Il castello di Kenilworth* and *Imelda,* and shows his concern for building a briskly forward-moving entity out of the whole opening episode up to the first curtain.

The five serious operas Donizetti wrote for Paris and Vienna – *Les martyrs, La favorite, Linda,* [10] *Maria di Rohan* and *Dom Sébastien* – all conform to the first and simplest type of *introduzione,* an opening chorus. Donizetti's experiments in creating dramatic momentum by extending the *introduzione* through several composite numbers seem to be confined to works intended for Italian stages; evidence of this is supplied by *Caterina Cornaro,* a score he wrote for Naples during the years of his activity in Paris and Vienna, where the first four numbers of the score are entitled: 1. 'Preludio ed Introduzione'; 2. 'Duettino'; 3. 'Scena e Cavatina'; 4. 'Seguito e Stretta dell'Introduzione'. On the other hand, however, the simplest type of *introduzione* is not restricted among Donizetti's late works to those intended for performance outside Italy: in *Maria Padilla* (La Scala, 1841) the *introduzione* consists simply of the opening mixed chorus. [11]

An economic fact of life helps to account for the persistence of numbers in Donizetti's scores, even when they really form episodes in a compound structure, as in the *introduzione* to *Caterina Cornaro.* The music-publishers of that day earned an appreciable proportion of their profits from the sale of individual excerpts to an eager public of musical amateurs. This financial concern is reflected in the widespread use of a system of double pagination – one sequence for the whole score and separate sequences for each number – and, further, in the frequently occurring direction that 'anyone wishing to perform the opera entire should omit the final two measures', as the editors in such cases supplied cadences to round off numbers that the composer intended to succeed one another without interruption.

Since the third of the *introduzione* patterns is properly an extension of the first, it is possible to find some common characteristics in a number of Donizetti's opening choruses. Up through the time of *Lucia* the opening chorus is usually written for male voices alone, but in later works Donizetti often uses a mixed chorus. All his serious French operas, including the incomplete *Le duc d'Albe,* open with a male chorus, but this procedure was not then de rigueur at the

Opéra, since Auber's *La muette*, and Meyerbeer's *Robert* and *Les Huguenots* all begin with interaction between solo voices and chorus. For Paris Donizetti followed the example of Rossini, each of whose serious works for the Opéra begins with a choral unit.[12]

A simple but somewhat surprising chorus follows the *sinfonia* in *Belisario*. It consists of a main melodic period, *a b a* [1], totalling twenty-two measures, followed by a coda (fourteen measures) and an orchestral ritornello (twelve measures). The coda and the ritornello together are actually longer than the main period, suggesting that Donizetti abridged, or made a conscious choice not to compose, a chorus of balanced proportions in which the main period of the existing chorus would have formed the opening episode; here Donizetti clearly dispensed with formal symmetry to achieve dramatic impetus, and one can only suppose that he regarded the repetitive intensifications of the coda as an adequate counterpoise to the terse choral melody. The autograph of *Anna Bolena*[13] may help to explain Donizetti's procedure in *Belisario*: it shows that Donizetti first composed and later cut almost fifty measures from the opening chorus to *Anna*, and the deleted material is precisely a middle episode and a repetition of the opening (surviving) episode, leaving only the initial choral period followed directly by an extensive coda. Again Donizetti chose to place greater weight on forward movement than on leisurely formal balance. The opening chorus of *Belisario* is introduced by two unaccompanied vocal phrases sung off stage, while that to *Anna* has a lengthy orchestral introduction; the latter feature tends to make the chorus seem more asymmetrical as the introduction implies a choral section more ample than that which actually follows.

These unequally proportioned designs not only show Donizetti living up to the ideal of *brevità* that he so often urged on his librettists, but they are of considerable dramatic and aesthetic importance. Asymmetry, as opposed to regular formal balance, was attractive to the Romantic sensibilities of the 1830s, and it seems likely that the audiences of those days found these choruses refreshingly up-to-date.[14] The choral codas stress dramatic intensification through their quickened tempo, their heightened accentuation and their raised dynamic level, which combine to create a sense of emphatic affirmation and conviction. When in modern performances of Donizetti's operas conductors truncate these codas and their cadential figures, put off by what seems a succession of naive musical formulas unacceptable to contemporary taste, they extinguish their musico-dramatic function. Clearly, the composer had a purpose in writing extended codas, even if in time he came to curtail the cadential sequences.[15]

In *Ugo, conte di Parigi* and *Sancia di Castiglia* Donizetti extends the *introduzione* beyond the opening chorus to allow interaction between a single character and a group of courtiers. *Ugo* has the simpler, less satisfactory plan of the two: the male courtiers express their hopes for the new French king, Luigi V, in 'No, che in ciel de' Carolingi'; this is followed, without any introductory recitative,[16] by Folco's ominous cavatina, 'Vani voti', and the episode is completed by the return of the courtiers, accompanied now by their ladies, to repeat the opening chorus. The *Ugo* chorus is strikingly asymmetrical: fifty-eight measures of choral coda are appended to a thirty-measure main period, a ratio of nearly 2 : 1. While Donizetti establishes a brief sense of formal ambiguity by having the coda begin with the same melody as the main period (as though it were a second strophe), before it veers off on new harmonic paths, he divides the six-line text of this passage in such a way that the different functions are clear: the main period sets the first four lines without any repetitions, while the coda sets the final two lines with much reiteration. Even if the opening of the coda is regarded as an abbreviated second strophe, the remainder still equals the length of what precedes it – yet another indication that Donizetti did not regard codas as small tails to wag at the ends of larger forms.

The *introduzione* to *Sancia* consists of an opening chorus, a recitative dialogue between Ircano (bass) and the courtiers, a second chorus which is not a repetition of the earlier one, and a concluding double aria for Ircano. The first chorus has something of the ambiguity noted at the same point in *Ugo;* the coda begins as though it were a second strophe, but this brief episode (only twenty-eight measures) is nearly the same length as the main period. This ambiguity is missing from the second chorus, which is more traditional in its proportions, having a main period of thirty-two measures followed by a coda of twenty measures. These two choruses, taken as a unit, form a rough equivalent of a double aria, the recitative dialogue functioning as a *tempo di mezzo;* viewed in this way they may be seen as creating a forward impulse preferable to the stasis in *Ugo,* where the second chorus is merely a repetition of the first. Ircano's cabaletta has an unconventional design since it is not a solo, nor are its two statements identical.

Cabaletta (Ircano, Rodrigo, chorus): 'Rodrigo, va consiglio' (*moderato*)

first statement: Ircano (16 measures)
                Rodrigo (12 measures)

transition: chorus, with phrases for Ircano and Rodrigo (11 measures)
second statement: Ircano, with phrases for Rodrigo and chorus (16 measures)
coda (più allegro): combined forces (6 measures)
ritornello and cadences: orchestra (6 measures)

This irregular cabaletta produces a powerful sonic climax to the opening scene, the shortened second statement adding impetus and culminating in the heightened rhythmic and harmonic energy of the coda. It is somewhat dismaying, then, to discover that this introduzione is followed by three pages of recitative, ending with the defiant Rodrigo alone; for a ritornello there is a quotation of his melody from the first statement of the cabaletta. Musically, if not dramatically, this concluding recitative defuses the tension that has accrued throughout the introduzione.

In Lucia Donizetti perfected the pattern he had striven to establish in Sancia di Castiglia, with the dramatic momentum growing steadily from the opening chorus to the end of the scene.[17] The first, male, chorus in the parallel major to the prelude uses the comprimario Normanno as a chorus-leader; the second chorus, 'Come vinti di stanchezza', in the same key as the first, forms part of the materia di mezzo[18] between Enrico's two arias, instead of coming before the bass's cavatina, as in Sancia. Unlike Ircano's cabaletta, Enrico's 'La pietade in suo favore' consists of two statements identical except that the second is reinforced by phrases for Raimondo and the chorus, and it is followed by a coda equal in length to each statement; this produces the highest sonic point of the scene, which ends without any concluding recitative. While there is an interchange of recitative before Enrico's cavatina, Donizetti uses such incisive accompanying and punctuating figures and frequent passages of arioso that he keeps the scene advancing and building up. He evidently regarded the introduzione as carrying through to the end of Enrico's aria.

Donizetti experiments with other patterns of introduzione, some of them undeniably effective, but none perhaps equalling the release of dramatic energy in the opening of Lucia. In Il castello di Kenilworth, for instance, he introduces Lambourne in a dialogue with the chorus, which is followed by a double aria for the tenor without a tempo di mezzo and without participation from the others; the scene concludes with an extended concertato (practically a second cabaletta) of almost the same dimensions as the opening episode and in the same key. While there is a sense of formal balance here, the disparity of the ingredients impedes the regular building of tension.

Both *Anna Bolena* and *Il furioso* have a compound *introduzione* that ends with an aria for the leading characters, the attendant personnel reinforcing the coda. In *Fausta* there is a large-scale, multiform *introduzione* with the dimensions of a finale–concertato. It begins with a victory hymn, 'Dio dell'armi', sung by Fausta, Beroë, Costantino, Massimiano and mixed chorus, which has a second period for Massimiano and his conspirators (shades of *Un ballo!*); this is followed by a solo prayer for Fausta, 'Dio che siedi in terzo cielo', which serves as a middle section preceding an expanded and altered restatement of the victory hymn as Crispo and his army return. Crispo's request for Beroë's hand then precipitates a canon *a quattro* (*larghetto*, 6/8, A flat major) which is rounded off by a full-scale stretta (*allegro*, 4/4, C minor/C major); the finale concludes with exit music in the form of a reprise of the march, marked 'il tempo la metà più lento' (half as slow as the preceding stretta). In *Gemma di Vergy* an opening dialogue chorus, like those of *Il castello di Kenilworth* and *Parisina*, is followed by a double aria; during the *andante* of the aria the main vocal melody is set off against a whispered conversation between the *comprimario* bass and the chorus (about the exploits of Jeanne d'Arc), creating a simultaneous presentation of foreground and background, unlike the usual series of episodes that each have a single emphasis. In the variety of his *introduzioni* there is clear evidence of Donizetti's restless search for greater dramatic immediacy.

One of the conventions that exerted a strong influence upon Donizetti's scores through most of his career was that pertaining to the prima donna's cherished perquisites: her *aria di sortita* at her first appearance and her aria–finale at the end. During the years of Rossini's Italian career (to 1823) this convention was not as firmly established as it would later be; it lasted into the 1840s. In *Elisabetta* the heroine's initial and final appearances are fully served (the role was written for Colbran); but in Rossini's later operas he does not automatically grant the prima donna either or both these favors: Semiramide has neither, Elena in *La donna del lago* has only a cavatina at her first appearance but is given a full-scale scena at the end, and Zelmira starts out with a duet and finishes with her full complement. Clearly around 1820 the final position was regarded as the more important of the two. Two further aspects of Rossini's practise are relevant here. In *La Cenerentola* he moved away from the earlier convention of ending an opera buffa with a moralizing ensemble when he allowed Cenerentola a final *rondò*.[19] In those serious operas, such as *Tancredi* and *Semiramide*, where a contralto (*musico*) is the hero, this character is given the prominence of a full-scale *aria di sortita* in the middle of the opening act; but when *musico* roles began to lose favor during the later 1820s this opportunity was customarily annexed by the prima donna.

In the first of Donizetti's operas to be publicly performed, *Enrico di Borgogna*, his prima donna Eckerlin was a *musico*, taking the title role, and he supplied her with both an *aria di sortita* and an aria–finale. From the start of his career he recognized that a well-disposed prima donna exerted a powerful positive influence on behalf of an opera at its crucial *prima*. In the 1824 revision of *Zoraida di Granata* the title role was demoted to second place by the composition of a new florid *rondò* for the contralto Pisaroni in the *musico* role of Abenamet; the *rondò* replaced a moralizing ensemble, and its inclusion produces an imbalance between the two principal roles. Although after this Donizetti was to write other *musico* roles, he was never again to give this type of character such prominence.

In *Alfredo il grande* the prima donna participates in the *introduzione*, but she has no major vocal opportunity until the end of the score. (*Alfredo* was written as a vehicle for the tenor Nozzari, then near the end of his glorious career, and this accounts for the little prominence accorded to the prima donna in the score.) In the 1824 version of *Emilia di Liverpool*, the title role contained only one full-scale aria, directly after the *introduzione*, and the work ended with a *finaletto*; but in the 1828 revision her part was given greater prominence by the moving of her *aria di sortita* to follow the first change of scene and the addition at the conclusion of a *maestoso* and *rondò*, both borrowed from the corresponding point in *Alahor in Granata*. It was between the two versions of *Emilia* that the convention of including both these display pieces for the prima donna had begun to make its greatest impact.

Elvida is Donizetti's only one-act serious opera, and maybe because of its limited length the heroine has her double aria directly following the *introduzione*; also, she is forced to share the final *rondò*, which is, exceptionally, in duet form.[20] For *Le convenienze* in its original one-act form, Donizetti borrowed Elvida's *aria di sortita* and inserted it, as an episode, into the *introduzione*, which ends with a brief *finaletto*. *Olivo e Pasquale* (1827), *Il borgomastro* (1827), and *Gianni di Calais* (1828) all give the prima donna her expected due with both an entrance aria and an aria–finale. That Donizetti was beginning to chafe at this convention, particularly at the end of the opera, is clearly shown by the letter he wrote to Mayr after the success of the trio–finale to Act 1 of *L'esule di Roma:* 'Next year I will finish a first act with a quartet and the second act with a death, according to my intention. I want to shake off the yoke of the finales.'[21] This implies that Donizetti associated the final *rondò* with the jubilation of the happy ending and it is clear that he longed to get his teeth into stronger, more tragic meat.

With *Il paria* (1829) Donizetti did not fulfill all the hopes he had expressed to Mayr, but he did end the score with an extended quartet which gives no more prominence to the soprano than to the three male parts. The prima donna of *Il paria* was Adelaide Tosi, and if she felt that Donizetti had short-changed her by giving her only an *aria di sortita*, she was recompensed in the next role he wrote for her: Elisabetta in *Il castello di Kenilworth.* This is the first of his serious operas with two important female roles, and the division of their labor sheds some light on the relative positions of prima donna and seconda donna in the late 1820s. The latter, in the role of Amelia, is the first to appear, and her contribution consists of a duet with Warney, a duet with Leicester, a duet with the prima donna at the close of Act 2 which develops into a quartet, and a full-scale double aria, which does not occur until the middle of Act 3. Elisabetta has pride of place with both an *aria di sortita* and an aria–finale; otherwise she participates only in the duet–quartet sequence that ends Act 2, where hers is the upper and more brilliant line, and in a duet with Leicester at the opening of Act 3. *Il castello di Kenilworth*, with only nine numbers, is perhaps the shortest of Donizetti's full-length operas;[22] the pre-eminence of Elisabetta's role derives from (besides her royal station) the position of her elaborate arias – both of them preceded by a choral buildup – rather than from the total number of notes. *Il castello di Kenilworth* confirms that by 1829 the claims of the prima donna as to the number and position of her showpieces was fully established.

This convention is observed in many of Donizetti's serious operas written for Italy after the late 1820s, for instance, in *Anna Bolena, Ugo, Sancia, Il furioso, Parisina, Maria Stuarda, Gemma, Belisario, Pia, Roberto Devereux, Adelia* and *Maria Padilla.*[23] More illuminating than these corroborative examples, however, are the exceptions, for they show Donizetti's quest for greater dramatic power and impetus. Lucrezia Borgia's *aria di sortita*, 'Com'è bello', originally had only a single movement, one reason why Méric-Lalande, who sang the role at the *prima*, insisted that Donizetti write her a final cabaletta; but when in 1840 Donizetti managed to insert the *finale nuovo*, emphasizing the dying Gennaro and eliminating the disputed cabaletta, he made amends to Erminia Frezzolini, the Lucrezia of that production, by adding a cabaletta, 'Sì, volli il primo a cogliere', to her *aria di sortita*. The original arrangement at this point, the aria being immediately followed by a full-scale duet with the tenor, made for better dramatic progress.

In *Lucia* there is a double set of aria–finales, with Lucia's (the mad scene) preceding Edgardo's. One of Donizetti's letters reveals that this arrangement irked Persiani considerably while *Lucia* was in rehearsal,[24] although the work's incontrovertible success soon reconciled her to her absence from the stage during the final scene. In *Anna Bolena* there is a similar situation, although here the prima donna has pride of place in the matter of the aria–finale; it is interesting to see that Donizetti was even-handed with Pasta and Rubini, for it is the tenor's *aria di sortita* that occupies the important position at the beginning of the second scene, while the soprano's equivalent has been moved back to form the climax of the compound *introduzione*.

In *L'assedio di Calais,* as he confessed,[25] Donizetti was attempting an opera *alla francese,* and so the traditional deployment of the prima donna goes by the board. The plot, centering upon the patriotic efforts of the burghers to spare their city from the English, makes female roles secondary in importance. In point of fact there are three: Aurelio, the son of the mayor of Calais, a mezzo *musico* role, and Aurelio's wife, Eleonora, and the Queen of England, both sopranos. Aurelio has a full-scale aria, 'Al mio core, oggetti amati', at his second entrance in Act 1 (his earlier appearance consists of extensive pantomimed action during the *introduzione*). The original ending of the opera was not a *rondò,* for Aurelio or for anyone else, but a concertato. In 1837, the year after the *prima,* Donizetti inserted into this concluding ensemble a *rondò,* 'Questo pianto', seeking to make the score conform more to current Italian taste; it is assigned not to Aurelio, but to the soprano Eleonora, Aurelio's wife, whose participation up to this point is confined to two duets. In the revised version of *L'assedio,* therefore, the prima donna's traditional moments for vocal honors are shared between two singers. Possibly it was this division of labor that led later prima donnas to ignore this moving score.

Like *L'assedio, Poliuto* was composed with more than half an eye on Paris. Paolina has a double aria at her entrance midway through Act 1, but instead of a final solo she participates in the 'conversion' duet, which occurs just before the final tableau of the martyrdom in the Circus. When this score was converted into *Les martyrs* for the

Opéra, Donizetti retained the ending, but he moved further from the Italian convention by dividing Paolina's entrance arias into two discrete solos: the cantabile remains in Act 1, while the cabaletta was moved to the end of the first scene of Act 2.

The dramatic norms, established and maintained chiefly by Scribe that obtained during the days of Donizetti's activities in Paris, dictated that the final moments of the action be occupied by a coup de théâtre, as in *Les martyrs* and *Dom Sébastien*, or by a final duet in which one of the lovers dies, as in *La favorite*, rather than by the solo apotheosis with attendant figures then popular in Italy. The Italian tradition of Romantic endings, on the other hand, was a carry-over from the days of the supremacy of the *lieto fine*, but it had proved adaptable to tragic endings with their emphasis on suffering and death, often preceding an expected reunion in heaven – in effect, a delayed happy ending.

In France, furthermore, there was no particular feeling of obligation to give the heroine an entrance aria. When Paolina became Pauline she retained only half of hers. Léonor in *La favorite* was to have had one, an *allegretto*, 'Sous le ciel de cette île' (Example 10), as a manuscript in the Bibliothèque de l'Opéra shows, but it was replaced before the premiere by her duet with Fernand, 'Mon idole'. At Zaïda's first entrance in *Dom Sébastien*, she has a single aria that develops into a concertato, 'Ô mon Dieu sur la terre'. At no point in the original score has Zaïda anything like a double aria, but when the opera was introduced to Vienna in 1845, in Leo Herz's German translation, Donizetti added to Act 2 a second aria to follow 'Sol adorée de la patrie'; this cabaletta, 'So mög denn Gott die Sünde' (Example 11), is a fine vigorous aria for a mezzo-soprano with an easy high B flat and considerable agility; (it has been dropped from the Ricordi scores of *Don Sebastiano*).

Donizetti's Viennese operas, *Linda di Chamounix* and *Maria di Rohan*, lie somewhat closer than the Parisian works to his native conventions, as they were composed for the Italian seasons at the Kärntnertortheater; however, neither ends with a solo scene for the title character – evidence that here at least Donizetti had 'shaken off the yoke of the finales'. Indeed, Linda did not originally have even an *aria di sortita*, but that lack, or half of it at least, was soon filled with 'O luce di quest'anima', which Donizetti added for Persiani when *Linda* was first given at the Théâtre-Italien. *Linda* ends with a duet–finale. By contrast, *Maria di Rohan* has a double aria, 'Cupa, fatal mestizia' and 'Ben ful il giorno' at her first appearance, but her second double aria (the cabaletta of which was added only in 1843

Example 10. *La favorite*, Act 1 scene ii, Léonor's suppressed *aria di sortita*

ZAÏDA

So mög____ dennGott die Sün - de an mei - nem eig-nen Glük-ke

rä - chen! mein ar - mes Herz kann bre - chen____

doch__ ihm, dem Theu-ren ent - sag'____ ich nie!

Example 11. *Dom Sébastien* (German version), Act 2 scene i, cabaletta
added to Zaïda's aria

for Paris) occurs early in Act 3, as the melodramatic conclusion of the plot does not allow for an aria–finale. At the very end, Maria's participation is as an actress rather than a singer; the final stage direction bids her 'fall on her knees, looking toward heaven, her hands joined'.

A survey of the conventions relating to the prima donna's arias permits a view, from one angle, of Donizetti's whole career and practise, since the tradition was at its height during the period of his greatest activity. But these arias exercised a conservative restraint upon musical form and dramatic structure; as if to counteract this, through much of his composing life Donizetti worked to expand the expressive potential of duets. The broad spectrum of dramatic situations possible for duets appealed to his strong theatrical sense, and they came to occupy an increasingly important place in his designs. It is consistent with the rising tide of Romanticism in Italian opera during the 1830s and the growing emphasis on melodramatic elements that new prominence should be placed upon duets, especially those of confrontation.

Duets for two women's voices are relatively uncommon in Donizetti's output, partly because before *Il castello di Kenilworth* (1829) he wrote no operas with two important female roles, and partly because in many later scores that had this distribution he found other means of bringing them into conjunction – as in *Maria Stuarda* where the two queens confront one another and exchange insults during the *materia di mezzo* of the finale to Act 2. Two striking exceptions to this general observation are provided by the encounter between Anna Bolena and Seymour and the brilliant duet for the sisters in *Maria Padilla,* which may serve to mark the opposite poles of the musico-dramatic spectrum for duets.[26]

The duet for Anna and Seymour near the beginning of Act 2 is a dramatic interaction with surprisingly little overlapping of the voices until the final coda. The scene begins with Anna's praying alone; Seymour enters bringing Enrico's message that the queen must confess in order to save her life, which prompts Anna's outburst and her prediction that her ghost will haunt the King and his new consort. Seymour's poignant confession, which follows, moves Anna to decide that her rival is the less guilty party, and culminates in the joint expression of Anna's compassion and Seymour's remorse. Donizetti resisted the temptation to treat this text as a traditional double aria *a due,* with exchanges of identical material and cadenzas, and concentrated on greater dramatic immediacy. Up to Seymour's confession the dialogue proceeds in alternating passages of flexible arioso and accompanied recitative. In the first period of Seymour's revelation (*larghetto*, G major) her phrases are four syllables long, set off by rests, and marked by falling endings, moving into the parallel minor; the second period conveys passionate intensity by repeating three times a short motivic idea, its urgency increased by the raised fourth (C sharp) and by its syncopated rise to a more expansive phrase (Example 12) – a melodic idea that Donizetti would often resort to again, for instance during Lucrezia's 'M'odi, ah m'odi'. During this scene Anna has two grandiloquent outbursts, scalar passages with punctuating chordal accompaniment: the first occurs when she calls down divine wrath upon her still unidentified rival and the second when she bids Seymour rise so that she may absolve her of the chief share of blame; it is the second of these that introduces Anna's 'Va, infelice' (*moderato*, C major), which balances Seymour's confession and is related to it by its detached phrases and upward chromatic resolutions. Seymour begins the coda (*più mosso*), 'Ah, peggiore è il tuo perdono', with a phrase reminiscent of that in which she earlier confessed her remorse to Enrico in Act 1. This duet with its clear dramatic progression, its interrelationships heightened by motivic and rhythmic echoes, is one of the highpoints of *Anna Bolena*, revealing Donizetti's efforts to escape from formal convention toward dramatic truth.

The duet of the heroine and her sister Ines in *Maria Padilla* is constructed along more conventional lines. Deeply upset that her father may have cursed her for her liaison with King Pedro, Maria questions her sister about his state of mind, revealing her own unhappiness, and then to Ines's joy, resolves to lay bare her heart to him. The two main sections of the duet are a *larghetto* (C sharp minor) and an *allegretto* in the relative major. The opening period of the *larghetto* adds to almost every measure a restless cello figure that depicts Maria's uneasiness. This tempo presents the voices in dialogue form, only overlapping at the end of an occasional phrase; it shifts into the parallel major at Ines's sympathetic rejoinder. As the emotional temperature rises, Maria's melodic line becomes increasingly florid until it bristles with thirty-second-note scales, more lavish than any roulades in the *Anna Bolena* duet; here Donizetti was writing for Sofia Löwe, who was oriented toward the high tensions of Romantic melodrama, while in *Anna Bolena* he shaped his vocal line for the more dignified, less nervous art of Pasta. Maria

Example 12. *Anna Bolena*, Act 2 scene i, *larghetto* of the Anna–Seymour duet

begins the coda (Example 13) with phrases that show a stylistic
kinship to the *Anna Bolena* duet (see Example 12); more than a
decade after *Anna Bolena* Donizetti still created a sense of emotional
urgency by similar means, ending the phrase with a chromatic upward appoggiatura and following it immediately by an upward
interval of an accented second beat that introduces a descending

MARIA

To - gli-mi a es - tre - ma   or - ri - bil___ te - ma: di', nel fu -

ro - re   di   su - a ven - det - ta dal   ge - ni - to - re,   fui_ ma - le - det - ta?

Example 13. *Maria Padilla*, Act 2, *larghetto* of the Maria–Ines duet

phrase. This coda leads into the *tempo di mezzo* without any full
cadence. The cabaletta is a jaunty coloratura showpiece, written
throughout for the voices *a due*, most often in thirds. If there is any
dramatic justification for this abrupt change of emotional climate, it
could be Maria's unstable temperament, her febrile excitement. But
even the staunchest devotee of Donizetti's operas must admit that
this cabaletta (originally part of a duet for Léonor and Alphonse in
La favorite which Donizetti dropped from that score), for all its vocal
effectiveness, does not fit into its new context without a dismaying
wrench of mood.

While 4/4 common meter was conventional in cabalettas before
1830, Donizetti would employ other patterns especially when he
wanted to depict an aberrant mental state, as in the waltz movement
that concludes Lucia's mad scene or the 6/8 meter he employs in the
duet for the Padilla sisters. An earlier duet for two sisters, Bianca and
Adelia in *Ugo, conte di Parigi*, written for two sopranos, has for its
slow section, like the example from *Maria Padilla*, a *larghetto* in
dialogue that ends without a full cadence; but then, instead of the
usual *tempo di mezzo* before the cabaletta, there follow solo statements for both characters in turn, climaxed by a third statement *a
due* – a plan that Rossini had exploited earlier. In Donizetti's operas
the most familiar example of this format occurs in the 'Veranno a te'

section of the heroine's duet with Edgardo at the end of Act 1 of *Lucia*, where, in the joint statement, the voices sing in unison not harmony.

The simplest structure Donizetti employs for duets is a single movement, without even a preliminary recitative. The best-known example of this type is 'Tornami a dir' (*larghetto*, 6/8) from the final scene of *Don Pasquale*, with the voices chiefly *a due* in a miniature ternary form with coda. A duet of identical length occurs during the *introduzione* of *Caterina Cornaro*, but here the internal form is more free. The similarity between the opening measures of these duets is very marked (Example 14), and since they were composed within

Example 14a. *Don Pasquale*, Act 3 scene ii, *larghetto* of the Norina–
Ernesto duet

months of each other it seems not unwarranted to regard them as alternate workings out of the same number.[27] An antecedent for this sort of vocal writing can be found in *La favorite*, in the concluding section, 'O mon amour' ('Ah, l'alto ardor'), of the duet for Léonor and Alphonse that begins 'Dans ce palais' ('In questo suolo'); although even shorter than the examples from *Don Pasquale* and *Caterina* it is cut from the same piece of cloth, but here the low tessitura of the mezzo part gives the passage a vivid sensuality.

In *Poliuto* the 'conversion' duet just before the final tableau in the circus is the dramatic climax of the whole score, a prime example of the increasing importance Donizetti places upon these confronta-

Example 14b. *Caterina Cornaro*, prologue, *larghetto* of the Caterina–
Gerardo duet

tions in his later works. Paolina has come to Poliuto in prison to tell him that he may save his life by renouncing Christianity in favor of the old religion, but his confident refusal to risk his immortal soul so moves her that she declares her readiness to share his belief and his fate. The *larghetto* (E minor/E major) consists of four periods: Paolina's plea, Poliuto's proclamation of faith, her growing conviction that he is unafraid, and her declaration that she adores a God that could endow him with such radiance; the fourth period is then repeated in dialogue. As in examples already discussed, the voices do not overlap in the *larghetto* and the coda leads directly into the *tempo di mezzo* without a full cadence. Much of the time the diction moves syllabically, Paolina breaking into *gruppetti* of thirty-second notes only as she describes the shining strength of Poliuto's faith. The cabaletta, 'Il suon dell'arpe angeliche', (*allegro vivace*, E major) is begun by Paolina, Poliuto's voice joining to hers in unison for the coda; the second statement is unison throughout. This is the conventional format for a two-statement cabaletta, but since the voices are not deployed identically in both statements, it can also be seen as a foreshortened arrangement of the older pattern with the full melody repeated three times (each voice separately and then in unison–*assieme*, as in the Lucia–Edgardo duet). When Donizetti revised the *Poliuto* duet for its inclusion in *Les martyrs*, he added episodes to the introductory recitative and to the *larghetto*. The necessity for this revision resulted from Scribe's discarding of Cammarano's awkward invention of Poliuto's jealousy and in part from the greater explicitness permitted in France in dealing with a religious experience; further, a close adherence to the original plot was advisable since Corneille's play was a revered classic to the Parisian audience.[28] The additions to the duet include several orchestral anticipations of the opening phrase of the cabaletta and a brief arioso prayer for Polyeucte, 'Seigneur de vos bontés', beginning in the key of A flat minor, an unusual one for Donizetti; further he expands Pauline's moment of decision from one measure to six, accompanying it now with the opening phrase of the Christians' hymn, first heard in the *sinfonia*. This scena, particularly in its expanded French version, shows Donizetti's keen awareness of the superior impact of a duet at this point in the work over the older aria–finale.

In Donizetti's later operas this shift from aria to duet near the conclusion of a work can be seen as an aspect of his conscious internationalization of style, looking backward toward *Les Huguenots* and forward to *Aida*. The most familiar example is the *larghetto–moderato* sequence in Act 4 of *La favorite*, culminating in

'Viens, viens, je cède'. Originally this cabaletta consisted of two solo statements; the third, in unison, was added only to the Italian version of 1843 for Alboni at La Scala.[29] The inconspicuous accompaniment of the *moderato*[30] focuses attention almost entirely upon the vocal melody, which repeats a basic rhythmic pattern (♩ ♫♫) in most measures, achieving eloquence by surprisingly simple means. As a rule these late, climactic duets rely on impassioned cantilena rather than embellished melody.

A very different mood but even greater intensity is found in the Maria–Chevreuse duet near the end of Act 3 of *Maria di Rohan*. In the *larghetto*, Chevreuse, believing Maria guilty of infidelity, greets her with intense irony in a suave melody posed over an implacably thudding rhythm (3/8 ♪ ♪♩♪ ♪ ♪ etc.); everything is suppressed, *piano*, until Maria bursts in, now in the relative minor, bidding him stop. Only at this point does the duet start to be a dialogue; Chevreuse, threatening now, takes over Maria's melody after four measures, reducing her participation to disjointed pleas (Example 15). This section ends abruptly on the dominant of B minor, which is followed by the clock's sounding the hour. Maria's gasp as she stares at the secret door tells her husband that she expects Chalais to return through it momentarily. The *moderato* of this duet, 'Sull'uscio tremendo', is short (*a b a'*, ten + seven + ten measures). The opening section is for Chevreuse who, first *mezza voce* and then with ferocious joy, presents balanced *declamato* phrases punctuated by ominous repeated chords; the middle section is for Maria, adopting a melody introduced in the coda of the overture, but here broken off in mid-word; the concluding section repeats the opening, but now with the pauses between Chevreuse's phrases answered by brief disjointed pleas from Maria, in the middle range. Again, there is no real cadence, as Chalais appears, and the concluding trio follows. This duet marks Donizetti's greatest achievement in creating and sustaining a mood of fierce dramatic intensity stripped down to its essentials.

The sextet from *Lucia* is far and away the best-known page from any of Donizetti's scores. Its immediate success helped to establish his pre-eminence as a master of ensemble writing, something more than a gifted melodist. It fulfilled the promise foreseen for him after the success of the trio that ended Act 1 of *L'esule di Roma*. A close look at this ensemble offers an appropriate point of departure for an examination of some of Donizetti's ensemble–finales. The *Lucia* sextet is the slow movement of the two-section finale to Act 2. In Italy this

Example 15. *Maria di Rohan*, Act 3, *larghetto* of the Maria–Chevreuse duet

passage is traditionally referred to as the 'quartet' from *Lucia* and with some justification, for the chief melodic content is carried by four voices; in the second half, when Alisa and Arturo start to sing, their function is chiefly to strengthen the harmony, along with the chorus who sing detached eighth-notes on each beat. The structure

Sextet (Lucia, Alisa, Edgardo, Enrico, Raimondo, Arturo, chorus): 'Chi mi frena in tal momento?' (*larghetto*)

a	duet: Edgardo and Enrico (16 measures)
*a*¹	quartet: Lucia and Raimondo repeat *a*, Edgardo and Enrico have subordinate phrases (16 measures)
b	sextet: dominated at the beginning by Enrico's 'Ah, è mio sangue', later by Lucia's 'Ah, vorrei piangere' (10 measures)
b	sextet repeated (10 measures)
coda	melodic cadences to dominant (4 measures)
	unaccompanied phrase for Edgardo and Enrico (2 measures)
	V⁷–I cadence for all (no other cadential figures) (2 measures)

of the ensemble could scarcely be more simple. The irresistible effectiveness of this passage is due to Donizetti's skill at transforming the rhetoric of confrontation into melody in such a way that it expands this moment so that the audience both feels and savors its pathos.[31] The opening section (*a*) of the sextet is dominated by the tenor and baritone singing in thirds or sixths; at the repetition of *a* these lines are taken by the soprano and the bass, and the greater distance between the voices (tenths or thirteenths) and the greater contrast of vocal timbre expands the range of emotion from raw confrontation to encompass Lucia's despair and Raimondo's forebodings. In the repeat of *a* the texture is richer, as Edgardo and Enrico contribute first isolated phrases and then full parts to the conclusion of the section. Enrico's 'Ah, è mio sangue', which opens the *b* section, is, unlike the declamatory material in *a*, broadly lyrical, and the frequent occurrence of triplets on second and third beats of the measure creates a sense of 9/8 that contrasts with the preceding 3/4. Section *a*, consisting of four pairs of balanced phrases, is longer than *b*, which is only ten measures long; *b* begins with Enrico's two-measure phrase, which is immediately repeated but now doubled by the bass. There follows a six-measure vocal arch, dominated by the tenor and soprano, over harmonies that move from II to V⁷ of the dominant key. This asymmetrical pattern, involving all six soloists and chorus and climaxing in the high B flats of the soprano, produces a moment of powerful tension. Although its structure is relatively simple the sextet possesses a keenly judged sense of forward momentum and organic development, effortlessly evolving out of itself; the effect it creates in performance is far greater than the sum of its parts.

The craftmanship that went into this ensemble was not learned overnight. Donizetti's knack for effective ensemble writing was admired early in his career. The quartet at the end of Act 1 of *Zoraida di Granata* and, particularly, the septet in the middle of Act 2 of *La zingara* were approved enthusiastically by the first audiences of these operas. A discussion of three ensemble–finales from various stages of Donizetti's career will allow some insight into his progress as a composer and afford a perspective on his manner of dealing with the conventions relating to the type. The *Lucia* sextet can serve as a touchstone for this survey.

Donizetti's ensemble–finales must be viewed against the background of older types. The episodic finale was grafted onto opera seria from the tradition of opera buffa, where it concluded the score with a concentrated tonal mass (in Handelian opera, for instance, the *finale ultimo* would be the chief ensemble passage of the whole score). These episodic finales in the later eighteenth century were characteristically built of connected units, bringing on the characters in pairs, or singly against the mass in the vaudeville pattern, to resolve the various misunderstandings and to match up the correct couples, and, more often than not, to point the moral of the piece. By the later 1820s this sort of denouement had been almost completely replaced by aria–finales, in which ensemble utterance was limited to commentary occurring in the *tempo di mezzo* and the coda, reducing all but the prima donna to the status of *pertichini*. The important feature is that the cast is subordinated to a single principal, usually the prima donna, as in the tower scene from *Anna*, but occasionally the tenor, as in the tomb scene from *Lucia*. When convention decrees that the final number of an opera should be an aria, then the point of greatest tonal mass is moved back from the denouement to the climax of the plot, a traditional ensemble spot. In a two-act structure this means that the chief ensemble will customarily be found at the end of Act 1, but in a three-act structure it might, as in *Lucia*, occur at the end of Act 2. Donizetti's practise, then, can be seen as a strengthening of the emphasis of the *finale primo*, as it had developed out of the old buffa tradition.

These midpoint ensembles in serious operas are the reverse side of the coin of the buffa finales of complication that are found, for instance, at the ends of the first acts of *L'italiana in Algeri* and *Il barbiere;* they pile up absurd responses to achieve at last an atmosphere of pandemonium, but they do not result in decisive events that clearly predicate further action. Such decisive events are common in the midpoint ensembles of serious or tragic operas. *Lucia* provides an example. The sextet is the slow movement of the Act 2 finale, the moment of confrontation; nothing happens, yet everybody reacts to Edgardo's arrival. At the start of the *materia di mezzo* of this two-part finale swords are drawn, but Raimondo separates the enemies. When Enrico tries to humble Edgardo by showing him the fait accompli of the marriage contract signed by Lucia, Edgardo offers more serious provocation by cursing Lucia for her apparent betrayal. At this point the *vivace* concluding movement begins: outraged honor must now be satisfied, and Lucia's reason has been dealt an irreversible blow. Everything that happens in the rest of the action is posited by this finale. For Donizetti such a plot, with its climax occurring more or less at the midpoint, had the particular merit of allowing him to devote the last part of his framework to exploiting its painful and frequently fatal consequences.

One of the most celebrated of the ensemble–finales that Donizetti composed during the first decade of his career was the trio that ends Act 1 of *L'esule di Roma*. What particularly pleased him about the situation at this point in the plot was that it allowed him to concentrate on the crucial interaction of only three characters, without even the intervention of the chorus;[32] and the first audience responded to it enthusiastically, applauding the composer's achievement in lending such comparatively slender resources the musical and dramatic weight normally achieved only by a crowded stage with everyone singing their heads off. This was a bold defiance of convention on Donizetti's part, for audiences were conditioned to expect a full ensemble at this point in the action. Five years after *L'esule di Roma*, the audience at the rowdy *prima* of *Norma* vented their displeasure when Act 1 of that opera ended with a trio rather than a full ensemble, and it was not until later performances, when the trio was better performed (Bellini had been nervously tinkering with it up to the last moment), that it was judged appropriate and effective.[33]

The trio in *L'esule di Roma* is touched off by Settimio's giving Argelia a scroll; reading it, she discovers that her father Murena has falsely accused Settimio of the crime of which he himself is guilty. Settimio is declaring himself ready to give up his life to save that of her father, when Murena enters, his reason shaken by remorse and guilt. At this unexpected encounter, all three cry out. Murena begins the *larghetto*, agitated by the sight of his victim (Example 16).

Example 16. *L'esule di Roma*, Act 1, *larghetto* of the trio–finale

Settimio takes Murena's hand and tells how, dying, Flavio had revealed Murena's complicity. Argelia observes them, praying to the
gods to spare both the man she loves and her father. As with the
Lucia sextet, the function of this ensemble is to expand the moment
of confrontation. Over the regular thudding of the accompaniment,
Donizetti keeps the three vocal lines admirably distinct, allowing
most of the text to emerge clearly. As the characters' emotions rise,
the harmony shifts to the parallel minor, reverting to B flat major
only for the eleven measures of incomplete coda, in which, exceptionally, Murena is interrupted in mid-word by the entrance of four
officials who come to order Settimio to prison. Their arrival
launches the *tempo di mezzo* (*allegro*, B flat major). Preparing to
obey them, Settimio tells Argelia to destroy the scroll; instead she
shows it to her father as evidence against him. Overcome with
shame, Murena falls to his knees and begs Settimio to escape with
Argelia and leave him his honor unsullied. Sternly, Settimio raises
him to his feet. For their different reasons, father and daughter beg
Settimio to live. The second movement of this trio (*moderato*, D
major) is begun by Settimio who sings the principal melodic period
alone; this is then repeated first by Argelia and afterward by Murena
(in the key of the dominant) (Example 17).

Example 17. *L'esule di Roma*, Act 1, *moderato* of the trio-finale

The pattern here is *a b c* (eight measures each, *b* in the relative minor), ending with four measures of codetta, derived from *c*. Settimio is ready to die and finds consolation in the thought of the tears that Argelia will shed for him. She tries desperately to prevent him, while Murena keeps urging him to flee. At the end, Settimio breaks loose and rushes off.

Certain aspects of this trio are worth noting. First of all, Donizetti was fortunate in dealing with a situation that is visually self-explanatory, like that of the finale to Act 2 of *Lucia* – the dramatic conflict being evident from the mere presence together on the stage of a certain group of characters. The *larghetto* is constructed less symmetrically than that of the *Lucia* sextet: the first six measures are introductory; the main melodic period begins with the entry of Argelia's voice and consists of two four-phrase units (major, minor); the last of these phrases is dilated and then is repeated just before the coda. After each of the three characters has stated the principal melodic period of the *moderato* in turn, there follows a middle section to heighten tension which leads into a repetition of the principal melody, now as an ensemble. The *moderato* ends with fifty measures of coda and four of cadential sequences. In this final movement of the trio Donizetti uses an expansion of the pattern he frequently adopted in the concluding sections of duets.

In *Maria Stuarda* Donizetti makes a significant modification of the conventions of the ensemble–finale. In the famous episode of the encounter of the two queens and their exchange of insults, he gives special prominence to the passage between the *larghetto* sextet and the stretta finale – the traditional position of the *tempo di mezzo* en and fashions out of it a striking piece of musical theater. Donizetti's intention of highlighting this episode is clear from his having given it a separate number (no. 10) in his score; most often he uses a single number for the whole finale, and while he would occasionally use two, three, as in *Maria Stuarda*, is exceptional. The sextet (*larghetto*, 3/4, B flat major) follows the same general pattern as that in *Lucia*, but here it is $a\ a^1\ b\ b^1$.[34] These sextets resemble one another, too, in that their first sections are relatively more declamatory than the second, which are lyrical with a strong feeling of 9/8; in both sextets the full complement of singers participates only in the second half. As before, in *Maria Stuarda* Donizetti expands the moment of confrontation as Elisabetta first lays eyes on Maria. But the *Maria Stuarda* sextet dispenses with the chorus and is only about half the length of its counterpart in *Lucia* (thirty-five measures against sixty-five). Donizetti kept it relatively brief because he did not want to delay the *scène obligatoire* between the rival queens.

The stretta finale to Act 2 of *Maria Stuarda* is more logically organized than the corresponding passage in *Lucia*.

Stretta finale to Act 2 of *Maria Stuarda* (*allegro vivace*, D major)

a	Elisabetta, with Cecil joining in the second half, 'Va, preparati furente' (32 measures)
b	Maria, with Leicester in unison and two subsidiary voices and chorus, 'Grazie, o cielo!' (40 measures)
c	interlude (the guards surround Maria) (24 measures, D minor to D major)

b   full repeat, with Elisabetta joining in the unison melody, but with new words
             for Maria, 'Or guidatemi alla morte' (40 measures)
coda   (40 measures, + 13 measures of ritornello and cadences)

Maria's being placed under arrest gives a dramatic focus and development to this stretta, while there is no such advancement in *Lucia;* there
the stretta begins with Edgardo's being ordered away, and he does not
leave until all the many notes of the stretta have been delivered. Instead
of beginning with a solo passage, the *Lucia* stretta starts out with a
unison tune for all the male soloists except Edgardo, and the male
chorus; a contrast of texture follows when the unison tune starts
again, but now for the soprano and leading tenor, other voices being
gradually added in contrasting phrases. This leads into a seemingly
interminable coda, which is usually drastically cut in performance.
That the second melodic period of a stretta was a unison passage for
the lovers was a rule that Donizetti generally adhered to; he did so,
for example, in the overall *a b a* pattern in the *vivace* of the finale to
Act 1 of *Maria di Rohan.*

The episode of the dialogue of the queens in *Maria Stuarda,*
which runs to 199 measures, is longer than the preceding sextet and
the concluding stretta combined. It begins with twenty measures of
preparatory material, hollow octaves and nervous brief figures. The
first main melodic period begins as Maria kneels before the English
queen to beg forgiveness (Example 18). It is introduced by a three-
note motif that recurs in almost every measure of the ensuing dialogue; Donizetti employs it to suggest the touchy pride and jangling
nerves of these royal ladies. The quoted passage illustrates how in-
geniously Donizetti expands this motivic idea into a countermelody;
then cunning syncopations (not shown) contradict the meekness
of Maria's words. Elisabetta icily rejects Maria's plea and, as the
connecting passage continues, now *più allegro,* a second more
intense little motif appears, this one characterized by trills and
a larger intervallic leap upward, leading into a *crescendo* that
ends on the dominant seventh. Suddenly, *piano,* the motif in Example 18 returns, introducing Elisabetta's charges of adultery and
other crimes and betrayals; these are set to substantially the same
music as Maria's plea, but this time there are more dynamic markings and the conclusion of the melody is marked *stringendo.* This is
followed by another connecting passage, moving from the parallel
minor, and introducing still another brief motif – a sinister five-note
figure heard first in the trombones and immediately echoed by violin
and oboe – as Leicester vainly tries to support Maria's case.
Elisabetta retorts that some reward must have prompted this defense,

Example 18. *Maria Stuarda*, Act 2, finale, Maria–Elisabetta dialogue

and her phrases are punctuated by granitic C major chords. The
opening three-note motif of Example 18 returns now as Maria
seethes at this insult, while Elisabetta swears that eternal shame has
fallen upon her rival's head. Only during this last exchange do the
queens sing simultaneously; otherwise their voices only briefly overlap. As the tension mounts the three-note motif is inverted, suggesting perhaps that Maria's hopes are henceforth overthrown. The concluding passage contains Maria's insults, the famous 'vil bastarda'
episode (Example 19). This tense declamation presents the text
with maximum clarity so that none of its outrageous import will be
lost. Confronted with a moment of such high dramatic tension,
Donizetti has avoided defusing it by conventional treatment. In one
sense this whole dialogue is a duet *manqué*; both queens have a
main melodic period using substantially the same material, but instead of a traditional *assieme* Donizetti has striven to give the
climactic moment something of the immediacy of the spoken theater. In any sense this dialogue is one of the most original and powerful passages that Donizetti ever composed.

Example 19. *Maria Stuarda*, Act 2, finale, Maria–Elisabetta dialogue

The Maria–Chevreuse duet from near the end of Act 3 of *Maria di Rohan* has been discussed above; the trio that follows it and the brief final passage following the coda provide a conclusion that in some ways anticipates the trio–finale that Verdi would write to conclude *Ernani* the next year, and in other ways looks forward to many Romantic melodramas. The entrance of Chalais through the secret door precipitates a declamatory passage (*maestoso*, E flat, fourteen measures), set over a march rhythm to which at intervals are added scalar triplet figures that suggest the underlying tension. Chalais throws down his sword, proclaiming his readiness to die. Maria starts to tell him of her fear, but a terrible glance from her husband cuts her short. The tempo quickens to *allegro* (beginning in G major, twenty-two measures) as a servant rushes in to announce the arrival of troops come to arrest Chalais, for whom all avenues of escape are now cut off. Next, Chalais attempts to take his own life, but Chevreuse stops him and thrusts a pistol into his hand, insisting upon a duel. This action takes place over a nervous motivic accompaniment that modulates energetically, coming to rest in F, the dominant of the subsequent trio.

Trio (Chevreuse, Maria, Chalais): 'Vivo non t'è concesso' (*moderato*, 4/4, B flat major)

a	Chevreuse (8 measures)
b	Maria and Chalais, unison melody (8 measures to D minor)
*b*¹	variant of *b*, with linking phrases and a part in the cadences for Chevreuse (10 measures to B flat major)
c	intermediate material (6 measures to F major)
b	as before but with increased participation for Chevreuse (8 measures)
*b*¹	as before but with increased participation for Chevreuse (10 measures)
coda	(12 measures)

This brief trio resembles the structure of a stretta to a finale more than that of the trio–cabaletta in Act 1 of *L'esule di Roma*; moreover the unison line for the soprano and tenor (*b* and *b*¹) (like that in the trio that ends Act 1 of *Il trovatore*) is also characteristic of a stretta. Considerably less extensive than Verdi's trio for *Ernani*, and without the tonal tug-of-war which Verdi uses to heighten opposing desires, Donizetti's resorts to restless modulation to sustain dramatic tension.

Maria di Rohan contains another thirty-three measures after the end of the trio. The vocal coda is broken off by insistent knocking, ignored by Chevreuse, who pulls Chalais out through the secret door. Fainting, Maria sinks into a chair, but almost at once the sound

Example 20. *Maria di Rohan*, Act 3, conclusion

of two pistol shots brings her back to her feet in terror. Meanwhile the knocking is resumed, and the door at the back is forced open to admit Fiesque and a detachment of the King's troops, come to arrest Chalais. Just then Chevreuse returns, his features deformed with rage because Chalais has evaded his vengeance by shooting himself. Fiesque and the soldiers rush off to see for themselves. Then:

Chevreuse (*advancing toward Maria*): Death to him!
Maria (*weeping*): Cruel man!
Chevreuse: A lifetime of infamy for you, faithless woman!

These final phrases are declaimed without any accompaniment at all, and suddenly we find ourselves in the world of Barnaba at the end of *La gioconda*. After this passage in B minor, the opera ends in B flat major (Example 20). With *Maria de Rohan* and particularly its final act, Donizetti opened vistas of Romantic melodrama that his successors would explore for years to come. From this passage it is clear that twilight had overtaken the conventions Donizetti had long hoped to see lose their prescriptive force.

9

The operas
1816–1830

Il Pigmalione. This one-act 'scena lirica',[1] as Donizetti called it, is his only attempt at a mythological subject; it tells the familiar story of the sculptor whose masterpiece is brought to life. The final page of the autograph states that it was 'begun on 15 September and finished 1 October at almost two in the morning, Tuesday, the day of the arrival of the new legate'; the year was 1816, when Donizetti was studying with Padre Mattei at Bologna. Most probably this score was composed for the experience, and since Mayr visited Donizetti in Bologna in September 1816, it would seem the project was either suggested by him or undertaken by Donizetti to demonstrate to his former teacher his current prowess. Since Donizetti's studies at Bologna were made possible only by contributions from Bergamo, he was scarcely in a position to commission a new libretto. Readily available to him was Sografi's text for Cimadoro's *Pimmaglione*, which was widely performed, especially in northern Italy.

Il Pigmalione, in every sense a modest work, contains only two characters (Pigmalione, tenor, and Galatea, soprano); the vocal writing is limited in range and discreetly embellished, and the work is scored for flute, oboe, two clarinets, two horns, two bassoons and strings. The autograph is unique among Donizetti's operas in not being divided into separate numbers – a strong indication that the work was written as an exercise, without expectation of performance or publication. Since Galatea's statue does not come to life until near the end, the chief burden falls upon the character of Pigmalione, who can only address himself, his statue, or the gods, with the result that the plot is deficient in dramatic tension. The finest moments in the work are a beguiling ritornello in ternary form for flute and strings that accompanies his contemplation of the statue, and the recitative in which he raises his chisel and is frightened to discover that some power deters his hand; here large intervals in the vocal line and unprepared dissonances in the accompaniment catch his agitation. The arias are brief and symmetrical; all the recitatives are accompanied, and the final duet is, unfortunately, the one feeble part of the score. The influence of Mayr's style is apparent in many places, that of Rossini scarcely at all.

Enrico di Borgogna. This is Donizetti's first full-length opera, and his first to be publicly performed. It is in two acts, each divided by several changes of scene. The score was composed sometime between the middle of May 1818, when Merelli signed a contract with the impresario Zancla to write a semiserio libretto derived from Kotzebue[2] for Donizetti, and the middle of October 1818, when Donizetti informed Mayr that he had 'to rewrite a few things'[3] owing to a change in the cast. The opera can be called semiseria only because it contains a buffo role (Gilberto); it is, in fact, an *opera eroica,* having a *musico* part for the title character, and the buffo role is quite extraneous.

Musically the most astonishing thing about *Enrico* is to discover that his Act 1 cabaletta contains substantially the famous melody of Anna Bolena's 'Al dolce guidami'. The opera is hampered by a libretto that wobbles between the turgid and the ludicrous.[4] The musical forms are more ample than in *Pigmalione,* but are conventional in design. The vocal melodies are usually fluent but rarely distinguished, with frequent coloratura passages (for all ranges) productive of vocal effect rather than illumination of character. The influence of Rossinian formulas can be found in many places, for example the *rondò* of Enrico, 'Mentre mi brilli intorno', with its symmetrical *gruppetti* of conjunct sixteenth-notes. This score contains the earliest examples of Donizetti's operatic ensembles, the best of which is a vigorous trio at the end of the first scene;[5] there is a full-scale finale of confrontation – Enrico disrupts the wedding procession of his beloved Elisa and the usurper Guido – at the end of Act 1 which has a brief *larghetto* and a longer *allegro,* and a sextet in Act 2 with an effective *largo* but a banal stretta. *Enrico* is a score that reveals mingled talent and inexperience, but it is not an interesting drama.

Una follia. This one-act farsa, to another libretto by Merelli, was composed, rehearsed and staged in the month following the *prima* of *Enrico di Borgogna.* Since neither the score (which was last heard of in the possession of the impresario Zancla who commissioned it) nor the libretto survives,[6] this work is an unknown quantity, except for eight measures that appear in the little anthology of tunes from his works that Gaetano assembled for Virginia not long before their marriage. Even though the context from which these measures come cannot now be determined, they are reproduced here as the earliest surviving example of Donizetti's operatic comedy (Example 21).

Example 21. *Una follia,* unidentified excerpt

Le nozze in villa. This opera buffa in two acts has a libretto by Merelli, derived from Kotzebue's *Die deutschen Kleinstädter.* On the whole this score is a routine and uninspired exercise in the compositional formulas of the period. The principal exception is the trio that opens Act 2, which boasts an attractive slow section and a stretta that is strikingly typical of Donizetti. The cabaletta of the aria–finale is shared with *Il falegname* and was later, at some unknown date, inserted into *La lettera anonima.* The copyist's score in the Bibliothèque Nationale, Paris, which is the only known copy, lacks the quintet in Act 2.

Il falegname di Livonia. 1819 saw the production of the opera buffa *Il falegname,* another uneasy mixture of naivete and incompletely

assimilated ingredients of the Rossinian idiom; but, dramatically
stronger than *Enrico*, it exercised sufficient appeal to survive for
some half-dozen subsequent stagings.[7] An example of Donizetti's
artless early style is Firman's solo passage, 'È 'l'interesse al mondo
principio, universale', in the second *allegro* of the *introduzione;* it
begins with a syllabic quarter-note melody emphasizing the tones
of the G major tonic triad. When Donizetti wants to achieve a
more imposing effect, as in the motivic phrases of Madama Fritz's
Act 1 aria, he burlesques Rossini's declamatory style (Example 22).

MADAMA FRITZ

Qual   ar - dir!   qual   bran - do   i - gnu - do!

Example 22. *Il falegname di Livonia*, Act 1, *maestoso* of Madama Fritz's
aria

Parody and mock seriousness were devices that particularly appealed to Donizetti, and he resorted to them throughout his comic
works. Yet not all the approaches to *rossinianismo* in *Il falegname*
were intended to be funny. The generous portion of roulades in
Pietro's music, appropriate to a tsar, contrasts sharply with the more
simple vocal writing that prevails in other parts. The most successful
imitation of Rossini occurs in the Act 2 sextet, which even has Rossinian echoes in its text, beginning: 'Ah, quel colpo!'[8] Unlike the
later serious sextets, which tend to introduce the participants singly
or in pairs, Donizetti employs the vocal mass throughout. In calling
this sextet Rossinian I do not intend to suggest that it approaches
Rossini's facility at linking and relating musical ideas, but Donizetti
has caught something of the external effect of his predecessor's
loquacious ensembles.

   The two-act structure of *Il falegname* demonstrates Donizetti's
competence at filling out the usual assortment of numbers. There is a
sinfonia that begins *moderato* 4/4 and ends *presto* 3/4, a combination of bustling and reiterated rhythmic figures in sonatina form; at
the end of the overture in the autograph, Donizetti wrote: 'If I do not
mistake, there are 368 measures.' The multiform *introduzione* (*allegro*, 6/8, G major) starts with a chorus declaring that true love
flourishes in the country rather than in the city. This is followed by a
recitative for the tenor hero Carlo leading into a *larghetto* strophe,
'Cara vezzosa immagine', which Annetta answers to the same music;
the *larghetto* expands into a duet with echo effects, and the whole

introduzione ends with the same 6/8 melody that opened it. Framing an *introduzione* by bringing back the first melody at the end is a static device that Donizetti rarely used afterward. The finale to Act 1 is in several contrasting movements; at the end of it Donizetti appended the date on which he finished it: 4 December 1819, just twenty-two days before the *prima*.

The second act is shorter, since the first-act finale has already provided the unraveling of the secret of Carlo's parentage and thereby all but wound up the plot. Act 2 chiefly consists of an engaging duet for Carlo's foster-parents, a full-scale aria and cabaletta with chorus for Carlo, the aforementioned sextet, and a concluding sequence of aria, chorus, *rondò* ('In quest'estremo amplesso') and second chorus. The final vocal honors go to the character of the Tsarina Caterina, not to Annetta the ingenue, a disposition that results from the strength of the tradition that demanded a tableau featuring noble condescension – the conclusion of an opera buffa could be indistinguishable from the *lieto fine* of an opera seria. All told, *Il falegname* is a work of promise rather than achievement, its most consistent shortcoming being that the melodic flow is at times impeded by the lack of supple harmonic movement to support it.

Zoraida di Granata. In its original form, with a libretto by Merelli, this two-act opera seria elicited for Donizetti his first really enthusiastic response from an audience when it was given at the Teatro Argentina in Rome on 28 January 1822. Owing to the death of the tenor Sbigoli, the role of Abenamet had to be revised for a mezzo-soprano at the last moment, and Donizetti's score was performed with some music omitted. Two years later the impresario Paterni invited Donizetti to revise his opera, expanding the role of Abenamet for the leading *musico* of the day, Rosmunda Pisaroni. The autograph score in the Ricordi Archives contains the materials used for this 1824 performance (Teatro Argentina, 7 January 1824) and lacks the supplanted music. In parts that were not replaced the indications of Donizetti's having changed the tessitura of Abenamet's part from the tenor range to the mezzo are clearly to be seen; in the Act 2 duet for Almuzir and Abenamet, for example, the introductory tempo shows such alterations, as well as some modifications by Ferretti to the text, but the duet proper, 'Là nel tempio, innanzi al Nume', is written on different paper with the heading, 'Duetto, Contralto e Tenore', and is obviously new. This duet was the most widely applauded piece in the 1824 production; it has a vigorous cabaletta, 'Più dell'usato rapido' (*allegro*, F major), full of bravura.

The principal changes between the two versions involve the ending
of Act 1 and the beginning of Act 2, and the replacement of Zoraida's
final aria by a formidable *rondò* for the *musico*, 'Da un eccesso di
tormento'; this consists of an eight-bar theme and three taxing variations which show that Pisaroni had a usable low G and could
sustain the G two octaves higher, as well as alternate it rapidly with
the A flat above. For some reason this vocal workout did not appeal
to the critic of *Notizie del giorno* (15 January 1824), who, besides the
duet already mentioned, singled out the Act 2 aria of Almuzir,
'Amarla tanto', the Act 1 quartet, and Zoraida's Act 2 aria, 'Rose che
un dì', all three left pretty much intact from the 1822 version.

That the 1824 *Zoraida* failed to match the eager reception accorded
it two years earlier reflects the restless taste for novelty of those days
rather than some marked deficiency in the music added to the score.
In acknowledging the lesser effect the opera produced in 1824, the
critic of the *Notizie del giorno* cannot decide whether to attribute it
'to a natural result of reproducing sensations no longer new, or to the
substantial change of color of certain pieces which had undergone
inevitable alteration to suit a different cast'. In 1822 the Romans had
experienced the excitement of discovering a 'new' composer, and by
1824 Donizetti had forfeited that advantage. The plot of *Zoraida*
belongs to that by then over-exploited category of heroic Spanish–
Moorish subjects, of which the elements are here predictably employed, and Donizetti's music, though serviceable (and in the numbers mentioned better than serviceable) could not really endow it
with sufficient vitality to warrant lasting interest.

La zingara. Donizetti's first opera for Naples is a rambling two-act
semiseria[9] in which the numbers are connected by spoken dialogue
in the Neapolitan fashion, rather than by recitatives as in *Enrico*. The
prelude begins with six measures of *maestoso* (chordal sequences)
succeeded by forty-six of *allegro*, chiefly confined to a single
motivic figure that builds up a *crescendo*, moving from the tonic of
G into E flat major. The extended *introduzione* is much better integrated than its counterpart in *Il falegname*, possessing a real sense of
forward movement; it presents first a male chorus and then two pairs
of characters in sequence, and finally combines these forces, ending
as it began in G major. The gypsy of the title, Argilla, introduces
herself in a cavatina (*allegro*, 3/4, E flat major), of which, after an
opening period, the main melody, set to the words 'La zingara
famosa, Argilla, l'indovina', is in bolero rhythm; suddenly a sharply
etched personality is revealed (Example 23). Unfortunately, this

Example 23. *La zingara*, Act 1, Argilla's *aria di sortita*

vividness is not really sustained in the rest of the rather loosely organized aria.

Besides Argilla, the chief interest of *La zingara* resides in the character of Pappacione, the earliest of the roles Donizetti wrote for the famous Neapolitan buffo, Carlo Casaccia. The traditional buffo idiom had long been firmly established when Donizetti first turned his hand to it with the extraneous Gilberto in *Enrico* and the bumbling Magistrate in *Il falegname*; in *La zingara* the buffo role is a manifestation of a character who was practically a comic folk hero to the Neapolitans. An example of Donizetti's writing for this vocal type in *La zingara* may be taken from the finale to Act 1 (Example 24). A first reaction to this passage is that it could have been composed by any of a large number of composers. Yet to dismiss it on these grounds alone is to miss much of its point: as the vehicle for a highly specialized style of performing the music is purposefully neutral so that it emerges as only one facet of a total comic performance. Carlo Casaccia's years of activity in the Neapolitan theaters extended from 1785 until 1826 and he belonged to the third generation of a comic dynasty that held sway there for over a century. Perhaps the most important point about Pappacione is that it provided Donizetti with the opportunity to study the buffo art at the hand of a master. Much of what is implicit in these bare-bone pages of *La zingara* he learned to make explicit in his great characters for this vocal type. Some of Casaccia's quality is captured by Stendhal, who elsewhere referred to him as the 'Le Brunet of Naples':[10]

The actual *city* of Naples, compared with Milan . . . has one peculiar glory of its own, the magnificent Casacciello,[11] and his individual artistry in performing a certain opera by Paisiello, which, I believe, together with *Nina*, is the only one which still survives in the modern repertoire. 'If you have ever

Example 24. *La zingara*, Act 1, finale

laughed in your life,' I might say to some clumsy English squire, whose solemn head is all one whirl of earnest arguments concerning the *Utility of Foreign Bible Societies* and the *Immorality of the French Nation*, 'go to Naples and see Casaccia in *la Scuffiara ossia la Modista raggiratrice*'.[12]

La lettera anonima. A little more than six weeks after the first performance of *La zingara* this one-act farsa was unveiled, its edifying libretto coming from the hand of one of the Neapolitan censors, Giulio Genoino. One of the most attractive pages of this otherwise rather dim score is the specialty number, apparently a later addition to the score as it is numbered 3 bis and is only remotely connected to the plot. Quite brief, it shows the French dancing-master Flagiolet (the part was written for the buffo Calvarola) giving a lesson; it consists of two *allegro* movements of old-fashioned dance music, one in 6/8 and one in 2/4, in the latter the melody occurring in the accompaniment. At the end of the first section old Flagiolet is illustrating the pirouette that was his star turn at the Opéra, singing a mock cadenza as he does so, and by mistake bumps into his pupil and breaks off to speak his apologies, explaining that he had not seen her. The other notable feature of this score is the substantial quartet, praised by the critic of the *Giornale del Regno delle Due Sicilie* (1 July 1822), wherein he saw 'made fresh again the old-time procedure of our so-called concerted pieces without those cabalettas, and [further] without that symmetrical repetition of motifs which obliges all the actors to repeat the same musical phrases no matter what very different emotions may agitate them'. The concluding *più allegro* of this long quartet (*moderato*, 4/4, C major; *andante mosso*, 2/4, B flat; *allegro*, 4/4, B flat; *più allegro*, 4/4, C) is not in two-statement form, although the opening phrase (unison for three voices) is largely repeated (against a sustained pedal in the fourth voice) at the beginning of the long coda.

Chiara e Serafina. This semiseria in two acts is most noteworthy in that it was Donizetti's first setting of a libretto by Romani (which he received only at the last minute) and in that its lack of success delayed his winning an audience in Milan for more than eight years. In Act 1 there is a storm scene (similar examples occur later in *Emilia di Liverpool* and *Il furioso*), but after a brief *crescendo* of *staccato* figures it is soon over. The most attractive aria in the score is the double one for Chiara: after an effective cor anglais introduction the cavatina (*maestoso*, 4/4, E flat), 'Queste romite sponde', has an ingratiating purling line. Chiara's ensuing cabaletta expresses her determination in a melody set to emphatic rhythmic patterns; the shape of these phrases reflects the Rossinian manner (Example 25). All through the autograph of Act 2 of *Chiara e Serafina* there are signs of Donizetti's working in haste, and from the traces of candle wax on some of the pages of the duet for Chiara and the buffo Don Meschino one surmises that he worked late into the night.

Example 25. *Chiara e Serafina*, Act 1, cabaletta of Chiara's *aria di sortita*

Much later, Romani turned over this same libretto, now retitled *I corsari*, to Alberto Mazzucato, but his version, which was first put on at La Scala on 15 February 1840, endured for only three performances.

Alfredo il grande. Donizetti's next opera, his first to be performed at the Teatro San Carlo in Naples, was a seria in two acts with a wildly improbable libretto by Tottola; it was first performed on 2 July 1823. There is little that mere music could do to introduce credibility into the unlikely meetings and furious confrontations that are liberally sprinkled through the tedious plot. There are two jaunty marches for stage band[13] and the chorus, comprising at various times English and Danish soldiers, armed shepherds and assorted rustics, is kept busy. The vocal writing is extremely florid, even for the minor characters. The role of Alfredo (written for the tenor Nozzari) has a vigorous *allegro* in Act 1, 'Non è di morte il fulmine', which seems to equate military prowess with vocal agility.[14] The Queen, Amalia, ends the opera with a long and busy *rondò*, 'Torna a gioir quest'alma', but all her exuberance cannot salvage this preposterous work. In composing a vehicle for a tenor long associated with Rossini's scores, Donizetti exposes with awful clarity the abyss that separates a *rossiniano* from his great model.

Il fortunato inganno. This two-act opera buffa was first performed at the Teatro Nuovo in Naples two months after the *prima* of *Alfredo*. Again the libretto is by Tottola, but he was more at home in comedy than in serious drama, even though his spoken dialogue is more than copious. Among the characters are two, the impresario Lattanzio (for Carlo Casaccia) and the poet Vulcano (for his son Raffaele), who speak and sing in Neapolitan dialect.

The *introduzione* contains a good deal of satire on the manners of opera personnel, a vein that Donizetti was later to explore more fully in *Le convenienze*. At the piano the composer Bequadro[15] sings an aria, 'Bella dea', from his newest opera, and the figurations of the melody are, to say the least, fulsome, particularly a rambling sequence (in *allegretto* 3/8) on the meaningless expletive 'deh!'. He explains to Vulcano his plans to orchestrate his aria, imitating the clarinet, oboe and trombone.[16] Later, the composer asks Vulcano's advice about writing roulades on the vowel 'U' (shades of Beckmesser!); Vulcano replies that while former taste forbade the practise, nowadays it is permissible to trill on 'I', 'O' and 'U'. Next, Fulgenzia del Folletto, the seconda donna, enters angrily and throws down her music, denouncing it as an *aria di sorbetto*[17] and refusing to sing nonsense (*frottole*). The bass now approaches to insist he must have his *rondò* in the key of A. Fulgenzia persists in her determination not to sing, prompting Vulcano to ask (in an aside): 'Since she cannot read notes, how can she sing?' The *introduzione* brings the members of this company vividly to life, and Donizetti takes obvious pleasure in the opportunities afforded by the satire, illustrating the musical ideas neatly and wittily.

L'ajo nell'imbarazzo. This was the first of Donizetti's buffa operas to establish itself; it is much helped by Ferretti's superior libretto which tastefully treats a rather risqué subject. *L'ajo* seems a marked improvement over its predecessors in that Donizetti finally succeeded here in creating real characters of more than one dimension, besides their comic function. Particularly successful are his portraits of Don Gregorio, the good-hearted tutor of the title, and Gilda, the enterprising heroine, who is secretly married to Enrico and has borne him a son. Donizetti's advance in supple and direct expressiveness, apparent at many points in the score, may be represented by Gilda's phrases in her Act 1 duet (Example 26). What is surprising, in the light of the regularity of melodies, common in his earlier scores, which often betray no particular sensitivity to the text, is the suppleness of the setting here, for example, the brief move into the relative minor at the word 'lagrime' and the drop of a seventh on 'sensibile'. Here, the tone of pathos foreshadows what will prove one of the keynotes of Donizettian comedy. While Gilda's pathos is to some extent assumed (a moment earlier, in an aside, she has announced her intention of playing on Don Gregorio's sympathies), she is such a genuinely appealing character, and her plight is so pitiable, that her fundamental sincerity and need are never in doubt. The superiority of Ferretti's libretto, a genuine comedy of character, undoubtedly helped Donizetti to reveal his true aptitude as a composer of opera buffa. Honesty requires the admis-

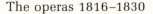

Example 26. *L'ajo nel'imbarazzo*, Act 1, *larghetto* of the Gilda–Gregorio duet

sion that *L'ajo* contains patches where the traditional formulas are in the foreground rather than the background, but what principally distinguishes it from its comic predecessors in the Donizetti canon is the improvement in the content of the non-concerted numbers – he had always composed the *introduzione* and the finale with flair. The welcome result is that *L'ajo nell'imbarazzo* is the most consistently characterized opera buffa to Donizetti's credit so far. It may not be the equal of *L'elisir*, but at least it opened the road that led in that direction and beyond to *La fille du régiment* and *Don Pasquale*.

Emilia di Liverpool. Like *Zoraida*, this score exists in at least two versions (the original of 1824 and the revision of 1828), but, as with *Zoraida*, the second, tighter, version of *Emilia* cannot correct its fundamental faults. Neither version of *Emilia* lives up to the promise of *L'ajo*, chiefly because the work belongs to the bastard semiseria genre. The intrusion of a buffo character, with his traditional musical idiom (compounded in the 1824 version when his Neapolitan dialect added still another level of stylization), into a serious, here a crudely Romantic action, especially when he is not integrally related to it, fatally short-circuits dramatic consistency and momentum. That Donizetti kept tackling this flawed genre, can be attributed to the glorious Neapolitan buffo tradition, stretching straight back to Pergolesi; by the mid-1820s this tradition was in its twilight years, but local audiences were still content with their beloved Pappacione Casaccia (who played the buffo in the 1824 *Emila*) in most contexts. However, since the 1824 *Emilia* survived at the Nuovo for only seven performances, the Neapolitan audiences evidently found their comic hero resistible in this context, for the Romantic elements of *Emilia* (storms, tombs, blasted heaths) proved an inhospitable environment for Casaccia's eccentricity. As the dramatic temperature grew increasingly warmer in the plots of the later 1820s, with their concomitant insistence upon greater emotional intensity and conviction, the basic artificiality of the semiseria grew increasingly difficult to tolerate.[18]

Yet Donizetti's belief that this mixed type was still viable, if the right proportions could be arrived at, is demonstrated by his reworking of *Emilia* in 1828. Clearly he hoped that the work was somehow salvageable and, further, he aspired to extend its appeal beyond Naples by dropping the buffo's dialect to make him a less local character. The dialect was not the only thing to go; along with it went three numbers for the buffo: his Act 1 duet with the tenor, his two-section aria, and the Act 2 trio; Donizetti compensated for this last omission by adding a new trio in Act 1, this one for male voices. The net result is to demote the buffo to a purely ensemble character. The Romantic and melodramatic elements of the plot gain prominence by the increased emphasis on the title role; Emilia's *aria di sortita* is moved to follow the first change of scene, and she occupies the center stage at the end in a *maestoso* and *rondò* borrowed from *Alahor in Granata* (to replace the old *finaletto*). All this reshaping, which involved the discarding of seven numbers and the two culminating movements of the finale to Act 1, the addition of three complete numbers as well as a new ending to the first finale, and the reshuffling of the seven numbers common to both versions, could not save a work whose basic weakness was generic. Perhaps the most significant thing about the second version of *Emilia* is that it shows Donizetti, as late as Lent 1828, to have been still unable to conceive the right vehicle for his own brand of Romanticism; but the time when he could was then not far distant.

Alahor in Granata. This two-act opera seria, a sort of first cousin to *Zoraida* through the source that is common to both librettos, was produced in Palermo during Donizetti's uncomfortable year at the Carolino. Until recently the score (except for the aria–finale preserved as part of the 1828 *Emilia*) was thought to be lost, but first a copyist's manuscript was found in Boston, and more recently the autograph itself was discovered in Palermo. If the Romans had found the cardboard *spagnuolismo* of the second version of *Zoraida* passé in 1824, the *palermitani* of 1826 were little more enthusiastic about it in this incarnation; nor did the Neapolitans like *Alahor* in the summer of 1826 when it served as a vehicle for Méric-Lalande and Lablache. The Spanish connections of the Bourbons of the Two Sicilies encouraged a vogue for such plots in court circles, but their appeal extended little further. Donizetti's own opinion of this score as a lost cause is clear from his use, six years later, of its Moorish march to serve the very different requirements of Sergeant Belcore's platoon.

Elvida. Donizetti's only opera seria in one act was designed to form part of a mixed bill at the San Carlo for the royal gala of 6 July 1826, the queen-mother's birthday. *Elvida* contains probably the most florid vocal writing of his whole oeuvre. He realized that the creaking plot – another dose of the Moors in Spain – was hopeless, and he gambled the success of the work upon the agile throats of Méric-

Lalande, Brigida Lorenzani in a *musico* role, Rubini and Lablache. Barblan has aptly described this score as having an 'atmosphere of abstract musicality', devoid of dramatic interest.[19] The tenor, for instance, has a ferociously difficult aria, 'Atra nube al sole intorno', in which the black clouds around the sun are described in a welter of roulades, all in bright C major! The best number in the score is a very craftsmanlike quartet that serves as the *adagio* of the two-movement ensemble before the finale. The final *rondò*, in G major, is a tenor–soprano duet, a forest of figurations in thirds and sixths, that confounds vocal activity with sincerity. Not surprisingly, *Elvida* survived for only four performances.

Gabriella di Vergy. The tangled history of this score (the original 1826 version, the 1838 revision by Donizetti, and the 1869 *rifacimento* by Giuseppe Puzone and Paolo Serrao) has been largely and convincingly explicated by Don White.[20] Donizetti decided on his own to set this tragic subject, adopting the text Tottola had written for Carafa's opera of the same title (1816). His choice speaks volumes about the generally inhospitable climate in Naples toward operatic tragedy and about his hunger to tackle subjects of greater emotional intensity than those he had hitherto composed. (The survival of Carafa's tragic score, given annually until 1826–27 in spite of the censors' distaste for such fare, is as much a tribute to Carafa's aristocratic connections as to its musical efficacy.)

In the original *Gabriella* Donizetti made the apparently backward-looking choice of a *musico* for the role of the lover, Raoul de Coucy; this decision seems the more retrogressive because the corresponding role in Carafa's opera was written for a tenor, the elder David.[21] But Donizetti was providing, for 1826, an up-to-date solution to both the musical and dramatic problems posed by the revolution in vocal types that resulted from the discarding of the castrati: he found the female contralto's emphatic sound more dramatically effective than the unavoidably effete tones of a falsetto-topped Rossinian tenor like David. The vocal line for the 1826 Raoul abounds in figurations, but they are written in such a way as to exploit the more powerful middle and lower registers of the female contralto range. Up to this time Donizetti's principal experience with a Rossinian tenor hero had been with Nozzari, nearing the end of his distinguished career, in *Alfredo il grande*, and it had proved unsuccessful. Carafa's *Gabriella* had employed two leading tenors, Nozzari creating the part of the villainous Fayel; in Donizetti's version that role was conceived for a baritone. Thus he completely banished the Rossinian tenor from his score, apparently feeling that that type of vocal sound and style was ineffective in a 'strong' subject; further, he wanted to avoid the monotony resulting from all the principal roles being written for high voices and to take advantage of contrasting vocal timbres in his ensembles.

To keep the first *Gabriella* in perspective, it is crucial to remember that it is the product of the year preceding the emergence of a new type of Romantic hero – a Byronic figure – created by Rubini in Bellini's *Il pirata*. Practically concurrently with his work on *Gabriella*, Donizetti had written the purely decorative role of Alfonso in *Elvida* for Rubini. It was the sterility of just such parts as this that made Rubini eager to co-operate with Romani and Bellini in breaking down the old barriers between the vocal virtuoso and the character he was supposed to impersonate.

Donizetti was no less dissatisfied than Rubini with the stiltedness of *Elvida*, and his composition of *Gabriella* represents his expression of that dissatisfaction. It also indirectly suggests one reason a composer of his undoubted talent took so relatively long to prove his mettle: this tardiness may be attributed partly to his long sojourn in Naples, and it was as a mute protest against the theatrical restrictions in force there that Donizetti wrote *Gabriella*. Bellini did not make a major mark until he had escaped from Naples into the more stimulating climate of Milan, and neither would Donizetti. Another reason for his slowness in reaching maturity is that Donizetti was not instinctively a reformer. There was precious little in the conservative climate of Naples, clinging fondly to its memories of the glories of the preceding century, to make him one. In *Gabriella* there are the first indications of his recognizing that his true forte was Romantic tragedy with strongly melodramatic situations, but it was not until he found an environment favorable to such plots that he came into his own. He retained his genuine flair for comedy and it grew richer as he came to deal more with believable characters and less with stereotypes.

1826, the middle year of his Neapolitan apprenticeship, saw him established in Naples as scarcely more than an estimable routineer, whose musical training was sounder than that of most of his contemporaries. So far only *L'ajo nell'imbarazzo*, introduced to Naples in 1826 in a revised form under the alternate title of *Don Gregorio*, had given substantial indications of his true capabilities. *Zoraida di Granata*, which had won him the engagement with Barbaja in the first place, had proved a flash in the pan, a fortuitous success that could not sustain itself.

Olivo e Pasquale. Three years after *L'ajo,* Donizetti and Ferretti collaborated again, but without matching the results of their earlier successful comedy. The problem lies, at least in part, in Ferretti's libretto, because his source was a prolix comedy contrasting general types of personality. Without a text that deeply involved his emotions throughout – and it is pertinent in this context to remember his admission that it was his susceptibility to words that released his musical imagination – Donizetti wrote a score that comes to life only fitfully, at the moments of deepest sincerity.

Donizetti was further handicapped by the limitations of the company at the Teatro Valle in January 1827, because he was forced to write the lover's role of Camillo for a mezzo-soprano.[22] The use of *musico* roles in opera buffa was rather uncommon, and although they would continue to occur in serious or tragic operas for at least a decade, it seems clear that the Roman audience in 1827 found the intrusion of this type into the relatively more realistic bourgeois world of opera buffa chilling. Maybe this was one instance where the audience's sensibilities demanded that the sexual personality of a character be matched by an appropriate vocal type: the generally lukewarm press for the first performance did not refer particularly to this problem, but it is difficult to imagine that the first hearers were not to some extent disturbed by the spectacle of Isabella striving so hard to attain what to the ears at least was an unconsummatable union. In opera seria, which maintained a greater aesthetic distance than buffa, the spectacle of a mezzo Romeo, for instance, would not seem as strange as a mezzo lover in a comedy, where the tenor was almost a sine qua non in romantic leading parts. The only other important transvestite role in Donizettian comedy is the redoubtable Mamm'Agata in *Le convenienze,* but she is the classic put-down of the stage mother and not a romantic hero. Donizetti rectified the absurdity of the mezzo Camillo later the same year when for its production at the Teatro Nuovo in Naples he adapted the role for the tenor Regoli.

The memorable numbers of *Olivo e Pasquale* are the male quartet (for tenor, baritone, two basses) that precedes the first change of scene in Act 1, and the duet for Isabella and the sympathetic Le Bross (more or less the Dr Malatesta of this plot), 'Isabella, voi scherzate?', in Act 2. In the quartet, Le Bross, a wealthy merchant from Cadiz, introduces himself, while the gruff Olivo, father of Isabella, and his timid brother Pasquale boast of her carefully guarded education, and the busybody Columella adds his comments; the music inspired by the opposing character types is beautifully organized, and the interplay of the overlapping lines creates a genuine sense of exhilaration. In her Act 2 duet Isabella confesses to Le Bross that she loves Camillo, and wins the merchant over to help in convincing her father and uncle of the genuineness of her affection. This situation contains the element of pathos that could move Donizetti to compose genuinely affecting music.

Otto mesi in due ore. The autograph of this work has the original score of 1827 bound in with the revision of 1833, making it very difficult to tell which version of those numbers present in two different guises belongs to which date. For instance, there are two ensemble Benedictions in Act 1, both settings of the same text, and both with the same general layout, the tenor Potoski leading off the melody which the soprano Elisabetta then repeats. But one version, borrowed from the quintet in Act 1 of the 1826 *Gabriella*, was later used again as the basis of the quintet 'Io sentii sulla mia mano' in Act 1 of *Anna Bolena* (which had its Neapolitan *prima* at the San Carlo on 6 July 1832); this, then, is evidently the earlier setting, which Donizetti was obliged to replace for the production of *Otto mesi* in 1833. Such useful evidence is not always available to unknot the problems posed by this autograph.

In *Otto mesi*, which is based on the hit play of Luigi Marchionni's 1820 season in Naples, *La figlia dell'esiliato* (itself derived from a French play by de Pixérécourt), Donizetti takes an important step in trying to reproduce the immediacy of the action of a drama. One of the favored episodes in Marchionni's play was a piece of pantomime for the heroine. In Act 2 of the opera there is a comparable scene, headed 'Discesa di Elisabetta', which depicts Elisabetta's journey across Siberia; the action is accompanied by simple descriptive music (*andante*, 4/4, E flat major), brief figures suggestive of the various movements and emotions specified in the stage directions: 'Elisabetta appears at the summit of a hill, walking slowly . . . she weeps . . . she stops . . . she starts walking again . . . she stumbles and almost falls . . . she raises her hands to heaven . . . she walks . . . stumbles . . . prays to heaven, weeps, and continues to walk.' Pantomimic action, quite a feature of the spoken stage of the period, was an expressive device that Donizetti would use again later, as in Aurelio's descent from the walls of the besieged city during the *introduzione* to *L'assedio de Calais*, and, most notably, at Linda's third-act entrance when Pierotto's hurdy-gurdy-playing leads the demented girl back to Chamounix.

Otto mesi contains indications of Donizetti's increasing sensibility to emotional atmosphere. In the *moderato* of the first finale there is a beautiful hushed effect of whispering voices floating above muted strings. In contrast, the finale to Act 2 takes place during a raging storm and the flooding of the River Kam; it builds gradually and threateningly, a note in the autograph stating 'Se è tamburo la pelle molla' (If a bass drum is available, the head should be slack), until the tempest reaches its full fury. The work ends with an aria–finale, for which Donizetti adapted once more the music first heard at this point in *Le nozze in villa*. The title of *Otto mesi in due ore* is presumably a gesture of defiance against the old concept of the unity of time tacitly observed in most of the librettos Donizetti had set up to this time; the score is also forward-looking in its responsiveness to emotional climate, though this is somewhat diffused by the unsubtle melodrama of the dutiful daughter who trudges from Siberia to the Kremlin to enlist the Tsar's aid in freeing her unjustly exiled father. The vocal writing is frequently florid, more so in the 1827 version than the tighter 1833 version. Like *Gabriella di Vergy*, *Otto mesi* underwent a *rifacimento* after Donizetti's death, when Uranio Fontana added some music of his own to replace the Donizettian originals; this version was first given in French at the Théâtre-Lyrique in 1853, and was then performed the following year in Milan in Italian.

Of the operas written earlier, only *L'ajo* was to continue to be produced fairly regularly; but starting with *Otto mesi*, Donizetti's operas, with some exceptions, were to begin to enjoy wider circulation. In 1831 at Modena the march that introduces the Tsar in Act 3 provided a rallying tune for a popular uprising. Even though the melody came from an autocratic context in the score, political exiles were much on peoples' minds in Italy just then and would become even more so the following year with the publication of Silvio Pellico's *Le miei prigioni*, the harrowing account of his days as a political prisoner of the Austrians in the fortress of Spielberg (near Brünn), from which he was released in 1830. Some credit for the upswing in Donizetti's career during the years between 1827 and 1830, besides that due to his greater experience and confidence, must go to Gilardoni's librettos, which if not major models of their kind, are at least more felicitous than the flawed texts of Tottola and Schmidt. Gilardoni remained Donizetti's favored Neapolitan librettist until his untimely death in 1831.

Il borgomastro di Saardam. The plot of this two-act opera buffa, which followed *Otto mesi* after only three months, has the same general background as that of *Il falegname di Livonia* and once more celebrates an act of generosity by a tsar. The haste with which this score was composed is apparent in its penmanship and numerous shortcuts, although the expressive markings are always clear; it is also apparent in the music itself, which is excessively regular and predictable, the melodies being often built up of obvious sequences. Though one cannot help but be struck by the easy competence and geniality of the work, one looks in vain for anything to catch hold of. The opening of Act 2 contains a clear (if unintentional) echo of Rossini's *Il barbiere di Siviglia* – the music that accompanies Almaviva's entrance disguised as a drunken soldier.

Le convenienze teatrali. Donizetti made two versions of this work: the first, in one act, was named after the play by Sografi on which he based his libretto; later when he expanded the opera into two acts, drawing on Sografi's sequel, *Le inconvenienze teatrali*, he altered the title to *Le convenienze ed inconvenienze teatrali*. Of all the many operas of this fecund period of Donizetti's career, none has more firmly re-established itself upon the stage today than this satire upon an operatic rehearsal. The title, which refers to propriety and impropriety in the theater, has been altered recently to *Viva la mamma* and, regrettably, *The Prima Donna's Mother is a Drag;* hopefully something closer to the original sense will soon be found. For this opera Donizetti provided his own libretto, and its clarity, concision and humor almost match those of the comic librettos of the admirable Ferretti.

Besides the Sografi comedies that are the source of Donizetti's titles at least, links with three roughly contemporary operas can be identified. One is Donizetti's inane heroic opera *Elvida*, which appears disguised as *Romulo ed Ersilia*, the opera the troupe in *Le convenienze* is rehearsing; it would have been readily identifiable to the original audience because the aria, or cavatina and cabaletta, sung by Corilla, the Prima Donna during the *introduzione,* is Elvida's *aria di sortita*, which had been heard at the San Carlo sixteen months earlier. A second link is with the *introduzione* to *Il fortunato inganno*, for many of the same matters (discussions of setting text, imitations of instruments, complaints about music) are dealt with there as, more fully exploited, in *Le convenienze*. The third link concerns the idea of using a baritone *en travesti* for the harridan role of Mamm'Agata; this may well have been suggested by Tamburini's famous exploit in Mercadante's *Elisa e Claudio*, which took place at the Teatro Carolino in Palermo, probably during Donizetti's year there.[23] Tradition has it that Tamburini, singing the role of Arnoldo, in order to make himself heard by the excessively noisy audience started singing in falsetto, having unusual facility and agility in that range; this prompted such applause from the audience and subsequently such disapproval of what were apparently the more limited attainments of the prima donna of the evening (Caterina Lipparini) that she left the theater in a fury. So that the opera might proceed, Tamburini put on her costume, which came nowhere near his wrists or ankles, and performed her role in falsetto, even carrying off a duet between Arnoldo and Elisa; such was his success that he was prevailed upon to appear in the evening's ballet, purportedly dancing a *pas de quatre* with the Taglionis and la Rinaldini. If even half this account is true, here was a motif – the *musico* convention in reverse – that could not help but have appealed to Donizetti's robust sense of humor.

Donizetti's fondness for this opera was sustained, as is proved by his expanding it into two acts and visiting other modifications upon it.[24] As a farsa, in contrast to opera buffa, its humor comes entirely from its hilarious situations, yet there is an appropriate moment of contrast in the tenderly flirtatious duet for the Composer and the Prima Donna (only in the one-act version). The parody in *Le convenienze* remains successful because the characters, for all their preening, their protesting, and their boasting, are the early-nineteenth-century Italian equivalents of types that abound in opera houses and opera studios today. Mamm'Agata is a buffo's dream part with its self-important entrance aria, replete with instrumental imitations, detailing just the sort of aria the Composer should write for her daughter the Seconda Donna; for her own audition she essays the 'willow song' from Rossini's *Otello* – here the text is misremembered, the tonal relationships of one phrase to another distorted, and for the original figurations banalities are substituted, making this the epitome of the unmusical audition – to which Donizetti added the cabaletta that Giuseppe Nicolini composed for Pasta to introduce into Rossini's *Tancredi*,[25] adapting it so as to make it seem inept and supplying it with many passages to be sung in falsetto (Example 27).

Example 27. *Le convenienze teatrali*, cabaletta of Mamm'Agata's aria

This cabaletta appears only in the original version, but it makes an indirect though heartfelt criticism of singers who dragged in show-piece cabalettas regardless of context. The parody reaches its height in the rehearsal of the pseudo-seria *Romulo ed Ersilia* with its fatu-ous march and limp chorus. Allowing *Le convenienze* to make its own points by playing it as a genuine satire of its period (which means resisting the temptation to bury the work in slapstick) permits the genuine humor, and Donizetti's humor is never arch, to emerge.

L'esule di Roma. Of all Donizetti's operas written for Naples during the period of his emergence, this two-act *melodramma eroico* won him the greatest acclaim. Except for the effective *larghetto* in the trio–finale of Act 1 (see pp. 267–76) and the episode of Murena's madness, it is difficult to find much to enthuse about in this chilly, posturing score. Everywhere there is evidence that Donizetti was trying to achieve a neo-classic spaciousness of effect, but the unfor-tunate result all too often is mere laboriousness. The chorus is given great prominence in this opera, its function ranging from the cere-monial to the actively dramatic; it even at times participates in an interlocutory way (as the chorus does in the *introduzione* of the later *Sancia*), and there is interaction among its members, for example at the opening of Act 2. In writing for it Donizetti uses a whole catalogue of devices – canon, imitation and unprepared modulation – which create a 'learned' effect that he only rarely attempted. The inescapable impression is that he composed this score for Mayr: there are many echoes of his teacher's style in the decorative dilation of phrases that have a decidedly eighteenth-century contour. It is as though he had temporarily exhausted his humor and sense of pro-portion on *Le convenienze*, and what he had left to put into *L'esule* comes across too often as long-winded earnestness.

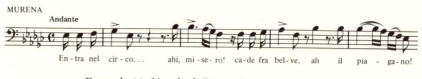

Example 28. *L'esule di Roma*, Act 2, Murena's aria

But *L'esule* is not totally a lost cause. The slow movement of the trio welds the disparate responses of Argelia, Settimio and Murena into an ensemble that is genuinely moving. Murena is Donizetti's first portrait of a deranged character and as such has particular im-portance in his oeuvre. His Act 2 aria, 'Entra nel circo' (*andante*, 4/4, E flat minor) presents a hallucinatory image of Settimio being torn to pieces by wild beasts; Donizetti sets the text clearly, in detached phrases with harshly regular accents, vivifying Murena's guilty conscience by expanding the phrase-ending on 'piagono' as Murena imagines the wounds inflicted on his innocent victim (Example 28).

Alina, regina di Golconda. Since *Le convenienze* has attracted the Donizetti revivalists of today, it is surprising that *Alina* has not yet tempted them. This two-act opera buffa was written for the opening season of the Teatro Carlo Felice, Genoa, in 1828 and then substantially revised[26] for a production at the Valle the following year with Annetta Fischer and Pietro Gentili; it was, up to that time, Donizetti's most carefully worked-out comedy. The score is rather long and elaborate and makes greater use of the chorus than was his custom in buffa works. To judge from the quality of the music with which he invested it, Donizetti was sincerely taken with this rather old-fashioned subject; it goes back to the narrative of de Boufflers (1761) which Sedaine subsequently adapted as a libretto for an opera-ballet by Monsigny (1766).

Something of the quality of Alina can be surmised from the passage, superbly evocative of rural Provence, that accompanies Volmar's awakening to behold an illusory landscape contrived by Alina to remind him of the days when they first fell in love. He looks about him, beguiled by the scene and by the music (provided by an offstage female chorus) (Example 29). The folk-song drone at the beginning is counterbalanced later by sinuous chromatic movement. In the enchanting introductory orchestral passage there occurs one of the rare examples of Donizetti's writing landscape music, here a soothing pastoral. For surety of effect and exquisite balance this whole episode ranks as a special achievement. Elsewhere in *Alina*, the admirable craftsmanship Donizetti lavished on this score is evident. The quartet in Act 1 for two sopranos, baritone and buffo, where Alina and Fiorina confront their long-lost husbands, sustains a fine sense of poise between subjects and countersubjects, and the canonic effects, unlike those in *L'esule*, seem wholly spontaneous.

Although the formal structure of *Alina* makes Donizetti's deployment of musical ideas frequently predictable, the quality of these ideas is consistently high. A case in point is the large-scale finale to Act 1. It begins with an attractive chorus for women's voices (*allegro*, 6/8, B flat major) which is soon followed by a *largo* (A flat major), precipitated by Alina's revelation to the astonished Seide that Volmar is her husband. This *largo*, 'Tace sorpreso e attonito' (Example 30), exploits exactly the same kind of situation as the famous 'Fredda ed immobile' episode from the first finale of Rossini's

Example 29. *Alina, regina di Golconda*, Act 2, Volmar's aria with chorus

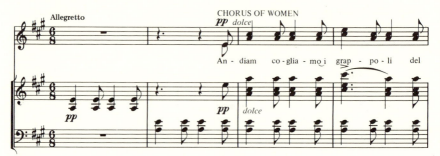

Il barbiere. Since Donizetti's rossinianismo in the operas of this period is more often talked about than examined, a comparison of these two episodes would seem to be in order.

Both ensembles are in the same key and similar rhythm (Alina, 6/8; Il barbiere, 12/8). Rossini's consists of two balancing periods, the first repeated three times, the second twice (a a¹ a² b b codetta). Rosina states the melody, which is repeated in full by the Count and then Bartolo canonically; the second period is dominated by Figaro in a new melody, the other parts functioning harmonically. In Donizetti's ensemble, the canonic beginning is limited to two voices, of which the second (Volmar) is identical with the first neither in harmony – for it moves from V to I – nor melody – it is extended an extra measure by a protracted cadence. Nor is it as strict a canon as Rossini's, since a third voice (Belfiore) accompanies the second statement. The second period of Donizetti's ensemble consists of three episodes, each only four measures long: the first comprises two agitated phrases for the tenor, Seide, echoed sotto voce by the chorus; the second uses the material of the first, on which is superimposed a variant of part of the first period of the ensemble, now sung by Alina and Fiorina; in the third this material is further developed in a tutti. Donizetti's procedure here is to thicken the texture progressively, giving a sense of climax and increasing complexity. The larghetto closes with a codetta consisting of four measures of vocal cadences followed by four more for orchestra. Donizetti's ensemble is less symmetrical than Rossini's, it employs the voices with greater independence and builds to a more emphatic, more contrapuntal climax. In fact, little more of the Rossinian epi-

Example 30. *Alina, regina di Golconda*, Act 1, *largo of the finale*

sode is imitated here than the general situation and the canonic
entrance of the second voice; 'Tace sorpreso e attonito' can more
legitimately be labeled Donizettian than Rossinian.

Gianni di Calais. This three-act semiseria was composed and produced three months after *Alina*. Its genial but sprawling text, by
Gilardoni, lacks any suspense because every event is foretold and
every prediction exactly fulfilled. The most attractive aria in *Gianni*
is Rustano's barcarolle in Act 1, 'Una barchetta in mar solcando va',
an interesting example of Donizetti's adapting to operatic purposes
the vein of the popular Neapolitan song, which he exploited further
in later comic scores. *Gianni di Calais* ends with an aria–finale, the
rondò in variation form, 'Dopo tante e tante pene', being a depressingly mechanical example of that type. When Donizetti was
preparing the Italian version of *La fille du régiment* he rifled *Gianni
di Calais*, taking Gianni's Act 2 aria, 'Fasti? Pompe? Omaggi?
Onori?', to serve as Tonio's *aria di sortita*.

Il paria. Although Donizetti was later to dismantle the score of this
two-act opera seria, using parts of it in *La romanziera e l'uomo nero*,
Anna Bolena, *Tasso* and *Le duc d'Albe*, the opera in its original form
must stand as Donizetti's finest achievement up to this point. None
of his scores so far had included so much expressive detail. The

accompanied recitatives boast highly evocative introductory figures that often move chromatically, and the recitative itself often develops into expressive arioso. The vocal writing responds vividly to textual values and dramatic situations: in Idamore's entrance aria, 'Lontano...io più...l'amai', the line moves down the scale from the dominant to the tonic of F minor, the phrases broken into short gasps that illustrate his sorrow and despair at learning that his father has arranged a marriage to an unknown woman when he wants only to wed Neala. And Donizetti had as yet composed nothing to match the honeyed sensuousness of the opening of the Act 2 love duet (Example 31). The scale in the accompaniment up to D flat (the flattened sixth) hints straight away at the ambiguity between major and minor (a favored terrain for Donizetti), and this ambiguity is exploited in the latter half of Idamore's solo. The persuasiveness of the supple vocal line in Example 31 stems in large part from the chromatic sequence in measure 7, and the rising appoggiatura (G sharp to A) at the end of that phrase. One could cite most of this score for its attractive features and for the pervasive evidence of Donizetti's care and sense of proportion, this last allowing characters who could so easily have been stereotypes to be depicted in large measure convincingly. These merits are found almost everywhere from the spacious multiform *introduzione* (which consists of Akebare's solemn phrases, prefiguring the style of Oroveso, an energetic mixed chorus, and Neala's fine double aria) to the concluding quartet, a signal example of Donizetti's 'shaking off the yoke' of the aria–finale.

Il paria, then, is the first of Donizetti's scores to give an adequate and consistent preview of his mature style. And if one were to fall back on the cliché of dividing a composer's output into periods – seldom useful because it tends to place some scores outside an imaginary pale – one would be tempted in Donizetti's case to single out the obscure *Il paria* as marking one sort of watershed. Part of the credit for its virtues, but also the blame for its short success, must go to Gilardoni's libretto: on the one hand this is a relatively clear and succinct reduction (probably assisted by the libretto of Carafa's opera, 1826, and the book of Salvatore Taglioni's ballet, 1827) of Delavigne's prolix tragedy, but on the other it preserves the latter's flawed dramaturgy, which makes it a tragedy manqué. There is no ultimate catharsis in the situation that leaves Idamore exposed as the son of a pariah, his father Zarete bewailing his fate as an outcast, Neala's father fulminating against impiety, and the poor girl foreseeing her own death and promising soon to belong to her lover forever. All

Example 31. *Il paria*, Act 2, *larghetto* of the Neala–Idamore duet

this, presented as a quartet, makes an effective musical climax but not a satisfactory dramatic ending because it lacks the intensity of focus upon a single victim; Donizetti only later discovered the importance of this element and the efficacy of the aria–finale in a genuinely tragic situation.

Il giovedì grasso. Among Donizetti's short romantic comedies this one-act farsa is one of the better examples, and it has recently come successfully through several revivals. The *introduzione* begins as a farewell duet for Nina and Teodoro and develops into an engaging quintet after Sigismondo has outlined his plan for foiling the intention of Nina's father to marry her to a stranger. There is a delightful trio in which the unwanted suitor, Ernesto, turns the tables on Sigismondo and his wife; here the easy handling of the melodic ideas testifies to Donizetti's increasing fluency – not that the ideas in themselves are remarkable, but they succeed one another with a natural facility that is most attractive. Sigismondo's aria in Neapolitan dialect, 'Cola Cò non fa zimeo', written for Lablache, turns once again to the world of Neapolitan song, this time in the shape of a tarantella. The aria–finale of *Il giovedì grasso* consists of an elaborate *maestoso* for Nina, which lead directly into an *allegretto* – three verses for different characters separated by a refrain in praise of Carnival. Donizetti's fondness for this score caused him later to write an aria, 'Che prego per riuscita',[27] for Tamburini, to take the place of Sigismondo's dialect tarantella.

Il castello di Kenilworth. Originally entitled *Elisabetta al castello di Kenilworth*, the shorter form of the title of this work became current after the season in which it was first performed. A three-act opera seria, following *Il paria* after about six months, it marks no clear line in Donizetti's development. Because it was composed to be performed at the royal gala on the queen's birthday it has the regulation happy ending – the stage queen's clemency at the end apparently constituting, in spite of the resulting unprepared volte-face, an acceptable compliment to the cheerily amoral Maria Isabella in the royal box. The frustration of *Il paria*'s ineffective conclusion had not weaned Donizetti from the idea of a quartet–finale, but in *Il castello* he placed it as the climax to Act 2, making of it the finest number in this short score.

Il castello is far from the negligible work it is often said to be, although, admittedly, it suffers from a melodramatic plot that is unclearly motivated, and the vocal embellishments of Elisabetta's melodies, unlike those of Neala in *Il paria*, are, especially in her aria–finale, extrovert and ceremonial rather than expressive of deep personal emotions. The Act 1 duet, 'Non mentir!', between Amelia (Amy Robsart) and Warney opens with rhetorical flourishes of a distinctly Rossinian cast for each participant, as though Donizetti, barely recovered from a serious illness and writing in haste to meet his deadline, fell back on formulas of proven effect; what makes this duet more than a mere reinvocation of the past is its fine, if crude, dramatic energy, especially in the cabaletta, 'De' tuoi rifiuti pentirai', where Warney's striding F major contrasts with Amelia's cowering D minor.

As has been pointed out, this is the first of Donizetti's serious operas to contain two opposing female roles. And this is just one indication of Donizetti's continuing desire to enlarge his repertory of musico-dramatic situations. He wrote to Mayr: 'I would not give one piece of *Il paria* for all of *Castello di Kenilworth*',[28] and one cannot help but substantially agree with his judgment. The Neapolitan public did not, however, for *Il castello* made at least a temporary place for itself at the San Carlo. In 1830, the year following the first production, Donizetti revised the role of Warney, changing it from the tenor range to the baritone; but the traces of the former arrangement are plain to see, as in Warney's duet with Amelia, where his melodic periods are in the same keys as hers and not in the dominant, which would be the normal key relationship in a duet between soprano and baritone.

I pazzi per progetto. This one-act farsa, composed to fill up the bill at Donizetti's benefit night at the San Carlo, is set in an asylum for the insane; with its feigned mad scenes it creates an uncomfortably ironical sense of humor. Musically, it is a predictable series of numbers, seven in all, from chattering *introduzione* through the usual series of aria, quartet and various duets to the aria–finale. The comedy is externalized and brittle, made monotonous by the presence of five basses, all of whom adopt the same buffo clichés, and lacking in those moments of pathos that in his best comedies give Donizetti's humor its humanity. It is difficult to feel much sympathy for this contrived and, at heart, tasteless piece.

Il diluvio universale. The term 'azione tragica-sacra', used to define this three-act work, denotes a staged oratorio; Rossini's *Mosè* is of the same ilk. *Il diluvio* had its *prima* only twenty-two days after *I pazzi per progetto*, suggesting that Donizetti may have dashed off that unfortunate comedy, in the intervals between bouts of working on this grandiose score. *Il diluvio* is built upon a crude contrast between the sacred and the profane: the unswerving faith of Noè and his family is set against the hedonistic court of Cadmo, satrap of Sennaar; these opposing attitudes are brought into conflict by Sela, Cadmo's wife, who wishes to share in the belief of Noè. Donizetti's tackling of this mixed genre, of which *Il diluvio* is the lone exemplar among his works, is further evidence of his campaign to broaden his expressive horizons, and his belief in this work is demonstrated by his revising it for the Carlo Felice in 1833–4.[29] If *L'esule*, written two years earlier, can be seen as his attempt to assimilate the style of Mayr, *Il diluvio* appears as an effort to absorb the manner of Rossini at the Opéra with *Moïse*.

The influence of Rossini can be conveniently illustrated by the role of Noè written for Lablache. Since one of the most famous pages of Rossini's score was the prayer, 'Dal tuo stellato soglio', it is not surprising to find a prayer for Noè in Act 2 of *Il diluvio*, 'Dio tremendo onnipossente' (*andante religioso*, 3/4, G flat minor/G flat major); it is introduced by a harp cadenza, marked 'a piacere', and accompanied by harp arpeggios against sustained harmonies for winds and horns. Noè's recitatives are solemn and hortatory, made emphatic by large intervals, and punctuated not by chords for the strings, but for trumpet, horns and bassoon. His fervent faith is established in the *introduzione*, another prayer, now in the form of a quintet with chorus, where the orchestral color seems to suggest an organ-like resonance. The Rossinian effect of *Il diluvio* is clinched by the final tableau which is reminiscent of both *Moïse* and *Guillaume Tell*; it is just forty-seven measures long, beginning in G minor and ending in E major, and shows an inundated landscape with a few survivors huddling on a still unflooded peak while the ark floats safely on the waters.

Il diluvio is, in part at least, an impressive achievement, but the profane elements of the plot rarely rise above the conventional. Although this mixture of oratorio and opera does not have an impressive performance history, it was, in spite of the contretemps of the Neapolitan *prima*, a respectable success. Toto Vasselli, asked by the busy Gaetano to forward to Mayr the news of its initial reception, had this to say:

After a long silence I find myself constrained to announce to you that the sacred opera of our Gaetano, *Il diluvio*, had an outcome fortunate beyond any description. I do not want to embroider eulogies because I could not do it adequately. It will suffice that the bitterest of his enemies, the journalist Prividali, praises it, and therefore I am sending you his review.[30]

Imelda de' Lambertazzi. In contrast to *Il diluvio*, the very slim performance history of this two-act tragedy is no measure of its significance in the Donizetti canon. There were no Italian performances after its first production (though there were two in Spain during the 1840s) until a single remounting at Sinigaglia in the summer of 1856.[31] With *Imelda* Donizetti for the first time had an opera produced that ended with onstage deaths, thereby fulfilling the prophecy he had made to Mayr in 1828, at the time of the encouraging reception accorded to *L'esule*: 'Next year I will finish a first act with a quartet and the second act with a death, according to my intention.'[32] *Imelda* misses this prediction by eight months and three weeks, but otherwise it holds true. The structural significance of the quartet has been pointed out in discussing the conclusion of *Il paria* and the Act 2 finale of *Il castello di Kenilworth*; at the end of *Imelda* the baritone hero, Bonifacio, is stabbed by the heroine's brother, who though himself fatally wounded in the duel, manages, in a *Forza*-like gesture, to run his sister through before he dies.[33] Deaths with a vengeance! The suffering of the scene is not minimized, as can be seen from this passage:

> Imelda: Padre...son...rea...lo vedo!
> (*between her death rattles*) Ma son tua figlia ancora!
> Almen...nell'ultim'ora...
> Non...mi scacciar...da te. (*she dies*)

(Father...I am guilty...I see it! But I am still your daughter! At least...in my final hour...do not drive me away...from you.)

This is dying in the spotlight, a vast difference from, for example, Semiramide's single cry of 'Oh, Dio!' before she collapses out of sight behind Ninus's tomb. Unlike the heroines of later Romantic melodramas, whose last thoughts are apt to be of a delayed reunion in heaven, Imelda confesses her guilt and seeks to be reconciled to her father; it was probably this note of confession and desire to come to terms with authority that made her death acceptable to the Neapolitan censors, who were as concerned with public morality as they were with matters of lèse majesté and possible affronts to the Church. (The activities of the censors can be clearly detected in the considerable divergence between the text of *Imelda* as it appears in the autograph and the libretto printed for the *prima* by Flautina.)

There is a crude, noisy energy rampant in many of the crowd scenes in *Imelda*: in the *introduzione* Lamberto whips up the followers of the Lambertazzi to rabid fury against the Geremei, and the finale to Act 2 begins with the mercenaries of the opposing Guelph and Ghibelline houses skirmishing before the terrified townspeople.

The disposition of the vocal parts is interesting: for the first time Donizetti wrote a romantic role for a baritone hero, casting for tenors the important roles of the hero's bloodthirsty adversary and the head of the house of Lambertazzi; then, also unusually, the tessitura of Imelda's part, designed for Antonietta Galzerani, is that of a high mezzo-soprano. During the first run of *Anna Bolena*, the following winter, Donizetti adapted the cabaletta, 'Restati pur, m'udrai', of Imelda's and Bonifacio's Act 1 duet to serve as the second episode of a 'new' duet for Anna and Percy (that which begins, 'Sì, son io'); though he retained the original text, he extended each melodic statement with new material and transposed the duet up from E flat to B flat, giving the opening statement to Anna, where originally it had been the baritone's.

In many ways and in spite of its crudities and bombastic libretto, *Imelda* can be seen as a logical climax to this phase of Donizetti's career, when his activities were mainly centered in Naples.[34] The works of this period fall comfortably into two disparate groups. The first group, ending with *Elvida*, covers a period during which Donizetti regarded himself as learning on the job; as he frequently admitted, with perfect sincerity, to Mayr, he felt at this stage that his lack of knowledge was detrimental to his work. Of these nine scores only *L'ajo* made any lasting impression. In the second group, which begins with the 'closet' *Gabriella* of 1826, there is a marked gain in confidence and a fairly sustained reaching out toward different styles and larger-scale subjects, apparently according to some inner-directed program, as the sequence of *L'esule*, *Il paria*, *Il castello*, *Il diluvio* and *Imelda* corroborates. Certainly, two features of *Imelda*, its baritone hero and its tragic conclusion, are clear indications of directions that Donizetti would later explore more fully.

10

The operas
1830–1835

Anna Bolena. With this opera seria in two acts Donizetti emerged at long last as one of the leading operatic composers of his day. The traditional view of *Anna Bolena* as a sudden leap into excellence, as the point at which, all at once, Donizetti discarded his older derivative style, is highly misleading. Rather it is the logical culmination of all his previous experience. The appreciable amount of his earlier music that he adapted for *Anna Bolena*, music from *Otto mesi*, *Il paria* and *Imelda* as well as *Enrico di Borgogna*, argues for a consistent and steady development rather than a radically new departure.

Anna Bolena richly deserved its success, and part of it was due to the exceptionally favorable circumstances under which it was composed. For the first time Donizetti had a satisfactory libretto from Felice Romani. The two Romani texts he had set earlier, the hopeless semiseria *Chiara e Serafina* and the elegant but old-fashioned buffa *Alina*, were not in the same class as the libretto for *Anna*, whose superiority lies in its clear focus upon its tragic heroine and in its opportunities for pathos and for clearly motivated interaction. A great advantage to Donizetti during the period of composing *Anna* was the friendly co-operation of Pasta who was to be the prima donna. It could well have been she who saw the possibilities of adapting Enrico's cabaletta as Anna's final cavatina: Donizetti's normal practise in using borrowed music was to preserve its original function, however greatly he modified it, but this is not the case with the *Enrico–Anna* material. The greatest advantage, and perhaps the most difficult to assess, was Donizetti's own sense of the degree to which his own future depended on winning over the previously hostile, or at best indifferent, Milanese.

The merit of *Anna Bolena* lies not in any radical departures from Donizetti's previous norms of structure, but rather in the generally higher level of expression to which his imagination was stimulated by the well-realized characters he was bringing to life. About a

month after the *prima* at the Carcano, *Anna* was temporarily withdrawn while Donizetti replaced three numbers: Percy's cabaletta in
Act 1, both parts of the Anna–Percy duet in the final scene of Act 1,
and the cabaletta of the trio in Act 2. His desire to improve the work
was not restricted to substituting one section for another. The autograph score shows deletions of fully orchestrated passages, which
may have been eliminated during the process of composition, or
while the rehearsals were in progress, or perhaps during the overhaul
of January 1831 – since they involve no change of text it is now
impossible to tell. The common denominator in these deletions (as
opposed to the substitutions) is that they increase the forward
momentum of the opera. Among the passages cut out were eight
measures of Anna's cavatina, 'Come innocente giovane', just before
the coda, and an orchestral statement of the melody of Giovanna's
'Per questa fiamma indomita', which leaves one measure of string
arpeggios to precede her vocal line.[1] The total effect of these minor
adjustments, which range from dropping a single measure in some
places to eliminating the second and third periods of the opening
chorus so that it moves directly from opening period to the extensive
coda, is to de-emphasize predictable resolutions and formulas of
structure so that they do not impede dramatic progress. Not that
many of the forms used in this score are not perfectly regular, but the
autograph shows Donizetti's increasing sensitivity to keeping the
drama alive and moving.

One of the most important improvements to be found in *Anna
Bolena* is that for the first time Donizetti created a final scene sufficiently expansive to bear all the weight of the musical and emotional
climax of the work. Its effect is infinitely more telling than any
Donizetti had achieved in the operas that conform to the tradition of
the *lieto fine,* which has the almost unavoidable consequence of
trivializing the preceding action; and it is more deeply moving than
the implicit tragedy of the *Il paria* quartet, or the garish, gasping
vignette of a death scene presented in *Imelda.* The scope of the
aria–finale is expanded to fill almost an entire scene; combining
aspects of the mad scene and the death scene, it vividly presents the
stages of Anna's retreat from unendurable reality, through longing
for release, to triumph, once her reason is restored, as she finds the
spiritual strength not to curse but to forgive those who have brought
her to her death. In this splendid episode Donizetti provided sopranos with a classic test of their vocal and dramatic powers.

Anna's scene is prefaced by a prelude of twenty-five measures
which serves to introduce, briefly, the melody of the succeeding F

minor chorus but also, more extensively (by means of a fine oboe solo), to establish the tragic atmosphere. The chorus for Anna's attendants, 'Chi può vederla', has a middle section twice the length of the opening period (sixteen measures), but the latter is repeated before the (even shorter) coda, which resolves into the parallel major only in the final cadence. A noble melody in the strings accompanies Anna's entrance, recalling that she is still a queen even though her mind is now disoriented and her dress in disarray. Each of her disjointed moods is characterized by a short melodic idea, among them the second theme of the overture, a reference not otherwise exploited in the score, when she thinks of adorning herself for her marriage to Percy.[2] A solo cor anglais introduces the purling opening phrases of Anna's 'Al dolce guidami' (larghetto, 2/4, F major, a a^1 b b^1), and it provides an obbligato at many points, frequently emphasizing the interval of the descending major and minor second, as she withdraws into a dream of adolescent yearning. This aria really does not end with Anna's final note, although in performance the singer is customarily applauded at this point, for it closes with four brief phrases for the chorus in their key of F minor, coming to rest on the dominant to provide a transition to the next episode.

The materia di mezzo is unusually extensive, running to more than 220 measures. It consists of: a march (maestoso, A flat major), as the other prisoners, Smeton, Percy and Rochefort, are brought in; recitative, developing into arioso (G minor); Anna's cantabile, 'Cielo a' miei lunghi spasimi' (lento, 2/4, G major), in effect an extra aria (twenty-four measures) for her, upon a variant of the tune familiar as Home, sweet home, the latter part with three harmonizing voices; a section for offstage band (allegro, 2/4, E flat major), punctuated by cannon shots and bells, depicting the premature wedding procession of Enrico and Seymour; recitative introducing the cabaletta. The cabaletta, 'Coppia iniqua', which is regular (moderato, E flat major), is energetic and exploits the extremes of vocal register, overwhelmingly conveying the ultimate expression of Anna's passion. And with it, the full tragic catharsis is achieved. Throughout this remarkable scene the vocal embellishments, at least those written out by Donizetti, are anything but empty decorations, rather they communicate the dilations of deep feeling. While the subtly inflected, seamless melody of 'Al dolce guidami' has suggested to many commentators the influence of Bellinian melos, the differences between the aria–finales of Bellini's Il pirata (1827) and La straniera (1829) and the final scene of Anna Bolena are significant. In Anna the whole complex of structures making up the aria–finale expands to fill most of the scenic unit. 'Al dolce guidami' is in binary form, while Bellini's corresponding sections employ the more usual ternary pattern. The contrast between the main parts in each of Bellini's double arias[3] is single and drastic, while Donizetti's scene involves a gradual development through contrasting moments of withdrawal and rationality to Anna's hard-won spiritual victory; and for all his success at exploiting the pathos of the scene, Donizetti has not ignored its dramatic irony.[4]

Though the closing scene contains the finest pages of *Anna Bolena*, it does not contain the only ones of lasting value in this opera. The fine duet for Anna and Seymour in Act 2 has already been discussed (see pp. 256–8). Remarkable in another way is the duet for Seymour and Enrico at the close of the opening scene. Even though its overall format is only slightly innovative, and less so than the Anna–Seymour duet, it contains some interesting detail.[5] The contrast between the remorseful Seymour and the King, a fascinating combination of wooer and tyrant who will brook no opposition, is maintained through the opening section and through the *larghetto*, where their melodic lines retain a surprising independence even when, in the last third of the movement, they overlap. Donizetti adopts the unusual device of repeating one of Seymour's melodies from the *larghetto*, 'Di un tripudio avrò la pena', a tone higher in the *moderato*, where her words are 'Ah! più rimorsi, più rimorsi, per pietà'. The two statements of the *moderato* are equal in length, but that equality is arrived at by eliminating Seymour's opening period, 'Ah, qual sia', the second time round and compensating for it by adding the same number of measures of vocal cadences at the end.

One particular feature of the score of *Anna Bolena* is the high quality of the ensembles, particularly their slow sections. The quintet in Act 1 scene ii, 'Io sentii sulla mia mano', which was borrowed from *Otto mesi* and revised, begins with a canonic entrance for three of the five voices which is both skillful and expressive; but its concluding stretta, of which the second period is begun by the tenor and soprano, again with a hint of canonic treatment, is on a lower level of achievement. The sextet 'In quegli sguardo impresso', which forms the slow section of the ensemble–finale in Act 1 scene iii, can produce a fine effect. The finale begins with Anna's plea for recognition that she has been innocently compromised, and continues with Enrico's furious threats in the parallel minor; the solo passages are succeeded by the sextet, the voices deployed in imitation, and Donizetti's characteristic modal ambiguity is maintained almost to the final cadence. The trio in Act 2 scene ii, 'Fin dall'età più tenera' (*larghetto*, 2/4, G minor/G major), which begins as if it were an aria for Percy, contains in its C major second half a particularly Rossinian luxuriousness of figuration; in the superbly energetic cabaletta, 'Salirà d'Inghilterra sul trono' (*presto*, 2/4, C major), the opening statement is divided between Enrico (solo) and Anna and Percy (in unison), but in the second statement the passage for Anna and Percy lacks its first half and the three voices sing together, continuing through the long coda. This cabaletta is one of Donizetti's exploitations of the rhythmic formula ♩ ♫ ♩ ♫ ♩ ♫ which here succeeds in generating and sustaining passionate intensity to the point of obsessiveness.

This discussion of *Anna Bolena* began by insisting upon it as the culmination of Donizetti's previous experience rather than a new departure. The high degree of accomplishment evident in many parts of this score is the hard-won result of his efforts to find, largely within the inherited syntax, a broadly expressive vocabulary, appropriate to a dramatically satisfactory libretto. *Anna Bolena* is truly a Janus-like work, for it opens up the main path leading toward the very considerable operas Donizetti was to write later. Its success strengthened his self-confidence in a beneficial way, and proved to him that the vogue for Romantic tragedy was established. Best of all, it set important theaters clamoring for his services, and although Naples would remain for nearly a decade the hub of his activities, much of his future would be spent in the relatively less conservative atmosphere of the north.

Gianni di Parigi. Donizetti wrote this two-act *opera comica*[6] for Rubini (setting a libretto by Romani originally written for Morlacchi in 1818), in the hope that the tenor would use it for a benefit evening at the Théâtre-Italien in Paris. His gesture bespeaks both his goodwill toward Rubini and his eagerness to catch the attention of a Parisian audience. Rubini failed to avail himself of this favor, much to the composer's disappointment, both because Boieldieu's opera on the same subject was a long-established favorite in Paris, and because in the French capital the chief focus of Rubini's career was upon star-crossed romantic heroes like Gualtiero and Percy rather than outmoded chivalric figures like Gianni. Donizetti's wellintended, but undeniably naive, gesture stems perhaps from his nostalgic memories of collaborating with Rubini on another opera in the same old-fashioned vein, *Gianni di Calais*. Rubini did sing the latter work at the Théâtre-Italien and its scant success may have discouraged him from making a second, similar experiment.

Gianni di Parigi has a limited performance history: its *prima* took place at La Scala in 1839, but this production, not authorized by Donizetti who was then in Paris, lasted for only four performances; it was given only once again at the San Carlo (from 10 March 1846), when Donizetti was already a patient at Ivry, and there its run was limited to a single season. Obviously, since neither of these productions was supervised by Donizetti, someone else made the changes in the score that emerge from a comparison of the two librettos[7] and from the considerable amount of non-autograph material mixed in with the autograph at Naples.[8]

For all its little success, the opera contains some agreeable surprises. For instance, there is the lovely lyrical passage in an episode of the duet between Gianni and the Princess in Act 2 (Example 32). Notable here is the freedom with which the melody develops. Instead of the usual pattern according to which the third phrase substantially echoes the first, here it is the fourth phrase which echoes the third; and instead of the first four phrases forming a subdivison of a melodic unit, the forward movement of the harmony keeps the line moving on to the cadences at the ends of the fifth and seventh phrases. This passage merits attention, too, as an example of Donizetti's own brand of *bellinianismo*; it is one of those ecstatic melodies in which Rubini could command the rapt attention of an audience with a whisper. One of Gianni's arias is well known to contemporary audiences in a different guise: his Act 1 cabaletta, 'Tutti qui spero', is the source of Don Pasquale's 'Un fuoco insolito', which is transposed down a fifth from the original. The buffo duet between the innkeeper Pedrigo and the self-important Seneschal shows Donizetti's easy verve in combining cunning and pomposity with irresistible results – particularly fine is the section in 12/8 meter. Vocal challenges abound in Gianni's role, especially in the Act 1 terzetto, and also in the music for the Princess, although neither her Act 1 double aria nor her final *rondò* is in Donizetti's hand.

Francesca di Foix. To judge by the autograph in Naples, Donizetti originally wrote this one-act semiseria with the title *Il paggio e l'anello*, which he then crossed out and replaced with the present title. The eight numbers of the score are separated by unusually lengthy string-accompanied recitatives; changes in the words of the recitative preceding the Duke's aria and of the aria itself suggest that the aria was borrowed from some other context.[9] The apportionment of the male roles to vocal types in this opera is rather unusual,

Example 32. *Gianni di Parigi*, Act 2, *larghetto* of the Gianni–Princess
duet

perhaps because its subject is jealousy rather than romantic love: the King, whose only aria forms part of the multiform *introduzione*, is a baritone role, written for Tamburini; the Count, Francesca's jealous husband, is a basso buffo; the Duke, a character who is largely peripheral to the plot, is the leading tenor and participates in a duet as well as his one-section aria. The score also contains the *musichetto* role of the page, Edmondo, sung by a mezzo, whose actions precipitate the plot; his song, 'È una giovane straniera', is reminiscent of a Neapolitan song with its jaunty 6/8 rhythm and minor–major sequence. All told, however, *Francesca di Foix* is a largely inconsequential score – more of a postscript to his earlier Neapolitan one-acters than a post-*Anna Bolena* work.

La romanziera e l'uomo nero. It is difficult to say much about this one-act farsa, which appeared not long after *Francesca*, because no copy is known of the libretto containing the spoken dialogue. The plot is a satire on Romanticism: in the *rondò*–finale Antonina assures her father that she will give up willows, cypresses, urns and ashes, and take up more appropriate pursuits like singing and dancing and going to the opera. The most notable thing about the rather routine music is the borrowing of the melody of the final quartet from *Il paria* to be parodied by Antonina in the terzetto, 'Dopo tante e tante pene'. Even more obvious is the parody of the Gondolier's song from Rossini's *Otello* in Filidoro's canzonetta: 'Non v'è maggior dolore che aver vuota la pancia e far l'amore nella miseria.' (There is no greater grief than to have an empty belly and to make love in time of distress.)[10] That Romanticism by 1831 in Naples was a subject for this sort of satirical treatment says a great deal about its spread as a literary movement, which paved the way for its dominance in the opera house during the 1830s and after, and it is a reassuring measure of Donizetti's objectivity and sense of humor that he set such a text. One can only hope that the full text of *La romanziera e l'uomo nero* will be rediscovered, for this brief work (only seven numbers) deserves to participate in the Donizetti revival.

Fausta. Donizetti's first opera seria after *Anna Bolena* shows him applying his new assurance to a tragic pendant to *L'esule di Roma*. The assurance takes the form of a larger-scale approach: a trio–finale to Act 1, the compound *introduzione* (described on p. 249), the extensive participation of the chorus, and a superfluity of martial and ceremonial music. This opera attempts to set up a contrast between the public life of ancient Rome and the private emotions of its characters; not surprisingly, the latter come off better than the former, the portrayal of which, with its rhythmic monotony, soon becomes chillingly redundant. The character of Fausta is a sort of Roman equivalent of Phèdre; she lusts for her stepson, accuses him of improper advances after he repulses her, and, when she learns of his execution, poisons herself. Obviously, Donizetti was attracted to the passionate possibilities of this character, and equally obviously he was attracted to the vocal possibilities of Ronzi who was to sing it. This was the first of the great parts he tailored to Ronzi's abilities, and it is worthwhile to remember that, in 1832 at least, Donizetti preferred Ronzi as an all-around artist to Malibran. A precious insight into Ronzi's vocal manner is given by Cottrau, even though he is voicing an unfavorable opinion: '[Ronzi's] voice displeases me completely and her expression always seems to me a little outrageous. I should say over-nuanced – do you understand me? – on every word and almost every note.'[11] Indeed, in Fausta's aria–finale, 'Tu che volli già spirto beato' (*cantabile*, 4/4, E flat minor/E flat major) (Example 33), not only the sweep of the opening phrases (already heard in the *maestoso* opening of the overture –

Example 33. *Fausta*, Act 2, cavatina of Fausta's aria–finale

though there in E minor) but also the sixteenth-note figurations at the words 'Te lo chiedo per quanto io t'amato' are accented to produce an alternating effect that fits Cottrau's word 'nuanced'.

'Tu che volli', with its vigorous cabaletta, 'No, qui morir degg'io' (*maestoso*, 4/4, E flat major), is the great moment of a curiously uneven score. So great was the celebrity of this double aria in the succeeding two decades that when Marianna Barbieri-Nini, famous for her association with Verdi's operas, particularly the 1847 version of *Macbeth*, wrote to him to describe her vocal style, she mentioned that these pages from *Fausta* were especially well suited to her voice. The potency of these arias indicates that Donizetti recognized, after the success of *Anna Bolena*, the importance of an overwhelming conclusion; in fact, Fausta's scene, relative to the rest of the rather sprawling score, is more concise than Anna's, and Donizetti evidently gained some advantage from setting his own text (Gilardoni had died before completing this libretto and the composer himself had supplied the missing passages).

Early on Donizetti recognized that *Fausta*, for all its powerful depiction of the title character, was an uneven work, and he subsequently made some efforts to strengthen it. First he adapted Tamburini's role of Costantino, Fausta's husband, for the bass Lablache in preparation for the revival of *Fausta* at the San Carlo (which was banned before any performances could be given). Then he revised the work for Pasta and Donzelli when they sang it at the Fenice in Venice in 1834; on this occasion he wrote a new duet, 'Per te vi nunzio al soglio', (later transferred to Act 2 of *Maria Stuarda*), and altered the parallel key relationships of the final arias for Pasta, moving 'Tu che volli' up to F minor/F major and transposing the cabaletta down to D. Perhaps the greatest lesson that Donizetti learned from *Fausta* emerges in the next of his operas to be set in the classical past, *Belisario*; it is an altogether more economical score than *Fausta*.

Ugo, conte di Parigi. This opera was Donizetti's ill-fated contribution to the 1831–2 Carnival season at La Scala – the season that saw *Norma*, after a contested opening night, establish itself as an almost instant classic. *Ugo* employed the same cast of singers as *Norma* (Pasta, Giulia Grisi, Donzelli and Negrini), and, in addition, Corradi-Pantanelli (in the *musico* role of Luigi V of France) and Felicita Baillou-Hillaret (as the queen-mother, Emma); but even these luminaries could not save the work. Part of the blame must go to the censors, who reduced Romani's libretto to a puzzle, and to the unsympathetic nature of Pasta's role of Bianca, whose jealousy is incessant and insatiable; with these disadvantages Donizetti's prevailingly somber score, which concentrates more on ensembles than brilliant showpieces, failed to establish itself.

Ugo was Donizetti's first new score for Milan after *Anna Bolena*, and like that opera it contains some music that had been written earlier.[12] Clemente Verzino has observed of *Ugo* that before Donizetti arrived in Naples 'the music was already almost completely written, composed bit by bit as the poet sent on his verses piecemeal to Naples';[13] in fact, for some of these verses Donizetti spliced old music into his new score. He based the chorus, 'No, che in ciel' (see p. 247), which opens the *introduzione,* upon a chorus from *Imelda,* and he used the prelude to a duet for Imelda and Lamberto for the introduction to the Act 2 duet for Bianca and Ugo, changing the obbligato instrument from clarinet to the more plaintive oboe. *Francesca di Foix* provided some music and, after *Fausta* was banned in Naples, he adopted fifteen measures from Fausta's final cabaletta to serve in a similar location in Bianca's aria–finale. (*Fausta* would not be introduced in Milan for another nine months.)

These self-borrowings formed part of the standard practise of the time and represent not laziness but a laudable concern not to waste worthwhile material from some score that had had its brief day.[14] Once Donizetti had decided that *Ugo* was a fiasco, it would serve in its turn as a source of passages for future scores. Jeremy Commons makes an important point about much of Donizetti's later self-borrowing:

the nature of Donizetti's borrowings can be seen to be changing. No longer is he transferring whole movements or even major movements; now he is resorting to minor sections, bridge-passages and the like. Thus the introductory chorus in Ugo, *No, che in ciel* ... becomes a bridge-passage between two sections of Parisina's Act 1 cavatina; and the presto bridge-passage between the larghetto amoroso and the moderato pendant of the Part III trio in Ugo becomes the bridge-passage between the two parts of [the tenor's] Act 2 aria in Parisina. By now, too, we find Donizetti reworking isolated ideas: a theme, a single phrase. The melody, for example, to which he set the words 'L'orifiamma ondeggi al vento' in the 'Seguito dell'Introduzione' of Ugo (which already shows an interesting process of evolution and revision in the autograph of Ugo) reappears as 'Dall'Eridano si stende', Azzo's Act 1 cabaletta in Parisina. But it is only the opening phrase that is used: all that follows has been reworked and rethought.[15]

'L'orifiamma ondeggi al vento' is one of Donizetti's most impressive martial passages. He believed in the importance of launching a melody with a clearly defined opening phrase, a goal he certainly achieved in this case, and it is significant that it is precisely this part of an effective musical idea that he adopted for re-use (Example 34). The salient character of Ugo's patriotic rallying-cry is here worked out in an unsubtle but telling way. Ugo's melody is repeated by Luigi V (contralto *musico*) in the key of the dominant and restated yet again by Folco (bass) in the tonic, but with alterations to the second and fourth phrases to bring them within his range. Usually it is the bass who repeats a melody in the dominant tonality, but Donizetti obviously preferred to reserve a vibrant masculine sound for the concluding statement, so arranging his melody that the all-important opening phrase lies within the bass compass. These three statements

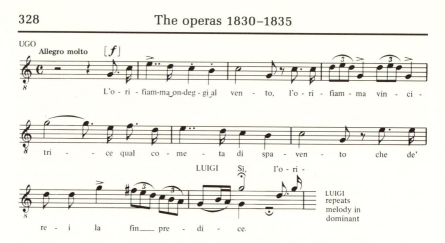

Example 34. *Ugo, conte di Parigi*, Act 1, *allegro molto* of the 'Seguito
dell'Introduzione'

are followed by a *più mosso,* with choral intervention, which builds
up a *crescendo* that leads into a unison reprise of just the opening
phrase of the original melody, and this introduces an ensemble coda:
the same procedure is observable in other asymmetrical expository
structures in Donizetti's operas of this period. But the number does
not end with the ensemble coda; it closes with a reprise of the second
period and coda of the opening chorus, 'No, che in ciel'. This trio
leading into an ensemble is labeled 'Seguito dell'Introduzione'
('seguito' in the sense of continuation); the recurrence of the opening
chorus in its original key confirms that everything up to this point
forms a cohesive part of the *introduzione* complex.

The autograph of *Ugo* (in the Conservatorio di San Pietro a
Majella) is eloquent testimony to Donizetti's difficulties with this
score. These range from textual changes – almost always made in
response to the demands of the censors – which include the rechris-
tening of Carlo as Folco (the Austrian emperor had a brother named
Karl and Milan was then the capital of an Austrian province), and
the many alterations and excisions in Bianca's music. The Carnival
season of 1831–2 at La Scala, running from 26 December to 20
March, was an almost unbelievably strenuous one for Pasta: in less
than three months she participated in thirty-four performances as
Norma, thirteen as Rossini's Desdemona, eight as Anna Bolena, and
five as Bianca in *Ugo,* to say nothing of the rehearsals for these
appearances. The role of Bianca was much altered to satisfy Pasta
and to reduce the demands on her: one section of an aria was entirely
removed after it had been fully orchestrated, some things were made

easier, a few made more grandiloquent, and others were adapted to include the descending scale passages she found most congenial. For instance, the cabaletta, 'No, che infelice appieno', of Bianca's *aria di sortita* is an *andante* rather than the usual *moderato*, and her Act 1 duet with her sister Adelia was extensively revised. Donizetti had originally planned, not surprisingly, that Bianca's final scene would be as spaciously designed as the comparable episode in *Anna Bolena*, but apparently the exigent Pasta decided to forego such drawn-out exposure as the first unit of her *larghetto* is entirely eliminated in the autograph, although it had even been orchestrated. (Donizetti did not throw this music away; he later found a place for it in *Il furioso* as Cardenio's 'Raggio d'amor', his Act 1 *aria di sortita*.)

Ugo can serve as a classic example of an opera of this period that suffered 'birth defects' because the composer's intentions carried less weight than those of the censors, the prima donna, and even the theater management which scheduled four *prime* in a short season, of which *Ugo* was the last. But if with this score he appears to have been the loser, Donizetti managed to exceed even the most sanguine expectations with his contribution to the *primavera* season at the Canobbiana, one day short of two months after the *prima* of *Ugo*.

L'elisir d'amore. With this two-act *opera comica* (so-called in the score) Donizetti demonstrated for the first time his full mastery of the buffa form. He was favored by having in his hands Romani's finest libretto in the comic genre, and it not only gave him a clear, graceful text and sharply realized characters, but, most important, it contains a deep vein of sincere sentiment. To consider first this matter of sentiment: such moments as Nemorino's 'Adina, credimi' in the first finale and his famous 'Una furtiva lagrima' from Act 2 are moments of genuine pathos, where Donizetti, instead of discussing his character's feelings objectively, presents their essence. To contrast Rossini's *Il barbiere* with *L'elisir* on the level of sentiment is to see that *Il barbiere* contains so much whirling wit and ingenuity, such sheer exuberance, that one scarcely notices that it characteristically defines situations in terms of external description. For all its masterful comedy, *Il barbiere* stems from a style and approach that takes matters of the heart for granted and wastes little time evoking them. *L'elisir*, on the other hand, is a romantic opera buffa, wherein the conflict is ultimately resolved not through trickery or any outward circumstance, but through Adina's coming to appreciate the true value of Nemorino's constancy.

In *L'elisir* the comic *introduzione* of the earlier Neapolitan *farse* – an ensemble built up by the entries of the characters, usually in pairs, and extended through a number of contrasting movements – is replaced by one that approaches the layout of the opening of *Anna Bolena* though on a slightly smaller scale. The opening chorus has Nemorino's one-movement cavatina, 'Quanto è bella', as a middle section. This is followed directly by Adina's 'Della crudele Isotta', which consists of two not quite identical strophes (*larghetto/poco più*), the first tempo a waltz and the second a mazurka. Immediately after, the march begins that brings on Belcore and his soldiers, and this serves as a prelude for Belcore's double aria, 'Come Paride vezzoso'; unlike a conventional cabaletta, in which both statements are sung by the same character, Belcore has the first and Adina the second (in the same key) and the section develops a concertato conclusion.

The superiority of *L'elisir* over Donizetti's earlier comic operas lies in its vivid melodic characterization. Each of the characters has his own idiom: Dulcamara is all garrulity, Belcore swaggering virility, while Adina's flirtatiousness never quite conceals her innate tenderness. Consider how she progresses melodically from the highly figured, coquettish phrases of her Act 1 duet with Nemorino, 'Chiedi all'aura', to her much more straightforward and sincere 'Prendi, per me sei libero' in Act 2, where her embellishments are principally cadential. Nemorino's idiom is dominated by a simplicity that does not disguise his depth of feeling, and it is this masterly portrait that has done more than anything else to keep *L'elisir* in the active repertory. A representative passage like his 'Adina, credimi', from the Act 1 finale, shows how Donizetti uses carefully balanced and interrelated phrases over inflecting harmony to bring to life Nemorino's utter sincerity (Example 35). The quoted passage shows the first half of the period which consists of eight phrases ($a\ b\ a\ b\ c\ c\ d\ d'$), moving from the tonic of F minor to C major in the eighth measure; C major, anticipated in the accompaniment of the second and fourth phrases, provides the pivot for the modulation to A flat for the second half of this period. The fifth and sixth phrases (over the dominant seventh of D flat) are an intensification of the first phrase, as Nemorino tries harder to persuade Adina to wait one day (until the elixir can take effect) before she marries Belcore. The second half of this period, in the relative major, is essentially a variation on the first half. This careful attention to detail exemplifies the art that conceals art, for the listener is convinced by this passage, which moves so inevitably and builds so logically, and rarely pauses to wonder why.

Example 35. *L'elisir d'amore*, Act 1, *larghetto* of the finale

In the discussion of *La zingara* it was noted that at one moment in
Argilla's cavatina (Example 23) the character of the heroine comes
into vivid focus; but the rest of that aria degenerates into a rather
mechanical exploitation of formulas because in 1822 Donizetti
lacked the skill to sustain the immediacy. Such skill is everywhere
apparent in 'Adina, credimi', which forms the main building-block
of the *larghetto* to the Act 1 finale of *L'elisir*; after Nemorino's solo
Adina takes up his melody, to which Belcore's muttered threats to

his rival now form a counterpoint, and Nemorino's voice is added to harmonize the cadential phrases. The second phase of this *larghetto* is dominated by unison phrases for the soprano and tenor – an identical pair followed by a varied pair. The whole movement sustains and expands the emotion launched by Nemorino's plea.

Dulcamara's *aria di sortita* is one of the great buffo arias in the literature of Italian opera. It begins with a solo trumpet call that will return as the main melody of the final *allegro vivace*. As the chorus gathers, to see what the trumpet announces, their music builds a *crescendo*, starting out with phrases borrowed from *Il castello di Kenilworth* (where they introduced Elisabetta) and going on to a new extended coda. According to the libretto Dulcamara arrives in an open landau (some modern productions have him descend by balloon, a maneuver that makes the chorus's reference to his gilded carriage apply to its basket). His aria is a glorification of the pitchman's spiel and provides a compendium of the traditional modes of buffo expression: recitative, monotone declamation over accompanying motifs, melodic phrases, free unaccompanied declamation and melody supported by chorus, all of them arranged to give the aria a sense of structure and to avoid monotony. The chief component of the *andante* is a twenty-measure period, beginning 'È questo l'odontalgico liquore'; here the accompanying figures embellish the vocal line without doubling the voice or interfering with the words and give the reiterated notes for the singer the impression of variety; these figures intensify until flutes in thirds, chattering in the high register, mark the climax of exuberant good humor. This period has the effect of a carefully controlled *crescendo* so that the text can always project clearly. Later this passage is repeated in the dominant, with the vocal line varied and the harmony changed. Dulcamara's aria shows an extension of the devices at work in the Pappacione episode in *La zingara* (Example 24), but what was meager there is here so enriched that the cumulative effect is like that of a rhetorical tidal wave.

Adina's Act 2 duet with Dulcamara, 'Quanto amore', neatly opposes the varied levels of action and meaning in this plot. Dulcamara comes to admit frankly that a woman's charm is more potent than any elixir, and as his playful humbug turns to honesty, Adina in her moment of self-awareness realizes that she must use her wiles to win Nemorino. Once more Donizetti demonstrates his skill at characterization through simple melody and harmony. As the intermediate material ends, just before the final *allegro*, Adina's commitment to Nemorino is coloured by an abrupt modulation to C (Example 36).

Example 36. *L'elisir d'amore*, Act 2, *tempo di mezzo* of the Adina–
Dulcamara duet

Her phrases, with the interval of the minor seventh, possess a seduc-
tiveness, as opposed to her flirting, that adds a new dimension to her
character. In Dulcamara's answering phrases, which lead back to his
home key of E major, Donizetti briefly retains the G natural that
Adina had reiterated, implying that the doctor has indeed understood her. A tiny detail, perhaps, but it is the accumulation of such
apt touches that helps to make *L'elisir* the fine opera that it is.

Sancia di Castiglia. In November 1832 Donizetti brought out his
next work, a two-act *seria* written for the San Carlo with a title role
designed for Ronzi. Donizetti dedicated this score to Mayr, a gesture
that demonstrates both his abiding gratitude to his old teacher and
his own belief that the music of *Sancia* was a worthy offering. *Sancia di Castiglia* is one of the more obscure titles in Donizetti's list: it
made little impression in its own day, and has not yet attracted the
attention of the revivalists; but it has its interesting features.

The reasons for its obscurity are not far to seek. The leaden libretto
by Pietro Salatino offers some promising situations but little in the
way of characterization. The old-fashioned air that permeates the
plot – another on the Spanish–Moorish theme – is also reflected in
Donizetti's disposition of vocal types: Sancia (dramatic coloratura
soprano), her son Garzia[16] (contralto *musico*), Sancia's lover and
intended husband, the Moorish prince Ircano (bass), and her prime
minister Rodrigo (tenor). The greatest weakness of *Sancia* is the
absence of any reciprocated love. Ircano turns out to be motivated by
vengeance, first urging Sancia to poison her son, and then, when she
has drunk the poison herself and is dying, revealing that he had only

pretended to love her. The interest of the opera, then, resides almost exclusively in the figure of Sancia and her internal conflict.

Sancia first appears, not in the *introduzione* as do Anna and Fausta, but after the opening scene for male voices; the delaying of the prima donna's entrance is a device used again in *Parisina* and *Lucia*, and Verdi employed it in, among other works, *Ernani* and *Il trovatore*. Prefaced by a female chorus in dance rhythm, Sancia's obligatory *aria di sortita* is routine: her *larghetto* (6/8) and *allegretto* (3/4) are not divided by a *tempo di mezzo*, and there is no great harmonic contrast between them as both are in G major; the first is overripe with vocal filagree, the second is more declamatory, expanding into flourishes in the final cadence. The relative brevity of these arias implies that Donizetti was almost eager to get them out of the way so that he could concentrate on Sancia's duet with Rodrigo. By 1832 Donizetti had come to appreciate the greater potential for musico-dramatic interest in duet situations as opposed to arias, and from that time on ensembles came to assume increasing importance in his scores; the same direction can be seen in Verdi's operas if *Attila*, say, is compared with the later *Rigoletto*.

The Sancia–Rodrigo duet concerns the minister's attempt to dissuade the Queen from making an impulsive marriage by reminding her that both her husband and apparently her son have been slain by the infidels. The duet is in three main sections: *allegro*, *larghetto* and *moderato*. In the first the participants have nearly identical statements, each prefigured by an orchestral anticipation of the first vocal phrase; this melody recurs in the *materia di mezzo* between the *larghetto* and *moderato*, where Sancia repeats her first two phrases in the original key of G, but the tenor answers her with urgent new material, made more emphatic by a sudden shift to E flat. This repetition of material in different sections of the duet does not equal the effectiveness of Seymour's echo of herself in her duet with Enrico, but it serves the same purpose of indicating that one character has not really been influenced by the words of the other. In the *larghetto*, at the modulation from E minor to the parallel major, Sancia has a fine ascending phrase, 'Sento a quei detti orrore', but the succeeding one, 'Ma li contrasta amore', is only a trite series of descending figurations; this unevenness, typical of the score, seems to show that Donizetti was more moved by the idea of Sancia as a suffering woman than as a deluded lover. The *moderato* section, 'Cessa, Rodrigo, ah lasciami', contains two back-to-back statements of the same material in G minor; then, to provide a major-mode conclusion to the duet, Donizetti introduces a different melody, starting off with the two voices in canon. This passage is based on six measures borrowed from *Ugo* (from the tenor's narrative before 'L'orifiamma ondeggi al vento'), but the material is altered: a three-note anacrusis to the first phrase has been dropped and a canonic treatment added.

The first finale is the repository of much more of *Ugo*. It opens with an eloquent chorus, 'Castiglia, il tuo lamento' (*moderato*, 4/4, F minor/A flat major), the orchestral introduction to which is in F minor while the choral entry is in A flat major and has slightly different contours from those of the tune announced by the orchestra; the arpeggiated accompaniment against dotted rhythms gives a distinctly Bellinian flavor to this chorus. It is followed by a march of embarrassing triviality that comes almost unchanged from *Ugo*, where it introduces and accompanies the choral interlude in Bianca's aria–finale. Also from *Ugo* comes the whole *larghetto* (B flat minor/B flat major) of the *Sancia* finale; the minor section is reduced by half, and in the major section a unison male chorus takes the place of the fifth voice in what was a quintet of soloists in *Ugo*. Oddly enough the borrowing does not end with the cadences of the quintet, but continues through the first orchestral figure which introduces the recitative before the stretta. The stretta is launched by the raging Ircano, whose vigorous 3/4 (in much the same vein as Enrico's 'Salirà d'Inghilterra sul trono') creates an impetus that is sustained to the end.

The final scene is the highpoint of the score, for here Donizetti is able to exploit the tragic nuances of his heroine's dilemma. The long introduction is given over chiefly to an elaborate and well-written clarinet solo in D minor, and that instrument provides further melodic commentary in the opening recitative. This 'instrumental aria' brings to mind Bellini's introduction for cor anglais and harp to Imogene's aria–finale in *Il pirata*. Sancia's *larghetto* (12/8, E flat major), 'Al figlio tuo', is addressed to her late husband's portrait (which she has just described as a 'squallido immago'); its broad opening phrases are contrasted with detached words that insistently repeat certain intervallic patterns. The melodic structure is relatively free, advancing through pairs of related phrases, but without any formal repetition, to fulfill a long arch of emotion. After she has drunk the poison, Sancia has a second *larghetto*, 'Vanne Ircano', which begins in G minor; the phrase after the modulation to the parallel major, to the words 'Ah! troppo barbaro, t'amai', recurs in slightly expanded form after the modulation to the major in her *andante* cabaletta (Example 37).

Example 37a. *Sancia di Castiglia*, Act 2, second *larghetto* of Sancia's aria

Example 37b. *Sancia di Castiglia*, Act 2, cabaletta of Sancia's aria

From Example 37b it can be seen that these phrases are a clear anticipation of Carlo's 'A consolarmi affrettisi' in *Linda di Chamounix*; in that score they serve as a sort of love motif. The expanded layout of Sancia's final scene suggests that Donizetti was seeking to emulate the finale of *Anna Bolena*. Garzia's entrance is accompanied by a little march that is at least a first cousin to the one that brings on Percy, Smeton and Rochefort. Though the closing pages are not the equals of those in *Anna Bolena*, they nevertheless possess a considerable degree of eloquence.

Il furioso all'isola di San Domingo. This three-act semiseria was unveiled at the Roman Teatro Valle less than two months after the *prima* of *Sancia* in Naples. Donizetti had begun to compose the work in Naples as Ferretti sent installments of the libretto to him. The text for *Il furioso*, based on a play itself derived from an episode in *Don Quixote*, shows Ferretti's knack for clear characterization and effective interaction. The most notable thing about the opera is that Donizetti, following the example of Rossini with *Guillaume Tell*, made the hero and title character a baritone. That the management of the Valle wanted a starring vehicle for the young baritone Giorgio Ronconi, who had been extraordinarily successful there the previous year, provided Donizetti with a reason for this casting in addition to his personal inclination, which is already apparent in earlier scores. In *Imelda* the baritone is the romantic hero, indeed the only sympathetic male role in the opera; and in *Sancia*, while Ircano (a role written for a bass, but more accurately described as a baritone part – the nominal distinction between the two ranges was not yet clearly established) is not exactly sympathetic, he is, in Sancia's eyes at least, an *objet d'amour* for most of the action.

The role of Cardenio in *Il furioso* may be viewed as the first of Donizetti's major baritone parts, and therefore as a first precursor of Verdi's great baritone roles; its importance stems not only from the fact that it was written for Ronconi, an artist of great stature whom it was Donizetti's good fortune to have available, but from Donizetti's dissatisfaction with many of the tenors of this period of transition between the falsetto-topped voices, whose principal strength was their facility in *canto fiorito,* and those better adapted to the more intense emotional expressiveness of Romantic tragedy. Since for much of the action of *Il furioso* Cardenio is represented as driven mad by the thought that his wife is unfaithful, it is understandable that Donizetti wanted the masculine sound of the baritone to convey the character's sexual anguish, rather than the more ambiguous vocal color of a *tenore contraltino* like Lorenzo Salvi (the leading tenor of the company at the Teatro Valle during the season in which *Il furioso* had its *prima*). It is relevant to remember here that Donizetti's only previous presentation of a deranged male character (Murena in *L'esule di Roma*) was written for a bass; he seems therefore to have judged this kind of vocal sound appropriate to the expression of the sufferings of a deeply troubled mind. Not until *Maria Padilla* (1841) did Donizetti write a mad scene for a tenor, and then the character was that of an aged father; in the vocal distribution of that score he assigned the active amative role to the baritone.

The first signs of Donizetti's dissatisfaction with the Rossinian tenor can be pinpointed in the 1826 *Gabriella,* when he had no one to prescribe to him what voices to write for; since this was before he began to explore seriously the great expressive potential of lower male voices, he chose a *musico* for his romantic hero rather than a tenor (the range that Carafa had found appropriate for this role in 1816). In Donizetti's operas of the years preceding *Il furioso* he underplayed the importance of the *primo tenore* roles, except when he was writing for singers of the calibre of Rubini or Donzelli. The tradition of the tenor hero was then of long standing, deriving to a considerable extent from the prominence that the voice assumed in ensemble passages; but the observing of that tradition no longer seemed obligatory to Donizetti. One of the reasons why Pasta, Rubini, Ronconi and Lablache stood out in the public's mind was undoubtedly that beyond their formidable technical resources they possessed the artistic intuition to adapt themselves to the new Romantic tendencies; but it would be mistaken to assume that, because these outstanding singers flourished in these years, their adaptability was shared by most of their contemporaries. The singers who emerged in the mid-1830s, Strepponi and Moriani for example, were prized for their aptitude for the greater emotional intensity demanded by the Romantic melodramas of Donizetti.

Il furioso stands, along with *Linda,* as one of Donizetti's most successful *semiserie,* and for this a fair share of the credit must go to Ferretti. The two requirements of this genre were that it have a happy ending and that one of the characters be a buffo: the latter reveals the origins of this genre as a compromise in the days when the personnel of any given company was usually limited, and if two bass roles were needed, one would have to be sung by the buffo, whose vocal abilities were apt to be limited to patter without much sustained singing.[17] *Il furioso* succeeds as a *semiseria* because for once the serious and the comic elements reinforce one another with an almost Shakespearean harmony. The buffo character of Kaidamà is analogous to the Fool in *King Lear,* being set against the noble hero whose reason is clouded; all the ironic resonances of that juxtaposition are implicit in *Il furioso.* Some modern productions have tried to turn Kaidamà into a farcical character, but such an approach succeeds only in straining this genre at its not very strong seams; besides this, the role of Kaidamà contains a fair share of Donizettian comic pathos. The Act 2 duet for Cardenio and Kaidamà, 'Fu l'error del tradimento', is a highpoint of the score: while Cardenio asks forgiveness of the poor fellow he has so frequently mistreated, Kaidamà's fear that the poor madman may hurt himself with the pistols cannot quite overcome his instinct for self-preservation. (The cabaletta of this duet, 'Ho deciso seco spento', borrows the beginning of the opening chorus of *L'elisir* and then goes on to new material, later combining it with Kaidamà's lines.)

The other ingredient that contributes to the success of *Il furioso* is the element of Romanticism, which helps to give a cohesiveness of tone. Besides the madness of the hero, who is unbalanced by fear that his wife has betrayed him, there are storms, the exotic setting of a tropical island, and Eleonora's sacrificial gesture in pointing her pistol at her own heart. Furthermore, this cohesiveness is reinforced by Donizetti's music, for by this time he was sufficiently in command of the expressive resources of harmony and melody to be able to control both the underlying structural and more superficial decorative ingredients of the score, but so discreetly that the music still seems spontaneous and direct.

The unconventional organization of the compound *introduzione* exemplifies Donizetti's skill at keeping the action moving without sacrificing the formal logic expected by an audience in 1833. He begins not with a chorus but with a duet for the subsidiary characters Marcella and Bartolomeo, which, after imparting a good deal of expository information, settles down to discuss the *furioso*: 'Coi capelli dritti in fronte' (*allegro*, 6/8, C major) contrasts Bartolomeo's fear of Cardenio with Marcella's more sympathetic view. The chorus gathers at Kaidamà's offstage cries for help and soon the terrified Fool enters to give a vivid account of his encounter with Cardenio and the resulting drubbing he has received: 'Scelsi la via brevissima' (*allegretto*, 6/8, G major) is essentially a solo in which the choral intervention is limited to brief questions or to laughter at Kaidamà's plight and his grotesque way of relating it. Cardenio now appears, but he seems not to be the violent lunatic Kaidamà has described, for he begins by speaking of love, 'Raggio d'amor parea'. (It is significant, in the light of Romantic dramaturgy, that he makes his first appearance at the top of a cliff and later descends to the playing area of the principal action.)[18] It is only when he sings his first phrase complete (earlier he sang only the first two words) that he reveals that his vision of love ('raggio d'amor') was deceptive – a neatly ironical touch (Example 38).

This melody (reclaimed from a passage discarded from Bianca's aria–finale, 'Nelle tue braccia stringimi', in *Ugo*, with only a few notes changed) establishes a noble, elegiac tone.[19] Its suppleness is matched by the harmony that moves from E minor through the parallel major to the dominant minor. Cardenio's grief and tension are mirrored in the alternation of *legato* and broken phrases, which succeed each other without disturbing the overall coherence and balance. The triple repetition of text at the end suggests an *idée fixe*. Cardenio delivers both verses of the soliloquy from the cliff, separated from, yet overheard by, the assembly below and reducing to tears those who had, a minute before, been laughing. After his second, almost identical, strophe, Cardenio slowly descends, his movement accompanied by an expressive ritornello in G major. Unable to relate to those who surround him, he announces that it would be better if he killed himself (*allegro*, D minor). After a brief struggle with those who seek to restrain him he breaks free and escapes up the cliff and disappears; this episode forms the *materia di mezzo* of the double aria. The remainder of the scene is a two-statement cabaletta, 'A quale squallido ferale aspetto' (*allegro*, F minor/F major), sung not by the character who sang the slow aria, but by the ensemble. The storm that rages during this section is no mere decoration: on the symbolic level it reflects the violence of Cardenio's aberration and on the practical level it causes the shipwreck from

CARDENIO

Example 38. *Il furioso*, Act 1, *andante* of Cardenio's aria

which Eleonora, Cardenio's wife, is washed ashore. The unconventional disposition of ingredients throughout this *introduzione* make it seem both fresh and dramatically effective.

Il furioso contains much else that is notable. In many passages of arioso in Cardenio's recitatives Donizetti creates a tone of noble pathos with a single expressive phrase of an almost Verdian force and conciseness. Good examples of this abound in the recitative preceding Cardenio's Act 1 duet with Eleonora, where he believes himself struck blind. The slow movement, 'Ah! un mar di lagrime' (*largo*, 4/4, A flat major), of the first finale is another of Donizetti's moving sextets; it begins as a solo melody for Cardenio, and then a particularly skillful buildup – Cardenio on a sustained dominant pedal, the basses in ascending chromatic thirds, the three other voices sustaining the dominant one after another – leads into a harmonized restatement of the melody, which, after the first two phrases, continues with new material, the vocal parts moving with admirable independence. In performance this sextet produces a powerful impression. The chief structural weakness of the work is the dramatically gratuitous arrival of the primo tenore, Ferrando, Cardenio's brother, who appears, one inevitably feels, simply to add his line to the sextet.

Parisina. This three-act opera seria followed *Il furioso* by only two and a half months. Since Romani was late in producing his libretto, the work was composed in a matter of a few weeks, and it stands, along with *L'elisir, Lucia* and *Don Pasquale* to name only the most prominent examples among Donizetti's operas, as eloquent proof that there is no correlation between the length of time spent in composition and the value of the opera; indeed, on more than one occasion Donizetti lamented that scores he had labored long over turned out less well than those he wrote in haste. *Parisina* was Donizetti's own favorite among his operas, though its relatively modest nineteenth-century performance history indicates that audiences did not share his preference. It is a tragedy, accentuating both the heroine's suffering and her husband's furious jealousy, but as Barblan has rightly observed, it is 'more a psychological novel in music than a theatrical opera'.[20] It is true that much of the score deals with the lyrical analysis of emotions, and here Donizetti's maturing expressiveness is deeply impressive.

Parisina was the first score Donizetti composed for Lanari's touring company at its Florentine headquarters, where its main wing performed during Carnival. It was a significant encounter for him because it brought him into contact with two important singers: Carolina Ungher, at her peak as a tragic singing-actress,[21] and the French tenor Gilbert Duprez. Ungher had sung in Vienna as a mezzo-soprano, and then, after Barbaja had brought her to Italy around 1825, she extended her range upward; her high notes were hard-pressed ('dagger-thrusts' was Bellini's word for them), but she had a fine low voice and considerable agility in the upper middle range. What particularly appealed to Donizetti, however, was her intense acting. Chorley sheds some light on this aspect of Ungher when he compares her to Giulia Grisi in the role of Lucrezia Borgia. Ungher was 'less splendidly gifted by nature . . . [her] serpentine and deep malevolence, subtly veiled at the moment when its most diabolical works were on foot . . . Madame Grisi had less astuteness, more violence'.[22] Duprez is best remembered as the first tenor to popularize the *do dal petto* (the high C sung in chest voice rather than falsetto), but at the time of *Parisina* he was still using the technique of the haut-contre, the falsetto-topped tenor voice. His role of Ugo contains many Cs and a D flat, and in the autograph there is written out a variant for him containing a high E flat. The most significant result of Donizetti's working with Duprez was that this intelligent and gifted singer was able to reconcile him to the traditionally important place of the tenor persona in Romantic melodrama. To think of the roles Donizetti wrote for Duprez, which include Edgardo, Polyeucte (a very different part from Poliuto), Fernand and Dom Sébastien, is to appreciate the importance of their meeting. The emergence of Moriani and Fraschini are later landmarks along the path cleared by Duprez.

The discussion of singers is an apt approach to *Parisina* because a glance at any part of the score reveals the distinction of the vocal writing. Parisina appears in the second scene; her pair of arias, preceded by a chorus of women,[23] consists of the cantabile 'Forse un destino che intendere' (*larghetto*, 6/8, B flat major) and a cabaletta, in the form of an aside, 'V'era un dì' (*moderato*, 4/4, B flat major). The cantabile is in *a b a'* structure, the concluding section much modified by descriptive embellishments on such words as 'ruscello' and 'etere'; the cabaletta is notable for its mood of restless melancholy. The influence of Ungher's voice is apparent in these arias, for the cantabile only once briefly touches on a high B flat (otherwise the highest note is G), while the cabaletta is only slightly more adventurous in the *acuti*. Of a very high order is her Act 2 romanza (a term Donizetti almost always used to mean a cantabile without an ensuing cabaletta), 'Sogno talor di correre' (*larghetto*, 2/4, A flat major). This aria has been likened to the 'Willow Song', and not only because

Parisina's jealous husband will soon enter her bedroom, for the heroine's melancholy and innocence are memorably evoked. In the middle section, where she speaks of heaven as the only harbor for an embattled spirit, the music modulates with telling effect into C major. The line is much embellished but here the figurations express her inner uneasiness. Imelda and the women's chorus provide an interlude before Parisina's vocal cadences; the ritornello is a poignant variation upon the opening phrase of her aria, treated sequentially, and it functions as the exit music for her attendants. Parisina's aria–finale consists of the austerely economical *andante*, 'Ciel, se' tu che in tal momento', and the highly dramatic cabaletta, 'Ugo è spento!', prompted by the opening of the windows to permit a view of Ugo's corpse; in this the emphasis on the upper register would seem to capitalize upon Ungher's stridency in that part of her range.

Undoubtedly the dramatic highpoint of the score is the scene where Azzo, Parisina's husband, comes to her bedroom and overhears her, in her sleep, utter Ugo's name. There is a lengthy introduction for muted strings and woodwinds that suggests Parisina's troubled slumber. In recitative, interspersed with patterns from the introduction, Azzo has almost quietened his suspicions when he hears Parisina's voice from the curtained alcove, her phrases nostalgic, modulating into constantly flatter keys. When she mentions Ugo's name, Azzo shouts it to sudden E major chords, followed by E minor ones. Parisina appears from the alcove and her husband's jealous fury explodes, accompanied by driving string figures over a striding bass and an upward-swirling phrase that punctuates his line. This protracted scene of confrontation, before the duet with its more regularly co-ordinated phrases begins, has a fine dramatic energy unequaled by anything Donizetti had composed up to this time; in its strength and drive it looks forward clearly to Verdi. The jealous Azzo is convincing (on a level that Enrico VIII is not) because his arias in the opening scene and his recitative in this scene before Parisina speaks have already made clear that he loves his wife and wants her love in return. There is no ulterior motive, no Seymour, to compromise Azzo's spontaneous fury at feeling himself rejected for another.

Ugo is a less striking character than either the desperately melancholy Parisina or the murderous Azzo, but Donizetti succeeds in making him a plausible object for his stepmother's love.[24] In his Act 1 duet with Ernesto (bass) he confesses his love for Parisina, against the older man's warnings, to phrases in 6/8 (G minor/B flat major) that combine the artlessness of the Neapolitan song with Idamore's honeyed style in *Il paria* (see Example 31). Ugo comes even more sharply into focus in his duet with Parisina, 'Dillo, dillo', in the following scene. Here his melody has a symmetrical elegance – the pairs of phrases in conjunct relationships – that again looks ahead to Verdi. In the cabaletta to this duet, 'Quando più grave' (allegro, 3/4, B flat major), Parisina's statement is followed directly by one for Ugo; then a new melody, 'Angiol celeste e santo', is introduced to form the coda, and here one can detect the seeds of some of the ideas that would later flower in Lucia in 'Veranno a te'. Ugo's aria in Act 2, however, especially the larghetto, 'Io sentii tremar la mano', has a melody so encrusted with figurations that today its chief interest is as documentation of Duprez's vocal prowess at this stage of his career.

Parisina marks a decided advance in Donizetti's progress as a musical dramatist. Its highpoints are more than adequate compensation for some tediously overextended passages, such as the protracted finale to Act 1. Parisina contains some of Donizetti's most vivid musical portraiture, and it is not difficult to understand his own fondness for this score.

Torquato Tasso. For his next work, a three-act semiseria, Donizetti returned to the Valle in September 1833, hoping to equal the earlier success of Il furioso with this new vehicle for Ronconi. In some ways 1833 can be regarded as Donizetti's year of the baritone, for to it belong the portraits of Cardenio, Azzo, Tasso, and Alfonso in Lucrezia Borgia (though this part is of intermediate range so that both baritones and basses could cope with it). The idea of an opera celebrating the author of Gerusalemme liberata and Rinaldo had attracted Donizetti for some time, particularly because the poet had connections with his native Bergamo; the completed score was dedicated to three cities associated with Tasso: Bergamo, Sorrento and Rome.[25]

In Ferretti Donizetti had a librettist undismayed by this assignment, but unfortunately, owing to the restrictions of the company at the Valle, Ferretti was obliged to write another semiseria text. Although this genre had worked well with a plot located on an exotic Caribbean island, it proved a serious liability in the context of cinquecento Ferrara with supposedly historical figures. The worst miscalculation of all was to make the buffo figure, Don Gherardo, a jealous, scheming rival to Tasso, without a redeeming feature; the result is an uneasy discrepancy of tone between the jauntiness of his idiom and his antipathetic function in the plot. Donizetti was aware of this blemish, but even two years later he felt helpless to correct it:

'Concerning *Tasso*, I told you that transforming the role [of Don Gherardo] into a serious one would make it more difficult to have the opera performed, because then you would need another *primo basso cantante*; and who would do Gherardo when there is the role of Tasso?'[26] That the poet who had contrived the neatly articulated and clearly characterized plots of *L'ajo, Olivo*, and *Il furioso* should create an action which contains only two sympathetic characters, Tasso and Eleonora d'Este, while all the others are either repellent or dim, or both, is a real disappointment.

There is another problem in the operas of these years that have a baritone in the central role; that arrangement produces a dislocation between the musical and dramatic functions of the tenor who, as in *Il furioso*, tends to seem more important to the musical fabric than to the dramatic action. In *Tasso* the tenor character, Roberto Geraldini, is not an amatory rival of Tasso, he is jealous of his poetical gifts and fame, and he resorts to contemptible and petty means to betray him; this role is the least effective exploitation of the *primo tenore* persona in Donizetti's long list of works. How much more satisfactory is the deployment of the tenor in the more traditional triangle of *Parisina*, with the heroine at the apex and the tenor and baritone in lethal competition for her.

To point out these weaknesses of plot in *Tasso*, which largely derive from the theatrical conditions of the period, is by no means to dismiss it as an inconsequential opera. One of the most fascinating things about it is that it is the sole presentation by Donizetti of the artist as hero – an assignment not undertaken by Rossini, Bellini, or Verdi; this puts *Tasso* in the same category, if not quite in the same league, as operas such as *Benvenuto Cellini* and *Die Meistersinger*. Constrained to work within the conventions, Donizetti makes a valiant effort, more successful than one might expect, to make Tasso credible as a working poet. He is first observed in the act of creation, composing a poem that conveys his ardent longing for some sign that Eleonora d'Este reciprocates his love. The setting of the text here reveals Donizetti's keen sensitivity to verbal values (Example 39).[27] The opening phrase repeats a violin melody from the prelude accompanying his entrance. The movement from the major beginning to the relative minor underscores the deeply felt emotion of these lines.

Oddly enough this *sortita* recitative leads not into a pair of arias but into a double duet with the tenor. Tasso as poet comes to the fore again in the next scene, where, in answer to her summons, he reads Eleonora a passage from Canto II of his *Gerusalemme liberata*. Dur-

Example 39. *Torquato Tasso*, Act 1, recitative to the Tasso–Roberto duet

ing the recitative before the duet Eleonora makes it clear in an aside that she identifies Tasso and herself with his characters of Orlindo and Sofronia. His reading from the manuscript begins the *andante commodo* (4/4, A flat minor/A flat major), 'Colei Sofronia, Orlindo egli si appella', another demonstration of Donizetti's subtle and persuasive setting of Tasso's verses. The baritone's vocal period ends with the idea that Sofronia disdains Orlindo's love, but this charge Eleonora promptly denies;[28] her melody is that with which Idamore begins the final quartet in *Il paria*[29] (the *allegro* section of this earlier ensemble provides the melodic material for the stretta of the finale to Act 2 of *Tasso*).

The apotheosis of Tasso occurs in the short third act, the portion of the opera that had an independent life in the later nineteenth century after the opera as a whole had had its day. Act 3 of *Tasso* consists of a double aria for the hero (his only one in the whole score) with interventions by the chorus; no other characters appear. Seven years have passed since Act 2 (a pointed departure from the old principle of the unity of time), which ended with Tasso ordered to prison, his reason unhinged by his enforced separation from Eleonora. There is a C minor prelude, an opening recitative, and then the deeply touching *larghetto* aria, 'Perchè dell'aure in sen', introduced by a notable flute solo which combines the customary virtuoso elements of the ritornello to a final aria with the first two phrases of the vocal melody. The first unit of this aria is ten measures; the second unit is expanded by repeating the last two phrases from the first. The coda begins with a variation of the opening phrases and closes with cadences to the refrain 'mio dolce amor'. This simple but uncommon structure produces a moving sense of the poet frozen in time by his all-consuming love. The chorus enter and greet Tasso to the A major *vivace* that dominated the prelude to Act 1 (again, it is uncommon to find material from a prelude – though not from a *sinfonia* – repeated later in the score); they tell him that he is to be crowned with Petrarch's laurels. Overjoyed, Tasso inquires for Eleonora, exulting that now he is to have a crown and become her equal; but he is shocked when the chorus (in A minor with thudding figures) tells him that she has died. In a typically Donizettian choice of tonality, the poet's grieving eulogy and vision (*cantabile*, 2/4) is cast in C major. The cabaletta, 'Tomba di lei, che rendermi' (*moderato*, 4/4, C minor/C major), beginning over *marcato* chords, conveys something of the irony of the poet's belated triumph. The overall structure of this aria–finale that functions as a separate act, with its two slow movements and choruses before the cabaletta, is similar to the expanded form found at the conclusions of *Anna Bolena* and *Sancia di Castiglia*.

Lucrezia Borgia. Romani's libretto, adapted from Hugo's play, is, in effect, cast in the three-act form that became usual for Romantic melodrama, even though Romani described it as having a prologue and two acts; the librettist's classical training caused him to label the opening episode a prologue, as it is separated in time and place from the balance of the action, which opens in Venice and concludes in Ferrara. Besides being the year of the baritone, 1833 may also be thought of as Donizetti's *ferrarese* year, since all of *Parisina* and two-thirds of both *Tasso* and *Lucrezia* take place there.

Lucrezia Borgia marks the clear emergence of a manner that can be labeled distinctly Donizettian for all his retention of structures that were by now traditional; this individuality was already present in the finest passages of *Anna*, *Il furioso*, *Parisina* and *Tasso*, but it invests the whole of *Lucrezia*. Donizetti's appetite for strong situations has already been alluded to, but none of his earlier operas contains a more striking series of coups de théâtre than this score: the unmasking of Lucrezia in the prologue, the offstage tolling bells and grisly chanting that interrupt Orsini's bumptious brindisi, and the dying Gennaro's horror when he learns that Lucrezia is his mother. At each of these moments Donizetti creates a musical frisson that effectively heightens the dramatic effect.

The high dramatic voltage of *Lucrezia* focuses attention on an important aspect of Donizetti's style. It was he who urged the subject of Hugo's play, itself a product of 1833, upon the unenthusiastic Romani, and in the following year he directed the seventeen-year-old Bardari in concocting a dramatically explosive text from Schiller's *Maria Stuart*. While Donizetti, as his letters attest,[30] was concerned with maintaining a high level of vocal competence – the sort of polished execution that is assumed by the phrase 'bel canto' – he also wanted dramatic conviction and powerful acting. With *Lucrezia* and *Maria Stuarda* Donizetti moved a step ahead of his audience: for all its successful opening run at La Scala and its subsequent popularity, *Lucrezia* did not establish its vogue until the end of the 1830s, and *Maria Stuarda* would not enjoy frequent productions until the 1840s and 1850s; but it did not take the audience long to catch up, for, as Chorley reports (referring to the failure, despite a star-studded cast, of Rossini's *Guillaume Tell* at Her Majesty's Theatre in 1839), by the end of the 1830s the public 'preferred any musical melodrama of Donizetti because of the scope for acting afforded by the story'.[31] The impetus given to the present Donizetti revival by such interpretations as Callas's Anna Bolena, Gencer's Maria Stuarda, Caballé's Parisina, Sutherland's Lucrezia and Sills's Elisabetta (*Roberto Devereux*) results from the ability of these singers to project dramatic personalities and not from vocal prowess alone.

Méric-Lalande, the original Lucrezia, is famous for having created problems during the rehearsal period of the opera at La Scala. It is important, however, not to miss the reason for her contrariness. Essentially what she objected to were the unconventional aspects of the opera: she did not like the idea of entering masked in the middle of the prologue to sing a one-movement cavatina because she was afraid the audience would not immediately recognize her as the prima donna of the evening; and, all dramatic logic aside, she had to have her final *rondò*. She clearly underestimated the dramatic potential of her role, put off perhaps by its partly unsympathetic traits, and hoped to compensate for its novelty by bouts of good old-fashioned florid singing. In spite of her initial reluctance and the mixed reaction to the opening night, she went on to make a success of *Lucrezia* for a run that almost equaled Pasta's in the first production of *Norma*.

The unorthodox elements of *Lucrezia*, which are almost without exception the result of Donizetti's concern for maintaining dramatic momentum, afford one explanation for the opera's survival, for it has a consistent dramatic atmosphere compounded of nocturnal scenes, blatant dance rhythms and passionate cantilena. Lucrezia's romanza in the prologue is prefaced by a prelude the theme of which is later associated with her concern for her son. Her aria, 'Com'è bello' (*larghetto cantabile*, 4/4, E flat major), in its original form, is constructed like a cabaletta, consisting of two statements, the second (beginning

'Mentre geme') a repetition of the first with embellishments supplied by the composer;[32] when Donizetti later added the cabaletta, 'Sì, voli il primo a cogliere', to the romanza (the description of which was changed at that point to 'cavatina') he omitted the second statement so as to avoid using the same structural pattern in two consecutive arias. The succeeding duet is unconventional in that the *larghetto* is not the usual dialogue with barely overlapping voices, but a romanza for the tenor Gennaro, which (appropriately, in light of its text, 'Di pescatore ignobile') has the flavor of a Neapolitan song, but is in two neatly varied (rather than identical) strophes. This solo, following shortly after Lucrezia's *aria di sortita*, contrasts Gennaro's youthful ingenuousness with the more mature deviousness of his, as yet unacknowledged, mother. The *moderato* that concludes this duet is cast in a typical pattern: a statement for the soprano is repeated by the tenor; the soprano starts the third statement, now with the tenor interjecting isolated phrases, and the two voices join for the quicker conclusion. The prologue ends with a stretta which consists of an *andante* tune alternating with excited passages of *allegro;* during the slower tempo Orsini and his friends taunt Lucrezia with her crimes, while in the faster sections she begs for mercy and bemoans her fate, the whole episode culminating in the snatching away of her mask to the climactic dissonance of a diminished seventh on the leading-tone of the dominant key.

Not the least novel aspect of *Lucrezia* for its time is the importance given to a large cast of minor characters. (The problems of casting this opera played at least some part, along with the sensational subject matter, in the time lag that delayed any further performances of it for nearly three years after the *prima*.) In Act 1, for example, the extended dialogue between the *comprimario* characters Rustighello and Astolfo, floated over a striking orchestral melody (essentially the device later used by Verdi in the first encounter between Sparafucile and the hero at the opening of the second scene of *Rigoletto*), draws these 'bit' parts from the shadows to the prominence of center stage. The tendency represented by this episode can best be understood as the transferral to Romantic melodrama of the opera buffa device of presenting individual vignettes of lesser characters (as in *L'ajo*, for example). In many but not all of Donizetti's later operas, the *comprimario* roles become more than functional or stock parts, as the opportunistic Normanno and the complaisant Arturo in *Lucia* well illustrate.

It is not only its relative unconventionality that raises *Lucrezia Borgia* far above the norm of Romantic melodrama of its decade, but also the musical distinction and expressive power of many of its pages. The terzetto–finale to Act 1 can be seen as the fruition of the experiment Donizetti made nearly six years earlier with a similarly placed trio in *L'esule di Roma*. The entrance of Gennaro is accompanied by a courtly dance-like tune (*andante*, 3/4, A major), one of several passages where the aristocratic aplomb of *galanteria* provides an ironic outer surface to Alfonso's jealous and murderous rage (the same note would later be struck by Ponchielli in Alvise's confrontation with Laura (*La gioconda*), and, more memorably, by Verdi in Otello's questioning of Desdemona near the start of Act 3). The urbanity of Alfonso's music is occasionally punctuated by *fortissimo* chords and broken by shuddering figures. The succeeding *larghetto* (12/8, A flat major), 'Guai se ti sfugge un moto', is one of the finest passages in the score. Alfonso's terse first phrases in sixteenth-notes, seethe with barely restrained emotion; dispensing with any prolonged exposition of material, Donizetti brings in Lucrezia in the third measure, repeating Alfonso's opening in the same key, and in the fifth he introduces Gennaro with a broad melody set against the conspiratorial mutterings of the other characters – innocence pitted unaware against evil. The tension is maintained by the increasing overlapping of voice parts over a restless series of modulations marked 'crescendo a poco e stringendo'; only at the coda is the dynamic level allowed to drop from *fortissimo* and the original tempo reinstated. In no ensemble he had written up to this time had Donizetti so successfully created the expansion of a dramatic moment or more memorably indicated its many-sidedness. The intensity continues through the cabaletta, 'Infelice il veleno bevesti' (*allegro vivace*, 4/4, F major), a duet (since Alfonso has withdrawn after Gennaro has drunk the poison) in which musical distinction is replaced by raw hysteria; as Lucrezia gives Gennaro the antidote her climactic phrase, ascending chromatically to the top A, is marked by stabbing syncopations. Verdi was in Milan as a student during the first run of *Lucrezia* and not the least of the lessons he absorbed was contained in this finale.

Lucrezia's Act 2 *largo*, 'M'odi, ah m'odi', must rank as one of Donizetti's finest accomplishments. The situation could easily be rendered ludicrous since it parallels that at the end of Act 1: again Gennaro has drunk poison unwittingly, and again Lucrezia offers him an antidote. But now other factors have been added: Gennaro knows that his friends are poisoned too and he refuses the antidote; moreover he knows his true relationship to his poisoner. Donizetti creates a genuine sense of development in this scene starting from

the melodramatic entrance, without any introductory music, of Lucrezia, arrayed in black, who informs her victims where they have
come (Example 40). As she realizes that her son, whom she thought

Example 40. *Lucrezia Borgia*, Act 2, scena preceding the finale

she had persuaded to leave Ferrara, is among her victims, maternal
love urges her to agonized persuasiveness (Example 41).

This aria provides a locus classicus of dramatically expressive
coloratura as opposed to mere vocal display. Every flow and ebb of
Lucrezia's emotion as she gathers her strength to save her son and to
appease her guilt is tellingly reflected. Here the idiom of Romantic
opera acquires an intensity of expressiveness that would be hard to
match. The version of the aria printed as Example 41 is that of the
finale nuovo, which differs from the original only in starting the
descending scales from high B and high C sharp (instead of G sharp
and A).

Peculiar to the *finale nuovo* (which dispenses with Lucrezia's
concluding cabaletta, 'Era desso il figlio mio') and to the Paris version[33] (which is a composite containing the new *materia di mezzo*
added for La Scala in 1840 as well as an abridgment of Lucrezia's
cabaletta) is Gennaro's dying cantilena, 'Madre, se ognor lontano'.
Although composed in G major, it has a characteristic ambiguity of
mode owing to the stress placed on the augmented fifth (D sharp),
which resolves onto the adjacent sixth (E), the tonic of the relative

Example 41. *Lucrezia Borgia*, Act 2, *largo* of the finale (*finale nuovo*)

pre - go... ah te - co almeno ah! ____ non vo - le - re in - cru - de -

- lir. ____ Be - vi, be - vi... il rio ve - le - no ah! ____ t'af -

LUCREZIA

- fret - ta, deh! t'af-fret-ta a pre - ve - nir. Il tem - po vo - la, deh! ce - di,

GENNARO

So - no un Bor - gia!...

rinforz.

p

p

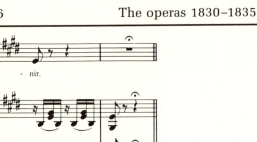

minor. This unadorned melody has a light accompaniment: simple arpeggios, slight doublings that highlight the modal ambiguity and an occasional extension of the vocal phrase (Example 42); it makes an eloquent contrast to the intricacies of line in 'M'odi, ah m'odi'.

Example 42. *Lucrezia Borgia*, Act 2, *larghetto* of the finale (*finale nuovo*)

The idiomatic difference between the soprano arias and the succeeding 'Di pescatore ignobile' is here maintained. The role of Gennaro in *Lucrezia*, especially with the ending of the *finale nuovo*, shows Donizetti fully discovering a tragic persona for the tenor; left behind are the ineffective solutions of a number of the operas between the 1826 *Gabriella*, which eliminates the tenor, and *Tasso*, which overexposes him in a shallow part.

Rosmonda d'Inghilterra. This two-act opera seria was the second of Donizetti's operas for Lanari's company in Florence; it contains the first role he wrote for Fanny Persiani. *Rosmonda* followed *Lucrezia* after an interval of almost exactly two months. Romani's libretto, an excursion into twelfth-century England, is a treatment of the story of 'Fair' Rosamond Clifford and her ill-fated love for Henry II which aroused the jealous wrath of Eleanor of Aquitaine; it had originally been written for Carlo Coccia in 1829, but for Donizetti Romani made a few adjustments in the text, shortening the introduction, plumping up the *musichetto* role of Arturo for Giuseppina Merola and rearranging a trio.[34] None of the other operas of this period has a slimmer performance history: the *prima* was given at the Teatro della Pergola in Carnival 1834, another production was mounted at Livorno in 1846 and one modern revival has taken place, in Britain in 1975. Coming on the heels of the major accomplishments of 1833, *Rosmonda* seems to mark a lessening of the composer's creative energy, if not of his customary craftsmanship; it moves along, but it rarely moves the audience.

The most fetching pages of the score are Rosmonda's *aria di sortita*, but these arias are better known from their later context at the same point in the French version of *Lucia di Lammermoor*. There is an effective duet for Rosmonda and Eleonora, 'Tu morrai, tu m'ha costretto', where the accents on unstressed beats suggest the contortions of Eleonora's jealousy; but the overall impression is ultimately that of the working out of predictable formulas rather than of true distinction. The biggest disappointment about *Rosmonda* is that just where one would expect Donizetti writing for Persiani to produce a sensational aria–finale, the first movement is an ensemble and the largely solo cabaletta that follows is earthbound. Significantly, this ending is the one part of the score Donizetti replaced in his partial revision of 1837. In his operas of the preceding year Donizetti had demonstrated his ability to bring his characters into sharp musico-dramatic focus, but this trait is only very fitfully present in *Rosmonda*.

Maria Stuarda. This three-act opera seria, banned before its *prima* could take place in Naples[35] and banned again during its opening run at La Scala with Malibran, has, since World War II, established itself after almost a century of neglect,[36] becoming one of Donizetti's most frequently performed operas. It is a highly significant work in the Donizetti canon because it illustrates so effectively many of the dominant tendencies in his development: most obviously, the confrontation of two powerful female figures in the notorious 'Dialogo delle due regine' (see pp. 277–80), and the exploitation of the spiritual longing and final suffering of a victim–heroine. It was Donizetti's own desire for strong subjects that caused him to turn to Schiller's drama, which he knew in Maffei's translation of 1830, rather than to Alfieri's more classical treatment (1778), which deals not with Mary's death but with her tribulations in Scotland. The importance of Schiller to Italian operatic composers of the nineteenth-century can scarcely be overstressed; in choosing one of Schiller's works Donizetti had before him the persuasive example of *Guillaume Tell*, so promptly acknowledged as Rossini's masterpiece. If *Gianni di Parigi* had provided Donizetti's first feeble rocket in the direction of Paris, his choice of *Maria Stuarda* as a subject can be interpreted as a second more forceful attempt to attract the attention of the French capital; if he could make a success of this opera on a plot by the author of *Tell*, how better to demonstrate his fitness to follow Rossini's path to Paris?

If Donizetti's insensitivity to the hullabaloo that *Maria Stuarda* would cause in Naples seems surprising, it should be remembered that he had been absent from Naples for over a year and was unaware of the increasingly conservative stance of the court and censors. Further, he had returned from the north with a surprisingly high average of successes to his credit with works that convinced him that the audience's appetite for melodramatic tragedy was keen and increasing. So confident was he that he believed he could carry the public with his new style; and after the initial setback over *Maria Stuarda* in the autumn of 1834 he still retained some measure of confidence that Milan would prove more hospitable to this score, but there too he was doomed to be disappointed. *Maria Stuarda* was, quite simply, ahead of its time.

Maria Stuarda is a fascinating score because one can detect Donizetti's increasing involvement in his subject as it progresses. It begins conventionally enough with an opening chorus, and an *aria di sortita* for Elisabetta that would not seem very out of place in the context of *Il castello di Kenilworth* – the new Elisabetta belongs to the same termagant stereotype as the old, she is only outlined more boldly. The succeeding pair of arias for Leicester shows some quickening of interest. His ardent impetuousness is indicated by a surging rhythmic figure as he looks at Maria's picture. Although these arias are labeled 'cavatina' in the score, they turn out to be a quasi-duet as Talbot's voice joins the tenor in the concluding passage of each of the three tempos. Noteworthy here is the fact that Leicester's cabaletta, 'Se fida tanto' (somewhat modified, for the first performance of *Maria Stuarda* in 1835, from the version in *Buondelmonte*), contains a curious anticipation of Verdi's 'Di quella pira'.[37] Leicester, however, is at best a sort of halfway hero; while he provides a means of focusing sympathy upon the heroine, who does not appear until Act 2, he always remains at a certain psychological distance from her, even in their duet, and at the end he is a grieving figure on the sidelines, helpless to intervene. The first flickers of interplay between the characters, one of the strongest aspects of this opera, occur in the duet between Elisabetta and Leicester that concludes this short first act. The opening *allegro* admirably depicts the queen's peremptory anger at Leicester's unresponsiveness to her obvious attempts to elicit flattery, while he single-mindedly can think only of pleading Maria's cause. The *larghetto* of the duet (partly borrowed from the Venetian *rifacimento* of *Fausta* for Pasta), 'Era d'amor l'immagine' (6/8, B major), begins with Leicester's balanced phrases praising Maria's beauty, then moves from B to G major. Elisabetta wrenches the tonality back to the tonic in splendidly energetic phrases as she comments with bitter irony on Maria's talent for winning over supporters, even when she is in prison. The concluding *vivace*, in E major, mercifully avoids the usual wholesale repetitions and maintains the vivid contrast between Elisabetta's vengefulness and Leicester's pleas in the Scottish queen's behalf.

The second act, in the park at Fotheringay, introduces Maria, and the prelude (in C major) is motivic, with scurrying triplets and *fortissimo* tonic chords; there is an ironic contrast between the tensions of the previous act at Westminster and the delusive sunniness here. Maria's first aria, 'Oh! nube che lieve per l'aria ti aggiri' (*larghetto*, 3/8, D flat major), conveys her nostalgia for France and freedom in a melody both elegant and simple; the opening phrase consists of a scalar ascent from the dominant through a seventh and a balancing descent, the return to the dominant being emphasized by means of a raised subdominant (Example 43).

This aria has the structure $a\ a^1\ b\ a^2$. The melody floats over inconspicuous harp arpeggios and rhythmic string chords, which

Example 43. *Maria Stuarda*, Act 2, *larghetto* of Maria's *aria di sortita*

creates a focus on a vocal line of Bellinian intensity; Maria's underlying anxiety is suggested only by the irregular length of the melodic sections. The *tempo di mezzo* features an offstage chorus and fanfares from two offstage trumpets (it was more usual to use horns at this point); unlike similar episodes in *Anna Bolena* and *Parisina*, this one carries the dramatic suggestion that the quarry is Maria herself. The cabaletta, 'Nella pace, nel mesto riposo', is marked 'moderato e fiero' and, although conventional in design, it reveals in its upward-surging line that this queen will know how to defend herself staunchly. Again, conventional structure dominates the melodically grateful duet for Maria and Leicester, but here, uncommonly, one is aware of how the regular deployment of periods creates suspense for the heralded arrival of Elisabetta.

The basic structure of the finale to Act 2 has been described in Chapter 8, but here a few comments may point up some of the finer details of this scene. For instance, the triplet figures that accompany Elisabetta's entrance reflect back to the prelude of this act, but since they are now in C minor it is as if a cloud has obscured the sun. The orchestration of the sextet, with its alternation of *pizzicato* and bowed notes for the strings and the menacing addition of horns and trumpets as Elisabetta first utters the word 'terror', depicts the subsurface tension as the rivals (both speaking aside) take each other's measure. The famous dialogue expands the *materia di mezzo* into the climactic moment of the opera and shows Donizetti's intuitive understanding that too much music could interfere with a moment of flaming drama. Hearing it today, one does not have to strain one's ability to believe that Ronzi and del Sere were carried away by it to the point of physical combat at that Neapolitan rehearsal in 1834!

The opening scene of Act 3, which deals with Elisabetta's signing of Maria's death warrant, is on a lower level than much of the rest of the score. Indeed, Donizetti thought so little of this trio that he suggested that it could be replaced by recitative for a production at Faenza in 1837 with Carolina Ungher.[38] Notable in this scene, though, are the brief prelude with its restless modulations, and Leicester's exact repeat, at the words 'libero è il tuo volere', of the opening phrase of both statements of the *larghetto* of his duet with Maria in Act 2 – such a cross-reference being relatively uncommon in Donizetti's operas. Notable, too, is the music Donizetti left out of this scene: Bardari's libretto shows that it was originally intended to end with a monologue for Elisabetta, which apparently Donizetti never set, feeling the need to shift the emphasis back to Maria as soon as possible. The second scene of Act 3, Maria's confession to Talbot, moves to an altogether higher plane. The tragic torment of Maria's conscience is emphasized by the interval of the minor second, falling and rising, that occurs in the prelude and in the accompaniment of the opening recitative. Having received news of her sentence from Cecil, Maria, to an expressive clarinet phrase, bids Talbot remain. When she kneels for her confession, 'Quando la luce rosea' (*larghetto*, 4/4, G minor/G major), the woodwinds play a descending scale, broken into groups of two notes. At the midpoint of this movement the music shifts to the parallel major as Maria addresses the memory of her murdered husband Darnley and bids him pray for her soul (Example 44).

Such changes of mode in the course of an aria ('Una furtiva lagrima' and Marie's 'Il faut partir' contain familiar examples of this device) possess an effectiveness beyond the relatively simple means used to achieve them; usually prepared by a linking note, the melody in the new key signifies the arrival at a new emotional plateau and requires a different vocal color. The usage is not, of course, peculiar to Donizetti, but he understood how to highlight these moves from minor to major, and the emphasis he places upon them can be counted as one characteristic of his style. In the coda to Maria's aria, Talbot's voice joins hers; again, as in Leicester's arias in Act 1, Donizetti proves his ability to combine features of the aria and duet without losing his main emphasis or wasting time over the wholesale repetitions that a literal adherence to the conventions would require. The *moderato*, 'Lascio contento al carcere', is more usual in its layout, except that Maria's melody, starting in the tonic G major like Talbot's opening period, is a variation of his melody, and the two are combined for the passage *a due*.

The final scene, which culminates in Maria's execution, is the finest in the work, continuing and elaborating the emotional catharsis begun at her confession. After a solemn E minor prelude, full of

MARIA

Om - bra a-do-ra-ta ah! pla - ca-ti... nel sen___ la_ mor - te io

sen - to. Ti ba - stin le_____ mie la - gri -me, ti

ba - sti il mio_____ tor - men - to il mio_____ tor - men -

to il mio tor - men - to.

Example 44. *Maria Stuarda*, Act 3 scene ii, *larghetto* of Maria's aria

insistent iterations and shuddering figures, has established a mood of ominous tragedy, the chorus, who up to now have been used more sparingly than in most of Donizetti's serious operas of this period, have an 'Inno di morte' that ends with a broadly elegiac tune in E major. The chorus also take a noteworthy part in Maria's famous prayer, 'Deh! Tu di un umile preghiera' (andante commodo, 3/4, E flat major), which has a melody derived from Il paria and later to be inserted, with further modifications, in both Linda di Chamounix and the uncompleted Le duc d'Albe. The structure of the prayer is basically binary though its sections are never repeated in exactly the same way; piano statements alternate with fortissimo ones, the second climax presenting the original melody in slightly varied form. Particularly striking is an episode in C major, where Maria sustains an inverted pedal point on the dominant for seven measures and at the end ascends chromatically to top B flat, overlapping there with the chorus in the tonic key. Donizetti sustains and expands the emotion of this moment by hammering away at a melody that features repeated notes, but arranging its movement so skillfully that insistence never becomes monotonous.

Similarly, in the larghetto of Maria's aria–finale, the touching 'Di un cor che more' (F minor/F major), where the text is built in units of three five-syllable phrases rounded out by one in four syllables, intensity is created by the insistence on a simple melodic idea (Example 45). The stark opening phrase, a descent from dominant to tonic poised over iterated string chords, is immediately repeated and conveys Maria's agony of contrition. Donizetti gave this aria a special heading: 'Aria del Supplizio' (Aria of the Execution).[39] This aria begins in F minor and in the second half moves through an extended D flat major episode before reverting to the opening minor key; the shift to the parallel major of the tonic is delayed until the second half of the substantial coda. In the D flat major portion the clarinet doubles the contour of Maria's first two phrases, later the horns sustain her series of conjunct descending phrases. In the F major section of the coda, Maria's voice ascends for the first time to A and B flat above the staff in pianissimo figures floating over the choral phrases, as she speaks of how her shed blood will cancel all her sins. During this aria her line moves from the declamato opening through increasing lyrical intensity up to this transcendent major conclusion. Her cabaletta, 'Ah! se un giorno da queste ritorte' (maestoso, 4/4), endows her with tragic grandeur as she renounces the idea of calling down on heretic England the wrath of a vengeful God. Here

Example 45. *Maria Stuarda*, Act 3, *larghetto* of Maria's aria–finale

Donizetti has sought to relieve the repetitiveness inevitable in a cabaletta by beginning the second statement in the parallel major instead of repeating the B minor/D major pattern of the first. The final scene of *Maria Stuarda* stands as a major accomplishment because Donizetti's own involvement with Maria's tragic fate moves him to communicate the drama with a searing directness balanced by moments of lyrical expansiveness that strike the listener with the force of truth.

Gemma di Vergy. Just as Donizetti's appetite for powerful subjects had lately led him to Hugo and Schiller, for his new opera, commissioned to open the Carnival season of 1834–5 at La Scala, he turned to Dumas *père* and his play, *Charles VII chez les grands vassaux.* Since Romani had taken up a career in journalism and was no longer interested in writing new librettos, Donizetti approached Emanuele Bidèra; the advantage of this choice was that Bidèra was then in Naples so that Donizetti could directly supervise the writing of the text. *Gemma* deals with the novel operatic subject of divorce from the repudiated wife's position; the topic was censorially 'safe' because the events depicted took place in early-fifteenth-century France and because Gemma's barrenness constituted legitimate grounds for the dissolution of her marriage to the Count di Vergy. It is not difficult to see why Donizetti was attracted to this plot with its possibilities for focusing on the torment of an innocent victim; tailoring the role to the nuanced and volatile throat of Ronzi, he produced one of his most vocally taxing roles. While Lilli Lehmann regarded one Norma as equal to three Brünnhildes, Montserrat Caballé, the only singer so far to undertake Gemma in the twentieth century,[40] is reported to have observed that one Gemma equals three Normas!

For all its challenges to a prima donna – and generations of nineteenth-century sopranos favored it as a showcase – *Gemma* contains an almost fatal flaw. The heroine suffers (there are stage directions such as 'convulsa e tremante' and 'disperatissima'), but her emotion is fundamentally self-indulgent and selfish. Unlike the repudiated Norma, whose sacrifice can rekindle Pollione's love and whose last thoughts are of her children, Gemma exists in too great an isolation from human relationships to engage our sympathies deeply; she is somehow exaggerated. True, she loves her husband and she manages to evoke his tears during the finale to Act 1, but when she is moved to murderous rage in the presence of her successor, Ida, and comes within an inch of stabbing her, it is only the fortuitous arrival of Tamas, her devoted Arab slave, that keeps her from murder, not the fundamental humanity that allows Anna Bolena to feel compassion for Seymour in a not dissimilar situation. Another part of the problem with *Gemma* is that Tamas, who loves his mistress enough to kill her ex-husband because he has brought her anguish and half destroyed her reason, is summarily dismissed by his mistress when she learns of his crime, whereupon he kills himself at her feet and is promptly forgotten. It is the absence of the kind of emotional catharsis that moves us at the suffering of Anna or Parisina or Maria Stuarda that ultimately fails to warm Gemma into life.

Musically, *Gemma* ranges between the genuinely impressive and the routine. An impressive episode occurs during the introduction where Donizetti achieves an unusual double perspective of foreground and background by superimposing Guido's recital of the Count's domestic problems upon a discussion between Rolando and the male chorus of recent events involving Joan of Arc. The routine aspects of the score are observable in the obsessive repetition of sequences that become glib and emptily rhetorical. Example 46 is taken from the finale to Act 1 where Tamas justifies his murder of the henchman Rolando (who had taken him prisoner in Arabia years before) and defies the Count.

Donizetti's thumbprint of phrases that begin on an accented second beat of the measure can be seen here, and there is the artful variation of the phrases that begin in the sixth and tenth measures of the example (repeated from the Count's earlier period); but the pained eloquence achieved by the device of varied repetition in the Anna–Seymour duet or in Lucrezia's 'M'odi, ah m'odi' is missing. Instead there is an obtrusive loquacity – this passage would not sound seriously misplaced in a buffa setting. It would be a mistake, however, to judge all the tenor's music by this example. In his virile aria 'Mi togliesti a un sole ardente' (*allegro giusto*, 4/4, C major) at his entrance in the first scene, the vigorous march-like opening period is finely contrasted with a more nostalgic pendant. This moment is interesting structurally: while Donizetti underplays the *maestoso* brief first aria, giving it something of the weight of an arioso passage within the recitative, he highlights the cabaletta, 'Mi togliesti', with a catchily orchestrated introduction and choral reinforcement in the coda. *Gemma*'s early popularity was owed in part to Tamas and his yearning for liberty, and it was this cabaletta that precipitated an historic demonstration at Palermo in 1847.

An example of Donizetti's fitful involvement in this score may be found in the Count's almost fatuous A major cabaletta in Act 2, 'Questa soave immagine'. The line in which the Count, thinking of his second marriage, looks forward to hearing himself called 'father' might be expected to have touched Donizetti deeply; perhaps the no more than commonplace setting indicates that Donizetti, for personal reasons, was holding himself aloof from this emotion. The same sense of inhibition undercuts the later duet for Gemma and Tamas, which begins so promisingly with a fine oboe solo – one of the few places where Donizetti gives this instrument such prominence; a striking ascending chromatic movement in the accompaniment of the *larghetto*, 'Non è ver', creates a sense of urgency, but this

Example 46. *Gemma di Vergy*, Act 1, *moderato* of the finale

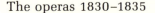

is soon dissipated in jogging dotted rhythms and thrown away in the
empty *vivace* that concludes the duet. The chief saving grace of this
score is the aria–finale for Gemma. The opening *maestoso*, 'Eccomi
sola alfine', a prayer in D flat, is introduced by the flute and clarinet
over a string bass; a declamatory *moderato*, 'Da quel tempio fuggite',
follows in which the vigorous descending phrases over a relentless
thudding accompaniment in E flat minor recall Mayr's *Medea*. In the
larghetto, 'Un altare ed una benda' (2/4, D flat major), a seamless bit
of vocal embroidery, Gemma speaks of her desire to end her days in a
convent; the low ending, rising to the tonic from the B flat below
middle C, was an exploitation of Ronzi's chest register. The *materia
di mezzo* is concerned with Tamas's confession and suicide, and it
precipitates the cabaletta, 'Chi m'accusa' (*moderato*, 4/4, E flat
major), in which Gemma protests her innocence. Here, the dotted
chromatic figures of the second period, where the tempo increases
and the music builds to a climax, are unhappily reminiscent of the
sequences in the closing pages of *Norma*. If *Gemma* is basically an
opera that affords only spasmodic delights, it is because while
Donizetti was composing it his mind was chiefly on its successor,
the opera that Rossini had invited him to compose for the Parisian
Théâtre-Italien.

Marin(o) Faliero. One of the most striking aspects of Donizetti's
musical dramaturgy is the way in which he tackles daunting subjects. In *Marin Faliero* he was composing an opera for Lablache, and
as a result he shifted the focus away from the prima donna; this was
noted as a shortcoming by Chorley,[41] who inevitably compared
Marin Faliero to *I puritani* in the prominence afforded to Giulia
Grisi – Bellini's and Donizetti's operas were the novelties performed

that season, by the same principals, in both Paris and London. Although *I puritani* had been performed before Donizetti's score in Paris, in London it was put on a week later so as to allow the somber tragedy of *Marin Faliero* to make its effect before the public heard Bellini's more vocally grateful score with its happy ending. Donizetti's opera produced an inevitable strain upon audiences habituated to the stereotyped presentation of operatic triangles because it placed the wronged husband, the bass, at the sympathetic apex.

Marin Faliero is an opera that poses particular problems to the researcher because of the discrepancy between the autograph score in Naples and printed scores such as that published by Ricordi;[42] the Ricordi score differs from the autograph in more than a third of the total material. To name just one instance, the autograph begins with a *sinfonia* while the Ricordi score starts with a prelude based on the Gondolier's song from Act 2. The whole question of *Marin Faliero* and its complicated evolution needs to be explored in depth, but the outline of these complexities can at least be indicated. Donizetti had composed most of the opera to Bidèra's text before he left Naples. At Paris Rossini, giving Donizetti the same assistance he had already tendered to Bellini over *I puritani*, made extensive suggestions for the better treatment of the opera, and Donizetti wrote a good deal of new music before the *prima*. What modifications were needed to the libretto were supplied by Agostino Ruffini, the brother of the poet of *Don Pasquale*, then living in exile in Paris.[43] When Donizetti returned to Italy in the spring of 1835, he informed Giovanni Ricordi[44] that he had entered into preliminary negotiations with Eugène Troupenas to publish the score, but it seems clear that he wanted Ricordi to bring it out, at least in Italy, for he could count on the publisher's help in combatting unauthorized and incorrect versions. Such a problem had already arisen by the following October. Donizetti was enraged to learn that the impresario Gennaro Fabbricatore had obtained a copy of the autograph of the music Donizetti had written in Naples and claimed he had rights of some sort to the opera; as a result the composer and the musical pirate faced each other in the prefecture of police in Naples. Donizetti reported to Ricordi the outcome of this confrontation: 'thank fortune, the many new pieces I had composed in Paris to *Faliero*, many of them I had added to the score, and thus, the modified libretto and my new music were witnesses to [Fabbricatore's] knavery and to my innocence'.[45] This problem explains why Donizetti kept the revised material distinct from the original autograph.

But the revisions did not stop with those Donizetti made in Paris.
When the opera was so successfully introduced to Italy by Lanari at
Florence in April 1836, new material was added and some old
material omitted: Lanari reported to Donizetti that Carolina Ungher
included the *aria di sortita* of Sancia di Castiglia and that the
baritone Paolo Ferretti omitted Israele's aria to keep the opera within
lengths tolerable to the Florentines. He also disclosed that 'The duet
between Elena and Ferdinando [*sic*]', the roles sung by Ungher and
the tenor Moriani, was 'sufficiently applauded, but the public recognized in its first two tempos those from the *Anna Bolena* duet many
times performed here.'[46] Yet the opening of the duet that appears in
the Ricordi score,[47] 'Tu non sai la nave è presta', does not come from
Anna Bolena; it is, in fact, a melody that is more familiar in modified
form as the cabaletta, 'Quest'addio, fatale, estrema', of the Sara–
Roberto duet from *Roberto Devereux*. Obviously there is much here
that needs sorting out. The following discussion is based upon the
Ricordi score, which, though it does not include all the materials
within the orbit of *Marin Faliero*, represents a version that had
Donizetti's sanction.

This opera inevitably invites comparison with Verdi's *I due Foscari*, not only because of their common Byronic antecedents, but
because they both portray elderly doges and both exploit Venetian
local color – a particular characteristic of Donizetti's score with its
gondolier's barcarolle and choruses in rollicking 6/8. (Donizetti's
plot is drawn not only from Byron but in part from Casimir Delavigne's 1829 play, which provided him with the intrigue between
Elena and her cousin Fernando; in Byron this motif is treated only as
the basis for an otherwise unsubstantiated insult.) Dramatically,
Donizetti's plot is the stronger; in *Foscari* the tenor and soprano
roles are those of the doge's son and his son's wife, all three, though
separated by fate, united in their suffering at the hands of the vengeful Loredano; but in *Faliero* these roles are assigned to the Doge's
wife and his nephew, who are enmeshed in an adulterous affair,
which creates a greater degree of conflict in the dramatic action. In
both operas the characters opposed to the doges are insufficiently
developed and individualized. And yet these works are most similar
in their tragic intensity and noble-heartedness; the adjective 'Verdian' may be applied to *Marin Faliero* with peculiar appositeness.

The Rubini role of Fernando provided opportunities for what
Chorley describes as one of that tenor's 'most incomparable and
superb vocal displays',[48] and indeed the difficulty of his music mili-
tates against an adequate revival of the opera today. Fernando's *aria*

di sortita in Act 1 is a double aria: 'Di mia patria, o bel soggiorno' (*cantabile*, 4/4, A flat major)[49] followed by the cabaletta 'Ma un solo conforto' (*allegro giusto*, 4/4, A flat major). Donizetti's affection for keys in the relationship of the major third can be seen in the C major orchestral introduction, and in the second half of the cabaletta's opening period, where the same tonality recurs. The cantabile is a nostalgic purling melody, revealing once more Donizetti's fondness for illustrative embellishment to color a text that includes such images as 'aure amiche' (friendly breezes). The cabaletta, which follows directly without a *tempo di mezzo*, is a vigorous aria with unrelentingly high tessitura that takes the tenor up to top D flat. In Act 2 Fernando has a second double aria, where one is surprised to encounter in the opening recitative the familiar words 'Tombe degli avi miei'.[50] Here the *larghetto*, 'Io ti veggio', which, uncommonly, both begins and ends in a minor key, moves in elegiac 6/8; it is followed by a dramatic *tempo di mezzo* and a most taxing G major cabaletta, 'Mi tornano presenti', which calls for high D naturals. These arias movingly convey both the anguish and desperation of Fernando, who is determined to die for Elena since he cannot live with her.

The Tamburini role of Israele, the sympathetic plebeian allied with the patrician Faliero, is highly effective. His Act 1 *maestoso*, 'Er'anch'io' (12/8, A flat major), is in the asymmetrical pattern observed elsewhere; the opening strophe is succeeded by a foreshortened second one that begins like the first but then moves to the climactic phrase before the vocal cadences, so that it is half the length. One of the great moments in the score, reworked for the Florence production, is the duet between Israele and Faliero in Act 1. As the outraged Israele tries to rouse the Doge into conspiring against his rival Steno, Faliero is first of all concerned with the security of Venice, but when the captain of the arsenal reminds him of his wife's impugned honor, the idealistic Doge abandons discretion. In three sections (*moderato*, A flat major; *larghetto*, C major; *moderato*, A flat major), the duet begins with a whispered colloquy that unexpectedly bursts out in sudden exclamations as suddenly choked back; this opening creates an immediate tension sustained by the determined march tempo. The concluding cabaletta, 'Sì! Trema o Steno', with its syncopated opening phrase has a vigor reminiscent of the young Verdi (Example 47). Notable, too, is Israele's Act 3 aria (cut in the performance at Florence), in which he voices his willingness to die for a righteous cause.

Grisi's role of Elena is exceptional in its neglect of the traditional perquisites of the prima donna. In the first scene of Act 1 Elena has

Example 47. *Marin Faliero*, Act 1 scene i, cabaletta of the Israele–Faliero duet[51]

only a duet with the tenor; in the second scene she participates in the finale. She is absent from Act 2. In Act 3 at long last comes her aria, a fine expressive prayer and cabaletta, 'Fra due tombe, fra due spettri' (*moderato*, 4/4, F major), in which her remorse is vividly projected and the image of a sea of blood rising around her feet is expressed in abrupt leaps of a tenth and swirling scalar passages. At the close of her confession–absolution duet with Faliero, he is led off to his execution, and she is left alone on stage for the final dramatic moment of the opera.

offstage voices: [basses in D minor]
  Let your face be raised to the Lord;
  Ask pity of the Lord.
Elena (*listening*): [her unaccompanied phrases are separated by pairs of upward-sliding chromatic chords]
  All is silent ...
  The priest ... prays for him ...
  And consoles him ...
  He has said one word ...
  Was it for me? (*she hears the blow of the axe, screams, and falls as though dead*)
Judges (*entering*): [tenors and basses in unison]
  Let the gates be opened so that the people
  May see the end of the traitor.
  (*curtain*) [D minor]

In such an episode as this, Donizetti has moved a long way from the convention of the aria–finale. And if the singer should feel slighted, the actress has a golden moment.

The delayed emphasis upon the prima donna, who comes into her own only in Act 3, is the result of Faliero's being the focal figure of the action. (One regrets that a Chaliapin never thought of this role as a vehicle, but in his time the notion of reviving a forgotten Donizetti opera would have seemed an almost certifiable eccentricity.) The composer has reached, in this score, such an advanced stage of development that he can endow the various ingredients of any part of a structure with sufficient emphasis to carry its dramatic importance. When Faliero first enters, after the soprano–tenor duet of the opening scene, his accompanied recitative immediately establishes, in a few motivic strokes, his imposing presence. The first impression is soon developed in his dramatic duet with Israele, which makes clear Faliero's internal conflict. Another instance where Donizetti takes a minor moment and transforms it into a dramatic highlight occurs near the beginning of the first finale. To offstage dance music (*larghetto*, 3/4, B flat major/B flat minor) Israele reports to the Doge about all the people who are willing to enter into their conspiracy; the ironic contrast between the old-fashioned dance tune and the terse dialogue, only thirty-two measures long, is musical theater that makes a memorable impact.

At the close of Act 2, Faliero dominates the ensemble of grief over Fernando's corpse; the ensemble is cast in cabaletta form, but with different texts for each statement, and ends with a rousing coda demanding vengeance – all of this, rather surprisingly for any composer other than Donizetti, in the key of C major. The emotional climax of the opera is the duet for Faliero and Elena in Act 3. Her confession of her liaison with Fernando takes place against an infinitely extendible accompaniment figure, syncopated and frequently insisting on the interval of the minor second; at the moment she mentions Fernando's name, Faliero's shocked recognition is expressed by a *pianissimo* descending figure, and then for a moment he struggles to repudiate her but finds he cannot. He begins the *larghetto* (2/4, F major) in an aside, 'Santa voce al cor mi suona', using the first phrase of Idamore's 'Da sì caro e dolce istante' from the opening of the final quartet from *Il paria;* but here the melody evolves along different and more expressive lines, particularly after the entrance of Elena's part.[52] There is a true sense of catharsis as the two, with their various griefs, seek to console each other, and pray for forgiveness. There is no cabaletta to this duet, only the dramatic action that leads to the Doge's offstage execution.

Marin Faliero marks a significant step forward for Donizetti. It provides clear evidence of his search to bend the conventions to his own dramatic needs. It is true that the betrayal of Faliero's conspiracy takes place off stage between Acts 2 and 3, but in other operas, such as *Il trovatore,* reversals of fortune are similarly relegated to the entr'acte. Donizetti sought to concentrate on the emotional consequences of the betrayal, and for an opera that makes the most promising fare.

11

The operas
1835–1838

Lucia di Lammermoor. Of all of Donizetti's operas, none has more resolutely resisted changes of operatic fashion than this seria in three acts, first given at the San Carlo on 26 September 1835, six and a half months after the *prima* of *Faliero* at Paris. It used to be a cliché of criticism to claim that *Lucia* was a direct result of Donizetti's exposure to *I puritani* at the Théâtre-Italien, as though otherwise he would have been incapable of composing it; some of the more extreme *belliniani* even went so far as to swear that *Lucia* was written in homage to Bellini's memory, when in fact Bellini died just three days before the delayed *prima* of Donizetti's opera. The advantage of taking a closer look at all Donizetti's operatic scores in turn is that it affords the opportunity to determine how directly *Lucia* stems from his preceding work and how it extends tendencies already observable there. No man who worked as consistently as he did inside a number of theaters could be impervious to what his contemporaries were about, yet by 1835 his manner was so thoroughly formed, if not at its fullest development, that he absorbed outside influences into his own practise, which was, quite simply, the most wide-ranging and solid of any Italian operatic composer of his generation.

The resemblances between *Lucia* and *I puritani*, other than those unavoidably resulting from the conventions of the period, are superficial ones. True, they both contain mad scenes and are set in the British Isles during the seventeenth century. But *Lucia* is a tragedy with its outcome implicit from the beginning, while *I puritani* depends upon a series of fortuitous events that ultimately turn out well. A deeper-lying distinction can be found in the differing ways in which the two composers present characters in these operas. Donizetti regularly presents the people of his drama more concretely, more literally, while *I puritani* shows a more abstract approach: the emotion is converted into a *melos* that transcends and makes emblematic its motivation. The bass arias that precede the mad scenes in both operas illustrate this point, despite the fundamental difference in the circumstances they describe: Giorgio Walton's 'Cinta di fior', in four balanced strophes, evokes a mood of sincere but diffuse pathos, while Raimondo's 'Dalle stanze', with its restless modulations and jolting chromatic movement in the bass seeks to convey immediately, and to particularize, the ghastly scene in Lucia's bridal suite.

Recently there appeared a recording of Lucia[1] that discharges the useful service of performing the score exactly as it appears in the autograph. The original tonalities are employed: that is, Lucia's aria di sortita is in E flat and A flat, her duet with Enrico is in A, and the mad scene is in F.[2] The orchestration has been corrected and many minor discrepancies have been eliminated.[3] While all that is very much to the good, there is a distortion of one feature of the opera simply because it does not appear in the autograph. The role of Lucia was composed for Fanny Persiani, probably the most accomplished vocal technician of her generation. Chorley wrote of her: 'The perfection with which [Persiani] wrought up certain songs – such as . . . the mad scene in Lucia – if considered in respect to style, and to what style can do, has not in my experience been exceeded, has been very rarely approached.'[4] The cadenza that Donizetti wrote out at the end of the larghetto of the mad scene (an arpeggio on the dominant seventh that descends nearly two octaves and ascends to a flattened sixth which drops to the dominant), shows that he knew perfectly well that there was no point in writing out a full cadenza for this soprano, who was perfectly capable of improvising a new one at each performance if she put her mind to it. To suppose that the simple arpeggio figure represents Donizetti's true intentions, especially as it comes on the heels of a highly figured variation of the original melody, is to ignore the conventions within which he worked. Rather, it is clear that the composer is merely giving the singer some indication of the harmonic path he prefers her flight of fancy to end with, the most striking feature being the downward step near the end of a half-tone to the dominant.[5] Nor should it be assumed that the established tradition of a cadenza with flute obbligato at this point stems from Persiani; according to Chorley, she altered her cadenza depending on her vocal health and mood, and since the flute participation must be fixed in advance, it would be highly unlikely that she used it. One bit of traditional lore singles out Teresa Brambilla, Verdi's first Gilda, as the originator of the flute obbligato in the cadenza of the Lucia mad scene.[6]

Some passages of Lucia, the introduzione and the Act 2 sextet, for instance, have already been examined in Chapter 8, where their familiarity made them useful examples in the discussion of form and convention. One way to appreciate the special qualities of *Lucia*, however, is to focus on the use of details, which might pass by almost unnoticed, but which, in their multiplicity, add to the total effectiveness. A few examples will serve. Most usually, Donizetti introduces an aria either with a forthright orchestral anticipation of the opening phrases, or with a measure of orchestral accompaniment, depending on whether he wants to establish a mood or to avoid losing dramatic momentum. The orchestral introduction to 'Regnava nel silenzio' creates a most uncommon dramatic effect (Example 48). Here Donizetti fulfills the functions of an introduc-

Example 48. *Lucia di Lammermoor*, Act 1 scene ii, introduction and opening of Lucia's *aria di sortita*

tion – establishing the opening tonality (E flat minor in this case) and the rhythmic motion – but, more important, he presents a vivid sense of Lucia's character. In the preceding recitative she has told her companion Alisa that she has seen in the fountain a hallucinatory vision of her ancestress, who was murdered in a fit of jealous rage by one of Edgardo's forebears; in her aria she relives this experience for Alisa. In the orchestral introduction Lucia's opening vocal phrase is encapsulated in a motif with a distinctive interval of the ascending minor sixth, which occurs twice in the winds and a third time, with *crescendo,* in the lower strings. This *crescendo* leads to a reverberating silence in the fourth measure, out of which begin soft clarinet arpeggios. This reduction of Lucia's opening phrase to a repeated motif is quite different from the usual decorative foretaste of the vocal melody in the introduction to an aria; it confronts the audience immediately with Lucia's obsession with the vision and her inhibited character, which will later prevent her from behaving decisively until she goes mad and herself commits a murder. Into these few bars, then, Donizetti has compressed considerable evidence of Lucia's unstable condition.

The end of the first strophe of 'Regnava nel silenzio' contains another instance of Donizetti's skill as a musical dramatist (Example 49). The second word of the text, 'ecco', is repeated, and

Example 49. *Lucia di Lammermoor,* Act 1 scene ii, *larghetto* of Lucia's
aria di sortita

this decision was clearly Donizetti's rather than Cammarano's as it breaks the regular pattern of eight-syllable lines (*ottonarii*) of the metrical scheme. On the other hand the repetition of the text in the last phrase is formal rather than specifically dramatic, as it provides a conventional extension of the cadence to mark the end of the strophe. Disturbing the metrical scheme by repeating 'ecco' allows the composer to emphasize that it was exactly here that the ghost appeared, and he further seeks to show how even the memory of that experience has shattered Lucia's self-control by marking this passage *presto* and by breaking up the regularly balanced phrases into compulsive chatter. In the third measure of the example, where Lucia first sings the words 'l'ombra mostrarsi' (the ghost shows itself), he sets the first syllable to the lowest note in the whole aria, to give it a special color, and he places accents above each syllable of the word 'mostrarsi', to stress the intensity with which Lucia relives her encounter. Unfortunately these last two points are almost invariably lost in performance, because the soprano, seeing a scale passage on the last syllable of 'margine' (almost always sung 'margin'aaaah', so that the frightened 'e' vowel that Donizetti emphasized is destroyed) takes it as an invitation to embellish *a piacere*, and alters the emphatic contour of the succeeding phrase for a showier, less interesting one; in doing so she erases the composer's dramatic pointing. This close look at the passage may offer some reason why Persiani later subsituted the far more conventional arias from *Rosmonda* for Lucia's *aria di sortita*: perhaps she found the dramatic realism demanded here by Donizetti uncongenial to her virtuoso style.

This type of dramatic description is not confined only to Lucia's first appearance. For instance, her entrances in the two scenes of Act 2 are both accompanied by expressive phrases. When she appears in Enrico's room (scene i) four measures of oboe solo,[7] over the tonic chord of B minor, depict her dread and languor as she hesitates in the doorway; her brother orders her to approach, and this melody is repeated (now over a seventh chord on the leading-tone) with its arch intensified, as she advances silently into the room. All through this introductory recitative Lucia's mute responses are indicated by solo instrumental phrases, When she reappears in the following scene to sign the marriage contract, her helplessness is characterized by an off-beat descending motif in the cellos in C minor, immediately echoed by the violin and oboe in octaves, this sequence being repeated five times (Example 50a). A variant of this motif occurs

Example 50a. *Lucia di Lammermoor*, Act 2 scene ii, Lucia's entrance

with powerfully ironic effect during Lucia's recitative before the mad scene; she mistakes the tune as it twists irresolutely from major to minor, and, suppressing its former context, turns it in her imagination into the hymn that heralds her marriage to Edgardo (Example 50b).

Example 50b. *Lucia di Lammermoor*, Act 3 scene ii, recitative to Lucia's
mad scene

At the end of this recitative, there is still another instance of Donizetti's willingness to modify convention for dramatic effect. By superimposing the final measures of the recitative 'Splendon le sacre faci' over the orchestral introduction to 'Alfin son tua' he once more offers an indication of Lucia's disorientation. Or again, at the beginning of the second statement of the tenor's cabaletta, 'Tu che a Dio spiegasti l'ali', in the tomb scene, he gives the opening melody to the cello, while the dying Edgardo declaims isolated phrases, only taking up the full melody at the seventeenth measure. Duprez claimed that he was responsible for suggesting this effect to Donizetti.

Although the accumulation of these touches contributes to the freshness and spontaneity of *Lucia*, the continuing appeal of this score rests on other foundations as well. One is the almost consistently high level of Donizetti's melodic inspiration – in such passages as 'Veranno a te', Lucia's 'Soffriva nel pianto' or Edgardo's 'Fra poco a me ricovero'. Another is the Romantic color of the orchestration – the prominence given the horns from the prelude at the beginning of the work through the final scene, and the participation of the solo woodwinds as 'characters'. Like so many of Donizetti's operas, *Lucia* looks both forward and backward: in the finale to Act 2 Donizetti employs the same orchestral pattern in both the *tempo d'attacco* and the *tempo di mezzo*, as Rossini was wont to do; but in Enrico's 'Se tradirmi, tu potrai', from the concluding section of his duet with Lucia, it is no strain to hear a clear anticipation of the hectoring tone of Verdi's Count di Luna. But the principal reason for *Lucia*'s vigorous survival where many other operas from this period have proved less durable may well be that its dramatic immediacy manages to survive routine performance in such a way as to convey *sui generis* early-Romantic sensibility.

In 1839 Donizetti created a French version of this opera, *Lucie de Lammermoor,* for the Théâtre de la Renaissance in Paris, and in this form *Lucia* became a factor in nineteenth-century French culture. The score is considerably changed, principally to accommodate the limited resources, financial as well as artistic, of the company at the Renaissance. The first scene explains the background to the plot more clearly than in the Italian score: the recitatives on each side of Henri's *larghetto* are rewritten, and Arthur enters after Henri's cabaletta, to a repetition of the opening chorus, after which they go off hunting. There is no change of scene before Lucie's appearance and no harp solo, and she makes her entrance with the *Rosmonda* arias, now become 'Que n'avons nous des ailes' and 'Toi par qui mon coeur rayonne'. The character of Alisa is omitted, her part in the sextet being taken over by a new character, Gilbert, who functions as a composite of Normanno and Alisa. He leaves before Lucie's arias, which have no *tempo di mezzo,* after she has given him a purse in exchange for his promise to watch over her. There are no other significant changes in Act 1. The recitative that precedes the Lucie–Henri duet is new, making clear Gilbert's duplicity. The scene between Lucia and Raimondo is omitted. Just before the sextet some of the ensemble outcries are recast as solo passages, and the concluding stretta is much abbreviated.

Act 3 is somewhat rearranged to reduce the number of sets required. It begins with the wedding chorus, followed by Edgard's arrival chez Ashton to put his challenge. The tenor–baritone duet is followed by a reprise of the wedding chorus, but when Raimond appears with his dreadful news, it is delivered not in an aria but in eight measures of recitative. The connecting link between the choral reaction to Raimond's tidings and the recitative before the mad scene (here in its original key of F) is modified: two phrases for Raimond without comment by the chorus. The opening recitative of the mad scene is slightly shortened, but the arias are substantially the same, the chief change being the elimination during the *tempo di mezzo* (here in E flat major) of the commentary by the other characters during Lucia's music, and a sizable cut before the cabaletta. After the cabaletta the recitative for Raimondo and Normanno is omitted. During the tomb scene everything remains the same until the moment at which Edgard stabs himself; here three measures are added as Henri arrives to fight the duel:

Henri: Me voilà!
Edgard: J'expire...
       Henri, tu viens trop tard.

The second statement of the cabaletta follows as in the Italian score. The final alteration is the addition of a part for Henri during the closing *più allegro*. Except for recitative passages, Donizetti wrote almost no new music for *Lucie de Lammermoor* and cut the Italian score extensively to make the opera feasible for a small company. Except for its clearer exposition of the plot, *Lucie* cannot be regarded as a satisfactory substitute for the original Italian version.

Belisario. This three-act seria was the first Donizetti opera composed for the Fenice, where it was first given on 4 February 1836. It is the third of Donizetti's operas in which the baritone role is the title character and, as I have noted before, this arrangement involves a realignment of the customary relationships: here the element of romantic love is dispensed with. Antonina, Belisario's wife, the role taken by the prima donna, becomes the *donna antipatica*, demanding vengeance for the death of their son, for which she believes her husband to be responsible. The other principals are Belisario's daughter and Alamiro (tenor), who turns out to be his long-lost son. The father–hero is a new character in the Donizettian gallery.

Barblan has called *Belisario*: 'one of the better balanced and more expertly managed scores in the maestro's immense production, but also one of the most impersonal'.[8] The chief counter to the charge of impersonality is found in the Act 2 duet for Belisario and Irene. Belisario, blinded, has been released from prison to go into exile, and Irene has come to serve as his guide (shades of Oedipus and Antigone). At first she does not reveal her identity and the opening recitative is notable for the simple elevation of Belisario's declamation and for the expressivity of its accompanying figures. Grand, yet touching, are the eight measures of B flat minor that accompany Belisario's being led out into the daylight; here the bass line does not so much stride as grope. As the case of *Lucia* has already demonstrated, Donizetti had learned the knack of writing brief passages of descriptive music that characterize stage entrances in sure, vivid strokes. Belisario urges the still-unknown young woman to go in search of his daughter, whereupon Irene weeps. At the moment of recognition, Donizetti modulates through progressively flatter keys, in a series of syncopated and agitated figures (Example 51). This melody has already been established when Belisario requests that his daughter be fetched, but its recurrence here, after the musical and dramatic suspense built up in arriving at this point, reinforces the idea of recognition. The use of the raised dominant and subdominant notes in the phrase 'il padre abbraccia' exemplifies

Example 51. *Belisario*, Act 2, *tempo d'attacco* of the Irene–Belisario
duet

Donizetti's fondness for this device to express tender insistence. The
heightened emotion released by this moment is sustained throughout the ensuing *larghetto*, 'Ah! se potessi piangere' (3/4, F major),
where Irene's answering period, though it begins by repeating Belisario's opening phrase in the tonic, continues by altering the contours of his succeeding phrases, gathering harmonic momentum as it
briefly moves into the parallel minor. Here is a prototype of the
father–daughter duet that Verdi was to make particularly his own,
and Donizetti notably anticipates the intense tenderness that is such
a feature of those later duets.

Effective in a different way is the Act 1 duet for Belisario and
Alamiro. The General offers his captive his freedom, but the young

man feels drawn to remain at his side. The *larghetto*, 'Quando il sangue tinto', shows Donizetti's newfound ability to advance a dramatic situation through a logical structural format (periods for each, excited interchange, a new period for the baritone, culmination in a joint proclamation of 'ah, sì! uniti ognor!') that carries the situation from the slow movement into the *tempo di mezzo* without any sense of psychological separation, and most naturally motivates the ensuing cabaletta, 'Sul campo della gloria' (*allegro moderato*, 4/4, A flat major), where each statement is sung *a due* to an exuberant march rhythm. The tenor is well favored, too, by his pair of arias near the outset of Act 2. The first of these, 'Ah sì tremendo annunzio' (*larghetto*, 4/4, A flat minor), is notable for its declamatory vigor and unusual in that it maintains the minor mode throughout. His cabaletta, 'Trema, Bisanzio! sterminatrice' (*allegro vivace*, 3/4, A flat major) has been likened to 'Di quella pira' (*Il trovatore*, Act 3 scene i) for its impetuous bolero rhythm, but where the *gruppetti* at the ends of Verdi's phrases express barely suppressed excitement, here the more extensive scalar passages are a typically Rossinian expression of determination. Verdi knew this cabaletta, for he once cited Donizetti's setting of the word 'sterminatrice' as a lapse in truth of accentuation;[9] while Verdi's charge has merit, such a lapse in Donizetti's word-setting is relatively rare, particularly in his later works. 'Trema, Bisanzio!' (Example 52) creates a genuine (if old-fashioned) air of heroic excitement, which, though it lacks the elemental simplicity of Manrico's rallying-cry, produces a very satisfactory propulsive effect. And perhaps it would not be totally facetious to point out that Alamiro is but a youth and that 'sterminatrice' is a hard word.

Example 52. *Belisario*, Act 2, cabaletta of Alamiro's aria

The role of Antonina, who appears only in the first act and the final scene of the third, suffers from the character's being largely unsympathetic. Barblan's charge of impersonality applies best to her music, for with her predictable and symmetrical arias and her overemphatic line in the stretta of the first finale, she seems more a prima donna function than a developed character. Only in the splendid quartet 'Ah da chi son'io tradito?' (*larghetto*, 4/4, A flat), the most effective section of the first finale, where her voice, having an expressive variant of Belisario's opening melody, is the last to enter, does she arouse sympathy. In point of fact this 'quartet' calls for six solo voices and chorus, but there are only four distinct melodic lines.[10]

Belisario is an imposing score, if not a totally appealing one. There is a certain brash extroversion about much of the choral music and marches, both frequent in this military ambience, that does not accord well with the more personal and human aspects of the drama, such as the duet for Irene and Belisario. In spite of Cammarano's success with the libretto of *Lucia*, he was still relatively inexperienced as a theater poet, and his excessively episodic treatment of this plot and his fitful characterization burdened Donizetti with liabilities he could not fully surmount. Donizetti gave his candid opinion of the opera to the publisher Pacini in Paris: '*Belisario* is less studied, but I know that in the theater it made an effect and it could not deceive a public without having some merit. Anyway, for myself I place it as a work below *Lucia*.'[11]

Il campanello. For this one-act farsa Donizetti adapted a French vaudeville and located it in Naples. If at first it seems strange that Donizetti should turn to writing a comedy within months of the death of both his parents and the delivery of his stillborn daughter, it must be remembered that theatrical activity was Donizetti's principal mode of maintaining his equilibrium, and also that during that strained summer of 1836 the Nuovo was the only Neapolitan theater open. *Il campanello* stands apart from the rest of Donizetti's comic oeuvre because it leaves a bitter aftertaste. The fixed rictus on the comic mask of *Il campanello* contains more than a hint of cruelty.

This opera presented Donizetti with the challenge of providing a bravura comic role for the intense Ronconi, the singer who was to be the first Chevreuse. The part is that of a frustrated suitor who visits worse frustrations upon the ancient apothecary and his nubile bride on their wedding night: after an initial appearance as a French dandy, he returns disguised as an opera singer who needs a remedy for hoarseness – a situation that gives Donizetti opportunities for parody of vocalization and for quotation of the Gondolier's song from *Marin Faliero;* he returns again, as a patient with a prescription that entails the entire pharmacopoeia. His second duet with Don Annibale carries the humor of loquacity to the limits; and, incidentally, it contains ironies that Donizetti may not consciously have intended, for one of the ingredients in the prescription is 'roba antisifilitico' (anti-syphilis stuff). Musically and dramatically, the role of Enrico is an irrepressible tour de force.

What is absent from *Il campanello* is the hint of pathos, the furtive tear, that lends human warmth to most of Donizetti's comedies. The duet for Enrico and Serafina, 'Non fuggir', a one-sided love duet, significantly lacks a slow movement, and the opening periods, for the baritone first and then the soprano, are full of Rossinian rhetorical flourishes. Beneath the caricature of Enrico's protestations one glimpses a man who is in love with his image of his own irresistibility, and to thwart him is to make him determined to get even. *Il campanello* is hilarious, uproarious even, and the recitatives are frequently as funny as the numbers themselves; but all the humor is, at bottom, heartless.

The music of *Il campanello* is fluent and hard-edged, resourceful and cutting. The brief prelude features the obligatory night-bell, which a Neapolitan apothecary is legally bound to heed; it connects directly with the opening chorus, and the *introduzione* is completed by Annibale's cavatina, in which he prefigures Don Pasquale's notion of being surrounded by progeny. The tone of urban bourgeois comedy is firmly established at the outset. Enrico makes his first appearance, dancing a galop with Serafina. The brindisi, 'Mesci, mesci',[12] which Enrico uses as another delaying device to prevent the newlyweds' bedding, has the folk-like character of an incidental song, and its coda, being a reprise of the opening, gives the illusion of a circular, unending form. The *terzettino finale* (in which everybody sees Annibale off at crack of dawn on his journey to Rome, where he must witness the reading of his aunt's will) is a model of economy. It begins with a cantabile for Serafina, 'Da me lungi' (*larghetto*, 4/4, E major), very much in the style of the opening sections of the aria–finales in the comedies of the previous decade; to this is appended a relatively brief *moderato* – in effect, a two-statement vaudeville, in which the eight-measure statements of Enrico and Annibale are separated by identical choral comment – and all culminates in a more extensive *vivace* in 3/8. *Il campanello* has repeatedly demonstrated its stageworthiness, and it remains notable as Donizetti's nearest approach to black comedy.

Betly. Although not quite three months separate *Il campanello* from *Betly*, first given at the Nuovo on 21 August 1836, they are worlds apart. While *Il campanello* reveals its *napolitanità* by a wealth of local allusions and by evoking now and again the style of Neapolitan songs, *Betly* is a Swiss idyll, for which Donizetti himself adapted the Scribe–Mélesville libretto of Adam's *Le chalet*, which was derived in turn from a Goethe Singspiel, *Jerry und Bätely*. With its capricious heroine, timid tenor and baritone soldier, *Betly* has some obvious resemblances to *L'elisir*, and it also provides a link between that score and the later *La fille du régiment*.

There are some touches of local color in *Betly*, a sort of *ranz des vaches* that precedes the opening chorus and the yodel-like figure in the refrain of Betly's tyrolienne, 'In questo semplice modesto asilo' (Example 53). These effects are also to be found in Adam's score (which had had its first performance at the Opéra-Comique on 25 September 1834, and which Donizetti undoubtedly heard when he was in Paris at the time of *Faliero*), but Donizetti handles them more memorably. Particularly, a comparison between the *couplets*[13] Adam wrote for his Betly and Donizetti's tyrolienne (*andante mosso*, 3/8, E flat major) shows the French aria to be altogether plainer and more modest in overall dimensions and far less venturesome harmonically; moreover Donizetti's *aria di sortita* presents a vivid portrait of an engaging personality.

The first measures of Example 53 slightly vary the soprano's opening phrases, used as a link to introduce the rhythmically contrasting *Schwung* of the refrain. Again there springs to mind the only fitfully realized evocation of Argilla in *La zingara* (see Example 23) of 1822; in Betly, written fourteen years later, the high-spirited heroine is admirably portrayed with great charm and surety. To revert to the comparison of Adam's *Le chalet* and *Betly*: the differing endings of the two operas reveal the diverse traditions they represent. The finale to *Le chalet* begins with a trio built in a number of episodes – during which the wedding contract acquires its full complement of signatures – and ends with a reprise for Max of his military song, which quickly works into an ensemble and concludes with a chorus. In *Betly*, on the other hand, the signing of the contract is carried on in recitative and motivates Betly's aria–finale, the cabaletta of which, 'Ah non posso esprimere', supplied the second theme to Donizetti's *sinfonia* to the opera.

In September 1837 Donizetti expanded *Betly* into two acts by a process of expansion similar to that he had used earlier with *Le convenienze*. The added material comes mostly in the middle: a first-act finale develops the confrontation between Betly and her as

BETLY

Oh li-ber-tà gra-di-ta, che in-fio-ri que-sta vi-ta,

re-gne-rai sem-pre qua, ah sem-pre, sem-pre, sem-pre qua.

tra___ la la la tra___ la la la tra___ la

tra___ la la___ la la la la la la

Example 53. *Betly*, Act 1, *andante mosso of Betly's aria di sortita*

yet unidentified brother Max and his soldiers into an imbroglio of a Rossinian cast but relatively modest proportions. Among other additions there is a trio in Act 2. Common to both versions is a delicious example of Donizetti's sense of humor which has no counterpart in Adam's score: in the duet 'Dolce istante inaspettato', in which Betly places her reliance on Daniele's protection while he vainly tries to stay awake, there is a concluding cadenza for Betly to which the tenor contributes notated yawns. I must confess to a personal preference for the one-act version of *Betly*: it shares all the best numbers with the more expanded score and, besides, it is better paced, not stretching the slender but beguiling material to the limits. It is worth noting that Donizetti's method of expanding a one-act comic work into two acts[14] by adding material in the middle is quite different from the procedure he followed in enlarging serious three-act works into four; when he transformed *Poliuto* into *Les martyrs* he chiefly expanded the opening acts, fleshing out the exposition of the drama.

L'assedio di Calais. In this three-act *melodramma lirico*, first given at the San Carlo in November 1836, Donizetti sought to write an opera *alla francese*, which would be transportable to the stage of the Opéra, just as Rossini had with *Maometto II–Le siège de Corinthe*. Regrettably, the propitious moment for the revision of *L'assedio di Calais*, which would have entailed among other things Donizetti's recasting a *musico* role[15] for tenor, just as Rossini had done, never arrived, but the work bears many indications of its appropriateness for export to France: the choice of subject, the heroic choruses, and the suite of dances in Act 3.[16]

Donizetti himself described *L'assedio di Calais* as his 'l'opera più travagliata' (most carefully worked-out score)[17] and the indications of his attention are frequent. It begins in a way unlike any other Donizetti opera: a cursory seven-measure prelude (simply a *crescendo* and *decrescendo* followed by three suspenseful chords) is followed by forty measures of *larghetto* (E flat major) for woodwinds, designed to accompany mimed stage action. According to Cammarano's stage directions, Aurelio descends from the walls of the besieged city by means of a rope ladder and stealthily approaches the English camp. He steals some loaves of bread from the sleeping soldiers and then ties the loaves to the end of the rope so that they may be raised into the starving city. In spite of all his precaution he arouses some of the English troops, who give the alarm, and Aurelio escapes only by leaping into the sea. It is significant that Cammarano's immediate source was Luigi Marchionni's adaptation of a French play,[18] as was *Otto mesi in due ore*, also based on a French-derived hit in the Marchionni repertory; both of them demonstrate the prominence pantomime enjoyed in the popular dramaturgy of the day.

Aurelio's descent from the walls is accompanied by a broad melody obviously associated with his heroism and that of his fellow citizens; but as he approaches the sleeping troops (measure 26 of the *larghetto*) the music abruptly changes (Example 54).

Example 54. *L'assedio di Calais, introduzione*

Here, instead of creating a generalized impression of mood, the music is designed to accompany specific action. The abrupt unprepared dissonances, heightened by anxious *pianissimo* echoes, describe Aurelio's wariness as he filches the bread. At the resolution to the tonic, he goes to secure it to the rope, as yet unaware that his presence has been detected. This unconventional *introduzione*, with its long-delayed opening chorus, gives yet another indication of Donizetti's restless search for dramatic novelty and effectiveness, closely allied to acting as then practised in spoken drama.

The *introduzione* comprises the short opening scene. The second scene of Act 1, which takes place in a vestibule in the *hôtel de ville* of Calais, begins with an extensive duet for Eustachio de St-Pierre, Aurelio's father and Mayor of Calais, and Eleonora, Aurelio's wife. The role of Eustachio is the first that Donizetti wrote for the French *bariton-noble* Paul Barroilhet,[19] a singing-actor of great distinction then under contract to Barbaja. Among Donizetti's baritone roles, Eustachio is a figure to set beside Simon Boccanegra, for, like the Genoese doge, he is a noble-hearted self-sacrificing leader who cares deeply about the welfare of his people. The duet begins with an expressive string introduction, dominated by a solo cello melody that goes on to provide the principal underpinning of the *tempo d'attacco*. In the recitative Eustachio's grief for the tragic plight of his city is nobly set out, and soon he is joined by Eleonora, who is filled with foreboding about Aurelio's failure to return from his foraging. The *larghetto*, 'Le fibre, o Dio, m'investe' (6/8, B minor/B major), finely contrasts the father's grief and the wife's fears, and in the *assieme* there is a twice-repeated sequence, modulating through fifth-related keys and introducing a Neapolitan chord, that forms the codetta; this phrase appeared earlier, in Eustachio's statement, at the word 'patria'. The introduction of rapidly shifting modulations just before the final vocal cadences is a regular feature of Donizetti's style. When the news arrives that Aurelio is safe Eustachio launches the cabaletta 'Un istante i mali obblio', which has contours similar to Alphonse's 'Léonor, mon amour brave', the pendant to 'Léonor, viens' at the beginning of Act 2 of *La favorite*.

Soon Aurelio appears, and his *aria di sortita* takes the expected form of a double aria, which gives him pride of place in the exposition; it consists of 'Al mio core, oggetti amati' (*larghetto*, 9/8, F major) and a cabaletta, 'Giammai del forte' (*moderato*, 4/4, F major), where the second statement is turned into a mini-ensemble by the addition of *pertichini*[20] halfway through. The first finale is touched off by the entrance of Un Incognito, really an English spy, who tries to arouse the citizens against their Mayor. Eustachio begins the *largo* (4/4, C major) by inviting them to slay him on the spot; his solo passage introduces 'Plebe ingrata', an ensemble statement with, at its repetition, a melodic line added for the Mayor. The ensemble builds to a climax by the gradual increasing of the vocal sonorities, a rising line and a *stringendo* – a fine example of Donizetti's easy skill in such moments. The stretta, 'Come tigri di strage anelanti' (*allegro feroce*, 4/4, D major), pits a hard-driving melody against a series of sustained notes to create a truly savage effect; later the same text is set to a different tune that chatters away in even faster tempo. This stretta that unleashes a Verdian level of raw energy is one of Donizetti's finest achievements in this section of a finale, where all too often he unwound a series of conventional formulas.

Act 2 is divided into two scenes. The first is concerned mainly with a duet for Aurelio and Eleonora, where, against the opening recitative, an offstage chorus of women praying is used with telling effect to heighten the concerns of the principals. This duet is one of the pages Donizetti would have to have revised had he revamped the role of Aurelio for tenor, for the vocal deployment is clearly designed for two women's voices. The *larghetto* (12/8, D major) is begun by the mezzo, the soprano following with a modulating transition (half as long) to the reprise of the opening, now *a due*. The *tempo di mezzo*, during which d'Aire bursts in with the news that an English envoy has arrived with a peace proposal, motivates the dance-like cabaletta, 'La speme un dolce palpito' (*allegretto*, 2/4, D major), which is *a due* throughout; this is in the same vein as Norma's and Adalgisa's 'Sì, fine all' ore', and it contains no suspicion of the possibility of duplicity on the English side.

The second scene of Act 2 of *L'assedio di Calais* is a fine achievement. It begins with an eloquent chorus, 'D'un popolo afflitto' (*maestoso*, 2/4, F minor/F major), where the repeated rhythmic motif, ♪ ♫♪♫ ♪, establishes a sense of solemn earnestness. In a recitative the English general Edmondo delivers the demand for six hostages to die in order that their city be spared. The envoy's fatal word precipitates the *larghetto* of the finale, where the shocked reaction of the Calais citizens is expressed in alternating *fortissimo* and *pianissimo* chords; against a string *tremolando* an oboe weaves a quiet chromatic line, which is interrupted by the sudden irruption of a chord on the leading-tone of the dominant key as a sense of outrage takes over. After another soft unison expression of horror, the chief melodic building-block of this movement is introduced by Aurelio and the tenors of the chorus to the words 'Di rio destin siam vittime'; where the motivic echoing between parts achieves a truly grand effect. Donizetti's visceral response to the dramatic situation is everywhere apparent in this section. The *tempo di mezzo* has independent melodic weight and consists primarily of two solo passages – first Aurelio's indignant rejection of the English proposal and then Eustachio's acceptance; although both are based upon the same material, they are clearly distinguished, not only in tonality (Aurelio in A flat major and Eustachio in F major), but also in figuration – the impetuous scales of the mezzo being replaced by more expansive phrases in the baritone's shortened period. Such an episode as this reveals Donizetti's keen sensitivity to dramatic rhetoric as an expression of character. Eustachio's words dismiss Edmondo, who leaves. There follows a *presto* (3/4, E major), 'Di scampo ogni via', in which Eustachio justifies his decision by declaring that it will save the entire city; his line is juxtaposed against the shocked comments of the others, and the whole rapid episode gains in intensity as his arguments win them over. His announcement that he will be the first to sign the hostage list starts off another intermediate episode. Against the choral comments as four others sign, and then against an orchestral melody occasionally echoed in the vocal parts, Aurelio and Eustachio argue, each wanting to save the other but neither giving way, and both finally committing themselves to die. Eustachio's bidding the doomed men to pray leads to the concluding episode of the finale, 'O sacra polve' (*largo*, 2/4, E major) (Example 55).

The hostages' opening phrases are largely unaccompanied; later the other soloists, beginning in the parallel minor, express their grief, and the interplay between the two vocal groups heightens the solemn emotion. The hostages go, kissing the flag as they depart, while those who are left dissolve in tears. It was unusual to conclude a finale with a slow movement, and this one achieves a real dramatic catharsis; more unusual still is that the whole finale to Act 2, with its inspiring patriotism, creates a sense of ongoing musical theater that sustains itself and builds from one musical unit to the next. Donizetti's nearest approach to this effect (if not the actuality) of through-composed opera had been in the second finale to *Maria Stuarda*.

Speaking of *L'assedio di Calais*, Donizetti wrote to Ricordi: 'The third act is the least felicitous (see my sincerity).'[21] It is difficult not to agree with this judgment. At the beginning of the act the arias for the English King, Edoardo III, separated by bouncy ceremonial music to accompany the arrival of his Queen, are fluent and, somehow, fatuous. Even worse, if anything, is the blatant ballet music, which gives no hint of Donizetti's achievement seven years later in the divertissement for *Dom Sébastien*. With the exception of the vigorous and efficient march that serves as prelude to the act, everything up to this point comes as an anticlimax after the fine finale to Act 2, demonstrating once again that when Donizetti's sympathies were not actively engaged by a dramatic situation his music subsides to a level of routine competence. There is an improvement, however, with the arrival of the hostages in the English camp; they enter to a fragmented funeral march that vacillates between A minor and D

Example 55. *L'assedio di Calais*, Act 2, *largo* of the finale

minor, and this leads to a reprise of the melody that followed their signing of the document in the preceding scene. The *adagio* of the third finale, 'Raddoppia i baci tuoi' (2/4, E minor), is begun by Aurelio, who addresses his grieving wife; at the words 'invan represso', the music modulates to the parallel major, and here the recurrence of the tonality and meter of 'O sacra polve' (see Example 55) creates a musical association that intensifies the emotion of this moment.[22] In the *tempo di mezzo* the English Queen intervenes on the hostages' behalf, and the concluding *allegro vivace*, 'Fin che i secoli vivranno' (4/4, A major), a *marziale*, brings the opera to a joyful, if not exactly an elevated, conclusion.

L'assedio di Calais, although not without flaws, contains some of the most attractive and genuinely moving music that Donizetti ever wrote. It shows the composer tackling a new kind of subject matter – sacrificial patriotism – and treating it, particularly in the finale to Act 2, with the dramatic immediacy that was his strongest suit as a man of the theater. The work seems rather old-fashioned in some ways, particularly in the use of a *musico* for the prominent role of Aurelio; and the 1837 version was even more so since Donizetti added a *rondò* for Eleonora into the third finale. But these symptoms are adventitious, and in many more important ways, such as the portrait of Eustachio and the many passages of fine ensemble writing, *L'assedio di Calais* is very much a forward-looking work. It is cause for regret, I believe, that the opportunity to revise it for Duprez and the Opéra never arose.

Pia de' Tolomei. This two-act opera seria had its *prima* in Venice in February 1837. At the time of *L'esule di Roma* Donizetti had somewhat rashly chosen the Ugolino passage from Dante's *Inferno* to set for Lablache, and now, nearly a decade later, he turned again to Dante, this time for an opera subject; *Pia* is derived ultimately from the end of Canto V of the *Purgatorio*.[23] Donizetti first mentioned *Pia* to Lanari in a letter of 31 May 1836: 'I propose *Pia* to you as a subject well adapted to the company.'[24] This proposal was based on Donizetti's familiarity with Giacinto Bianco's play *Pia de' Tolomei*, which was given at the Teatro dei Fiorentini, Naples, on 19 April 1836.[25] The better-known play of the same name by Carlo Marenco was not given its first performance until almost three weeks after Donizetti first wrote about *Pia* to Lanari, and therefore it played no part in their original decision.[26] Both plays derive from Sestini's novella *Pia de' Tolomei* of 1822. Obviously Cammarano's task was much easier when he could work from a dramatization rather than a narrative.

It is not surprising that *Pia* has attracted the attention of the twentieth-century Donizetti revivalists, primarily because much of the motivation for that movement has been soprano-oriented, and the attractions of a title role tailored to Persiani, renowned as the first Lucia, raised hopes that this work might prove a worthy companion to that famous score. And yet, in spite of some fine and memorable passages, *Pia* is disappointingly uneven. The trouble with *Pia*, at heart, is that the structure is geared to the traditional emphasis on the prima donna and her aria–finale, when Donizetti's chief interest lies not in Pia herself but in the tenor role of Ghino degli Armieri and, almost as intensely, in the jealous husband, Nello della Pietra. The structural problem was exacerbated for Donizetti by the extraneous circumstances that forced him to plump out the *musico* role of Pia's brother, Rodrigo, for Rosina Mazzarelli; Rodrigo is only briefly essential to the plot, since he merely provides a figure round whom Ghino can build his imputation of Pia's faithlessness so as to inflame Nello. His only dramatically necessary appearance occurs during the first finale, yet Rodrigo has a double aria in both Acts 1 and 2, each of them involving a scene-change;[27] these episodes drag the audience back to the world of *opera eroica* vintage 1818. Worst of all, Pia is the most passive victim imaginable, except when she repulses Ghino's advances; since the only relationship that arouses her from misery to joy is her love for her brother Rodrigo, her character is too limited for the function assigned to her in the plot. Significantly, Persiani was never tempted to sing Pia again after the first run of performances in Venice was over.

The most interesting character in *Pia* is Ghino, Nello's cousin, a man tortured by his consuming love for Nello's wife. As he himself describes his condition in his Act 1 aria:

Ah! L'incendio che mi strugge
È delirio e non amor!

(Ah! The fire that destroys me is frenzy and not love!)

From the point of view of Donizetti's prefiguring Verdi, the most striking passage in *Pia* consists of two phrases of arioso in the recitative that leads up to Ghino's first aria (Example 56). Put into the key of F and with the note values doubled, this becomes Violetta's 'Amami, Alfredo' from Act 2 scene i of Verdi's *La traviata*.[28] Although Verdi could have known about Ghino's passage from hearing *Pia* (in which his wife-to-be, Strepponi, sang) at La Scala in June 1839, surely the resemblance is no more than coincidence.[29] The differences between Donizetti's and Verdi's use of the idea quoted in Example 56 are more significant than the similarities. Verdi's soprano sings 'Amami, Alfredo' as the irrepressible climax of a tense scene; Donizetti's tenor sings the quoted phrases immediately upon his first appearance, breaking off into recitative as he describes the destructive passion that obsesses him. The underly-

Example 56. *Pia de' Tolomei*, Act 1 scene i, recitative to Ghino's aria

ing significance of this passage is the indication it gives of the re-markable extent to which Donizetti in 1837 approached the expressive idiom of Verdi's middle works, or, to turn it around, the extent to which Verdi, at his most characteristic, may be seen to evolve directly out of Donizetti.

Donizetti evidently found the character of Ghino the most challenging, and indeed the finest music in the score is his. His introductory pair of arias, 'Non puo dirti la parola' and 'Mi volesti sventurato?', both convey Ghino's obsessive energy: both are in B flat major, and both have melodies that have a way of getting stuck and repeating notes, often marked with accents. Even better is his duet with Nello in the second scene of Act 1, where he arouses his cousin to murderous jealousy; the headlong cabaletta, 'Del ciel che non punisce', laid out in the conventional three statements (one for each participant, and one *a due*), is especially fine. Best of all is his death scene, which has been called the finest of such passages that Donizetti composed for the tenor. The structure of the scene is similar to that in the Paris version of *Lucrezia Borgia*, where Gennaro's death constitutes the *tempo di mezzo* between the heroine's final arias; but Ghino's death forms an even more extended episode, separating Nello's *andante sostenuto* from his cabaletta 'Ciel pietoso' in the penultimate scene of the opera. Ghino's easing of his troubled conscience by his dying confession is set to broken phrases, and he dies in the middle of a word (like Riccardo in *Un ballo in maschera*). The eloquence of this moment possesses the powerful immediacy and sense of inevitability that characterize Donizetti's finest writing.

Pia's music contains some interesting features, even though it lacks the dramatic force of Ghino's. Her least effective page is the cabaletta of her *aria di sortita*, 'Di pura gioia in estasi' (*moderato*, 4/4, G major), where her emotion at the thought of being reunited with her brother expresses itself in a surprisingly stiff-jointed melody, and the embellishments seem obligatory rather than spontaneous. She most nearly comes to life in her duet with Ghino in the opening episode of Act 2, but here most of the conflict is suffered by her adversary, while she declares that she would rather die than yield to him. This duet crystallizes the fundamental dislocation of the work: our sympathy and interest are more actively engaged by the villain and his expressive music than by the heroine. This defect is all too plain in what ought to be the musical climax – Pia's death scene. It begins with an extended and very promising prelude: portentous chords for full orchestra are followed by touching solos for clarinet, oboe and flute in sequence; but the promise is not fulfilled because Pia's arias lack true melodic distinction. Her cabaletta, 'Ah! di Pia...che muore...e geme...', has a measure of dramatic realism in the second statement, set to a different text from the first, where the vocal line breaks up and the accompaniment thins out and becomes correspondingly disjointed; but the positive effect of this is badly undercut by the conventional coda in which the apparently moribund heroine must dominate the *pertichini* and orchestral tutti.

The orchestral introduction to the final scene of *Pia* is not the only instance in this opera of Donizetti's providing effective atmospheric music. The opening description of Rodrigo's dungeon in Act 1, where powerful chords lead into an oddly clammy melody, conveys a strong sense of (distasteful) place. The second scene of Act 2 begins with a thunderstorm. This scene also contains the unison prayer 'Divo spirto' for Piero the hermit and his fellows, a passage of real grandeur that bears a certain resemblance to the idiom of Balthasar in *La favorite* and Zaccaria (*Nabucco*) and even Padre Guardiano (*La forza del destino*); but instead of being central to the action, it merely serves, though most effectively, to set the background against which Ghino will soon die. All in all, *Pia* must be accounted one of Donizetti's most frustrating operas, because, along with a considerable amount of music that testifies to a composer of dramatic power, it contains an almost equal amount that is pedestrian.

Roberto Devereux. First performed at the San Carlo on 28 October 1837, this three-act seria is the last of the operas Donizetti composed for Ronzi in which she actually appeared.[30] The chain of Ronzi roles – Fausta, Sancia, Maria Stuarda, Gemma and now Elisabetta in *Roberto Devereux* – reveals the growth of this collaboration between singer and composer. It is all too easy to think of fat, aggressive Ronzi, *maîtresse sans titre* at the Neapolitan court and quondam combattant with del Sere, as rather a comic figure, but when one looks, even for a moment, at the music Donizetti composed for her, from the aria–finale of *Fausta* to the extraordinary effusion of the last pages of *Roberto Devereux*, one realizes her serious artistic worth, for hers was the instrument with the expressive capabilities he needed.

Cammarano's libretto had the advantage of being at least in part derived from Romani's 1833 text for Mercadante's *Il conte d'Essex*,[31] and that source may help to account for the clearly motivated and well-paced plot, which has none of the loose connections and side-tracks that weaken his text for *Pia*. The dominant figure in the drama is Elisabetta, and this is by far the most complete portrait of the three Donizetti made of her, for in *Roberto Devereux* her regal power and her womanly vulnerability are in conflict and are movingly contrasted. In *Il castello di Kenilworth* Elisabetta's shift from menace to magnaminity is largely unexplained; in *Maria Stuarda* her imperiousness and tetchiness are admirably caught, but her secondary function to the title character keeps her necessarily from the prominence she enjoys in *Roberto Devereux*.[32] This third Elisabetta changes from a wary but loving woman at the start to a furious queen who is traumatized by her sense of betrayal both as a sovereign and as a woman, and at last she almost disintegrates as she is consumed by remorse and beset by avenging visions.

Elisabetta's *aria di sortita* occurs early in Act 1, after the opening choruses and Sara's romanza. She enters to fifteen measures of orchestral introduction that set out at once her dual character of Queen and lover: loud chords and dotted rhythms (G minor) alternate with a conjunct string melody that comes to rest in B flat major, which will be the key of her ensuing *larghetto*. Near the end of her recitative, at the words 'la mia vendetta', her ruthless energy is expressed in a scalar sweep up to high A and back down to middle C – no empty flourish, but a direct expression of her peremptory character. Her first aria begins with a limited melodic arch (Example 57). Over an inconspicuous accompaniment, the vocal line unfurls gradually until in the fourth phrase it encompasses an octave and a fourth as her tender mood grows expansive; in the contrasting second period, where she mentions her grief should she find her love betrayed, the aria touches both G minor and C minor before coming

Example 57. *Roberto Devereux*, Act 1 scene i, *larghetto* of Elisabetta's
aria di sortita

to rest in the tonic. Word that Devereux (Essex) will soon arrive
precipitates her exuberant cabaletta, 'Ah, ritorna qual ti spero' (*allegro*, 4/4, G major), with its upward leap of a tenth at the end of the
third phrase and growing inward at the *poco meno* that begins the
second vocal period, quickening again for the final flourishes – a
perfect expression of her radiant anticipation.

When Elisabetta orders the courtiers to leave, a warm A flat melody on the strings accompanies their exit, but here the emphasis is not upon them but upon the Queen's hope that Roberto's emotion will match her own. (This brief passage has a similar contour to that in the triumphal scene of *Aida,* when Amneris, whose hopes at that moment are analogous to Elisabetta's, places the laurel crown on Radamès's head.)[33] There is no clear separation between the *materia di mezzo* and the succeeding duet for Elisabetta and Roberto, 'Un tenero core' (*andante,* 3/8, D major), in which Elisabetta becomes increasingly uneasy at Roberto's restraint and indifference. Early on, Donizetti supplied this duet with a new cabaletta, notably different from its predecessor: the beginning is common to both versions but instead of repeating Elisabetta's headlong 'Un lampo, un lampo' Roberto has a different melody, which passes restlessly through a number of keys before reasserting the tonic of D major.[34] The opening scene concludes with a double aria for Nottingham, another role designed for Barroilhet. His cavatina, 'Forse in quel cor sensibile' (*larghetto,* 4/4, E minor/G major), is a representative example of Donizetti's dignified and easy declamation, but beneath the suave surface of the melody, particularly in the more agitated second period, lurks the Duke's nameless suspicions that all is not right in his marriage with Sara. The opening phrases of his cabaletta, 'Qui ribelle ognuno ti chiama', offering his friendly support to Roberto, recur at the opening of Act 3 scene i, as Sara awaits her husband's return.

The second scene of Act 1 is concerned with the duet of leave-taking between Roberto and Sara. The *allegro* orchestral introduction, studded with nervous iterative figures and sudden *sforzandi,* paints Sara's agitation as she waits for Roberto. If the character of Roberto has been overshadowed in the opening scene by his having to mask his true feelings, here he comes into his own. The *larghetto* of their D flat major duet, 'Dacchè tornasti, ahi misera!' (in 6/8), bears a certain resemblance to the duet for Stuarda and Leicester, 'Da tutti abbandonata', but the internal relationships of phrases within the periods are quite different. The cabaletta of the Sara–Roberto duet, 'Ah! quest'addio fatale estremo' (which had made its first appearance in the Paris version of *Marin Faliero*), with its impetuous detached phrases, anticipates to a surprising degree the urgency of the parting of Gilda and the Duke of Mantua, 'Addio, addio, speranza ed anima', in the second scene of *Rigoletto.*

Act 2 of *Roberto Devereux* consists of a single scene and just three numbers, but it achieves both consistency and accumulative tension as musical drama. The chorus, less in evidence in this than in Donizetti's other 'English' operas, comes to the fore in the introduction to this act. The initial comments of the courtiers, assembled to learn the results of the council's trial of Roberto, ride over an orchestral statement of a broad E major melody, which they take up and sing at the words 'misero Conte!'. This melody recurs again in the orchestra, but now in A flat, to accompany their exit. Then, Donizetti adopts the unconventional procedure of teaming Elisabetta with one character in the recitative (Raleigh, who reports on Roberto's arrest and gives the Queen the incriminating scarf), and another in the ensuing duet (Nottingham, who enters at the beginning of the *larghetto* to beg the Queen not to sign Roberto's death warrant); this makes a fine economical effect and lends the scene an appropriate ironic urgency, since the evidence that will disabuse Nottingham is lying in plain sight. Nottingham begins the *larghetto*, 'Non venni mai sì mesto', in regularly shaped phrases, but this melodic period breaks down into freer declamation as his pleas for Roberto's life expand over sustained chords that allow his words to project with maximum clarity. Barely controlling her jealous fury, Elisabetta takes up his opening phrase in the same key, over the same accompaniment, but the contours of the phrases are heightened; her melodic period is partly in dialogue form, as Nottingham exclaims at her recital of Roberto's betrayal. The voices overlap in a brief *più mosso*, forming the *tempo di mezzo*, and then in the second half of the duet, Nottingham renews his pleas, beginning 'Su lui non piombi il fulmine', to lengthening phrases that gain in rhythmic insistence; each phrase of Elisabetta's reply begins with a peremptory octave interval, her inflexibility contrasting forcefully with Nottingham's persuasiveness.

Roberto's entry immediately after the duet recalls that of Pollione at an analogous point just before the trio at the end of Act 1 of *Norma*; this resemblance grows when Elisabetta's sense of outrage irrupts in volcanic scales, like Norma's in 'No, non tremare, o perfido!'. Elisabetta shows them Sara's scarf, which both Roberto and Nottingham recognize and react to in different ways, but both are too stunned to reveal their feelings at once. The *largo* of the trio, 'Alma infida, ingrato core' (4/4, E flat major), is begun by Elisabetta, her bitter phrases separated by *pizzicato* chords; only when she mentions her father, 'il tremendo ottavo Enrico', does her syllabic incisive line expand to paint the adjective with a two-octave arpeggio from top B flat. The second period is dominated by Roberto and Nottingham who sing together, the betrayer feeling himself betrayed by Sara's scarf and Nottingham inwardly exploring the seething rage that is soon to explode; at the beginning of the coda Elisabetta's voice is joined to theirs in a wide-ranging line that encompasses top C. This *largo* shows all of Donizetti's mature mastery at sustaining the tension of the moment of recognition, and at building suspense before the unavoidable detonation. In the *materia di mezzo* first Nottingham's jealous fury bursts out as he demands a sword, and then Elisabetta offers to spare Roberto if he will name the woman who gave him the scarf; Roberto declares that he would rather die, whereupon Elisabetta signs the death warrant and summons the court to return. Now she rounds on Roberto, her wrath fully unleashed (Example 58).

Example 58. *Roberto Devereux*, Act 2, stretta of the finale

This hard-driving melody with its wide intervals and emphatic declamation shows Donizetti moving beyond the decorative expression of rage in roulades to the naked emotion itself. Earlier Nottingham had spoken to Elisabetta of 'the lightning' of her cruel wrath and her top A in the opening phrase of the stretta recalls that metaphor vividly; the effect is heightened in the second half of the stretta when the harmony moves from F sharp minor to F sharp major, shifting the top A up to an A sharp. As with the *largo* prayer that ends Act 2 of *L'assedio*, the concluding episode of this finale is its true climax; the stretta eschews the working out by formula that chills the ending of Act 2 of *Lucia*, and with its relative brevity and its force sustains the dramatic tension right up to the curtain. The second act of *Roberto Devereux* achieves, in its own very Italian way, the Wagnerian ideal of music drama.

Act 3 is divided into three short scenes. The first is a duet between Sara and Nottingham that develops into a powerful cabaletta, unconventional in that each character has a different melody and at the second statement only Nottingham's is repeated. In the course of this

scene the jealous husband refuses to allow Sara to take to the Queen
the ring that would spare Roberto's life. (One of the excellent things
about this plot is the way the two tokens – the ring the symbol of life
and the scarf of death – encapsulate the tragedy.)[35]

The second scene shows Roberto in his cell in the Tower. There is
a splendid introduction that in its classic sense of gloom looks
backward to the opening of Act 2 of *Fidelio*;[36] the echo of the
Viennese style, which Donizetti had absorbed from Mayr, is particularly strong in the elegiac melody for violin and oboe. This introduction also looks forward, as Winton Dean has pointed out,[37] to the
opening of the Ulrica scene of *Un ballo in maschera*, where the little
woodwind figure that in *Roberto Devereux* follows the opening
chords (Example 59) recurs in the same key and near-identical form.

Example 59. *Roberto Devereux*, Act 3 scene ii, introduction

The role of Roberto has been overshadowed till now by the dominat-
ing figure of Elisabetta, but in this scene, where he appears alone, he
has ample recompense. His very inward aria 'Come un spirito angeli-
co' (*cantabile*, 9/8, A major) begins with a brief orchestral statement of
the opening melody, and continues with two phrases of recitative – a
simple modification that intensifies the spontaneity of the aria; the
second period opens with the third and fourth phrases of the first,
which creates a sense of integrated onward movement. Vocal ornament is restricted to the link between the two periods and the final
vocal cadence. The cabaletta, 'Bagnato è il sen di lagrime' (*alleg-*

retto, 4/4, A major), expresses Roberto's eagerness to die so that he may swear to Sara's innocence before the throne of heaven; the melody gains impetus by recurring in dotted form. Donizetti later employed this melody as the second subject in the overture he wrote for the Paris *prima* of *Devereux* at the Théâtre-Italien in 1838; there it appears first in F major and returns, foreshortened, in D major.

The concluding scene belongs to Elisabetta. In the brief expressive prelude which exploits the ambiguity of mode so characteristic of Donizetti, the second melodic idea begins with a *sforzando* flattened leading-tone (C natural in the key of D major) lending an air of pathos to this passion-ravaged Queen who contemplates a loveless future. In her recitative she says:

Io sono donna alfine.
Il foco è spento del mio furor.

(At last I am just a woman. The fire of my wrath is out.)

The recitative is broken by a brief choral interlude for her ladies, and Elisabetta's voice briefly joins theirs, sustaining a *pianissimo* high A as an inverted pedal. She is increasingly troubled by thoughts of Roberto's imminent execution, and she is moved to renunciation. In an aria of great melodic freedom, 'Vivi, ingrato', her phrases lengthen as her mood intensifies (Example 60).

Donizetti's sensitivity to textual values and dramatic inflection is clear in this aria, as he never sets the word 'sospirar' the same way twice, and he increasingly protracts the desolate 'o' vowel of the word 'm'abbandona' as it recurs. In the second half of the melody the flattened sixth becomes increasingly prominent. In the *materia di mezzo*, through Raleigh's intervention, Sara arrives with the ring, too late, and with her comes Nottingham to gloat over his rival's spilt blood. Outraged at their pettiness, Elisabetta breaks into her awesome cabaletta, 'Quel sangue versato', which, with its wide-ranging intervals and insistent progressions, is a worthy pendant to her *larghetto*. Uncommonly, the second statement has a different text as Elisabetta envisions the bloodstained block on which Roberto has died, and in the coda she has yet another new section of text, announcing her surprising decision to abdicate in favor of James I.

Every number of *Roberto Devereux*, save Sara's romanza at the beginning, has its cabaletta, which makes for a certain predictability of structure, felt most strongly in Act 1 before the drama generates its full momentum; yet the appropriateness of the melodic ideas to the drama and Donizetti's frequent success in modifying the conventions and in varying the internal forms makes this one of his most

ELISABETTA

Example 60. *Roberto Devereux*, Act 3 scene iii, *larghetto* of Elisabetta's
aria

powerful and affecting operas. And in Elisabetta he created a complex tragic portrait that can, without any embarrassment, be placed beside Bellini's Norma.

Maria de Rudenz. Increased familiarity has altered my original dim impression of this three-act tragedy. At first *Maria de Rudenz* seems a violent and repulsive melodrama, but on reconsideration, while it is undeniably overdrawn, it shows a fine sense of musical proportion, and it is strewn with highly expressive effects which show that Donizetti's appetite for 'amore violento'[38] remained undiminished. Further, *Rudenz* stands in a significant relationship to tendencies that dominate Donizetti's output of the 1830s.

It is possible to imagine a graph with two divergent lines: an ascending one that shows the generally increasing Romanticism of the serious subjects that attracted Donizetti – dramas that turn on violent emotions and deeds; and a descending one that shows the growing disenchantment of the Italian censors, particularly those in Naples, with these more extreme manifestations of Romanticism, which they regarded as unsettling to the public in a time of social unrest. For instance, *Pia de' Tolomei,* written for Venice, presented no problems for the censors there, but when the work was produced in Naples the following year the censors visited upon it changes that infuriated Donizetti. Some other plots that attracted Donizetti contained nothing overtly challenging to the representatives of authority – *Lucia,* for example – yet even an apparently 'safe' work,[39] *L'assedio di Calais,* contained details that caused the Neapolitan censors to draft (and possibly send) the composer a letter of reprimand. Undeniably, Donizetti valued freedom of expression and kept pressing at the limits of the censorially acceptable in his desire for strong subjects. As a result he produced a number of works that the censors regarded as distressingly 'modern'. For the proposed performance of *Lucrezia Borgia* in Naples the title of the work was to have been changed to *La cena della vendetta* and Lucrezia's filial relationship to a pope disguised by altering the characters' names, the time and the place; one of the censors, Francesco Ruffa, reported on it to the Minister of Police in terms of such indignation that the effect is almost one of self-parody: 'To remain silent about the other horrors of the plot, it ends with the death of six individuals, five of whom are poisoned at one table, where they have been enticed by the blackest perfidy disguised as polite and chivalrous hospitality.'[40] *Maria Stuarda* is another such work: forbidden in Naples, it was finally given in Milan, where, without Donizetti's express approval

but probably with his tacit consent, Malibran sang the original text
and not the 'vil bastarda'-less version approved by the local censors.
Maria de Rudenz stands alongside these operas as, in one respect at
least, an extremely 'challenging' work.

Cammarano contrived for *Maria de Rudenz*, a plot, derived from the
French play *La nonne sanglante*, in which past events shape the
present action. Some years before the time at which the action begins Corrado di Waldorff eloped with the not unwilling Maria de
Rudenz, but, believing her unfaithful, abandoned her in the catacombs of Rome, where it is supposed that she died. Maria's elope-
ment sent the Count de Rudenz into a fatal decline, and he left
a will specifying that, if Maria failed to return within one year of his
death, his property was to go to his niece Matilde, who was free to
choose a husband. Corrado, who has kept his true identity a secret
from Matilde, has fallen in love with her and she with him. The
action of the opera occurs on the date specified for Matilde to enter
into her inheritance, the day on which she plans to marry Corrado.
Baldly told, these antecedent details would seem to make for great
problems of exposition, but Donizetti and Cammarano are surprisingly successful in making the plot sufficiently clear: they set out the
motives of the various characters one at a time, and always keep the
present conflict in the foreground, later bringing the opposing forces
into violent collision.

The opera begins with a deceptive blandness. One of Donizetti's
longer preludes, sixty-two measures of insistent alternation of D
minor and D major that come to a quiet 'dissolving' conclusion in C
major, lead directly into the *introduzione* (in F major); this is exceptional since it is entirely for female voices (an offstage prayer for
Matilde and her ladies, scored for organ, band, and, in the orchestra,
harp and *pizzicato* strings) and is shorter than the prelude. Corrado
is the first character to appear, and his once famous romanza, 'Ah,
non avea più lagrime' (*larghetto*, 2/4, B flat major), expresses his love
for Matilde, which makes him forget his guilty past. This romanza is
in two strophes, the already elaborate line of the first being further
embellished in the second; the whole piece is a demonstration of the
composer's regard for Ronconi's vocal suavity at this period. Here
Donizetti uses the seductive charm of elegant melody to manifest the
sexual charisma that explains Corrado's success with both Maria and
Matilde.

The opening scene ends with a duet for Corrado and Enrico, who
suppose themselves to be brothers. In their lengthy recitative Corrado relates his past involvement with Maria; Donizetti does nothing

to emphasize the gruesomeness of Corrado's tale, preferring to proceed quickly to the conflict between the two men. In the *tempo d'attacco* (*vivace*) Enrico reveals that he loves Matilde himself but hopes to hide his true feelings from his brother. The *larghetto* contrasts Corrado's expansive good humor with Enrico's melancholy in different melodies. Their cabaletta has an unusual structure: Corrado's 'Fratello! Enrico! Abbracciami' is answered by a different melody of equal length (twenty-six measures) for Enrico; after a brief transition Enrico repeats the first half of his melody to which Corrado appends two phrases from the middle of his corresponding passage, and this leads directly into two sixteen-measure statements *a due*, forming in effect a second cabaletta that is regular and shorter than the first.

The second scene of Act 1 takes place within the castle of Rudenz. An old family retainer, Rambaldo, discovers a woman weeping in front of the late Count's portrait and is amazed to discover that she is Maria, who has arrived undetected by a secret passage. Material from the orchestral introduction recurs as underpinning of their recitative, which frequently expands into melancholy arioso. When Rambaldo informs her that Matilde will shortly be married, Maria wishes her cousin well, and adds that she will hide her shame in the convent of Arau. Her *larghetto*, 'Sì, del chiostro penitente', is notable for its long, restless phrases and uneasy modulations (Example 61). At the cadence of the third phrase, where Maria speaks of her 'smania ardente' (her unextinguished love for Corrado), the aria moves into the parallel minor. Her phrase 'chiederò gemente a Dio' (moaning I shall ask God) is first intensified by being echoed by the oboe and then made more explicit by her descending chromatic scale, in effect one of the moans she has just mentioned. This cavatina is only twenty measures long, but in its wealth of expressive detail it surpasses many longer arias. In her cabaletta, 'Sulla mia tomba gelida' (*moderato*, 4/4, G major), Maria, in a typically Romantic posture, envisions the remorseful Corrado weeping at her grave. By this point in the opera all the characters have been presented sympathetically; this has been made possible by the suppression of Corrado's true identity, but all this smoothly-handled preparation has laid the fuse for the charge about to be detonated in the first finale. Between Maria's *aria di sortita* and the finale, there is a brief chorus, which creates a sense of necessary space around the ensemble.[41]

The finale (*moderato*, 4/4, C major) opens with fanfares and at once there begins a series of confrontations. Matilde, dressed as a

MARIA

Example 61. *Maria de Rudenz*, Act 1 scene ii, *larghetto* of Maria's aria

bride and attended by her pages, advances to meet Corrado, who is accompanied by Enrico. Matilde and Enrico are surprised to encounter each other again, while Rambaldo and the vassals are enraged to recognize Corrado. Corrado orders a chamberlain to read the terms of the Count's will, and, without impediment, the wedding procession re-forms. Matilde and Corrado look forward to future bliss in an *andante* (D major), set against one of those jaunty tunes that Donizetti liked to use just before happy prospects turn to ashes (the figure that insinuatingly supports the dialogue between Enrico and Arturo in Act 2 of *Lucia* is a familiar example of this device). As Corrado publicly affirms his affection for Matilde, Maria suddenly appears (recalling the effect produced by Lucrezia's abrupt entrance in her final scene) and orders him to desist. Maria's first word, 'Empio!', overlaps the end of Corrado's phrase, and the sense of dramatic clash is heightened by the *fortissimo* chord of the seventh on the leading-tone of the dominant key, Maria's voice ringing out on high A. Everyone exclaims in astonishment, over harmonies that slide toward D minor, and there follows one of those portentous pauses that Donizetti used in order to allow the surprise to register before the big musical moment begins (there is just such a pause before the *Lucia* sextet.)

The succeeding *larghetto*, 'Chiuse al dì per te le ciglia', begins the movement that Donizetti first transported to *Poliuto* and later to *Les martyrs*, and which, in some ways, is not quite so effective in its original context as its later ones.[42] After a formidable glance at Matilde, Maria denounces Corrado in a melody of great dignity and pathos, while he, to the same phrases in the same key, defies her and wonders why God does not incinerate her on the spot. These two melodic statements are followed by new material for the tenor, which is introduced at a shift from minor to parallel major that propels the movement forward; it now expands into a quintet with increased rhythmic impulse and more sustained vocal lines.[43] The whole passage has the same formal structure as the *Lucia* sextet (*a a b b*), but here the change of key in the second half gives a sense of greater development and expansiveness (Example 62). Donizetti always had a sure hand for capping a modulation with the release of a new and welcome melodic idea. Example 62 clearly anticipates the kind of big tune that Verdi used in *Il trovatore*, particularly di Luna's 'Ah! l'amor, l'amor ond'ardo', but it has a peculiarly Donizettian mellowness, contributed by measures 4–6 of the musical quotation, where the dominant-seventh harmony freezes and the melody is colored by a flattened sixth (B flat).

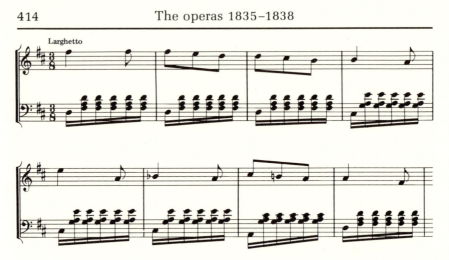

Example 62. *Maria de Rudenz*, Act 1, *larghetto* of the finale

In the *moderato* that divides the *larghetto* from the stretta, the jaunty tune from the *andante* recurs (Rossini style)[44] to accompany the vassals' attestation of loyalty to Maria. Maria orders Corrado to leave and then commands Matilde to enter a convent. Corrado blusters, Matilde tries to kill herself and is restrained by Enrico, while Maria exults in her triumph, and the chorus repeats her order that Corrado depart. The characters keep up a harmonic tug-of-war, their phrases frequently overlap, headlong scalar passages maintain the tension, and the melodic link to the stretta is provided by the threatening voice of Corrado ascending chromatically to his top F sharp. The concluding movement of the finale is launched by the solo voice of Maria (Example 63).

Starting with a thrice-repeated F sharp, Maria's melody has a clear musical relationship to the passage quoted in Example 62; at each recurrence of this melody additional voices are added to it, and the whole stretta sustains admirably the sense of conflict between obsessed characters – yet another instance of Donizetti's having outgrown the rhythmic formula of ♩. ♫ | ♩. ♫ that had dominated the concluding sections of so many of his finales earlier in the 1830s. Of this finale to *Maria de Rudenz*, he transported to *Poliuto* and *Les martyrs* only the *larghetto*; the *materia di mezzo* and stretta, admittedly on a lower level of eloquence, are peculiar to *Maria de Rudenz*.

The first act of *Maria de Rudenz* is no inconsiderable accomplishment. Corrado's romanza, Maria's cavatina and the *larghetto* of the finale are the musical jewels in its crown, but unlike some other scores where gems shine fitfully against a duller background, this

Example 63. *Maria de Rudenz*, Act 1, stretta of the finale

act is built with a keen sense of proportion by a very sure hand. Unfortunately the momentum so carefully built up is not consistently maintained in the balance of the score. Only the duet for Maria and Corrado at the end of Act 2 and Maria's aria–finale are outstanding.

Act 2 is very short, consisting only of a prelude with an uncommonly effective bass clarinet solo, a double aria for Enrico and the soprano–baritone duet. In Enrico's arias Maria appears as a subordinate character, informing him that she knows a secret that will ease his misfortunes – prospect enough to motivate his cabaletta. Enrico leaves to send Corrado to her, and as she waits she explores, in an expressive recitative accompanied by a short motif that modulates incessantly, her conflicting emotions and decides that her love for Corrado is the strongest of them. When Corrado enters, Maria reveals to him that he is truly the son of the outlaw and assassin, Ugo di Berna, and at the climax of this disclosure the short motif of the opening recitative returns. Maria offers to suppress the evidence of his birth if only he will love her as once he did (Example 64).

Example 64. *Maria de Rudenz*, Act 2, *larghetto* of the Maria–Corrado
duet

Maria's expressive melody, in which she swears sacrilegiously to
adore him as much as heaven itself, expands gradually through a
wealth of subtle inflections. The third phrase with its detached elements (which prefigures Leonora's 'È deggio è posso crederlo' from
the *Il trovatore* quintet)[45] is a variant of the opening phrase. Corrado's statement, portraying his troubled conscience, moves
chromatically; just before the two voices join for the coda the rate of
modulation increases markedly, then the duet concludes with a
cadenza *a due*. The *materia di mezzo* never loses its melodic impulse, although it grows increasingly rhetorical, as Maria furiously
reacts to Corrado's abiding love for Matilde in soaring *sostenuti* and
scales that touch high C. Maria opens a trap door, proclaiming that it
is the mouth of Matilde's tomb, and cries out to Corrado 'The only
way you can save Matilde is to swear you love me!' The 4/4 *marcato*
cabaletta, 'È d'altra il cor nè franger', is of the same type as Violetta's
intense and insistent 'Gran Dio, morir sì giovane!', and it builds up
to the moment of Corrado's stabbing Maria. Rambaldo and the vas-

sals rush in, horrified; in an unaccompanied phrase Maria announces that she has stabbed herself and that Corrado should live, and she falls back apparently dead. By appending this brief coup de théâtre to the formal duet structure, Donizetti creates in ten measures a mini-finale.

Act 3 opens with a chorus, followed by a scene in which Enrico challenges Corrado to a duel. Corrado is reluctant until Enrico tears the order from his chest; they pause for a full-scale cabaletta before they rush out. The brief second scene begins with a lilting 'Valzer svizzero' (to which Donizetti added 'that means it is not *presto*') for chorus and dancers, which makes a strong contrast with Maria's aria–finale. She is not dead, of course, only mortally wounded, and she has sufficient strength to sustain what is possibly Donizetti's most original solution to this convention. Before she enters she stabs Matilde, whose dying shriek is heard from the wings. Maria confronts Corrado in her *larghetto*, 'Mostro iniquo'; its second statement is a variant of the first, to a new text, and later the *andante*, 'Al misfatto enorme e rio', presents yet another variant. Here Donizetti avoids the stasis common in the usual cabaletta, with its initial contrast and subsequent repetition, and creates an unusually unified and moving effect that increases in pathos up to Maria's death as she forgives Corrado, who is left to exclaim that he is condemned to live.

Maria de Rudenz is a fascinating and frustratingly uneven instance of Donizetti's deep penetration into Romantic melodrama – a world that he would re-enter later when his experience had been tempered by composing for non-Italian stages. In spite of its inequalities and the strain it puts upon an audience's credulity, *Maria de Rudenz* stands as a subject that Donizetti took seriously, and on which he lavished some passages of sincere and genuinely moving music.

Poliuto was the last score Donizetti composed before his departure from Naples in the fall of 1838, but as its performance was banned, because it dealt with the martyrdom of a saint, and since it substantially formed the basis for Donizetti's first work for the Paris Opéra, it will be most conveniently discussed in the following chapter in conjunction with its French metamorphosis.

12

The operas
1838–1841

Poliuto and Les martyrs. Although *La fille du régiment* had its first performance at the Opéra-Comique in February 1840 and *Les martyrs* would not be performed until the following April, the roots of the latter work go back to 1838. Donizetti composed *Poliuto* before his departure from Naples, where it had advanced as far as preliminary rehearsals before the king's prohibition forestalled its actual performance. Donizetti wrote *Poliuto*, like *L'assedio di Calais*, with more than half an eye to its potential for being recast as a French grand opera. He expanded and altered the score into *Les martyrs* in 1839 in Paris. Since about eighty percent of the French version in four acts is made up of *Poliuto*, and since the three-act Italian score enjoys the greater currency, it makes sense to discuss *Poliuto* before examining the alterations and change of emphasis it later underwent.

The literary source of *Poliuto* is Corneille's *tragédie chrétienne*, *Polyeucte* (1641–2). Cammarano's libretto converts Corneille's spiritual drama, with its carefully observed unities, into a Romantic melodrama, adding the motive of Poliuto's jealousy (which does not occur in the French original) to turn the action, at least in part, into a stock tenor–soprano–baritone triangle. Donizetti may have played some part in this emendation of Corneille, for he had complained in a letter to Toto Vasselli, speaking of *Poliuto:* 'there is little love interest in it'.[1] Moreover since the religious aspect of the plot had to be treated circumspectly in Naples – and this was a matter not merely of blunting nouns in the text, but of restricting the religious theme to a relatively few episodes – the resultant gap in the fabric demanded some other intensification of the conflict, and jealousy provided the needed patch. It should be mentioned, too, that the religious aspect of the play was transformed in the opera libretto into a Romantic transcendence, an escape from amorous predicaments and suffering; religion functions in much the same way in the

418

Rivas–Piave–Verdi *La forza del destino,* especially in the revision of 1869 with the addition of the final trio of reconciliation. Cammarano's chief coup in his libretto (and the idea may well have come from Nourrit, who had the greatest direct experience of the specialties of the Opéra), was to convert what in Corneille's play is a narrative by Stratonice (Pauline's confidante) of the events at the temple into a scene that shows them directly. The result of this alteration is not only to bring to life before the audience the most dramatic action in the plot – Poliuto's upsetting of the altar to Jupiter – but to afford the opportunity for exactly the sort of mass confrontation in an imposing setting that French opera reveled in.

Donizetti's score shows everywhere that he intended it to have a weight and spaciousness that would lend itself to export across the Alps. The *larghetto* of the overture, with its famous passage of twenty-six measures for four bassoons, is clearly intended to have the emphasis of a separate prelude to the *allegro vivace* of the overture, and it establishes at once an atmosphere of distinctive solemnity. The autograph of *Poliuto,* dating from 1838, shows that the use of four bassoons was part of Donizetti's original intention; in a work written for Naples at that period one would not expect to find such orchestral resources. The largely unaccompanied hymn, 'O nume pietoso' (*larghetto,* 4/4, E major), directed to be sung 'from behind the curtain', supplants the normal repetition of the second subject of the overture (the cabaletta of the 'conversion' duet) and dispenses with the *crescendo* that is usual at this point in the traditional structure. In *Poliuto,* but not in *Les martyrs,* the overture is followed by an additional *preludio,* twenty-eight measures of *allegro vivace* (E minor), to which is appended a modulating passage, marked *largo,* to connect it to the opening D flat major chorus. Since Donizetti did not live to see *Poliuto* performed, much less published, it cannot be decided now what were his final intentions for this *preludio.*[2] Most likely it antedated the present overture and was supplanted by it, as its tempo and tonality are those of the first subject of the overture, and its present position makes it seem anticlimactic. As it appears among the manuscript materials of *Poliuto,* it has been printed in the Ricordi scores.

The male chorus of the *introduzione,* 'Ancor ci asconda', consists of two asymmetrical statements, prefaced by an introductory period and followed by a dissolving postlude that accompanies the Christians' silent entrance into their cavern. Poliuto enters with Nearco, and their expository recitative expands into arioso when Poliuto confesses his jealousy of Paolina; then, at Nearco's injunction, he prays for peace of soul in 'D'un alma troppo fervida' (*larghetto*, 3/8, D flat major), in which the two voices join for the final phrases before the men also enter the cavern. A long and technically arduous clarinet solo forms the introduction to Paolina's *aria di sortita*. She has followed Poliuto, fearful that he may be tempted to embrace the proscribed religion, and Nearco confirms her dread. From the cavern comes the sound of Poliuto's voice in the hymn from the overture, accompanied by three solo voices vocalizing wordlessly.[3] Paolina is strangely moved, and in her aria 'Di quai soavi lagrime' (*lento assai*, 12/8, F major) she explores this novel emotion through a wide-ranging melody, dilating on key words with arpeggiated and scalar figures. The unexpected news that Severo is not dead as she had believed but is even now arriving in Armenia in his new capacity as proconsul, fills her with excitement. In 'Perchè di stolto giubilo' (*allegro giusto*, 3/4, F major) the brilliant vocal effects give the lie to the conflict her words express; this is the only place in the work where the prima donna swamps the character.

The second scene of Act 1, which takes place in the main square of Melitene, consists of a march and welcoming chorus, both genuinely rousing, followed by Severo's *aria di sortita*, 'Di tua beltade immagine' (*cantabile*, 9/8, A flat major) and 'No, l'acciar non fu spietato' (*moderato*, 4/4, A flat major). His cabaletta is motivated by his learning that Paolina is now married; between its statements there is a brief trio for men's voices and chorus, and it ends with a short, assertive coda that is thoroughly conventional.

Act 2 is divided into two scenes. The first is set in the atrium of Felice's house; Callistene brings in Severo, knowing that he may encounter Paolina, and he plans also to bring Poliuto there so that he may observe his wife with the proconsul. The *tempo d'attacco* of the Paolina–Severo duet features a nervous seven-note motif in the accompaniment which is incessantly repeated to build up a *fortissimo* climax; this contrasts strongly with the spare chords of the latter part of the duet, as Severo comments on Paolina's terror at finding herself alone with him. He opens the duet, 'Il più lieto dei viventi' (*allegretto*, 4/4, E minor), with a persuasive melody, punctuated by rising phrase-endings and syncopated accents (Example 65a). Paolina begins her melodic period in the parallel major, her phrases having an obvious relationship to Severo's, but in many of the contours of her line the thumbprints of Donizetti's style are clearly recognizable (Example 65b).

This movement ends with an extended series of cadential figures, both alternating and *a due*. Much of the *tempo di mezzo* is carried

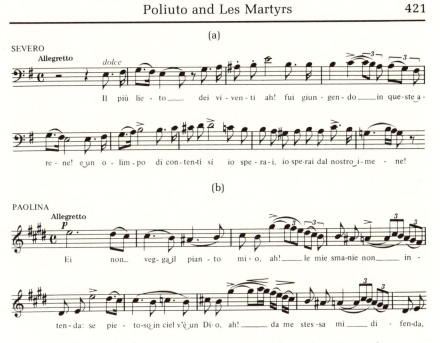

Example 65. *Poliuto*, Act 2 scene i, *allegretto* of the Paolina–Severo duet

on against an impetuous scalar figure, as Severo tries to get Paolina
to confess her love for him. Their cabaletta, 'Quest'alma è troppo
debole', is in a slower tempo (*andante*) than the first main movement, an effect Donizetti had a fondness for, and it is set to one of
those quarter-note chordal accompaniments that he favored in the
pendant sections of soprano–baritone duets. Only at the coda does
the pace quicken to an *allegro*. Callistene has brought in Poliuto to
overhear the conclusion of his wife's encounter. When the others
have left, Poliuto sings a double aria which begins 'Fu macchiato
l'onor mio' (*allegro giusto*, 4/4, F minor/A flat major); the opening
section is accompanied by a driving figure of great energy, but,
rather inconsistently, the same figure recurs in the *materia di mezzo*
in a different emotional context. Here Poliuto receives word that
Nearco has been seized and dragged to the temple of Jupiter; his
resolution to spare his coreligionist is expressed in his cabaletta,
'Sfolgorò divino raggio' (*allegro*, 4/4, F major), in which the
gradually increasing tempo generates a sense of mounting excitement.[4] The cabaletta begins *allegro* and then bears these subsequent
directions in both statements: *poco più*, *1⁰ tempo*, *poco più*, *più
allegro* and then again *più allegro*. Indications of adjustments of

tempo are especially frequent in the score of *Poliuto*, and they should be appreciated as a characteristic that Donizetti himself thought central to his style. As early as 1824 he had written to Mercadante to ask his help in preparing one of his scores: 'You are familiar with my manner of composing, and you understand well where sometimes an alteration of tempo is needed.'[5] Throughout his career he insisted upon this point.

Act 2 scene ii, which is set in the temple of Jupiter, is one of Donizetti's major accomplishments and it stands in the same relationship to the rest of his theatrical output as does the triumphal scene of *Aida* to Verdi's oeuvre; indeed the earlier scene must be counted among the direct antecedents of the later one. It begins with a startling *fortissimo*, an imposing unison over a chromatically descending bass, which is answered by a softer series of resolutions to the dominant key; these seven measures, succeeded by a moment of absolute silence, constitute a prelude that is both arresting and economical. The priests in unison sing a hymn to the god 'in a tone of fanatic zeal' (Example 66).

This imposing melody, the main building-block of the opening of the scene, is strikingly asymmetrical, consisting of ten phrases – a unit of six completed by a unit of four. The second unit begins with what is, in effect, the third phrase of the opening unit, which (since it is also the same as the first phrase) gives a momentary sense of ternary form; but it leads now to a deceptive cadence on C natural, accompanied only in the bass, which lends this outburst a tinge of barbaric strangeness. The hymn is then echoed softly by the women's chorus, accompanied by warm string figurations and without the deceptive cadence. It returns again, now *fortissimo*, all the voices joining in a thundering tutti; this leads to a quiet coda that ends on a whispered monotone. Callistene and Severo begin the interrogation of Nearco, and when he refuses to name the neophyte, Poliuto suddenly (in a moment that inevitably calls to mind *Norma*) declares 'Son io!'. This disclosure motivates the *larghetto*, borrowed with slight modification from *Maria de Rudenz*; here it is the baritone who has the first horrified statement, 'La sacrilega parola', followed by Paolina, before Poliuto sings the passage quoted in Example 62. From the *materia di mezzo* onward the scene is new. As the guards move forward to seize her husband, Paolina begs Felice, Callistene and Severo in turn to spare him, but Poliuto advances to the altar of Jupiter and, calling down imprecations on the lying, infamous god, overturns it. Amid the general horrified reaction Poliuto repulses his wife and the stretta of the finale begins (Example

Example 66. *Poliuto*, Act 2 scene ii, opening chorus

che può dai cardini svel - ler la terra, le stelle in -
nu - me - ri strap-pa - re al ciel!___ le stelle in - nu - me - ri strap - pa - re al ciel!

67). As with the stretta at the same point in *Maria de Rudenz*, this (different) melody harks back to the F sharps of the major key tune of the *larghetto* (see Example 62). Paolina's voice joins Poliuto's for the second half of this statement, in the parallel minor. A contrasting melodic idea in an insistent pattern of ♩ ♫ | ♩ ♫ ♩ ♫ is launched by Severo as he thinks how Paolina will hate him when he sheds her husband's blood, while the tonal mass thickens in a big chromatic *crescendo*. The voice of Callistene, alone, summons the priests and lictors, and with them he repeats the opening hymn (see Example 66); this forms an implacable bass line against which the other voices move in overlapping motivic phrases, and the finale ends in a coda that is directed to move faster and then faster still.

For sheer power and massiveness this finale surpasses all of Donizetti's efforts so far. He has moved far from the sense of under-

Example 67. *Poliuto*, Act 2, *allegro non troppo* of the finale

nourishment that afflicted the big moments of his operas in the 1820s, for he now clearly controls the resources needed to fill an outsize scene convincingly, keeping the personal conflict and the public opposition in equilibrium. With this scene he imposed a much enlarged scale upon Italian opera, for which reason *Poliuto* can be seen as standing at the head of the line of Italian grand operas that stretches down the years to Verdi's *Otello*.

Act 3 opens in the sacred wood next to the temple of Jupiter. People can be heard off stage making their way to the circus. Callistene and his priests enter, and he vents his fury at the news that other Christians have confessed so that they may share in Poliuto's fate. His aria 'Alimento alla fiamma si porga'[6] (*larghetto,* 12/8, E flat major) is routine and was obviously included simply to flesh out the bass's part. It is later restated in unison with the chorus, *poco più,* and a more urgent accompanying figure somewhat increases its effectiveness.

The setting changes to Poliuto's cell, and the scene begins with a prelude based on the Christian hymn from the overture. Dreaming, Poliuto thinks of Paolina, and in an expressive arioso, 'Bella e di sol vestita',[7] imagines that he hears a heavenly voice proclaim her virtuousness. Paolina arrives and begs him to recant to save his life. When Poliuto mentions his suspicions and Callistene's part in provoking them, Paolina explains her past relationship with Severo, attests her innocence, and claims that Callistene was motivated by his own frustrated desire for her. Again she begs Poliuto to save his life, beginning the *larghetto* of their duet, 'Ah! fuggi da morte', in E minor; he answers her to a serene melody in the parallel major, stating his belief in eternal life. Moved by his radiant certainty, Paolina, in a new melody embellished with short shimmering scales, to the words 'Un fulgido lume', is herself convinced and announces her willingness to share his fate. This is a notable example of a duet that advances dramatically, the whole in dialogue form. Their cabaletta, 'Il suon dell'arpe angeliche', brings back the tune already familiar as the second subject of the overture (though since Donizetti's usual practise was to compose the overture last, it would be more accurate to regard the overture as using the cabaletta). Here it has all the easy assurance of a 'big' tune, if lacking a little in genuine elevation (Example 68). In the middle of the century this was one of Donizetti's melodies that everyone knew and could whistle. In its contour, tonality and accompaniment, it looks forward to *La forza del destino* and Leonora's 'Tua grazia, o Dio' in the concluding section of her duet with Padre Guardiano. Early critics of *Forza*, oddly enough, chastised Verdi for imitating Donizetti's cabaletta in a different part of his score; the Leonora–Alvaro duet, 'Seguirto fino agli ultimi', in the opening scene.

The doors at the back of the prison open to reveal the adjacent circus, thronged with an eager crowd, who launch the finale with a barbaric, G minor outburst, 'Alle fiere'. Severo pleads with Paolina, begging her to think not so much of his love for her as of her father's grief, and the unusual key of C flat adds impetus to his insistent phrases; but the martyrs reply 'Ah! insieme si muoja', to the main melody of the *maestoso,* their four-square phrases growing more flexible in the second half of this increasingly eloquent quartet with

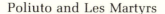

Example 68. *Poliuto*, Act 3 scene ii, cabaletta of the Paolina–Poliuto duet

chorus. The Christians are heard off stage singing their hymn, which leads into an *allegro vivace* that reaches a climax in Paolina's and Poliuto's reaffirmation of their faith (see Example 68) against Callistene's and the priest's curses (see Example 66). The contrapuntal collision of these two melodies symbolizes the opposing forces of the drama. The opera ends in E major, the key that dominates the whole of the final scene; since it began with an E minor/E major overture, it is evident that Donizetti felt the need of a greater degree of tonal coherence in this score than is usually found in his music.

In reworking *Poliuto* as *Les martyrs* Donizetti had to adjust his score to Scribe's new French text. Since the librettist wanted to preserve some of Corneille's original text, he cast parts of the recitative in Alexandrines, with the result that all the recitatives had to be newly composed, although sometimes they retain the original harmonic sequences. But not all the onus of adaptation was upon the composer's shoulders; Scribe found himself in the position, uncommon for him, of tailoring his text to fit the large amount of music that Donizetti retained from the Italian score. Scribe's text differs in its general tone from Cammarano's not only because he could permit himself such specific references as 'baptism' and 'martyrdom', which the Neapolitan poet could not, but because he substituted for the prompt emotionalism of the first text a more spacious and self-contained diction.[8] Scribe abolished the motive of Poliuto's jealousy, which had never fitted very comfortably into Cammarano's plot, and reverted to religious conflict as the dominant issue of the drama. Since the Opéra wanted the compass of the work enlarged to four acts, Scribe had to provide some new material, most of which is to be found in the latter part of Act 1 and the opening of Act 2, it being easier to extend the exposition than to modify other sections of the plot.

Later a musical alteration was made in the overture. The choral hymn sung at the Opéra was dropped and the melody played by horns. This change was probably prompted by what for provincial theaters was the unconventionality of a choral passage to be sung behind the curtain. The subsequent *preludio* is dropped, except for the *largo* modulation at the end, which is retained to connect the last bars of the overture (in E major) to the opening chorus (in D flat major). The motivation of Pauline's entrance in Act 1 is modified: now she comes to pray at her mother's tomb, and the final section of her opening recitative is an arioso hymn to Proserpina. This is followed by a female chorus (new), 'Jeune souveraine' (*andante*, 4/4, F major), of no particular distinction. Pauline dismisses her companions, who exit to a brief clarinet solo that recalls the extensive prelude that accompanies her entrance; then comes Pauline's aria, 'Qu'ici ta main glacée' ('Di quai soavi lagrime', with a slightly more complex vocal line), but now she prays to her mother to remove from her heart her feeling for Sévère. Next, the singing of the Christians' hymn by the chorus, which in *Poliuto* preceded and motivated Pauline's *larghetto*, leads into the completely new ending to Act 1. Polyeucte, entering, is surprised to find Pauline, and their interchange develops into a brief duet. In a lengthy and rather static *vivace* Pauline expresses first her grief and then her horror at finding her husband one with the Christians, while they remonstrate with her. The act now closes with a very beautiful and finely worked trio, 'Objet de ma constance' (*larghetto*, 6/8, E major), in which the interweaving of the parts is exceptionally felicitous (Example 69). The high C sharp in the tenor part in Example 69 calls attention to another major difference between the two versions of this score. While the role of Poliuto was fashioned for Nourrit, whose effective (i.e. non-falsetto) range went no higher than A, that of Polyeucte was written for Duprez, who was famous for his C from the chest and who could sing still higher *en fausset*; the tessitura of this role is therefore much more demanding in the French score.

The first scene of Act 2 begins with new material. The role of Félix, Pauline's father and Governor of Armenia, has been enlarged from a *comprimario* tenor role in *Poliuto* to a part for principal deep bass. (With the removal of the element of Poliuto's jealousy, the part of Callisthènes has been demoted to a secondary position, but it is still for a bass.) In a brief recitative Félix signs an edict proscribing Christianity, and then in the aria 'Dieux des Romains' (*larghetto*, 3/4, E flat major) he dedicates himself to serving the wrath of the Roman divinities. Pauline enters and her father forces her to read aloud the fatal edict, which causes her considerable anguish for Polyeucte's sake, but she seeks to disguise her feelings from Félix. His second aria, 'Mort, mort à ces infâmes' (*allegro vivace*, 4/4, E flat major), expresses his fanatical hatred in a driving melody in ternary form, reinforced by a unison male chorus in the cabaletta; this cabaletta is in modified form since the two statements are not identical – the second deploys the chorus more fully than and differently from the first and adds a contrasting soprano line for Pauline. Callisthènes brings the news of Sévère's arrival with his legions, which provides the cue for Pauline's 'Sévère existe!'; this was formerly Paolina's cabaletta at the end of the opening scene, but here it occurs as a separate aria though it is practically unchanged.

The second scene of Act 2, in the public square, begins with a march (slightly amplified over the corresponding passage in *Poliuto*) and triumphal chorus. Sévère's cantabile is only slightly modified from the original but now it is separated from his second aria by a ballet, a divertissement of three numbers. The dance music

Example 69. *Les martyrs*, Act 1, trio–finale

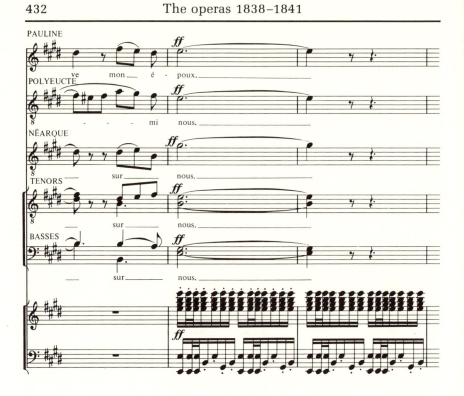

is vigorous and competent, but without anything approaching distinction; only in the first *entrée*, a gladiatorial combat, is there any effort to dramatize the situation. The baritone's second aria, now 'Je te perds que je t'adore', has undergone some elaboration in an effort to disguise its original function as a cabaletta. Donizetti altered and improved the first four phrases of the vocal line, while retaining practically unchanged the second period – this is the only case where he drastically modified an aria in moving it from *Poliuto* to *Les martyrs*. Originally the intermediate material between the two statements was a brief twelve measures, but in the French score they have been extended to 105 and now consist not only of recitative but an arioso that is expanded into a quintet. Sévère's opening melody returns, but this time the second half turns into a sextet with a newly elaborated coda. What in *Poliuto* had been a simple baritone cabaletta has in *Les martyrs* become a cross between an aria and a finale.

The third act of *Les martyrs* corresponds very closely to the second act of *Poliuto*, but it contains a few significant alterations. There is a new woodwind passage that leads into Pauline's brief prayer, 'Dieux immortels' (*larghetto*, 4/4, E flat major), in which she asks the Roman gods to banish her dishonorable thoughts of Sévère. The *tempo d'attacco* has the same accompaniment as its counterpart in *Poliuto* but different vocal phrases. The baritone launches the duet which, except that it opens in E major instead of the parallel minor and has a new arpeggiated accompaniment, is much as before. The biggest change in this scene is the substitution of two new tenor arias for Poliuto's 'Fu macchiato l'onor mio' and 'Sfolgorò divino raggio'. Since Donizetti was writing for a different sort of tenor voice and since the theme of the hero's jealousy has been dropped, this new material produces a very different effect. The first aria, 'Mon seul trésor' (*cantabile*, 6/8, B flat major), is a tender melody with a more animated middle section, which concludes with a slightly modified repeat of the opening period to a new text. It is Félix now that brings Polyeucte the news that Néarque has been seized. Polyeucte's resolution to go to Néarque is expressed in the vigorous 'Oui, j'irai dans leurs temples' in cabaletta form; in the coda at the phrase 'Dieu m'inspire' Donizetti supplied the otherworldly effect of an optional F above high C on the penultimate syllable. In the temple scene, little in the music except the recitatives has been changed; but the shift of emphasis in the text becomes clear when Polyeucte begins the stretta not by dismissing his wife (see Example 67) but by proclaiming 'Je crois en Dieu, roi du ciel et de la terre'.

The opening scene of Act 4 is completely changed. To take the place of Callistene's old-fashioned *aria con coro* there is a trio for Félix, Sévère and Pauline, in which the distracted wife begs them to have pity on her husband. This trio utilizes the accompaniment and some of the melodic material of 'Fu macchiato l'onor mio', to which is appended a new ending, an extensive unaccompanied passage *a tre*. The concluding section of the trio begins with a reprise of Félix's 'Mort, mort à ces infâmes' to a new text, but soon goes onto a different track. The addition of this trio makes the role of Pauline longer and more demanding than that of her Italian counterpart. The second scene of Act 4 contains a few amplifications. At the opening Polyeucte's dream has been expanded, and after it there appear in the orchestra anticipations of the passage quoted in Example 68. Pauline's recitative has been enlarged to permit her to deliver Corneille's famous line: 'Je suis...Je crois...Je suis désabusée!' The opening chorus of the finale, with its tempo marking intensified to *féroce*, has been doubled in length. The later ensemble passages have a fuller texture that increases the level of sonority to conclude the work.

Les martyrs possesses an amplitude at once greater and yet, paradoxically, both emptier and more encumbered than that of *Poliuto*. Undeniably it has greater consistency but at the same time it has less human interest than the more impulsive Italian version. With the exception of the fine trio that concludes Act 1 of the French score,[9] all the most memorable music is common to both versions. An adherent of the values of Romantic melodrama will prefer *Poliuto*; a mystic will find *Les martyrs* more to his taste.

Le duc d'Albe (Il duca d'Alba). Donizetti composed approximately half of *Le duc d'Albe* in 1839 and then put it aside in order to compose *L'ange de Nisida* and *La fille du régiment*. In succeeding years he periodically hoped that it would be scheduled for production at the Opéra, where it had been intended originally to follow *Les martyrs* as a vehicle for Dorus-Gras. However, the condition of the autograph shows that after his original spate of work upon it he could not have devoted more than a few additional hours to it.

The prelude is lacking, but the autograph contains an indication of the point at which the curtain should rise; and the rest of the first act is complete except for the dances; that these were intended is clear from the three pages left blank to accomodate them and the heading on next number 'Après la danse'. All of Act 1 is completely orchestrated save for two brief choral passages, which possibly were intended to be unaccompanied. Act 2 is only slightly less complete: missing are a few passages of recitative, the accompaniment of the drinking chorus and the *allegro* of the conspirators' oath. Of the last two acts, Donizetti wrote little more than the voice parts and the bass lines, with an occasional indication of the entrance for an instrument. Even these sketches are not consistent because there are no indications at all for such important passages as the Duke's recitative at the beginning of Act 3, the tenor aria in Act 4 (which was moved to the final act of *La favorite* and its text modified to become 'Ange si pur'), and the sailors' chorus in the final scene.

The subject of *Le duc d'Albe* (libretto by Scribe and Duvéyrier), is a Flemish uprising against the Spaniards in the sixteenth century. (It was this libretto, with the action shifted to twelfth-century Sicily that Scribe, never a man to waste his work, supplied to Verdi for *Les vêpres Siciliennes*.) Rosine Stolz did not find the role of Hélène or the subject to her taste and refused to appear in it when Le duc d'Albe was proposed as the opera for Donizetti's December 1840 'turn' at the Opéra; her refusal was the principal reason why Donizetti was obliged to cobble L'ange de Nisida into La favorite for that occasion. Since her sway at the Opéra lasted until her contretemps in Robert Bruce on 30 December 1846, and her opposition to Le duc d'Albe remained unwavering, there were no prospects for that score at the one theater for which it was intended until after Donizetti's physical condition had deteriorated to the point at which he could not resume work upon it. Stolz's opposition resulted in Léon Pillet's paying a fine of 15,000 francs to Donizetti and Scribe for failing to produce the work in the time allowed by their contract for it.

The incomplete state of the manuscript resisted all hopeful efforts to produce the work. Pillet's successors at the Opéra, Duponchel and Roqueplan, wanted to mount it in 1848, but after an examination of the score Dietsch declared their plan to be unfulfillable. Again in 1875, at the time the remains of Donizetti and Mayr were moved to Santa Maria Maggiore in Bergamo Alta, there were plans to put it on, but once again the pitiful evidence of the score resisted that generous gesture. In September 1881 the incomplete score was sold to Giuseppina Lucca, that indefatigable rival of the Casa Ricordi, and she put together a panel consisting of Antonio Bazzini, Cesare Dominceti and Ponchielli, all of the faculty of the Milan Conservatory, to supervise the completion of the score by Matteo Salvi, who had studied privately with Donizetti for two seasons in Vienna; the French libretto was translated by Angelo Zanardini and the names of the chief characters were changed from Henri and Hélène to Marcello and Amelia to minimize the resemblance of the plot to that of Les vêpres. The result of this commission was produced at the Teatro Apollo in Rome on 22 March 1882, with Abigaille Bruschi-Chiatti (Amelia), Gayarré (Marcello di Bruges) and Leone Giraldoni (Alba) and conducted by Marino Mancinelli. Four productions in two years was all the immediate history of that effort, but it has since been revived in the theater and on RAI. The best-known item from this score, the tenor aria, 'Angelo casto e bel', is not by Donizetti at all but was written by one or more members of Lucca's group of composers.

In 1959 Le duc d'Albe was completed a second time, by Thomas Schippers for the Spoleto Festival. Schippers made a conscientious effort to orchestrate passages in the style of the 1840s, to a greater extent at least than had the collaborators on the earlier version, but he did not seek authenticity to the extent of restoring Scribe's original French text over Zanardini's Italian one. A feature of this realization, which has its own subsequent performance history, was to restore 'Ange si pur' as 'Spirto gentil' to the position from which Donizetti had taken it during the summer of 1840.

La fille du régiment. No other score composed by a non-Frenchman for the Opéra-Comique has come even close to matching the record of *La fille du régiment* on that stage; since it was originally composed to a French libretto, it falls into a different category from those operas first performed elsewhere before gaining popularity on the stage of the Opéra-Comique in French translations – works like *Il barbiere di Siviglia* and *Tosca*. Donizetti's aptitude for opera in French had been demonstrated in 1839 with his *Lucie* for the Théâtre de la Renaissance, and now, in the form that the Parisian public regarded as most characteristically their own, he produced a score they accepted as native. His ready sensibility and his knack for promptly assimilating stylistic elements into his musical vocabulary allowed him to catch the true Gallic tone at many moments in *La fille,* and yet the score remains at heart deeply Donizettian. To put his achievement here in an accurate perspective it must be acknowledged that during the 1820s and 1830s the influence of Rossini's works had made itself felt on the repertory of the Opéra-Comique, as in the tenor aria 'Ô ma tendre amie' in Hérold's *Le pré aux clercs* (1832). But granted that the alien soil Donizetti tilled contained some familiar elements, it is nevertheless remarkable that with *La fille* he created his own international style at his first attempt.

One of the most famous episodes in *La fille* is the singing lesson in Act 2, where the Marquise on the one hand is trying to instill into her 'niece' the art of sentimental French song as perfected by Pierre Garat, while Sulpice, on the other, keeps reminding his 'daughter' of the military songs that had enlivened their encampments. The situation, particularly since the conflict demands the contrast of two types of singing, is one that drew on all of Donizetti's longstanding delight in musical parody, which stretched back to *Il fortunato inganno* and *Le convenienze;* the affected air 'Le jour naissait dans le bocage' undergoes a series of witless embellishments, until Marie, first tempted into the regimental song by the bored Sulpice and then recalled by the Marquise to the *air du salon,* becomes so frustrated with its insipidness that she breaks out in a lather of scales and arpeggios before launching into a rataplan and giving up propriety as a bad job. The comic exploitation of coloratura singing could scarcely go further, and the trio, each section of which is well proportioned, is full of clear contrasts of rhythm and tempo; this episode is thoroughly integrated with the plot (even more so than the lesson scene in *Il barbiere*), and it stands as one of the most successful comic ensembles of nineteenth-century opera.

Another strand that connects *La fille* to its predecessors among Donizetti's comedies is the injection of pathos; Donizetti understood well that comedy needs a touch of human warmth, for without a moment that moves the listener humor soon seems mere contrivance. This moment occurs during the *larghetto* of the first finale, when Marie takes leave of Tonio and her 'fathers' in 'Il faut partir'. What could easily have been a scene of exaggerated sentimentality is saved by Donizetti's restraint and melodic refinement. Introduced by the cor anglais, which continues with an understated obbligato, the melody evolves syllabically and seamlessly through its F minor verse and then, with one of Donizetti's best-judged modulations to the parallel major, expands into a brief refrain, 'Ah, par pitié, cachez vos larmes'.[10] There are two strophes, and the aria ends with a coda, heard twice, which is a further expansion of the refrain, and in which Marie's voice, entering in A major, soars over the ensemble. Structurally 'Il faut partir' is a cross between a strophic romanza and the French *couplets*, to which a melodically related, rather than contrasting, coda has been appended. Besides giving *La fille* its requisite moment of pathos, this aria lends the score one of genuine distinction.

Traditionally this opera has provided a vehicle for coloratura sopranos who have a flair for comedy and who have mastered, if not paradiddles exactly, at least some dexterity upon the drum. Besides the trio and her important part in the first finale, where Donizetti constricts the usual ensemble *larghetto* to an aria *con pertichini* so as to fit the modest proportions of an opéra comique, Marie has two other moments of prominence: these are her regimental song, 'Chacun le sait' (which, in one of Donizetti's more improbable self-borrowings, stems from *Il diluvio universale*),[11] and her brilliant cabaletta in Act 2, 'Salut à la France', which during the Second Empire became almost an unofficial national anthem, and a reprise of which ends the opera.[12]

In striking contrast to Maria, Sulpice has no aria of his own, which would be an unthinkable act of neglect in an Italian opera buffa. The joviality beneath his crusty exterior is well established in his *marziale* duet with Marie, following the episodic *introduction*. This duet, 'Au bruit de la guerre', is in two parts; the second, instead of being a cabaletta, repeats the opening of the first (*moderato mosso*) and at the fifth phrase turns into a crisp rataplan. A number of Donizetti's operas were staged at La Scala during the first years of Verdi's activity, and many prominent features from them have a way of showing up, usually thoroughly assimilated, in his successor's works. *La fille*, transformed into an opera buffa and translated into Italian, made its debut at La Scala on 3 October 1840; it was preceded, a month earlier, by the fiasco of *Un giorno di regno* and would be followed two weeks later by the revival of *Oberto*. One of the many effects that Verdi assimilated from Donizetti's music to use later in his own way was that of this rataplan, which is recalled in the encampment scene in *La forza del destino*; Verdi's Preziosilla is a direct lineal descendant of Marie.

The role of Tonio illustrates clearly the way in which Donizetti adapted the Italian conventions to serve French ends. His Act 1 love duet with Marie, 'Depuis l'instant' (*andante non mosso*, 3/4, A flat major), has two identical four-phrase periods separated by transitions in dialogue with Marie; there follows a contrasting melodic idea in faster tempo, to the words 'De cet aveu si tendre' (*allegretto*, 2/4, A flat major). The duet continues with Marie's taking up Tonio's *andante* tune, but now in A major, the key in which here (and elsewhere in the opera) she expresses the sincerity and depth of her feeling for Tonio, and it ends with the return of the *allegretto* in expanded form. The structure of this duet (a a b a¹ b¹) is clearly distinct from the Italian double forms with their sequence of discrete tempos. Tonio's enlistment (so that he can be a proper regimental husband to Marie) is celebrated in a double aria, but once again the structure is unconventional in the second and longer section. The opening, 'Ah! mes amis, quel jour de fête' (*allegro vivace*, 2/4, E flat major), is in ternary form; then, after an extended *tempo di mezzo* between Tonio and the soldiers, the soldiers begin the second tempo (*allegro*, 3/4, F major). Not until after sixty or so measures does Tonio's voice enter, with 'Pour mon âme quel destin!', and instead of repeating this melody, Tonio uses the same text to a new tune, which indicates his growing exuberance with a succession of high Cs (Example 70).

In Act 2, after an Offenbachian trio for Marie, Tonio and Sulpice, 'Tous les trois réunis', in which Donizetti captures the note of Gallic élan with remarkable precision, comes Tonio's *romance*, 'Pour me rapprocher de Marie' (*larghetto*, 2/4, A major); this consists of two strophes, subtly varied in melody, harmony and tempo (unlike Corrado's romanza in Act 1 of *Maria de Rudenz*, where the variants are principally melodic), so that the second strophe is a

Example 70. *La fille du régiment*, Act 1, Tonio's *allegro*

logical intensification of the first. 'Pour me rapprocher de Marie' is one of Donizetti's most tender and spontaneous arias; that he omitted it from the Italian version of the work that he created in the summer of 1840 suggests that he felt its French sentiment was somehow inappropriate to the more extrovert world of opera buffa.[13]

La figlia del reggimento contains other modifications of the original opéra comique, which demonstrate Donizetti's sense of the distinction between the two national forms. The couplets of the Marquise, 'Pour une femme de mon nom', are dropped from the introduzione. Gone, too, is Tonio's 'Pour mon âme' (see Example 70), probably because of its tessitura (it is one thing to touch a high C in a cadenza and quite another to repeat it as part of the main melody); the earlier sections of the aria are grafted on to the beginning of the first finale in the Italian version. To compensate Tonio for the loss of so much material, Donizetti gave him a 'new' aria, placed early in Act 1 to serve as an aria di sortita, borrowing without modification the C major tenor aria from Gianni di Calais. Since there was no reason to exploit the French patriotic motif in Italy, Donizetti dropped the reprise of 'Salut à la France' from the end of the opera, replacing it with a soprano–tenor duet, 'In questo sen riposati', an indication that by this date Donizetti felt that the prima donna's aria–finale had long since ceased to be a sine qua non for an opera buffa score. His other modification that needs to be mentioned is, of course, the replacement of the French spoken dialogue in compressed form with recitatives.

La favorite. Although this four-act grand opera was the third of Donizetti's operas to appear on Parisian stages in 1840, receiving its premiere at the Opéra on 2 December, only about a third of the score was actually composed after Les martyrs was given in April of that year. The balance of the score dates from 1839, but substantial sections of it were taken from a work probably written in 1834. No other score of Donizetti's, especially one that has continued to demonstrate its vitality as has La favorite, possesses a more mixed parentage, and at the same time no work proves more forcefully that a miscellaneous parentage need not be a handicap.

To clear this matter up briefly: La favorite is substantially based on the score of L'ange de Nisida; the production of this opera, written for the Théâtre de la Renaissance, was prevented by the bankruptcy of the theater's management, and the score was returned to Donizetti early in 1840. Parts of L'ange had used passages from a still earlier opera, the incomplete semiseria Adelaide, that Donizetti had started and then put aside perhaps in 1834. These varied origins make the autograph of *La favorite* a challenging palimpsest, for the pages that stem from *Adelaide* have the original Italian words crossed out and supplanted by the French text of *L'ange*; this in turn has been frequently superseded by the different French text of *La favorite*, which imposes what is in large part a different story with different characters upon the music of *L'ange*. Donizetti's unusual knack for assimilating external influences and imposing his own distinctive personality upon them has been mentioned in other contexts, but in the case of *La favorite*, this knack emerges in a different light, for here he takes disparate ingredients from works of markedly different genres and adds to that mixture his most recent compositions and still succeeds in imposing a severe and coherent logic upon them.

The parts of *La favorite* that go all the way back to *Adelaide* include Inès's solo with women's chorus 'Doux zéphir' early in Act 1 scene ii, the main melody of the first Léonor–Fernand duet later in that scene, and the two big finales to Acts 2 and 3. From *L'ange* come most of scene i of Act 1, the Léonor–Alphonse duet in Act 2, the men's chorus with Don Gaspar in Act 3, and all of Act 4, save 'Ange si pur' ('Spirto gentil') borrowed from *Le duc d'Albe* and Léonor's prayer, 'Fernand, imite la clémence' ('Pietoso al par del Nume'), added shortly before the premiere. Music belonging exclusively to *La favorite* consists of Fernand's martial aria at the end of Act 1, Alphonse's double aria at the beginning of Act 2, the divertissement, Alphonse's 'Pour tant d'amour' in Act 3 and Léonor's double aria, 'Ô mon Fernand' that directly follows it. If the presence of Enrico di Borgogna's cabaletta at the heart of Anna Bolena's 'Al dolce guidami' can be taken as an argument for a hitherto unappreciated core of consistency in Donizetti's music, the composite nature of *La favorite* is further evidence of that consistency, as one would hesitate to claim that the finest music of the opera is the exclusive property of any one of its layers.[14]

While *L'ange de Nisida* had been designed for the limited resources of the Théâtre de la Renaissance, *La favorite* was intended to meet the more lavish demands of the Opéra, where spectacle and a ballet divertissement were regarded as essential; the superimposition of the story of the historical Leonora de Guzman[15] upon the earlier plot not only provided a milieu more consistent with the traditions of the Opéra's current repertory, it also permitted the possibility of performances in Italy where *L'ange*, which featured the extra-marital activities of a King of Naples, could never have been given. But in spite of its advantages, the new story of *La favorite* possesses the disadvantage of certain implausibilities. Most of these relate to Balthasar, who is the Superior of the Monastery of Santiago de Compostela; it transpires that he has two children – Fernand and a daughter, who does not appear in the action, but is the wife of King Alphonse. This problem is, at least, obscurely explicable. Balthasar is a member of the Cistercian Order of Calatrava, a mixed religious and lay order of soldiers and monks dedicated to driving the Moors from Spain and allowed by papal dispensation to marry without relinquishing membership in the order. The particular rules of this order explain Fernand's desire to leave it and seek the hand of the beautiful unknown lady who fills his thoughts. A concomitant problem, however, resists explanation. The plot of *La favorite* turns upon Fernand's falling in love with Léonor without having an inkling of her actual status as Alphonse's mistress, and yet, as Balthasar's son he is the king's brother-in-law, a relationship that makes his ignorance scarcely credible.

The musical adaptation of *L'ange* into *La favorite* was complicated by the fact that the role of Sylvia, the heroine of the earlier work, had been composed for Anna Thillon, the English high soprano who had triumphed at the Renaissance as the first Lucie, while the role of Léonor had to be designed, in view of the political facts of life at the Opéra, for Rosine Stolz (the mistress of Pillet, the director), whose voice was a wide-ranging mezzo-soprano. Of the roles composed for her in her heyday, which include the heroines of Marliani's *Xacarilla* and Halévy's *La reine de Chypre* and *Charles VI*, only Donizetti's Léonor made a lasting impression. It was this prominent use of a mezzo-soprano for a serious romantic role, in a work that was widely circulated throughout Italy, that helped to pave the way for parts like Eboli[16] and Amneris. (Mezzo roles like Azucena and Ulrica, on the other hand, are in the tradition of Fidès in Meyerbeer's *Le prophète*.)

Another lesson that Verdi learned from Donizetti came from the overture to *La favorite*, which, as Winton Dean puts it, 'must surely have been at the back of Verdi's mind when he wrote the overture to *Forza* more than twenty years later'.[17] The *larghetto* opening is dominated by a theme in the minor that is put through some contrapuntal paces, and which has a somewhat similar contour to Alvaro's 'Le minaccie, i fieri accenti'. The first subject (C minor) of Donizetti's *allegretto mosso* both looks backward to the similar figure in *Roberto Devereux* (see Example 59) and anticipates all but the driving force of the later Leonora's fate motif. The second subject, a

broad ascending theme, forms a lower (and less distinguished) arch
than the famous phrase at the end of the later Leonora's aria in the
convent scene, but these two themes fulfill a similar function, both
returning for a *fortissimo* major promulgation at the climax. To say
this is by no means to urge that in any sense the overture to *La forza
del destino* is a copy of that to *La favorite*, or that the latter matches
the distinction of the former. To look at both of them side by side,
however, is perhaps to come to a clearer understanding of how much
Verdi reaped in a field that had first been turned over by Donizetti. It
is helpful to note a significant difference of practise here; all of
Verdi's thematic material recurs prominently later in the opera, but
Donizetti re-uses only the broad ascending motif, which emerges in
altered form as the opening phrase of Fernand's 'Une ange, une
femme inconnue' (*larghetto*, 6/8, A major). The beginning of this aria
returns to form the brief prelude to Act 3, but on the whole *La
favorite* employs far less cross-reference of music than does *Les martyrs*.

Fernand personifies the ideals of courtly love with his unworldly
idealism, prompt courage and punctilious sense of honor. The last
trait shines out in one of the famous episodes of the opera – the early
critics were unanimous in their praise of Duprez when he broke his
sword and threw down the pieces at the King's feet (Example 71).

Example 71. *La favorite*, Act 3, recitative before the stretta of the finale

With their clear rhythmic impulse,[18] the heroic declamation of these
phrases (first accompanied by a string tremolo on diminished
sevenths and later by stabbing chords) constitutes a new note in
Donizetti's expressive arsenal, for without any lyric softening of outlines these phrases present the dramatic climax of the opera in a
moment of recitative, but heightened in impact so that it over-
shadows the stretta that immediately follows it. The stretta does

have the interest of a rather gingerly pitting of 6/8 against 4/4, but for all its hard-driving emphasis it comes as an anticlimax after the passage quoted in Example 71.

The royal Alphonse is one of Donizetti's most fascinating portraits. He is every inch a king, but the other side of his nature – sardonic, sensual and corrupt – is always in evidence. He first appears at the beginning of Act 2, where his broadly declaimed recitative 'Jardins d'Alcazar' combines sustained phrases and fastidious embellishments – another instance of Donizetti's search for a French equivalent to Italian arioso – as the King confesses the sexual stimulation he receives from nature. His subsequent *larghetto*, 'Viens, Léonor', with its prominent clarinet introduction and obbligato, is a forthright expression of Alphonse's physical desire; unfortunately the perfumed eroticism of this aria is dispelled by the old-fashioned cabaletta. The amorous note, however is fully recaptured in his subsequent duet with Léonor, in which their opposing responses to the bond that unites them is clearly established; but at the end the King's persuasiveness prevails. In Romantic opera love is usually treated as a fait accompli, but in the characterization of Alphonse in Act 2 Donizetti creates its presence with astonishing success.[19] In Act 3 Alphonse is presented in an even more surprising way. At the end of the preceding act he was delivered a papal bull ordering him to put by his mistress, and now he is faced by a naive young hero who quite sincerely asks for that lady's hand in marriage. All the irony of this situation is positively relished by the half-angry Alphonse in his *andante* 'Pour tant d'amour' ('A tanto amor'), the melody of which is a model of sophisticated double entendre, alternating suavity with ironic insistence (Example 72).[20] This aria is called a trio in the

Example 72. *La favorite*, Act 3, Alphonse's *andante*

score, and the contrasting reactions of Léonor and Fernand to the King's apparent *noblesse* are brief but devastatingly clear. The influence of a baritone like Barroilhet, whose elegant finesse was so different from the melodramatic intensity of Ronconi, becomes clear when a role like Alphonse – the least Verdian of the great baritone parts of Donizetti – is compared with Chevreuse.

Léonor's great scena 'Ô mon Fernand' follows directly on the heels of 'Pour tant d'amour'. The familiar opening phrase of the *largo* can serve as still another example of the stark simplicity of the melodic ideas that Donizetti consistently favors in this opera (Example 73).

Example 73. *La favorite*, Act 3, *largo* of Léonor's scena

This classic restraint is even more apparent in the original French version of this aria than in the better-known Italian translation in which note values are altered and notes are even changed. Léonor's cabaletta, 'Mon arrêt descend du ciel' (*moderato mosso*, 4/4, E major), in which she foretells her death, includes a fully written-out cadenza (just before the coda), which is omitted in Italian scores. Since she is alone on stage for both arias, the motivation for the second reflects her internal conflict, rather than her reaction to some messenger's tidings. In this revealing test of the mezzo-soprano, Donizetti's deep understanding of the particular weight and color of that vocal type stands out; the broad melody exploits the singer's lower middle register, and in the second aria, the single bravura episode of the entire score, the energy of the insistent rhythms and the brilliant scale passages that crest on high A allow her to shine.

Most critics have traditionally held Act 4 of *La favorite* to be among Donizetti's finest accomplishments, and it is not to detract from their judgment to maintain that the earlier acts have their conspicuous merits as well. The prelude to Act 4 alternates a solemn organ melody and a broad cello tune that reappears at the climax of the final duet. After a brief A major chorus, Balthasar sings his evening prayer, 'Les cieux s'emplissent d'étincelles' ('Splendon più belle'), a dignified melody of the utmost simplicity that exposes the serene core of his faith, and at the end, when the bass voice combines with the chorus, there is something very like an allusion to Sarastro's 'O Isis und Osiris'. Fernand's celebrated *romance*, 'Ange si pur' ('Spirto gentil') could scarcely be simpler with its opening sequence of repeated notes on successive steps of the scale, but Donizetti avoids a sense of scantiness by his adroit control of melodic and harmonic rhythm and by varying the accompaniment at the return to the beginning, where the arpeggios become triplets echoed by *pizzicato* strings. A satisfactory performance of this aria requires the utmost vocal refinement and security of technique; the range (up to high C), the long linked phrases, and the repeated upward and downward movement through the tenor's passage notes all provide challenges, but the most important requirement is the singer's ability to cast a spell over the audience so that he holds them suspended and silent, alive to every expressive nuance.

The concluding duet for Fernand and Léonor moves through a whole series of melodic episodes, the keys gradually brightening from A flat minor to the parallel major and finally culminating in C major for their expansive 'Viens, je cède éperdu'. With its relative freedom of structure and wealth of melodic ideas it seems like a composition of a later date than 1840. Performance practise in Italy has been for many years contrary to the letter of Donizetti's original score, and it is high time this abuse came to a halt. The conclusion of *La favorita* as printed in the current Ricordi score (plate no. 46268) adds a brief unison reprise of the 'big' tune (in effect rather like Aida's and Radamès's unison 'Vieni meco, fuggiamo insieme' in the Nile scene), for which there is no counterpart in the autograph. In the French version Balthasar and the monks enter at the very end to hear Fernand's last words, 'et vous priez pour moi demain!', after which the opera closes in B flat minor; but in the Ricordi score Balthasar and the monks are left out and the opera ends in F minor with Fernando's exclaiming, 'È spenta!' over Leonora's corpse. To the best of my knowledge, Donizetti had no hand in these 'improvements'.

For a work designed for the Opéra with its fondness for lavish spectacle, *La favorite* is positively spartan. Except for the obligatory ballet in Act 2, it contains no public or ceremonial music, and it is in every way a more intimate music drama than *Les martyrs*. The contrast between the sobriety of the monastery scenes and the central acts set in Alphonse's hedonistic court imposes a formal balance upon this work. Some of its music is almost austere, as in the chorus that opens Act 1, where the monks sing an ascending and descending C major scale, a setting saved from banality by the subtle handling of the accompaniment. C major is to *La favorite* what E is to *Les martyrs*: the tonality of the minor/major overture and of key episodes in the final act (although at the end of *La favorite* Léonor's death brings the opera to a close in an alien minor key).

In spite of its mixture of sources, *La favorite* must rank among Donizetti's best works, although it slips from its high standard in a few instances, such as the merely efficient ballet music. In some modern productions the opera has been found rather chilly, but this stems from a wrong approach. It is not just another Italian Romantic melodrama, but an elegant French grand opera, and it needs the focus and incisiveness of Donizetti's original setting of the French text to allow its controlled passion to show through its polished surface; further, it needs to be acted with a clear projection of the grand manner.

Adelia. Donizetti's first opera for Italy after his departure from Naples in 1838 was this three-act opera seria, first given at the Teatro Apollo, Rome, on 11 February 1841. The libretto Donizetti was assigned for the work was a vintage 1817 text by Romani; it ended with Adelia's leaping from a balcony, thereby incapacitating herself for a final *rondò*, and several composers who had set it had replaced the last act so as to allow Adelia to participate in the closing moments of the opera. For instance, for Carlo Coccia's *La figlia dell'arciere* (San Carlo, 19 January 1834) a certain Domenico Andreotti had supplied a new ending in his version; Adelia swallows poison, believing that her fiancé, Count Oliviero, has been beheaded by the Duke, but Oliviero appears, inexplicably pardoned, ready to marry her just as she expires. In the early 1840s the Roman ecclesiastical censors would not permit suicide to be enacted on stage, nor would they countenance a tragic ending; therefore Donizetti, unenthusiastically, had to resort to Girolamo Marini's last act for Romani's text, which supplies a *lieto fine*. Later Donizetti blamed himself 'for having accepted a libretto not to his liking, without situations, without passions, without effects, and without verses designed to excite inspiration'.[21]

It is difficult not to share Donizetti's opinion of the poem for *Adelia*. Even the first two acts by Romani are among his dimmer

efforts: the chorus is obtrusive and smug, interminably so, and it is
hard to recognize the poet of *La sonnambula* or *L'elisir* in the turgid
diction. But at this stage of his career Donizetti could not be completely extinguished by a bad libretto, and this score has a fair share
of splendidly orchestrated pages, where the action, however improbable, takes on impetus and life. He even managed to put to good
effect those verses that were designed for the musical structures in
vogue at the time he was writing his first operas. This point is well
illustrated by the first finale. After a chorus in praise of Carlo, Duke
of Burgundy (a full reprise, with new text, of the chorus that opens
the *introduzione*), the material that leads up the *larghetto* gives each
of the four principals a solo passage; at this point in operas such as
Maria Stuarda and *Lucia* the characters engage in dramatic dialogue, make delayed entrances and interact promptly. The older disposition in *Adelia* is more static, but Donizetti is not put off his stride.
In the first of the solo passages, 'Miei prodi' (*maestoso*, 4/4, A
major), the Duke accepts his subjects' gratitude for his victory in
old-fashioned rhetorical terms, but in the latter half of this period the
fleet accompanying figure and the vigorous phrases counteract the
initial impression. Next, Arnoldo, Adelia's father, who believes
that his daughter has been seduced by Oliviero, begs for justice:
'Una figlia, un sol sostegno' (*moderato*, 4/4, F major); against
an urgent, infinitely extendable orchestral melody, Arnoldo's
denunciation is splendidly spirited and emphatic (Example 74).
(As the old soldier thinks of his daughter seduced by an aristocrat,
one cannot help but be reminded of Verdi's Miller and his concern
for his Luisa.) Just as Arnoldo is about to name the object of his
vengeance, Oliviero steps forward with the words 'Io l'amai del
primo istante' (*cantabile*, 4/4, D major). The tenor's protestation of
his sincere attachment to Adelia, over a regular chordal accompaniment, is lyric, syllabic, alternating impetuous dotted rhythms with
even phrases, so that he convinces his hearers of his sincere desire to
marry the girl. Motivic scraps of the melody that accompanies Arnoldo's denunciation bind together the intermediary passages between the solos, but it returns in full to accompany Adelia's 'Se
funesto a' giorni suoi', in which she offers to go far away if this will
save Oliviero's life. Her phrases, however, have a different contour
from those her father sang to the same accompaniment; Donizetti
characterizes her desperation with insistent repeated notes and
half-coherent duplications of text.

So far the interest in the scene and its dramatic momentum have
been maintained because neither the Duke nor Oliviero has appeared

Example 74. *Adelia*, Act 1, first *moderato* of the finale

before, and because Donizetti's music is coherent and reasonably
economical. His most telling effect, however, is to link all the foregoing with the ensuing *larghetto* (9/8, D major) by introducing it with
yet another solo passage for Arnoldo. Furious because his daughter's
offer may prevent his vengeance, he now insists that Oliviero marry
Adelia, knowing the Duke's edict that for a noble to marry a commoner is to be sentenced to death. To a dignified tune of regular

shape, Arnoldo begins his plea, reminding the Duke of his soldierly accomplishments; but then, as he demands that the marriage take place, the tune dissolves into a shuddering *tremolo* with a *staccato* bass figure, and finally he bares his scars to demonstrate that he has earned this favor. The tune is now combined with a countermelody and commenting chorus in a full ensemble. The rest of the finale is on a lower level, as the Duke's granting of Arnoldo's wish is misinterpreted by all but Arnoldo to mean his blessing on the marriage, and the stretta of rejoicing is set to bouncy 6/8.

While the first act is compromised by a slow start and the conclusion to the finale, Act 2 is significantly better. It begins with a beguiling female chorus in dance rhythm as, to the most poetic piece of Romani's verse, the ladies compare Adelia to the jewels they place upon her as she readies herself for her marriage. A clear example of Donizetti's economy in this score is his replacing of a first aria for Adelia with sixteen solo measures that make up the third period of the opening chorus. Oliviero sends her a countess's tiara to wear, and in her cabaletta, 'Ah, non è tal nome' (*allegro giusto*, 4/4, G major), she gaily claims that it is her bridegroom not his title that she cherishes. Oliviero arrives in a somber mood as he has seen a scaffold being erected outside the Duke's palace (Example 75a). This passage comes from the Act 1 duet for Gabriella and Raoul in the 1838 *Gabriella,* but Donizetti adapted it freely, capturing Oliviero's unsettled mood in the nervous rhythmic pattern abetted by the potentially ominous accompanying figure as he confesses to Adelia what troubles him. When Adelia seeks to soothe him, she sings a lyric variant of the passage quoted in Example 75a, without the stressed accents and with the jittery sixteenth-notes smoothed into even eighths so that the music increases in warmth as Oliviero regains his tranquillity in her presence. This whole passage is an object lesson in Donizetti's skill at characterization through modification of melodic pattern (Example 75b).

After Adelia has received a letter[22] that informs her of the Duke's fatal intentions, she is confronted by her father, and in an extensive and highly dramatic *tempo d'attacco* she declares her readiness to die herself rather than go through with this ill-fated wedding; Arnoldo takes her anguish as proof of her guilt. Their duet, 'Ah, non posso, o figlia mia', consists of a *larghetto* section only, in which Arnoldo realizes that he cannot shed Adelia's blood even though he dies of shame, while she remains firm in her determination; structurally, the duet consists of two lyric units for Arnoldo, followed by four agitated measures for Adelia, and then a repetition of the second

Example 75. *Adelia*, Act 2, *andante* of the Adelia–Oliviero duet

(a)

(b)

unit of Arnoldo's melody in which the two voices combine in harmony. The arrival of Oliviero turns this duet into a trio. In a
moderato (4/4, E flat major), 'Ardon le tede', the bridegroom announces that all is in readiness for the ceremony; Arnoldo has
threatened to slay Oliviero on the spot if Adelia retracts now, and in
the trio section that follows the opposing responses of the three are
clearly indicated by the variety of accompanying motifs and by the
contrasting tonality of A flat major. Oliviero salutes his bride in a

beautiful *larghetto*, 'Vieni a' miei voti arrenditi' (9/8, B flat major), which looks forward to the contours of the Norina–Ernesto duet; the melody is first presented as a tenor solo and is then repeated as a trio with Adelia taking the principal part and, at the third phrase, drooping into the parallel minor. The chorus streams out of the church to learn the reason for the delay; their inquiries are made in an *allegro* in B flat, which, as they begin to realize that something is amiss, turns to A minor. Still in that key Oliviero, in an *andante* episode, offers to release Adelia if she does not love him, and then in a sudden shift to *allegro giusto*, the girl loses hold of her reason and bursts out 'Io non l'amo, o ciel, lo senti?' to the main melody (in A major) of the stretta that brings this act to a dramatic conclusion.

The brief last act consists of just three numbers: a superfluous rataplan for male chorus, a double aria for the tenor, and Adelia's aria–finale. The tenor's arias are introduced by a prelude that is imaginatively orchestrated; it ends with a string *tremolando* combined with softly sustained trombone notes against a repeated trumpet pedal and this leads into a brief cello theme accompanied by the basses *tremolando* and barely audible timpani rolls. His shapely *larghetto*, 'M'ingannò la mia speranza', gains coherence because the melodic idea of the second half is anticipated in a figure that punctuates the first half. After a rather four-square cabaletta he is led off, presumably to his execution. Adelia's final scene begins better than it ends. After a brief, impetuous orchestral introduction she enters, still bereft of her wits; her agitated recitative is soon smoothed out into an arioso passage as she imagines herself at Oliviero's feet, declaring her undying love for him. After more expressions of despair for her hopeless situation on earth, her thoughts turn to heaven for her *larghetto*, 'Chi le nostr'anime' (3/8, F major) (Example 76). Her first phrase bears a surprising similarity to the opening of the hymn to Jupiter from *Poliuto* (Example 66), but here the change in meter and the arpeggiated accompaniment produce an otherworldly effect. As the aria progresses the vocal line becomes increasingly florid, but without ever obscuring the basic shape of the melody. Here, one suspects, Donizetti was attempting to reproduce the effect of Anna's 'Al dolce guidami', but, by however little, he missed his mark. The *materia di mezzo* brings the news that the Duke has relented and Oliviero can marry her without fear of reprisal; this development launches Adelia's headlong cabaletta, which bears the self-defeating stage direction that she is to sing it 'breathless with joy'. The reversal is too abrupt and too little explained, and one can only doubt the future happiness of a couple who live in such an unstable environment. The unfortunate libretto of *Adelia* may cause

Example 76. *Adelia,* Act 3 scene ii, *larghetto* of Adelia's aria

dismay, but the music is by no means contemptible and that in Act 2 reaches quite considerable heights of expressivity.

Rita. Although this one-act opéra comique was written in the summer of 1841 after Donizetti's return to France from Rome and *Adelia,* it was not performed until more than a dozen years after his death, being given at the Opéra-Comique on 7 May 1860. An alternate title for the work, *Deux hommes et une femme,* describes the whole singing cast[23] for this amusing farsa on the subject of 'maistrie', as the Wife of Bath puts it. The score consists of eight numbers connected by spoken dialogue. *Rita* is, therefore, a slender work, but in its completely unpretentious way it is as comely as the charming bigamist of its title.

Each of the characters has his own aria, each of them participates in two of the three duets, and all join forces for the penultimate trio and the finale. In this splendidly economical and symmetrical score, Rita's entrance music is the *introduzione*, and motivic figures from the prelude (which, though brief, is in two tempos) overflow into her introductory recitative. The final section of this aria utilizes an effect often found in the closing arias of earlier Italian *farse*, for the heroine addresses the ladies in the audience (as Gilda in *L'ajo* had done, for instance); Rita explains to them that married happiness depends upon having a husband not overburdened with brains, like her Peppe. The plot arises from the unexpected arrival of Gaspar, Rita's first husband, whom she believed had been drowned. Peppe sees Gaspar's return as a heaven-sent opportunity to escape Rita's habit of dealing out slaps, and the sailor Gaspar (who, in a touch designed to spare the sensibilities of the audience at the Opéra-Comique, had sailed away on his wedding day, leaving his marriage apparently unconsummated) has found a girl in Canada he hopes to marry; each husband is therefore anxious to see Rita end up with the other. In the most delightful number of the score, 'Il me vient une idée' (which combines felicitous music with ongoing action), Peppe challenges Gaspar to a game of *morra* (a game for two played by extending their fingers) to see who must have the wife neither of them wants; the recurring refrain of this duet is the ironic notion that the loser is the winner, and these words are set to an engaging E major tune in 2/4 that the two utter separately and then together in canon. The simple but spontaneous idiom of this score can be clearly illustrated by Peppe's aria, 'Je suis joyeux comme un pinson', (*allegro*, 3/8, E major), where his lighthearted relief at thinking himself a bachelor again and free as a lark is expressed in rondo form (Example 77). This aria is not as simple as it looks: its range extends to high B and once even to C sharp (originally intended to be sung *en fausset* – that vocal tradition lasted longer at the Opéra-Comique than elsewhere), and its contrasting periods require considerable finesse. Peppe is rather like a French cousin of Nemorino, and in this aria he brings to mind his Italian relative at that moment when Nemorino has grown tipsy on Dulcamara's elixir.

The resolution of the plot also has analogies with *Betly*. The more worldly Gaspar realizes that the way to resolve this dilemma is not

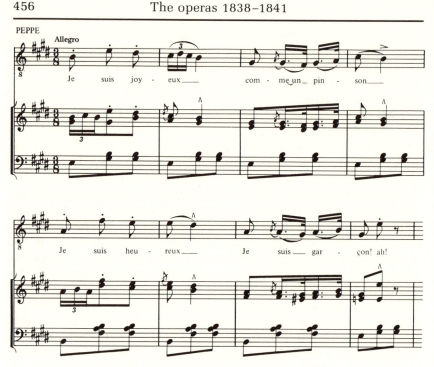

Example 77. *Rita*, Peppe's aria

merely to get his hands on his old wedding contract, but to make Peppe cut a better figure in Rita's eyes. In the trio, 'Je suis manchot', he pretends to have an injured arm and provokes Peppe to the point where he declares, to Rita's delight, that he loves her and wants to stay with her. The brief finale[24] begins with a reprise of Gaspar's entrance aria and ends, as the happy couple bid Gaspar *adieu*, in engaging 3/8 and E major, the meter and tonality in which Rita addressed the audience at the close of the *introduction*.

The basic integrating tonality of Rita is E major, the same key that unifies *Les martyrs*; this unexpected resemblance should discourage anyone who jumps to the conclusion that particular keys had particular associations for Donizetti. *Rita* is an unassuming comedy of character, and Vaëz's libretto, apparently an original plot, makes its slender point with deceptive guilessness. To impose a broadly farcical tone upon this domestic comedy is to endanger the equilibrium of a finely attuned work.

Maria Padilla. The Carnival season of 1841–2 at La Scala saw both Donizetti's return to that stage and the astonishing emergence of

Verdi's *Nabucco*. Verdi's spectacular debut has thrown the other events of that season into eclipse, and the chief victim has been one of Donizetti's richest and most original scores. Sofia Löwe, best remembered today as the first Elvira in *Ernani*, made her first appearance at La Scala in *Maria Padilla*; in December 1841 she was a singer of redoubtable accomplishments, and the vocal demands of her long role have tempted few singers since those of her generation. Donizetti began work on the opera believing that his prima donna would be Erminia Frezzolini, who had triumphed at La Scala the year before as Lucrezia Borgia; but he learned in August that she was pregnant[25] and, as the many altered fioriture in the autograph show,[26] during the rehearsal period he modified, rather than simplified, Maria's music to suit the driving dramatic style of Löwe. To find the prototype of the propulsive, highly figured style of vocal writing for the soprano voice that Verdi provided for his Abigaille and other prima donna roles in the early years of his success one need look no further than *Maria Padilla*.

Maria Padilla, although different in the effect it produces from *La favorite*, is in one sense a pendant to that French grand opera, for it continues the action into the next generation. English-speaking audiences have developed a special interest in Donizetti's Tudor operas, and certainly *Anna Bolena*, *Maria Stuarda* and *Roberto Devereux* amply recompense the effort of reviving them, but Donizetti also provided a panoramic view of fourteenth-century Castille which affords its own fascination.[27] His Castillian Ring-let is if anything less inhibited by any notion of fidelity to fact than are his Tudor operas, but he may be excused as historical accuracy was a post-Romantic preoccupation that emerged only later on in the nineteenth century. Donizetti wrote even more operas on Spanish subjects than on English ones. In the earlier examples a trite brand of *spagnuolismo* emphasized crusading against the Moors, while the Romantic focus was largely nullified by the convention of the *lieto fine*, as *Zoraida*, *Alahor* and *Elvida* illustrate. The first of his Spanish operas to end tragically is *Sancia*, and here the Moorish war motif is increasingly pushed into the background by dynastic concerns. This tendency is carried further in *La favorite* and *Maria Padilla*; in the former the war against the Moors keeps Fernand off stage for the whole of Act 2, while the dynastic issue is raised by Balthasar's delivering of the papal bull at the end of that act, and at the end the emphasis is focused upon the romantic tragedy of Léonor and Fernand. In *Maria Padilla* the Moorish wars are mentioned briefly en passant and the romantic conflict and the dynastic issue are entwined as the principal subject. And finally *Dom Sébastien de Portugal* re-examined these motifs in what for Donizetti was their definitive form.

The rather ambiguous romantic hero of *Maria Padilla* is Pedro el Cruel, the son of Alfonso XI and of his queen, Maria of Portugal. Pedro's reign was dominated by civil war, not against the Moors, but against his bastard half-brother, Enrique di Trastamara, one of the nine children that Leonora de Guzman bore Alfonso. Fifteen years after the events portrayed in *Maria Padilla*, Pedro was defeated, slain, and succeeded by Enrique (the great-grandfather of Ferdinand, the husband of Isabella). Enrique viewed Pedro's death as his vengeance for the murder of his mother Leonora, arranged by Pedro and his mother Maria. La Padilla was Pedro's favorite mistress among many, and she was the daughter of Don Ruiz Padilla, who had been a stalwart follower of Alfonso XI.

Musically *Maria Padilla* has all the Italian exuberance that the comparatively restrained *La favorite* significantly lacks. While the French score has only two cabalettas, *Maria Padilla* is full of double aria structures, and some of the arias that originally did not have two movements acquired them early on. The vocal writing of this Italian opera has more extrovert emotionalism and panache than has *La favorite*: the cabaletta of the duet for the Padilla sisters[28] is the last great virtuoso duet and perhaps the most demanding in the tradition that extends all the way back to *Tancredi*. A more forward-looking example is Pedro's buoyant and virile cabaletta, 'Quitter Marie, toujours chérie', which appears only in the 1842 French printed score, but which, because of the contour of the melody and the pattern of its embellishments, I strongly suspect to have been composed to satisfy some Italian baritone in one of the later productions of the opera; (the autograph of the aria is apparently lost).

If certain aspects of *Maria Padilla* were already old-fashioned when the opera was first performed, many passages reveal a broad sweep and dramatic effectiveness considerably ahead of their time. The orchestration of this score has an overall richness and dramatic allusiveness that reveal Donizetti's development in this aspect of composition. None of his scores makes greater use of the stage band, but here instead of leaving its constitution to chance as he sometimes did, he was careful to specify what he wanted, frequently calling for horns, alone or in conjunction with bassoons. The trumpet sketches Pedro's dynamic personality at his first (disguised) appearance. Motivic ideas recur in varied guises much more frequently than in Donizetti's previous scores and lend many scenes a peculiar sense of homogeneity. For instance, the prelude to Act 3 (*andante*,

6/8, B minor) is dominated by a melody for cello and bassoon, already prefigured in the introduction to the closing scene of Act 1; it also provides the germ of Don Ruiz's offstage romanza a little later in Act 3, and only then does it become clear that the momentary obliteration of the melody by chords in the prelude is an indication of Don Ruiz's derangement and obsession. When the theme takes its definitive shape in his romanza, 'Sento ad ogn'ora estinguersi' (*andante mosso*, 6/8, B flat minor), it is introduced by a cor anglais over harp arpeggios, but when the tenor voice begins to sing, the vocal line is sustained by *tremolandi* on the lower strings combined with chords for the horns (Example 78). This melody returns once again

Example 78. *Maria Padilla*, Act 3 scene i, Don Ruiz's romanza

mi - se - ro!

fa che u - na vol - ta strin - ge - re,

in an episode of the finale to Act 3. Another unexpected ingredient in this score is the introduction of genuine Spanish color by means of the dance rhythm in the dashing introduction to Act 2, and in the opening and closing choral periods of 'Nella reggia d'amore' (*moderato mosso*, 6/8, E flat major).

For all its obvious merits, *Maria Padilla* unfortunately possesses a major flaw at the most sensitive point in the drama – its resolution. In Ancelot's play of 1838, the source for Rossi's and Donizetti's libretto, Maria believes she is secretly married to Pedro, but when she discovers that for political reasons he is about to marry Blanche de Bourbon, she snatches the crown off her rival's head and, declaring that she is Pedro's real wife and queen, stabs herself. The Milanese censors of 1841 were no more tolerant of suicide enacted on stage than their Roman counterparts had been at the time of *Adelia,* and much to Donizetti's displeasure, ironically expressed, ordered that Maria 'die of joy'. Certainly by the time of the second production at Trieste on 1 March 1842, and perhaps even during the initial run at La Scala the ending was converted into a *lieto fine* that left Maria alive and in Pedro's arms, publicly acknowledged as his bride, and the silent Blanche publicly insulted and repudiated.[29] Though this modification makes the ending itself more satisfactory, it negates the important theme of the political machinations of Don Ramiro who hopes to counteract Maria's influence on the King by stirring up the courtiers against her as he advocates the advantages of a marriage with a French princess and the concomitant alliance between France and Castille. The new ending really does not resolve the conflicts of the plot because the obvious, grave consequences of Pedro's marrying Maria and jilting Blanche are simply ignored. Nor would it really improve matters as the libretto stands to substitute Ancelot's denouement with Maria's suicide and Pedro's espousal of Blanche, because then Pedro's decision would lack motive and give the lie to all we have seen and heard from him, making him, finally, despicable.

This serious flaw in the opera's basic dramaturgy should not, however, be allowed to eclipse the great merits that *Maria Padilla* does possess. One of the most effective scenes is that of the abduction of Maria at the end of Act 1, an episode that unavoidably recalls the analagous episode in another opera with a Spanish locale, *La forza del destino*. Donizetti's prelude to this scene, which has a prominent chromatic bass line – Donizetti uses chromatic lines a great deal in *Maria Padilla*, sometimes in inner voices too – introduces Maria, alone in her bedroom, thinking of Mendez, whom she secretly loves. Francisca (the equivalent of Verdi's Curra in this scene) comes to alert her mistress that a plot is afoot to abduct her, adding the startling information that Mendez in reality is Pedro, the King's son. A vivid succession of agitated figures accompanies this revelation, and a stealthy string passage describes their apprehensive glances through the double windows. Maria draws a dagger, claiming that she has the courage of the Padillas, and dismisses Francisca so that she will confront her abductor alone. A *maestoso* passage of self-confident scalar motifs in F brings on Pedro; he is taken aback at the sight of Maria, dagger in hand, who greets him by his true name. They carry on a dramatic exchange over a series of short rising figures that suggest fiery Spanish pride (*allegro*, D flat major), which leads into Maria's ironical *larghetto* (Example 79). The level melodic line, the intervals indicating her scornful inflections, is accompanied by *staccato* figures that characterize her bravado and her excitement. Pedro's answering period is more lyrical and less declamatory, but the continuation and later the intensification of the *staccato* accompaniment sustains the uneasy tension. In the *tempo di mezzo* (*allegro*, 4/4, F minor) Maria's thoughts swing to her father and his undoubted response to this disgrace, and she moves as though to stab herself. 'Live and be my bride', says Pedro, a proposition that she forces him to swear to upon the cross-shaped hilt of her dagger; once his oath is made Maria rejoices at the prospect of a throne in coruscating roulades that introduce the exultant cabaletta, 'A me, o cara, t'abbandona' (*moderato mosso*, 4/4, D flat major).

The vocal distribution in *Maria Padilla* is unconventional in that,

MARIA

Example 79. *Maria Padilla*, Act 1 scene ii, *larghetto* of the Maria–Pedro
duet

since the hero is a baritone, the chief tenor part is that of Maria's father, Don Ruiz; this role was designed for the 51-year-old Donzelli, who had shared Donizetti's first success with *Zoraida* nearly twenty years earlier. Don Ruiz is the most dramatically original of all Donizetti's leading tenor parts, and it gave Donzelli the opportunity to play his own age; the relatively low tessitura – it hardly ever rises above A flat – allowed him to utilize the effective range still left him. In Act 2 Don Ruiz has a double aria, a bitter major cantabile, 'Il sentiero di mia vita' (4/4, B flat major), in which he contrasts his prestige under Alfonso XI with his shame in the days of his successor, while his cabaletta, 'Ma una gioia mi resta', voices his desire for vengeance to an energetic bolero.[30]

It is, however, the mad Don Ruiz of Act 3, particularly in his very touching duet with Maria, who engages one's sympathies most deeply. Maria hopes to earn her father's forgiveness, but when he appears she realizes from his distracted and disconnected observations that he does not know who she is. In an impassioned *allegro giusto*, 'Padre, ah padre, o rio dolore' (B minor), she tries to get through to him and then, at the modulation to the parallel major, where the driving, skittish accompaniment subsides to an even lyrical pulse, she swears she is innocent. Don Ruiz tells her that her beauty reminds him of his daughter and then his mind wanders to a song about an Andalusian fisherman which his daughter used to sing. Don Ruiz begins the song 'Della sera la brezza leggera' (*larghetto*, 6/8, B major) (Example 80). His memory fails him, and Maria takes up the song and weeps at the memories it brings back. In a second *larghetto* (9/8, F major), he marvels that she can weep, while such comfort is denied him, and she repeats his melody, now broken into sobbing phrases, as she cannot restrain her grief at the anguish she has caused him. In the *tempo di mezzo* she reads him a letter that proclaims Maria Padilla to be the legitimate consort, which is signed by Don Pedro of Castille. Hearing that name, Don Ruiz grows furiously angry and snatches the letter from her, tears it up and tramples the pieces beneath his feet. In a cabaletta, 'Uno sguardo', that begins *vivace* (4/4, D major) and grows progressively faster, Maria pleads with him not to repulse her but to accept her as his daughter, while he answers her to a different melody (D minor) made up of broken phrases over a disjointed accompaniment, demanding that he be left alone. An offstage chorus is heard hailing Blanche of Bourbon, which rouses Maria to an even more desperate plea (again *poco più*) not to cast her off as she confronts the possibility of her death and his vindication. This long scene contains a masterly de-

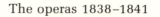

Example 80. *Maria Padilla*, Act 3 scene i, first *larghetto* of the Maria–
Don Ruiz duet

velopment of musical intensity. Clearly, too, this duet is designed to lead toward a tragic resolution of the plot, and its point is blunted by the revised denouement.

Some of the details of the two big concertatos that end Acts 2 and 3 show Donizetti working to lend new expressive effect to the finale. The conclusion of Act 2 develops directly out of the duet of confrontation between the obsessed Don Ruiz and the touchy Pedro, who is supposedly unaware of the true identity of this furious old man who has slapped him in the face with his glove. The *tempo d'attacco* begins in C and moves toward B flat minor as the chorus express their shock, and Maria enters, aroused by the sounds of argument she has heard. Don Ramiro reveals the identity of the challenger to the astonished Pedro and the horrified Maria. But instead of the expected *larghetto*, the stretta follows at once, launched by Maria and Ines in unison in old-fashioned stretta meter, as they deplore the events. Soon Don Ramiro and the chorus are foreseeing the end of Maria's sway, but unfortunately their opposition is superimposed so that their words rarely emerge out of the increasingly hectic and headlong momentum of this movement. This condensed finale comes to a surprisingly energetic, if rather mystifying, conclusion.

The finale to Act 3 combines ingredients of the old-fashioned aria–finale with the dimensions of an enlarged ensemble. The opening section is a full-scale chorus, introduced by alternate phrases for stage band, here enlarged to include trumpets, and orchestra, which hails the bridal cortège of Blanche. After Maria has snatched away the crown, to Pedro's angry reaction she protests her legitimate status in her *maestoso*, 'Giurata innanzi a Dio', while Don Pedro's shocked interjections and the chorus's hostile comments increasingly thicken the texture. The normal sequence of the aria–finale is broken up by the appearance of Don Ruiz in a reprise of his romanza (see Example 78), in which the vocal mass joins (Donizetti pointed out in a note in the autograph that they must be subordinate to the tenor line); in the revised version Don Pedro is moved to contrition by the pathetic spectacle of Maria's father. To this minor-key episode is now appended a broadly diatonic melody in the parallel major; this has an effect rather like that of the tenor's solo line in the *Maria de Rudenz* finale (see Example 62), but here instead of a single voice, the whole ensemble is involved, dominated by Maria's line. In the *materia di mezzo* Pedro publicly acknowledges Maria's claims upon him and defies his political opponents. This proclamation leads naturally into the brilliant cabaletta for Maria, 'O padre, tu l'odi, sua sposa mi chiama' (*moderato mosso*, 4/4, D flat major), which is quite regular in its format, save that in the second statement the ensemble is added at an earlier point than in the first. The finale of Act 3 of *Maria Padilla* then to some extent expands and liberalizes the old traditions of the aria–finale, by giving more prominence to other vocal parts.

As a mixture of new and old this finale points up the strengths and weaknesses of *Maria Padilla*; in fact much of the opera generates enough interest and momentum to disguise most of its liabilities. Yet however lenient one is tempted to be, nothing can disguise the fact that until the final scene this work is aimed toward a tragic conclusion, and the *lieto fine* connects uneasily and contradicts a great deal of what has gone before. Some of the individual scenes, particularly that between father and daughter in Act 3, must rank among Donizetti's outstanding accomplishments. And not for the first time, one finds oneself wishing that Donizetti had worked in a period when the censors were less demanding.

13

The operas
1842–1843

Linda di Chamounix. For this, the first of the two operas he was to compose for the Kärntnertor in Vienna, Donizetti obviously lavished great attention to detail upon a score intended to please the most musically experienced audience in Europe. *Linda* is an opera of *demi-caractère*, contrasting *contadini* and aristocrats in an atmosphere of tenderness and ironic humor tinged with pathos. It is the last and best of Donizetti's semiserie. In this plot the buffo role is that of a Marchese who is an irrepressible advocate of the droit du seigneur in spite of his advanced years; his music has such charm and sparkle that he appears an integral part of the whole fabric rather than the tiresome intruder that such figures all too often seem to be. Unusually for a buffo in a semiseria, the Marchese is, after the leading tenor part, the longest male role in *Linda*.

Linda was written to an Italian libretto by Gaetano Rossi to serve as the highlight of the three-month Italian season at the Kärntnertor, the *haute-saison* of the Viennese musical year. It is difficult not to believe that Donizetti, eager to win acceptance and his court appointment from the Habsburgs, deliberately chose a plot that not only contained nothing to upset the most susceptible censor, but one which positively reinforced those virtues now regarded as Victorian. *Linda* is an opera of sentiment rather than emotion, a celebration of simple domestic virtues, and it results in the triumph of innocence. The plot is dated and demands from the audience a remarkable suspension of disbelief, yet such is Donizetti's skill at creating a forthright and intimate musical atmosphere, at finding just the guileless note of musical rhetoric for his characters' sentiments, that much of the strain upon one's credulity is eased. With *Linda* Donizetti produced an opera quite different in effect from the overt emotionalism of his Italian Romantic melodramas and the massiveness and severity that mark his French grand operas.

One of the clearest signs that Donizetti is on a new tack with *Linda* is the frequency with which he dispenses with either the cantabile or the cabaletta section of the traditional double forms. For instance, the *aria di sortita* of Antonio, Linda's father, consists simply of a *moderato*, 'Ambo nati' (12/8, G major), laid out in three asymmetrical strophes; each begins with the same contour but their individual differences are achieved by extending the melody or by adding a second voice (that of Maddalena, Linda's mother), not by figurations, and the coda consists of simple cadential figures *a due*. At the Viennese *prima* Linda's first entrance, astonishingly, assigned her only an 'introductory' recitative that did not lead into an aria at all; but for Persiani at the Parisian premiere Donizetti supplied a tyrolienne, 'O luce di quest'anima', at this point, which is not a double aria but a typical two-statement cabaletta standing by itself. When Pierotto (a contralto *en travesti*) enters in Act 1, he has two arias, which Donizetti calls a romanza followed by a ballata, but this pair does not form a conventional double aria structure. Both are *couplets*, consisting of two verses with a repeated refrain; both are in the same tempo (*larghetto*), the same meter (6/8), and even the same tonality (D minor, although the refrain of the ballata modulates to D major). The chief difference between them and the justification for their difference in nomenclature concerns their texts: the romanza, 'Cari luoghi ov'io passai', describes Pierotto's own feelings, whereas in the ballata, 'Per sua madre', he tells a sad story that foreshadows obliquely Linda's later predicament. That Donizetti should cast both of Pierotto's simple songs in the form of *couplets* speaks of his experience in writing for the Opéra-Comique, while the terms 'romanza' and 'ballata' relate them to an Italian tradition of nomenclature.

The omission of one or the other part of the traditional double form occurs regularly but not invariably throughout the rest of *Linda*. The first finale is a one-movement prayer, which uses an adaptation of the melody of the prayer from the final scene of *Maria Stuarda*, and the ensemble ends without the customary stretta. The Linda–Pierotto duet near the beginning of Act 2 consists of a cabaletta structure preceded only by a *tempo d'attacco*. Carlo's arias in Acts 2 and 3 are both single-movement cantabiles. The duet–finale is yet another example of cabaletta structure without its full complement of antecedents. Traditional double structures are interlarded between the single ones; only seldom are double structures found in succession. For instance, the Marchese's arias in Acts 1 and 3 and his duet with Linda in Act 2 are double, as are Antonio's duet with the Prefect in Act 1 and the duet between Carlo and the Prefect in Act 3. Donizetti had never in his earlier Italian scores so fully availed himself of the freedom to chose between one- and two-unit forms, although one-movement arias do, of course, occur. Some advantages accrue to Donizetti from his greater exercise of this freedom. He can achieve a more spontaneous sense of dramatic pacing since this score is not generally predicated upon forms requiring an equal dilation of time. He found the cabaletta-sans-cantabile useful to express happy anticipation, as in Linda's *aria di sortita* where she thinks of Carlo, her joyful reunion with Pierotto at the beginning of Act 2, and the duet at the *lieto fine*.

Another feature of *Linda* that deserves particular mention is Donizetti's success at establishing with considerable, though not unfailing, consistency a distinctive tone for each of his characters. Obviously, the buffo Marchese has a traditional idiom that distinguishes him, but the other characters also have their own individual traits. Pierotto's music even has a characteristic instrumental color, that of his hurdy-gurdy (*ghironda*), and in addition the first notes of his ballata serve him as an identifying leitmotif. A useful illustration of this device is provided by the famous pantomime episode in Act 3, where Pierotto leads the poor deranged Linda back to her native village (Example 81). Donizetti begins this passage with the first two phrases of the ballata, intensifying them contrapuntally; later in the episode, which extends to forty-five measures, he uses as a bass figure the characteristic whole-tone interval with its off-beat stress

Example 81. *Linda di Chamounix*, Act 3, Linda's entrance

that begins the ballata, and later still inverts it. In the older dispensation such an entrance would suggest that Linda would now have a
full-scale mad scene, but she has already demonstrated the loss of
her reason in 'No, non è ver, mentirono' at the end of Act 2, a
cabaletta structure appended to her *larghetto* duet with her father.
Not surprisingly, Linda has the greatest variety of expressiveness,
from the gaiety of 'O luce di quest'anima', through her dignified yet
spirited rejection of the Marchese's importunities in their Act 2 duet,
to her participation in Act 3, which, until her mental equilibrium is
restored for the final duet, is limited to occasional pathetic phrases,
exemplifying the restraint that characterizes much of this score.

The tenor role of Carlo is the least well defined, chiefly because of
the ambiguous figure he cuts in Act 2, the most contrived and least
satisfactory part of Rossi's dramaturgy. But even here, where
Carlo appears muddle-headed, Donizetti manages convincingly to
convey his substratum of sincerity (Example 82). At this point in
the plot Carlo has come to the lavish apartment in which he
has innocently set up Linda Manon-style in the hope that soon he
can persuade his aristocratic family, who are trying to force him to
make a more appropriate match, to let him marry this pure peasant
girl. Example 82 is the opening eight-phrase unit of his romanza,
which employs the condensed ternary form that Donizetti often favors; in this form the final section consists of the first two phrases
followed directly by the seventh and eighth phrases, a procedure
that leaves room for the expanded coda. In the opening unit the first
and third phrases are identical (as is the case more often than not),

Example 82. *Linda di Chamounix*, Act 2, Carlo's romanza

CARLO

Cantabile

Se tan - to in i - ra a - gli uo - mi - ni   è __ l'a - mor no - stro, o

ca - ra,   il   du - ro lac - cio in fran - ga - si

di   que - sta vi - ta __ a - ma - - ra: las - sù   nel cie - lo un

ter - mi - ne la no - stra guer - ra a - vrà,   las - sù nel cie - lo un

but the fourth phrase modulates into C minor so as to arrive at B flat minor for the dynamic and harmonic climax before a quiet tonic cadence. This passage, which bears a certain resemblance to 'Ah! nulla di più perfetto' from *Gianni di Parigi* (quoted in Example 32) of eleven years earlier, is striking for its overall spontaneity and unaffected expression. For a composer who ten years or more previously had often subordinated the tenor to other male vocal types – principally the baritone – Donizetti had now come to write for tenors music of real distinction and effectiveness.

The character of Linda's father Antonio is first established in his Act 1 aria, 'Ambo nati', where the familial concerns of this upstanding *contadino* are straightforwardly and gently expressed. His sudden outburst in his duet with the Prefect later in the act catapults the work into the world of Verdian social consciousness (Example 83). Antonio's outrage is unleashed by the revelation of the Marchese's

Example 83. *Linda di Chamounix*, Act 1, *moderato* of the Antonio–
Prefect duet

dishonorable designs upon Linda. His outcry that the privileged
believe the poor to have no sense of honor irrupts with vehement
conviction. It is rather discouraging, then, to encounter the initial
servility of Antonio's approach to the fine lady in Act 2 whom he
fails to recognize as his daughter, but in the *larghetto* of their duet,
'Ah! che il ciel vi benedica', the concerned father begins to reassert
himself and he resumes the idiom of a Verdian parent (Example 84).
Linda as yet does not dare to reveal her identity, though her generosity has already reminded Antonio of his daughter whom he believes
lost. Antonio's broad phrases gain in intensity at the chromatic upward modulation into unexpected D major (the key of the Neapolitan
to the dominant of G flat major), and the contours of their melody are
more than a little reminiscent of the musical language of Rigoletto
and Gilda.

From the foregoing discussion of *Linda* the importance of duet
scenes to the dramaturgy will be strikingly evident. In this opera
episodes of togetherness or of confrontation between two characters

Example 84. *Linda di Chamounix*, Act 2, *larghetto* of the Linda–Antonio
duet

carry a greater weight than the solo episodes. This is the result of a gradual shift of emphasis, which began as early as *Lucrezia Borgia*, away from a principal focus upon vocal display (although this ingredient never disappeared entirely from Donizetti's scores) toward the increasing dominance of dramatic interaction.

Some further aspects of these duets should be explored for the light they shed upon Donizetti's practise at this stage of his career. Probably the best-known duet in *Linda* is the Act 1 love duet, where Carlo launches the cabaletta, 'A consolarmi affrettisi' (*allegro moderato*, 4/4, G major), with an ear-catching phrase that assumes motivic importance later on (Example 85).

Example 85. *Linda di Chamounix*, Act 1, *allegro moderato* of the
Linda–Carlo duet

Of the double duets in Linda this is the only one to employ the
three-statement pattern; each of the characters sings the opening
statement as a solo and then they join to sing it *a due*. Donizetti
creates a striking effect in this third statement by having Linda and
Carlo look around to see if they are overheard before beginning to
sing *pianissimo* and surreptitiously (*come di soppiatto*); the

dynamic reaches *forte* only in the codetta and coda. By the time the duet is over the melody is firmly established, so that at its later recurrences it is immediately recognizable, as when Linda quotes it just before 'No, non è ver, mentirono' at the end of Act 2, when she repeats it not long after her return to Chamounix in Act 3, and most importantly when Carlo sings it to her and restores her reason. In *Lucia* Donizetti made a slight thematic allusion to the melody of the Act 1 duet 'Veranno a te' in the recitative of Lucia's mad scene, and his use in *Linda* of the melody quoted in Example 85 can be seen as a considerable musical and dramatic extension of that device. The only one of the duets that is primarily exhibitionistic in its vocal demands is that of Linda and Pierotto in Act 2, 'Al bel destin che attendevi' (*larghetto*, 6/8, D major); the first half of each statement is a contralto solo, the line growing increasingly elaborate, while the second half puts the two voices through their ensemble paces in figurations of a Rossinian luxuriance. This is the most backward-looking number in the score, and the only one in which Pierotto's simple vocal idiom is not consistently maintained.

The influence of Verdi upon Donizetti, rather than the other way round, might seem to be suggested by the figures of the Prefect in *Linda* and Zaccaria in *Nabucco*, which had made its first appearance a little more than two months before. Both roles were written for the same singer, the French bass Prosper Dérivis who had an extensive vocal range. In the *tempo d'attacco* of his act 1 duet with Antonio the Prefect describes the Marchese's lascivious intentions toward Linda in tones of majestic indignation, which, though they may lack the full thunder of Zaccaria's prophecy, certainly approach it. The same monumental accents pervade the Prefect's description of approaching winter just before the finale to Act 1, in which he prays for the safety of the troop of mountain youths going off to seek work in France.[1] Yet over the shoulders of both these figures looms the shadow of Rossini's Mosè, who had already mastered the same hortatory style.

The merits of *Linda* obviously far outweigh its shortcomings, most of which can be blamed upon the libretto. From the first-rate overture to the buoyant duet–finale there is hardly a page lacking in some distinction. The choral episodes in the *introduzione*, and at the beginning of Act 3, when most of the migrant workers return to their village, are genre scenes that create a sense of the patterns of rural life and produce an entirely different effect from that of the courtiers who populate the Romantic melodramas. The most significant thing of all about *Linda* is the evidence it affords of the mature

Donizetti modifying convention in the interests of dramatic pacing and of exercising his growing skill at individualizing his musical characters.

Caterina Cornaro. Although this opera seria was the last of Donizetti's operas to have a *prima* during his lifetime (at the San Carlo on 18 January 1844), more than half the score was composed in the eight months or so that separated the *prime* of *Linda* and *Don Pasquale*, and therefore this seems the most appropriate point in the survey of Donizetti's works to examine it. *Caterina Cornaro*, like *Lucrezia Borgia*, is divided into a prologue and two acts, and this terminology seems to have the same significance in both cases: the action of the prologue takes place in a location (Venice) a significant distance from the scene of the rest of the action (Cyprus) and is separated from it in time.

The prelude to the opera is a barcarolle (*andante mosso/larghetto*, 6/8, A major); near its close some sense of the approaching conflict arises from an ascending figure leading into an unexpected Neapolitan chord, horns clashing against the tonic timpani roll in the bass. This raw juxtaposition of the minor second prefigures Donizetti's surprising harmonic vigor in this score, in which he often sets out a protracted modulating series and then for particular emphasis reproduces it in a terse sequence of encapsulating chords. After an introductory chorus for the wedding guests, with a coda much longer than the single melodic period, a solo flute over sustaining strings leads into the single-movement love duet for Caterina and Gerardo, 'Tu l'amor mio', which has already been shown to be an alternate version of 'Tornami a dir, che m'ami' in the final scene of *Don Pasquale* (see pp. 260–1). The guests return, but on Mocenigo's orders they are sent away again; the rather lumbering melody of his cavatina, 'Dell'empia Cipro il popolo' (*larghetto maestoso*, 3/4, G major), manages to catch both his egotism and his menace, as he reveals the will of the Council of Ten that Caterina's wedding be halted, for she is to become the bride of Lusignano, King of Cyprus. The alternative to obedience is death, and this last word is shouted against an unprepared series of E flat major chords (the key that stands in the Neapolitan relationship to the dominant of G); abruptly returning to the tonic key, Mocenigo repeats the word 'morte' in his lowest register, and stalks out to a ritornello that is a shuddering reprise of his opening phrase. The puzzled guests return once more, only to be told by Caterina's father that the wedding will not take place; his announcement produces reactions of dismay and anger that are the subject of a hard-driving stretta to the *introduzione* and conclude this opening scene of the prologue.

The second scene takes place in Caterina's bedroom later that evening. Through her windows are heard a chorus of gondoliers singing the barcarolle from the prelude. Caterina is brought a letter from Gerardo informing her that he will return to elope with her. Caterina's romanza, 'Vieni, o tu che ognor io chiamo' (*larghetto*, 6/8, D flat major), expresses her desire for Gerardo in two four-phrase units that are almost identical, and to which is appended a coda of sequences repeated in increasing diminution as her impatience mounts, ending in a (written-out) cadenza. This romanza, to cite one uncommon feature, has a cabaletta, and, to cite another, the cabaletta is connected to the *larghetto* not by a *tempo di mezzo*, but simply by a pair of dominant-seventh chords in the new key (B flat). Caterina's increasing impatience is motivation enough for the *allegro*, 'Deh! vieni, t'affretta'; her headlong melody is built upon a repeated series of brief motivic ideas and bears the uncommon direction that it be sung 'without slowing down or stopping' (that is, to insert more extensive embellishments). In the subsequent recitative her father Andrea and Mocenigo come to tell her that any attempt to escape with Gerardo will result in the latter's instant death, and she is to send him away by telling him that she no longer loves him. The duet between Caterina and Gerardo that follows has a conventional multiple structure; the opening recitative contrasts Caterina's agitation, accompanied by restless figures or incisive chords, with Gerardo's ardent arioso, 'Dolce amor mio'. Misunderstanding the reason for her distress, he seeks to calm her in his *moderato*, 'Spera in me' (4/4, D major); her answer is just half as long and uses a heightened version of his melody. When she sees the threatening figure of Mocenigo in the doorway she forces herself to tell Gerado that she no longer loves him; her words prompt his short but telling *andante*, 'Dunque è vero, bugiardo core', which begins in thudding E flat minor but is cut off after ten measures by a warning word from Mocenigo. Swearing the truth of her words, Caterina precipitates Gerardo's routinely propulsive 'Va, crudel' (*vivace*, A minor/A major), to the rhythmic pattern ♩ ♫ | ♩ ♫ | ♩ which runs its predictable course. The autograph of *Caterina* at the Conservatorio di San Pietro a Majella, Naples, shows abundant signs of the haste with which it was composed; it consists of odds and ends of paper, some of them smudged and in quite a few places nearly indecipherable; the musical results of that haste do not afflict the whole score by any means, but they are clearly to be heard in this disappointing conclusion to the prologue.

The prelude to Act 1, which opens in a piazza of Nicosia, Cyprus, is a *vivace* in A minor, dominated by a folklike melody over a drone bass which creates an atmosphere generally redolent of the Levant.[2] The usual tendency in the preludes that Donizetti provided for particular scenes was to create a sense of mood rather than of place. But the prelude to Act 1 of *Caterina* is an example of the evocation of local color that Donizetti attempted in a number of scores: by using *Home, sweet home* in *Anna Bolena*,[3] a chorus of the gondoliers at the beginning of Act 2 of *Marin Faliero*, a Swiss waltz in Act 3 of *Maria de Rudenz*, a tyrolienne in *La fille du régiment*, and a genre scene at the opening of Act 3 of *Linda*. All these cases show Donizetti's interest in giving a geographical or social ambience to the action he is dramatizing, above and beyond his use of setting and atmosphere to reveal the emotions of his characters. This interest is more often encountered in his later operas than in the earlier ones.

That the prelude to Act 1 is meant to be descriptive is confirmed by Mocenigo's first words immediately succeeding it: 'Sei bella, o Cipro!' As Venetian ambassador to Cyprus he is determined to seize control of the island for the Doge. From Strozzi, the chief of his armed *sgherri* or thugs, he learns that Gerardo has come to Cyprus, and he looks forward to bringing about that young man's death as he sings 'Credi che dorma, o incauto?' (*andante*, 3/4, A major), an aria in that heavy, ominous tone already associated with him. Strozzi joins in for the coda of this aria, and they speak of the sea as a fit tomb for traitors, before they hurry off to foment rebellion. Lusignano now enters, aware of the Venetian threat to his rule and grieving that the unhappy Caterina has been made an implement in the plot against him, but determined to resist to the utmost. His aria 'Da che sposa Caterina' (*andante mosso*, 3/4 bolero, B flat minor/D flat major, ending in B flat major) effectively explores his varied moods in a structure that much resembles a cabaletta. There are different words to each statement, and each ends in a broadly lyrical codetta that occurs first in D flat and at its second appearance ends the aria in B flat major. Here Donizetti adopts the unusual procedure of allotting the first limb of the double aria to Mocenigo and the cabaletta to Lusignano for his *aria di sortita*; moreover, instead of some traditional key relationship between the two arias, the A major of Mocenigo and the B flat minor of Lusignano stand in the Neapolitan relationship that is prominent in this score and which seems to have represented for Donizetti the opposing forces of his conflict.

This aria is followed by a chorus for the *sgherri* with Strozzi, 'Core e pugnale!' (*larghetto/allegro*, 12/8, D major), which through a variety of tempos builds up to a pitch of ferocity and abruptly dies away. As a refrain, throughout, there are shouts of 'Sangue ci vuole!' (Blood must be shed!) set to an unprepared dissonance (a movement from the tonic of C major to a diminished seventh on the leading-tone of A minor). Compared to the ruthless intensity generated by this chorus, the assassins in Verdi's *Macbeth* sound like picnickers.

The thugs move off and soon confused sounds of fighting are heard. Gerardo's voice calls for assistance and Lusignano saves him from his attackers. In the dialogue that follows their relationships to Caterina are revealed. Lusignano asks Gerardo why he does not dare to attack him, and Gerardo replies 'Vedi, io piango' (*cantabile*, 3/4, B flat major) to one of those melodies common in Donizetti's scores, in which an ambiguity of mode is created by an emphasis on the flattened sixth; he tells Lusignano that suffering has taught him compassion. Lusignano's contrasting melody is equal in length but broader, and is decorated with turns – an embellishment that Donizetti usually associated with magnanimity. During the *tempo di mezzo*, as Lusignano's night patrol crosses the back of the stage, there appears a subdued march tune of the type that Donizetti so often used to create an ominous effect (Example 86). (Earlier examples of marches occur in *Anna Bolena*, *Sancia*, and *L'assedio di Calais*.) The cabaletta, 'Sì, dell'ardir dell'empi' (*moderato mosso*, 4/4, B flat major), is *a due* throughout; Gerardo promises to protect Lusignano like a brother, while the King affirms his steadfastness and wishes that Caterina were not the victim of these troubled events. The tenor–baritone friendship duet had proven its popularity with audiences for Donizetti from the Alamiro–Belisario duet in Act 1 of *Belisario* onward.

The second scene of Act 1 of *Caterina* unfolds in the Queen's apartment in the palace at Nicosia; it opens with the customary chorus of ladies-in-waiting who here pay their compliments in 12/8 and E flat major, varied by a different accompaniment for the second strophe. When Lusignano enters, Caterina dismisses the women. The King is weak and ill because, unknown to him, he is being systematically poisoned by his enemies. In the romanza 'Ah non turbarti' (*andante*, 3/8, D flat major) he informs her, in a noble, eloquently inflected melody, that he now knows the cause of her grief (Example 87).

Lusignano's line, so well suited to the baritone's voice, is a classic example of how the mature Donizetti uses embellishments

Example 86. *Caterina Cornaro*, Act 1 scene i, *tempo di mezzo* of the
Gerardo–Lusignano duet

for expressive intensification without disturbing at all the fundamental flow of the melody. This single-movement romanza is connected tonally with Lusignano's cabaletta-like *aria di sortita* in the
preceding scene, and marks again, as does *Linda*, the composer's
increasing interest in single-movement forms. Another effective fea-

Example 87. *Caterina Cornaro*, Act 1 scene ii, Lusignano's romanza

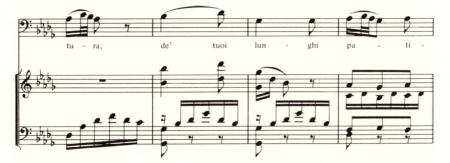

ti   so   la   sto - ria   a - cer - ba   e   du - ra.

ture of this aria is the addition of a second voice (Caterina's), but here in a much more understated way than Talbot's participation in Leicester's Act 1 arias in *Maria Stuarda*; Caterina dominates only in the brief cadenza as she finds Lusignano's tragic generosity almost too much to bear. The eloquence and economy of this romanza inspire admiration.

Shortly after, Caterina and Gerardo find each other unexpectedly in each other's presence. Gerardo reveals to her that he is now a member of the quasi-monastic order of Knights Hospitalers at Rhodes. The lovers' *larghetto*, 'Da quel dì' (6/8, F sharp minor/A major), moves in dialogue form, progressing without a full cadence directly into their *moderato*, 'T'amo ancora' (3/4, A major); here Caterina's opening statement is substantially repeated by Gerardo, but then, instead of a recapitulation *a due*, they both sing a new, more lyric melody. The outcome of this meeting is that they both understand how their unextinguished love must be sublimated because of the obligations they have assumed. It has become clear that from the early 1830s Donizetti was increasingly interested in plots with a powerful love interest, a tendency that reaches its climax in *Maria de Rudenz*; here, however, he explores the dramatic implications of love that cannot be fulfilled, exactly the situation that Verdi would depict so movingly in *Don Carlos*.

In the following recitative Gerardo reveals to Caterina Mocenigo's plot to poison Lusignano, but the Ambassador himself now bursts in and is soon boasting that he will condemn Caterina as an adulteress and accuse her of disposing of her husband, asking 'Who will defend you then?' 'I will', says Lusignano, and this dramatic confrontation begins the quartet (*maestoso*, 2/4, F minor/A flat major) that serves as the finale to Act 1. The first half is a solo passage set in Lusignano's characteristically dignified tone; the second utilizes all four voices, Gerardo's being associated first with Mocenigo's in defiance and then with Caterina's in commiseration. Only near the end is the conflict expressed in brief solo phrases (Example 88). Instead of building up melodic propulsion as it develops, as the *Lucia* sextet does, this ensemble advances by juxtaposing different vocal textures – two voices echoing a single one, or unison pairs deploying contrasting rhythms – to create a powerful sense of opposition, which is emphasized by the sudden separation of the texture shown in Example 88, where the voices are supported only by isolated string figures. In the agitated and harmonically active *materia di mezzo* both sides declare open warfare. The precipitate stretta begins conventionally, but later countermelodies are set effectively against the opening line and surging chromatic figures are added to bring this act to a rousing conclusion.

The brief final act begins with a prelude that vividly describes the fighting raging in the streets outside the palace. Gerardo now comes forward to sing a double aria: a *larghetto*, 'Io trar non voglio', in which he expresses his selfless devotion (*ben spianato* – very

Example 88. *Caterina Cornaro*, Act 1 scene ii, quartet

smoothly – is Donizetti's direction here), and a cabaletta (*moderato marziale*), 'Morte! morte!', in which he rallies the forces of Lusignano with different texts for each statement, ending the coda with cries of 'All'armi!' As the men rush out to join in the fighting, the ladies of the court enter in confusion to sing a vigorously contrapuntal description of the battle. This chorus, 'O ciel! che tumulto!' (*vivace*, 4/4, B minor throughout), with its relentless rhythm and canonic surges that sometimes place the two parts at the interval of a major second, produces anything but the *grazioso* atmosphere common in Donizetti's female choruses, and it makes a powerful and novel effect.

The finale of the opera exists in two forms: the original conclusion provides what is essentially a double aria for Caterina, but with a touching C major *larghetto* for the dying Lusignano as the centerpiece of the *materia di mezzo*; and a *finale nuovo*, first sung at Parma in February 1845, which shifts the main emphasis to the dying King and dispenses with Gerardo (who in the original version had little more to do than to sing 'Addio' twice before the cabaletta, and who now dies in the fighting).[4] In both versions the final tableau features the widowed Caterina, left alone to rule her victorious people. The *finale nuovo* is to be preferred, as it represents Donizetti's considered thoughts on this scene.

In spite of some very striking passages, *Caterina Cornaro* cannot be counted an unmitigated success. Donizetti convincingly projects the noble and generous-spirited Lusignano, but Gerardo and Caterina are much more conventional figures, and a good deal, if not all, of their music suggests that the composer was only fitfully interested in them. (Exceptions to that judgment are Caterina's two-movement romanza in the prologue and her prayer, 'Pietà, Signor', with its somber accompaniment for four horns near the end of the opera.) The passages that really stand out in one's memory are the violent chorus of the *sgherri* and that of the ladies in Act 2, along with the vivid touches of local color and descriptive music. The total effect of *Caterina Cornaro* is dark and tumultuous, and it shows Donizetti's striving to invoke greater brevity, incisiveness and vigor in his score in response to the dynamic Zeitgeist of the 1840s.

Don Pasquale. This three-act opera buffa is unquestionably the most familiar and the most frequently performed of all Donizetti's many operas. If at first glance it seems strange that he should have been involved in operatic comedy at this late stage of his career, it is as well to remember that he had never gone longer than four years without turning his hand to humorous works, and that psychologically they seemed to provide him with a needed relief from the tragic plots that occupied so much of his time.

Donizetti exerted a formative influence upon the libretto of this work but an inhibiting one upon his librettist, Giovanni Ruffini.[5] The composer himself selected the subject and the source for the text – Anelli's libretto to Stefano Pavesi's *Ser Marc'Antonio* (Milan, 1810). Donizetti's adaptation was designed to flatter the particular strengths of the leading quartet at the Théâtre-Italien, with most of whom he had already worked many times: his association with Tamburini and Lablache stretched back twenty years, and that with Giulia Grisi more than ten; only the tenor Mario was a relatively unknown quantity. During their collaboration over the libretto, the poet Ruffini grew increasingly annoyed with Donizetti's apparent intransigence, reaching such a climax of exasperation when the composer preferred what Ruffini regarded as the poorest of a number of versions of the text he had made for the final ensemble that he refused to allow his name to appear upon printed librettos or scores; his identity is hidden under the misleading initials 'M.A.'.[6] Donizetti had neglected to explain to Ruffini that for this final ensemble he was borrowing the music from a song, *La bohémienne*, that he had composed some time previously, and that what he needed was not the most literate text but one that would fit the existing phrases. Nor is this the only self-borrowing to show up in *Don Pasquale*, a fact that further explains Donizetti's apparent high-handedness with poor Ruffini.

It is a further sign of Donizetti's consistency as a composer that he could take a tenor cabaletta, 'Tutti qui spero', from *Gianni di Parigi* (1831) and adapt it, transposed down a fifth, to form the basis for Don Pasquale's 'Un fuoco insolito' (Act 1) without any sign of stylistic uneasiness. In another sense too he was drawing upon a whole lifetime's experiences in composing *Don Pasquale*, for his first exposure to the music of Stefano Pavesi (1779–1850) had been at Mayr's school in Bergamo.[7] Not that he consciously imitated Pavesi in *Don Pasquale*; rather, he applied all he had ever learned about operatic comedy, beginning with those green and topsy-turvy days of the late Napoleonic period when buffa was the dominant genre on Italian stages. While one can argue that *Don Pasquale* is a deliberate exercise in nostalgia on Donizetti's part, it makes more sense to regard it as the culmination of his experience, a representative example of his current practise. To a great extent the comedy of this work results

from the characters' being intensely themselves, and the chief contrivance of the plot, Norina's disguising herself as 'Sofronia', never
entirely obscures her own personality. *Don Pasquale* is remarkably
free of the multiplicity of stratagems and the abuse of coincidence
that are the staple fare of many opere buffe. To an exceptional degree
the traditional comic types (the *senex amans*, the schemer, the soub-
rette and the young lover) are humanized in *Don Pasquale*, and this
emphasis on character and the triumph of character over artifice is
precisely the common denominator between it and such comedies as
L'ajo, *Alina* and, particularly, *L'elisir*. It is out of these comedies, in
all of which at some point the fun is dignified by pathos, that *Don
Pasquale* legitimately springs.

In some ways *Don Pasquale* is not a typical opera buffa structure,
and the often repeated description of it as a mixture of common
ingredients poured into a nearly worn-out mold which by some accident of chemistry turns out a masterpiece obscures more than it
illuminates. *Don Pasquale* is, rather, a fascinating mixture of conventional and unconventional solutions to traditional situations. For
instance, the recitative is distinctly secco in effect, yet it is scored to
be accompanied by occasional sustaining string chords, not by the
keyboard. Then, in Act 1 there is a similar sequence to that in
Caterina Cornaro (a single-movement aria for one character followed
by a cabaletta-type structure for another) when Malatesta's romanza
is succeeded by Pasquale's 'Un fuoco insolito' – a division of labor to
which Tamburini as Malatesta took exception. The most extended
example of Donizetti's turning a double aria into a continuing duet
occurs at the end of the opening scene. Ernesto begins his nostalgic
'Sogno soave e casto' in a lyric vein, but after his fourth phrase Don
Pasquale begins to make *parlando* asides and continues during the
rest of this tempo, even to the extent of having the final word.[8]
Ernesto's cabaletta, 'Mi fa il destino mendico', has a solo first statement, but his irrepressible uncle takes over the middle, connecting
passage, and during the second statement (which omits the first
eight-measure unit of the melody), he keeps up a running commentary against the tenor's phrases, and then shares the coda. In essence,
this is a tenor double aria with extensive buffo commentary.

Not only does Donizetti modify expected practise in these ways,
but he deals even more radically with two staples of opera buffa: the
introduzione and the midpoint finale of imbroglio. Instead of beginning with an introductory chorus, or the sequential arrival of most of
his cast to build up an ensemble in several tempos (as he had done in
Il giovedì grasso and other comedies he wrote for Naples in the

1820s), he provides *Don Pasquale* with only seventy-four measures of *introduzione*, connected almost seamlessly to the rest of the scene. It involves only two characters, Don Pasquale and, later, Dr Malatesta, and consists of soliloquy and then dialogue (the voices never overlap) largely carried on over a rolling orchestral melody[9] that depicts the gait of a fat man restlessly walking up and down; it is briefly interrupted by recitative and ends with a new *staccato* idea that serves as a transition to Malatesta's slyly ironical romanza, 'Bella siccome un angelo'. This *introduzione*, then, more nearly resembles a through-composed episode than the conventional opening of an opera buffa. Instead of the customary midpoint finale using principals, *comprimarii* and chorus, Act 2 of *Don Pasquale* ends with a quartet that dispenses with choral reinforcement. Donizetti manages to make a satisfactory climax with this quartet because he has built up carefully graduated comic tension, underlining and intensifying the continuous action so successfully that the intrusion of any additional forces would only be a distraction. This quartet exemplifies to what an extent *Don Pasquale* is a comedy that concentrates its energy rather than diffusing it.

That there should be a chorus at all in *Don Pasquale* – it appears only in Act 3 – seems to have been decided only late in the composition of the score; Donizetti had to send posthaste to the Countess Merlin to retrieve a waltz he had jotted down in her album so that it might form the basis of the adroit choral interlude in Act 3 scene i. Even though this chorus, 'Che interminabile andirivieni', seems to have been almost an afterthought, Donizetti nevertheless to some extent humanized and individualized the gossiping servants. The only other major part the chorus plays is to accompany Ernesto's offstage serenade, 'Com'è gentil!' at the beginning of the second scene in Act 3. They add a few measures to the final ensemble, but they only reinforce solo lines.

Don Pasquale has been called the most Mozartean of Donizetti's comedies, but that comparison can easily be misunderstood: *Don Pasquale* derives from nineteenth-century Italian conventions and not from the more cosmopolitan eighteenth-century modes practised in Vienna. Although Donizetti had first been exposed to Mozart's scores in Mayr's library, he rarely encountered them in performance. One of those infrequent occasions occurred as early as 1811, when at Mayr's urging the Teatro della Società in Bergamo Alta staged *Don Giovanni* in one of its earliest performances in Italy. Although there was a very successful flurry of Mozart performances at La Scala in 1815–16, shortly after the Austrian annexation of Lombardy, they took place while Donizetti was a student in Bologna. Nor would he have had the opportunity to hear Mozart's works in Bologna, for *Don Giovanni*, the first of Mozart's major scores to be performed there, was not put on at the Teatro Badini until some months after Donizetti's departure.[10] During the sixteen years he spent in Naples, apparently only one opera by Mozart was staged at the San Carlo:[11] *Don Giovanni* received its local *prima* on 6 July 1835, the day that Donizetti completed *Lucia*. While he was in Vienna and associated with the Kärntnertortheater he could have encountered Mozart's comedies on that stage during the German-language seasons, but they did not form part of the repertory of the Italian seasons which were his principal concern.

There is an element of social commentary in *Don Pasquale*, but it takes a rather different form from that in Mozart's comedies. Instead of mingling the landed aristocracy with other strata of society, *Don Pasquale* plays off the old-fashioned ideas and attitudes of the urban middle class against more up-to-date ones. There are, however, traits in *Don Pasquale* that can be said to be Mozartean: vivacity, humanity, a finely attuned sense of proportion, and most of all a rare knack for transmuting the timely into the timeless.

The opening scene of Donizetti's score, as has been pointed out, establishes right away that *Don Pasquale* is no run-of-the-mill opera buffa. The second scene of Act 1 starts with Norina's introducing herself in her two-part cavatina, 'Quel guardo il cavaliere' (*andante/allegretto*, 6/8 then 2/4, G major/B flat major), which compares the old-fashioned world of romances, with their artificial diction and situations, with the outlook of a resolute woman who understands the uses of charm. There is no introductory recitative; the *andante*, in miniature ternary form (four + two + four phrases), fills that purpose, and it connects to the *allegretto*, an asymmetrical cabaletta, without any intervening material. The infectious melody and dance-like rhythm of this *allegretto* are already familiar, for it has served as the first theme of the overture and to introduce its coda, appearing there in 4/4 and D major, first as a *moderato* then as an *allegro*. Norina's double duet with Malatesta, in which she rehearses the role she will play to gull Pasquale, welds both tempos into the most cohesive organism of any of Donizetti's compound structures: both sections are in the same key, they share some thematic material (an effect Donizetti had already used in the Seymour–Enrico duet in Act 1 of *Anna Bolena*), and a single situation advances from the *maestoso* through the *allegro*.

The prelude to Act 2 consists of a trumpet solo[12] (*maestoso*, 4/4, C minor) which anticipates the melody (though not in exactly the same form), that Ernesto will shortly sing in F minor as 'Cercherò lontana terra' (*larghetto*, 4/4).[13] Since it is on an odd page in the autograph, it seems likely that the prelude was composed after the aria; both of them belong to that rather sparse category of Donizetti's movements that end in the same minor key in which they began. There is, oddly, no shift of mood between Ernesto's cantabile and his cabaletta (he remains disconsolate that his uncle has disinherited him and he must give up his hopes of marrying Norina), and no *tempo di mezzo* separates them. The lyrically straightforward phrases of both these arias have a tessitura that most tenors find uncomfortably high, particularly the cabaletta, for it stresses the top fifth of the tenor's range with little respite, repeatedly ascending to the high B flat (though no higher); moreover Ernesto's music rarely descends further than the A flat a ninth below, and from this range it is possible to form some notion of the vocal placement and resistance that Mario possessed at the age of thirty-two.

The comic heart of the opera begins with the entrance of Don Pasquale in Act 2; he comes on to eight measures of scurrying string figures that settle down into jocular wisps of melody and set before us the preening bridegroom. The arrival of the veiled Norina and Malatesta shortly after produces not further recitative but the opening of a trio (*larghetto*, 4/4, E major); the dialogue moves over a rising and falling bass figure, its intervals echoed on the off beats, that suggests the bride's supposed timidity. The main melodic period of this terzetto begins with Norina's 'Sta a vedere', which is divided into three four-measure units: in the first her line is lyric, then as she experiences difficulty in maintaining her composure she breaks into dotted rhythms, finally dissolving into irrepressible roulades. Nothing could be more apt than Donizetti's depiction of the successive stages of her amusement. During the intermediate section (G major back to the tonic of E) Malatesta introduces Don Pasquale to 'Sofronia', and now upon the timid bass line from the opening is superimposed a countersubject that suggests the bridegroom's ingratiating approach. Norina feigns horror at finding herself in the presence of a strange man and wants to escape at once, but her agitated line only provides the link leading back to the repetition of 'Sta a vedere', and the contradiction between these words ('wait and see') and her previous talk of flight produces just the sort of absurdity that Donizetti loved to exploit.

The following recitative, sparsely accompanied save for the *tremolandi* and agitated figures that depict Pasquale's eagerness, is

filled with little touches of parody, with references to earlier music
and even with puns. When Pasquale simpers over Norina's hand the
violins repeat a languishing figure used frequently in the accompanied recitatives of older operas; it serves here to locate the source
of his manners that seemed old-fashioned in 1843. When Malatesta
orders Norina to remove her veil, he deliberately plays upon the
word 'velo', saying 'Ve lo commando'. The languishing figure recurs
as Malatesta turns to Norina to encourage her to reply to Pasquale's
proposal. Norina's one word, 'Sì!', is set to F natural against the G
orientation of the recitative at this point and catches 'Sofronia's'
gaucherie in a single note.

The quartet (beginning *moderato*, 12/8, C major) opens with
Malatesta dictating the terms of the marriage contract to the Notary
(really Malatesta's cousin Carlotto in disguise) all on a dominant
monotone against an almost blowsily sentimental melody in the orchestra. The need of a second witness for the contract is met by
Ernesto's untimely arrival (a comic counterpart of Edgardo's irruption into Act 2 of *Lucia* at the signing of that contract), and this sets
off the richest parody of the act. A vigorous *allegro* (A major) featuring a brusque descending figure that alternates between the basses
and the violins, accompanies Ernesto's scornful address to his uncle,
'Pria di partir, signore'. The contrast between this moment of broad
declamatory style and the *parlando* that has dominated much of this
scene produces just the note of exaggeration that Donizetti sought.
Not that Ernesto is not perfectly in earnest, but since the audience
has always been aware of Malatesta's scheme as the scene has un-
folded, the effect of his indignation is undercut and seems to be a
parody of itself.

After this moment of 'serious' relief, Malatesta restores the comic
equilibrium with 'Ah, figliuol non mi far scene', in which again vol-
uble roulades are equated with barely restrained mirth. This section
of the quartet (*allegro moderato*, 4/4, C major) consists of just twenty
measures dominated by Malatesta's figured line. It is succeeded by a
moderato (6/8, F major), a lengthy *tempo di mezzo* that exploits
'Sofronia's' volte-face once the contract has been signed. Donizetti
supports the vocal parts with a wealth of accompanying figures,
emphasizing them now and again by doubling them in the vocal
line. The most important of these is a four-note ascending sequence
that formed Norina's line to the words 'Vado, corro' at the beginning
of the *allegro* of her duet with Malatesta. Norina's increasingly outrageous behavior ultimately has the effect of turning Don Pasquale
rigid with amazement. Seeing the old man's condition, Malatesta

sings a broad phrase, 'È rimasto là come impietrato' (*adagio*, 4/4, E major), which is variously imitated in the other parts and is finally sung in unison. The situation is one that Donizetti had already employed in *Alina* (see Example 30), but behind it stands the example of Bartolo in Rossini's *Il barbiere* at the moment of 'Fredda ed immobile'. For its spontaneity and musical grace this *adagio* stands as the crown of the second act.

During another intermediate section Norina behaves even more outrageously, planning to hire a staff and refurnish the house; much of her music is accompanied by a droll figure that perfectly reflects her restless imagination. This transition to the stretta is built upon a protracted modulation to D major from the dominant side. The stretta, 'Son tradito, son tradito',[14] possesses considerably more rhythmic and melodic variety than Donizetti usually lavished on this section of his finales. Particularly striking is a five-note phrase, first sung by Ernesto ('Sono, o cara'), which recurs in each of the parts always in real rather than tonal imitation. The extended coda of the stretta begins as though it were going to be a second statement of 'Son tradito' but it soon veers off into the vocal cadences, less excessive in their profusion here than in some of Donizetti's strettas. Among the works of a composer whose talent as a writer of ensembles had early been recognized as far above the ordinary, the terzetto and quartet from Act 2 of *Don Pasquale* assume a very high place, both for their air of spontaneity and the refinement of the part-writing.

Act 3 begins with a brief scene for the chorus, which is labeled '*introduzione* to Act 3' in the score, and which more closely resembles a traditional opening than does the *introduzione* to Act 1. It begins with several solo parts for choristers, and then the whole group shout as they rush around doing Norina's bidding; in the middle of them Pasquale observes that his well-ordered home has become a madhouse. Soon Norina appears, elaborately dressed, to go to the theater, her entrance launching the *tempo d'attacco* of her duet with Pasquale, 'Signorina, in tanta fretta'. Her determination to have her way and his opposition create a confrontation that culminates in Norina's slapping the old man's face. A little A minor tune in detached phrases makes Pasquale's disillusionment palpable, and the spectacle of his shocked awareness of the consequences of his folly is touching (Example 89).

This melody returns, extended, in the relative major at Norina's 'È duretta la lezione' as the emotion expands and in an aside she reveals that she too is touched by Pasquale; one of the devices that makes her feeling convincing is Donizetti's use of the Schubertean

Example 89. *Don Pasquale,* Act 3 scene i, *larghetto* of the Norina–Don Pasquale duet

procedure of modulating from C to D flat and back again. The concluding section of this duet is in ternary form ending in a coda: the framing sections are formed by Norina's 'Via, caro sposino', which derives from a cabaletta Donizetti wrote for Tadolini to introduce into *L'elisir* at Naples; the contrasting middle section, Pasquale's 'Divorzio, divorzio', is as emphatic as Norina's melody is serene and lilting.

After an interlude in which the servants gossip, Don Pasquale returns with Malatesta to decide what course of action he should take as a result of a note he has found indicating that 'Sofronia' plans a rendezvous in the garden that evening. The two men plot their moves to catch the lovers in 'Cheti, cheti, immantinente', in which Malatesta persuades the old man that it would more tactful if the two of them alone sprang their surprise.[15] Pasquale's melody is repeated by Malatesta and leads into one of the most naturally handled of all of Donizetti's *tempi di mezzo*; it seems to continue unabated the dialogue of the opening and its motivic accompaniment derives in modified form from the melody of the first unit. Their cabaletta,

'Aspetta, aspetta, signorina' (*moderato mosso,* 6/8, F major) has the standard three statements, two solo and one *a due* and in unison, each consisting of a melodic idea followed by whirlwind *parlando;* but Donizetti introduces variety into this structure by using new material to lead into the climactic unison delivery of the *parlando.* The sight of these two grown men plotting like naughty little boys and getting carried away by their own ingenuity (even though Malatesta is perfectly aware that 'Sofronia's' note is simply part of the plot) is reinforced by the exuberant music and the canny exploitation of the buffo afflatus. (This duet, by the way, did not assume its definitive form until the production that Donizetti mounted at the Kärntnertor in 14 May 1843, four months after the Parisian *prima.*)

The second scene of Act 3 takes place in the garden of Pasquale's villa; it begins with Ernesto's offstage serenade, 'Com'è gentil!' (*andante mosso,* 6/8, A major), which introduces the romantic aura that has been conspicuously absent up to this point. Until now even the apparently sad or pathetic or serious moments of the plot have been modified by the audience's awareness of the underlying ruse, but as the tenor's voice, accompanied by chorus, guitars and bass drum, floats over the empty stage the comic tension is relaxed and supplanted by youthful longing. The serenade consists of two asymmetrical strophes, the second lengthened and the harmony enriched by the choral imitation of the guitar parts. The romantic atmosphere is heightened by the immediately succeeding *notturno,* Norina's and Ernesto's duet, 'Tornami a dir, che m'ami' (*larghetto,* 9/8, A major), which is introduced by woodwinds in sixths, accompanied by arpeggios in the second clarinet against sustained chords for the bassoons. The double vision of events that this comedy provides – the simultaneous view through the eyes of Norina and Pasquale – lends sincerity to this duet, which after all has its musical roots in an opera seria since it derives from the prologue to *Caterina Cornaro.* The finale opens with recitative and the brief *tempo d'attacco* (G major) begins at the point at which Pasquale agrees to allow Ernesto to marry Norina; it leads directly into the *rondò*–finale, 'La morale in tutto questo' (*allegro moderato,* 6/8, B flat major), in which two phrases for Malatesta introduce the theme of Norina's cabaletta. The finale reconciles the old-fashioned and the up-to-date by setting an eighteenth-century pointing-up of the moral to a nineteenth-century dance rhythm.

Maria di Rohan. This three-act seria is the second of the two operas Donizetti composed for Vienna, and it received its *prima* at the

Kärntnertortheater on 5 June 1843. During the half-century from the 1830s to the 1880s Romantic melodrama was the dominant type of Italian opera, and the foregoing discussions of Donizetti's works have demonstrated the major part he played in establishing this dominance. His earliest experiment with Romantic melodrama was *Gabriella di Vergy* in its first version of 1826. His last is *Maria di Rohan*, the most legitimately melodramatic in his long list and the one which contains the most cumulatively powerful solution he ever provided to the aesthetic problems posed by this type of plot.

Simply put, the basic demand for Romantic melodrama is that the composer give musical coherence and credibility to an intense plot whose denouement is tragic and inevitable. To attain this Donizetti had gradually been moving in three related directions. First, his arias, particularly *sortite*, became more concerned with the revelation of character than with vocal display; this tendency can be illustrated by the sequence of Elisabetta's *aria di sortita* in *Il castello di Kenilworth*, Lucia's 'Regnava nel silenzio' (see Examples 48–9), and Maria de Rudenz's, 'Sì, del chiostro penitente' (see Example 61), where the shift from embellishment as a gracing of melody to an illustration of a dramatic idea can be clearly seen. Second, he increasingly subordinated arias to duets and larger ensembles. This tendency was already well-developed in Act 1 of *Lucrezia Borgia*, where the Lucrezia–Alfonso duet (with its forward-looking diversity of statements in the cabaletta) is capped by the trio. A corollary to this point is his inclination in his later operas to combine aria units with ensembles. Two different approaches to this solution may be exemplified by the aria–ensemble–finale to *Maria Padilla* and by the aria-cum-quartet in the Act 1 finale to *Caterina Cornaro*. Third, he became increasingly concerned not just with mounting dramatic tension (as in the last act of *Roberto Devereux* where each of the three scenes contains only one double form and requires about the same playing time), but with a quickening of dramatic pacing; this is especially clear in *Maria di Rohan* where the passage of time is a function of the plot. In his last operas Donizetti moved toward more streamlined forms and greater use of single structures, even sometimes dividing double ones between two different characters. All these tendencies can be seen by a quick comparison between *Lucia* and *Maria di Rohan*. The more episodic structure of the former is spread out over three acts with a total of seven scenes; the latter undergoes what might be described as a vortical compression, being in three undivided acts, each shorter than the last.

As always with Donizetti, the singers for whom he wrote played a significant part in the shaping of *Maria di Rohan*; writing with particularly gifted interpreters in mind, to judge by his letters, stimulated his creative imagination. The cast on this occasion was to include Eugenia Tadolini and Giorgio Ronconi. As a singing-actor, Ronconi had proved a fruitful challenge to Donizetti's imagination since the time of Il furioso, a decade earlier. In Chevreuse, the composer presented him with a towering role; the chief characteristic of that impersonation as Ronconi appeared at the end of Act 3 was what critics of his day were fond of describing as 'terribilità'. Chorley left a vivid vignette of Ronconi in this role which is particularly worth quoting because it not only describes the impact of the performer but reveals a Victorian critic's response to the dramatic values of the opera itself:

> There have been few such examples of terrible courtly tragedy in Italian opera as Signor Ronconi's Chevreuse, the polished demeanour of his earlier scenes giving a fearful contrast to the later ones when the torrent of passion nears the precipice . . . the terror of the last scene, when (betwixt his teeth, almost) the great artist uttered the line, "Sull'uscio tremendo lo sguardo figgiamo", clutching, the while, the weak and guilty woman by her wrist, as he dragged her to the door behind which her falsity was screened, was something fearful, a sound to chill the blood, a sight to stop the breath.[16]

The original Maria di Rohan was Tadolini, for whom Donizetti had written a very different sort of role in Linda the previous year. More people know about a letter Verdi wrote to Cammarano protesting about Tadolini's selection for the role of Lady Macbeth than that she actually sang the role in spite of his remonstrance. Part of this letter deserves quotation in this context, since the traits that Verdi objected to are precisely those that five years earlier had made her a cherishable Maria di Rohan.

> If the part of Lady Macbeth is given to Tadolini, and I am amazed that she could have agreed to play that role – you know how much esteem I have for Tadolini and she herself knows it – . . . in our common interest I believe it is necessary to make some observations to you.
> Tadolini has too many great qualities to play that part! Perhaps this will strike you as an absurd thing to say!! . . . Tadolini has a fine and beautiful figure, and I would want Lady Macbeth to be ugly and evil. Tadolini sings to perfection, and I would prefer the Lady not to be able to sing. Tadolini has a stupendous voice, clear, pure and powerful; and I would prefer in the Lady a voice that is harsh, choked and somber. The voice of Tadolini has angelic qualities; the voice of the Lady Macbeth that I would want would have diabolic ones.[17]

Donizetti's own estimate of Tadolini at the time of Linda was: 'She is a singer, she is an actress, she is everything.'[18]

In the discussion of Linda, it was noted that the heroine's aria 'No, non è ver, mentirono' underplayed the mad-scene tradition, reducing it to a cabaletta without, save in the codettas, any demand for virtuosity. Even more striking is the starkness of expression in Maria's *aria di sortita*, 'Cupa, fatal mestizia' (*andante mosso ma non troppo*, 3/4, A minor/A major), where a brief cadenza before the final vocal cadence is her single flourish. Maria is torn between love and duty, her conscience is deeply troubled with the painful awareness that Chalais is ignorant of her secret marriage to his rival. The introduction to the aria makes no reference to the singer's melody, but simply announces a bass *pizzicato* figure that rises in a *crescendo* and falls growing softer; this figure dominates the accompaniment. Maria's first phrase is the tragic counterpart of the pathos of 'Una furtiva lagrima', beginning with the same interval of the descending fifth. The succeeding phrases are inexorably regular until Maria mentions that the hours of her life (the first allusion to the recurring motif of the passage of time) are filled with grief; the expansion of the melody on the word 'dolore' vividly conveys that her life passes in a blur of sadness (Example 90a). In the context of the major key (the music has moved from A minor to C) the chromatic contrary motion accompanying 'dolore' suggests that she has lost her emotional bearings. The *pizzicato* bass of the opening is repeated and the second strophe varies the first in every phrase; but it takes a new direction, modulating into the parallel major and expanding in quite a different way from that shown in Example 90a (Example 90b). The nervous accompaniment is replaced by string *tremoli* with sustaining woodwinds, and Maria's arching melody both heightens and distills her emotion.

To some extent it seems that Maria is here approaching the expressive vocabulary of Amelia in *Un ballo in maschera*, yet what remains peculiarly Donizettian about this coda is that the modulation to the major does not dissipate the tragic tone of the minor opening but, rather, intensifies it, for as Maria says, to reveal her grief would be a serious error. There is a remarkable dramatic irony in this major ending; it portrays the discrepancy between the external beauty and poise of the lady at court and the miserably unhappy woman she is at heart. 'Cupa, fatal mestizia' is one of Donizetti's highest achievements as a psychological portraitist. The reappearance of the scalar figure in the bass after Maria's last phrase makes for a finely economical ritornello. The ensuing cabaletta, 'Ben fu il giorno' (*allegro giusto*, 12/8, G major), is motivated by Maria's gratitude that Chalais has used his influence with the King to secure a pardon for Chevreuse, who has killed Richelieu's nephew in a

Example 90. *Maria di Rohan*, Act 1, *andante mosso ma non troppo* of
Maria's *aria di sortita*

(a)

duel; it follows a conventional path until the expansive *dolce*
codetta where the melody broadens and moves into the key of the
dominant.

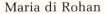

The whole first act of *Maria di Rohan* has a spaciousness that results from the seriatim introduction of four characters, each with his *aria di sortita;* it creates a slowpaced beginning that contrasts with the faster-moving later parts of the opera. Maria is the second of the characters to enter, but her aria has been described first because the *larghetto* exemplifies the dramatic incisiveness that animates this opening act, which at first glance seems discouragingly episodic. After the opening chorus, the first solo character to appear is Chalais, who has been summoned by a note from Maria, once his mistress, begging his assistance. Chalais's *sortita* consists of a somewhat unconventional double aria: 'Quando il cor da lei piagato' (*larghetto*, 6/8, B flat major) is followed without any *tempo di mezzo* by the cabaletta, 'A te, divina immagine' (*moderato*, 4/4, D flat major). The *larghetto* is asymmetrical (first quatrain of text: eight measures; second quatrain: sixteen measures), but the melody expands so spontaneously, relying more on motivic intensification than on exact repetition of phrases, that it can be said to be a single-unit form. The material separating the two statements of the cabaletta is accompanied by a descending scalar passage which returns first in the coda and again to depict the agitated entrance of Maria. Here Donizetti streamlines the conventional aria patterns and uses musical ideas to form interconnections between succeeding episodes.

The third of the characters to be brought forward is Armando di Gondì, a womanizing gallant whose chief mode of expression is effrontery. This part was sung at the Vienna *prima* by a *comprimario* tenor, but for Paris Donizetti sought to add a note of ironic relief to the work by enlarging the role of Gondì and reworking it for contralto *en travesti*; in this form it was designed for Marietta Brambilla, who had been the first Maffio Orsini. Gondì's revised *aria di sortita*, 'Per non istare in ozio' (*moderato*, 4/4, C major) is in the form of *couplets*, in which the jaunty tune of the refrain is echoed by the male chorus. Gondì's one-movement aria provides the scherzo for this act, but it has serious consequences, for when he reveals that the woman whose pursuit he has mockingly described is Maria herself, Chalais promptly challenges him to a duel. Moments later Chevreuse enters, having come straight from prison to court to thank Chalais for securing his freedom. His *moderato*, 'Gemea di tetro carcere' (4/4, C minor/E flat major), consists of two contrasting strophes: the first is impulsive and energetic, while the second, a lyrically expansive melody that moves into the key of the dominant, is marked *dolce*. Unlike those minor–major arias that delay the modulation until a climactic phrase near the end, here Donizetti places it inconspicuously in the middle of the first strophe. Chevreuse's cabaletta, 'Se ancor m'è dato stringerti' (*moderato assai*, 4/4, A flat major), an aside addressed to Maria, contains a clear example of Donizettian *morbidezza* (Example 91). The raised appoggiaturas (A natural and B natural) at the cadences of the first two phrases are balanced by the

CHEVREUSE

Example 91. *Maria di Rohan*, Act 1, cabaletta of Chevreuse's aria

descending chromatic movement at the end of the third, giving the
melodic movement a sensuous intensity. The tessitura of this cabaletta,
never lower than A flat at the top of the staff and rising to F above it,
reveals how far Donizetti had come in exploiting the baritone's brilliant upper register.

After Chevreuse has volunteered to serve as his friend's second in
the duel with Gondì, he discloses that for a year he has been married
to Maria, and that he has had to dissemble hitherto because
Richelieu's nephew wanted to marry her himself. This disclosure
prompts the mixed response of the *andante* to the finale. It is built
up in twelve-measure units (*a a' b* coda), and the texture is gradually enriched. The first unit is a solo for Chevreuse, 'D'un anno
il giro', which is followed by a variant of the opening melody sung
by Maria who is at a few points joined by the baritone; then Chalais,
stunned by the unexpected news, takes up a second melodic idea,
his line reinforced by Maria's at climactic points. Only in the coda
does the full quintet sing together and the chorus join. In the brief

materia di mezzo a courtier announces that Richelieu has been supplanted as prime minister by Chalais. In the succeeding stretta of rejoicing (*vivace*, 6/8, D major) an eloquent unison melody is set off against a second subject in the minor for Maria and Chalais and the stretta ends in a brief coda of phrases in chromatic sequence. Just before the final cadences a terse exchange between Chalais and Gondì recalls their approaching duel. This stretta succeeds very well in suggesting the disparity between the external appearance that all is well and the conflicting forces hidden beneath the surface.

In his room, Chalais writes a letter, to the accompaniment of a *cantabile* melody for the strings in C minor, and gives it to his confidant Aubry, with orders to deliver it if he fails to survive the duel. Chalais's dying mother lies in an adjoining room, and in an eloquent arioso passage in A minor he thinks of the eternal sleep awaiting them both. Then he begins a splendid one-movement aria, 'Alma soave e cara' (*cantabile*, 3/4, A major), which is similar in some ways to Leonora's 'Mira d'acerbe lagrime' in *Il trovatore*.[19] The melody of the opening of the final section (Example 92) is that of the opening of the aria, but then with the unexpected movement into B minor at the beginning of the third phrase it takes a new course. The harmonic contrast between the third and fourth phrases, beginning with G natural and G sharp respectively, colors the distinction between love on earth and love in heaven. A variant of the opening melody in the orchestra introduces the two cadential phrases, and the vocal line ends, uncommonly for Donizetti, on the note of the mediant rather than the tonic. This passage is a model of the type of Donizettian expressivity that has nothing to do with exhibitionism.

Gondì now pushes his way in to demand an hour's delay in the duel so that he can keep a rendezvous; he sings a purposely fatuous one-movement cavatina, 'Son leggero è ver', in which his liberal roulades bespeak his affectation and create a marked disparity of tone with Chalais's immediately preceding cavatina. Maria enters masked, and Gondì retires upon an ironic allusion to the refrain of his Act 1 *couplets*. Maria has come to tell Chalais that he must flee for his life, as Richelieu has returned to power. She has barely given him this news when Chevreuse's voice is heard outside, coming to second Chalais in the duel, whereupon Maria is hidden in a nearby arms store.

The scene between Chevreuse and Chalais consists of two main sections, an *andante* in free form, and a *moderato* that disguises their conflicting concerns under the idiom of a conventional friendship duet; a connecting bridge that leads from one to the other alter-

Example 92. *Maria di Rohan*, Act 2, Chalais's aria

nates *vivace* with slower tempos. The *andante* is particularly notable for the way in which much of it floats upon one of those sinuous,
extendable motifs that continually modulates. Dramatic irony is developed here in a number of ways. Chalais cautions Chevreuse to
speak softly so as not to disturb his mother, but when he tries to
prevent Chevreuse from entering the armory to select a sturdier
rapier Chevreuse takes up his words humorously, assuming that
Chalais's extreme agitation is caused by the presence of some other
lady nearer his age; more ironical still, Chevreuse does not suspect
that the woman concealed in the armory is his own wife. The complexity of motivation in this scene leads Donizetti to treat it with
great flexibility, particularly in the *andante* and in the dissolving
coda to the *moderato* conclusion, where the sinuous chromatic harmonies convey the implicit danger of this encounter (Example 93).
The finale to Act 2 (which Donizetti revised after the Viennese
prima), takes the form of a protracted duet for Maria and Chalais, in
which the pressure of time is forcibly felt. Chalais's sense of honor
insists that he go to fight the duel with Gondì, but Maria uses every
argument she can to detain him. The tolling of the clock from the
nearby Louvre marks the passing of time. Only at the end of the
scene, when word comes that Chevreuse is prepared to fight in his
place, does Chalais tear himself away. The *tempo d'attacco* (*allegro*,
4/4, B flat minor) is cued by the clock's striking, and it consists of
agitated dialogue over detached motifs that drive toward a coherent
surging melody. The centerpiece of this duet is Maria's declaration
of her unextinguished love for Chalais, 'Ah, s'io pur mi disonoro'
(*larghetto*, 3/8, B flat major), where her arching melody, simply accompanied by arpeggios, urges its sincerity in a series of drooping
suspensions. Not since the first aria of her *sortita* have the true
feelings of Maria, whom circumstance has forced to dissemble
much, been so clearly and movingly revealed.

Act 3 begins with a thirty-measure prelude in two tempos; first a
larghetto in which four horns intone a sad melody that begins and
ends in C major but keeps straying into the minor mode; then an
allegro that restates the first theme of the overture in a *crescendo*
surge that is abruptly cut off as the horns return for the cadence,
pianissimo. The curtain rises on a room in Chevreuse's *hôtel*, from
which, it is later revealed, a secret passage connects with the city
walls. Chevreuse has fought the duel in Chalais's place since Chalais
arrived late at the appointed place, and he has sustained a wound on
his arm, which he dismisses as slight. Chalais and Maria are with

Example 93. *Maria di Rohan*, Act 2, *moderato* of the Chalais–Chevreuse
duet

(When CHEVREUSE exits, CHALAIS closes the door and hastens to the closet where MARIA is hiding.)

him, but he soon leaves them alone. In another duet Maria begs
Chalais to escape, her line in the opening *larghetto* combining
gruppetti with insistent repetitions of notes and intervals as she urges
him to get away while there is still time. In his reply he takes over
her melody in the key of A flat, instead of the original F, before
reverting to her key and a simplified version of her phrases as he
declares he would rather live or die with her than leave her. The
second section of this duet, with the voices entirely *a due*, involves
no shift of tempo or key or meter. Aubry arrives to tell Chalais that
his papers have been seized, among them his letter confessing his
relationship with Maria. Chevreuse returns to show Chalais the secret passage, telling him that all arrangements have been made for
his escape. Chalais follows him out, but not before he can whisper to
Maria that if she does not join him in an hour he will return for her.

Left alone, Maria prays in her aria, 'Havvi un Dio che in sua
clemenza' (*larghetto*, 6/8, beginning and ending in F minor). A cor
anglais introduces her melody and later reinforces it, lending a particular elegiac color to an aria which develops with great expressive
freedom. It provides another instance of Donizetti's sensitivity to the
ideas behind the text, for he expands with figurations only words
such as 'involarmi' and 'mai chiuso', where some dilation amplifies
their sense. This eloquent aria is followed by a cabaletta, 'Benigno il
cielo arridere' (*moderato*, 4/4, A flat major), in which Maria's delusive sensation of hope finds expression in accented syncopations
and driving scales. The effect here is quite different from that of

Verdi's decisive cabalettas, such as Abigaille's 'Salgo già del trono aurato', for here Donizetti is portraying Maria's inner hysteria and contradicting by her feverishness the optimism of her text. What looks on the page like a routine air of parade turns out from details like the *presto* final cadence (where a singer would normally retard the melody) to be a subtle example of dramatic characterization.

Chevreuse returns and is soon left alone, as Maria is summoned by the Queen. (The comings and goings of characters in this act make for stilted dramaturgy, but the intensity of the scene to a considerable extent compensates for that awkwardness.) No sooner has she left than the captain of the Royal Guards delivers Chalais's letter and a casket containing a portrait of Maria. As Chevreuse realizes the meaning of this evidence, his rage and disillusionment are expressed in contrasting outbursts and whispers, alternating *allegro* and *lento*. His cantabile, 'Bella e di sol vestita' (3/4, G flat major) continues this sense of warring emotions, the suave grief of his opening phrases contrasting with ferocious jealous outbursts, while the harmony is wrenched from G flat to unprepared D major. Donizetti rarely surpassed this achievement in the direct depiction of a soul in crisis. Nor is there any falling off in the succeeding aria, 'Ogni mio bene' (*andante moderato*, 4/4, B flat major); this cannot be called a cabaletta for Chevreuse's thirst for vengeance keeps exploding the expected structure so that the *moderato* melody, 'Sì, ma fra poco di sangue un rio', recurs with the force of an obsessive refrain rather than as a section of a symmetrical two-statement form.

The denouement of the opera begins with a tense and shattering duet for Chevreuse and Maria; the first section of the duet, 'Se per prova il tuo bel core' (*larghetto*, 3/8), uncommonly begins in D major and ends in B minor, while the second is that passage which Chorley so vividly described, 'Sull'uscio tremendo' (*moderato*, 12/8, D major). The remarkable freedom of this duet, the voices rarely overlapping in either section, has already been remarked on in Chapter 8 (see Example 15) as showing the extent to which the mature Donizetti subordinated formal convention to obtain a sense of dramatic immediacy. A further detail to corroborate that point occurs at the end of the *larghetto*, where instead of a chord there is an irrepressible cry from Maria as the clock (on stage) strikes the hour, causing her eyes to turn instinctively toward the secret door in fear that Chalais will return. This duet leads directly into the trio–finale, which has also been discussed in Chapter 8 (see pp. 280–2) to illustrate the economy of the dramaturgy and the device of the final tableau: Chevreuse rages because Chalais's suicide in the secret passage has deprived him of his victim, while Maria falls to her knees, her hands joined in prayer.

That the dramatic action of *Maria di Rohan* is period melodrama has not prevented the opera's being revived from time to time. It is a score that deserves to be more widely known than it is because anyone who is unfamiliar with it has not experienced the full range of Donizetti's power as a musical dramatist. The roles of both Chevreuse and Maria should be in the repertory of modern singers who could identify themselves with the splendid tradition of Ronconi and Tadolini.

Dom Sébastien. This last towering opera by Donizetti is a five-act French grand opera, a genre that is both aesthetically and economically out of fashion today because of a prevailing supposition that the intrinsic merits of such works do not justify the cost of a production that would accurately realize the settings, costumes and spectacle. While *Dom Sébastien* is the grandest of Donizetti's three operas in this style, it should not be automatically lumped with all those other behemoths of the *école de Meyerbeer*. It presents less of a problem to produce today than does a work like *Les Huguenots*. While *Les Huguenots* calls for a cast that includes seven front-rank singers, three women and four men, *Dom Sébastien* requires but five: a high mezzo for the Stolz role of Zaïda; a high *spinto* tenor for the title part, written for Duprez; two baritones, a medium one for the sympathetic part of the warrior–poet Camoëns and a higher one (listed in the French score as 'baryton ou ténor grave') for the fanatic Moorish king, Abayaldos; and a true bass for the Levasseur role of the Grand Inquisitor, Dom Juan de Silva, Sébastien's implacable enemy. The vocal writing in Donizetti's score relies much more on expressive singing than on the exhibitionistic features that abound in Meyerbeer's, and *Dom Sébastien* looks positively chaste in the matter of *points d'orgue* and incidental embellishments compared to *Les Huguenots*. Uncut, the two works are very nearly equal in length, which is to say very long indeed. The divertissement in Act 2 of Donizetti's opera ranks as his finest achievement in the field of ballet music, for it has enjoyed a life independent of the rest of the opera in the repertory of dance companies. One quality which *Dom Sébastien* possesses in a greater degree than *Les Huguenots*, in spite of having a less 'effective' Scribe libretto, is greater forward momentum, a result of Donizetti's craftsmanship as a composer and his more subtle approach to dramatic values. *Les Huguenots* contains great moments and even whole scenes (those of Act 4 for instance) that possess cumulative power, but not even the most objective critic of Meyerbeer would deny that it suffers from inequalities and that many scenes have a curiously disjunctive effect. As these pages have pointed out, Donizetti himself could be an unequal composer, but in *Dom Sébastien* the balance is very much in his favor.

There is scarcely an opera by Donizetti that does not raise some editorial problems, because of later revisions or discrepancies in manuscript sources. In this respect *Dom Sébastien* may very well prove to be the most problematical of all. Some initial indication of these problems must precede any discussion of the opera as a whole. The autograph is in the Bibliothèque Nationale, and unfortunately it is not only incomplete but in a rapidly deteriorating condition.[20] The manuscript copies in the library of the Opéra are fuller but do not agree with any of the printed editions; all of them show variations, with some of which Donizetti most probably had nothing to do. There with some of which Donizetti must probably had nothing to plate no. L-1807) seems to have been prepared just before the premiere so that its appearance would coincide with that event; it contains textual details that were shortly altered and music that was later replaced. The second French edition reveals the modifications made during the first Paris run, changes that were probably made by Donizetti between the premiere (13 November 1843) and his departure for Vienna on 20 December. The score published in Vienna by Mechetti, with a German translation by Leo Herz and an Italian translation by Giovanni Ruffini, reflects the state of the score as Donizetti modified, condensed and even added to it for the Viennese production in German which he prepared and first conducted at the Kärntnertor on 6 February 1845. The Ricordi scores stem from the version of the opera which was first given at La Scala on 14 August 1847, and which achieved a total of forty-two performances that season; but the provenance of the modifications shown in these scores is in some doubt as Donizetti had been a helpless invalid for a year and a half at the time his opera was introduced to Milan. While the Italian scores are generally closer to the Viennese than to the Parisian, retaining for instance most of Ruffini's translation, they differ in some points. One of the new elements in the Viennese score is the abridged conclusion to the final scene, which ends with a new passage in C major; the Italian scores do not perpetuate this change, but revert to the original, more extensive, French ending in G major. Clearly, a full bibliographical study of *Dom Sébastien* is badly needed.

One further illustration reveals the kind of problem posed by this work. There is a famous anecdote told by the Parisian music-publisher Léon Escudier with considerable factual detail in his *Mes souvenirs* (1863), about an incident he witnessed during one of the rehearsals of Act 5 of *Dom Sébastien* at the Opéra. Apparently Rosine Stolz objected to standing around on stage with nothing to do while Barroilhet as Camoëns sang two strophes of his barcarolle, 'Pêcheur de la rive'.[21] If she had to remain on stage, according to Escudier, she insisted that one of the verses of the baritone's aria be cut, and since she was Léon Pillet's mistress and her power with the management was unassailable, her demands were acceded to by the administration in spite of Donizetti's furious objections.[22] Escudier goes on to relate that Donizetti's tantrum took the form of a seizure of some sort and he had to be assisted home, incoherent and barely able to stand unaided. Corroboration of this may be found in an important letter from Donizetti to Leo Herz, who was to make the German translation of this opera for Vienna. Writing on 9 November 1843, just four days before the premiere of *Dom Sébastien*, he reports among other things: 'In Act 5 – a little cavatina (nothing much), a big duo will attract attention; the succeeding barcarolle, of which I must cut half because of the situation, will be lost.'[23] By 'the situation' Donizetti refers to the fact that the barcarolle is sung from off stage by Camoëns, while Zaïda and Sébastien on stage listen.

The Escudier score (L-1807) does not reflect the cut in the barcarolle, for there it appears in two strophes (unless, of course, – which seems highly unlikely – it originally consisted of four strophes!). The barcarolle also has two strophes in the Viennese score published by Mechetti and in the Ricordi score (plate no. 15988), but both of these differ from one another and from the Escudier score in some details; the barcarolle may therefore be used to illustrate the divergences among scores of *Dom Sébastien*. In the Escudier score a chorus concludes each strophe, and the chorus, without solo intervention, sings a four-bar coda that is a reprise of Camoëns's introductory 'Ô matelots, ô matelots!' There are no phrases for either Zaïda or Sébastien. The Mechetti score contains two slight modifications: near the beginning Sébastien sings the name 'Camoëns!' to identify the offstage singer, and the baritone doubles the melody line of the brief coda. In the Ricordi score these changes are found: two orchestral measures at the beginning are omitted, and at the tenth measure of the first strophe Zaïda interjects the words 'O suddito fedel!', which appear in no earlier version; the choral refrain after the first strophe is cut, but over the orchestral ritornello between the strophes the tenor and the mezzo have two short phrases apiece.

These divergences are puzzling. To what extent they reflect Donizetti's post-Parisian modifications of his score is unclear, and must remain so unless some further specific evidence emerges to shed some needed light on this matter. Under the circumstances, it seems wisest to base the following discussion of the work primarily upon the Escudier score as this seems to stand closest to Donizetti's original intentions. Indeed, it seems to match some of the alterations that Donizetti describes elsewhere in his letter to Herz of 9 November 1843.

An *adagio* has been cut in the finale of Act 3 in order to move it to the fourth act, and this poor finale is now only *bavardage*. Thus the finale of Act 3 is lost because M. Scribe (conceitedly) said that the scene will gain from this change. There will always be sufficient pieces of music and *de luxe*, but I complain about my finale.[24]

In the Escudier score the finale to Act 3 consists only of a *vivace* movement, and the later addition of an E major aria for Dom Juan to round off Act 3 had not yet, to judge from this letter, been proposed. The *adagio* that was moved to Act 4 would be the famous septet, although in the Escudier score the tempo is *larghetto*. To broaden the perspective that the Escudier score gives on the opera references will be made to later editions where they seem particularly germane.

The prelude to Act 1 anticipates the funeral march of Act 3, presenting the main thematic material in the same order in which it is encountered later; it is scored principally for drums *voilés*, solemn horns, and marching strings with the cellos interlarding lamenting sequences of minor seconds. The coda provides a brief lyric peroration with cadences that expand the lamenting sequence. Lasting fifty-two measures, this prelude is Donizetti's longest, and it sets forth the elements of somber spectacle and Romantic tragedy that will dominate the later action. It is in the key of C major with strong leanings toward A minor, and indeed at times the keys literally overlap. Like a breath of invigorating fresh air, the sailors' chorus, 'Nautoniers, mettez à la voile' (*vivace*, 6/8, D major), creates with its rhythmic dash and bold harmonies a *genre* scene as the flotilla, visible in the distance, prepares to depart on the King's African expedition. It is followed by a recitative for Dom Antonio, the King's uncle who will be Regent during his absence, and Dom Juan, the Inquisitor, who reveals his plot to betray Portugal to Philip II of Spain. Donizetti handles this cumbersome chunk of Scribean exposition as expeditiously as possible, keeping it largely unaccompanied save for the string *tremolandi* that underline Dom Juan's treachery. In the French score this dialogue is followed by an abridged reprise of the sailors' chorus, but this repetition is omitted from both the Viennese and Ricordi scores, where the last note of Juan's recitative is raised a half-tone (to A sharp) to overlap with the introductory figure of the passage preceding Camoëns's cavatina.

Dom Antonio contemptuously dismisses a poor soldier who has asked to speak to his king. Sébastien himself appears, his impetuous entrance accompanied by a vigorous motif for violins, flutes and clarinets over string harmony, asserting that a soldier has every right to address his king and asking the man who he is. (It would be unthinkable in a nineteenth-century Italian opera between *Tancredi* and *Rigoletto* that a title character would make his entrance only to provide another character with his aria cue!) Camoëns's cavatina, 'Soldat, j'ai rêvé la victoire' (*moderato*, 4/4, F major) explains that he has faithfully served his ungrateful country as soldier, sailor and poet. The martial figure of the opening recurs at the end to frame two extensive contrasting sections – a lyric one in which he speaks of *The Lusiads*, and a stormier passage, over rising chromatics, as he tells how he cried out to the gale to spare his verses even if he should be lost at sea. This aria provides a fine example of Donizetti's forthright characterization.[25]

Sébastien accepts Camoëns as a volunteer, but they are soon interrupted by a procession of inquisitorial judges leading a female captive to the stake. They enter to the words 'Céleste justice' (*largo molto*, 6/8, G minor), accompanied by brass and with strokes of the tam-tam to emphasize the cadences; originally Dom Juan sang the first statement as a solo, but at least by the time of the Viennese production of 1845 it had been assigned to the basses of the chorus as well. It is repeated with frightening force, the ominous orchestration suggesting that these fanatics already see the flames flickering (Example 94).

Sébastien intervenes, ordering that the captive be freed; he learns that she is Moorish but she does not reveal her royal descent. Zaïda's gratitude is expressed in a *romance*, 'Ô mon Dieu, sur la terre' (*cantabile*, 3/4, G major), a one-movement aria that turns into an ensemble, for her melodic statement leads into a quartet of only slightly longer proportions. This whole episode, the first moment of great lyric expansiveness in the score, contrasts with the strenuous music quoted in Example 94, but is related to it through the parallel tonality and the continued rumblings of the holy wrath of the frustrated inquisitors carried on beneath the contrapuntally related lines of Zaïda, Sébastien and Camoëns.

Example 94. *Dom Sébastien*, Act 1, inquisitors' chorus

DOM JUAN and INQUISITORS

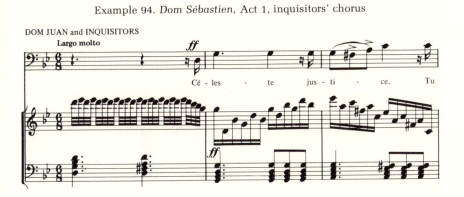

Cé - les - te jus - ti - ce, Tu

veux leur__ sup - pli - ce, Et le saint of -

fi - ce Pu - nit les per - vers,___ Sau -

vons les in - fâ - mes; Qu'i-ci-bas les

Onstage trumpets announce the impending departure of the flotilla, but before the forces embark the King asks Camoëns to use his vatic powers to foretell the outcome of the expedition. Camoëns's prophecy, 'Oui, le ciel m'enflamme' (andante/moderato, 6/8, G minor/G major), sung as the sky portentously darkens, constitutes one of the most evocative passages in the score (Example 95). Beginning with a strange undulating rhythm and figures that emphasize the Neapolitan sixth, and occasionally interrupted by fortissimo allegro passages, this aria creates an uncanny, at times an awesome, effect. The baritone's chiefly declamatory phrases alternate with a refrain in the major key, for which he is joined by the male chorus; in the Viennese and Italian scores this chorus is a battle hymn which replaces the far less effective 'En avant!' of the Escudier score. Camoëns's vision grows more violent (at one point he is interrupted by Donizetti's availing himself of the Opéra's thunder-machine) as he foresees disaster represented by the bloody Portuguese flag in the dust. In the French score this aria concludes with a brief coda of apology (in C major), but this was later cut and a connection made to the orchestral description of the brightening

Example 95. *Dom Sébastien*, Act 1, Camoëns's *andante*

sky. The concertato–finale (*vivace*,[26] 4/4, E flat major) starts off with
renewed trumpet fanfares, and contrasts well the varied emotions of
the characters: the enthusiasm of the departing troops, the good
wishes of the women who stay behind and the ill wishes of Dom
Juan and his party are all combined contrapuntally in the course of
the ensemble. The original coda in the French score, a reprise of the
static 'En avant!' refrain from the prophecy, is replaced by conventional sequences and cadential figures in both the Italian and German scores.

The second act of *Dom Sébastien* takes place in Morocco and is
divided into two scenes, the first in the palace of Zaïda's father, King

Ben-Selim, near Fez, and the second on the battlefield of Alcazar Kebir. The prelude to this act, one of the most beguiling pieces of local color Donizetti composed, was apparently added after the premiere, for it is missing from the Escudier score (Example 96).

Example 96. *Dom Sébastien*, Act 2, prelude

In contrast to the prelude to Act 3 of *Maria di Rohan,* which serves to anticipate the approaching conflict, this passage powerfully evokes an atmosphere, carrying even further the effect of the prelude to Act 1 of *Caterina Cornaro.* Donizetti's orientalism here shares something of the strange elegance and placidity of Ingres's odalisques, and reveals his susceptibility to cultural traits, for he seems to catch the flavor of that interest in harem subjects that inundated France on the heels of expansionism in North Africa during the 1830s. The chorus of Zaïda's Arab attendants, 'Les délices de nos campagnes' (*andante*, 6/8, G major), is graceful and full of unexpected harmonic nuances, but it is less overtly exotic than the prelude. The germ from which the prelude developed can be found in the orchestral introduction to the recitative before Zaïda's second *romance*, 'Sol adoré de la patrie' (*larghetto*, 6/8, C major). This aria, with its introduction for flute and oboe in thirds, unfolds in skillfully contrasted pairs of phrases, the modal shifts conveying a haunting sense of nostalgia; the coda, in which new melodic ideas are introduced, is particularly eloquent. (This coda is eliminated in the Viennese score, but there it is more than compensated for by a dashing, full-scale cabaletta (see Example

11).) The succeeding ballet consists of a *pas de trois*, a *pas de deux* and a finale; the items occur in that order in the Escudier score, but later, the order of the first two sections was reversed. In the customary way, each of these sections is divided into a sequence of contrasting tempos, rhythms and keys. The *pas de trois* opens with a beautiful *largo* in E flat major, notable not only for its distinguished melody, reminiscent of a Beethoven slow movement, but also for its apposite scoring: two clarinets and two basset-horns. The finale of the divertissement concludes with a fetching galop (Auber out of Rossini), much more suggestive of the Parisian music halls than the plains of Morocco. After the dance, Abayaldos appears to announce the approach of the Christian army and to rally his forces in the name of the prophet, with the whirlwind 'Levez-vous, levez-vous' (*vivace*, 3/4, G major); this culminates in a coda for three solo voices, one of them Zaïda's, with full chorus, which forms a pocket concertato–finale.

Act 2 scene ii opens, after a surging minor prelude, upon the plain of Alcazar Kebir strewn with corpses after the battle. Wounded, Sébastien is sustained by the loyal Dom Henrique Sandoval, and they take refuge behind a boulder when Abayaldos and his followers sweep down to exterminate the survivors. The opening period of the ferocious victory hymn (*vivace*, 4/4, C major), is a unison pentatonic melody that shows Donizetti attempting to achieve a sense of local color. Abayaldos offers to spare the survivors if they will point out their king. Dom Henrique, claiming that he is the king, is killed, and after the Moors leave the field, his companions carry away his corpse.

Sébastien is left alone and unconscious. Zaïda appears, to a grandiose introduction that describes both her urgency and her apprehension; knowing Sébastien's fate, she hopes at the very least to spare his remains from vandalism. She hears a faint voice naming his fallen companions and discovers Sébastien, barely alive. The first section of their duet, 'Grand Dieu! sa misère est si grande', with its expressive accompaniment, possesses a largeness of rhetoric that is used to particular effect in this score (Example 97). Having set all the cumbersome mechanics of the work in motion and established his characters, Donizetti is at last able to bring his protagonists together for an extended episode in which their private emotions can be expressed and allowed to dominate. Sébastien's statement, over much the same accompaniment as Zaïda's, uses a more harmonically venturesome variant of her melody, but the softened contour of his phrases reflect his weakened condition. She

Example 97. *Dom Sébastien*, Act 2 scene ii, *larghetto* of the Zaïda–Dom Sébastien duet

identifies herself in a second *larghetto*, 'Quand le sort t'abandonne' (3/4 G major), which is not so much a quotation, although there are liberal melodic and textual references, as a sublimation of her Act 1 *romance*, in which she expressed her gratitude that the King had spared her life from the inquisitors. Sébastien's reply is a counter-melody, which at the words 'aux accents de ta voix' quotes one of his phrases from the quartet pendant to Zaïda's Act 1 *romance*. These musical allusions, by no means mere repetitions, supply a needed ingredient of musical and dramatic coherence to a rather sprawling work; now the positions of the two characters are reversed from the situation in Act 1, in which the love Zaïda feels for Sébastien clearly had its origins.

Abayaldos and the Moors return once more ('Du sang! du sang!' (*vivace assai*, 3/4, F sharp minor)), and Zaïda pleads with them, over orchestral allusions to her *romance*, to spare Sébastien's life, since hers was spared by a Christian. Consenting, Abayaldos and his cohorts leave, singing 'Partez, partez' – the repetition of words is part of a consistent idiom Scribe assigned to the Moors; this passage, however, is not their usual *vivace* type, but an expansive *larghetto* (3/4, D major), that develops into a short ensemble for four solo voices and full chorus. As Zaïda leaves with the others, Sébastien is left alone for his *romance*, 'Seul sur la terre' (*larghetto*, 6/8, D flat major), perhaps more familiar in its Italian translation as 'Deserto in terra'. This aria provided Duprez with one of his most celebrated moments – but not just for its three high Cs and even a top D flat, marked to be sung *doux*, because these notes are all melodic, in the sense that they form part of complete phrases; the aria is a poetic evocation of a moment in which the hero appears to have lost everything but a woman's love and his own soldier's courage. The principal melody is simple and regular, supported over subtly inflected arpeggios; the exposed vocal line, an Italianate feature, relies upon the singer's art to mould it and to relate each phrase to the next. The contrasting middle section is more expansive and declamatory, and it moves into F minor before leading back into a restatement of the last four phrases only of the opening; the coda consists of a melodic sequence repeated and the vocal cadences, and there follows a ritornello that alludes to the principal melody. This is the most spacious of all of Donizetti's tenor arias in one movement and provides the only instance of his ending an act with a single character in a solo without *pertichini*.

The first scene of Act 3, set in a room in the royal palace in Lisbon, is chiefly concerned with the duet for Zaïda and Abayaldos; the latter has come to Lisbon as an ambassador seeking peace, and has brought his fiancée with him because his jealousy will not permit him to leave her behind. Their *larghetto*, 'C'est qu'en tous lieux' (3/8, F minor/F major), is dominated at the start by a rhythmic figure ♪♪♪ ♩ ♪♪♪ ♩ descriptive of Abayaldos's jealous fixation. At the modulation to the major, Zaïda claims that she would rather he killed her than that she should remain subject to his cruel suspicions; her line here gives a more lyrical emphasis to the earlier rhythmic pattern (♪♪♪ ♪♪♪ ♪♪♪ ♪ ♪ ♪♪♪♪ ♪ etc.). This section concludes with a conventional cadenza *a due*. In the *tempo di mezzo* (*allegro*), Abayaldos berates Zaïda for naming another man in her sleep. In their cabaletta, 'En vain pour te soustraire' (*moderato*, 4/4, F major), Abayaldos sings the first statement, but instead of repeating it Zaïda has a contrasting one; in the third (unison) statement the opening melody is cut in half and a new, more urgent, *poco più* completes it.

The scene changes to the main square of Lisbon. Camoëns enters

to a lengthy and expressive horn melody that leads into his famous
romance, 'Ô Lisbonne' (*larghetto*, 4/4, E flat major), in which his
opening phrase is prefigured by two cors anglais in thirds. His noble
melody modulates to G minor before the end of the first melodic
period and moves into E flat minor in the middle section; the coda
cuts off the restatement halfway through. His patriotic awe at finding
himself once more at home prefigures the dramatic situation of Pro-
cida at the beginning of Act 2 of *Les vêpres siciliennes*. 'Ô Lisbonne',
however, was not Donizetti's original intention for this point in the
score; the autograph contains a different baritone aria, also in E flat,
which is linked to the opening of the scene by the continuation of
the horn accompaniment and of their 6/8 meter (Example 98).
Although the discarded aria (Example 98a) contains some effective
modifications of phrase patterns, it lacks the directness and large-
heartedness of the final one. It is illuminating, too, to see how
Scribe's text was improved by the process of revision, and how his
new verse clarifies and advances the emotion by the end of the first
sentence. Reduced to poverty Camoëns must beg. He begins the
duet, 'C'est un soldat qui revient de la guerre' (*largo*, 6/8, G minor),
and the stranger he asks for alms replies to the same tune, now in B
flat minor, that he too was wounded during the African wars. The
regular patterns of the duet break down in an excited dialogue as
they exchange information, and soon Camoëns realizes that he is
addressing none other than Sébastien himself. A brief *vivace* in 3/8,
leads into the even brisker tempo of their recognition duet, 'Ô jour de
joie, ô jour d'ivresse', which is merely routine and seems even longer

Example 98a. *Dom Sébastien*, Act 3 scene ii, Camoëns's original aria

Example 98b. *Dom Sébastien*, Act 3 scene ii, Camoëns's *larghetto*

than it is because all three statements are sung *a due*. In the intermediate section before the third statement, they exchange some dialogue in which it is revealed that Sébastien is believed to be dead,
has been replaced on the throne by his uncle, and supposes himself
to have no popular support. (Scribe's usual historic license here
permits him to overlook the awkward fact that Sebastião did indeed
die on that African battlefield, and to associate the King with one of
the pretenders – there seem to have been three of them – who came
forward to claim the throne.)

The joyful reunion of King and poet is interrupted by the awesome
sound of draped drums, funereal trumpets, and distant chanting.
Slowly a massive funeral procession appears, the catafalque bearing
the royal arms, attended by a huge throng and followed by Sébastien's warhorse, members of the royal family and other dignitaries.
This massive scene makes for a chilling spectacle; the march, already familiar from the prelude to the opera, conveys a lugubrious

atmosphere, rendered macabre by the fact that the supposed occupant of the catafalque is present, wrapped in his cloak, watching the whole procession.[27] This episode produced an unforgettable effect on all who saw it at the Opéra, for it marked the culmination of spectacular effect as practised in that theater.

Camoëns steps forward to protest the treason of this mock funeral, winning a strong protest from Dom Juan, 'Pour ameuter ici la discorde et la haine' (moderato, 4/4, c sharp minor), the old man's fury irrupting over a seething accompaniment that features sequences of major sevenths. Sébastien now reveals himself, and this precipitates what in the Escudier score is the concluding movement of Act 3, a conventional vivace stretta, 'Il faut qu'il périsse' (6/8, E major). The relative ineffectiveness of this ending was soon apparent because it did not make clear, musically at least, that Sébastien was being arrested as a heretic and would be haled before the Inquisition. Donizetti later decided to halt the vivace at the forty-sixth measure, to bring Dom Juan forward for a maestoso denunciatory aria in E major; this passage was obviously designed to exploit Levasseur's low range, for it culminates on bottom E.[28] In this version Act 3 ends with Dom Juan's climactic phrases reinforced by Abayaldos and the chorus of inquisitors (in the Viennese score, however, Abayaldos does not participate here).

Act 4 is set in the court of the Inquisition. There is a brief prelude, for brass in unison, introducing a motif that will recur in a faster tempo during the vivace section of the finale to the act. A somber chorus, 'Ô voûtes souterraines' (andante con mosso, 4/4, B minor), first heard with a unison accompaniment and then with a marcato bass, creates an almost palpable atmosphere of inexorable treachery. Unlike earlier unison choruses where vocal harmony is introduced primarily in the coda and cadence sequences, Donizetti here uses choral part-writing developmentally, reinforced by imitation (devices common in his sacred music) to suggest the implacable conservatism of the inquisitors (Example 99).

When Dom Juan attempts to interrogate Sébastien, the King challenges his right to do so. Suddenly Zaïda appears among them to recount the true events of the battlefield of Alcazar Kebir, her revelation producing an abrupt tutti followed by a moment of silence. Zaïda begins the septet, 'D'espoir et de terreur' (larghetto, 3/4, B major); the other parts enter canonically after her four-phrase statement, and then the main melodic idea is launched by the full ensemble (Example 100).

Example 99. *Dom Sébastien*, Act 4, inquisitors' chorus

Example 100. *Dom Sébastien*, Act 4, septet

This septet develops with far greater freedom of part-writing than is found in earlier ensembles in slow tempos, and without their exact repetitions of whole episodes. After the strict contrapuntal opening, the structure is built up in pairs of phrases with related contours, and an increased sense of organic unity is contributed by Dom Juan's part, which repeats one of the phrases from the initial canon. (The personnel for this septet is at first glance a little confusing; originally Zaïda, Sébastien, Abayaldos and Dom Juan were joined by parts identified as the first and second inquisitors and the Grand Inquisitor – patently an error since the Grand Inquisitor is Dom Juan who is already a participant in the ensemble. A note in the front of the Escudier score explains that the parts of the three inquisitors are to be performed by the singers of the roles of Dom Antonio, Dom Henrique and Ben-Selim, who would not be recognized in their monastic regalia.)

The *materia di mezzo* of the Act 4 finale is dominated by an outburst from Abayaldos, who rejects Zaïda as an adultress (in the generally toned-down Italian translation, this charge is modified to 'una spergiura' – a woman disloyal to her faith). Abayaldos's 'Va, parjure, épouse impie' (*moderato*, 4/4, B flat major) turns out to be a modified cabaletta, for after some intermediate dialogue, the opening melody is restated, more or less, in unison by three and then more voices. The cabaletta does not, however, complete the finale, for it is followed by a stirring recitative for Zaïda who throws in her lot completely with Sébastien, prompting a vigorous *vivace* stretta. The first statement, which draws on material from the prelude to the act, but now in much brisker tempo, voices the ecclesiastics' vigorous denunciation, and the second, dominated by Zaïda and Sébastien, in usual stretta fashion, proclaims their belief that divine justice will ultimately vindicate them. This short fourth act, consisting of little more than an opening chorus, some powerful dialogue and an extensive finale, marks one of Donizetti's peaks as a musical dramatist.

Act 5 opens with a prelude that anticipates the melody of Camöens's barcarolle, 'Pêcheur de la rive'. A brief recitative between Dom Juan and the Spanish legate reveals that the Duke of Alba's army is already drawn up outside Lisbon to seize the country for Philip II. Zaïda is brought in and Dom Juan offers her a letter of abdication for Sébastien to sign, assuring her that if he does so, his life will be spared. Left alone, Zaïda sings what is identified in the score as a 'récit et cabalette', and certainly 'Mourir pour ce qu'on aime' (*allegro moderato*, 4/4, C major) is structurally a two-statement cabaletta; its strange lack of a preceding aria for Zaïda or anyone else, suggests that at some stage Donizetti may have intended a double aria for Zaïda at this point. Perhaps the overall length of the work, together with the fact that a full-scale duet follows, caused him to discard the first part of it. Sébastien appears and in a *tempo d'attacco*, 'Du moins dans ma misère' (*vivace*, 4/4, A flat major), the two give a rather conventional expression to their emotions at their reunion, but their subsequent dialogue, carried on over urgent accompanying figures, as she gives him the letter of abdication, which he rejects as dishonorable, is forceful and dramatically apt. Their *larghetto*, 'Son âme noble et fière' (3/4, D flat major), is a short and energetic affirmation of their determination, accompanied only by punctuating chordal figures. In an adaptation of a device from *Lucrezia Borgia*, an offstage voice, against a chiming clock, warns of the passing of time. The concluding section of the duet, 'Sans regret, sans remord' (*vivace*, 4/4 D flat major), uses a vocal melody that repeats the rhythmic pattern ♩ ♩ ♩ | ♩ ♩ ♩ ; it is structurally a modified cabaletta in which the voices share the statements and combine for the codettas and the cadence figures. There is an indomitable sweep to this concluding movement which seems to symbolize Donizetti's own efforts to bring his massive work to a conclusion, for he had struggled hard against the unsympathetic attitude that prevailed in many quarters at the Opéra, and he was fighting the ominous signs of his own failing health.

Camoëns's barcarolle, sung from the wings, makes an effective juxtaposition of the tonic key of A flat major with A minor. At the conclusion Camoëns climbs up a rope ladder into their cell in the Tower of Lisbon to help Zaïda and Sébastien to escape. This first scene ends with a largely unaccompanied trio, 'De la prudence', (*allegro moderato*, 4/4, B flat major) as they prepare to flee.

The brief final scene, 'for which', Donizetti said, 'music can do nothing',[29] shows the Tower of Lisbon in the background; in the foreground on the shore are Dom Juan, Abayaldos, Dom Antonio and guards. Camoëns starts to lead Zaïda and Sébastien down the rope ladder, but the guards fire two shots and the bodies of the lovers fall into the sea. Dom Antonio now proclaims himself King, but Dom Juan dismisses his claim by swearing allegiance to Philip II. But Camoëns, brought in by the soldiers, who have captured him, has the last word: 'Gloire à Dom Sébastien!' Musically, the final scene consists of just fifty measures; the first part, a contrapuntal prelude marked *moderato*, starts out in D major; in the second part, *allegro vivace*, the sound of the shots is followed by a sudden sweep of unprepared B flat major, and after Camoëns's salute to Sébastien the work ends in D major cadences. As noted earlier, the final scene is even shorter in the Viennese version; the second tempo of the French version is dropped and is replaced by thirteen measures of C major *vivace*, which alter the harmonic scheme of the episode but allow the opera to end in the key in which it began.

It is to be hoped that before too long a major company, with the capacity for mounting an opera of these proportions, will turn its attention to a revival of *Dom Sébastien* in French. The work has the reputation for being gloomy, as one might expect since its best-known excerpt is a funeral march, but it contains greater variety (for instance in the African scenes and the ballet), than it is usually given credit for. In their discussion of this opera, Clément and Larousse praise Donizetti's score and mention the initial enthusiasm with which it was greeted; they blame its subsequent disappearance upon its sodden libretto, claiming that Donizetti was 'a victim of Scribe'.[30] Granted the libretto is cumbersome, yet in spite of it Donizetti frequently managed to bring his five leading characters vividly to life. *Dom Sébastien* enjoyed more than two decades of success in Italy, but as has been shown the Italian score is not always faithful to Donizetti's musical intentions, and, even more damaging, the Italian translation often does violence to the shape and emphasis of his carefully wrought phrases. It was this opera that Donizetti hoped would prove his masterpiece, and had his health permitted it he would, to judge by his ongoing attentions to his other scores, quite likely have revised it. It remains a most noble and frequently eloquent work that testifies to the penetration of Donizetti's tragic vision. It preceded Verdi's *Don Carlos* by a quarter of a century, but the dark beauty that pervades much of Donizetti's work most frequently calls to mind that score. A scrupulous, well-prepared revival of *Dom Sébastien* would do more than anything to reveal Donizetti's importance as Verdi's great and influential predecessor and should do much to raise him to the position of respect that he fully deserves to occupy.

Appendix I
Synopses

Il Pigmalione opera ('scena lirica')[1] in 1 act
Composed: 15 September – 1 October 1816
First performed: Teatro Donizetti, Bergamo, 13 October 1960, with Oriana Santunione-Finzi (Galatea), Doro Antonioli (Pigmalione), conducted by Armando Gatti.
Librettist: unknown
Libretto: based on Antonio Simone Sografi's libretto for Giambattista Cimadoro's *Pimmaglione* (Venice, 1790), itself a translation of Jean-Jacques Rousseau, *Pygmalion* (Lyons, 1770) but following Ovid, *Metamorphoses*, Book X.
Synopsis: Pigmalione, King of Crete (tenor), has renounced women and turned sculptor in order to create his ideal of female beauty. He becomes so enamored of his statue that he can no longer raise his chisel to it for fear of hurting it. In torment he prays to Venus, through whose intervention Galatea (soprano) is brought to life and reciprocates Pigmalione's love.
Manuscript score: Bibliothèque Nationale, Paris (autograph)

Enrico di Borgogna opera semiseria ('opera eroica')[2] in 2 acts
Composed: 1818
First performed: Teatro San Luca, Venice 14 November 1818, with Fanny Eckerlin (Enrico), Adelaide [Adelina] Catalani (Elisa), Adelaide Cassago (Geltrude), Giuseppe Fosconi (Pietro), Giuseppe Spech (Guido), Andrea Verni (Gilberto), Giuseppe Fioravanti (Brunone), Pietro Verducci (Bruno).
Librettist: Bartolomeo Merelli
Libretto: based on August von Kotzebue, *Der Graf von Burgund* (Vienna, 1795), via an unidentified Italian intermediary.
Synopsis: In exile, Enrico (contralto) learns that his father's murderer has died and that Guido (bass), the usurper's son, has succeeded to his dukedom. Enrico sets off to regain his rights and marry his beloved Elisa (soprano), whom Guido plans to wed. Enrico arrives in time to disrupt the wedding procession. Later, he heads a successful assault on the castle and wins Elisa.
Manuscript score: Bibliothèque Nationale, Paris (non-autograph copy)

Una follia farsa in 1 act
Composed: November–December 1818
First performed: Teatro San Luca, Venice, 17 December 1818, by Zancla's company who sang *Enrico di Borgogna* (exact cast unknown).
Librettist: Bartolomeo Merelli
Libretto: probably based on Andrea Leone Tottola's libretto for Giacomo Cordella's *Una follia* (Naples, 1813).
Manuscript score: no copy of this work is known

Le nozze in villa opera buffa in 2 acts
Composed: in great part by summer 1819
First performed: Teatro Vecchio, Mantua, Carnival 1820–1, with Fanny Eckerlin (Sabina) (others unknown).
Librettist: Bartolomeo Merelli
Libretto: based on August von Kotzebue, *Die deutschen Kleinstädter* (Vienna, 1802) via an unidentified Italian intermediary.
Synopsis: The plot turns on the wooing of Sabina (mezzo-soprano) by two suitors: Claudio (tenor), a wealthy landlord, and Trifoglio (buffo), the village schoolteacher, whose suit is favored by her father, Petronio (bass). After many misunderstandings, Trifoglio renounces his claims to Sabina when he learns that her dowry consists of fifty-eight wigs, one aerostatic globe, six dozen pairs of spectacles and no money at all. Claudio wins Sabina's hand when he accepts her without a dowry.
Manuscript score: Bibliothèque Nationale, Paris (non-autograph copy)

Il falegname di Livonia, ossia Pietro il grande, Tsar delle Russie opera buffa in 2 acts
Composed: fall – 4 December 1819
First performed: Teatro San Samuele, Venice, 26 December 1819, with Amati, Giovanni Battista Verger, Luigi Martinelli, Vincenzo Botticelli.
Librettist: Marchese Gherardo Bevilacqua-Aldobrandini
Libretto: based on Alexandre Duval's comedy *Le menuisier de Livonie, ou Les illustres voyageurs* (Paris, 1805), via Felice Romani's libretto for Giovanni Pacini's *Il falegname di Livonia* (Milan, 1819)
Synopsis: A young carpenter (*falegname*) named Carlo (tenor) loves Annetta (soprano), who is the young friend of Madama Fritz (mezzo), an innkeeper in the province of Livonia. Carlo defends Annetta when a usurer, Firman (baritone), tries to cheat her out of a bracelet. This altercation is halted by the arrival of two impressive strangers, later revealed to be Tsar Pietro (bass) and his wife Caterina (soprano), who are searching for the Tsarina's missing nephew. Pietro questions Carlo about his parentage, but when the youth fails to give satisfactory answers, he is turned over to a bumbling Magistrate (buffo). Carlo is about to be led away when Madama Fritz produces an old letter found with the infant Carlo, revealing him to be the son of Carlo Stravonski, the Tsarina's brother. Carlo is released, recognized by his aunt,

ennobled by his uncle and granted permission to marry Annetta. The populace cheers the imperial couple for their generosity.
Manuscript score: Ricordi Archives, Milan (autograph)

Zoraida di Granata opera seria in 2 acts
Composed: August 1821 – January 1822
First performed: Teatro Argentina, Rome, 28 January 1822, with Maria Ester Mombelli (Zoraida), Mazzanti (Abenamet), Gaetana Corini (Ines), Domenico Donzelli (Almuzir), Gaetano Rambaldi (Almanzor), Alberto Torri (Alì Zegri).
Librettist: Bartolomeo Merelli
Revised: October–November 1824
First performed in revised version: Teatro Argentina, Rome, 7 January 1824, with Luigia Boccabadati (Zoraida), Benedetta Pisaroni (Abenamet), Rosalinda Ferri (Ines), Domenico Donzelli (Almuzir), Giacomo Galassi (Almanzor), Domenico Patriozzi (Alì Zegri).
Librettist: revision of Merelli's libretto by Jacopo Ferretti
Libretto: based on Jean-Pierre-Claris de Florian, *Gonzalve de Cordove, ou Grenade reconquise* (Paris, 1793), via Luigi Romanelli's libretto for Giuseppe Nicolini's *Abenamet e Zoraide* (Milan, 1805).
Synopsis: Almuzir (tenor) has murdered the King of Granada and usurped his throne; he hopes to secure his position by marrying the late King's daughter Zoraida (soprano), but she loves Abenamet (*musico*), leader of the Abencerrages. To rid himself of his rival, Almuzir makes him leader of the Moorish army, charging him to bring back a banner. Since Almuzir has already arranged for the banner to be seized by the Spaniards, he arrests Abenamet for treason when he returns without it. Zoraida determines to marry Almuzir to save Abenamet's life. Guessing the price of his freedom, Abenamet comes to Zoraida and accuses her of infidelity. When the lovers are discovered together, Zoraida is arraigned for faithlessness – a capital offense – to the King and is to be executed unless a champion comes forward to defend her. Appearing as an unknown knight, Abenamet wins the combat and forces a confession from Almuzir. Enraged by the usurper's perfidy, the populace turns against him, but Abenamet defends the King, who is so moved by this noble behavior that he bestow's Zoraida's hand upon Abenamet.
Manuscript score: Ricordi Archives, Milan (autograph, 1824 version)

La zingara opera semiseria (with spoken dialogue) in 2 acts
Composed: February–May 1822
First performed: Teatro Nuovo, Naples, 12 May 1822, with Giacinta Canonici (Argilla), Caterina Monticelli (Ines), Giuseppe Fioravanti (Don Sebastiano), Marco Venier[3] (Ferrando), Carlo Moncada (Don Ranuccio), Carlo Casaccia (Pappacione), Alessandro Busti (Duca di Alziras), Raffaele Sarti (Alvarez), Raffaele Casaccia (Sguiglio).

Librettist: Andrea Leone Tottola

Libretto: based on Louis-Charles Caigniez's *La petite bohémienne* (Paris, 1816) ('imitated from Kotzebue' according to its title-page), probably via an Italian intermediary, as yet unidentified.

Synopsis: The gypsy Argilla (mezzo-soprano) is the focal character. She brings the lovers Ferrando (tenor) and Ines (soprano) together; she foils a plot of Ranuccio (baritone) to assassinate the Duke of Alziras (tenor); she reunites the Duke with his brother Ferrando; she secures the freedom of Don Sebastiano (baritone), unjustly imprisoned by Ranuccio; she tricks a foolish servant, Pappacione (buffo), into exploring an old cistern in search of gold; and at the end she turns out to be Don Sebastiano's long-lost daughter.

Manuscript score: Conservatorio di San Pietro a Majella, Naples (non-autograph copy)

La lettera anonima farsa in 1 act

Composed: May–June 1822

First performed: Teatro del Fondo, Naples, 29 June 1822, with Giuseppina Fabré (Contessa), Teresa Cecconi (Melita), Raffaela de Bernardis (Lauretta), Giovanni Battista Rubini (Filinto), de Franchi (Don Macario), Giovanni Pace (Giliberto), Calvarola (Flagiolet).

Librettist: Giulio Genoino

Libretto: based on a farce by Genoino himself, ultimately derived from Pierre Corneille, *Mélite, ou Les fausses lettres* (Paris, 1630).

Synopsis: Melita (mezzo-soprano) writes an anonymous letter to the Countess (soprano), hinting that the Count, Don Macario, has been unfaithful to her. By chance the letter is read by Rosina (soprano), who interprets it to mean that her fiancé, Filinto (tenor), has been untrue. Before Melita's trouble-making is exposed, a servant Lauretta (soprano) is accused of having written the letter, but she is exonerated when she proves she can neither read nor write. When Melita finally confesses, Rosina and Filinto are reconciled, and the Countess forgives both Melita and her husband.

Manuscript score: Ricordi Archives, Milan (autograph)

Chiara e Serafina, ossia I pirati opera semiseria in 2 acts

Composed: October 1822

First performed: La Scala, Milan 26 October 1822, with Isabella Fabbrica (Chiara), Rosa Morandi (Serafina), Maria Gioia (Lisetta), Carolina Sivelli (Agnese), Savino Monelli[4] (Don Ramiro), Antonio Tamburini (Picaro), Nicola de Grecis[5] (Don Meschino), Carlo Poggiali (Don Fernando and Gennaro), Carlo Pizzochero (Don Alvaro), Carlo Dona (Spelatro).

Librettist: Felice Romani

Libretto: based on René-Charles-Guilbert de Pixérécourt's melodrama *La cisterne* (Paris, 1809).

Synopsis: Don Alvaro (bass), father of Chiara and Serafina (both sopranos), and Chiara are captured by Algerian pirates. At the Spanish court, Don

Fernando (bass), Alvaro's secret enemy, explains this absence as treason, hoping to become Serafina's guardian and gain control of her wealth. Serafina has fallen in love with Don Ramiro, a Majorcan gallant. In an attempt to dispose of Ramiro's suit, Fernando has his rascally servant Picaro (baritone) pretend to be Alvaro who is supposed to have returned secretly after a ten-year absence and to be opposed to the match. Meanwhile, Alvaro's faithful friends arrange his release from slavery. On his way to Spain he is driven by a sudden storm to Majorca, but arrives in time to save Serafina from Fernando's schemes.

Manuscript score: Ricordi Archives, Milan (autograph)

Alfredo il grande opera seria in 2 acts
Composed: 1823
First performed: Teatro San Carlo, Naples, 2 July 1823, with Elisabetta
  Ferron (Amalia), Teresa Cecconi (Enrichetta), Andrea Nozzari (Alfredo),
  Giovanni Botticelli (Edoardo), Michele Benedetti (Atkins), Gaetano Chizzola (Rivers), Antonio Orlandini (Guglielmo).
Librettist: Andrea Leone Tottola
Libretto: perhaps based on Bartolomeo Merelli's libretto for Johann Simon
  Mayr's *Alfredo il grande* (Rome, 1818).
Synopsis: This unexpected action occurs on the island of Athelney, which is 'ringed with pleasant hills overlooking a lake', with 'rustic houses ... scattered over the mountain and plain'. Queen Amalia (soprano) and the General, Edoardo (bass), come in disguise to Somerset in search of Alfredo (tenor). Guglielmo (tenor), a loyal shepherd, offers them shelter, unaware that the fugitives are being tracked by the Danish general, improbably named Atkins (bass). Amalia is delighted to discover that Guglielmo's hut is Alfredo's hiding-place. In disguise, Atkins informs Alfredo that his refuge is known to his enemies. At this news Guglielmo volunteers to lead them to safety. A Danish force surprises the royal refugees (who according to the libretto make their entrance 'on all fours'), but Guglielmo opportunely arrives with a band of armed shepherds. His foes outnumbered and at his mercy, Alfredo generously offers to meet them in fair fight on open ground. A large army gathers around Alfredo, who urges them on to victory. After the defeat of the Danes, Atkins and a few survivors happen upon Queen Amalia, whom they seize as hostage. The intrepid Amalia draws a dagger and holds off the Danes until the arrival of the English, who duly free their Queen. All hail Alfredo as the savior of England.

Manuscript scores: Conservatorio di San Pietro a Majella, Naples (autograph); Bibliothèque Nationale, Paris (non-autograph copy)

Il fortunato inganno opera buffa (with spoken dialogue; i.e., strictly a farsa), in 2 acts
Composed: 1823
First performed: Teatro Nuovo, Naples, 3 September 1823, with Teresina

Melas (Aurelia), Francesca Checcherini (Fulgenzia del Folletto), d'Auria (Eugenia), Clementina Grossi (Fiordelisa), Carlo Casaccia (Lattanzio Latrughelli), Giuseppe Fioravanti (Francheschetti), Marco Venier (Tenente Edorado), Carlo Moncada (Bequadro), Raffaele Casaccia (Vulcano), Giuseppe Papi (Biscaglino), Raffaele Sarti (Ascanio).

Librettist: Andrea Leone Tottola

Libretto: source unidentified

Synopsis: Lattanzio Latrughelli (buffo) manages a troupe of singers, headed by his wife, Aurelia (soprano). She practises a series of deceptions on Colonel Franceschetti (baritone) to try to overcome his scruples against people of the theater so that he will permit his nephew Edorado (tenor) to marry Aurelia's niece Eugenia (soprano), a junior member of the troupe. At length, Aurelia, who has posed as a countess, routs the Colonel, who gives his consent to the young couple's wedding.

Manuscript score: Conservatorio di San Pietro a Majella, Naples (autograph)

L'ajo nell'imbarazzo opera buffa in 2 acts (revised as *Don Gregorio*, Neapolitan farsa in 2 acts)

Composed: 1824

First performed: Teatro Valle, Rome, 4 February 1824, with Maria Ester Mombelli (Gilda), Agnese Loyselet (Leonarda), Savino Monelli (Enrico), Antonio Tamburini (Marchese Don Giulio), Nicola Tacci (Don Gregorio), Giovanni Puglieschi (Pipetto), Luigi de Dominicis (Simone).

Revised: between 1824 and summer 1826

First performed as *Don Gregorio*: Teatro Nuovo, Naples, 11 June 1826, with Giacinta Canonici (Gilda), Francesca Checcherini (Leonarda), Antonio de Bezzi (Enrico), Felice Pellegrini (Marchese Don Giulio), Carlo Casaccia (Don Gregorio), Giovanni Pace (Simone).

Librettist: Jacopo Ferretti

Libretto: based on Giovanni Giraud's comedy *L'ajo nell'imbarazzo* (Rome, 1807).[6]

Synopsis: The puritanical Don Giulio (baritone) has brought up his two sons, Enrico and Pipetto (both tenors), so strictly that they know nothing of diversions, especially women. This rigorous but limited education has been in the hands of Don Gregorio (buffo), the tutor (*ajo*), but the system soon goes askew. Pipetto falls in love with the only woman he has ever seen, the old housekeeper, Leonarda (mezzo-soprano), who is senile and takes him seriously. The elder son, Enrico, has secretly married a charming neighbor, Gilda (soprano), and their union is already blessed by an infant son, Bernardino. Through Gilda's skillful maneuvers, Don Giulio is brought to admit the folly of his educational system and blesses the marriage of his heir.

Manuscript score: Conservatorio di San Pietro a Majella, Naples (non-autograph copy)

Emilia di Liverpool (also given as *L'eremitaggio di Liverpool*) opera semiseria in 2 acts

Composed: February–July 1824

First performed: Teatro Nuovo, Naples, 28 July 1824, with Teresina Melas (Emilia), Francesca Checcherini (Candida), Clementina Grossi (Luigia), Domenico Zilioli (Federico), Giuseppe Fioravanti (Claudio), Carlo Casaccia (Don Romualdo), de Nicola (Il Conte).

Librettist: unidentified

Revised: 1828

First performed in revised version: Teatro Nuovo, Naples, 8 March 1828, with Annetta Fischer (Emilia), Francesca Checcherini (Bettina), Marianna Checcherini (Candida), Manzi (Villars), Giuseppe Fioravanti (Claudio), Gennaro Luzio (Asdrubale), Muraglia (Giacomo).

Librettist: revision of original libretto by Giuseppe Checcherini

Libretto: based on an anonymous libretto for Vittorio Trento's opera semiseria *Emilia di Laverpaut* (Teatro dei Fiorentini, Naples, 1817), itself derived from Stefano Scatizzi, *Emilia di Laverpaut*, which in turn has its source in a melodrama by August von Kotzebue given as *Emilia, ossia La benedizione paterna* (1788).[7]

Synopsis of revised version (the original plot is condensed slightly, and the characters are renamed as follows: Federico becomes Villars, Don Romualdo becomes Don Asdrubale, Candida becomes Bettina): Emilia (soprano) grew up in Naples where she had the misfortune to be seduced, which caused her mother's death. Now she does penance for her unsavory past by caring for the poor at a hospice in the mountains near Liverpool. There one day in a furious storm a carriage overturns and a tattered stranger helps three passengers to safety. The passengers are Don Asdrubale (buffo), a Neapolitan roué searching for his long-missing fiancée, his niece Bettina (soprano) and Colonel Villars (tenor), who later turns out to be Emilia's betrayer, but who now amuses himself by flirting with Bettina. The tattered stranger, lately escaped from the Barbary pirates, is Claudio, who recognizes in Emilia the daughter he has for years dreamed of punishing. When Villars is revealed as Emilia's seducer, Claudio challenges him to a duel. Villars confesses his error and resolves to make Emilia an honest woman. Overjoyed, Claudio forgives Emilia.

Manuscript score: Conservatorio di San Pietro a Majella, Naples (autograph of the 1828 version superimposed on the 1824 original)

Alahor in Granata opera seria in 2 acts

Composed: 1825

First performed: Teatro Carolino, Palermo, 7 January 1826, with Elisabetta Ferron (Zobeida), Maria Gioia-Tamburini (Muley-Hassem), Carlotta Tomasetti (Sulima), Berardo Calvari Winter (Alamor), Antonio Tamburini (Alahor), Salvatore Patti (Ismaele).

Librettist: identified only as M.A.[8]

Libretto: Jean-Pierre-Claris de Florian, *Gonzalve de Cordove, ou Grenade reconquise* (Paris, 1793), via Étienne de Jouy's libretto for Luigi Cherubini's

Les Abencérages (Paris, 1813) and Felice Romani's libretto for Giacomo Meyerbeer's *L'esule di Granata* (Milan, 1821).

Synopsis: The late chief of the Zegri faction, Aly, has slain all the family of the leader of the rival Abencerrages but Alahor (baritone) and Zobeida (soprano). Alahor has fled into exile, but Zobeida remains behind because she loves Muley-Hassem (*musico*), who has succeeded his brother Aly to the throne. The honorable peace Hassem has arranged with the Spanish foe seems an act of betrayal to the fiercely partisan Zegris. Their leader, Alamor (tenor), conspires to overthrow Hassem. Returning in disguise to avenge his father's murder, Alahor joins the conspiracy and volunteers to slay Hassem. Hassem learns of the plot and forgives Alahor, who defends him against an attack led by Alamor. The attack fails and Alamor is led away. Zobeida rejoices at the reunion of her brother and her beloved Hassem.

Manuscript scores: private collection, Palermo (autograph); Boston University (non-autograph copy of 1830 revival, at Palermo)

Elvida opera seria in 1 act
Composed: 1826
First performed: Teatro San Carlo, Naples, 6 July 1826, with Henriette [Enrichetta] Méric-Lalande (Elvida), Brigida Lorenzani (Zeidar), Almerinda Manzocchi (Zulma), Giovanni Battista Rubini (Alfonso), Luigi Lablache (Amur), Gaetano Chizzola (Ramiro).
Librettist: Giovanni Schmidt
Libretto: source unidentified
Synopsis: Elvida (soprano), a Spanish noblewoman captured by the Moorish chieftain Amur (bass), spurns the suit of Zeidar (*musico*) because she is faithful to her fiancé, the Spanish prince Alfonso (tenor). Alfonso knocks down the walls of Amur's stronghold with catapults, causing the chieftain to hide Elvida in a cave. Alfonso's sudden arrival there provokes Amur to try to stab Elvida, but Zeidar knocks the dagger out of his father's hand. The Spaniards seize Amur and drag him away, followed by Zeidar who hopes to save his father. Elvida and Alfonso are happily reunited.
Manuscript score: Conservatorio di San Pietro a Majella, Naples (autograph)

Gabriella di Vergy opera seria in 2 acts
Composed: 1826
Revised: 1838
First performed in a *rifacimento* by Giuseppe Puzone and Paolo Serrao entitled *Gabriella*: Teatro San Carlo, Naples, 29 November 1869, with Marcellina Lotti della Santa (Gabriella), Carolina Certoné (Almeide), Giuseppe Villani (Fayel), Gottardo Aldighieri (Raoul), Marco Arati (Filippo II), Memmi (Armando).
First performed in revised (1838) version: for recording, London, August 1978, by Opera Rara, with Milla Andrew (Gabriella), Joan Davies (Almeide), Christian du Plessis (Fayel), Maurice Arthur (Raoul), John Tomlinson (Filippo II), John Winfield (Armando), conducted by Alun Francis.

Librettists: Andrea Leone Tottola and Gaetano Donizetti (?)
Libretto: taken from Andrea Leone Tottola's libretto for Michele Enrico Carafa's *Gabriella di Vergy* (Naples, 1816), ultimately derived from a fourteenth-
century *roman Le chastelain de Couci.*
Synopsis: Gabriella (soprano) has married Fayel, Count of Vermand (or
Vergy) (tenor, 1826; baritone, 1838), believing her beloved Raoul (*musico,*
1826; tenor, 1838) to have died on the crusades. An unknown knight
comes to Fayel's castle to announce the arrival of King Filippo II of France
(bass). Gabriella is overcome to recognize the stranger as Raoul de Coucy,
who reproaches her for infidelity. When the King appears he proposes to
reward Raoul, for having saved his life, by marrying him to Fayel's sister
Almeide (soprano). Raoul's silent shock at this proposal stings Fayel's
touchy pride. Secretly Gabriella sends for Raoul, but their interview is overheard by Almeide, who summons Fayel. He rushes in to find Raoul kneeling
at Gabriella's feet. Furious, he challenges Raoul to a duel and banishes
Gabriella to a dungeon. There, Fayel presents her with an urn containing the
still warm heart of Raoul. Gabriella dies of grief and horror.
Manuscript scores: Museo Donizettiano, Bergamo (autograph, 1826 version);
Sterling Library, University of London (non-autograph copy, 1838 version)

Olivo e Pasquale opera buffa in 2 acts
Composed: September–December 1826
First performed: Teatro Valle, Rome, 7 January 1827, with Emilia Bonini
    (Isabella), Anna Scudellari-Cosselli (Camillo), Agnese Loyselet (Matilde),
    Giovanni Battista Verger (Le Bross), Domenico Cosselli (Olivo), Giuseppe
    Frezzolini (Pasquale), Luigi Garofolo (Columella), Stanislao Prò (Diego).
Revised: 1827
First performed in revised version: Teatro Nuovo, Naples, 1 September 1827,
    with Annetta Fischer (Isabella), Francesca Checcherini (Matilde),
    Vincenzo Galli (Olivo), Gennaro Luzio (Pasquale), Francesco Regoli
    (Camillo), Manzi (Le Bross), de Nicola (Columella), Giuseppe Papi (Diego).
Librettist: Jacopo Ferretti
Libretto: based on Antonio Simone Sografi's comedy, *Olivo e Pasquale*
    (Venice, 1794).[9]
Synopsis: Olivo (baritone) and Pasquale (bass) are brothers, merchants in
Lisbon; the former is rash and intemperate, the latter easy-going. Olivo's
daughter Isabella (soprano) loves a young apprentice, Camillo (*musico,*
Rome; tenor, Naples) but her father is anxious that she marry a wealthy
merchant from Cadiz, Le Bross (tenor). Isabella confesses to Le Bross that she
loves someone else, but when asked to identify him, she is too shy to tell the
truth and says it is Columella (buffo), a vain and foolish old man. Olivo flies
into such a rage when he finds that Isabella opposes his wishes that the
shocked Le Bross becomes Isabella's active ally and promises to help her
marry Camillo. When Olivo refuses to heed the threat that unless he consents to the marriage by five o'clock the lovers will kill themselves, the clock

strikes and shots are heard. Pasquale faints and Olivo declares he would rather Isabella wed Camillo than kill herself. The smiling couple appear at the door to be embraced by the much relieved Olivo.

Manuscript score: Conservatorio di San Pietro a Majella, Naples (non-autograph copy)

Otto mesi in due ore (also given as *Gli esiliati in Siberia*), opera romantica in 3 acts

Composed: January–May 1827

First performed: Teatro Nuovo, Naples, 13 May 1827, with Caterina Lippa-
    rini (Elisabetta), Francesca Checcherini, Servoli (Potoski), Vincenzo Galli
    (Gran Maresciallo), Giuseppe Fioravanti (Ivano), Gennaro Luzio, Giuseppe
    Loira, Raffaele Scalese.

Librettist: Domenico Gilardoni

Revised: 1833

First performed in revised version: Livorno, 1833

Librettist: revision of Gilardoni's libretto by Antonio Alcozer

Libretto: based on Luigi Marchionni, *La figlia dell'esiliato, ossia Otto mesi
    in due ore* (Naples, 1820), adapted from René-Charles-Guilbert de
    Pixérécourt, *La fille de l'exilé, ou Huit mois en deux heures*, itself based
    on Sophie Cottin's prose narrative *Élisabeth, ou Les exilés de Sibérie*
    (Paris, 1806).

Synopsis: The father of Elisabetta (soprano) has been exiled unjustly to Siberia. Convinced of her father's innocence, she undergoes all sorts of hardships on her journey on foot toward Moscow. The River Kam is in flood; Tartar hordes harry the land. She gains access to the Tsar and once the plots against her father are exposed she gains a full pardon for him.

Manuscript score: Conservatorio di San Pietro a Majella, Naples (autograph consisting of a confusing and disordered combination of the original, but with pieces missing, and the 1833 revision)

Il borgomastro di Saardam opera buffa in 2 acts

Composed: summer 1827

First performed: Teatro del Fondo, Naples, 19 August 1827, with Carolina
    Ungher (Marietta), Almerinda Manzocchi (Carlotta), Celestino Salvatori
    (Tsar Pietro), Berardo Calvari Winter (Pietro Flimann), Carlo Casaccia
    (Borgomastro), Raffaele Casaccia (Timoteo), Giovanni Pace (Leforte),
    Gaetano Chizzola (Ali Mahmed).

Librettist: Domenico Gilardoni

Libretto: based on Anne-Honoré-Joseph Mélesville, J.-T. Merle and E.-C. de
    Boirie, *Le bourgmestre de Sardam, ou Les deux Pierre* (Paris, 1818).

Synopsis: Under an assumed name, Tsar Pietro (baritone) works as a ship-wright in the yards at Saardam, where his constant companion is Pietro Flimann (tenor), a deserter from the army turned carpenter. Flimann loves the Burgermaster's daughter Marietta (soprano), but in his humble position he has small hopes of winning her, even though the disguised Tsar has promised his help. The Burgermaster (buffo) has heard a rumor that the Tsar works in the shipyard in disguise; he holds an interrogation but succeeds only in getting identical, evasive answers from Pietro and from Flimann. Wambert (bass) assumes that Flimann is the true Tsar, but after an argument with Pietro, suddenly finds himself with two Tsars on his hands. The problem is resolved when news of a revolt comes from Russia, making it imperative for the true Tsar to resume his throne. Before Pietro leaves Saardam he appoints Flimann to high rank, thereby removing the obstacles to his marriage with Marietta.

Manuscript score: Ricordi Archives, Milan (autograph)

Le convenienze teatrali farsa in 1 act (revised as *Le convenienze ed inconvenienze teatrali* in 2 acts)
Composed: October–November 1827
First performed: Teatro Nuovo, Naples, 21 November 1827, with Gennaro
  Luzio (Mamm'Agata) (others unknown).
Librettist: Gaetano Donizetti
Libretto: based on Antonio Simone Sografi, *Le convenienze teatrali* (Venice,
  1794).
Revised: spring of 1831
First performed as *Le convenienze ed inconvenienze teatrali*: Teatro Canob-
  biana, Milan, 20 April 1831, with Fanny Corri-Paltoni (Prima Donna),
  Giuseppe Giordano (Guglielmo), Giuseppe Frezzolini (Mamm'Agata).
Librettist: Donizetti revised his own libretto
Libretto: new parts of the plot were based on Antonio Simone Sografi, *Le
  inconvenienze teatrali* (Padua, 1800).
Synopsis of the original version: At a rehearsal in a provincial opera house, Luigia, the Seconda Donna (soprano), complains of the insignificance of her role and wishes her mother would come to her support. The Impresario (bass) announces that the rehearsal will resume at five; this is greeted by a storm of excuses as to why the cast cannot attend. Into this disagreement bursts Mamm'Agata (baritone), Luigia's mother, ready to do battle to protect her daughter's interests. She insists that Luigia should be given a rondò to sing and gives the Composer (tenor) explicit instructions how to orchestrate it. This effrontery is too much for Proclo (bass), the basso of the troupe and the Prima Donna's father, who boasts of his daughter's vocal prowess and her many admirers and protectors. Mamm'Agata now insists that her daughter be given a duet to sing with the Prima Donna; when Corilla (soprano), the Prima Donna, protests, Mamm'Agata rudely reminds her that not so long ago she was a chorus singer in Milan. Soon the singer and the virago are threatening one another with physical violence. When Corilla storms out, vowing never to return, Mamm'Agata assures the Impresario that she is perfectly capable of singing the leading role. She offers a sample of her singing, and when the Composer reproaches her with being off pitch, she

blandly replies that the prompter threw her off. Now that Mamm'Agata has joined the cast, a new rehearsal is called. Everyone, but Agata, foresees a great fiasco.

Scores: published score (Paris: Schoenenberger, c. 1855) (original 1-act version); Bibliothèque Nationale, Paris (autograph of 1-act version, revised); Conservatorio di Musica, Milan (non-autograph copy of the 2-act version of 1831); Bibliothèque Nationale, Paris (non-autograph copy of a 2-act version)

L'esule di Roma, ossia Il proscritto (also given as *Settimio il proscritto*), opera seria ('melodramma eroico') in 2 acts
Composed: winter 1827
First performed: Teatro San Carlo, Naples, 1 January 1828, with Adelaide Tosi (Argelia), Edvige Ricci (Leontina), Berardo Calvari Winter[10] (Settimio), Luigi Lablache (Murena), Giovanni Campagnoli (Publio), Gaetano Chizzola (Lucio), Capranica *figlio* (Flavio).
Librettist: Domenico Gilardoni
Libretto: based on Luigi Marchionni, *Il proscritto romano, ossia Il leone del Caucaso* (Naples, 1820), derived from Louis-Charles Caigniez and Debotière, *Androclès, ou Le lion reconnaissant* (Paris, 1804).
Synopsis: Settimio (tenor), who has been banished by Tiberius, braves death by returning to Rome to see his beloved Argelia (soprano). Her father Murena (bass) has caused Settimio's exile by falsely accusing him of treason; Murena's conscience is troubled by the knowledge that Settimio possesses clear proof that the charge is false. Though able to spare his own life by revealing Murena's treachery, Settimio remains silent because of Argelia. Settimio's noble behavior plunges Murena into such depths of remorse that he is driven to confess his guilt.
Manuscript score: Ricordi Archives, Milan (autograph)

Alina, regina di Golconda opera buffa in 2 acts
Composed: March–April 1828
First performed: Teatro Carlo Felice, Genoa, 12 May 1828, with Serafina Rubini (Alina), de Vicenti (Fiorina), Giovanni Battista Verger (Seide), Antonio Tamburini (Volmar), Giuseppe Frezzolini (Belfiore).
Revised: 1829
First performed in revised version: Teatro Valle, Rome, 10 October 1829, with Annetta Fischer (Alina), Teresa Cecconi (Fiorina), Pietro Gentili (Seide), Federico Crespi (Volmar), Filippo Spada (Belfiore).
Librettist: Felice Romani
Libretto: based on Michel-Jean Sedaine's libretto for Pierre-Alexandre Monsigny's *Aline, reine de Golconde* (Paris, 1766), derived from Stanislas-Jean de Boufflers's prose narrative *La reine de Golconde* (Paris, 1761).[11]
Synopsis: Alina, the Queen of Golconda (soprano), is urged by her people to choose a husband, an honor that young Prince Seide (tenor) hopes to win.

He tries to force the issue, but the sound of cannon announces the arrival of the French ambassador, Volmar (baritone), and his aide, Belfiore (buffo), who are in reality the long-lost husbands of Alina and her maid Fiorina (soprano). The women disguised as slaves visit their husbands, an interview observed by the jealous Seide, who tells the people that Alina plans to betray them to the French. When Volmar comes to arrange an alliance, Seide claims that only a king can sign such a pact and insists that Alina choose one of her subjects as her consort. Seide stirs the people to revolt, but the French troops form a protective ring about Alina.

With the help of a sleeping-potion, Alina and Fiorina arrange an elaborate fantasy for Volmar and Belfiore. First, Alina appears to her husband in a reconstruction of the Provençal setting where first they met; then Fiorina deceives Belfiore into believing he is back in their French farmhouse. This illusion is interrupted by shouting, as the enraged Seide seizes Alina and drags her to prison. Alina renounces the throne but Seide forbids this move. Led by Volmar, the French attack the palace and free Alina. After Seide has been captured all hail Alina as their queen.

Manuscript score: Conservatorio di San Pietro a Majella, Naples (autograph)

Gianni di Calais opera semiseria in 3 acts
Composed: summer 1828
First performed: Teatro del Fondo, Naples, 2 August 1828, with Adelaide Comelli-Rubini[12] (Metilde), Maria Carraro (Adelina), Edvige Ricci (Arrigo), Giovanni Battista Rubini (Gianni), Antonio Tamburini (Rustano), Michele Benedetti (Il Re), Filippo Tati (Ruggero), Giovanni Pace (Guido), Gaetano Chizzola (Corrado), Capranica *figlio* (un officiale).
Librettist: Domenico Gilardoni
Libretto: based on Louis-Charles Caigniez, *Jean de Calais* (Paris, 1810).
Synopsis: Princess Metilde (soprano) and her young son return to her old home, the port of Seelanda. Some years before she had been captured by pirates and later rescued by the freebooter, Gianni of Calais (tenor), whom she subsequently married. Metilde is befriended by the Duchess Adelina (mezzo-soprano), who promises to help her win her father's approval for her marriage. Gianni's ship comes to port, flying a flag with Metilde's portrait on it. A sailor Rustano (baritone) advises Gianni and accompanies him to the palace, where the King has summoned him to explain the flag with its portrait of the long-missing Princess. At the palace Ruggero (bass) considers Gianni's actions insulting, but his anger really stems from his own thwarted design to marry Metilde. The King tells Gianni that the peers of the realm must give their consent to Metilde's marriage, approval that Ruggero plots to prevent. Rustano exposes Ruggero's treachery, and the King welcomes Gianni, Metilde and their son to his court as his legal heirs.

Manuscript score: Conservatorio di San Pietro a Majella, Naples (autograph)

Il paria opera seria in 2 acts
Composed: winter 1828

First performance: Teatro San Carlo, Naples, 12 January 1829, with Adelaide
   Tosi (Neala), Edvige Ricci (Zaide), Giovanni Battista Rubini (Idamore),
   Luigi Lablache (Zarete), Giovanni Campagnoli (Akebare), Gaetano Chiz-
   zola (Empsaele).
Librettist: Domenico Gilardoni
Libretto: based on Casimir Delavigne's tragedy, Le paria (Paris, 1821), via
   Gaetano Rossi's libretto for Michele Enrico Carafa's Il paria (Venice,
   1826), and Salvatore Taglioni's scenario for his ballet of the same name
   (Milan, 1827).
Synopsis: Neala (soprano) is the daughter of Akebare (bass), the high priest
of the Brahmins; she has fallen in love with Idamore (tenor) without knowing his true identity. Akebare decrees that his daughter is to marry a military
hero. In a sacred grove, Neala and her priestesses encounter an exhausted
fugitive, who reveals that he is Zarete (bass). When Idamore returns victorious from the wars to greet Neala, she tells him that her father has determined
that she must marry someone else. Zarete reveals himself to his son, Idamore, and flies into a rage when he learns that his son loves the daughter of
his enemy. When Idamore next sees Neala, knowing that Akebare has chosen him as his son-in-law, he tells her that he is a pariah's son and manages
to persuade her that the Brahmins' fear and loathing of his caste is only
superstition. Hearing the nuptial hymn for Neala and Idamore, Zarete becomes convinced that his son has betrayed him by consenting to marry the
daughter of the man who is responsible for the death of Zarete's wife. He
interrupts the marriage ceremony, whereupon Akebare orders him to be
killed at once, but Zarete proudly tells him that they are born of the same
dust, children of the same god. Both Idamore and Neala plead for the old
man's life to be spared, but Akebare is implacable. When Idamore swears
that he will die with his father, Akebare orders that they both be executed.
The fanatical priest even orders the execution of his daughter Neala for
having loved a pariah. Led to their fate, the lovers pledge that their love will
transcend death. Zarete dies cursing the Brahmins.
Manuscript score: Conservatorio di San Pietro a Majella, Naples (autograph)

Il giovedì grasso (also known as *Il nuovo Pourceaugnac*), farsa in 1 act
Composed: winter 1828–9
First performed: Teatro del Fondo, Naples, probably 26 February 1829, with
   Adelaide Comelli-Rubini (Nina), Maria Carraro (Camilla), Rosalinda
   Grossi (Stefania), Giovanni Battista Rubini (Ernesto), Luigi Lablache
   (Sigismondo), Giovanni Arrigotti (Teodoro), Giovanni Campagnoli (Il
   Colonello), Giovanni Pace (Cola).
Librettist: Domenico Gilardoni[13]
Libretto: based on Eugène Scribe and Charles-Gaspard Delestre-Poirson, *Le
   nouveau Pourceaugnac* (Paris, 1817).
Synopsis: Nina (soprano) loves the timid Teodoro, but her father the Colonel
(baritone) has arranged a marriage for her with a certain Ernesto Roustignac
(tenor) and will not heed her protests. Monsieur Piquet and his wife are

sympathetic to Nina's plight, and the former suggests that they bamboozle the intended bridegroom, whom nobody has seen, by adapting the plot of Molière's *Monsieur de Pourceaugnac* (Paris, 1669), in which a city-bred suitor is discomfited by quick-witted country people. Ernesto duly appears and Monsieur Piquet, now playing the part of Sigismondo (bass), greets him as an old friend, but Ernesto turns the tables on the would-be tricksters by treating Madame Piquet, now pretending to be Camilla, as an old flame with whom he went riding in a closed cabriolet and walked home arm-in-arm after the theater – inventions that reduce Piquet–Sigismondo to a jealous fury. When all is explained, Ernesto persuades the Colonel to allow Nina to marry Teodoro and the Piquets are reconciled.

Manuscript score: Conservatorio di San Pietro a Majella, Naples (autograph)

Il castello di Kenilworth (given at the *prima* and throughout its first production as *Elisabetta al castello di Kenilworth*), opera seria in 3 acts

Composed: spring–summer 1829

First performed: Teatro San Carlo, Naples, 6 July 1829, with Adelaide Tosi (Elisabetta), Luigia Boccabadati (Amelia), Virginia Eden (Fanny), Giovanni David (Leicester), Berardo Calvari Winter (Warney), Gennaro Ambrosini (Lambourne).

Revised: 1830

Librettist: Andrea Leone Tottola

Libretto: based on Gaetano Barbieri, *Elisabetta al castello di Kenilworth* (1824), adapted from Eugène Scribe's libretto for Daniel-François-Esprit Auber's *Leicester, ou Le château de Kenilworth* (Paris, 1823), itself ultimately derived from Walter Scott, *Kenilworth* (1821).

Synopsis: The news that Queen Elisabetta will soon come to Kenilworth worries Leicester (tenor) because he fears her wrath when she learns that he is married to Amelia (soprano). When Warney (tenor, 1829; baritone, 1830) tries to take advantage of Amelia's ambiguous position, she spurns him and Warney vows vengeance. To Leicester's relief Elisabetta arrives without any suspicions of his marriage. Amelia later confronts Leicester and reproaches him for his shabby treatment, declaring that she would rather die at his hands than be ignored. Warney enlists Lambourne (bass) to help him wreak his vengeance on Amelia. In the castle grounds Amelia unexpectedly encounters Elisabetta and throws herself at the Queen's feet. Elisabetta's suspicions of Leicester's infidelity are confirmed by his obvious agitation at seeing Amelia in her power. After Elisabetta orders Amelia to confinement, she worms from Leicester the confession that he is indeed married to Amelia. Furious, the Queen demands revenge; but when Leicester offers himself as her victim, she dismisses him contemptuously. Warney comes to Amelia's cell to administer a cup of poison to her, but Leicester appears in time to save her. When Elisabetta unexpectedly arrives in the cell, she gives orders that Warney and Lambourne be led away and forgives Leicester and Amelia, blessing their marriage. The chorus acclaims Britain's fortune in having such a Queen.

Manuscript score: Conservatorio di San Pietro a Majella, Naples (autograph)

I pazzi per progetto farsa in 1 act

Composed: winter 1829–30

First performed: Teatro San Carlo, Naples, 6 February 1830, with Luigia
  Boccabadati (Norina), Maria Carraro (Cristina), Luigi Lablache (Darlemont), Gennaro Luzio (Venanziano), Gennaro Ambrosini (Frank).

Librettist: Domenico Gilardoni

Libretto: adapted from Giovanni Carlo di Cosenza, *I pazzi per progetto*
  (Naples, 1824), derived from Eugène Scribe and Charles-Gaspard Delestre
  Poirson, *Une visite à Bedlam* (Paris, 1818), via the libretto to Bertini's *Una
  visita in Bedlam* (Naples, 1824).

Synopsis: Darlemont (bass) directs an insane asylum at Paris. His niece
Norina (soprano) is married to Blinval (baritone), but having been separated
for a long time by his military service, they pretend off and on to be patients
at this clinic to discover if in spite of their past differences, they still love
each other. The other characters are the outspoken servant (Frank), a military trumpeter who has deserted and is now posing as an alienist named
Eustachio (baritone), Cristina (mezzo-soprano), with whom Blinval has had
an affair, but who is now trying to evade Venanziano (buffo), her guardian,
who hopes to have Cristina certified mad so that he can get his hands on her
inheritance. At the resolution of the plot Norina and Blinval are reconciled.

Manuscript score: Conservatorio di San Pietro a Majella, Naples (autograph)

Il diluvio universale *azione tragica-sacra* in 3 acts

Composed: winter 1829–30

First performed: Teatro San Carlo, Naples, 28 February 1830, with Luigia
  Boccabadati (Sela), Maria Carraro (Ada), Fabiani (Tesbite), Edvige Ricci
  (Asfene), Cecilia Grassi (Abra), Luigi Lablache (Noè), Lorenzo Salvi (Cam),
  Berardo Calvari Winter (Cadmo), Gennaro Ambrosini (Iefte), Giovanni Ar-
  rigotti (Sem) and Gaetano Chizzola (Artoo).

Revised: winter 1833–4

First performed in revised version: Teatro Carlo Felice, Genoa, 17 January
  1834, with Edvige Claudini, Palmira Michel, Margherita Rubini,
  Domenico Cosselli (Noè), Lorenzo Bonfigli (Cadmo), Pietro Novelli (Iefte).

Librettist: Domenico Gilardoni

Libretto: based on Francesco Ringhini's tragedy, *Il diluvio* (Venice, 1788),
  but some details from Lord Byron's verse play *Heaven and Earth* (1822)
  and Thomas Moore's narrative poem *Loves of the Angels* (1823).

Synopsis: For building the ark, Noè (bass) and his sons are persecuted by
Cadmo (tenor), even though Sela (soprano), Cadmo's wife, tries to protect
them. Ada (mezzo), Sela's handmaiden, covets her mistress's place and tells
Cadmo that his wife is infatuated with Iefte (bass). To Ada's delight, Cadmo
casts off his wife and orders the execution of Noè, his sons, and Sela, who
has taken refuge with them. Noè warns Cadmo; thunder rumbles ominously
as Noè describes the coming inundation. As the marriage of Cadmo and Ada
is being celebrated, Sela burst in to bid farewell to her son. Cadmo offers to
take her back if she will renounce Noè's god. Desperate, she renounces

Jehovah and falls dead at a great clap of thunder. As a furious storm breaks, all rush out in confusion. In the final tableau of a sumberged landscape, a few survivors huddle on the remaining high ground as Noè's ark floats unharmed.

Manuscript scores: Conservatorio di San Pietro a Majella, Naples (autograph, 1830 version); Ricordi Archives, Milan (autograph, 1834 version)

Imelda de' Lambertazzi opera seria in 2 acts

Composed: May–August 1830

First performed: Teatro San Carlo, Naples, 5 September 1830, with Antonietta Galzerani (Imelda), Berardo Calvari Winter (Lamberto), Giovanni Basadonna (Orlando), Antonio Tamburini (Bonifacio), Michele Benedetti (Ugo), Gennaro Ambrosini (Ubaldo).

Librettist: Andrea Leone Tottola

Libretto: based on Sgricci's *Imelda* (Naples, 1827) and Defendente Sacchi's *I Lambertazzi e i Geremei: cronache di un trovatore* (Milan, 1830), both derived from Bombaci, *Historia dei fatti d'Antonio Lambertacci* (Bologna, 1532).

Synopsis: Although the Lambertazzi and Geremei families of Bologna are feuding,[14] Imelda (soprano) loves Bonifacio Geremei (baritone). They fall victims to the bad blood between the factions, fomented in large part by Imelda's father, Orlando (tenor) and her brother Lamberto (tenor). When Bonifacio fails to persuade Imelda to go away with him, he comes to the Lambertazzi to beg for peace and proposes that he marry Imelda to spare the city further bloodshed. Lamberto takes this offer as a dire insult. When Bonifacio tries to see Imelda once more, the alarm is raised, and Lamberto stabs him. In the midst of the fighting Imelda tries to flee, but she is run through by her dying brother.

Manuscript score: Conservatorio di San Pietro a Majella, Naples (autograph)

Anna Bolena opera seria in 2 acts

Composed: November–December 1830

First performed: Teatro Carcano, Milan, 26 December 1830, with Giuditta Pasta (Anna Bolena), Elisa Orlandi (Giovanna Seymour), Enrichetta Laroche (Smeton), Giovanni Battista Rubini (Percy), Filippo Galli (Enrico VIII), Lorenzo Biondi (Rochefort), Antonio Crippa (Hervey).

Librettist: Felice Romani

Libretto: based on Ippolito Pindemonte's *Enrico VIII, ossia Anna Bolena* (Turin, 1816), which is a translation of Marie-Joseph de Chénier's *Henri VIII* (Paris, 1791); and Alessandro Pepoli's *Anna Bolena* (Venice, 1788).

Synopsis: the King's neglect of Anna (soprano) bothers the conscience of Giovanna Seymour (mezzo-soprano), who has yielded to his royal importunities, and the King's dark hints about Anna's future only increase her distress. Rochefort (bass), Anna's brother, is amazed to see Percy (tenor), Anna's first love, returned from exile. The thought of seeing Anna again fills Percy with agitation. The royal hunting party approaches and Enrico (bass), who has planned Percy's return as a trap for Anna, is grimly amused at their emotion at encountering each other. When Smeton (*musico*), Anna's household musician, who is in love with his mistress, tries to return a miniature of her that he has stolen, he is forced to hide as Anna hears Percy's confession of love. When Percy draws his sword to kill himself, Smeton rushes forward just as Enrico bursts in and orders their arrest. Smeton creates a counter-disturbance, and in his flurry the miniature slips out of his tunic and lands at the King's feet. In spite of their protests, Anna, Percy and Smeton are ordered to prison.

Seymour tells Anna that the King will spare her if she will confess. Anna refuses. Hoping to persuade her, Seymour admits that Enrico loves another; but when Anna demands to know her rival's identity, Seymour confesses it is she. Anna's repugnance is overcome by Seymour's sincere remorse. At Anna's trial Smeton lies and admits to being her lover, believing his confession will save her, whereas it seals her fate. When Anna and Percy are summoned before the council, Seymour rejects the King's offer of a crown and pleads for Anna's life. In the Tower, Percy and Rochefort (Anna's brother) refuse clemency when they learn it does not extend to Anna. In her cell, Anna's mind wanders as she recalls her girlhood love for Percy. When cannons announce the King's new marriage, Anna calls on heaven not to curse the royal couple but to have mercy on them.

Manuscript score: Ricordi Archives, Milan (autograph)

Gianni di Parigi opera buffa ('opera comica') in 2 acts
Composed: 1831
First performed: La Scala, Milan, 10 September 1839, with Antonietta Rainieri-Marini (Principessa di Navarra), Felicita Baillou-Hillaret (Oliviero), Marietta Sacchi (Lorezza), Lorenzo Salvi (Gianni), Ignazio Marini (Il Siniscalco), Agostino Rovere (Pedrigo).
Librettist: Felice Romani[15]
Libretto: based on Godard d'Aucourt de Saint-Just's libretto for François-Adrien Boieldieu's *Jean de Paris* (Paris, 1812).
Synopsis: A provincial inn has been rented by the Princess of Navarre (soprano), daughter of the King of Navarre. To this hostelry comes a page, Oliviero (*musichetto*, mezzo-soprano), to arrange supper for his master, Gianni of Paris, a rich and honest burgher. The host Pedrigo (bass) explains that his establishment is already engaged, but Oliviero insists that an inn should be open to all comers. Gianni (tenor) shortly arrives and bids the page not to reveal his true identity nor the purpose of his journey. Gianni is really the Dauphin of France, hoping to discover whether his fiancée, the Princess, whom he has never seen, is as good and beautiful as reports have made her out. Gianni secures accommodations by paying Pedrigo double. When the Princess's self-important Seneschal (bass) arrives, he is irritated by Gianni's presumption. The Princess drives up and is not at all displeased to find Gianni ensconced in the inn and graciously accepts his invitation to

dinner. Later, she reveals to Gianni that she has seen through his ruse and is delighted to marry such an enterprising young man.

Manuscript scores: Conservatorio di San Pietro a Majella, Naples (autograph); Ricordi Archives, Milan (partial autograph)

Francesca di Foix opera semiseria in 1 act
Composed: spring 1831
First performed: Teatro San Carlo, Naples, 30 May 1831, with Luigia Boccabadati (Francesca), Marietta Gioia-Tamburini (Edmondo), Lorenzo Bonfigli (Il Duca), Antonio Tamburini (Il Re), Giovanni Campagnoli (Il Conte).
Librettist: Domenico Gilardoni
Libretto: based on Jean-Nicolas Bouilly's and Emanuel Mercier-Dupaty's libretto for Henri-Montan Berton, *Françoise de Foix* (Paris, 1809).
Synopsis: The King of France (baritone), the Duke (tenor) and Edmondo, a page (*musichetto*, mezzo-soprano) form a conspiracy to teach the jealous Count (bass) a lesson. The Count keeps his lovely young wife in seclusion, afraid to expose her to the temptations of the court, and he has spread word that she is too ill and too ugly to be seen in public. By a ruse the plotters get Francesca, the Countess (soprano), to court, where the Count recognizes her but dares not acknowledge her for fear of being caught out in his lies. But when the King offers the Countess's hand to the victor of a tournament, the Count can control himself no longer. As he confesses his falsehoods, the others moralize on the folly of jealousy.
Manuscript score: Conservatorio di San Pietro a Majella, Naples (autograph)

La romanziera e l'uomo nero farsa in 1 act
Composed: spring 1831
First performed: Teatro del Fondo, Naples, 18 June 1831, with Luigia Boccabadati (Antonina), Antonio Tamburini (Carlino), Gennaro Luzio (Fedele), Gennaro Ambrosini (Il Conte) (others unknown).
Librettist: Domenico Gilardoni
Libretto: lost, possibly based on Eugène Scribe and Jean-Henri Dupin, *L'homme noir* (Paris, 1820).
Synopsis: (Since the original libretto, containing the spoken dialogue, is lost the following description can be only brief.) Antonina (soprano), the daughter of the Count (bass), has taken up the fad of extreme Romanticism, abetted by the flamboyant Tommaso (bass) and the others. Finally, Antonina comes to see the folly of attitudinizing and swears to her father 'Mai più romanticismo!' (Never again romanticism!)
Manuscript score: Conservatorio di San Pietro a Majella, Naples (autograph)

Fausta opera seria in 2 acts
Composed: August–September 1831
First performed: Teatro San Carlo, Naples, 12 January 1832, with Giuseppina Ronzi-de Begnis (Fausta), Virginia Eden (Beroë), Edvige Ricci (Licinia),

Giovanni Basadonna (Crispo), Antonio Tamburini (Costantino), Giovanni Campagnoli (Massimiano), Giovanni Revalden (Albino).

Librettists: Domenico Gilardoni, completed after his death by Gaetano Donizetti (according to Zavadini)[16]

Libretto: source unidentified

Synopsis: Fausta (soprano) is the second wife of the Emperor Costantino (baritone) and loves her stepson Crispo (tenor). Although she tries to conceal her passion from her husband, she cannot restrain herself from confessing it to Crispo. When Costantino discovers them together, Fausta accuses Crispo, who is speechless, of making improper advances to her. Costantino orders Crispo into exile. Fausta's father, Massimiano (bass), leads a conspiracy against the Emperor. Crispo overhears their plotting and starts after them sword in hand; suddenly finding himself before his father, he drops his sword. The Emperor's suspicions seem confirmed when Massimiano hypocritically accuses Crispo of intended parricide. When Crispo is tried before the senate, Costantino can hardly bring himself to sign the death warrant of his son, although the senate insists upon it. Massimiano hurries off to have Crispo executed without delay. When Fausta realizes that she is powerless to save Crispo, she drinks poison from her ring. Learning of Massimiano's plot, Costantino hurries to save his son but he is too late. Dying, Fausta confesses her guilt to the horrified Emperor.

Manuscript score: Conservatorio di San Pietro a Majella, Naples (autograph)

Ugo, conte di Parigi opera seria in 2 acts

Composed: winter 1831–2

First performed: La Scala, Milan, 13 March 1832, with Giuditta Pasta (Bianca), Giulia Grisi (Adelia), Clorinda Corradi-Pantanelli (Luigi V), Felicita Baillou-Hillaret (Emma), Domenico Donzelli (Ugo), Vincenzo Negrini (Folco d'Anjou).

Librettist: Felice Romani

Libretto: source unidentified

Synopsis: King Luigi V (*musico*), the last of the Carolingians, has lately ascended the throne, upon the recent (and unexplained – at least as the censors left the libretto) death of his father King Lotario. Folco d'Anjou (bass) plans to play off the weak king against the powerful soldier Ugo (tenor). Ugo (perhaps more recognizable as Hugues Capet, the first of the Capetian kings of France) remains loyal to Luigi in spite of the pressure to win the crown for the house of Anjou. Luigi's fiancée, Bianca of Aquitaine (soprano), secretly loves Ugo and despises Luigi, but she is stunned to learn that her sister Adelia (soprano) also loves Ugo. Luigi sanctions a match between Adelia and Ugo, but this prospect enrages the jealous Bianca, who declares her love for Ugo and insists that he confirm it. Horrified, Ugo draws back, but Luigi is so angered by Ugo's apparent faithlessness that he orders his arrest. Bianca comes to Ugo in prison and urges him to lead a revolt

against Luigi. Ugo refuses, but soon learns that his troops have revolted without him. Ugo puts down the rebellion and informs Luigi that he has no designs either on his throne or his fiancée. Luigi returns Ugo's sword and conducts him and Adelia to the chapel. Folco insinuates to the jealous Bianca that poison might be her revenge upon Luigi; as she decocts a lethal dose, she is interrupted by the remorseful Emma (soprano), widowed mother of Luigi. Then the sounds of nuptial jubilation from the nearby chapel drive Bianca into a frenzy. Emma summons the guards and, as everyone pours in from the chapel, Bianca drinks the poison herself, declaring it her revenge, and dies, bequeathing both her hatred and her love to those about her.
Manuscript score: Conservatorio di San Pietro a Majella, Naples (autograph, incomplete)

L'elisir d'amore opera buffa ('opera comica') in 2 acts
Composed: spring 1832
First performed: Teatro Canobbiana, Milan, 12 May 1832, with Sabine Heinefetter (Adina), Giambattista Genero (Nemorino), Henri-Bernard Dabadie (Belcore), Giuseppe Frezzolini (Dr Dulcamara).
Librettist: Felice Romani
Libretto: based on Eugène Scribe's libretto for Daniel-François-Esprit Auber's *Le philtre* (Paris, 1831), derived from Silvio Malaperta, *Il filtro*.
Synopsis: Nemorino (tenor) is hopelessly in love with Adina (soprano), but she is put off by his lack of self-assertiveness. The arrival of Sergeant Belcore (baritone) provides a diversion, and the capricious Adina seems in danger of being swept off her feet. Dr Dulcamara (buffo) peddles his cure-all, selling Nemorino a bottle and assuring him that he will be irresistible to the ladies – after twenty-four hours. The elixir gives Nemorino a rush of self-confidence, but his spirits are crushed when Adina agrees to marry Belcore that very evening. Thoroughly dejected at these wedding plans, Nemorino hopes to buy more elixir but he is penniless. When Belcore returns, chagrined because at the last moment Adina has refused to marry him, Nemorino volunteers for the army, planning to spend the bounty money on elixir. The village girls have heard that Nemorino's rich uncle has died, having made his nephew his heir, and they crowd around him provocatively – attentions that Nemorino attributes to the elixir he has just drunk. The sight of all the girls fawning over Nemorino, just when she expected to see him downcast, astonishes Adina. From Dulcamara she learns that Nemorino truly loves her and has drunk the elixir to help him win her, but she claims she has a more potent art than Dulcamara's to make him hers. Seeing a tear upon her cheek, Nemorino is deeply moved. After Adina tells him that she has bought back his enlistment, she confesses she loves him. The whole village celebrates the happy couple's betrothal.
Manuscript scores: Conservatorio di San Pietro a Majella, Naples (autograph, Act 1); Museo Donizettiano, Bergamo (autograph, Act 2)

Sancia di Castiglia opera seria in 2 acts

Composed: September–October 1832

First performed: Teatro San Carlo, Naples, 4 November 1832, with Giuseppina Ronzi-de Begnis (Sancia), Diomilla Santolini, (Garzia), Edvige Ricci (Elvira), Giovanni Basadonna (Rodrigo), Luigi Lablache (Ircano).

Librettist: Pietro Salatino

Libretto: source unidentified[17]

Synopsis: Ircano (bass), a Moorish prince, hopes to marry Sancia (soprano) as a reward for his military assistance. The Queen's principal minister, Rodrigo (tenor), is completely opposed to the marriage. Believing her son Garzia (*musico*) has died in battle, Sancia hopes to quench her grief in spite of the council's opposition. Garzia returns after a lucky escape from death and demands the throne. Ircano tries to persuade the passionate but weak-minded Sancia to poison her son. Just as Garzia raises the fatal cup prepared by Ircano, Sancia snatches it from his hand and drains it.

Manuscript score: Conservatorio di San Pietro a Majella, Naples (autograph)

Il furioso all'isola di San Domingo opera semiseria in 3 acts

Composed: August–winter 1832

First performed: Teatro Valle, Rome, 2 January 1833, with Elisa Orlandi (Eleonora), Marianna Franceschini (Marcella), Giorgio Ronconi (Cardenio), Lorenzo Salvi (Ferrando), Filippo Valentini (Bartolomeo), Ferdinando Lauretti (Kaidamà).

Librettist: Jacopo Ferretti

Libretto: based on a five-act play, *Il furioso nell'isola di San Domingo* (Rome, 1820),[18] ultimately derived from Miguel Cervantes, *Don Quixote*, Part I (1605), chapters 23–7.

Synopsis: Cardenio (baritone), driven mad by his wife's unfaithfulness has come to San Domingo, where he is cared for by Bartolomeo Mergoles (bass) and his daughter Marcella (soprano). Their servant Kaidamà (buffo) lives in terror of the madman. A tropical hurricane shipwrecks Eleonora (soprano) on the island; for years she has searched for her missing husband. Cardenio tells Kaidamà of his tormenting memories, but Kaidamà, uncomprehending, flees. After the storm, Ferrando (tenor), Cardenio's brother, disembarks; he, too, has long been looking for Cardenio. Bartolomeo persuades Cardenio to talk of his suffering, but at the climax of his story the madman suddenly recognizes Eleonora and tries to stab her. Only Ferrando's swift action prevents a tragedy. Later, Eleonora tries to unburden her conscience to Cardenio, but he is seized with delusions of blindness. At last he recognizes her and rushes off to leap into the sea. Ferrando runs after him and saves him. This shock restores Cardenio's reason, but he believes his suffering can be resolved only by death. Ferrando brings Eleonora to him, and she, weeping, confesses her intolerable guilt. Cardenio hands her a pistol, telling her they will shoot each other. Eleonora takes the weapon willingly, but when the others appear carrying torches, in the flickering light Cardenio sees that

Eleonora aims the pistol at her heart. Convinced at last that Eleonora truly loves him, he welcomes her to his arms.

Manuscript score: Ricordi Archives, Milan (autograph)

Parisina opera seria in 3 acts

Composed: February–March 1833

First performed: Teatro della Pergola, Florence, 17 March 1833, with Carolina Ungher (Parisina), Teresa Zappucci (Imelda), Gilbert Duprez (Ugo), Domenico Cosselli (Azzo), Carlo Ottolini Porto (Ernesto).

Librettist: Felice Romani

Libretto: based on Lord Byron's *Parisina* (1816), derived, according to Byron, from 'a circumstance in [Edward] Gibbon's "Antiquities of the House of Brunswick"' (1814 edn).

Synopsis: Azzo d'Este (baritone) correctly suspects that his wife Parisina (soprano) loves Ugo (tenor), his first wife's son.[19] At one time Parisina and Ugo had planned to marry, but Azzo had forced her to become his wife instead. When Ugo wins a tourney, Parisina gives him the victor's crown, and this nearness to the man she loves troubles her deeply. That night Azzo comes to her bedchamber, consumed by jealousy, desperately hoping to have his doubts settled. In her sleep, Parisina murmurs Ugo's name, and Azzo, enraged, swears vengeance. When Ugo and Parisina attempt to flee, Azzo intercepts them and orders Ugo's execution. At the sight of her lover's corpse, Parisina dies of grief.

Manuscript score: Museo Donizettiano, Bergamo (autograph)

Torquato Tasso opera semiseria in 3 acts

Composed: summer 1833

First performed: Teatro Valle, Rome, 9 September 1833, with Adelina Spech (Eleonora d'Este), Angiolina Carocci (Eleonora di Scandiano), Giorgio Ronconi (Tasso), Antonio Poggi (Roberto Geraldini), Ferdinando Lauretti (Don Gherardo), Antonio Rinaldi (Alfonso d'Este), Luigi Garofalo (Ambrogio).

Librettist: Jacopo Ferretti

Libretto: based primarily on Giovanni Rosini, *Torquato Tasso* (Pisa, 1832); and secondarily on Carlo Goldoni, *Tasso* (1755), Johann Wolfgang Goethe, *Tasso* (published 1790; acted 1809), and Lord Byron, *The Lament of Tasso* (1817).

Synopsis: At the Ferrarese court, Tasso (baritone) has two rivals: Roberto (tenor), who envies his fame; and Don Gherardo (buffo), who believes that Tasso loves Eleonora di Scandiano (mezzo-soprano), whom he himself adores. Tasso, however, loves another Eleonora (soprano), the Duke's sister. Don Gherardo steals a poem Tasso has written in praise of his beloved Eleonora. Together, the Duchess and Tasso read from his *Gerusalemme liberata*, and she is moved by it to confess her own love for him. They learn that the Duke is in possession of a poem by Tasso that compromises the

Duchess. Roberto announces the Duke of Mantua's ambassador, who is bringing a marriage proposal to the Duchess Eleonora. The Duke (bass) feigns indifference to these matters and orders all to accompany him to Belriguardo. There, the Duchess, believing Roberto is loyal to Tasso, begs him to arrange a final interview with the poet, but Roberto informs the Duke. When Tasso approaches the Duchess, they are spied upon by Don Gherardo and Eleonora di Scandiano (herself in love with Tasso), and by Roberto and the Duke. The Duchess Eleonora begs Tasso to forget her, but he urges that they go away together. The Duke comes forward, declaring that Tasso has gone mad and orders that he be confined. After seven years in the madhouse Tasso has forgotten where he is and why. Courtiers come to announce his freedom as he is to be crowned laureate on the Campidoglio. Thinking his crown of bay might bridge the gap that has separated him from a Duchess, he asks for news of Eleonora. He is shattered to learn that she died five years before. His mind wanders and he imagines he sees her again, as the courtiers urge him to think of his future glory.

Manuscript score: Ricordi Archives, Milan (autograph)

Lucrezia Borgia[20] opera seria in a prologue and 2 acts

Composed: October–December 1833

First performed: La Scala, Milan, 26 December 1833, with Henriette Méric-Lalande (Lucrezia Borgia), Marietta Brambilla (Maffio Orsini), Francesco Pedrazzi (Gennaro) Luciano Mariani (Alfonso d'Este), Napoleone Marconi (Jeppo Liverotto), Giuseppe Visanetti (Don Apostolo Gazella), ismaele Guaita (Ascanio Petrucci), Giuseppe Vaschetti (Oloferno Vitellozzo), Domenico Spiaggi (Gubetto Belverana), Raineri Pochini (Rustighello), Francesco Petrazzoli (Astolfo).

Revised: 1839

First performed in revised version (with *finale nuovo*): La Scala, Milan, 11 January 1840, with Erminia Frezzolini (Lucrezia Borgia), Rosina Mazzarelli (Maffio Orsini), Napoleone Moriani (Gennaro), Ignazio Marini (Alfonso), Gaetano Rossi (Gubetta).

Revised: 1840[21]

First performed in second revised version: Théâtre-Italien, Paris, 31 October 1840, with Giulia Grisi (Lucrezia Borgia), Luigia Bianchi (Maffio Orsini), Mario (Gennaro), Antonio Tamburini (Alfonso).

Librettist: Felice Romani

Libretto: based on Victor Hugo, *Lucrèce Borgia* (Paris, 1833).

Synopsis: In Venice, Gennaro (tenor) enjoys the Carnival festivities with his friends, especially the loyal Maffio Orsini (*musico*). He meets a beautiful woman and is attracted by her tender concern; later he is horrified to learn from Orsini and the others that she is the infamous Lucrezia Borgia (soprano).

In Ferrara, Duke Alfonso (bass), Lucrezia's fourth husband, hopes to avenge his honor, believing Gennaro to be Lucrezia's lover. Gennaro and his friends have come to Ferrara for adventure, but when he sees Lucrezia's crest, he disfigures the emblem to read 'ORGIA'. For this insult, Alfonso orders that Gennaro be seized. In the *palazzo* Lucrezia, unaware of the perpetrator's identity, insists that Alfonso punish the culprit. When he produces Gennaro, Lucrezia hides her fear and consents to Alfonso's poisoning the young man. When Alfonso leaves, Lucrezia promptly supplies Gennaro with an antidote and bids him leave Ferrara at once. Before Gennaro can depart, Orsini insists that he attend a ball at the Princess Negroni's. There in the midst of the jollification, sinister voices are heard singing of death. Orsini and his friends rush to the doors but find them locked. Lucrezia suddenly appears, clad all in black, and declares she has had them all poisoned for their insults. Horrified to see Gennaro among them, for she believed he had left the city, she swears she never meant her vengeance to extend to him. Gennaro refuses her proffered antidote and recoils in loathing when she confesses that she is his mother. When he dies, she collapses by his corpse.

Manuscript score: Ricordi Archives, Milan (autograph; including both finales)

Rosmonda d'Inghilterra opera seria in 2 acts (revised as *Eleonora di Gujenna*)

Composed: January–February 1834

First performed: Teatro della Pergola, Florence, 27 February 1834, with Fanny Tacchinardi-Persiani (Rosmonda Clifford), Anna del Sere (Eleonora di Gujenna), Giuseppina Merola (Arturo), Gilbert Duprez (Enrico II), Carlo Ottolini Porto (Clifford).

Revised: summer 1837

Librettist: Felice Romani.[22]

Libretto: Romani's libretto for Carlo Coccia's *Rosmonda d'Inghilterra* (Venice, 1829); the immediate source of that libretto is not known, but it was probably the same as that used for the ballet *Rosemonda*, music by Francesco Schira and choreography by Giovanni Galzerani, danced at La Scala on 26 December 1828.[23]

Synopsis: Enrico II of England (tenor) has returned from the wars tired of his jealous wife Eleonora (mezzo-soprano) and longing to see Rosmonda Clifford (soprano), whom years earlier he had wooed under the alias of Edegardo. When the King confesses his grief at his loveless marriage, Clifford (bass) tells him he must not act dishonorably. Rosmonda eagerly awaits a reunion with 'Edegardo', but when her father tells her that this suitor is married, Rosmonda is shaken. The jealous Eleonora suspects that Rosmonda is her rival and tries to win back Enrico's love by reminding him that he owes his power to her. All the King desires is peace. Clifford hopes to get Rosmonda away to safety, but she manages to see Enrico once more to say farewell. When Enrico promises to make her his Queen, Rosmonda is horrified. Eleonora comes to Rosmonda's tower room to have her revenge, since she has arranged for Rosmonda's poisoning. Dying, Rosmonda welcomes the release of death.

Manuscript score: Conservatorio di San Pietro a Majella, Naples (autograph)

Maria Stuarda opera seria in 3 acts (revised as *Buondelmonte* in 2 acts)
Composed: July–August 1834
First performed: La Scala, Milan, 30 December 1835, with Maria Malibran (Maria Stuarda), Giacinta Puzzi-Tosi (Elisabetta), Teresa Moja (Anna Kennedy), Domenico Reina (Leicester), Ignazio Marini (Talbot), Pietro Novelli (Cecil).
Librettist: Giuseppe Bardari
Libretto: based on Andrea Maffei's translation (1830) of Friedrich Schiller, *Maria Stuart* (Weimar, 1800).
Synopsis: Leicester (tenor) and Talbot (bass) are concerned for the imprisoned Maria. Leicester shows Queen Elisabetta (soprano) a letter he has received from Maria, hoping to arouse sympathy for her, but the irascible sovereign's jealousy flares; yet she does not refuse to visit Maria in her detention at Fotheringay. Leicester tries to prepare Maria there for this interview. Elisabetta is so infuriated at the sight of the youth and dignity of the Scottish Queen that she insults her. Stung, Maria calls Elisabetta her father's bastard and a stain on England's honor. For these words Elisabetta threatens her with death. At Westminster Elisabetta has prepared a death warrant for Maria, but she hesitates to sign it until Cecil persuades her to rid herself of her dangerous rival. When Leicester comes to plead for Maria's life, Elisabetta tells him he is too late. At Fotheringay, Maria receives her sentence from Cecil without flinching. Talbot, wearing a priest's cassock beneath his cloak, offers her the consolations of her faith and grants her absolution. Maria asks her friends to join her in a prayer of forgiveness for all those who have wronged her. Leicester watches helplessly as Maria is led to the block.
Manuscript score: Conservatorio di San Pietro a Majella, Naples (non-autograph materials)
Revised: September–October 1834
First performed as **Buondelmonte:** Teatro San Carlo, Naples, 18 October 1834, with Giuseppina Ronzi-de Begnis (Bianca degl'Amadei), Anna del Sere (Irene), Anna Salvetti (Eleonora dei Donati), Teresa Zappucci (Giovanna), Francesco Pedrazzi (Buondelmonte), Federico Crespi (Lamberto), Achille Balestracci (Oderigo Fifanti), Signor Sparalik (Stiatta Uberti).
Librettist: Pietro Salatino
Libretto: source unidentified
Synopsis: The action takes place in Florence in the mid-thirteenth century. Buondelmonte, a native of Florence, has gone back on his promise to enter into an arranged marriage with Bianca degl'Amadei, thereby precipitating local warfare between the Guelphs (the party of the pope) and the Ghibellines (the supporters of the Holy Roman Emperor).

Manuscript score: Conservatorio di San Pietro a Majella, Naples (partial autograph)

Gemma di Vergy opera seria in 2 acts
Composed: October–December 1834
First performed: La Scala, Milan, 26 December 1834, with Giuseppina Ronzi-de Begnis (Gemma), Felicita Baillou-Hillaret (Ida), Domenico Reina (Tamas), Orazio Cartagenova (Il Conte di Vergy), Ignazio Marini (Guido), Domenico Spiaggi (Rolando).
Librettist: Emanuele Bidèra
Libretto: based on Alexandre Dumas père, *Charles VII chez les grands vassaux* (Paris, 1831).
Synopsis: Gemma (soprano) discovers that her husband Vergy (baritone) has had their union annulled because she has borne him no children; he has done this so that he will be free to marry again. Tamas (tenor), an Arab slave faithful to Gemma, has quarreled with the retainer Rolando (bass), and Gemma temporarily quiets the arguments. She is so stunned with grief and also troubled by jealousy that she insists on a final interview with the Count to try to dissuade him from his decision. Tamas murders Rolando, but when the Count sees the bloody dagger, he fears that Gemma has attempted to take her own life. Tamas is sentenced to die, but Gemma pleads for him. The Count is much stirred by her eloquence, but the news that his new bride Ida (mezzo-soprano) is arriving moves him to eager expectation, agitates Gemma, and prompts Tamas to swear vengeance for her.

Posing as her own servant, Gemma confronts Ida and soon threatens to kill her; the Count's opportune arrival does not deter her. Tamas takes the dagger from her and tries to get her to escape with him. While the wedding of Ida and the Count is in progress, Gemma urges Tamas to kill her. He snatches up the dagger and rushes off instead to stab the Count at the altar. Gemma, unaware of his act, tries to pray. Tamas returns to confess his crime, saying he could not bear to see Gemma suffer and stabs himself. Overwrought, Gemma swears her innocence and her abiding love for her husband, but looks forward to the release of death.
Manuscript score: Ricordi Archives, Milan (autograph)

Marin(o) Faliero opera seria in 3 acts
Composed: summer 1834 – February 1835
First performed: Paris, Théâtre-Italien, 12 March 1835, with Giulia Grisi (Elena), Giovanni Battista Rubini (Fernando), Antonio Tamburini (Israele Bertucci), Luigi Lablache (Marin Faliero), Nicholas Ivanoff (Gondoliere) (others unknown).
Librettists: Emanuele Bidèra, with revisions by Agostino Ruffini
Libretto: based on Casimir Delavigne's tragedy, *Marino Faliero* (Paris, 1829), derived from Lord Byron's tragedy of the same name (London, 1829).
Synopsis: Israele Bertucci (baritone), captain of the Venetian arsenal, is pub-

licly insulted by a young patrician, Michele Steno (bass), who has recently aroused the old Doge's ire by impugning the chastity of the young Dogaressa Elena (soprano). Israele enlists the support of Marin Faliero, the Doge (bass), in a conspiracy against the council. There is, however, some justification for Steno's charge; Elena has fallen in love with the Doge's nephew Fernando (tenor). She has decided to part from him and gives him a scarf as a token. At a masked ball where the conspirators meet, Elena complains of a masker (Steno) who dogs her steps and insults her. Fernando challenges Steno, setting the square before SS. Giovanni e Paolo as their duelling ground. There Fernando waits, willing to die for Elena's honor. As the conspirators gather, the sound of fighting is heard, and Fernando is borne in; dying, he asks that his face be covered with Elena's scarf. The conspirators go off to their appointed tasks, unaware that one of them, Beltrame (bass) has betrayed them. While the Doge tells Elena of Fernando's death, the guards come to arrest him. In the council chamber when the Doge is condemned he tears off his doge's cap and tramples it. He is granted a final interview with Elena. He shows her the scarf and asks that it be used to cover his face and Fernando's when they are buried in the same tomb. Shaken, Elena confesses her adultery. The Doge rages, but realizing that his death is near, he forgives Elena. After the Doge is led away, she waits shuddering at the window. At the sound of the blow of the headsman's axe, she screams and collapses.

Manuscript score: Conservatorio di San Pietro a Majella, Naples (autograph, not including the revisions made in Paris in January and February 1835)

Lucia di Lammermoor opera seria in 3 acts (revised as *Lucie de Lammermoor*)

Composed: June – 6 July 1835

First performed: Teatro San Carlo, Naples, 26 September 1835, with Fanny Tacchinardi-Persiani (Lucia), Teresa Zappucci (Alisa), Gilbert Duprez (Edgardo), Domenico Cosselli (Enrico), Carlo Ottolini Porto (Raimondo Bide-the-Bent), Balestrieri[24] (Arturo Bucklaw), Anafesto Rossi (Normanno).

Librettist: Salvatore Cammarano

Revised: summer 1839

First performed as *Lucie de Lammermoor*: Théâtre de la Renaissance, Paris, 6 August 1839, with Anna Thillon (Lucie), Achille Ricciardi (Edgard), Hurteaux (Henri), Zelger (Raimond), Gibert (Arthur), Joseph Kelm (Gilbert).

Librettists: Cammarano's libretto translated and revised by Alphonse Royer and Gustave Vaëz

Libretto: based on Walter Scott, *The Bride of Lammermoor* (1819) via Giuseppe Balocchi's libretto for Michele Enrico Carafa, *Le nozze di Lammermoor* (Paris, 1829), Calisto Bassi's libretto for Luigi Rieschi, *La fidanzata di Lammermoor*, and Pietro Beltrame's libretto for Alberto Mazzucato, *La fidanzata di Lammermoor* (Padua, 1834).

Synopsis: Enrico Ashton (baritone), is outraged to learn from his gillie Normanno (tenor) that Lucia (soprano), his sister, has been secretly meeting with Edgardo (tenor), his enemy. Lucia waits with the apprehensive Alisa (mezzo-soprano) for a rendezvous with Edgardo, who tells her that he must leave Scotland for France, but not before they exchange rings and pledge vows. Some time later Enrico shows Lucia a forged letter, supposedly proving Edgardo's infidelity. Grief-stricken, Lucia consents to a political marriage, arranged by her desperate brother. The presbyter Raimondo (bass) further persuades her. The wedding guests assemble, and Lucia comes numbly forward to sign the contract. Just then Edgardo bursts in, unexpectedly returned from France, and denounces Lucia's breach of faith. The miserable girl faints. Enrico comes to Edgardo's dilapidated castle to challenge him to a duel. Raimondo interrupts the wedding festivities with the appalling news that Lucia has gone mad and stabbed her bridegroom Arturo (tenor). Still carrying the knife, Lucia appears and it is soon apparent that she is unaware of her crime and is hallucinating that this is the day appointed for her marriage to Edgardo. In his family burying-plot Edgardo waits to duel with Enrico, thinking bitterly of his fate. When Raimondo brings news of Lucia's death, he stabs himself.

Manuscript score: Museo Teatrale alla Scala, Milan (autograph)

Belisario opera seria in 3 acts

Composed: October 1835 – January 1836

First performed: Teatro La Fenice, Venice, 4 February 1836, with Carolina
   Ungher (Antonina), Antonietta Vial (Irene), Amalia Badessi (Eudora),
   Celestino Salvatori (Belisario), Ignazio Pasini (Alamiro), Saverio Giorgi
   (Giustiniano), Adone dell'Oro (Eutropio), Giovanni Rizzi (Eusebio and
   Ottarino).

Librettist: Salvatore Cammarano

Libretto: based on Luigi Marchionni's adaptation of Eduard von Schenk,
   Belisarius (Munich, 1820).

Synopsis: When Belisario (baritone) returns to Byzantium in triumph, his wife, Antonina (soprano), believing he is responsible for the death of their son, plans to denounce him to the Emperor Giustiniano (bass). Belisario asks freedom for his captives, but one, Alamiro (tenor), elects to stay at his side. Belisario is summoned to the senate, charged with filicide and condemned on forged evidence. Outside Belisario's prison, Alamiro is enraged to learn that Belisario has been sentenced to exile and blinded, and he swears vengeance on Byzantium. Belisario's daughter Irene (mezzo-soprano), disguised as a boy, comes to lead her father into exile. On their wanderings, Belisario and Irene hide in a cave at the sound of an army and overhear Alamiro and Ottarino (bass) plan an assault on Byzantium. Belisario rushes out of hiding and denounces them. Alamiro is overjoyed to see Belisario again; by a cross on the young leader's neck, Irene recognizes him as her long-lost brother. Alamiro goes off with Belisario to prepare the defence of Byzantium. In the resulting victory, Belisario is fatally wounded. Antonina is overcome by remorse and confesses her guilt to her dying husband.

Manuscript score: Ricordi Archives, Milan.

Il campanello di notte farsa (with recitatives) in 1 act

Composed: spring 1836

First performed: Teatro Nuovo, Naples, 1 June 1836, with Amalia Schütz-Oldosi (Serafina), Giorgio Ronconi (Enrico), Raffaele Casaccia (Don Annibale).

Librettist: Gaetano Donizetti

Libretto: based on Léon Lévy Brunswick's, Mathieu-Barthélmy Troin's and Victor Lhérie's vaudeville, *La sonnette de la nuit* (Paris, 1836).

Synopsis: Among the guests at the wedding of an aged pharmacist, Don Annibale Pistacchio (buffo), to Serafina (soprano) is Enrico (baritone). Enrico is a great practical joker and wants revenge on the hoary bridegroom because he has toyed with the idea of marrying Serafina himself. According to a Neapolitan statute, any apothecary who does not fill prescriptions at any hour is liable to imprisonment. No sooner has Don Annibale got rid of his lingering guests and escorted Serafina to their nuptial chamber than the night-bell rings. Enrico embarks on a series of disguises and pranks, an extended charivari, to prevent the old man from bedding his bride. First Enrico appears as a French dandy, then as an opera singer out of voice, and last as a rheumatic old man with an endless prescription to fill. Believing he has at last rid himself of these importunate customers, Annibale starts up to bed but steps on some torpedoes (which Enrico has left there) and arouses the whole household. Enrico and all the wedding guests burst in to speed Annibale on his way, as he has to take an early diligence for Rome to see about an inheritance. Enrico wishes the frustrated bridegroom a whole life as happy as the night he has just passed – a sentiment endorsed by everyone but Don Annibale.

Manuscript score: Conservatorio di San Pietro a Majella, Naples (autograph)

Betly, o La capanna svizzera opera buffa ('opera giocosa') in 1 act (revised in 2 acts)

Composed: summer 1836

First performed: Teatro Nuovo, Naples, 21 August 1836, with Adelaide Toldi (Betly), Lorenzo Salvi (Daniele), Giuseppe Fioravanti (Max).

Revised: September 1837

First performed in revised version: ? Teatro del Fondo, Naples, 29 September 1837.

Librettist: Gaetano Donizetti

Libretto: based on Eugène Scribe's and Anne-Honoré-Joseph Mélesville's libretto for Adolphe Adam's *Le chalet* (Paris, 1834), ultimately derived from Goethe's Singspiel, *Jery und Bätely* (1780), first set by Peter Winter (Munich, 1790).

Synopsis: Daniele (tenor) arrives at Betly's chalet overjoyed because he has received a letter in which Betly (soprano) accepts his proposal. Since the letter has been written by local pranksters, Betly denies any knowledge of it, stoutly proclaiming she prefers her independence. Betly's brother Max (baritone), who has been away in the army for years, returns home and decides to keep his identity secret and help Daniele's cause. Max's scheme, involving turning his soldiers loose in Betly's house and even challenging Daniele to a duel, has the desired result of making Daniele show some spunk and of persuading Betly that her independence leaves her vulnerable. Gratefully, she agrees to marry the faithful Daniele.

Manuscript score: Conservatorio di San Pietro a Majella, Naples (non-autograph materials for both versions)

L'assedio di Calais opera seria ('melodramma lirico') in 3 acts

Composed: July–October 1836

First performed: Teatro San Carlo, Naples, 19 November 1836, with Almerinda Manzocchi (Aurelio), Caterina Barili-Patti (Eleonora), Paul Barroilhet (Eustachio de St-Pierre), Federico Lablache (Edoardo III), Nicola Tucci (Edmondo), Pietro Gianni (Un Incognito), Ferdinando Cimino (Giovanni d'Aire), Freni (Giacomo de Visants), Giovanni Revalden (Pietro de Visants), Giuseppe Benedetti (Armando).

Librettist: Salvatore Cammarano

Libretto: based on Luigi Marchionni, *L'assedio di Calais* (also known as *Edoardo III*; Naples, c. 1825) with details from Luigi Henry's ballet *L'assedio di Calais* (Naples, 1828), itself based on Marchionni's play; both of these derived ultimately from Dormant de Belloy (pseudonym of Pierre-Laurent Buirette), *Le siège de Calais* (Paris, 1765), almost certainly via Hubert (pseudonym of Philippe-Jacques Laroche), *Eustache de St Pierre, ou Le siège de Calais* (Paris, 1822).

Synopsis: Aurelio (*musico*), son of Eustachio, Mayor of the besieged city of Calais, narrowly escapes capture on a reconnaissance and foraging expedition outside the city's walls. (The English king, Edoardo III (bass), longs for the day that the French capitulate.)[25] On the city walls Eustachio (baritone) muses sadly on the state of his starving city. He is joined by Eleonora (soprano), both of them alarmed by the news that Aurelio's sortie outside the city had been detected. Aurelio returns and tries to hearten his fellow citizens by reminding them that they can still die for Calais. An English spy (bass) bursts into the *hôtel de ville* at the head of a mob, demanding that the Mayor capitulate and allow his people to avoid certain death. Eustachio exposes the spy and bravely rallies the citizens.

Women praying for the city awaken Eleonora. Aurelio has a nightmare in which he believes their young son Filippo is harmed. Aurelio and Eleonora seek to retain some optimism. An English envoy comes to the audience hall to announce that the English King will grant clemency if six citizens of noble blood will die for their city. When Aurelio rejects the offer, Eustachio tells the envoy that the victims will be ready at sunset and declares that he will be first to volunteer. Others come forward, but when Aurelio attempts to sign, his father vainly tries to prevent him. The six doomed men pray for God's guidance while the citizens mourn. All are reduced to tears as the hostages leave.

The English soldiers celebrate the arrival of their Queen. The six captives are led in, followed by their weeping wives, who beg for mercy. The Queen is aghast at the King's cruelty and persuades him to pardon the burghers of Calais. The King accedes and all rejoice solemnly.

Manuscript score: Conservatorio di San Pietro a Majella, Naples (autograph)

Pia de' Tolomei opera seria in 2 acts

Composed: June 1836 – January 1837

First performed: Teatro Apollo, Venice, 18 February 1837, with Fanny Tacchinardi-Persiani (Pia), Rosina Mazzarelli (Rodrigo), Marietta Bramati (Bice), Antonio Poggi (Ghino), Giorgio Ronconi (Nello), Alessandro Meloni (Piero), Alessandro Giacchini (Ubaldo), Alessandro Cecconi (Lamberto).

Librettist: Salvatore Cammarano

Revised: spring 1837

First performed in revised version: Sinigaglia, 31 July 1837, with Eugenia Tadolini (Pia), Letizia Suddetti (Rodrigo), Napoleone Moriani (Ghino), Giorgio Ronconi (Nello).

Librettist: Cammarano revised his original libretto

Revised: September 1838

First performed in second revised version: Teatro San Carlo, Naples, 30 September 1838, with Giuseppina Ronzi-de Begnis (Pia), Eloisa Buccini (Rodrigo), Rizzano (Bice), Giovanni Basadonna (Ghino), Paul Barroilhet (Nello), Anafesto Rossi (Piero), Timoleone Barattini (Ubaldo).

Librettist: unknown

Libretto: based on Bartolomeo Sestini's novella *Pia de' Tolomei* (1822), and two plays derived from it – Giacinto Bianco, *Pia de' Tolomei* (Naples, 1836), and Carlo Marenco, *Pia de' Tolomei* (Naples, 1836); the ultimate source of all three is Dante, *Purgatorio*, Canto V.

Synopsis: Ghino (tenor) lusts after Pia (soprano), the young bride of his cousin Nello of Maremma (baritone). When Pia spurns Ghino, Ghino accuses her of adultery. Her suspected suitor is her brother Rodrigo (*musico*), whose freedom from prison Pia has purchased. Ubaldo (tenor) betrays a secret meeting between brother and sister, and Rodrigo barely escapes before Nello and Ghino burst in. Nello orders Pia to prison. Ghino offers to free Pia, but she tells him that she is a faithful wife and that her nocturnal visitor was her brother. All this she wants Ghino to relay to Nello. Ubaldo has received a letter from Nello ordering the death of Pia if he should not survive the coming battle against the Guelphs. During a storm Piero (bass) and the other hermits pray for peace. Nello has been defeated in the latest foray, and Ghino, fatally wounded and tortured by his bad conscience, confesses before he dies his part in making Pia seem to be guilty. Nello rushes to Pia's cell, but arrives too late; Ubaldo has already administered the poison. She forgives him, and when the victorious Rodrigo arrives, she begs them to settle their differences peacefully, and dies.

Manuscript score: Conservatorio di San Pietro a Majella, Naples (autograph)

Roberto Devereux opera seria in 3 acts

Composed: 1837

First performed: Teatro San Carlo, Naples, 28 October 1837, with Giuseppina Ronzi-de Begnis (Elisabetta), Almerinda Granchi (Sara, Duchessa di Nottingham), Giovanni Basadonna (Roberto Devereux, Il Conte d'Essex), Paul Barroilhet (Il Duca di Nottingham), Timoleone Barattini (Lord Cecil), Anafesto Rossi (Sir Gualtiero Raleigh), Giuseppe Benedetti (Un Servo).

Librettist: Salvatore Cammarano

Libretto: based on François Ancelot's tragedy, *Élisabeth d'Angleterre* (Paris, 1832), and Felice Romani's libretto for Saverio Mercadante, *Il conte d'Essex* (Milan, 1833).

Synopsis: Though Elisabetta (soprano) is upset that Roberto, the Count of Essex (tenor) has been avoiding her, she resists the efforts of Cecil (bass) and Gualtiero Raleigh (bass) to charge him with treason. The Queen greets Essex ardently, but he is reserved and noncommittal, and his cool response immediately arouses her suspicions. Nottingham (baritone) is suspicious because his wife Sara (mezzo-soprano) is sad and has tried to hide a blue scarf; he confides in Essex, who, unbeknownst to the lady's husband, is much in love with her. Essex visits Sara to reproach her for having married Nottingham during his absence, while she reproaches him with wearing the Queen's ring. Essex tears off the ring and gives it to her, while she presents him with the blue scarf as a memento of their parting. The council has condemned Essex and informs the Queen of his arrest. Though Nottingham begs that his friend be spared, Elisabetta, her jealousy apparently confirmed by the scarf that Raleigh has brought her from Essex's apartment, will not be deterred from signing the death warrant. When Elisabetta shows Nottingham the scarf, the enraged husband tries to slay Essex on the spot, but he is restrained and Essex is led to the Tower.

Sara receives from Essex a letter informing her of his fate, but before she can take the ring that would save him to the Queen, Nottingham restrains her and, refusing to listen to her protestations of innocence, orders her to be confined. In his cell Essex wishes that he might clear Sara's name before he is executed. Elisabetta, in spite of all the signs of Essex's infidelity, wishes that his life could be spared. She hears the cannon shot announcing his execution, and a moment later Sara hurries in with the ring, confessing to the Queen that she has been her rival. Convulsed with rage, the Queen accuses Sara of perversely keeping until too late the token that would have saved Essex. Nottingham declares that he prevented her coming in order to have his revenge. The Queen orders their arrest, and then, oppressed by visions of Essex's ghost and her approaching death, she presses the ring to her lips. Her final words announce her abdication: 'Dell'anglia terra sia Giacomo il re; dell'Anglia Giacomo e re.' (Of the English realm let James be king; of England James is king.)

Manuscript score: Conservatorio di San Pietro a Majella, Naples (autograph)

Maria de Rudenz opera seria in 3 acts

Composed: October–December 1837

First performed: Teatro La Fenice, Venice, 30 January 1838, with Carolina Ungher (Maria de Rudenz), Napoleone Moriani (Enrico), Giorgio Ronconi (Corrado di Waldorff).

Librettist: Salvatore Cammarano

Libretto: based on Anicet Bourgeois, Cuvelier and Mallian, *La nonne sanglante* (Paris, 1835), derived from an episode in *The Monk*, the gothic novel of Matthew G. Lewis (1795).

Synopsis: After a violent youth, during which he eloped to Rome with Maria, whom he subsequently abandoned in the catacombs, Corrado di Waldorff (baritone) hopes to settle down to marriage with Matilde (soprano), heiress of the late Count de Rudenz. Since the Count's daughter Maria is presumed dead, his niece Matilde will come into her inheritance one year after his death. Corrado's brother Enrico (tenor) also loves Matilde and is torn between jealousy and fraternal loyalty. Secretly, Maria has returned to Rudenz, planning to hide her shame in a convent, until the news of Corrado's matrimonial venture turns all her thoughts to vengeance. As the bride and groom approach the church, Maria suddenly appears and orders away the usurping Corrado and sends Matilde off to become a religious. Enrico begs Maria to give Matilde into his protection. Maria hints that Corrado is not his brother. She confronts Corrado with the proof that his father is really the assassin, Ugo di Berna; but none of this matters, for she still loves him in spite of everything and will forgive him if only he will give up Matilde. When Corrado refuses, she suddenly opens a trapdoor, announcing that there gapes Matilde's tomb. Corrado hurls himself at her and stabs her. When the retainers rush in, Maria declares, with what is apparently her last breath, that she has stabbed herself. Enrico challenges Corrado to a duel and is slain by him. In Corrado's absence, Maria, who has only feigned death, steals into the bridal chamber and stabs Matilde. Maria confesses her crime to Corrado and tells him she has reopened her wound and is dying in earnest, still loving him and still forgiving. Corrado is left to live with his conscience.

Manuscript scores: Teatro La Fenice Archives, Venice (non-autograph copy), Conservatorio di Musica, Milan (non-autograph copy)

Poliuto opera seria in 3 acts (revised as *Les martyrs*, grand opéra in 4 acts)

Composed: May–July 1838

First performed: Teatro San Carlo, Naples, 30 November 1848, with Eugenia Tadolini (Paolina), Carlo Baucardé (Poliuto), Filippo Colini (Severo), Marco Arati (Callistene), Domenico Ceci (Nearco), Anafesto Rossi (Felice).

Librettist: Salvatore Cammarano

Revised: mainly April–May 1839

Fitst performed as *Les martyrs*: Opéra, Paris, 10 April 1840, with Julie Dorus-Gras (Pauline), Gilbert Duprez (Polyeucte), Jean-Étienne Massol

(Sévère), Prosper Dérivis (Félix), Pierre-François Wartel (Néarque), Jacques-Émile Serda (Callisthènes), Molinier, Wideman.

Librettist: Cammarano's libretto translated and revised by Eugène Scribe

Libretto: based on Pierre Corneille, *Polyeucte* (Paris, 1642)

Synopsis of *Poliuto*: In third-century Armenia, Poliuto (tenor) has resolved to embrace Christianity. His wife, Paolina (soprano), suspicious of his secrecy, follows him to the hidden sanctuary and witnesses his baptism. Nearco (tenor), the Christian leader, warns her that, since their cult is proscribed, Poliuto will die under the law lately promulgated by her father Felice if she reveals what she has learned. Paolina is agitated to learn that the Proconsul Severo (baritone) is arriving; she once loved him but, believing him dead in battle, married Poliuto. When Felice (tenor) informs Severo of his daughter's marriage, Severo is deeply upset. Observing his emotion, Callistene (bass), the high priest, brings Severo to an interview with Paolina, having arranged that Poliuto should overhear it. (Callistene sets this trap, it later transpires, because Paolina has spurned his advances.) When she hears Severo's declaration of undiminished love Paolina is profoundly moved, but she begs him to leave her in peace. Poliuto has seen his wife with the Proconsul and is filled with jealous rage, but the news that Nearco has been seized by the authorities sends him off to try to save the Christian leader. In the temple of Jupiter, Nearco is threatened unless he tells the neophyte's name. To general astonishment, Poliuto reveals that it is he. When Paolina kneels and begs mercy from Severo, Poliuto overturns the altar. Both Poliuto and Nearco are seized and led away. Callistene meets his priests near the temple and tells them that the Christians have chosen martyrdom. With savage joy he foresees the day when priestcraft will control the Empire. In his cell, Poliuto dreams of Paolina, who soon comes to him and begs him to renounce his faith. Hearing his refusal to imperil his soul, she is moved to embrace his religion and to share his martyrdom. Singing of their faith in heaven, they advance into the circus where the beasts await them.

(For a summary of the modifications to the plot made for *Les martyrs* see pp. 428–34.)

Manuscript scores: *Poliuto*, Conservatorio di San Pietro a Majella, Naples (autograph);[26] *Les martyrs*, Bibliothèque Nationale, Paris (autograph)

Le duc d'Albe grand opéra in 4 acts (incomplete, completed and revised by other hands as *Il duca d'Alba*)[27]

Composed: April–October 1839

Librettists: Eugène Scribe and Charles Duvéyrier

First performed as *Il duca d'Alba*: Teatro Apollo, Rome, 22 March 1882, with Abigaille Bruschi-Chiatti (Amelia di Egmont), Julián Gayarré (Marcello di Bruges), Leone Giraldoni (Il Duca d'Alba), Giovanni Paroli (Carlo), Alessandro Silvestri (Daniele), Igalmer Frey (Sandoval), Romeo Sarti (Un Taverniere).

Librettist: Scribe's and Duvéyrier's libretto translated and revised by Angelo Zanardini

Libretto: source unidentified

Synopsis of *Le duc d'Albe* (names of characters as they were changed in *Il duca d'Alba* appear in parentheses); In Brussels, the Flemish seethe under Spanish tyranny. In an incident, Daniel (Daniele) (bass) is arrested, and Hélène (Amelia) (soprano), Egmont's daughter, refuses to bow before the Spanish governor. For her defiance, a Spanish officer asks her to sing a song praising the Duke of Alba; instead she breaks into a patriotic tune that rouses the Flemish to the point of attacking the soldiers. Only the arrival of the Duke (baritone) prevents bloodshed. Henri (Marcello) (tenor) comes from Bruges to tell his beloved Hélène of the unrest there. The Duke approaches Henri and questions him about his parentage and childhood. When Henri rejects the Duke's offer of pardon, he is led away under guard. Mysteriously Henri is set free and joins Hélène and the other conspirators in Daniel's brewery, where they are surprised by Spanish troops, who discover a cache of arms. All are arrested but Henri. Going to the Duke to plead for his friends' lives, Henri is stunned when the Duke claims him as his missing son. Henri refuses to acknowledge the relationship, until he realizes it is the only way he can save Hélène. Hélène accuses him of betrayal and refuses to listen to his protestations of innocence. He goes to Egmont's tomb, hoping to see her again. At first Hélène repulses him; finally she tells him she is resolved to murder the Duke. When he tries to dissuade her, she orders him away. At Antwerp Hélène comes, ostensibly as a suppliant, to the Duke, who is about to embark for Spain. When she draws her dagger Henri throws himself between her and his father and receives the blow. Dying, he begs the Duke to forgive Hélène.

Manuscript score: Ricordi Archives, Milan (incomplete autograph)

La fille du régiment opéra comique in 2 acts (revised, in Italian, as *La figlia del reggimento,* opera buffa in 2 acts)

Composed: summer–autumn 1839

First performed: Opéra-Comique, Paris, 11 February 1840, with Juliette Bourgeois (Marie), Marie-Julie Boulanger (Marquise de Berkenfeld), Blanchard (Duchesse de Crakentorp), Mécène Marié de l'Isle (Tonio), Henri (Sergent Sulpice), Riquier (Hortensius), Palianti (Un Caporal), Léon (Un Notaire).

Librettists: Jules-Henri Vernoy de Saint-Georges and Jean-François-Alfred Bayard

First performed in Italian version: La Scala, Milan, 3 October 1840, with Luigia Abbadia (Maria), Lorenzo Salvi (Tonio), Raffaele Scalese (Sulpizio).

Librettist: Saint-Georges's and Bayard's libretto was translated into Italian by Calisto Bassi

Libretto: source unidentified

Synopsis: Marie (soprano), a young girl found on the battlefield and brought up by the soldiers of the 21st Regiment as their 'daughter', confesses to Sergeant Sulpice (buffo) that she is attracted to Tonio (tenor), a young Tyrolean who has saved her life. Tonio has lurked around the encampments, hoping for a glimpse of Marie. When he is seized as a spy, Marie claims him as her personal prisoner. Learning that she may only marry a member of the 21st, Tonio promptly enlists, but the aged Marquise (mezzo-soprano) claims that Marie is her long-lost niece and takes her home with her. There, bored with the artificial manners of polite society and longing for her old freedom, Marie is being forced into marriage with a foppish young Duke. The 21st returns to the neighborhood of the Marquise's château, and Tonio, who has been searching out the facts of Marie's parentage, demands an explanation. The Marquise confesses that Marie is really her daughter and, her heart softened by renewed memories of the soldiery, consents to Marie's marriage to the upstanding Tonio.

Manuscript score: Conservatorio di San Pietro a Majella, Naples (non-autograph copy)

L'ange de Nisida grand opéra in 4 acts (reworked as *La favorite*, see below)
Composed: fall – 27 December 1839
Librettists: Alphonse Royer and Gustave Vaëz
Libretto: final scene based on François-Thomas Baculard d'Arnaud, *Les amans malheureux, ou Le comte de Comminge* (Paris, 1790), itself derived from the end of his prose narrative *Mémoires du comte de Comminge* (1764); some details have analogies with Gaetano Rossi's libretto for Giovanni Pacini's semiseria *Adelaide e Comingio* (Milan, 1818). Sources of the rest of the work are unidentified. (An autograph copy of the libretto is in the Archives Nationales, Paris.)
Synopsis: Leone de Casaldi (tenor), an exiled soldier, risks his life by coming to the island of Nisida to see the noble lady whom he loves and who is known to him only as Sylvia, 'the Angel of Nisida'. Leone meets Don Gaspar (buffo), Chamberlain to King Fernand of Naples, who hints that justice can be arranged for him and invites him to Naples. Sylvia de Linares (soprano), the King's mistress, enters and encounters Leone; she confesses that she loves him but begs him to leave and forget her. Steadfast, Leone remains and is discovered by the King (baritone) who, enraged that his orders have been disobeyed, turns over Leone to Don Gaspar as a prisoner.

In Sylvia's Neapolitan villa the King promises that she shall soon share his throne; when Sylvia reminds him that secret orders have come from Rome that she be banished, the King offers to grant her any favor, and she requests Leone's freedom. A Monk (bass) enters and produces the papal bull ordering that Sylvia be banished or else confined in a convent; she leaves, crushed. Don Gaspar and the King plan that Leone and Sylvia be married but that Leone be sent away as an ambassador and Sylvia remain in Naples and resume her relationship with the King. After the ceremony Leone learns from the Monk that he has married the King's mistress. When the King appears Leone reproaches him bitterly for having exacted such good fortune at the price of his honor, and he breaks his sword and casts it at the royal feet. The Monk leads Leone away.

At a monastery the monks are engaged in digging their graves in the hillside. Leone is about to make his vows, but he is still beset by the vision of Sylvia. Disguised as a novice monk, Sylvia has followed him there and she listens as his voice is heard from the chapel pronouncing his vows. When Leone appears she begs his forgiveness; her humility reawakens his love, and he urges her to escape with him, but knowing she is near to death she sadly realizes the futility of his hope. She falls dying at his feet. Leone calls for help. The Monk, father superior of the community, announces the death of the novice and bids the others pray for 'his' soul.

Manuscript scores: Library of the Performing Arts, New York (microfilm of the autograph of *L'ange–La favorite*; the autograph itself was formerly in private hands); Bibliothèque Nationale, Paris (8 or 10 numbers or parts of numbers, not used in *La favorite*, autograph)

La favorite grand opéra in 4 acts (largely a reworking of *L'ange de Nisida*, see above)

Composed: September 1840

First performed: Opéra, Paris, 2 December 1840, with Rosine Stolz (Léonor), Élian (Inès), Gilbert Duprez (Fernand), Paul Barroilhet (Alphonse XI), Nicholas-Prosper Levasseur (Balthasar), Pierre-François Wartel (Don Gaspar).

Librettists: Alphonse Royer and Gustave Vaëz, with contributions by Eugène Scribe

Libretto: based in part on the libretto for *L'ange de Nisida* (see above), upon which was grafted the story of Leonora de Guzman.

Synopsis: Fernand (a tenor), a novice, confesses to his father and Superior, Balthasar (bass), that a beautiful woman has caused him to lose his religious zeal. Sternly Balthasar orders him away from the monastery. Fernand is brought, blindfolded, to an island retreat, where Léonor (mezzo-soprano) tells him that although she cannot marry him, she will help him to advance his career, and she gives him a military appointment. Later, King Alphonse (baritone) hopes to reward Fernand for saving his life in battle against the Moors, and gives him noble titles. Léonor, the King's mistress, begs Alphonse to end their relationship. Balthasar comes to court to present the King with the papal bull issued against his liaison. When the King protests, Balthasar threatens him with excommunication. Fernand, ignorant of the bond between Léonor and the King, asks for the lady's hand, a favor to which the King gives his ironical consent. Léonor sends her confidante to inform Fernand of her true status, but Alphonse has the messenger arrested before Fernand learns the truth. After the ceremony, Fernand is stung by the courtiers' contempt. When Balthasar tells him he has married the King's mistress, Fernand defies the King, breaks his sword and casts it at the sovereign's feet, and then rushes back to the monastery to resume the life of a religious. There he is still haunted by memories of Léonor. Disguised as a postulant, she comes to beg his forgiveness, arriving at the moment at which

Fernand, inside the chapel, takes his final vows. She pleads with him for pardon, and at first he repulses her, but soon her despair arouses all his old passion for her. Before they can escape together, the exhausted Léonor sinks at his feet and dies.

Manuscript scores: Library of the Performing Arts, New York (microfilm of the autograph of *L'ange–La favorite;* the autograph itself was formerly in private hands); Bibliothèque de l'Opéra, Paris (partly autograph material, newly composed for *La favorite,* discarded during rehearsals)

Adelia opera seria in 3 acts

Composed: October–November 1840

First performed: Teatro Apollo, Rome, 11 February 1841, with Giuseppina Strepponi (Adelia), Clementina Baroni (Odetta), Lorenzo Salvi (Oliviero), Ignazio Marini (Arnoldo), Filippo Valentini (Carlo), Pietro Gasperini (Comino), Luigi Fossi (Uno Scudiere).

Librettists: Felice Romani (Acts 1 and 2),[28] Girolamo Marini (Act 3)

Libretto: Romani's libretto for Michele Enrico Carafa's *Adele di Lusignano* (Milan, 1817), with a new Act 3 by Marini; Romani's original text was based on an unidentified French play.

Synopsis: Arnoldo (bass), captain of the Duke of Burgundy's guards, resolves to kill a man in a red cloak who has been seen climbing out of the window of his daughter Adelia's room. When he discovers that the man is a noble named Oliviero (tenor) (as a commoner Arnoldo cannot avenge himself against an aristocrat), he determines to punish his daughter Adelia (soprano). Arnoldo seeks to persuade the Duke (baritone) to permit a marriage between Oliviero and Adelia, knowing all the while that his master will punish by death a noble who weds beneath his station. Adelia does everything in her power to postpone the ceremony, pitying her father's sense of his dishonor, wishing she could die herself, and hoping against hope somehow to save Oliviero. In turn, Arnoldo feels some compassion for his daughter, but his desire for vengeance is implacable. The wedding takes place. Adelia waits in her room, praying that Oliviero may be spared. She is amazed when Oliviero appears unscathed, the Duke having relented and spared his life by presenting Arnoldo with a patent of nobility, a gesture that resolves everybody's problems.

Manuscript score: Ricordi Archives, Milan (autograph)

Rita, ou Le mari battu (also known as *Deux hommes et une femme*) opéra comique in 1 act

Composed: June 1841

First performed: Opéra-Comique, Paris, 7 May 1860, with Caroline Lefebvre-Faure (Rita), Warot (Peppe), Barielle (Gaspar).

Librettist: Gustave Vaëz

Libretto: apparently an original plot.

Synopsis: Rita (soprano) has married an unassertive bumpkin, Peppe (tenor), believing that her first husband, Gaspar (baritone) has drowned at sea. Gaspar arrives unexpectedly at Rita's inn to check out a rumor that Rita has died. Peppe recognizes the name on his passport and sees in the stranger a means of escaping from his temperamental Rita. Gaspar, who was planning to marry a Canadian girl, cajoles Peppe into suggesting a game of *morra* and then into drawing straws to see which of them wins the wife neither of them wants. When Peppe accuses Gaspar of cheating, Gaspar shows him the long straw, and for a while Peppe has the illusion of freedom. Gaspar tries to persuade Peppe, apparently in vain, that a husband should stand up to his wife. By pretending to have a useless arm, Gaspar provokes Peppe into fighting him. At the sight of her husband asserting himself, Rita, who has not only dealt out blows to Peppe but received them from Gaspar, is as happy to be reunited with Peppe as Gaspar is contented, having gained possession of his old marriage-license, to return to Canada.

Manuscript scores: Conservatorio di San Pietro a Majella, Naples (autograph of the work in Italian translation entitled *Due uomini ed una donna*); Bibliothèque Nationale, Paris (partly autograph copy with alternate finale)

Maria Padilla opera seria in 3 acts
Composed: July–December 1841
First performed: La Scala, Milan, 26 December 1841, with Sofia Löwe (Maria Padilla), Luigia Abbadia (Ines Padilla), Teresa Ruggieri (Francisca), Domenico Donzelli (Don Ruiz de Padilla), Giorgio Ronconi (Don Pedro di Castillo), Gaetano Rossi (Don Ramiro), Raineri Pochini (Don Luigi) and Agostino Berini (Don Alfonso di Pardo).
Librettists: Gaetano Rossi and Gaetano Donizetti
Libretto: based on François Ancelot, *Maria Padilla* (Paris, 1838).
Synopsis: Maria Padilla (soprano) tells her sister Ines (soprano) that she hopes to become a royal bride. When the so-called Mendez comes to her room at night by stealth, she confronts him with his true identity, King Pedro the Cruel (baritone). By dissembling and angry talk of dishonor, she extracts his promise that he will marry her, even though reasons of state force him to keep their marriage a secret. They elope, in spite of Maria's certainty that her father, Don Ruiz (tenor), will insist on vengeance. Maria is troubled by the knowledge that a civil war forces Pedro to appear to be negotiating a marriage with Blanche, a Bourbon princess, and that a strong faction at the court, hostile to Maria, strongly favors this alliance. Don Ruiz comes to court, where his daughter is to all appearances the King's mistress and, his mind overwrought by his daughter's shame, challenges the King. The old man is led home in disgrace. Maria comes to beg his forgiveness and to reveal her true status, but her father will not understand her. When Blanche arrives and is hailed as Queen by Pedro's enemies, Maria is terrified by the thought that she is to be rejected, but at the last moment Pedro rejects Blanche and proclaims Maria as his Queen; overcome, Maria dies of joy. (In the original, uncensored, version of the text Maria snatches the crown from Blanche's head and then commits suicide.)

Revised: spring 1842[29]
First performed in revised version: Trieste, 1 March 1842, with Eugenia
Tadolini (Maria).
Synopsis of revised version: as above, except that Maria is alive at the end of
the opera, publicly acknowledged as his Queen by Pedro, who repudiates
Blanche.
Manuscript score: Ricordi Archives, Milan (autograph)

Linda di Chamounix opera semiseria in 3 acts
Composed: 31 December 1841 – 4 March 1842
First performed: Kärntnertorteater, Vienna, 19 May 1842, with Eugenia
Tadolini (Linda), Marietta Brambilla (Pierotto), Napoleone Moriani
(Carlo), Felice Varesi (Antonio), Prosper Dérivis (Il Prefetto), Agostino
Rovere (Marchese di Boisfleury).
Revised: winter 1842
First performed in revised version: Théâtre-Italien, Paris, 17 November
1842, with Fanny Tacchinardi-Persiani (Linda), Marietta Brambilla
(Pierotto), Mario (Carlo), Antonio Tamburini (Antonio), Luigi Lablache (Il
Prefetto).
Librettist: Gaetano Rossi
Libretto: based on Adolphe-Philippe d'Ennery and Gustave Lemoine, *La
grâce de Dieu* (Paris, 1841).
Synopsis: Antonio (baritone) and his wife Maddalena (mezzo-soprano) be-
come concerned for the virtue of their daughter Linda (soprano) when they
learn that the Marchese (buffo) intends to seduce her. Linda loves Carlo
(tenor), whom she believes to be a poor painter, but who is really the
Viscount of Sirval. Antonio, willing to do anything to protect his daughter,
goes to the Prefect (bass) for advice and is told to send Linda off to Paris,
along with the hurdy-gurdy player Pierotto (*musico*) and the other silk-
workers, to work in the factories. There, Linda lives in a richly appointed
apartment belonging to Carlo, but their relationship is strictly virtuous.[30]
The Marchese has recognized her, even in her fine clothes, and has come to
court her, but she spurns him. Antonio comes to Paris to learn of his daughter's whereabouts and mistakes her for a great lady. When he recognizes her
as Linda, he misconstrues her circumstances and curses her. Added to this
blow, Linda learns from Pierotto that Carlo has apparently married a girl of
his own station. Linda loses her reason. The faithful Pierotto leads her back
to Chamounix. Here Carlo, who has refused to go through with the wedding
in Paris that his mother was trying to insist upon, is able to restore Linda's
wits by offering her his heart and hand.
Manuscript score: Ricordi Archives, Milan (autograph)

Caterina Cornaro opera seria in a prologue and 2 acts
Composed: fall–winter 1842, 9 March – end of May 1843
First performed: Teatro San Carlo, Naples, 18 January 1844, with Fanny
Goldberg (Caterina), Anna Salvetti (Matilde), Gaetano Fraschini (Gerardo),

Filippo Coletti (Lusignano), Nicola Benevento (Mocenigo), Marco Arati (Andrea Cornaro), Anafesto Rossi (Strozzi), Domenico Ceci (Un Cavaliere).
Librettist: Giacomo Sacchèro
Libretto: based on Jules-Henri Vernoy de Saint-Georges's libretto for Fromental Halévy, *La reine de Chypre* (Paris, 1841).
Synopsis: In Venice, the approaching marriage of Caterina (soprano) to a young French knight Gerardo (tenor) is postponed when Mocenigo (bass) brings words that Lusignano (baritone), the King of Cyprus, wishes to marry her. Andrea Cornaro (bass) orders Gerardo to forget his daughter. Having learned from Mocenigo that Gerardo will be slain on the spot if she tries to escape with him, Caterina rejects him when he comes to her room, prepared to elope with her, and tells him that she does not love him.

In Cyprus, Mocenigo, the Venetian ambassador to Cyprus, with his henchman Strozzi (tenor) is trying to foment a rebellion to gain the island kingdom for Venice. Gerardo runs foul of these insurgents, but his life is saved by Lusignano, who does not realize until afterwards that this is the man his Queen Caterina has been pining for. Gerardo, for his part, has vowed to avenge himself on Caterina's husband, and is thunderstruck to recognize in Lusignano the man who had earlier saved his life. Lusignano is being slowly poisoned by Mocenigo, and in his weakened condition he learns that the Venetians will soon attack his kingdom. Gerardo, who has joined the Knights Hospitalers at Rhodes, comes with his companions to defend Lusignano and succeeds in turning the tide of the battle. In the fighting, Lusignano receives a mortal wound. As he dies he confides his people to Caterina's care. Gerardo returns to Rhodes.
Manuscript score: Conservatorio di San Pietro a Majella, Naples (autograph)
Revised: winter 1844–5
First performed in revised version: Teatro Regio, Parma, 2 February 1845, with Marianna Barbieri-Nini (Caterina), Nicholas Ivanoff (Gerardo), Felice Varesi (Lusignano).
Synopsis of revised version: as above, except that the opera ends with Lusignano, before he dies, telling Caterina that Gerardo has been killed in the fighting; the widowed Caterina is left alone to rule Cyprus.

Don Pasquale opera buffa in 3 acts
Composed: November–December 1842
First performed: Théâtre-Italien, Paris, 3 January 1843, with Giulia Grisi (Norina), Mario (Ernesto), Antonio Tamburini (Dr Malatesta), Luigi Lablache (Don Pasquale), Federico Lablache (Il Notaro).
Librettists: Giovanni Ruffini and Gaetano Donizetti
Libretto: based on Angelo Anelli's libretto for Stefano Pavesi's *Ser Marc'Antonio* (Milan, 1810).
Synopsis: The elderly Don Pasquale (buffo) is determined to marry a young wife and sire children of his own in order to disinherit his nephew Ernesto (tenor), whose infatutation with Norina (soprano) angers the old man. Don Pasquale consults Dr Malatesta (baritone) about his progenitive prospects

and is reassured and, later, delighted when Malatesta tells him of 'Sofronia', his 'sister', a paragon of demure femininity. Malatesta visits his friend Norina and together they concoct the role she must play to bring Don Pasquale back to reason. On the appointed day, Pasquale is delighted with his naive 'bride' and signs the mock marriage contract. Ernesto, who has appeared at that moment, is dismayed by Norina's apparent infidelity, but when she starts to act the shrew, he begins to relish the humor of the situation. Later, when Don Pasquale remonstrates with Norina for her extravagance and forbids her to leave the house, she boxes his ears and orders him to bed. She drops a note, indicating that she will keep a rendezvous that night in the garden. Outraged, Pasquale summons Malatesta and together they plot to surprise the lovers. Promptly at nine Ernesto and Norina play a love scene in the garden, as Don Pasquale and Dr Malatesta steal in. When the old man is so discomfited that he admits to wishing he were not married, he agrees to reinstate Ernesto as his heir and permit him to marry his Norina. When the supposed 'Sofronia' turns out to be Norina, he readily gives his blessing to Ernesto upon his forthcoming marriage.

Manuscript score: Ricordi Archives, Milan (autograph)

Maria di Rohan opera seria in 3 acts

Composed: January–February 1843

First performed: Kärntnertortheater, Vienna, 5 June 1843, with Eugenia Tadolini (Maria di Rohan), Carlo Guasco (Riccardo, Conte di Chalais), Giorgio Ronconi (Enrico, Duca di Chevreuse), Michele Novaro (Armando di Gondì), Friedrich Becher (Visconte di Suze), Gustav Hölzel (de Fiesque), Anton Müller (Aubry) and Friedrich Baldewern (Un Famigliare di Chevreuse).

Librettists: Salvatore Cammarano, with small adjustments probably by Giovanni Ruffini

Libretto: Cammarano's libretto, begun for Donizetti in 1837, was completed for Giuseppe Lillo and set by him as *Il conte di Chalais* (Naples, 1839); it was based on Lockroy [pseudonym of Joseph-Philippe Simon] and Edmond Badon, *Un duel sous le Cardinal de Richelieu* (Paris, 1832).

Synopsis: Maria (soprano) is secretly married to Chevreuse (baritone), but when her husband kills Richelieu's nephew in a duel, she begs Riccardo, Count of Chalais (tenor), whose mistress she had once been, to intercede for Chevreuse. Recognizing Chalais's noble nature, Maria feels her old love for him reawaken. Gondì (tenor; revised November 1843 as contralto *musichetto*) a young gallant, makes an insulting reference to Maria, and Chalais instantly challenges him to a duel. When Chevreuse is released from prison, he hurries to court to thank Chalais for his intercession and insists on seconding him in his duel with Gondì. Before the duel Chalais sends a farewell note to Maria, which is to be delivered only if he dies. Maria comes secretly to Chalais to warn him of his enemies, but she is forced to hide when Chevreuse arrives to accompany Chalais to the duelling ground. When Chevreuse departs, Maria emerges from her hiding-place, and having heard about the duel for the first time, implores Chalais not to run such danger and admits her love for him. Word comes that Chevreuse is about to take Chalais's place in the duel, and Chalais tears himself away from Maria's arms. Chevreuse sustains a wounded arm in the duel. Maria is with Chalais at Chevreuse's palace when Aubry (tenor) comes to warn him that Richelieu's men have pillaged his room and carried off his letter to Maria. Knowing that discovery is not far off, he urges Maria to escape with him. Chevreuse, still unaware of these developments, returns and shows Chalais a secret passageway, but before he leaves through it Chalais whispers to Maria that if she does not join him when the clock next strikes he will return for her. De Fiesque (bass), acting under Richelieu's orders, arrives and sends Maria away on a ruse and then hands Chalais's incriminating letter to Chevreuse. Swept up in a jealous rage, he treats Maria with ominous comments on her character, but Maria refuses to deny her guilt. The clock strikes and Chalais returns. Chevreuse challenges him to a duel and they rush off through the secret door. Soon Chevreuse comes back to tell de Fiesque that Chalais has turned his pistol on himself. When Maria begs him to kill her too, Chevreuse condemns her to a life of disgrace.

Manuscript score: Ricordi Archives, Milan (autograph)

Dom Sébastien grand opéra in 5 acts (revised, in German, as *Dom Sebastian*)

Composed: February–November 1843

First performed: Opéra, Paris, 13 November 1843, with Rosine Stolz (Zaïda), Gilbert Duprez (Dom Sébastien), Paul Barroilhet (Camoëns), Nicholas-Prosper Levasseur (Dom Juan de Silva), Jean-Étienne Massol (Abayaldos), Ferdinand Prévost (Dom Henrique Sandoval), Jean-Baptiste Octave (Dom Antonio), Hippolyte Brémont (Ben-Selim).

Librettist: Eugène Scribe

Revised (German version): winter 1844–5

First performed in revised version: Kärntnertortheater, Vienna, 6 February 1845, with Clara (Stöckl-)Heinefetter[31] (Zaïda), Josef Erl (Dom Sebastian), Eduard Leithner (Camoëns), Josef Draxler (Don Juan de Sylva), Franz Wild (Abayaldos), Karl Wolf (Don Antonio), Gustav Hölzel (Ben-Selim).

Librettist: Scribe's libretto was translated into German by Leo Herz

Libretto: based on Paul-Henri Foucher, *Dom Sébastien de Portugal* (Paris, 1838).

Synopsis: Dom Sébastien (tenor), King of Portugal, is ready to depart for a crusade against the Moors. During the King's absence, Dom Juan de Silva (bass), head of the council and in control of the Inquisition, hopes to betray the country to Philip II of Spain. Camoëns (baritone) asks to accompany the King. When Sébastien sees a Moslem beauty being led to the stake, he releases her and offers to return her to her father in Africa. Zaïda (mezzo-soprano) throws herself at the King's feet in gratitude. While the King and his troops sail, Dom Juan and the Regent, Dom Antonio the King's uncle (tenor), pray that the expedition will come to disaster.

Near Fez, Zaïda's father, Ben-Selim (bass) tells her that he plans to marry her to the Arab chieftain Abayaldos (baritone), who is even now preparing to meet the advancing Portuguese army on the plains of Alcazar Kebir. After the battle Dom Henrique (bass), one of the few Portuguese left alive on the disastrous field, pretends that he is Sébastien and is slain by Abayaldos. Though gravely wounded, Sébastien survives and is tended by Zaïda. Begging outside Lisbon Cathedral, Camoëns recognizes Sébastien, whose throne has been usurped by the Regent. Camoëns is loyally sure that the common people will stand with their true ruler. A solemn funeral passes, supposedly that of Sébastien. Sébastien reveals himself to the crowd, but Abayaldos (who has come to Lisbon as an ambassador) claims that he saw the King's corpse on the battlefield. Sébastien is seized as an imposter and condemned. At the trial by the Inquisition, Zaïda appears and reveals what she knows of the true events of the battle and of Sébastien's survival, but she is accused of treason. In the Tower of Lisbon, Zaïda has been told her life and Sébastien's will be spared if she can persuade him to sign a document legitimizing the Spanish claims to Portugal. Sébastien indignantly refuses to sign it, and he and Zaïda agree to die together. Camoëns's voice is heard from outside the window, for he is coming with some faithful sailors to try to engineer an escape for the King. As Sébastien, Zaïda and Camoëns descend from the tower on a rope, the Regent and Dom Juan observe their escape and order the soldiers to fire. The bodies of Zaïda and Sébastien pitch into the harbor below.

Manuscript scores: Bibliothèque Nationale, Paris (autograph, incomplete; facsimile published New York, 1981); Bibliothèque de l'Opéra, Paris (non-autograph copies) (for printed scores reflecting changes made by Donizetti during the initial run and for Vienna, see pp. 511–32).

Appendix II
Projected and Incomplete Works

The works listed here are of three types: those left incomplete; those that were projected but never carried out by Donizetti; and individual numbers mostly from librettos that he had no intention of setting as a whole.

Adelaide. Of the approximately 100 manuscript pages of this score now in the Bibliothèque Nationale, Paris (formerly part of the Malherbe Collection), many were incorporated into *L'ange de Nisida* and from there some of them found their way into *La favorite*. The autograph consists of vocal parts, a bass line to indicate harmony, and occasional proposals for instrumentation. *Adelaide*, an opera semiseria, has a libretto by an unidentified poet, but it is clear from references in the text of the autograph that the plot is to some extent derived from Baculard d'Arnaud's *Les amans malheureux, ou Le comte de Comminge* (Paris, 1790); it also bears some relation to Gaetano Rossi's libretto for Pacini's semiseria *Adelaide e Comingio* (Milan, 1818). The list of characters includes Adelaide (soprano), Roberto (tenor), Il Colonello (baritone) and Il Marchese (buffo). Zavadini (*Donizetti: Vita – Musiche – Epistolario*, p. 178) suggests a date of 1834 for this score, but it could have been composed at any time during the following four years. It is clear from the presence of some of the material in *L'ange de Nisida* that Donizetti took his unfinished manuscript with him to Paris in 1838.

La bella prigioniera. The autograph of two duets with piano accompaniment from this farsa is preserved in the Museo Donizettiano in Bergamo; they are a recitative and duet for soprano and bass (Amina and Everardo), 'Ella parlar mi vuole', and a recitative and duet for soprano and tenor (Amina and Carlo), 'Olà ... tosto discenda e a me si guidi Amina'. A further sixteen measures occur in the scherzo for violin and piano based on themes from his works that Donizetti wrote for his future wife, Virginia Vasselli, in 1826 (also in the Museo Donizettiano); Donizetti's annotations to the scherzo state that *La bella prigioniera* was a farsa and that it had not been performed ('non rappresentata' – that is, publicly). The inclusion of a passage from the opera in the scherzo implies strongly that the work was written or was under way in 1826. The piano accompaniment to the surviving duets may indicate that it was not intended for public performance but for the private enjoyment of a group of *dilettanti*.

Il castello degli invalidi. In a letter to Toto Vasselli (Z. no. 378) of 24 October 1841 Donizetti mentions this farsa as having been performed in Palermo, but gives no date; Zavadini (*Donizetti: Vita – Musiche – Epistolario*, p. 171) lists it as having been given at the Teatro Carolino in spring 1826, though this claim seems to have no foundation except in inference, and I regard it as incorrect. It seems most likely that the work was composed between 1835 and 1841. An opera with the same title by Giacomo Cordella was performed at the Teatro del Fondo, Naples, in 1823; it is possible that the libretto of Donizetti's work drew on this opera. To date not a note that may belong to a farsa with this title by Donizetti has been identified, and it is therefore the most mysterious item in his oeuvre.

Circe. This subject was the one proposed for an opera by Donizetti, with a libretto by Felice Romani, for the summer season of 1842 in London. In the fall of 1841 the English impresario Benjamin Lumley approached the composer and the librettist to write an opera for a large fee. The project fell through because Romani failed to submit even part of the libretto by the agreed date – much to Donizetti's chagrin. His commitment to Vienna for *Linda di Chamounix* prevented Donizetti from allowing a greater leeway to Romani for *Circe*.

Le duc d'Albe. Donizetti composed parts of this grand opera in the summer of 1839. He orchestrated most of Act 1 and some parts of Act 2; the rest of the score is a compositional sketch. It was completed by other hands in an Italian version as *Il duca d'Alba* (see pp. 434–6). For further details of the French original see Appendix I.

La fiancée du Tyrol. This was the title tentatively proposed for a reworking of *Il furioso* for the Théâtre de la Renaissance. Donizetti refers to it in a letter to Persico, dated 9 October 1839 (Z. no. 328, p. 503). He was then in the throes of composing *L'ange de Nisida* for Joly, and because the impresario's operations at the Théâtre de la Renaissance collapsed before *L'ange* could be performed, nothing came of the project for a further opera.

La fidanzata. One aria from what seems to have been a one-act farsa is in the Bibliothéque Nationale, Paris. It is possible that Donizetti, as in the case of *Olimpiade*, set one number from an already existing libretto without any thought of composing a complete work of this title.

Gli illinesi. In July 1835 Donizetti was engaged in correspondence with Giuseppe Consul, the impresario at Turin, about setting an old libretto by Romani, already the basis of operas by Francesco Basili and Feliciano Strepponi (the father of Giuseppina). Since the revisions of the text requested by Donizetti were not forthcoming from Romani nothing came of this project. Indeed, the tone of Donizetti's letters give the decided impression that he did not have any real expectations that anything would.

Gli innamorati. In Bergamo (Museo Donizettiano) there exists in Donizetti's hand, and from some undetermined date, a scenario for a three-act opera buffa based on Carlo Goldoni's comedy of this title (?Venice, 1759).

L'ira d'Achille. This title used to be listed among Donizetti's works as that of an incomplete opera, apparently in the hope that the whole score would be found. During his student years in Bologna Donizetti set the first act and a duet from Act 2 scene v of a libretto, perhaps by Romani, composed by Giuseppe Nicolini (Milan, 1814); in addition, the catalogue of the Museo Donizettiano in Bergamo (1970) lists a bass aria with chorus from this work, which exists in a copyist's full score. It seems probable that Donizetti composed a few numbers from the libretto for the practise or for performance among the musical amateurs of Bologna.

Jeanne la folle. In 1844 Donizetti briefly considered setting Scribe's text on this subject, which was eventually composed by Louis Clapisson and brought out at the Opéra in 1848.

Lara. A libretto on this subject from Byron was proposed to Donizetti by a gentleman from Verona, but the composer rejected it because he had little confidence in the plot. Donizetti's student Matteo Salvi set a text by Leopoldo Tarantini on this subject in 1843, but its production at La Scala met with no success. A long letter to Donizetti from Count Giulio Pullé, dated 1 March 1837, containing a synopsis and some lines from the projected libretto, is printed as *S.d.*, 1, no. 2, pp. 125–32.

Mlle de la Vallière. Nothing but the title is known of this projected work, dating from Donizetti's Paris years.

Ne m'oubliez pas. Most probably in 1843 Donizetti completed and orchestrated seven numbers, but nothing else, from this three-act opéra comique to a libretto by the Marquis de Saint-Georges. On 30 September 1842 he had signed a contract for the work with Crosnier, manager of the Opéra-Comique, but apparently it was allowed to lapse. The libretto has not been found. The seven numbers (autograph in the Bibliothèque Nationale, Paris) have been recorded by Opera Rara, but since they come from different points in an as yet unreconstructable story they produce no cumulative effect.

Olimpiade. This title, like *L'ira d'Achille,* used to form part of the Donizetti canon, on the basis of a single duet. The duet (in a copyist's full score in the

Museo Donizettiano, Bergamo) is all that is known to exist in Donizetti's hand of a setting of Metastasio's famous libretto. As there is only one duet in the text, and it was very well known, it seems most likely that Donizetti set it during his Bolognese student days for performance by friends.

Onore vince amore. Donizetti proposed to compose this opera, to a libretto by Giovanni Ruffini, for the Théâtre-Italien. The composer's declining health prevented the project from getting beyond preliminary discussions about the selection of members of the company to undertake the roles. This provides interesting evidence of the extent to which the personnel of his original cast determined from the start the plans for Donizetti's operas.

I piccioli virtuosi ambulanti. This is the title of one of the end-of-term pasticcios that Mayr put together for performance by the pupils at his school. Donizetti's contribution to this work, performed by Mayr's scholars in 1819, was limited to a scena and aria with chorus, borrowed from his score for *Le nozze in villa,* and the *introduzione.*

Ruy Blas. After Donizetti halted work on the score of *Caterina Cornaro* in the autumn of 1842 and was composing *Don Pasquale,* he for a time considered composing an opera for Naples to a libretto by Cammarano based on Victor Hugo's drama. The composition of *Maria di Rohan* for Vienna and the later resumption of work on *Caterina Cornaro* for Naples effectively supplanted any prospect of Donizetti's carrying out the project of *Ruy Blas.*

Sganarello. In 1845 Donizetti considered writing a vehicle for Lablache to perform at the Théâtre-Italien, deriving it from Molière's comedy. His physical decline prevented any serious work upon this project.

There survive a number of sketches and even some orchestrated passages that are evidently parts of stage works, but it is not now possible to establish for which works they were intended.

Appendix III
Librettists

Italian librettists during the first half of the nineteenth century were typically associated with the particular city in which they worked. More often than not the operas they contributed to were first performed in those cities. Exceptions to this practise attracted attention. Donizetti's use of librettos by the Neapolitan Cammarano for operas that were introduced in Venice was most unusual, and he was constantly under pressure to use a Venetian poet. On the other hand, Italian operas introduced outside of Italy, in Paris or Vienna for instance, characteristically employed texts written in Italy; that of *Don Pasquale*, however, was written in great part by an Italian émigré living in Paris.

More new operas were written and produced between 1800 and 1850 than in any other half-century since operas had been written at all. During this period the public's practically insatiable appetite for novelties meant that most operas were commissioned, conceived, composed and produced in a matter of a few months. For the librettist the pressure of time was a constant restriction. Even greater pressure was exerted, directly and indirectly, by the local censors; they were supposed to approve librettos even before the composers started to set them, but practical expediency often meant that this proviso was circumvented or ignored. The existence of censorship clearly affected the plots even at the stage of preliminary planning and discussion; for instance, weddings in operas of this period are represented by the signing of civil contracts rather than as religious ceremonies. But after 1830, with the growing ascendancy of Romantic melodrama, with plots turning on deaths and conspiracies of one sort or another, problems between librettists and composers on the one hand, and the *censura* on the other markedly increase.

Nor were these the only restrictions confronting librettists of this period. The poet was paid outright for his work either by the impresario commissioning the opera or by the composer; therefore he did not participate in any future profits or royalties from his work. Unless they were enormously productive librettists could scarcely survive by librettos alone, and many held other jobs. Obviously the librettist had to design his poem to fit the prevailing conventions of musical form; even his metrical patterns and rhyme schemes were subject to modification by the composer. And then he had to

582

construct his plot to allow the various singers their share of opportunities. Working within all these given limitations left him precious little space to please himself. In the hierarchy of operatic activity in Italy during the first half of the nineteenth century the librettists occupied a very low, even a debased, position. It is surprising, then, to find that some of their work is very good indeed.

How can one realistically gauge the merits of a libretto of this time? It seems only fair to judge it first of all as a period document, representative of the actual working conditions that shaped it and expressive of the sensibility of its times. Its function of providing a substructure for musical elaboration is more important than its abstract merit as an example of a sub-literary genre. For the listener, librettos have a way of existing in the mind as a composite of stray tags and highly-charged phrases rather than in discrete structural units. Yet one should not therefore ignore such criteria as individuality of characterization, plausibility of motivation, clarity, dramatic effectiveness and suspense. It is always more useful to judge a libretto in terms of what it is and how it assumed that form, than of something it is not.

In considering Donizetti's librettists one must also consider Donizetti himself. In the preceding pages there has been recurring stress on his participation in all stages of the evolution of the texts he set. Except for the letters he wrote to Ferretti during the composition of *Il furioso*[1] and those to Scribe (via Accursi) while he was working on *Dom Sébastien*,[2] there is not much documentary evidence of Donizetti's influence on the shaping of his librettos because as far as possible he preferred to work face to face with his librettists. There were many topics, such as potential censorial problems or the aptitudes and limitations of individual singers, that could not with any discretion be entrusted to letters; personal dealing allowed far greater freedom of discussion and could save valuable time. Understandably, then, there is not much concrete evidence of these exchanges, yet to interpret his few letters on the subject as indicating a lack of interest on Donizetti's part would be greatly mistaken: they simply represent the occasions on which it was impossible to hold the personal conferences that were a part of his routine. Unlike most of his contemporaries, Donizetti was perfectly capable of writing his own librettos when the occasion arose. As he gained in practical experience and self-confidence the extent of his participation increased. He must be regarded as an active collaborator in most of the texts he set, and in some cases (for example *Maria Padilla*) he even deserves to be listed as a co-librettist.

For easy reference, Donizetti's librettists are discussed in alphabetical order.

Bardari, Giuseppe (1817–61). Jeremy Commons has published information on this hitherto obscure figure.[3] Surprisingly, Bardari was only seventeen when Donizetti pressed him into service to provide the libretto for *Maria Stuarda*. Considering his relative inexperience as a theater poet and Donizetti's much greater familiarity with the composition of operas and the writing of texts, it seems logical to assume that Donizetti was the dominant partner in this collaboration, suggesting both the subject and the treatment, which follows (though it drastically simplifies) Maffei's translation of Schiller's play. The libretto is one of the most dramatically vivid Donizetti set, particularly in the famous 'Dialogo delle due regine', but exactly how much of this is due to Bardari and how much to Donizetti himself is difficult to determine with any surety. Bardari wrote no other librettos; he must have been discouraged by the banning of his text in Naples owing to the personal intervention of the king. In any event he later turned to the study of the law and became a magistrate; he lost his office for his participation in antigovernment activity in 1848.

Bevilacqua-Aldobrandini, Marchese Gherardo. This Bolognese aristocrat was an amateur librettist. His one text for Donizetti was that of *Il falegname di Livonia* (1819) which was probably an adaptation of Romani's libretto of the same title for Pacini (Milan, 1819). That Bevilacqua-Aldobrandini's chief modus operandi was the adaptation of another poet's work or collaboration with other poets, rather than the construction of an entire libretto by himself, is demonstrated by his work for Rossini: he adapted Romani's text *Il califfo e la schiava* for *Adina*; he contributed with Tottola and Schmidt, to the book for *Edoardo e Cristina*; and he added a trio to Rossi's text for *Semiramide*. As the Bevilacqua-Aldobrandini family were active supporters of the Liceo Musicale at Bologna, Donizetti probably made the acquaintance of the Marchese during his student days there. Bevilacqua-Aldobrandini was more highly regarded for his painting than for his versifying.

Bidèra (Giovanni) Emanuele (born Palermo, 1784; died ?). The years of his principal activity were between 1834 and 1844. For Donizetti he wrote two librettos, *Gemma di Vergy* (1834), the earliest effort of his that I have been able to trace, and *Marin Faliero* (1835). Donizetti turned to him when he could not procure texts from Romani for two important commissions: his opera to open the Carnival season of 1834–5 at La Scala, and his first opera for a Parisian theater. Once Donizetti began his series of works with Cammarano, starting with *Lucia* (1835), he had no further recourse to Bidèra as a poet, although they apparently remained on friendly terms. Naples was the chief scene of Bidèra's activity, where he provided librettos for a number of now forgotten composers: Giuseppe Balducci, Francesco Chiaromonte, Carlo Coccia, Henri de Ruolz, Giuseppe Lillo, Salvatore Sarmiento, Prospero Selli and Giuseppe Staffa. All these composers were active at the San Carlo and their works to Bidèra's librettos were introduced there in the years between 1835 and 1844; obviously Bidèra was a house librettist during this period, a position he may have gained on the strength of his two texts for Donizetti.

None of Bidèra's other texts came within a country mile of the durability of those he provided for Donizetti, which suggests either that Donizetti contributed to the treatment of the plots and perhaps even to the verses, or that in their discussions he stimulated Bidèra to produce work of a level that he did not later match. Certainly it seems clear from a letter written by Donizetti to Persico in 1842[4] that he regarded Bidèra more highly as a writer of verses than for his sense of dramatic effect.

Cammarano, Salvatore (born Naples, 19 March 1801; died Naples, 17 July 1852).[5] One of the most prominent theater poets of his time, Cammarano came from a family long associated with the Neapolitan stage and with painting. He was employed at the San Carlo as a scene-painter and later as a stage director, before he turned to libretto-writing in 1834. He made his mark collaborating with Bidèra on the book for Giuseppe Persiani's *Ines de Castro* (Naples, 1835), and it was on the strength of this creditable performance that Donizetti turned to him and not to Bidèra to furnish him with the text for *Lucia* (1835). This heady triumph and the mutual satisfaction they derived from working with each other kept them operating as a team as long as Donizetti remained in Naples, and during that time Cammarano worked with no other composer.[6] After *Lucia* their joint efforts include *Belisario* (1836), *L'assedio di Calais* (1836), *Pia de' Tolomei* (1837), *Roberto Devereux* (1837), *Maria de Rudenz* (1838), *Poliuto* (written in 1838, but not produced until 1848), and *Maria di Rohan* (1843).

Although Cammarano has been severely criticized as a librettist, Donizetti considered him second only to Romani as a writer and his superior as a man to work with. Many writers have deplored Cammarano's lack of fidelity to Scott's novel in his text for *Lucia*, but it would never have occurred to him that he owed any such fidelity to his source; he preserved the essential conflict by concentrating on a minimum of characters, the motivation is always clear and the plot moves rapidly yet allows space for the musical expansion of crucial scenes. In a word, he produced a highly effective libretto. Cammarano's great asset as a librettist was his knack for encapsulating dramatic conflict into a few words that instantly make sense; for instance, Lucia's 'Alfin son tua, alfin sei mio' in the *larghetto* of the mad scene. In this respect, he anticipated (as in the Lucia–Enrico duet) what Verdi later described as 'la parola scenica'. To those who dislike Camarano's diction, finding it high-flown and over portentous, one need only point out that it was never intended to be isolated from music and that it represents a conscious effort to invent a rhetoric appropriate to the emotional level of Romantic melodrama.

The best of Cammarano's librettos are those to *L'assedio di Calais* and *Poliuto*. The former is surprising for its period because it is a stirringly patriotic work and embodies a plea for liberty. The scene in which the burghers volunteer to die for their city and then join with their fellow citizens in prayer is a most eloquent achievement. Another highpoint is Eustachio's meditation on the besieged and starving city. His text for *Poliuto*, although not strictly faithful to Corneille's play, achieves a unique blend of Romantic sensibility and classic lucidity, which is probably indicative of Nourrit's counsel during the formative stages. On only a slightly lower level is his libretto for *Roberto Devereux* with its splendidly effective portrait of Elisabetta and the vigorous interaction of its characters; its only drawback is its depressingly conventional formal structure.

Cammarano's text for *Belisario* is frequently cold and one-dimensional, but it takes on human warmth in the scene between the blinded General and his daughter in Act 2. *Pia de' Tolomei* suffers from being too episodic and often unclearly motivated, but it has flashes of considerable power, as in Ghino's death scene. Violent and ill-explained melodrama makes *Maria de Rudenz* the weakest of the librettos, but even this has some redeeming features such as Corrado's 'Ah, non avea più lagrime' and Maria's aria–finale. His text for *Maria di Rohan* accumulates considerable dramatic power, working from a slow-moving and cumbersome exposition. In his overall competence at handling dramatic structure and in his mastery of effective verbal climaxes at the ends of stanzas (that part which underwent most musical repetition) Cammarano displays a level of skill that few of his contemporaries could match.

Checcherini, Giuseppe (born Florence, 1777; died Naples, 19 September 1840). Checcherini began his career in Rome, where he was connected with the Teatro Valle, and probably in 1807 moved to Naples, where he spent the rest of his life, primarily as a stage director at the Teatro Nuovo. His one libretto for Donizetti was the 1828 revision of *Emilia di Liverpool*,[7] in which he simplified and heightened the effectiveness of the earlier, more jumbled, text. Libretto-writing was only an occasional activity for Checcherini, as for example when he supplied the text for Giuseppe Mosca's *Federico II re di Prussia* (Naples, 1824).

Donizetti, Gaetano. The composer supplied his own texts for three of his scores, *Le convenienze teatrali* (1827), *Il campanello* (1836) and *Betly* (1836), besides participating actively in the development and execution of the librettos written for him by other poets. After the death of Gilardoni, he completed the libretto for *Fausta,* and his contributions to the texts of *Maria Padilla* and *Don Pasquale* were considerable enough to warrant listing his name as one of the poets for those works. Donizetti possessed in large measure that lively sense of practical and effective theater that is an essential attribute of a great opera composer.

As a poet Donizetti commanded a vein of easy, pungent, satirical verse. The fugitive lines that occur in many of his letters, such as that of 13 November 1832[8] which contains a passage beginning 'Se asmatico è Ferretti', exhibit the verbal nimbleness one would expect of a comic librettist. It is symptomatic of this adroitness that the complete librettos he wrote are a comedy and two *farse,* and that they are adaptations of existing sources rather than original inventions.

The satire of *Le convenienze* exposes the pretensions of theatrical people. The basso of the company is the Prima Donna's father and he boasts how his daughter sang chromatic scales in her mother's womb; Mamm'Agata, one of the great farcical roles in nineteenth-century comedy, combines sleazy aplomb with outrageous good humor. The digs at the outmoded aspects of opera seria during the rehearsal episode could come only from one who had been forced to take its tired premises seriously. The single weakness of *Le convenienze* is the ending; the joke wears out. *Il campanello* does not share that weakness, it builds irresistibly to the final ensemble. The whole text is truly a virtuoso display of sharp characterization and verbal dexterity, and Donizetti endowed it with a distinctive Neapolitan flavor that was no part of his source. A comparison of the libretto of *Le chalet* with that of *Betly* shows Donizetti's adaptive gifts to particular advantage. To set the text of the entrance *couplets* of Adam's heroine next to the *aria di sortita* of Donizetti's is to observe that while the general sense of their words is the same, the Italian text possesses a radiant charm and even a syntactical forward motion superior to that of its source. For *Betly* Donizetti recreated the world of *L'elisir;* a romantic aura surrounds the naive, timid youth who loves a good-hearted but resolutely independent girl. Increased familarity with Donizetti's texts proportionately increases one's respect for his skill with words that convey emotional responses; many full-time librettists of his day might have envied his competence.

Ferretti, Jacopo (born Rome, 16 July 1784; died Rome, 7 March 1852). Between 1807 and 1846 Ferretti wrote more than sixty librettos. His chief income, however, came from a post with the tobacco monopoly of the Papal States. He was a man of broad general culture and earned Romani's praise as 'the only one worthy of co-operating with the impulse already given to the Italian musical theater'.[9] While Ferretti's name is most familiar as the librettist of Rossini's *Cenerentola,* the worth of his four superior texts for Donizetti (*L'ajo nell'imbarazzo* (1824), *Olivo e Pasquale* (1827), *Il furioso* (1833) and *Torquato Tasso* (1833)) is more widely recognized today than it was not long ago. Ferretti's one other labor for Donizetti was less distinguished – his 1824 *rifacimento* of Merelli's text for *Zoraida di Granata.* Other composers that Ferretti served throughout his notable career were Mayr, Mercadante, Pacini and Luigi Ricci; he also wrote the text for Rossini's *Matilde di Shabran.*

Ferretti's librettos for Donizetti (to ignore his wasted effort on *Zoraida*) consist of two buffa and two semiseria books. The Roman poet possessed real literary gifts of a delicacy and charm that are striking, yet he was capable of implying true depth of feeling through understatement and apt juxtaposition, as in the episodes between the mad Cardenio and the buffo Kaidamà. These are scenes entirely beyond the range of Cammarano, who possessed other admirable traits as a librettist. Although for *Il furioso* Ferretti adapted a plot that relied too heavily on coincidence, he more than compensated for its structural weakness with sharply-etched characters and well-developed scenes of interaction. Quite as good in its own way is *L'ajo,* for which his source was a well-constructed comedy of character; here Ferretti presents a full cast of individuals instead of stock comic types. The text of *L'ajo* is especially commendable for its delicacy in the treatment of the plight of the heroine, whose marriage must be kept secret, and who it turns out is also a mother – a heavy hand would have been disastrous.

For different reasons the texts to *Tasso* and *Olivo*, in spite of fine moments, fall short of the expert equilibrium that sustains *Il furioso* and *L'ajo*. *Il furioso* is a success in the difficult genre of semiseria because it integrates the buffo character as a poignant extension of the main conflict. *Tasso* precisely lacks this organic unity because the buffo role is the 'chorus' of the piece, commenting on the action but never becoming an integral part of it. Yet the looseness of structure that afflicts *Tasso* does not prevent Tasso himself from emerging as a convincing poet and a genuinely tragic character. The last act of *Tasso* is very fine, and Ferretti's verses help make it so. To read the libretto of *Olivo* is to understand Donizetti's insistence on 'brevità' during the composition of *Il furioso*. *Olivo* is a comedy of humors, and although there are neatly pointed and effective moments, they are adrift in a diffuse plot which ends with a clumsy contrivance.

Genoino, Giulio (born Frattomaggiore, 13 May 1778; died Naples, 8 March 1856). Genoino was a monk, but when his order was suppressed by the French, he became a military chaplain. For many years he was one of the triad of Neapolitan censors; thus Genoino was a rare bird indeed – a censor turned librettist. He supplied Donizetti with one text, *La lettera anonima* (1822). This libretto, apparently derived from one of Genoino's own plays, is devoid of suspense: a slight misunderstanding produces an unnecessary reconciliation. The chief interest of Genoino's text is symptomatic rather than dramatic, for it reveals that the values prized by the censors had nothing much in common with the values of effective theater. Genoino turned out a number of dramas, including comedies, and an amount of occasional verse, in all of which the tone is relentlessly didactic. One suspects that his function as one of the censors, in view of his experience as a writer, was to supply substitute phrases and verses for unacceptable ones in librettos and plays.

Gilardoni, Domenico (born 1798; died Naples 1831).[10] Gilardoni's first libretto was *Bianca e Gernando* (1826), for Bellini's first professionally produced opera. Although he provided texts for Pacini (*Il connestabile di Chester*, 1829), Coccia, Pietro Raimondi (*Il ventaglio*, 1831) and Luigi Ricci, by far the greater part of his labor was devoted to Donizetti, whom he provided with eleven texts, and for whom he worked right up to the end of his tragically short life. The consistency of their collaboration over the space of four of Donizetti's most productive years reveals that the composer found in Gilardoni a poet with whom he could work harmoniously and efficiently. As this was one of Donizetti's periods of marked growth and experimentation it seems safe to assume that the composer and the librettist, both practically the same age, learned a great deal from one another.

The librettos Gilardoni supplied to Donizetti are those for *Otto mesi in due ore* (1827), *Il borgomastro di Saardam* (1827), *L'esule di Roma* (1828), *Gianni di Calais* (1828), *Il giovedì grasso* (1829), *Il paria* (1829), *I pazzi per progetto* (1830), *Il diluvio universale* (1830), *Francesca di Foix* (1831), *La romanziera e l'uomo nero* (1831) and *Fausta* (1832). That Gilardoni's work turns out to be uneven is not surprising considering the pressure of time under which he must have worked, but what is surprising is the range of subject matter and the different types of plot that he essayed in such a comparatively brief period. Still another reason for Gilardoni's unevenness is hinted at in a letter of Bellini, which describes him as pursued by bad luck.[11]

Gianni di Calais and *Fausta* (which he did not live to complete) both possess the merits of clear characterization and consistency of mood. In *Gianni* he achieved a sustained sense of romatic bonhomie, and even the potentially subversive device of Rustano's invariably accurate predictions of future events is managed in such a humorous way that the plot maintains its momentum. In *Fausta* he achieved the nervous energy and the intensity requisite to convincing tragedy. The tragic irony of the scene in which the Emperor must preside over the trial of his son, falsely accused of attempted parricide, is gripping. A comparison between the diction of Gilardoni's feebler librettos and his better efforts points up a striking difference. In *Francesca di Foix* the lines are awkward and unfocused, while in *Fausta* again and again one is impressed by their vividness and compactness; but this difference could well reflect the relative weakness and power of the sources from which he worked. The best of Gilardoni's one-act texts is that of *Il giovedì grasso*; although rather episodic in its working out, it is full of engaging humor and felicitous touches.

Gilardoni's best work is to be found in *L'esule di Roma* and *Il paria*. The former is cleanly constructed and the conflict is straightforward, but the effect of the obligatory *lieto fine* on an implicitly tragic plot is unsatisfactory. The character of Murena provides a penetrating study of a man driven by a guilty conscience beyond the edge of madness. *Il paria* is Gilardoni's most solid work; this is surprising considering the stultifying *longueurs* of Delavigne's play, but Gilardoni worked from Rossi's libretto for Carafa's opera (Venice, 1826) and the scenario of Salvatore Taglioni's successful ballet danced at La Scala in December 1827. Gilardoni develops the relations of his characters in convincing detail; the complexity of Neala's feelings for Idamore, her love for him and her superstitious fear of his caste, are clearly indicated. If he had been able to work consistently on the level he achieved in *Il paria*, Gilardoni would rank as an outstanding librettist.

Marini, Girolamo Maria (born Recanati, 4 November 1801; died Rome, 25 July 1867).[12] For Donizetti, Marini performed only the thankless task of supplying a new third act (a *lieto fine*) for Romani's old libretto of *Adele di Lusignano*, rechristened in its new guise *Adelia* (1841). He wrote ten librettos: the earliest was *Pia de' Tolomei* for Luigi Orsini, whose opera was performed at the Teatro Alfieri in Florence in July 1835; the last was *La duchessa de la Vallière*, composed by Francesco Petrocini and given at Venice during Carnival 1851–2.

Merelli, Bartolomeo (born Bergamo, 19 May 1794; died Milan, 4 April 1879). Before he became first a theatrical agent (in this capacity one of his assignments was to engage the company and commission the operas for the inaugural season at the Carlo Felice in Genoa in 1828)[13] and later a famous, even a notorious, impresario, Merelli wrote a number of librettos: two for Mayr, four for Vaccai, one for Morlacchi, and four for Donizetti. Those for Donizetti were the texts of the composer's first attempts at writing for the theater: *Enrico di Borgogna* (1818), *Una follia* (1818), *Le nozze in villa* (1819) and *Zoraida di Granata* (1822). It is difficult to believe that Donizetti ever set worse librettos than those provided for him by Merelli. They are compendia of clichés expressed in unalloyed bombast. Only one of the texts has any merit – *Le nozze in villa*, which contains several amusing situations, one of them a surprising anticipation of the scene of Beckmesser's serenade.

Romani, Felice (born Genoa, 31 January 1788; died Moneglia, 23 January 1865).[14] The most famous librettist of his time, Romani wrote nearly a hundred texts, some of which were set several times. His active period as a librettist falls between 1813 and 1834. Although Romani's superiority, both as a poet and as a fashioner of plots for music, was early acknowledged, he owes his greatest fame to the period of his collaboration with Bellini, beginning with *Il pirata* (1827). For Donizetti, Romani wrote seven librettos: *Chiara e Serafina* (1822), *Alina, regina di Golconda* (1828), *Anna Bolena* (1830), *Ugo, conte di Parigi* (1832), *L'elisir d'amore* (1832), *Parisina* (1833) and *Lucrezia Borgia* (1833); besides these Donizetti set two of Romani's librettos first used by other composers: *Rosmonda d'Inghilterra* (1834) and *Adelia* (1841).

Three of Romani's texts for Donizetti do nothing to justify the librettist's high reputation. Of these *Chiara e Serafina* and *Adelia* date from the first phase of his career. *Ugo*, even though it was maltreated by the censors, suffers because it generates insufficient sympathy for its characters and the verse rarely exhibits genuine elevation.

Anna Bolena, *L'elisir*, *Parisina* and *Lucrezia Borgia* have books that would add luster to any librettist's reputation. Although *Anna* is most famous for its very fine closing scene, there are many other dramatic episodes that Romani handles in superior fashion. The encounter between Seymour and Enrico at the end of the final scene sets off the conflict between the remorseful mistress and the King's alarming mixture of sensuousness and ruthlessness. Even better is the encounter between Anna and Seymour, where each disclosure increases both the tension and the poignancy of the scene, and at the same time the situation of both women holds the sympathy of the audience. Romani's superior grasp of characterization stands out even more clearly in his text for *L'elisir*. Although he was here adapting Scribe's *Le philtre*, Romani much improved upon the original. Scribe's naive Guillaume is no more than a pale sketch of Nemorino (literally 'Little Nobody'), who possesses a vein of tender melancholy along with his eager optimism, traits scarcely suggested by Scribe. Romani balances comic exaggeration and romance with innate good taste, especially in the duet between Adina and Dulcamara where the old charlatan admits the superiority of Adina's charms to his elixir. For dramatic power and accruing tragic intensity, *Parisina* is possibly the finest libretto Romani ever wrote. The Act 2 scene in Parisina's bedchamber and her aria–finale are on a high level of achievement indeed. His libretto for *Lucrezia Borgia* is a smooth condensation of Hugo's play and remarkably faithful to it. The ominous atmosphere is excellently sustained and heightened, and his command of moments of sudden dramatic contrast are particularly successful.

Romani once wrote that he tried to be neither a Classicist nor a Romanticist; he merely pursued the beautiful wherever it might lead him (Z. no. A31, dated 23 November 1841, p. 890, to Donizetti). However strong his sympathies may have been for earlier ways, he was extraordinarily successful in expressing the afflatus of the earliest Romantic melodrama, and it is in this vein that most of his best work is to be found. Romani always insisted that the poet deserved equal consideration with the composer and maintained that it perhaps took even longer to create a first-class text than it did to write the music for it. This attitude, coupled with his prickly pride, did not make him an easy collaborator for Donizetti to work with.

Rossi, Gaetano (born Verona, 18 May 1774; died Verona, 25 January 1855). The most prolific librettist of his time, Rossi wrote more than 100 texts between 1799 and shortly before his death. Although he was at one time associated with the Fenice, his works were brought out at many theaters. He supplied Rossini with two famous texts: *Tancredi* (1813) and *Semiramide* (1823). For Donizetti he wrote two librettos: *Maria Padilla* (1841) and *Linda di Chamounix* (1842). A good *routinier*, Rossi strove to keep abreast of changing tastes in operatic subjects, but his adaptability is in some measure responsible for the lack of a clearly defined personality in his texts. He co-operated agreeably with Donizetti's suggestions and countenanced his insertion of passages into the text of *Maria Padilla*. In *Linda* he apparently raised no objection to dropping from the libretto the essential detail that Linda had become Carlo's mistress in Act 2 – the relationship of their counterparts in *La grâce de Dieu* – which omission makes much of what occurs in that act scarcely credible. The most successful character in *Linda*, from the point of the view of the libretto, is the lecherous old Marchese, whose cynical hedonism blows like a breath of fresh air through the prevailingly sentimental atmosphere.

Royer, Alphonse (born Paris, 10 September 1803; died Paris, 11 April 1875). Before he embarked on a distinguished career as a director of Parisian theaters (Odéon, 1853–6; Opéra, 1856–62) and Inspecteur Général des Beaux-Arts, Royer, with his chief collaborator Gustave Vaëz, served Donizetti in a variety of ways. Royer and Vaëz were responsible for the French text of *Lucie* – a distinct version rather than just a translation as it involves a large number of modifications. They wrote the libretto for the never produced *L'ange de Nisida*, and along with Scribe managed the revision of that work into *La favorite*.

Ruffini, Giovanni (born Genoa, 20 September 1807; died Genoa, 3 November 1881). Giovanni Ruffini, along with his brothers Agostino and Iacopo, were early and enthusiastic followers of Mazzini. In May 1833, Giovanni and Iacopo were arrested for their revolutionary activities and condemned to death. While Iacopo committed suicide by slashing his wrists in prison, Giovanni managed to escape and fled first to Switzerland and later to France.

Accursi introduced Ruffini to Donizetti to perform for him various librettist's chores. The most important was the revision and adaptation of the text that Angelo Anelli (1761–1820) had written for Pavesi's *Ser Marc'Antonio*, from which Ruffini produced *Don Pasquale*. Although his dissatisfaction with the composer's treatment of that text caused Ruffini to have his name omitted from the work, the two collaborated again later. It was most probably Ruffini to whom Donizetti referred when he wrote to Toto on 27 November 1842: 'I called in a poet to make some little adjustments';[15] the work concerned was Cammarano's old libretto *Il conte di Chalais* which was the source of *Maria di Rohan*, and since the adaptation was carried out during the time of the creation of *Don Pasquale*, Ruffini is the most likely candidate. He certainly provided the texts for the new contralto arias for Gondì when *Maria di Rohan* was altered for the Théâtre-Italien. Ruffini's Italian translation of *Dom Sébastien* was completed by February 1845, for it appears, along with Leo Herz's German text, in the Viennese score published at that time by Mechetti.

For a good many years both Giovanni Ruffini and his younger brother Agostino (who in 1835 had helped Donizetti out by revising Bidèra's text for *Marin Faliero*) lived and wrote in Edinburgh. After the unification of Italy they were able to return home.

Sacchèro, Giacomo (born ?; died 1875). Little information about Sacchèro is available, save that he was active as a librettist in Milan between 1841 and 1845. His text for Federico Ricci's *Corrado d'Altamura* (Milan, 1841) was his only work to meet with much success. He wrote only one text for Donizetti, *Caterina Cornaro* (1844), a more serviceable libretto than the performance history of the score would lead one to expect. The situations are clearly handled, but in the poem the characters, except for Lusignano, are scarcely individualized.

Saint-Georges, Jules-Henri Vernoy de (born Paris, 1801; died Paris, 23 December 1875). Saint-Georges was probably, next to Scribe, the most productive libretto writer in France. Together with Jean-François-Alfred Bayard (1796–1853), he wrote the libretto for *La fille du régiment* (1840). The plot is well handled, the humor and sentiment neatly balanced, but the final resolution is a bit compressed. The original text was a good deal longer, but during the rehearsal period it was cut to its present length. A neat example of adroit craftsmanship, combining logic with charm, is the Act 1 duet for Marie and Tonio, 'Depuis l'instant'. Saint-Georges was also the poet for the never completed *Ne m'oubliez pas*, but on the basis of the surviving fragments one cannot form an opinion of the work.

Salatino, Pietro (dates unknown). Salatino was a Sicilian; he lived for a time in Messina, and went to Naples to study law. The only librettos he seems to have written for anybody are those of Donizetti's *Sancia di Castiglia* (1832) and the revision of Bardari's text for *Maria Stuarda* when it was reconstituted as *Buondelmonte*. Donizetti's opinion of Salatino as a librettist appears in a letter he wrote to his friend in Messina, Spadaro del Bosch, on 8 July 1835: 'Here there is a lack of comic poets, but don't let Salatino know; if you do he will put his knapsack on his back and roll from Messina to Naples.'[16]

Schmidt, Giovanni Federico (*c.* 1775–*c.* 1840). Pacini describes Schmidt as 'a man of some talent, but misery was his inseparable companion, so that his character, afflicting beyond all description, inspired melancholy just at the sight of him'.[17] Schmidt, whose prolific activity in the Neapolitan theaters was mainly carried on between 1802 and 1830, wrote for Donizetti the text for *Elvida* and the words for two cantatas. The talent that Pacini saw in Schmidt does not appear in the text for *Elvida*.

Scribe, Eugène (born Paris, 24 December 1791; died Paris, 20 February 1861). With the help of collaborators, Scribe produced an average of ten theater pieces a year over a span of fifty years. He wrote three texts for Donizetti: *Les martyrs* (1840), *Le duc d'Albe* (written in 1839), with Charles Duvéyrier's assistance, and *Dom Sébastien* (1843). Further, he made some contribution to the libretto of *La favorite*, for which Royer and Vaëz were chiefly responsible. Gautier's opinion of Scribe's wooden, anti-musical verses has already been cited. It is true that his texts are apt to be heavy, prosaic and monotonous, but in their dull way they are efficient, and he was notorious for his skill in putting together a stageworthy plot, the kind of work that is condescendingly referred to as a 'pièce bien faite'. Scribe's gloomy text to *Dom Sébastien* does a real disservice to one of Donizetti's most impressive scores.

Tottola, Andrea Leone (dates unknown). Tottola is often linked with Schmidt as an example of the wretched librettists active in Naples during the early years of the nineteenth century. He was perhaps the most uneven librettist whose work Donizetti ever set. Donizetti availed himself of Tottola's texts for five scores: *La zingara* (1822), *Alfredo il grande* (1823), *Il fortunato inganno* (1823), *Il castello di Kenilworth* (1829) and *Imelda de' Lambertazzi* (1830). Without a commission and for his own edification Donizetti also made a setting in 1826 of Tottola's libretto for Carafa's *Gabriella di Vergy*.

For sheer vacuity it is difficult to surpass such lines as this quatrain from *Alfredo il grande:*

> Il lasso fianco
> Chi vuol posar
> Sicuro e franco
> Qui può inoltrar.

(Who hopes to rest his weary side, with safety blest may come inside.)

Although Tottola's text for *Il fortunato inganno* runs on, it contains some genuinely funny lines and situations. There is a sharp sense of satire in the opening episode of the rehearsal, and in the extensive spoken dialogue the parts for the two dialect comics must have been thoroughly entertaining on stage. The best of Tottola's work for Donizetti is to be found in *Imelda,* a generally underrated work; his pointed way with this Romantic melodrama and the fine emotional tension he developed in it suggest that he had been bored for years by plots tailored to avoid any problems with the censors. When, as with his *Gabriella di Vergy,* he had a subject with some dramatic meat to it he came quite surprisingly to life.

Vaëz, Gustave (pseudonym for Van Niewenhuysen, Jean-Nicholas-Gustave) (1812–62). He collaborated with Royer on the French version of *Lucia* and on *L'ange de Nisida–La favorite,* the composite autograph of which testifies to his participation in the words 'Les changemens de paroles ont ils fait sur ce manuscrit par moi. Gustave Vaëz'. On his own he wrote for Donizetti the book for the genuinely amusing farsa *Rita, ou Le mari battu* (1841). The scene in which the two husbands resort to games of chance and cheat in their anxiety to lose the wife neither of them wants is very funny indeed.

Notes

1. 1797–1821: The beginnings

1 Z. no. 496, dated 15 July 1843, p. 679. References to letters in Guido Zavadini, *Donizetti: Vita – Musiche – Epistolario* (Bergamo, 1948) will be given in this form. Numbers without prefixes refer to letters written by Donizetti; numbers preceded by A refer to letters from someone else to Donizetti; numbers preceded by B refer to letters from someone else which mention Donizetti.

2 Ciro Caversazzi, *Gaetano Donizetti: la casa dove nacque, la famiglia, l'inizio della malattia* (Bergamo, 1924), p. 1.

3 Considering what little is known of the medical history of Donizetti's sisters, there is some possibility that venereal disease, which was to strike down both Donizetti and his nephew Andrea (Giuseppe's son), might have been a factor in their heredity.

4 Caversazzi, *op. cit.*, p. 4.

5 At one time it was conjectured that Donizetti had Scots blood in his veins, but Caversazzi demonstrates that the family had been in Bergamo since the seventeenth century at least. The Scottish hypothesis seems to have been the invention of George T. Ferris, *The Great Italian and French Composers* (New York, 1878), and it is as implausible as it is inaccurate.

6 'Clavicembalo' is an Italian term for harpsichord, but in the early nineteenth century it was applied indiscriminately to all keyboard instruments.

7 John Allitt has suggested (in a letter to the author, 28 January 1977) that some of the things Donizetti learned from Mayr came from the latter's adherence to the Masons, as he claims that Mayr was an initiate of the Order of Illuminati. At one point, Mayr found himself in difficulties with the Bergamo authorities over his Masonic connections.

8 Mayr's first opera, *Saffo* (Teatro La Fenice, Venice, 1794), was a success, and he composed almost seventy other stage works of all types during the next thirty years, until, with *Demetrio*, first given at Turin in 1824, his failing eyesight caused him to renounce the theater. After that he devoted his attention to Santa Maria Maggiore and to his school until a paralytic stroke halted his career.

9 Fire destroyed the Teatro Riccardi in 1797, but so great was local enthusiasm that, entirely rebuilt, it was in use again the following year. During Donizetti's youth the annual season at the Riccardi ran from

Easter through September; later on it was open only during the summer *fiera* (fair).

10 The Teatro della Società gave performances from October until the end of Carnival. After 1892 the structure fell into disrepair and performances were given there only sporadically. Today the building houses a *trattoria*.

11 Rossini's *Mosè in Egitto* (first version, Naples, 1818) was remarkable in that the title role was assigned to a bass.

12 Giacomo David (or Davide) (1750–1830), famous for the purity of his voice and as an improviser of embellishments and variations, and equally renowned as performer and teacher, retired from the stage in 1812 and return to Bergamo to serve as tenor soloist at Santa Maria Maggiore, where the young Donizetti heard him frequently.

Giovanni David (1790–1864), celebrated for his three-octave range, was chiefly active in Naples, singing in the *prime* (first performances) of five of Rossini's operas; his voice began to deteriorate in the mid-1820s, and later he became an impresario at St Petersburg.

13 Domenico Viganoni (1754–1823) achieved great celebrity during the 1790s in Milan, Vienna and London, before retiring to Almenno near Bergamo; his villa there was the scene of many an evening of impromptu music-making, and there Donizetti was a regular guest, performing and improvising to entertain the company.

14 Andrea Nozzari (1775–1832), a fine singing-actor, was still active on the Neapolitan stage when Donizetti moved to Naples in 1822.

15 Marco Bordogni (1788–1856), after a success at the Théâtre-Italien, was appointed professor of singing at the Paris Conservatoire at Rossini's urging, as part of the latter's campaign to improve the standards of French vocal technique. Bordogni was still actively teaching when Donizetti settled in Paris in 1838.

16 Domenico Donzelli (1790–1873) made his debut at Bergamo in 1808 in Mayr's *Elisa* and continued singing until 1844. He may be best remembered today as the first Pollione in Bellini's *Norma*, but ten years before he had done Donizetti important service, helping to ensure the success of *Zoraida di Granata*, the opera that established the composer in his chosen profession.

17 Giovanni Battista Rubini (1795–1854) initiated the great days of his career in Paris in 1825, but his contract with Barbaja kept him singing in Italy for six months of every year until 1831, an obligation that permitted him to take part in the *prime* of major works by Bellini and Donizetti. Rubini had started out in 1804 as a chorister at the Teatro Riccardi, Bergamo. After his retirement in 1844, he settled in a lavish villa near his birthplace at Romano Lombardo, an hour's journey from Bergamo. Shortly before Donizetti's death, Rubini visited him in Bergamo Alta, hoping to bring some glimmer of recognition to the composer's clouded mind by singing to him a passage from *Lucia*.

18 Donizetti used both Christian names only through his first year at Mayr's school. Thereafter he dropped 'Domenico' permanently.

19 This report and the subsequent ones pertaining to Donizetti's progress at Mayr's school appear in Giuliano Donati-Pettèni, *L'Istituto Musicale Gaetano Donizetti* (Bergamo, 1928), pp. 35ff.

20 Z. no. 1, dated 7 November 1810, p. 223.

21 Mayr's own printed copy of this libretto is in the Biblioteca Civica, Bergamo Alta.

22 Besides Donizetti's waltz, the score of *Il piccolo compositore di musica* drew on works by Sebastiano Nasolini, Stefano Pavesi and Mayr.

23 Z. no. B3, pp. 910–11.

24 Giovanni Ricordi (1785–1853) was first a violinist, then a copyist for the Teatro Carcano; in 1808 he established the music-publishing house in Milan that still bears his name. Ricordi published many of the works of Rossini, Bellini, Donizetti and the young Verdi, which gave the firm its highly successful foundation. He maintained, except for their brief difficulty over *Gianni di Parigi* in 1839, a friendly and supportive relationship with Donizetti.

For some years Mayr had served Ricordi as an editorial consultant. The direct result of his letter of 1815 was the first publication of any composition by Donizetti – a set of variations on a theme from Mayr's opera *La rosa bianca e la rosa rossa* – which Ricordi brought out that year.

25 Federico Alborghetti and Michelangelo Galli, *Gaetano Donizetti e G. Simone Mayr: notizie e documenti* (Bergamo, 1875), pp. 32–3.

26 Francesco Giorgi, *Gaetano Donizetti studente al Liceo Musicale di Bologna* (Bologna, 1928), p. 6.

27 Corrado Ricci, 'Donizetti a Bologna: appunti e documenti', *Gaetano Donizetti: numero unico nel primo centennario della sua nascità: 1797–1897*, ed. P. Bettoli (Bergamo, 1897), pp. 10–13. In popular tradition Bologna is a city preoccupied with sex.

28 Maroncelli married the mezzo-soprano Amalie Schneider.

29 Z. no. A38, pp. 895–6. One of the degli Antonj, to whom Maroncelli refers in this letter, could have been Clementina, the contralto soloist chosen by Rossini for the first Italian performance of his *Stabat mater*, conducted by Donizetti at Rossini's invitation in Bologna in March 1842.

30 Although composed in 1816, *Il Pigmalione* was not performed until 13 October 1960, at the Teatro Donizetti, Bergamo. The text Donizetti set for this opera was based on one by Sografi, adapted from Rousseau, and it had been set by several other composers during the 1790s.

31 The autograph of *Il Pigmalione* is in the Bibliothèque Nationale, Paris, and a photocopy of it is in the Museo Donizettiano, Bergamo.

32 I agree with Commons's conclusion that '*Olimpiade* has only the most dubious rights to be included in the list of operas at all. All that exists is one duet, obviously a student exercise. It is one of Metastasio's most famous duets, and the only one in *Olimpiade*. Nothing more likely, it seems to me, than that young Donizetti wanting to compose something chose it. But there's not one shred of evidence that he ever set anything more of the text and one duet hardly amounts to an opera. Personally, I think it's about time it was excised from the list.' (Letter to the author, 14 July 1976.)

33 V. Sacchiero and others, *Il Museo Donizettiano di Bergamo* (Bergamo, 1970), pp. 87–8.

34 Donizetti used for *L'ira d'Achille* an existing libretto (not being in a position to pay for a new one), already set by Giuseppe Nicolini

(1763–1842), and given at La Scala on 26 December 1814. The printed libretto does not identify the poet, but Carlo Gatti (*Il Teatro alla Scala*, (2 vols., Milan, 1964), vol. 2, p. 26) lists the librettist as Felice Romani.

35 Marco Bonesi, 'Note biografiche su Donizetti' (letter dated 16 July 1861, Biblioteca Civica, Bergamo Alta); ed. G. Zavadini, *Bergomum: bollettino della Biblioteca Civica*, 40/iii (1946), p. 87. Bonesi wrote years after the events he describes; his notes are apt to be discouragingly general and the quoted passage is untypically circumstantial. Those who turn to Donizetti's string quartets imagining they will find developmental passages in the manner of Haydn or Beethoven will be disappointed. At one time Bonesi gave Donizetti viola lessons so that after several sessions Donizetti could perform the second viola part in a quintet he had written; in return he gave Bonesi lessons in realizing figured bass. Bonesi became a prominent figure in the musical life of Bergamo; he directed the orchestra at the Teatro Riccardi from 1839 to 1847 and in 1850, conducting thirteen of Donizetti's operas there.

36 The misleading passage is quoted in Zavadini, *Donizetti: Vita – Musiche – Epistolario*, p. 13.

37 Giuseppina Ronzi-de Begnis (1800–53) was then eighteen and on the threshold of a distinguished and scandal-ridden career. In the early 1820s she sang successfully in Paris and London, but in 1825 she underwent a vocal crisis. In the summer of 1831 she re-emerged, now a dramatic soprano, and pursued for a decade, chiefly in Naples, a highly successful career as a lyric tragedian, taking part in important Donizetti *prime*. Donizetti described her to Melzi at the time of her return to Naples: 'She sang *par excellence* and also sustained well the dramatic side of her role [Desdemona in Rossini's *Otello*]. There are those who seek to compare her with Pasta, but such comparisons are always invidious.' (Z. no. 67, dated 30 July 1831, p. 284.) This comment reveals that Donizetti was concerned with the projecting of the text and its emotional coloring. His friend, the music-publisher Guillamme Cottrau, did not share his enthusiasm for Ronzi, objecting to her singing as 'over-nuanced' (*Lettres d'un mélomane* (Naples, 1885), p. 16). Giuseppe de Begnis (1793–1849) had sung the role of Dandini in the *prima* of Rossini's *Cenerentola* at Rome earlier in 1817. In time he separated from Ronzi and became an impresario at Bath and Dublin. He died in New York.

38 Luigi Pilon discovered this letter in the Biblioteca Civica, Bergamo Alta, and presented it at the 1° convegno internazionale di studi donizettiani, held at Bergamo in 1975.

39 The Teatro San Luca had formerly been known as the Teatro Vendramin.

40 In the Zancla–Merelli contract, dated 16 May 1818, also found by Luigi Pilon, Merelli speaks of adapting a play by August von Kotzebue, giving the title as *Giovanna di Monfalcor*; Merelli's handwriting is difficult to decipher, but he can only be referring to Kotzebue's *Johanna von Montfaucon* (Vienna, 1799). Between the time he wrote this letter and the time he came to write his libretto for Donizetti, the subject had been changed to one derived from another play by Kotzebue – *Der Graf von Burgund* (Vienna, 1795).

41 Angelo Geddo, *Bergamo e la musica* (Bergamo, 1958), p. 344, lists Merelli as *direttore d'orchestra* at the Teatro Riccardi for the seasons 1830–2, but I suspect Geddo has confused the function of lessee with that of conductor.

42 The first libretto Merelli wrote was for Mayr's *Lanassa* (Teatro La Fenice, Venice, Carnival 1817–18). Then followed *Alfredo il grande*, also for Mayr (Teatro Argentina, Rome, February 1818), and *Il lupo d'Ostenda* for Vaccai, written in April 1818, performed at the Teatro San Benedetto, Venice. Merelli's libretto for Donizetti, *Enrico di Borgogna*, was the fourth he had dashed off in a little more than six months!

43 Not to be confused with the famous Angelica Catalani (1780–1859).

44 Z. no. 7, p. 228. Unaware of the Merelli–Mayr letter of 18 April 1818, Zavadini assumed that Donizetti's letter to Mayr of 13 October 1818 was written from Venice.

45 The buffo Andrea Verni sang the role of Gilberto.

46 Quoted by Luigi Pilon in his paper 'Gli esordi operistici di Donizetti', delivered at the 1ᵒ convegno internazionale di studi donizettiani, Bergamo, 1975.

47 *Nuovo osservatore veneziano*, 17 November 1818.

48 Quoted by Pilon, *op. cit.*

49 This one-sided dialogue is reprinted in Giuliano Donati-Pettèni, *Donizetti* (Milan, 1930), pp. 40–1.

50 'Voi s'appreste invan' . . . 'Non mostrarmi in tale istante'.

51 See Jeremy Commons, 'The Authorship of *I piccioli virtuosi ambulanti*,' *Donizetti Society Journal*, 2 (1975), 199–207.

52 Bevilacqua-Aldobrandini may have drawn on Romani's libretto of the same name, which was set by Giovanni Pacini (Milan, 1819). Merelli turned to the same subject in a text for Nicola Vaccai (1824).

53 The libretto of this Verona production shows that Caterina's *rondò*, 'In quest'estremo amplesso', was replaced by an ensemble of soloists, without chorus. This change may well indicate that the *rondò* had already become widely known in a number of other contexts. For instance, it did not originate in the score of *Il falegname di Livonia*, for Donizetti had borrowed it from *Le nozze in villa*, where it had occupied a similar position. He later used it in several other scores to replace finales of less effect. It was inserted into *La lettera anonima* with new opening words ('Ricevi quest'amplesso') and a more subtle cadence to the first phrase. That it was also used or considered for both *Emilia di Liverpool* and *Otto mesi in due ore* is proved by the autograph of the latter work (in the Conservatorio di San Pietro a Majella, Naples), with which a copy of the *rondò* is bound as an alternate aria–finale: the name of the character who sings it has been altered from 'Emilia' to 'Elisabetta'. The continued reappearance of 'In quest'estremo amplesso' testifies both to its effectiveness and to the persisting popularity of the convention of the aria–finale.

54 'Musico' is the term Donizetti and his contemporaries used to refer to heroic male roles designed to be sung by female contraltos. By extension, the term was also applied to the singers (like Eckerlin and Pisaroni) who specialized in such parts. These contralto hero parts, common in the

early nineteenth century but pretty well disappearing during the late 1830s, derived from the castrato contralto heroes of eighteenth-century opera seria; after fashion and humanitarian considerations had banished the castrato from opera, the association of that vocal range with heroic characters survived for a time. This was also the period when tenors were expected to have well-developed falsetto ranges. Therefore, during the 1820s there was for the audience no strict correlation between a singer's vocal sound and the sexual characteristics of the role he or she sang. The related term 'musichetto' was applied by Donizetti's generation to roles sung by women who impersonated pages or male adolescents. Donizetti composed a number of roles of both these types.

55 Copyists' scores of both Enrico di Borgogna and Le nozze in villa are in the Bibliothèque Nationale, Paris.

56 Bonesi, 'Note biografiche'.

57 Z. no. 7 bis, p. 229.

58 Z. no. 323, dated 29 July 1839, p. 499.

59 A number of Donizetti's piano compositions of this period are dedicated to Marianna Pezzoli-Grattaroli.

60 Z. no. 8, dated 17 June 1821, pp. 229–30; S.d. 1, no. 1, dated 7 August 1821, p. 1 (in this and later references to published letters, 'S.d.' stands for Studi donizettiani); Z. no. 9, dated 9 August 1821, p. 230.

61 Giovanni Paterni (1779–1837) was a wealthy Roman industrialist.

62 Z. no. 8 begins as follows: 'By means of Sig. Corini I have received the contracts, one of which I am sending back to you by him.' The name Corini is the same as that of Donizetti's musician uncle who had lived next door in the Borgo Canale. If the Corini mentioned in the letter was this uncle or a member of his family, it could well have been that he helped to recommend Donizetti for this crucial engagement.

63 Z. no. B4, p. 912.

2. 1822–1830: *Zoraida di Granata* to *Imelda de' Lambertazzi*

1 Jacopo Ferretti (1784–1852) wrote librettos for Rossini (La Cenerentola and Matilde di Shabran), Pietro Carlo Guglielmi (whom Ferretti regarded as the most difficult composer he worked with), Niccolò Zingarelli (who never asked for changes), Giovanni Pacini, Saverio Mercadante, Luigi Ricci and others. For Mayr Ferretti never wrote an operatic text, but he supplied him with the oratorio Il voto di Jefte (1814). For Donizetti Ferretti would write the texts to the rifacimento of Zoraida (1824), L'ajo nell'imbarazzo (1824), Olivo e Pasquale (1827), Il furioso all'isola di San Domingo (1833) and Torquato Tasso (1833). Between 1807 and 1846 Ferretti wrote more than sixty librettos.

2 The Apollo was originally known as the Teatro Tordinona, but the name was changed in 1795 in the hope of ridding the theater of any association with the notorious Tordinona prison. In 1938 Alberto Cametti brought out a two-volume history of the Apollo, Il Teatro di Tordinona, poi di Apollo (2 vols., Rome, 1938).

3 Michele Enrico Carafa di Colobrano (1787–1872), a Neapolitan prince who turned opera composer, was a longtime friend of Rossini and upon occasion his collaborator. Carafa's best opera seems to have been Gab-

riella di Vergy (Naples, 1816). In 1827 he moved to Paris, where for a time he taught composition at the Conservatoire. Although his music obtained a passing popularity, he had a knack for choosing subjects better remembered in other composer's works: for example, *Le nozze di Lammermoor, I due Figaro* and *Masaniello*.

4 Luigi Lablache (1794–1858), then on the threshold of his career as the greatest bass of his time, made his Roman debut in Carafa's *La capricciosa e il soldato*. He sang in Vienna in 1824 and again in 1827, when he was a soloist in Mozart's Requiem at Beethoven's funeral, and he was one of the torch-bearers at Beethoven's interment. He was to sing in the *prime* of many of Donizetti's operas, most memorably in that of *Don Pasquale* (1843).

5 Giovanni Pacini (1796–1867) was one of the more prolific composers of operas among Donizetti's contemporaries, turning out nearly ninety. He was one of the *rossiniani*. His best-known work, *Saffo* (Naples, 1840), is evidence that he tried to keep abreast of post-Rossinian developments.

6 Pacini tells the story of Sbigoli's death in his *Le mie memorie artistiche* (Florence, 1875), pp. 28–9. He states in the same book that his enduring friendship with Donizetti dated from these days in Rome.

7 I have never succeeded in finding any further reference to Mazzanti.

8 Maria Ester Mombelli (1794–?), member of a famous family of singers, made her debut in the *prima* of Rossini's *Demetrio e Polibio* (Rome, 1812). She retired from the stage in 1827, when she married Count Gritti.

9 Vincenzo Puccita (1778–1861), composer of twenty-three operas, was chief conductor and contriver of music for the famous Angelica Catalani. Puccita exemplifies the subordination of composer to singer common during this period.

10 *Notizie del giorno*, 31 January 1822. Part of Celli's review is quoted in Alberto Cametti's *Donizetti a Roma* (Turin, 1907), p. 20.

11 Z. no. 10, p. 231.

12 Luigi Vasselli (1770 or 1771–1832) was a distinguished lawyer connected with the Vatican, and the author of *Formulario di tutti gli atti di procedura analogamente al Codice pubblicando con Notu proprio del 22 novembre 1817* (Rome, 1818). He and his family lived on the *piano nobile* (first floor) of Via della Muratte, no. 78. The family originally came from Riofreddo.

13 According to Cametti (*Donizetti a Roma*, p. 60), the nickname Toto is pronounced with the accent on the first syllable.

14 See Z. no. 20, dated 7 October 1823, pp. 239–40, beginning 'Amico del core'. Gaetano wrote this letter jointly to Toto and Ferretti about the proposed revisions in the libretto of *Zoraida*. He addressed it to Toto to spare Ferretti the expense of handling, for in those days the recipient, not the sender, paid for his mail.

15 There were two other brothers: Francesco, then twenty-two, who died in 1826; and Gaetano, a schoolboy of sixteen.

16 In S.d.1, pp. 133–4, there are three letters from Mercadante to Anna Carnevali. The first (4 October 1821) is from Milan, where Mercadante was rehearsing his very successful *Elisa e Claudio* for its *prima* at La

Scala on 30 October, and begins: 'I take the occasion of Signor Maestro Donizetti's trip to Rome (and I recommend him to you highly) to give you news of my excellent state of health.' This letter, by the way, helps to pinpoint the date of Donizetti's passage through Milan on his way from Bergamo to Rome, as he obviously took this letter with him. The third of the letters (8 February 1822) is from Venice and starts: 'With great satisfaction I hear that Maestro Donizetti has done himself honor in spite of the usual cabals and intrigues.' This letter shows how relatively quickly news of the operatic world traveled in those days.

17 Donizetti's friendship with the Carnevali family lasted at least until 1834. The latest of his letters to Anna (Z. no. 155, dated 3 November 1834, p. 366) is signed 'your eternal servant and friend, G. Donizetti', and the sheet contains a note in another hand: 'answered 19 December'. I mention this letter of 1834 because Barblan (see Guglielmo Barblan and Frank Walker, 'Introduzione alla lettura delle centotrentatrè nuove lettere di Donizetti', *Studi donizettiani*, 1 (1962), 1–20) has suggested (pp. 7–8), on not very convincing grounds, a possible romance between Anna Carnevali and Donizetti. He puts much stress on a letter of 18 July 1832 (*S.d.*1, no. 15, p. 13), in which Donizetti writes: 'Remember you said you would come to Naples, come on, and in October we will leave together.' There are two reasons that make Barblan's interpretation less than inevitable. For one thing, Anna Carnevali had daughters about Donizetti's age; for another, the Vasselli family and the Carnevalis were acquainted and almost certainly the invitation to visit Naples came from both Gaetano and Virginia, and then all three of them would travel to Rome, for whenever Gaetano left Naples to put on an opera, Virginia went with him as far as Rome to visit her family. An undated letter that Barblan, for no very persuasive reason, suggests is from 1833, contains some agitated phrases: 'I am beside myself . . . This treatment of me by you has humiliated me', but there is nothing to suggest that this necessarily refers to the end of an affair; it could, just as plausibly, mean that someone (one of the musicians Anna Carnevali cultivated, perhaps) had been spreading gossip about Donizetti.

18 Z. no. 12, dated 26 March 1822, p. 233.

19 Rossini had come to Naples in 1815 to put on *Elisabetta, regina d'Inghilterra*, with Isabella Colbran (1785–1845) in the title role. Rossini's tenth and last opera for the San Carlo, *Zelmira*, had been brought out shortly before Donizetti's arrival, on 16 February 1822, and had obtained only a succès d'estime. Rossini and Colbran were going to Vienna, where the impresario Barbaja had added the Viennese Kärntnertortheater to his managerial responsibilities; on their way, Rossini and Colbran were married (16 March) in a little town near Bologna.

20 Colbran had been offered and had refused the role of Atalia in Mayr's oratorio; that part was then assigned to Giuseppina Fabré (who was the daughter of Beaumarchais's cook). Since Fabré was a contralto, the soprano role of Atalia had to be extensively adjusted (*puntato*) to suit her voice.

21 Z. no. 11, dated 4 March 1822, pp. 231–2.

22 Domenico Barbaja (1778–1841) was the most astute and colorful impre-

sario of his day. He ran the San Carlo in Naples from 1809 to 1824, and again from 1827 to 1831, and finally from 1836 to 1840. He managed La Scala from 1826 to 1832. Further, he held the leases on two Viennese theaters, the Kärntnertortheater and the Theater an der Wien, from 1821 to 1828.

23 In those days composers were under contractual obligation to prepare an opera for its *prima* and to be present in the pit (usually at the *clavicembalo*) for the first three performances. If the work was sufficiently successful to be put on in other theaters, its preparation was in the hands of the local staff. On occasion a composer would be engaged to prepare a special revival, usually with some new music added to the score.

24 San Gennaro (St Januarius), the patron saint of Naples, was believed to protect the city from the eruptions of Vesuvius. Phials purporting to contain his blood were exposed for a double novena (eighteen days) each May and September, when it was hoped the contents would liquefy. The Neapolitan theaters were closed during these times.

25 Z. no. 12, p. 233.

26 The Teatro Nuovo ranked a poor third among the opera houses of Naples, the most important being the San Carlo, followed by the Fondo. The usual fare at the Nuovo consisted of *farse*, often with spoken dialogue.

27 The libretto to *La zingara* was based on a French melodrama, *La petite bohémienne*, by Louis-Charles Caigniez (Paris, 1816).

28 Andrea Leone Tottola was an impoverished *abate* and an errand boy for Barbaja and Colbran. He wrote for the Neapolitan stages between 1796 and 1831. Among his many librettos probably the best known are those he supplied Rossini for *Mosè in Egitto* and for *La gazza ladra*.

29 *Giornale del Regno delle Due Sicilie*, 13 May 1822.

30 In this period Neapolitan audiences were famous for their restraint, the result of the etiquette that prevailed when a member of the royal family was in attendance, for then applause was permitted only when initiated by the king or his representative.

31 Z. no. 13, pp. 233–4. The king was Ferdinando I (1751–1825), the Bourbon ruler of the Kingdom of the Two Sicilies.

32 *La zingara* was the first of Donizetti's operas to be given outside Italy, being staged in Germany in 1823. The most recent performance I have traced took place at Havana in 1859.

33 Francesco Florimo, *Bellini: memorie e lettere* (Florence, 1882), pp. 129–30. Florimo (1800–80) was a student with Bellini at the Naples Conservatory (Conservatorio di San Pietro a Majella) and became his dearest friend and most ardent partisan. The cited anecdote is all the more striking as Florimo rarely paid Donizetti compliments. He became director of the library at the Conservatory and later was to exert considerable influence in opposition to Donizetti's appointment as director.

34 Besides Genoino, the board was then made up of Marchese Puoti and Francesco Ruffa.

35 This singer was Teresa Cecconi, who, for a time at least, balked at singing the role of Melita.

36 *Giornale del Regno delle Due Sicilie*, 1 July 1822.

37 Z. no. 14, pp. 234–5.
38 The chief source of information about Donizetti's stay in Milan during 1822 is Clemente Verzino, *Le opere di Gaetano Donizetti* (Bergamo, 1897), pp. 20–48.
39 Unpublished letter, dated 28 September 1822, in the Biblioteca Civica, Bergamo Alta. Mercadante's *Adele ed Emerico* had its *prima* on 21 September 1822, but it went on to attain a run of fifty performances that fall season. Mercadante's opera of the year before at La Scala was his *Elisa e Claudio,* which received thirty performances during the fall season of 1821 and twenty-seven more the following spring.
40 In this period, the beginning of rehearsals did not necessarily mean that the score was complete, let alone orchestrated.
41 Z. no. 15, p. 235.
42 In the Ricordi Archives, Milan.
43 Fabbrica sang the leading role of Chiara.
44 Like many ballets of this period, *Gabriella di Vergy* employed a plot which had been successful as an opera – in this case Carafa's (Naples, 1816). Donizetti was to write an opera on this subject in 1826, and the ballet, which he must have seen, may well have played some part in his decision to write a *Gabriella* of his own.
45 Appendix of 27 October 1822, quoted in Verzino, *Le opere di Donizetti,* pp. 44–7.
46 Rosa Morolli Morandi (1782–1824) was the wife of the composer Giovanni Morandi (1777–1856). This couple participated in the first staging of a Rossini opera, *La cambiale di matrimonio* (Venice, 1810), when Rosa sang the soprano role of Fanny. By the time of *Chiara e Serafina* she was singing mezzo roles. She died two years after Donizetti's *Chiara,* still under contract to La Scala, where a memorial service was held for her.
47 *Chiara e Serafina* was sung at La Scala on 26, 27, 28, 29, 30 and 31 October, and 2, 21, 23, 24, 25 and 26 November. I have found no further record of performances of this opera.
48 Verzino, *Le opere di Donizetti,* p. 43.
49 Nicola Cartoni (?–1837) was one of the distinguished amateur singers then active in Roman society, moving in the circle of the Ferretti, Carnevali and Vasselli families. He died during the cholera epidemic of 1837.
50 Donizetti's fondness for these high-Romantic deathbed protestations persisted as long as he lived. A surprising number of the poems he set deal with some variation of this situation, among them *Malvina, Amore e morte, Le dernier chant du troubadour, Il rinnegato* and *L'amor funesto.*
51 'Rifacimento' is the term used to describe a version of an opera in which the original material may be reworked and new material (either specially written or borrowed and adapted from other contexts) added.
52 Giovanni Schmidt (*c.* 1775–*c.* 1840), his name notwithstanding, was born in Tuscany. Among his many librettos are those to Rossini's *Elisabetta* and *Armida.*
53 Z. no. 18, dated 4 June 1823, p. 237.
54 Z. no. 16, dated 1 April 1823, p. 236.

55 It is possible that Tottola's libretto for *Alfredo il grande* was originally intended for Mercadante: Donizetti mentions in a postscript to his letter to Ferretti of 26 March 1822 (Z. no. 12, p. 233) that Mercadante was writing an *Alfredo d'Inghilterra*, but no work of that title by Mercadante was ever performed.

56 Elisabetta Ferron (born Fearon) was a Londoner; she became active in the Italian theaters during the 1820s, when her husband Joseph Glossop briefly held the leases of the San Carlo and La Scala. She was the grandmother of Augustus Harris, director of Covent Garden from 1884 to 1896.

57 Z. no. 18, dated 4 June 1823, p. 238.

58 Zavadini errs in describing *Il fortunato inganno* as being in one act (*Donizetti: Vita – Musiche – Epistolario*, p. 170). The work is in two, as the libretto shows, and it contains a great deal of spoken dialogue, some of the characters speaking in Neapolitan dialect.

59 Leo XII was elected pope on 28 September 1823.

60 Benedetta Rosmunda Pisaroni (1793–1872) became the foremost contralto of her generation, celebrated for her bravura *musico* roles. She began her career in Bergamo as a high soprano, making her debut in 1811 in the title role of Mayr's *Ginevra di Scozia*. Later a severe case of smallpox took away her voice and left her badly disfigured. When her voice returned, it had deepened into a true contralto. Her astonishing technique enabled her in large measure to compensate for the handicap of her scarred face. Pisaroni retired from the stage in 1831.

61 Z. no. 20, dated 7 October 1823, pp. 239–40. Donizetti is complaining that he will receive only 500 *scudi* for the extensive revisions to *Zoraida* and his new opera (*L'ajo nell'imbarazzo*) together, while Mercadante got 700 for a single opera. Donizetti was always conscious of the size of fees as a measure of prestige.

62 Z. no. 21, p. 241. This *rondò*, 'Quando un'alma generosa', was published by B. Girard of Naples, probably *c.* 1824.

63 The revised *Zoraida* was to have been given on the traditional opening date of the season, 26 December (Santo Stefano), but the new pope's severe illness caused the Roman theaters to remain closed for a further two weeks.

64 Besides Pisaroni in the place of Mazzanti, Luigia Boccabadati sang Zoraida and Donzelli repeated his role of Almuzir.

65 *Notizie del giorno*, 15 January 1824.

66 Donzelli belongs to the group of tenors who sang in the chest register to their topmost notes; for Donzelli this was A. Stendhal here shows clearly his preference for another type of tenor who carried his voice upward by employing an extensively developed falsetto, the type of tenor voice Rossini usually wrote for. The modern tenor, who sings in the chest range up to high C or on occasion even D, was not to make an appearance for more than a decade after the time of *Zoraida*, and this type would eventually make those tenors, like Rubini, who specialized in falsetto *acuti* (high notes), as extinct as the dodo.

67 Princess Pauline Borghese (1780–1825), one of Napoleon's sisters, had her character epitomized in Canova's famous statue of her as Venus.

68 *Stendhal, correspondance inédite* (Paris, 1855), p. 257.

69 The revised *Zoraida* was performed at Munich and Lisbon (in Italian) in 1825.

70 In the first cast of *L'ajo* were Maria Ester Mombelli, who had created Zoraida in 1822, as Gilda, the baritone Tamburini as Marchese Don Giulio, and the buffo Nicola Tacci was Don Gregorio, the tutor.

71 Some of the reviews of the first *L'ajo* are reprinted in Cametti, *Donizetti a Roma*, pp. 39ff.

72 Tortoli then had the authority to sign contracts for the royal theaters in Naples, as Barbaja gave up his lease in April 1824, prior to his departure for Vienna; he was soon to be succeeded by Joseph Glossop, the husband of Elisabetta Ferron.

73 The anonymous text of Vittorio Trento's *Emilia di Laverpaut* (sic) (Naples, 1817) has characters with the same names as those in Donizetti's *Emilia*. This text apparently derives from Scatizzi's play, *Emilia di Laverpaut*, which, according to Franca Cella (in a paper given at the 1° convegno internazionale di studi donizettiani, Bergamo, 1975), has its source in a play by Kotzebue, which she identifies as *Emilia, ossia La benedizione paterna* (1788).

74 By 'new' here Donizetti means 'new to the score', not 'newly composed', as he continues 'the former ones were of lesser effect than these', clearly implying that 'these' had already been performed before an audience. In the Conservatorio di San Pietro a Majella, Naples, is a copy of the *rondò* from *Il falegname di Livonia* (which had already been the final number in *Le nozze in villa*), with the name 'Emilia' crossed out and 'Elisabetta' written in above; this manuscript is bound in with the autograph of *Otto mesi in due ore*. At one time, clearly, Donizetti intended to use this *rondò* in *Emilia di Liverpool*, most probably for the projected but never-realized Viennese production, since the original 1824 score ends with a tame *finaletto* (brief moralizing ensemble) and the revised *Emilia* of 1828 concludes with a different *rondò*, this one borrowed from *Alahor in Granata*. It seems quite likely that the *rondò* that had earlier been used in both *Le nozze in villa* and in *Il falegname* formed part of the 'new' material Donizetti sent along to Mercadante in Vienna.

75 Giuseppe Fioravanti (dates unknown), a baritone and later a buffo, was the son of a Valentino Fioravanti (1764–1837) who composed *Le cantatrici villane* (Naples, 1799). Near the start of his career he was a member of Zancla's company, appearing in the *prima* of Donizetti's *Enrico di Borgogna*. He first sang at La Scala in 1819, and in 1821 at Rome he sang in the first performance of Rossini's *Matilde di Shabran*. After 1822 his chief center of activity was Naples where he formed, with Raffaele Casaccia and Gennaro Luzio, a triad of successors to the inimitable Carlo Casaccia. During this phase of his career he sang in the *prime* of *La zingara*, *Il fortunato inganno*, *Emilia di Liverpool* and *Betly*. In 1836 Donizetti was obliged to alter his cavatina in *Betly* to suit his diminished vocal resources.

76 'Puntature' are changes in notes or figurations to accommodate the range or technique of a particular singer. Lablache was a bass, while Giuseppe Fioravanti was a baritone. Donizetti always preferred to change notes in a vocal part rather than to transpose a whole a number.

He referred to transposition as a '*horror*' (his italics; Z. no. 220, undated but assigned to September 1836, p. 418) because he was used to writing for wind instruments that could not play the full chromatic octave.

77 Z. no. 23, p. 242.

78 The chief authority on *Emilia di Liverpool* is Jeremy Commons, who played a significant part in resurrecting the opera for its 1957 revival at Liverpool. He discusses the revision in 'Emilia di Liverpool', *Music and Letters*, 40 (1959), 207–28, and is preparing a fuller discussion of that opera for publication.

79 The first performance of the revised version of *Emilia* was given on 8 March 1828 at the Teatro Nuovo, Naples. I am grateful to John Black who supplied the precise date (letter to the author, 1 February 1981). The role of Emilia in 1828 was sung by Annetta Fischer, about whom I gave some misleading information in my earlier book on Donizetti (*Donizetti* (London, 1965), p. 74, note 5), where I confused her with her aunt Josefa Fischer-Vernier. Annetta was the daughter of the Viennese regisseur Miedke and as a young child she was adopted by Josef Fischer, who taught her singing. She sang in Italy and Spain, retiring in 1836 and afterward teaching in Mannheim. I am indebted to Clemens Höslinger of Vienna for setting me straight about this.

80 The San Carlo briefly broke its period of mourning for Ferdinando I when it opened for a gala in honor of the new king, Francesco I. Donizetti's contribution to that evening of 6 March 1825 was a pastoral cantata, *I voti dei sudditi*, to a libretto by Schmidt, and it was sung by Adelaide Tosi and Nozzari.

81 Today the Teatro Carolino in Palermo is known as the Teatro Bellini.

82 The principal source of information about Donizetti's Palermitan adventure is Ottavio Tiby, *Una stagione lirica di 125 anni fa: Gaetano Donizetti a Palermo* (Rome, 1951).

83 Berardo Calvari Winter (dates unknown), a tenor, was of German extraction, but of Italian training and experience. He made his debut at Bologna in 1822 in Rossini's *Mosè in Egitto*. For Donizetti he sang in the prime of *Alahor di Granata*, *Il borgomastro*, *Il castello di Kenilworth*, *Il diluvio*, and *Imelda de' Lambertazzi*. In 1840 he sang in the first performance of Pacini's *Saffo*, that composer's chef d'oeuvre. In 1848 he was briefly associated with the management of the San Carlo. The figure of the German tenor that Donizetti added to the two-act version of *Le convenienze* was most likely inspired by Winter, whom the composer found endowed more with affability than brains.

84 Antonio Tamburini (1800–76) was a baritone whose active career lasted from 1818 until 1856. One of the supreme vocalists of his generation, he was an adequate actor but was incapable of the intensity that characterized such baritones of the next generation as Giorgio Ronconi and Varesi. Chorley sums him up as follows: 'He was a singularly handsome man, his voice was rich, sweet, extensive, and equal ... and in every part of it entirely under control. His execution has never been exceeded.' (Henry F. Chorley, *Thirty Years' Musical Recollections* (New York, 1926), p. 34.) For Donizetti Tamburini sang in the prime of *Chiara e Serafina*, *L'ajo*, *Alahor*, *Alina*, *Gianni di Calais*, *Imelda de' Lambertazzi*, *Francesca di Foix* and *Fausta*; after 1832 when his activ-

ity was confined principally to the Italian companies of Paris and London, he appeared in the *prime* of *Marin Faliero* and *Don Pasquale*. Tamburini was more of a bass-baritone than a typical baritone, as his range extended two octaves from the F below the staff to the F above it.

85 The Superintendent of Public Spectacles was the Duke di Serradifalco. The upshot of this meeting was the dismissal of three members of the orchestra and a promise to adjust the hood of the prompter's box to permit clearer vision between stage and pit. The prompter's box interfered with the singer's ability to see the conductor because in those days the conductor did not face the stage and orchestra, as he does today, but stood at the back of the pit facing out.

86 *Il trionfo della musica* was the alternate title of *Che originali!*, and it seems that music by a number of composers was inserted into Mayr's score. This pasticcio was Ferron's warhorse: she had sung it at La Scala six months earlier, and she would trot it out there again in 1827.

87 *La Cerere*, 8 September 1825.

88 Marietta Tamburini (1800–76) was the daughter of the dancer and choreographer Gaetano Gioia.

89 Z. no. 25, pp. 243–5. Besides *Il trionfo della musica* and *L'ajo*, the operas Donizetti was responsible for that year in Palermo were: *Il barone di Dolsheim* (Pacini), *L'italiana*, *Il barbiere*, *Il matrimonio segreto*, *Aureliano in Palmira*, *Tancredi* (Rossini), *La gioventù di Enrico V* (Pacini), *L'inganno felice* (Rossini), *La vestale* (Spontini), *Elisa e Claudio* (Mercadante), and his own new work, *Alahor in Granata*. Significantly, only one of these scores, *La vestale*, was more than fifteen years old.

90 James Freeman, 'Donizetti in Palermo and *Alahor in Granata*', *Journal of the American Musicological Society*, 25 (1972), 240–50. The score (in a copyist's hand) was found in the attic of Symphony Hall, Boston, and is now in the Special Collections Division of the Mugar Memorial Library, Boston University.

91 James Freeman explains that Romani's libretto to *L'esule di Granata* is, in turn, derived from Étienne de Jouy's text for Cherubini's *Les Abencérages*, which, in turn, was based upon Florian's romance *Gonzalve de Cordove* (Paris, 1793). Florian's romance is also the source that stands behind Merelli's libretto for Donizetti's *Zoraida di Granata*, by way of Romanelli's libretto for *Abenamet e Zoraide* by Giuseppe Nicolini (Milan, 1805). A tangled skein indeed.

92 This opera has never been performed to its original French text. I have used the French title throughout, however, to refer to the French grand opera that Donizetti was composing and left unfinished, and from which *Il duca d'Alba*, as completed by others, differs considerably.

93 It should be noted that the projected *prima* of *Rita* at the Teatro Nuovo did not take place; *Rita* was first given at the Opéra-Comique on 7 May, 1860).

94 Zavadini, *Donizetti: Vita – Musiche – Epistolario*, p. 171. *Il castello degli invalidi* appears as no. 18 in Zavadini's list of Donizetti's operas, identified as a 'farsa in one act by X, performed Teatro Carolino, spring 1826'.

95 *Il castello degli invalidi* is not mentioned by Ottavio Tiby in *Il Real*

Teatro Carolino e l'ottocento musicale palermitano (Florence, 1957),
which includes a *cronisteria* (theatrical chronicle) of works performed
at the Teatro Carolino from 1808 to 1896. In his *Una stagione lirica di
125 anni fa* (p. 33), Tiby details his vain searches for any news of this
score and concludes that Gaetano was either referring to some other
opera by an alternate title or had a lapse of memory when he wrote to
Toto.

96 Of the score of *La bella prigioniera* two duets, with piano accompaniment, are in autograph at the Museo Donizettiano, Bergamo. In addition, a passage sixteen measures in length occurs in the scherzo for
   violin and piano based on themes from his works that Donizetti dedicated to Virginia Vasselli, his future wife.

97 The autograph of this scherzo is in the Museo Donizettiano, Bergamo.
   The list needs some explanation. 'Ideale' (nos. 2 and 8) is not from an
   opera but is dance music, a movement in 2/4 time. Although Donizetti
   refers to *Aristea* (no. 20) as an opera, it is properly a cantata, but his
   identification suggests that he himself did not draw as fine a line in
   distinguishing these genres as those writing about him are wont to do.
   No. 24 represented all that was known – eight measures – from *Una
   follia* until Don White and Patric Schmid lately discovered a manuscript of the overture to that opera (information given in a letter to the
   author, 17 July 1978).

98 The *monferrina* comes from the region of Monferrato. Donizetti used
   only four measures as a coda, but marked it 'con sentimento'.

99 *Una stagione lirica di 125 anni fa*, p. 33.

100 *Il vapore*, 6 June 1835.

101 Z. no. 26, pp. 245–6.

102 The Neapolitan censors forbade the name Fernando because the late
    king's name and that of the current heir-apparent was Ferdinando.

103 This was Bellini's first work in a public theater. The year before, his
    Adelson e Salvini had been sung at the Conservatorio di San Sebas-
    tiano, Naples.

104 Z. no. 26, pp. 245–46.

105 Winter had also created the corresponding role of Alamar in Meyer-
    beer's *L'esule di Granata* (Milan, 1821). For the San Carlo production of
    Alahor the tenor role had originally been assigned to Bertazzi, but he
    was removed from it and the rehearsals were suspended until Winter's
    arrival. Donizetti has this to say about Winter: 'Theater people are orig-
    inal; in Palermo Winter had many heated discussions with me about
    this part, which in reality is not much, and now he is asking for it for
    his debut. And he does well, since the aria from Act 2 suits him, having
    been written for his voice.' (Z. no. 27, dated 15 June 1826, pp. 246–7.)

106 Z. no. 27, p. 247.

107 This *rondò* Donizetti later used as the conclusion to the 1828 version of
    Emilia di Liverpool.

108 Z. no. 28, dated 21 July 1826, p. 248.

109 Z. no. 27, p. 247.

110 The *Gabriella* that was sung at the San Carlo in 1869, after Donizetti's
    death, was a *rifacimento* by other hands.

111 Because of the similarity of the name of Raoul de Coucy in de Belloy's

play and that of Raoul, Sire de Créqui, hero of Boutet de Monvel's text for Dalayrac's rescue opera, *Raoul, Sire de Créqui* (Paris, 1789), some have mistakenly assumed that Italian operas based on Boutet de Monvel, like those of Mayr (Milan, 1810), Morlacchi (Dresden, 1811) and Valentino Fioravanti (Rome, 1812) are related to the plot of *Gabriella di Vergy*. They are not.

112 See Don White, 'Donizetti and the Three Gabriellas', *Opera*, 29 (1978), 962-70, and see also the booklet accompanying the Opera Rara recording (1978) of the 1838 *Gabriella di Vergy* (the first ever performance), both of which contain a number-by-number comparison of the three versions.

113 Z. no. 30, p. 249, to Mario Aspa, impresario at Messina.

114 *S.d.*1, no. 10, undated fragment assigned to August 1826, p. 9.

115 Z. no. A10, dated 15 August 1837, p. 870.

116 The autograph of this duet for two sopranos is in the Museo Donizettiano, Bergamo. The text begins: 'Sarà più fida Irene'; the dedication reads: 'Per la Sig.ra Virginia Vasselli/Donizetti nell'anniversario suo D. D. D. Sono 29. 30. Novemb. 1826'.

117 The opening of the season at the Teatro Valle had been postponed from 26 December 1826.

118 Z. no. 32, dated 14 May 1827, pp. 251-2. *Otto mesi* was given at the Teatro Carolino, Palermo, in 1828-9.

119 Luigi Marchionni (1791-1864) belonged to a famous Italian theatrical family, his sister Carlotta being the leading tragic actress of her day until the emergence of Adelaide Ristori. Luigi was an actor, writer and translator of plays, and for many years he was associated in one or more capacities with the Teatro dei Fiorentini at Naples. One of his best-known plays, written for Carlotta, was *Chiara di Rosemberg*, which subject was set as an opera in 1831 by Luigi Ricci and became widely successful. Other plays adapted by Marchionni include *La vestale* (from Étienne de Jouy's libretto for Spontini's opera), which was praised by the poets Vincenzo Monti and Ugo Foscolo, and *L'assedio di Calais*, also performed as *Edoardo III* (almost certainly from Hubert's *Eustache de St Pierre*), which Cammarano used as a source for his libretto for Donizetti's *L'assedio de Calais*.

120 *La figlia dell'esiliato, ossia Otto mesi in due ore* was sometimes referred to as *La figlia della terra d'esilio* and sometimes as *Elisabetta* (the latter may have been urged by the censors because they objected to the word 'esilio' in the title).

121 Domenico Gilardoni (1798-1831) is described by Pacini in *Le mie memorie artistiche* (p. 58) as 'a young man of some talent, too soon taken from the scene because of poor health, leaving a young wife'.

122 The autograph of the original *Otto mesi in due ore*, at the Conservatorio di San Pietro a Majella, Naples, is bound together with the 1833 revision in a most confusing way.

123 Although neither Donizetti's original nor revised *Otto mesi* was ever given in France, a *rifacimento* of the score made by a composer named Uranio Fontana, who wrote a new last act, was sung there in 1853, under the title *Elisabeth, ou La fille du proscrit*. An Italian version of Fontana's composite work was given in Milan at the Teatro Santa Radegonda on 24 July 1854.

124 Z. no. 33, pp. 252–3.
125 The possibility that a Marianna Donizetti, baptized 25 May 1815, was the daughter of Giuseppe and Angela Donizetti, born 'sub conditione', about three months after their marriage, is discussed by Herbert Weinstock in 'Chi era Marianna Donizetti?' *Studi donizettiani,* 2 (1972), 41–6.
126 Z. no. 28, p. 248.
127 The ducat was a coin then in use in Naples, while the *svantziche* (actually *zwanzigiste*) referred to the Austrian lira then current in Lombardy.
128 Z. no. 37, dated 5 December 1827, p. 256.
129 Carolina Ungher's name was customarily spelled so in Italy, where she pursued the major part of her career. She was born in Hungary in 1803, and studied singing in Vienna with Aloysa Lange, Mozart's sister-in-law. She made her debut as a mezzo-soprano, singing Dorabella in *Così fan tutte* (Vienna, 1821). In 1824 she was the contralto soloist in the first performance of Beethoven's Ninth Symphony, and it was she, according to tradition, who turned the deaf composer round so that he could acknowledge the applause. Barbaja took her to Italy in 1825, and she continued a brilliant career there, singing most frequently for the impresario Alessandro Lanari. She retired from the stage at her marriage to a painter, Sabatier, in 1840, and continued to sing in concerts, appearing at the Saturday Concerts at the Crystal Palace as late as 1869. She also taught singing at her villa in Florence. She died in 1877.

From all accounts her voice retained its basic mezzo-soprano orientation and, although she extended her range upward, the production of her high tones was not without effort. When she created the role of Isoletta in Bellini's *La straniera* at La Scala in 1829, the composer described her top notes as being like 'dagger-thrusts'. The beauty of her expansive middle and lower range was widely praised. As an actress, she produced a telling effect in romantic and tragic roles.

Duprez tells an anecdote concerning the opening run of Donizetti's *Parisina* at Florence in 1833. 'I asked her, in my role as lover, for a souvenir of the tender moments we had passed together. She held out to me her handkerchief which she had previously raised to her adored lips. I covered it with impassioned kisses. Horrors! she had spat in it! I could not hold back an exclamation: "Oh! *la malpropre!*" or something worse. La Ungher compressed her lips and continued her cabaletta.' (Gilbert Duprez, *Souvenirs d'un chanteur* (Paris, 1880), pp. 99–100.)
130 Luisa Cambi, ed., *Vincenzo Bellini, epistolario* (n.p. [Milan], 1943), no. I, dated 2 January 1828, p. 31.
131 Z. no. 36, dated 30 October 1827, p. 255.
132 Gennaro Luzio (1775–1855), a basso buffo, was the son of another buffo of the same name, and was consequently often referred to as 'Gennarino' or 'Pappone'. He made his debut in 1806 and pursued his career until at least 1851. Besides his role in *Le convenienze* he was also a member of the first casts of *Otto mesi in due ore, I pazzi per progetto* and *La romanziera.*
133 The buffo in female attire is a hilarious reversal of the *musico* tradition.
134 Hector Berlioz, *Memoirs,* ed. E. Newman, (New York, 1932) p. 170.
135 The first twentieth-century revival of *Le convenienze ed inconvenienze*

teatrali was at Siena in 1963; in 1969 it was revived in Munich, rather freely adapted, as *Viva la mamma*, and under that title was sung at San Francisco in 1975. In London it has been called both *Upstage and Downstage* and *The Prima Donna's Mother is a Drag*. In 1966 I prepared an English translation of the original 1827 version, performed first at Indiana State University, Terre Haute, Indiana, calling it *An Unconventional Rehearsal* for want of a better idea. For the University of New Mexico Thomas Phillipps in 1968 modified my version by adding a trio from the two-act score and replacing the original *finaletto* with the later one. There have been a number of subsequent productions of the Phillipps version.

136 At this period it was customary for the first act of a two-act opera seria to end with a concertato and the second with an aria–finale for the prima donna.

137 Z. no. 38, dated 2 February 1828, p. 257.

138 *L'esule di Roma* was the fourth of Donizetti's operas to be staged at La Scala. It received ten performances, and its reception was judged 'good' (Pompeo Cambiasi, *La Scala: 1778–1889* (Milan, 1889), p. 273).

139 Pezzi's review of *L'esule* at La Scala is quoted in Verzino, *Le opere di Donizetti*, p. 80. The Milanese superciliousness to a success gained elsewhere is plain to see in this review.

140 *Bellini, epistolario*, no. XI, dated 16 January 1828, p. 38. Le Roy was a formidable purgative of the period; originally intended for horses, its use was extended in the early nineteenth century to human beings.

141 Francesco Morlacchi (1784–1841) is chiefly remembered today as having been co-*Kapellmeister* at Dresden with Weber, and then his successor and Wagner's predecessor there. Morlacchi's most widely performed operas were *Le Danaidi* (Rome, 1810) and *Tebaldo ed Isolina* (Venice, 1822).

142 *Alina, regina di Golconda* was a comedy derived from Sedaine's French libretto for Monsigny's opera of the same name (Paris, 1766).

143 Z. no. 38, pp. 257–8.

144 The *prima* of *Alina* did not take place until 12 May 1828.

145 Z. no. 39, p. 259.

146 Donizetti's hymn, *Inno reale*, with text by Romani, was sung by Letizia Cortesi, the tenor G. B. Verger, Tamburini and the opera chorus.

147 Bellini's work had been first performed as *Bianca e Gernando* at the San Carlo on 30 May 1826; it was revised for Genoa.

148 The account of the opening gala comes from G. B. Vallebona, *Il Teatro Carlo Felice: cronisteria di un secolo (1828–1928)* (Genoa, 1928). The ballet that Vaque-Moulin appeared in was *Gli adoratori del fuoco*, choreographed by Giovanni Galzerani.

149 Adelaide Tosi (?1800–59) was the daughter of a prominent Milanese lawyer. After training with Girolamo Crescentini, a castrato renowned for his smooth vocal execution, she made her debut at La Scala on 26 December 1820, singing the *musico* role of Ippolito in Mayr's *Fedra*. She went to Naples where she made her debut in Pacini's *Alessandro nelle Indie* and sang for Donizetti in the *prime* of *L'esule di Roma, Il paria* and *Il castello di Kenilworth*. When she sang in London in 1840 she produced little impression, and shortly afterward she retired from the stage upon her marriage.

150 Francesco Pastura, *Bellini secondo la storia* (Parma, 1959), p. 132.
151 *Bellini, epistolario*, no. XXVI, dated 5 April 1828, p. 75.
152 *Bellini, epistolario*, no. XXVII, dated 16 April 1828, p. 84.
153 In my earlier book on Donizetti (*Donizetti*, p. 101), I followed Zavadini (*Donizetti: Vita – Musiche – Epistolario*, p. 172) in misidentifying the first Alina as Adelaide Comelli-Rubini, the French-born wife of the famous tenor, who pursued a career in Italy until her husband went to Paris in 1831. Vallebona's *Il Teatro Carlo Felice* (p. 25) identifies Serafina Rubini as appearing in this inaugural season.
154 Giovanni Battista Verger (1796–?). He sang in three Donizetti *prime*: *Il falegname di Livonia, Olivo e Pasquale* and *Alina*. His career, devoted almost exclusively to opera buffa, seems to have been principally confined to the decade 1819–29. He married Amalia Brambilla, daughter of the composer Paolo Brambilla, but no relation of the extensive family to which Marietta Brambilla belonged.
155 Z. no. 40, dated 15 May 1828, p. 259.
156 *Alina* was very successfully revived at the Carlo Felice in 1858 and 1868, marking thereby the thirtieth and fortieth anniversaries of its original production.
157 The Italian translation of *Le siège de Corinthe* (Paris, 1826), a *rifacimento* of *Maometto II* (Naples, 1820), had been introduced to Italy at Parma on 26 January 1828.
158 Mayr's *Medea in Corinto* (Naples, 1813) was for Donizetti the apex of his teacher's achievement.
159 Donizetti wrote *Ugolino*, a curious composition, in Naples during January 1828 and dedicated it to Lablache as a sort of 'thank you' for the bass's splendid Murena in *L'esule di Roma*. The vocal writing is scarcely equal to the power of the lines from Canto XXXIII of the *Inferno*. Rossini once wrote: 'I heard that Donizetti had the melancholy idea of setting a canto of Dante to music. It seems to me that this is much too proud. I believe that in such an undertaking not even the Eternal Father would succeed had he been a *maestro di musica*.' (Quoted from Giuseppe Radiciotti, *Rossini* (3 vols., Tivoli, 1927–9), vol. 2, pp. 321–2.) Donizetti was not the only Italian composer of his generation tempted by this passage, as some years later Morlacchi composed an *Ugolino*. For Donizetti, however, the choice of this subject at this particular phase of his career is significant because it reveals him turning his hand to something tragic, even grisly.
160 Z. no. 40, p. 260.
161 The marriage certificate, as Cametti reports in *Donizetti a Roma*, is difficult to find because the bridegroom's name is misspelled 'Bonizetti'.
162 The recipient paid the expense of postage. Here Donizetti is implying that if the cost of two letters would be a burden to his father then the expense of a trip to Rome had been out of the question. But he is not being particularly consistent, for later in this letter he urges his father to come to Rome the following October: 'To come to Rome requires only a few *bajocchi*.'
163 When Gaetano mentions Virginia's handwriting, he is making a play upon the word 'carattere'.
164 Z. no. 41, pp. 260–1. When Donizetti specifies that his invitation does

not include his brother Francesco it becomes clear that he had no desire to expose the Vassellis of Rome to his entire family.

165 Z. no. 42, dated 21 October 1828, p. 262.

166 *Gianni di Calais* was given at the Théâtre-Italien once in 1833 and once in 1834.

167 Z. no. 42, p. 262.

168 Z. no. 42, p. 262. Zavadini adds a note here that Donizetti could be alluding to either *Il giovedì grasso* or *Il paria*. It seems much more likely that he is referring to the full-length *Il paria*, which had its *prima* on 12 January 1829, rather than the one-act farsa *Il giovedì grasso*, which was not given until late the following month and quite possibly was not composed until after *Il paria* had been performed.

169 According to Carlo Gatti's tabulation of performances at La Scala in his two-volume *Il Teatro alla Scala*, Lablache was in the cast of almost every opera given that autumn season, including the final one, Coccia's *L'orfano della selva*, which had its *prima* on 15 November 1828 and ran for fifteen performances. Appearing most evenings and rehearsing many days, Lablache must have had precious little free time between July 1828 and the end of November.

170 Date supplied by John Black (letter to the author, 1 February 1981).

171 Signora Venturali was twice Mayr's mother-in-law; after the death of his first wife Angela in 1799, Mayr married Angela's sister Lucrezia in 1804.

172 Andrea, the son of Gaetano's brother Giuseppe, entered Mayr's school in 1828 at the age of ten to study voice and keyboard; he left the school the following year.

173 Z. no. 43, p. 263.

174 Andrea had been left behind in Italy when his parents settled in Constantinople so that he might continue his education at Bergamo. Subsequently he turned to the study of law at Genoa, receiving his degree in 1841. Andrea was to play a major role in his uncle's life at the time of Donizetti's breakdown in Paris.

175 Z. no. 40, dated 15 May 1828, p. 260.

176 The choice of this subject at this time was probably suggested by a ballet, *Il paria*, also derived from Delavigne's plot, which was danced on the opening night of the 1827–8 Carnival season at La Scala and performed there thirty-nine times. This ballet was choreographed by Salvatore Taglioni to music assembled by G. P. Brambilla; the leading roles were danced by Maria Conti, Antonio Ramacini and Pietro Trigambi.

177 Z. no. 44, dated 19 January 1829, p. 264.

178 Z. no. 305, dated 15 July 1838, p. 481.

179 Z. no. 44, p. 264.

180 This work was known as *Elisabetta al castello di Kenilworth* at its first performance and for the duration of the first production; thereafter the shorter form of its title, *Il castello di Kenilworth*, was used exclusively. Except in discussing the composition and *prima* of this opera I shall refer to it by the better-known title.

181 Z. no. 45, p. 264. Both 30 May (the birthday of King Ferdinando II) and 6 July (the queen-mother's birthday) were royal galas at the San Carlo.

New operas by the director of the royal theaters were the usual fare for such occasions.

182 Scott's *Kenilworth* had been translated into Italian in 1821.

183 Z. no. 49, p. 268.

184 The birth certificate is quoted in Cametti, *Donizetti a Roma*, p. 68. At the baptism Antonio Vasselli stood proxy for the godfathers; Countess Virginia Rusponi was the godmother.

185 This not a reference to either of the well-known Guglielmis, Pietro (?1727–1804) or Pietro Carlo (*c.* 1763–1817), but to an obscure Sicilian, Pasquale Guglielmi, whose *Teresa Navagero* was, in fact, first given at the San Carlo on 19 August 1829.

186 Z. no. 50, dated 11 August 1829, p. 269. The italics are in the original. Donizetti's figure of speech, referring to *Il castello di Kenilworth*, is, under the circumstances, poignant in the extreme.

187 Z. no. 51, p. 269.

188 I am particularly indebted to Professor W. H. Trethowan, of the Department of Psychiatry at the University of Birmingham (England), for his detailed interpretation of the evidence relating to Donizetti's health.

189 The balance of the music of *Il genio dell'armonia* was composed by two Roman *marchesi*, Vicenzo Castaguti and Domenico Capranica. The cantata celebrated the election of Pius VIII nine months after the event because, according to Cametti (*Donizetti a Roma*, p. 73), the Accademia had difficulties in finding an appropriate place for their performance.

190 Z. no. 52, dated 10 January 1830, p. 271.

191 Luigia Boccabadati(-Gazzuoli) (?1800–50), a soprano, was active between 1817 and 1845. She sang in four *prime* for Donizetti besides that of *Il diluvio*: *Il castello di Kenilworth*, *I pazzi per progetto*, *Francesca di Foix* and *La romanziera*. After *Il diluvio* Donizetti quarreled with Barbaja over Boccabadati, refusing to allow her to jeopardize the chances of *Fausta*; his obstinacy over this matter led to his breaking his contract with Barbaja, and the dismissal of Boccabadati opened the road for Ronzi to go to Naples. Boccabadati's career did not flourish after she left Naples, for she rarely sang at major opera houses after that. One of her daughters, Cecilia, became the wife of the baritone Felice Varesi.

192 Nicola Festa was the chief conductor at the San Carlo from 1793 to 1839, and therefore he would have directed the first performances of all Donizetti's operas given there during his long tenure.

193 The Schoenenberger printed score (Paris, *c.* 1855) of *Il diluvio universale* is of the revised version for the 1834 production at the Carlo Felice, Genoa.

194 Corrected date and theatre supplied by John Black (letter to the author, 1 February 1981).

195 The distinction between baritone and bass was not yet current, and both ranges were usually referred to by the single term.

196 Z. no. 53, dated 13 February 1830, p. 272.

197 Luigi Ricci (1805–59) is remembered today chiefly for *Crispino e la comare* (Venice, 1850), written in collaboration with his brother Federico (1809–77).

198 Z. no. 53, p. 272.

199 Z. no. 57, dated 24 June 1830, p. 276.
200 Precise date supplied by John Black (letter to the author, 1 February 1981). Cametti (*Donizetti a Roma*, p. 77) gives the correct date, but Zavadini (*Donizetti: Vita – Musiche – Epistolario*, p. 38) gives the date wrongly as 28 August. The reason for this inconsistency is apparently that the *prima* was postponed, for a letter dated 7 August 1830 from Donizetti to Mayr (Z. no. 60, pp. 278–9) shows that rehearsals for the work were then under way.
201 Franca Cella in her paper 'Il donizettismo nei libretti di Donizetti' given at the 1" convegno internazionale di studi donizettiani, Bergamo, 1975, does not identify a principal source, but cites as intermediary sources an opera *Imelda* by Sgricci, given in Naples in 1827, and a work that appeared in Milan in 1830, Defendente Sacchi's *I Lambertazzi e i Geremei: cronache di un trovatore*. Behind these stands a work by Bombaci, *Historia dei fatti d'Antonio Lambertacci* (Bologna, 1532). In any event, the plot is based upon actual events.
202 The autograph of *Imelda* is in the Conservatorio di San Pietro a Majella, Naples. Here is just one instance of Donizetti's setting an uncensored text, although the legal requirement in those days was that a libretto had to be submitted a full year in advance. This requirement frequently had to be overlooked for practical reasons, but that Donizetti composed an unsubmitted text argues not only haste but suggests a desire completely to circumvent local censorship.
203 *Imelda*, according to Tom Kaufman (letter to the author, 15 August 1978), was later performed at Barcelona (1840), La Coruna, Spain (1843), and Sinigaglia (1856). That seems to be the extent of its performance history.
204 The cabaletta from the Imelda–Bonifacio duet, for mezzo-soprano and baritone, was transposed and used as the concluding section of the 'new' duet Donizetti added for Anna and Percy during the opening run of *Anna Bolena* at the Teatro Carcano. Oddly enough, the cabaletta retains its original text (beginning 'Restati, pur m'udrai') in its new context. The complete 'new' duet for Anna and Percy ('Sì, son io' ... 'Restati, pur m'udrai') was published by Ricordi (Milan, *c.* 1831), not long after the first production of *Anna Bolena*.
205 Verzino, *Le opere di Donizetti*, p. 91. Verzino was writing in 1897.

3. 1830–1835: *Anna Bolena* to *Marin Faliero*

1 Giuditta Pasta, née Negri (1798–1865), studied at Como with Bartolomeo Lotti and the Milan Conservatory with Bonifacio Asioli. Although she made her debut in 1815, Pasta did not emerge from obscurity until she appeared at the Théâtre-Italien in Paris in 1821. An imaginative and authoritative singing-actress, with a powerful but not completely controlled voice, she managed to maintain her pre-eminence until her retirement in 1837, though in the last four years of her career her vocal decline was evident. Her final appearance, in London in 1850, in a special concert, revealed a splendid ruin. Her most famous creations were Anna Bolena, Norma, and Amina (in *La sonnambula*). Her final years were spent as a

teacher of singing, but none of her pupils made anything like the impression produced by their great *maestra*.

2 The 650 *scudi*, including the expenses of his travel and lodging at Milan, was not a lavish fee. Back in 1823 Donizetti had complained that Mercadante received 700 *scudi* for a single opera, while he was paid a total of 500 for revising an opera and composing a new one.

3 Z. no. 61, p. 280.

4 Donizetti's long absence from Bergamo should not be interpreted as disaffection. His attitude can be inferred from a few lines he had written to his father the previous year: 'Ah, if I could only have a full-scale view of Bergamo . . . there was one around at one time . . . I would pay for it, you know.' (Z. no. 47, dated 22 May 1829, p. 267).

5 Z. no. B7, dated 21 December 1830, p. 914.

6 Gaetano stresses the significance of the occasion by starting out with the formal 'Lei' form, but by the end he is addressing Virginia by the informal 'tu'.

7 Here Donizetti is poking fun at the old-fashioned 'poetic' style that Romani occasionally affected.

8 Zavadini, *Donizetti: Vita – Musiche – Epistolario*, pp. xvii–xviii, reprinted from Arnaldo Fraccaroli, *Donizetti* (Milan, 1945), p. 124. The whereabouts of the autograph of this letter, the only one from Donizetti to his wife to have been published, are unknown; its authenticity cannot therefore be proved.

9 Filippo Galli (1783–1853) the leading *basso cantante* of the day, had made his debut at Bologna in 1804 as a tenor, but a serious illness in 1810 deepened his voice to a true bass. In 1812 he made a second debut, in his new register, in the *prima* of Rossini's *L'inganno felice*, going on to create such important Rossinian roles as Mustafà, Maometto II, and Assur (*Semiramide*); in the last part he was the only bass whom Rossini judged to be fully satisfactory. The creation of Enrico VIII was the last of Galli's major creations; after 1832 his career began to slide, and when, after some years in Mexico, he returned to Milan in 1840, his vocal decline was so embarrassing that he was persuaded to accept the post of chorus-master at Madrid. When he went to Paris in 1842 in abject poverty, Donizetti used his influence to help him obtain a teaching position at the Conservatoire. During the 1820s Lablache was the only serious rival to Galli, both of them being effective in comic as well as serious roles.

10 The promising career of Elisa Orlandi (1811–34), who created the role of Seymour in *Anna Bolena*, was cut short by her early death at the age of twenty-three.

11 *Gazzetta di Milano*, 27 December 1830.

12 Many of the modifications in the autograph of *Anna Bolena*, which is in the Ricordi Archives, are illuminatingly discussed by Philip Gossett in '*Anna Bolena e la maturità di Donizetti*', 1° convegno internazionale di studi donizettiani, Bergamo, 1975.

13 The original version of the duet ('Ei t'abborre' . . . 'Per pietà del mio spavento') was replaced temporarily by 'Sì, son io' . . . 'Restati, pur m'udrai'; the first part of the replacement would later go into *Marin*

Faliero, and its cabaletta comes from *Imelda*. Looking through a number of nineteenth-century Italian librettos of *Anna Bolena*, one finds a clear preponderance of 'Ei t'abborre' over 'Sì, son io'. Other treatments of the Anna–Percy scene that occur in these old librettos are: the reduction of the whole scene to a brief recitative; or the substitution of a duet from another opera – at Bergamo in 1843, for example, Eugenia Tadolini and Carlo Guasco used a duet from *Roberto Devereux*.

14 Quoted in Herbert Weinstock, *Vincenzo Bellini: his Life and his Operas* (New York, 1971), p. 97.

15 *I Capuleti e i Montecchi*, as performed at La Scala on 26 December 1830, put Bellini in an ill humor: 'I did not write after the first performance because my poor opera could not have been more badly put on.' (*Bellini, epistolario*, no. CI, dated 3 January 1831, p. 264.)

16 The contrasting passage is found on p. 15 of the Schoenenberger score of *Il paria* (Paris, *c.* 1855) and on pp. 101–2 of the Ricordi score of *Anna Bolena* (Milan, 1957) [plate no. T45415 T].

17 Romani did not work from Shakespeare's *Henry VIII*, he drew on two more recent plays: Marie-Joseph de Chénier's *Henri VIII* (Paris, 1791), in an Italian translation by Ippolito Pindemonte, and Alessandro Pepoli's *Anna Bolena* (Venice, 1788).

18 At the end of the final scene of *Anna Bolena* it is clear that Romani originally intended that Anna die on stage, instead of being led off, fainting, to the block. The penultimate line of the libretto (later omitted) read: 'Sventurata! ella manca . . . ella muore.' (Unfortunate woman! she faints . . . she dies.) This line was followed by a stage direction (later cut): 'When the sheriffs enter, the bystanders point to Anna lying dead.' The omitted line and stage direction give real meaning to the final line of the libretto: 'Immolata una vittima è già!' (One victim has already been sacrificed!)

19 Robert Nicholas Charles Bochsa (1789–1856) was a harpist of unsavory reputation. In 1839 he eloped with the soprano Anna Bishop, wife of the composer Sir Henry Bishop, composer of, among other things, *Home, sweet home*.

20 Chorley, *Thirty Years' Musical Recollections*, pp. 17–18.

21 The wedding was celebrated at Turin on 27 February 1831. In 1842 Donizetti became *Hofkapellmeister* to Emperor Ferdinand, and the same year he dedicated *Linda di Chamounix* to the Empress Anna.

22 Z. no. 64, p. 281.

23 Giuseppe Mazzini, *Filosofia della musica*, ed. A. Lualdi, 2nd edn (Rome, 1954), p. 180. Mazzini writes: 'And when Lablache thunders these words: "Salirà d'Inghilterra sul trono/Altra donna più degna d'affetto" [(Another woman more worthy of my affection will ascend the throne of England)], etc., who has not felt his spirit contract, who has not in that moment understood the tyrant completely?'

24 In Z. no. 66, dated 19 May 1831, p. 283, to his father, Gaetano describes their apartment as 'after all not so sordid' (*indecente*).

25 Romani's libretto for *Gianni di Parigi* was originally written for Morlacchi, whose opera on that subject had its *prima* at La Scala in 1818.

26 Z. no. 95, dated 27 May 1833, p. 310.

27 Precise date supplied by John Black (letter to the author, 1 February 1981).

28 Neither of these operas has yet been revived in the twentieth century. Until a libretto of *La romanziera* is found, this work is irrecoverable in its original form, as the score, published by Schoenenberger (Paris, c. 1855), contains only the musical numbers and not the spoken dialogue.

29 Z. no. 68, dated 8 September 1831, p. 295. Donizetti's friendship with Count Gaetano Melzi (1786–1851), a Milanese bibliophile and a man of broad general culture, dates from the time of *Anna Bolena* and survived until the composer's death.

30 Z. no. 69, p. 286.

31 The Minister of Police was Marshal Marchese Francesco Saverio del Carretto.

32 Inappropriate to a royal gala because 'on such evenings . . . public exultation ought to be nourished by delightful spectacles, analogous to the feelings of the audience'. Quoted in Jeremy Commons, 'Donizetti e la censura napoletana', 1° convegno internazionale di studi donizettiani, Bergamo, 1975.

33 These two suspect letters are Z. no. 70, p. 287, to Teodoro Ghezzi, and Z. no. 71, pp. 287–8, to a Maestro Rubetti. The original autographs were not available to Zavadini, who states that he reprints the letters from other texts.

34 Weinstock shares my opinion of these two letters (see his *Bellini*, Appendix E, pp. 399–402). Let me offer a hypothesis as to how they might have been invented: starting from the knowledge that Donizetti was in Milan by the beginning of March 1832 to stage his *Ugo* at La Scala, the perpetrators of these letters, failing to discover that he was contractually engaged to be in Naples at the time of the first performance of *Norma*, assumed that he arrived in Milan early enough to attend La Scala on that historic night. Anyone who has waded through much nineteenth-century Italian material on composers knows that the principle 'se non è vero, è ben trovato' (if it is not true, it is a plausible invention) is frequently met.

   Probably Donizetti did hear *Norma* that season at La Scala, but not until after his arrival in March 1832. Yet we cannot assume that these letters are authentic and only misdated, for one (Z. no. 70) says: 'Yesterday evening *Norma* had its first performance' (*andata in scena*), and the other (Z. no. 71) speaks of the work's growing success 'after the 26th of the current month' (*dopo del 26 corrente*), clearly a reference to December 1831. At best, these letters, if authentic, have been severely tampered with. For all this, it does not do to think that Donizetti was ill disposed toward Bellini's operas. On 26 September 1831 he wrote from Naples: 'Tuesday they will give *I Capuleti*, today was the general rehearsal. I hope it goes very well indeed.' (Z. no. 69, p. 286, to Melzi.)

35 Zavadini, *Donizetti: Vita – Musiche – Epistolario*, p. 42.

36 Four of Donizetti's operas have a Roman ambience. *L'esule di Roma* (the time of Tiberius), *Fausta* (that of Constantine the Great), *Belisario* (Byzantium in the days of Justinian), and *Poliuto* (Roman Armenia during the middle of the third century A.D.). Except for *L'esule*, they all

come at significant points in his career: *Fausta* was the first opera he
contracted to write after *Anna Bolena; Belisario* followed on the heels
of the huge success of *Lucia;* and *Poliuto* was the fruit of the stimulation of his friendship with Nourrit, and, as *Les martyrs*, was his first
work given at the Opéra.

37 Z. no. 38, dated 2 February 1828, p. 257.
38 Back in 1828 (Z. no. 38) Donizetti had spoken of wanting to 'shake off
the yoke of the finales', but this does not mean that he intended to
dispense with them entirely. Donizetti was always praised for his writing of concertato passages and his success in adapting the big finale to
his varied musico-dramatic purposes can be clearly seen from *Maria
Stuarda* and *Lucia* right down to the powerful ensemble that concludes
Act 4 of *Dom Sébastien*.
39 I am grateful to David Rosen for calling to my attention the letter of
Barbieri-Nini to Verdi in which she speaks of the *Fausta* aria (letter to
the author, 12 September 1978).
40 *Fausta* showed more vigor at Naples than elsewhere. It had two productions at Palermo, one each at Genoa, Turin and Bologna. It has never
been given in Rome, most probably because of the censorship. Outside
Italy it was given in Madrid, Lisbon, Havana and Valparaiso. In London, at Her Majesty's Theatre in 1841, with Giulia Grisi, Mario and
Tamburini, the last repeating his original Costantino, it failed to make a
real impression; nor does it seem to have made one that same year in
Vienna, when Eugenia Tadolini was the Fausta. In German it appeared
briefly in Berlin. There have been to date no performances in France or
in the United States.
41 To replace the short prelude played at the *prima* in Naples.
42 Amelia's aria, 'Perchè mi dica ancora', from Act 2 of *Il castello di
Kenilworth*, was given new words, 'Ah, se d'amor potessi', but the text
of the cabaletta remained unchanged. Tosi had been in the original cast
of *Il castello di Kenilworth* at Naples, but as Elisabetta, not Amelia.
43 Cesare Pugni (1802–70) was principally a composer of ballets; he wrote
more than 300.
44 Verzino, *Le opere di Donizetti*, p. 103.
45 Donizetti had signed the contract for *Ugo* late in the summer of 1831.
He broke his old contract with Barbaja not just because of an argument
about who would sing in *Fausta* but to be free to accept this engagement at La Scala.
46 Donizetti's autograph of *Ugo* is in the Conservatorio di San Pietro a
Majella, Naples, and in it these last-minute revisions are clear to see.
47 Besides *Norma*, one of the operas given at La Scala in this Carnival
season was *Anna Bolena*, having its second Milanese production, the
first having been at the Carcano. It was sung for the first time at La Scala
by Pasta, Giulia Grisi (Seymour), Antonio Deval (Percy) and Vincenzo
Negrini (Enrico VIII).
48 Giulia Grisi (1811–69), a soprano, was the younger sister of the mezzo-
soprano Giuditta Grisi and the cousin of the ballerina Carlotta Grisi.
She made her debut in 1828. For Donizetti, besides Adelia in *Ugo*, she
created Elena in *Marin Faliero* and Norina in *Don Pasquale;* for Bellini, Giulietta in *I Capuleti*, Adalgisa in *Norma*, and Elvira in *I puri-*

tani. After 1834 her career chiefly centered on Paris (until 1849) and London (until 1861). Her second husband was the famous tenor Mario, with whom she made a tour of the United States in 1854–5. At the time of her London debut Chorley praised the evenness of her voice and her mastery over it. Of her dramatic ability he says: 'Madame Grisi's attitudes were always more or less harsh, angular and undignified, and when she was in her prime, and had no reason to manage or spare her resources, there was a fierceness in certain of her outbursts which impaired her efforts. In short, her acting did not show reflection so much as the rich, uncultivated, imperious nature of a most beautiful and adroit southern woman.' (*Thirty Years' Musical Recollections*, p. 79.)

49 Quoted in Verzino, *Le opere di Donizetti*, pp. 105–6.

50 After its run at Milan, *Ugo* had six other productions during the nineteenth century. At Pisa in the spring of 1835 and Trieste that autumn Donzelli repeated the role of Ugo, which he had created (Fanny Persiani was his Bianca at Pisa). In December 1837 it was given at Prague in German, in 1839 at Madrid and in 1846 at Lisbon. (In some of these productions the *musico* role of Luigi V was taken by a tenor.) The opera then lay dormant until it was recorded in London by Opera Rara in 1977; the recording proves that *Ugo* hardly deserves the neglect that has been its portion.

51 Parts of *Ugo* went into *Sancia di Castiglia*, *Il furioso*, *Parisina*, and the 1838 revision of *Gabriella di Vergy*. On the other hand, a chorus from the earlier *Imelda de' Lambertazzi* was used in *Ugo*.

52 Alessandro Lanari (1790–1862) would figure large in Donizetti's future. Although based primarily in Florence, where he managed the Teatro della Pergola and other theaters off and on for twenty-five years between 1823 and 1862, he was also active at various times in Milan, Rome, Naples and Venice, as well as being responsible for touring companies, several of which might be performing simultaneously. At various times Lanari held exclusive contracts with some of the most important singers of this period – such as Carolina Ungher, Fanny Persiani, Gilbert Duprez and his wife, and Giuseppina Strepponi; he would negotiate the use of their services with other impresarios if his stiff fees could be met. Lanari had a good reputation for the quality of the singers he handled and for his impressive productions, such as *Marin Faliero* in Florence in 1836, but he was also notorious for his tightness about money.

53 Although Auber's *Le philtre* was first performed at the Opéra (20 June 1831), it later entered the repertory of the Opéra-Comique. Scribe's plot was drawn from an Italian play, *Il filtro*, by Silvio Malaperta.

54 Thérésine, Guillaume, Jolicoeur and Fontanarose became Adina, Nemorino, Belcore and Dulcamara.

55 Henri-Bernard Dabadie (1797–1853) had a notable career at the Opéra, making his debut there in 1819 and appearing in such notable premieres as *Moïse* (Pharaon), *La muette de Portici* (Pietro), *Le comte Ory* (Raimbaut) and *Guillaume Tell* (title role). He retired from the stage in 1835.

56 The Teatro Canobbiana opened its spring season of 1832 on 23 April with Luigi Ricci's *L'orfanella di Ginevra*. The soprano Sabine Heinefet-

ter, the tenor Giambattista Genero and the buffo Giuseppe Frezzolini were in that cast and would appear in *L'elisir*.

57 Sabine Heinefetter (?1809–72). If her birthdate is correct, she made her debut at the unusually precocious age of thirteen (in Peter Ritter's *Der Mandarin* at Frankfurt am Main in 1822). In 1829 she broke a lifetime contract with Cassel and went to Paris to study with Davide Banderali and Giovanni Tadolini. In the same year she made debuts at the Théâtre-Italien and at the Kärntnertortheater in Vienna. As a member of the buffa troupe at the Canobbiana she sang Adina in the *prima* of *L'elisir*. Her only appearance at La Scala was in a single disastrous performance of Persiani's *Ines de Castro* (1837). In 1843 she followed some performances in Russia by singing in an Italian season at Berlin; she retired from the stage in 1845.

58 Giuseppe Frezzolini (1789–?1861) was a basso buffo whose active career lasted from 1819 to about 1840. He was the father of the soprano Erminia Frezzolini (1818–84). For Donizetti he created Pasquale in *Olivo e Pasquale*, Belfiore in *Alina*, and, most important, Dr Dulcamara in *L'elisir d'amore*. Something of the esteem in which he was held is indicated by his being a member of the blue-ribbon company at the Teatro Carcano in Milan in 1830–1, where he sang Rustano in *Gianni di Calais* with Rubini. He pursued his career chiefly in northern Italy, but he appeared at the San Carlo in 1835–6.

59 Z. no. 72, pp. 288–9.

60 The first production of *L'elisir* maintained itself throughout the season, being performed a total of thirty-three times. Berlioz saw the performance of 20 May 1832, but he says nothing about the music, claiming that the audience chattered so loudly and continuously that he could not hear one note. He left the theater before the performance was over (*Memoirs*, p. 183).

61 The method by which the 570 *scudi* would be paid was typical of the period. Donizetti received the money in three installments: a third when he arrived ready to rehearse his opera, another third when he gave the first act of his completed score to the impresario, and the balance after the third performance.

62 The first *Anna Bolena* in Naples was sung by Ronzi (Anna), Adelaide Toldi (Seymour), Nicholas Ivanoff (Percy) and Lablache (Enrico VIII).

63 Apparently the modifications and changes made for Lablache did not turn out well, for Donizetti reported to Ferretti early in September: '*Fausta* was ruined by Lablache.' (Z. no. 82, undated, p. 297.) Donizetti's remark here is one of the very few unfavorable comments recorded about Lablache throughout a long career.

64 Z. no. 84, p. 298.

65 Giovanni Basadonna (1806–after 1851), a tenor, was born in Naples. After study with Nozzari, he made his stage debut in 1828, soon establishing himself as the most famous exponent of the title role of Rossini's *Otello* of his generation. For Donizetti, who had a high regard for his musicianship, Basadonna sang in the *prime* of *Fausta*, *Sancia* and *Roberto Devereux*. In 1841 he first developed symptoms of the disease of the vocal cords that caused him to interrupt his career in 1845. He attempted (unsuccessfully) to make a comeback at the Teatro della Per-

gola in Florence in 1851 as Otello. (This final appearance contradicts the legend that he emigrated to Rio de Janeiro and died there of yellow fever in June 1850.)

66 Z. no. 86, dated 6 November 1832, p. 300.
67 Cervantes, *Don Quixote*, Part I (1605), chapters 23–7.
68 Donizetti gave his reactions to the libretto of *Il furioso* in the following five letters: Z. no. 78, dated 2 August 1832, pp. 292–3; Z. no. 79, dated 9 August 1832, pp. 293–4; Z. no. 80, dated 18 August 1832, pp. 294–5; Z. no. 82, undated, assigned to early September 1832, pp. 296–7; Z. no. 84, dated 16 September 1832, p. 298.
69 Donizetti's habit of working directly with his librettists is well illustrated by this note Cammarano sent him while they were working on *Roberto Devereux* in 1837. 'I shall wait for you in the Two Sicilies Café until two o'clock . . . The finale strikes me as not too bad. We will read it together: four eyes are better than two, or rather eight – counting my glasses and your two eyes which are equal to four.' The original of this note is in the Biblioteca Lucchesi-Palli, Naples.
70 Z. no. 82, undated, p. 297.
71 Z. no. 86, dated 6 November 1832, p. 300.
72 Giorgio Ronconi (1810–90) made his stage debut at Pavia in 1831. Following appearances at Milan (Teatro Re) Cremona, Bologna and Padua, he went to Rome for the fall season of 1832 at the Valle, where he appeared as the deranged Murena in the local stage *prima* of *L'esule di Roma*. A vivid description of Ronconi is preserved in Chorley's *Thirty Years' Musical Recollections* (pp. 209–12). Chorley admits to Ronconi's early vocal decline, but attests to his extraordinary powers as an actor, saying: "I owe some of my best opera evenings to Signor Ronconi.'
73 Bonifacio in *Imelda de' Lambertazzi* is a baritone romantic lead, but that role has scarcely the dramatic scope of Cardenio in *Il furioso*.
74 Z. no. 90, dated 3 January 1833, p. 305.
75 Z. no. 90, p. 305.
76 On one occasion Donizetti characterized the false orchestration of one of his works as 'super-Arabic' (*arciarabo*).
77 Giacomo Panizza (1804–60) was *maestro di cembalo* at La Scala from 1830 until his death, an ill-paid post that gave him access to scores. Panizza also tried his hand at writing operas; among his works is a *Gianni di Calais* (Trieste, 1834) that uses the same Gilardoni libretto earlier set by Donizetti.
78 The notice appears twice in *La rivista teatrale*, 8 June 1833 and 31 July 1833.
79 Z. no. 92, p. 306.
80 Published in Iarro (pseudonym of Giulio Piccini), *Memorie d'un impresario fiorentino* (Florence, 1892), p. 133. Lanari's reference to that traditional Latin symbol of cuckoldry should not be construed literally; since he was not married to Merola but to another lady, the 'horns' he complains of were, at best, proprietary. Giuseppina Merola was a member of Lanari's company from 1831 to 1835, perhaps longer. For her Donizetti wrote a cavatina, 'Ah, potessi un sol momento' to substitute for Smeton's 'Ah, parea, che per incanto' in Act 1 of *Anna Bolena*.
81 Z. no. 115, dated 22 August 1833, p. 333.

82 Z. no. 111, p. 328. Significantly, Donizetti uses the word *finito* (finished) and not *scritto* (written). Romani's delay was caused by the burden of work that swamped him when, in the fall of 1832, he assumed the post of staff librettist for La Scala. If Romani's tardiness was a hardship for Donizetti in Florence, it proved if anything more trying to Bellini, then in Venice impatiently awaiting the libretto of *Beatrice di Tenda*. Bellini's *Beatrice* came out in Venice on 16 March 1833; Donizetti's *Parisina* in Florence the following day.

83 Domenico Cosselli (1801–55) was one of the leading baritones of the period. He was a singer whom Donizetti particularly respected and he was a sufficiently convincing actor for Ronconi to regard him as a serious rival.

84 In Byron's poem, Ugo is the Duke's bastard; Romani makes him the Duke's son by his first wife. In the poem the lovers are beheaded, but in the opera Parisina dies of grief at the sight of Ugo's corpse.

85 Filippo Cicconetti, *Vita di Gaetano Donizetti* (Rome, 1864), p. 80, tells of Donizetti's suddenly excusing himself from a group of assembled friends and reappearing half an hour later with the finale to Act 2 of *Tasso* complete. This feat of rapid composition assumes a different aspect when we realize that this finale uses the same music as the final quartet from *Il paria*.

86 Adelina Spech (1811–66) was a prima donna of some prominence during the 1830s, but she caused Donizetti trouble during the rehearsals of *Tasso*. He informed Ricordi that 'La Spech, a contralto who has pulled herself up by the teeth to mezzo-soprano, has caused me to turn half my opera inside out.' (Z. no. 116, dated 27 August 1833, p. 334.) The following year Spech married the tenor Lorenzo Salvi (1810–79), who sang in a number of Donizetti *prime*. Salvi was a tenor with the Rubini type of vocal production and pursued a long career, singing in England, France, Austria, and the United States (with Jenny Lind).

87 On 12 November 1835 Donizetti wrote to Ferretti: 'Concerning *Torquato* I told you that transforming the role [of Don Gherardo] into a serious one would make it more difficult to have the opera performed, because then you would need another *primo basso cantante*; and who would do Gherardo when there is the role of Tasso?' (Z. no. 185, p. 391).

88 When the fall of Charles X in 1830 caused all official appointments to lapse, Rossini was cut off from his official connection with the Opéra; he became an advisor, an *éminence-pas-encore-grise*, to the Théâtre-Italien.

89 Z. no. 101, dated 15 June 1833, p. 316.

90 Albert Soubies reports this incident in *Le Théâtre-Italien de 1801 à 1913* (Paris, 1913), p. 72.

91 At least two of these 'new' pieces were only new to the score of *Il furioso*: the tenor Winter inserted a cavatina and aria from *Il castello di Kenilworth*, while Eugenia Tadolini adopted 'Ah, fu un sogno' from *Il borgomastro di Saardam* as her aria–finale. As Donizetti was preparing the production he would have approved or even suggested these changes. The orchestration was augmented by increasing the horns and trombones to four of each. An overture replaced the former prelude, but this too seems to have been borrowed from an earlier score; it was

never, to my knowledge, printed with *Il furioso* and is not now identifiable.

92 Henriette (known in Italy as Enrichetta) Méric-Lalande (1798–1867) was born in France and studied with Talma and Garcia (the father and teacher of Malibran and Viardot). She went to Italy in 1823. In her best days she had fabulous vocal agility, as may be seen from the music Donizetti composed for her in *Elvida* (1826). In 1827 she sang at La Scala in the *prima* of *Il pirata*, but Bellini complained that she was incapable of 'delicate sentiments', and the critic of *I teatri* at that period spoke of her as 'dal genere grande agitato' (a highly emotional type) (see *Bellini, epistolario*, no. XI, dated 16 January 1828, p. 27). When she appeared in London in 1830, Chorley dismissed her debut as 'too late' (*Thirty Years' Musical Recollections*, p. 4). By the time of *Lucrezia Borgia* she had reached that nerve-racking point in her career when she felt she could take no chances with the unfamiliar, insisting on what she believed would show her off to the best advantage. She retired from the stage in the late 1830s.

93 Mercadante had recently assumed the post of *maestro di cappella* at Novara, succeeding Pietro Generali. Mercadante's next opera at La Scala was not a *Saffo*, but *La gioventù di Enrico V* (7 November 1834), to a libretto by Romani derived from Shakespeare. It is probable that the anti-Donizetti faction in Naples, headed by Florimo, believed Donizetti to have schemed to supplant Mercadante to obtain the opening night position for *Lucrezia*; they bore a grudge over this situation and it may well have formed some part of their motivation in urging Mercadante over Donizetti for the directorship of the Naples Conservatory after 1837. There is obvious bias in the Neapolitan newspaper *Omnibus*, which reported Bellini's successes and Donizetti's failures at Milan and made no single mention of the *prima* of *Lucrezia Borgia* at La Scala or of its subsequent run of thirty-three performances.

94 Quoted in Verzino, *Le opere di Donizetti*, p. 141.

95 An exception was Romani's response (Z. no. A31, dated 23 November 1841, p. 890) to the idea of writing with Donizetti an opera for Benjamin Lumley in London (where the censorship problems were far less acute); but this project ultimately fell through.

96 There is a certain similarity between Parisina's rondò 'Ugo è spento!' and Lucrezia's 'Egli è spento!', with the significant difference that the first is sung over a lover's corpse and the second over a son's by his mother, who is responsible for his death.

97 Marietta Brambilla (1807–75) was the chief florid contralto in the generation separating Rosmunda Pisaroni from Marietta Alboni. She made her debut in London in 1827 as Arsace in *Semiramide*, and made *musico* roles her specialty. Besides her participation in *Lucrezia Borgia* she sang Pierotto in *Linda* and Gondì in *Maria di Rohan* when it was introduced to Paris. Brambilla came from a musical family; five of her sisters were also singers, among them Teresa, who was the first Gilda in *Rigoletto*. Chorley remarks of Marietta Brambilla on her return to London in 1835 that her voice was not what it had been eight years before, but goes on to say: 'in the interim ... Mdlle Brambilla had learned how to sing [and] her choice and variety of ornaments carried

her through the season to the satisfaction of the public' (*Thirty Years' Musical Recollections*, p. 66).

98 In 1832, when Pedrazzi (dates unknown) made his debut at La Scala in the local first performance of *Fausta*, Donizetti wrote to Ricordi (Z. no. 88, dated 6 December 1832, p. 302) about the tenor's tendency to sing a half-tone sharp. This problem would seem to have been largely overcome for he sang again for Donizetti, not only in the *prima* of *Lucrezia Borgia*, but in *Buondelmonte* in 1834. Another tenor, Luigi Pedrazzi, was active at the same time as Francesco, but his career appears to have been more limited.

99 Luciano Mariani (dates unknown), a bass, first appeared at La Scala in 1820. In 1823 he created Oroe in Rossini's *Semiramide*, and in 1831 Rodolfo in Bellini's *La sonnambula*; his role in Donizetti's *Lucrezia Borgia* makes an illuminating link between these composers. Mariani was one of the soloists in the cantata *In morte di Maria F. Malibran*, to which Donizetti contributed, when it was performed on 17 March 1837; this was apparently Mariani's last appearance at La Scala.

100 Pezzi's review is reprinted in Verzino, *Le opere di Donizetti*, pp. 144–7. He thought Lalande badly out of voice and close to panic. The settings he judged disgraceful. (The great scene designer Sanquirico had died the previous year, and he was sorely missed at La Scala.)

101 The prominence given the large number (larger than usual) of lesser characters in *Lucrezia Borgia* was an innovation.

102 The role of Noè had originally been composed for the bass Lablache.

103 Amalia Schütz-Oldosi (1804–52) had appeared in opera buffa as a contralto at the Odéon in Paris as early as 1825. Extending her voice upward, she converted herself into a serviceable prima donna for tragic works, appearing at many important Italian theaters during the 1830s. The only Donizetti *prima* she appeared in was *Il campanello di notte* (Naples, 1836), an uncharacteristic work for that stage of her career.

104 Z. no. 131, dated 31 January 1834, p. 344.

105 Z. no. 131, pp. 343–4. Donizetti also hoped that Visconti would not give *Parisina* at La Scala during the season, as the company was ill adapted to it. He offered to stage it himself when he returned to Milan the following year, but this offer went unheeded. *Parisina* was given at La Scala on 6 February 1834, with the 'emotional' Lalande in the title role and with the baritone role of Azzo adapted (*puntato*), by somebody other than Donizetti, for the tenor Winter. This production of *Parisina* was judged 'mediocre' (Cambiasi, *La Scala: 1778–1889*, pp. 276–7) and eked out only nine performances.

106 Fanny Tacchinardi-Persiani (1812–67) was the daughter and pupil of the tenor Nicola Tacchinardi, one of the great vocal technicians of his time. In 1830 she married the composer Giuseppe Persiani (1804–69). Donizetti had tried her voice in Milan in October 1833 and described her to Lanari as 'more than a little chilly [*freddina, freddina*] but precise and absolutely on pitch'. Severini of the Théâtre-Italien found her difficult and complained that 'she cries a lot'. Writing of her great days in Paris and London (1837–48), Chorley speaks of her voice as 'acrid and piercing . . . and always liable to rise in pitch', but allows that this defect was more than compensated for by her mastery of vocal art. 'She

was never careless, never unfinished; always sedulous – sometimes to the point of strain... in the employment of her vast and varied resources, rising to an animation which, if not sympathetic as warmth kindling warmth, amounted to that display of conscious power which is resistless.' (*Thirty Years' Musical Recollections*, pp. 99–100.)

107 Donizetti was obliging too. One of the changes he asked for from Romani was an amplification of Merola's role of Arturo.

108 *S.d.* 1, no. 26, dated 8 March 1834, p. 22.

109 Persiani had started inserting the *Rosmonda* scena into Italian productions of *Lucia* at least by May 1837, performing it as part of the *Lucia* score in both Paris and London. Jenny Lind followed that practise when she sang *Lucia* in London. Part of the *Rosmonda* cabaletta was heard at the Metroplitan when Lily Pons used it to amplify the proportions of 'Salut à la France' in the 1940 revival of *La fille du régiment*. Joan Sutherland recorded the entire scena from *Rosmonda* as an annex to her first complete recording of *Lucia* for Decca of London.

110 Donizetti's reply to Rossini is in *S.d.* 1, no. 25, dated 22 February 1834, pp. 21–2. Donizetti engaged in an elaborate bit of scheming with his Milanese publisher Ricordi to try to ensure that his new opera for La Scala would open the season, allowing him plenty of time to get to Paris. He was anxious that Visconti should not know of his Parisian engagement, for fear the impresario would be put out by his ulterior motives in wanting the opening date. For further help in getting his way, Donizetti enlisted the support of Ronzi, who had been engaged as prima donna for that Carnival season of 1834–5 at La Scala.

111 On 15 April 1834 Donizetti wrote to Ricordi that he was 'renewing' his offer to Romani 'for the text for 6 July if he wants to do it, and if he can do it or not' (Z. no. 132, p. 345).

112 Quoted from Jeremy Commons, '*Maria Stuarda* and the Neapolitan Censorship', *Donizetti Society Journal*, 3 (1977), 151–67. Much of the story about the prohibition of this opera has been unearthed by Commons.

113 Quoted from a letter, dated 7 September 1834, from Prince di Torella, then head of the royal commission in charge of the Neapolitan theaters, to Prince di Ruffano, the Superintendent of the Royal Theaters and Spectacles. See Commons, *op. cit.*

114 The previous year when Ronzi was singing at the San Carlo in competition with Malibran, Donizetti facetiously described her 'as having more going for her (because actually she has the bigger ass – that adds weight – besides more flesh elsewhere)' (Z. no. 80, dated 18 August 1832, p. 295). The account of the battle between the singers comes from *Teatri, arti e letteratura*, 23 October 1834.

115 Z. no. 150, dated 7 October 1834, p. 362.

116 I repeated it myself twice in print, along with almost every writer on Donizetti, but Commons (*op. cit.*) has demonstrated that the tale of the queen's fainting at the dress rehearsal began to be told about 1865, more than thirty years after the event and after the Bourbons had been forced to leave Naples.

117 King Ferdinando himself was also descended from the Scottish queen.

118 Significantly, the *prima* of *Fausta* occurred before Ferdinando married

Maria Cristina. Donizetti had left Naples in November 1832, a few weeks before the royal wedding, and when he returned after an absence of almost a year and a half he may well have been insensitive to the new prudery emanating from the royal palace. The queen-mother was well known for her uninhibited ways.

119 I use the term 'royal commission' to refer to the Society of Industry and the Fine Arts, also sometimes referred to as the 'Company of Industry and the Fine Arts'; these terms seem to have been used interchangeably.

120 The need for a new opera by Donizetti was compounded by the banning of *Parisina* in October 1834 at the San Carlo. *Parisina* had aroused real enthusiasm when it was introduced to Naples on 10 July 1834 with Ungher and Duprez. Lanari's company was then appearing at the San Carlo, having been engaged by the royal commission.

121 The transformation of *Maria Stuarda* into *Buondelmonte* has been explored by Patric Schmid, '*Maria Stuarda* and *Buondelmonte*', *Opera*, 24 (1973), 1060–6.

122 S.d.1, no. 31, dated September 1834, p. 26, to Innocenzo Giampieri (or Giampietro), librarian of the Biblioteca Palatina, Florence.

123 Z. no. 311, dated 25 August 1838, p. 486.

124 Z. no. 311, p. 486.

125 In Z. no. 148, dated 4 October 1834, p. 360, Donizetti asks Ricordi: 'What is Romani doing? Why has he denied himself to me four times? Does he feel such antipathy toward me?'

126 Z. no. 149, undated, pp. 260–1. This letter must have been written somewhat earlier than the position given it by Zavadini suggests. Zavadini places it between a letter dated 4 October 1834 and one dated three days later, yet it is clear from the letter (Z. no. 150) that by 7 October Donizetti had completed all of *Marin Faliero* but one duet.

127 All performances at the Théâtre-Italien were given in Italian.

128 Z. no. 146, dated 27 September 1834, p. 358.

129 Z. no. 153, p. 364.

130 Domenico Reina (1797–1843) had made his debut by 1825 when he sang Norfolk in Rossini's *Elisabetta, regina d'Inghilterra*, with Lalande in the title role, at the Teatro Comunale, Bologna. He appeared at La Scala from 1829 to 1836 and at the San Carlo in Naples from 1832 to 1834 and again from 1837 to 1841. He seems to have retired from the stage in 1841.

131 Orazio Cartagenova (1800–41), an effective singer and actor, is not so well remembered today as he deserves. He made his debut at La Scala in the autumn season of 1823. He sang at the Fenice in the *prima* of Bellini's *Beatrice di Tenda*. When he sang Cardenio in *Il furioso* at La Scala in 1833 he was regarded as Ronconi's peer. He sang in Spain in 1826, in Vienna in 1835, and in 1836 he appeared in London. His last appearances were in Vicenza, where he died of 'melancholia', still a relatively young man.

132 Dumas's *Charles VII* had been given in Italy as *Berengaria*, and Bidèra probably worked from this translation. In the opera the names of the principal characters are changed from the French originals: Berangère becomes Gemma; de Savoisy, Vergy; and Yaquob, the Arab slave, Tamas.

133 Teresa Parodi was the favorite pupil and protégée of Pasta, but contemporary accounts suggest that she was better at imitating her mentor's vocal defects than her dramatic genius.

134 The lines of Tamas: 'Mi togliesti e core e mente/Patria, Numi e libertà [*sic*]!' (You deprived me of both heart and mind, native land, gods, and liberty!), particularly the last irresistible word, touched off the incident. The story is vividly told in Harold Acton, *The Last Bourbons of Naples* (New York, 1961), p. 189.

135 Donizetti's music had already been heard at the Théâtre-Italien, where *Anna Bolena* had been given twenty-five times by the end of the 1834 season, *Gianni di Calais* twice, and *L'ajo nell'imbarazzo*, twice.

136 Z. no. 157, undated, p. 367, purports to be a letter from Donizetti to Romani, describing his reactions to *I puritani*. The only known source of this letter is Francesco Florimo's *Bellini: memorie e lettere* (Florence, 1882), p. 57, and until the original autograph turns up (an unlikely prospect I believe), it should be regarded as highly suspect. Donizetti is supposed to have written to Romani in French, and at this period he still consistently wrote to his Italian correspondents in their native language. On 4 October 1834 Donizetti had written to Ricordi about Romani (Z. no. 148, p. 360): 'Why has he denied himself to me four times? Does he feel such antipathy toward me?' Under the circumstances it is unlikely that Donizetti would be sending Romani news from Paris. Moreover the tone of the letter Florimo prints is dubious because it has nothing of Donizetti's hasty vividness. And then it closes with this mealy-mouthed sentiment: 'Je ne mérite point le succès des *Puritains*, mais je désire ne point déplaire.' (I do not at all deserve the success of *I puritani*, but I hope that I do not displease in any way.) Donizetti had a realistic view of his own worth and a sense of humor. In the light of all this, one cannot help but feel that Z. no. 157 says exactly what Florimo would want it to say about the relative standing of his idol Bellini and Donizetti.

137 *Bellini, epistolario*, pp. 443–543, contains many biased references to this season at the Théâtre-Italien. At one point (p. 482) Bellini has the self-awareness to instruct Florimo: 'Tear up this letter as it is full of bile.'

138 An illuminating sidelight on Rossini's estimate of Pacini (as recorded by Bellini) is shed by Pacini's frank admission in his memoirs (*Le mie memorie artistiche*, p. 72), referring to this year 1834, after the fiasco of *Carlo di Borgogna* at the Fenice:

> My orchestration had never been careful enough. If sometimes it went well and brilliantly, it did not occur from reflection, but rather from the natural taste God had given me. I was often slovenly in my treatment of the strings, and I did not pay sufficient attention to the effects that could be drawn from the other families of instruments. I was always concerned with the vocal part above everything, and most of all I sought to investigate the capacities of the particular performers to whom I entrusted my compositions.

139 *Bellini, epistolario*, no. CLXXXVII, 4 October 1834, p. 443.

140 *I puritani* was Bellini's eleventh opera; Donizetti, by the time of *Marin Faliero*, had composed more than four times as many stage works.

141 *Bellini, epistolario*, no. CCII, dated 30 November 1834, p. 482.
142 *Bellini, epistolario*, no. CCXXIV, dated 27 February 1835, p. 529.
143 Z. no. 180, dated 20 October 1835, p. 387. Donizetti is here reporting to
    Ricordi how he was able to expose an illegally obtained score of *Marin
    Faliero* because it had been copied from the autograph left behind in
    Naples and contained none of the changes made in Paris. Presumably
    some of these changes were the result of Rossini's advice. *Faliero* gives
    the lie to the story that Donizetti always composed in haste, but, with
    typical irony, Donizetti pointed out that music he sweated over rarely
    had the great success of music that had come easily to him.
144 Nicholas Ivanoff (also known as Nicolai Ivanov; 1810–77), whose fam-
    ily name was Kuzmich, accompanied Glinka to Italy in 1828 and, after a
    period of study, made his debut in 1832 in the Neapolitan *prima* of
    Anna Bolena. He was subsequently engaged at the Théâtre-Italien as an
    understudy for Rubini, whose vocal style he approximated fairly effec-
    tively. He returned to Italy about 1840 and remained active there until
    his retirement in 1852.
145 Donizetti was sufficiently fond of the Gondolier's barcarolle in Act 2 to
    use it in the score of *Il campanello di notte*.
146 *I puritani* has a happy ending, while *Faliero* is a tragedy.
147 Z. no. 160, pp. 368–9.
148 Donizetti's diploma is dated 2 February 1836.
149 Chorley, *Thirty Years' Musical Recollections*, p. 65.
150 Sofia Löwe replaced Grisi as Elena in 1841; the rest of the principals
    were as before.
151 Z. no. A7, dated 19 May 1836, pp. 867–8, from Lanari to Donizetti.
    Lanari's letter begins: 'Furore! Fanatismo! Entusiasmo!' Everything
    went well, apparently, with a single exception: 'The duet between
    Elena e Ferdinando [sic], sufficiently applauded, but the public recog-
    nized in its first two tempos those from the *Anna Bolena* duet many
    times performed here.'
152 *Faliero*, dealing with a conspiracy against a Doge of Venice, has obvi-
    ous points of resemblance to *I due Foscari*, nor are these points merely
    dramatic ones.
153 Mazzini discussed the opera, having seen Lanari's production at Flor-
    ence in 1836. He mentions the tenor aria 'Di mia patria, o bel soggiorno'
    as something 'that only an exile can understand'. The duet between
    Israele and Faliero he describes as 'that alternation, irate, incomplete,
    excited, of melodic phrases which is not song because the orchestra has
    the melody, but real, palpable plotting', finding in it an 'admirable
    mastery of musical science and of the science of human psychology'
    (*Filosofia della musica*, pp. 182–3).
154 Chorley, *Thirty Years' Musical Recollections*, p. 107.
155 Michele Accursi posed as a political exile – Paris was full of fugitive
    Italians in those days – but he was really a counterspy who sent de-
    tailed reports to the Vatican of the activities of his fellow countrymen in
    Paris. There is a distinct possibility that Donizetti met Accursi through
    the Vassellis.
156 *La juive* was first given on 25 February 1835.

4. 1835–1838: *Lucia di Lammermoor* to *Poliuto*

1 On 1 August 1835 Donizetti sent the librettist Salatino a poem describing his new quarters. (See *S.d.*1, no. 35, p. 30).

2 Guillaume Cottrau (1797–1847), a partner in the music-publishing firm of B. Girard, was a close friend of Donizetti. Cottrau's interests were not limited to opera; he also encouraged the publication of Neapolitan songs. His son Teodoro (1826–79) composed the ubiquitous *Santa Lucia*.

3 Cottrau, *Lettres d'un mélomane,* pp. 30–1.

4 Lanari had been engaged as impresario by the commission in the fall of 1834, but the situation in Naples deprived him of the authority necessary to achieve his usual satisfactory results.

5 Z. no. 164, dated 3 May 1835, p. 372.

6 This contract is in the Museo Donizettiano, Bergamo.

7 Z. no. 165, p. 373.

8 Salvatore Cammarano (1801–52), who came of a family of actors and painters active for three generations in the Neapolitan theaters, had been associated with the scenic department of the San Carlo, and then about 1831 became what today would be called an assistant stage director. Cammarano made his debut as a librettist at the Fondo in 1834 with *La sposa* to music by Vignozzi. His first chance to write a libretto for the San Carlo came when he collaborated with Bidèra on the text of Giuseppe Persiani's *Ines de Castro* (Naples, 1835), composed for Malibran. In Cammarano Donizetti found the librettist responsive to the values of Romanticism whom he had been seeking. It is somewhat misleading to compare Romani and Cammarano because their careers scarcely overlapped (Romani had almost completely given up writing librettos by 1835) and because they represent different generations and different parts of Italy. Cammarano became the most considerable librettist of his day. (See John Black, 'Cammarano's Libretti for Donizetti,' *Studi donizettiani,* 3 (1978), 115–29.)

9 Internal evidence suggests that Cammarano had to hand three earlier Italian librettos derived from Scott's *Bride of Lammermoor* (1819): Giuseppe Balocchi's for Carafa's *Le nozze di Lammermoor* (Paris, 1829); Calisto Bassi's for Luigi Rieschi's *La fidanzata di Lammermoor;* and Pietro Beltrame's for Alberto Mazzucato's *La fidanzata di Lammermoor* (Padua, 1834). (See Jerome Mitchell, *The Walter Scott Operas* (Tuscaloosa, 1977), pp. 105–44.) Obviously, Cammarano could work more expeditiously with the help of existing dramatic reductions of Scott's sprawling plot than he could from the novel itself. There is little likelihood that Cammarano was even aware of Hans Christian Andersen's poem set by the Danish composer Ivar Frederik Bredal, with spoken dialogue, as *Bruden fra Lammermoor;* the work was first performed at Copenhagen on 5 May 1832.

10 Z. no. 166, pp. 373–4. Donizetti's earlier letter, of 25 May, to the commission, referred to in this letter, has yet to be found.

11 It is significant that Donizetti completed *Lucia* on 6 July, the traditional date of the royal gala for the queen-mother's birthday, the date *Lucia*

would probably have had its *prima* if the commission had not been dilatory in the execution of its responsibilities. It is not hard to believe that Donizetti found the queen-mother a more sympathetic figure than her prudish daughter-in-law.

12 Z. no. 170, dated 16 July 1835, p. 378, to Gaetano Cobianchi.

13 Z. no. 172, dated 24 July, p. 381.

14 Z. no. 174, p. 383.

15 *S.d.* 1, no. 37, undated, p. 33. The editors of *S.d.* 1, while giving the date 28 September 1835 for this letter (based on the phrase 'Today the 28th'), comment that Donizetti mistook the date and should have written '26th'. Oddly enough, he had earlier made the identical error in a letter of 16 September 1835 to Ferretti (Z. no. 175, p. 384), in which he announced that *Lucia* would be given on the '28th'. It does seem strange that Donizetti should make the same mistake twice, yet the 28th is an impossible date, for no performances whatever were scheduled on that day for either the San Carlo or the Fondo. Further corroboration of the 26th may be found in a letter from Cottrau (who seems to have been more reliable about dates than Donizetti) to his brother: on 24 September 1835 he wrote that *Lucia* would be given 'the day after tomorrow' (*Lettres d'un mélomane*, p. 35).

16 I am extremely grateful to John Black for pointing out to me the evidence that confirms the date of 26 September (letter to the author, 1 February 1981).

17 Gilbert Duprez (1806–96) is regarded as the first 'modern' tenor; with his high C from the chest he revolutionized the public's expectations of what a tenor should sound like. He studied with Choron at the Institution Royale de Musique Classique et Religieuse in Paris, and sang first in 1826 at the Odéon as a *tenor contraltino*. In 1828 he went to Italy for further study, making his Italian debut at Varese in *Le comte Ory* with Pasta. He was soon engaged by Lanari, along with his wife Alexandrine Duperron-Duprez, and appeared in several Donizetti *prime: Parisina, Rosmonda* and *Lucia*. He returned to Paris in 1837, making his debut at the Opéra as Arnold in *Guillaume Tell* and producing a sensation with his top notes. He remained at the Opéra until 1849 and appeared there in the premieres of *Les martyrs, La favorite* and *Dom Sébastien*. He taught at the Conservatoire from 1842 until 1850, and in 1853 founded his own school. A product of his old age is his delightful *Souvenirs d'un chanteur*.

18 Carlo (Ottolini) Porto (dates unknown), a bass, is first heard of singing in London in 1827, where Chorley judged his voice as both 'hard' and 'deep' (*Thirty Years' Musical Recollections*, p. 86). He was a frequent member of Lanari's companies in the 1830s and appeared in the *prime* of *Parisina, Rosmonda, Buondelmonte* and *Lucia* (as Raimondo). He seems to have been a true basso profondo.

19 Z. no. 177, p. 385.

20 The title of *Gli illinesi* refers to a tribe of Indians living in India, not in Illinois.

21 As Consul explains to Donizetti on 1 July 1835: 'You will see that the old libretto has a happy resolution. And I would want the new version to end the same way, because now such an opera is desired here and it

will please all the public. Understand that the ending cannot be foreseen until the final scene and that the anxiety of the audience cannot be dissipated until almost at the very'end of the opera, and then in a flash.' (Z. no. A3, pp. 860–2.) Consul's remarks show that the predilection for old-fashioned happy endings lasted well into the 1830s.

22 Romani was by then living in Turin, being the editor of the *Gazzetta ufficiale piemontese*.

23 Z. no. 168, undated (but probably about 10 July 1835 as it is a direct reply to Consul's letter of 1 July), p. 376.

24 'What! Donzelli in love? But you know that Donzelli must be fifty! [Donzelli was then forty-five.] and with fifty years on his back to play the lover, or *per Bacco* at my age, no! [Donizetti was not yet thirty-eight] I know that Donzelli in 1822 already played tyrant roles [in *Zoraida di Granata*]; I know that at Milan in *Norma* he already seemed over the hill [*grandicello*] as he seemed in *Ugo*.' (Z. no. 168, p. 375.) It is important to realize that, in Donizetti's day, a man of fifty was regarded as elderly; the obsession with youthful appearance and behaviour is a comparatively recent phenomenon.

25 Z. no. 168, p. 376. Giuditta Grisi (1805–40) was the elder sister of the more celebrated Giulia. Giuditta had been the first Romeo in Bellini's *I Capuleti*, a role she introduced at a number of important theaters. That she was plain and had an unfortunate figure we understand from Consul's comment that while 'not made' to play a European lady in skirts, she would be acceptable as an Indian heroine (Z. no. A3, 1 July 1835, p. 861). Donizetti's suggestion of using a *musico* for the hero followed Feliciano Strepponi's example, as Carolina Ungher had sung the role of Guido in Strepponi's *Gli illinesi*.

26 The limited size of a company of singers in those days helps to explain the perpetuation of that compromise genre, the semiseria. Since most impresarios would not think of hiring both a leading baritone and a leading bass for serious roles, the only available singer for an additional male role would be the basso buffo. But after 1840 companies containing both baritone and bass became more usual as the usefulness of the distinction between them became more widely appreciated in Italy.

27 Z. no. 171, dated 21 July 1835, p. 379.

28 Consul's reply to Donizetti's letter of 24 September 1835 is dated 12 October 1835, and is in the Conservatorio di San Pietro a Majella.

29 A correlation of the text of Coppola's *Gli illinesi* with the earlier versions used by Basili and Strepponi would provide helpful evidence of Romani's activity at this stage of his career.

30 With *Fausta* and the prime of *Lucrezia Borgia* and *Gemma di Vergy*.

31 Maria Malibran (1808–36), mezzo-soprano, was the daughter of the Spanish tenor Manuel Garcia, who was her teacher. She made her debut as Rosina in *Il barbiere* in London in 1825. Later that year she accompanied her family to New York, where she was the prima donna of the first company to perform opera in Italian in the United States, and where she married a New Orleans businessman named Malibran, from whom she soon separated. Upon her return to Europe she initiated the enormously successful phase of her career with her debut at the Théâtre-Italien on 14 January 1828. In 1830 she became the mistress of

Charles de Bériot, a Belgian violinist, by whom she had a son before she was able to marry him in 1836 on the granting of her divorce from Malibran. She first appeared in Italy in 1832, where her brilliant singing and piquant personality aroused unbounded enthusiasm. She sang in Naples from mid-November 1833 until mid-March 1834, moving next to Bologna and then to Milan, where she made her debut at La Scala on 15 May 1835. Engagements followed at Sinigaglia, Lucca, Milan, Naples, Venice, London, and again Milan, where she appeared once more at La Scala between 12 September 1835 and 20 March 1836; it was during this stay that she created the role of Maria Stuarda. In April 1836 she was thrown from her horse and when she died the following September it was said to be as the result of her injuries.

Malibran was an extraordinarily accomplished vocalist whose basically recalcitrant voice was wrought up by her father until its range extended from contralto low D to D above the staff, a range of three octaves. As an actress when she was in a good mood or when she felt deeply challenged she was capable of moving an audience profoundly; but when she was out of sorts, for she seems to have been a creature of whims, she would produce little or no effect. Her younger sister was the famous contralto Pauline Viardot (1821–1910).

32 Cottrau, *Lettres d'un mélomane*, p. 30. Malibran was obviously only interested in *Maria Stuarda* in its original form, not the *rifacimento* as *Buondelmonte*.

33 Z. no. 180, dated 20 October 1835, p. 388.

34 In 1836 Donizetti put together a third memorial for Bellini, *Sinfonia per orchestra sopra motivi di V. Bellini*. The autograph of this work is in the Bibliothèque Nationale, Paris.

35 Z. no. 180, p. 388.

36 The Requiem for Bellini remained unpublished and unperformed until 1870, when Lucca brought out a vocal score with organ, and the work was sung at Santa Maria Maggiore, Bergamo, under Alessandro Nini. Its only other recorded nineteenth-century performance, and apparently an unsatisfactory one, was in 1875 as part of the ceremonies accompanying the transferral of the remains of Mayr and Donizetti to Santa Maria Maggiore, Bergamo. Gavazzeni revived it in 1948 to mark the centenary of Donizetti's death. Since then it has become recognized as one of the most important of Donizetti's non-operatic works. A facsimile of the Lucca score has been issued by Egret House, London (1974). The manuscript of the Requiem is in the Conservatorio di San Pietro a Majella, Naples.

37 Z. no. 164, p. 372. Donizetti offered to write a new overture for *Maria Stuarda* because the overture performed with *Buondelmonte* in Naples was one the Milanese public had already heard (see Z. no. 174, dated 5 September 1835, p. 383). It seems likely that Donizetti decided to help justify the extra fee he was receiving for the adaptation of *Maria Stuarda* into *Buondelmonte* by providing a 'new' overture, but because he had to do the job hastily he borrowed an overture from one of his recent operas that had not yet been given in Naples.

38 It was to effect a similar change of text that the Neapolitan censors had summoned Bardari to a meeting on 4 September 1834. According to

Verzino (*Le opere di Donizetti,* p. 159), the Milanese censors approved the libretto of *Maria Stuarda* on 12 November 1835.

39 Actually the contract for *Maria Stuarda* at La Scala was signed after the rehearsals had begun. The signatures were affixed to it on 16 December 1835, apparently confirming an already existing verbal agreement. It specifies that the opera was to be ready to go on during the first days of the season and not later than 4 January 1836, that Donizetti would direct rehearsals, that he would adjust his score and add an overture to it, and for these labors he would receive 250 *bavare.* The original contract was in the mysterious Visconti archives, to which Verzino refers so often and whose whereabouts are unknown, but it is reprinted in Verzino, *Le opere di Donizetti,* pp. 160–1, and in the *Donizetti Society Journal,* 3 (1977), 212.

40 Z. no. 169, dated 8 July 1835, p. 377.

41 Z. no. 183, dated 29 October 1835, p. 390; Z. no. 187, undated but written shortly after 9 December 1835, p. 392; Z. no. 189, dated 28 December 1835, pp. 393–4.

42 The contract for *Maria Stuarda* lists the cast, but after the names of the characters Elisabetta and Anna (Maria's confidante) no names of singers appear.

43 *I puritani* was also given at Palermo on the night of 26 December 1835, under the title *Elvira e Arturo.*

44 The manuscript of the 'Malibran' version of *I puritani,* partly autograph, is in the Museo Belliniano, Catania.

45 After further reflection, I feel I somewhat overstated the case in an article on *Maria Stuarda* I wrote for *About the House* (vol. 5, no. 4, (1977), p. 21), where I stated that Donizetti 'deliberately hoodwinked' the censors. I think now that the idea of performing the uncensored text probably originated with Malibran and is consistent with what we know of her capricious, devil-may-care character; but Donizetti was undeniably an accessory to Malibran's defiance of authority.

46 Z. no. 190, dated 3 January 1836, p. 394.

47 Pietro Cominazzi, 'Sorsa attraverso le opere musicali di Gaetano Donizetti: Reminiscenze', *La fama,* no. 38 (21 September 1875), 150.

48 Z. no. 199, dated '8 or 9 March' 1836, p. 400. I am indebted to Jeremy Commons for many discussions about the events surrounding the Milanese *prima* of *Maria Stuarda.* The dates of the six performances are derived from the *Gazzetta privilegiata di Milano.* Since it was published by the authorities, that newspaper did not allude to the violation of the censorship or to the banning of further performances; it merely recorded that Malibran on 16 January began a series of performances of *La sonnambula.* Her other roles at La Scala that season were Romeo in Bellini's *I Capuleti* and the title character in Vaccai's *Giovanna Gray.*

49 *Gianni di Parigi,* composed in 1831, had a belated and unauthorized *prima* at La Scala on 10 September 1839. It was given as the third opera during the fall season, a far less important position than the opening night of the Carnival season. During the years between the banning of *Maria Stuarda* and the *prima* of *Maria Padilla,* other operas by Donizetti, which had been introduced elsewhere, continued to be performed regularly at La Scala.

50 See Jeremy Commons, Patric Schmid and Don White, '19th Century

Performances of *Maria Stuarda*', *Donizetti Society Journal*, 3 (1977), 217–42.

51 Z. no. 235, dated 13 May 1837, pp. 427–8.

52 Z. no. 185, dated 12 November 1835, p. 391.

53 Donizetti's reference here illustrates the confusion that remained until the term 'baritone' came into general usage, about 1850. Salvatori, who would sing the title role of Belisario, was, in fact, a baritone. The role of Giustiniano, for which Donizetti needed 'an excellent second bass' is a genuine bass part. Although Donizetti assigned no arias to Giustiniano, the character sings imposing recitatives and important parts in ensembles, and he was anxious to have a singer with the vocal presence to make a creditable emperor on stage.

54 *S.d.*1, no. 38, pp. 33–4.

55 Pietro Beltrame wrote the libretto for *Ida della Torre*, music by Alessandro Nini, performed at La Scala in April 1838, and that for Mazzucato's *La fidanzata di Lammermoor* (Padua, 1834).

56 Cammarano had written *Belisario* at least a few years earlier, in the hopes of persuading Barbaja to engage him as a house librettist. What Donizetti means in this letter is that Cammarano had begun revising his existing text to the composer's satisfaction. Cammarano's autograph with marginal annotations by Donizetti is in the Conservatorio di San Pietro a Majella, Naples. In his preface to the first edition of the *Belisario* libretto (Venice, 1836), Cammarano states that his work is based upon Luigi Marchionni's Italian adaptation of Franz Ignaz Holbein's play *Belisario*; in fact the original of Marchionni's work is Eduard von Schenk's *Belisarius* (Munich, 1820).

57 Z. no. 181, p. 389.

58 Antonio Poggi (1808–75), a tenor, made his debut in 1827, and he, Salvi and Ivanoff came to be recognized as the direct *epigoni* of Rubini. Poggi appeared in the first casts of both *Tasso* and *Pia de' Tolomei*. In 1840 he married Erminia Frezzolini, with whom he sang in the *prima* of Verdi's *Giovanna d'Arco* (Milan, 1845), but shortly afterward they separated and Poggi retired from the stage. Tradition has it that he was jealous of Verdi's attentions to his wife.

59 The season opened with an opera by Granara, entitled *Giovanna di Napoli*, and a ballet, *Gismonda*, choreographed by Antonio Cortesi.

60 Celestino Salvatori (sometimes spelled Salvadori) (dates unknown) was a baritone. Although he was first associated with Donizetti at the *prima* of *Il borgomastro*, he had the success of his career with Belisario, a role he created and one in which Donizetti sincerely admired him. One of the outstanding baritones of the 1830s, ill-health plagued him from 1837, when he was forced to withdraw from the *prima* of *Pia*; he was past his prime when he went to London in 1851 and was not allowed to fulfill his contract.

61 *S.d.*1, no. 40, dated 14 January 1836, pp. 34–5.

62 See *S.d.*1, no. 41, dated 5 February 1836, p. 35, to Ricordi.

63 Two years later when Mercadante, whom Lanari was paying 6000 francs for a new opera, discovered that Donizetti was receiving 10,000 francs for *Maria de Rudenz*, he put pressure on the impresario and succeeded in getting his fee raised so that it equaled Donizetti's.

64 *S.d.*1, no. 41, p. 35.

65 *S.d.*1, no. 41, p. 35.

66 The total of performances of *Belisario* that first season would have been even greater had not the *prima* taken place when the season was already well advanced.

67 It is not clear exactly when Gaetano heard about Virginia's miscarriage, but he mentions it in a letter to Giampieri written from Livorno on 18 February 1836, while he was in transit from Genoa to Civitavecchia. (*S.d.*1, no. 42, p. 36.)

68 Z. no. 197, dated 5 March 1836, p. 399.

69 'I announce to you that our royal theaters are still closed and that la Scholz [Schütz] is singing at the Nuovo; now the public applauds her, now they whistle her to death and now they ignore her.' (Z. no. 205, dated 19 April 1836, p. 407, to the publisher Pacini.) Zavadini mistranscribed the name of Amalia Schütz as 'Scholz'.

70 Z. no. 204, p. 406. In this letter Donizetti also tells Ricordi that he is awaiting material for *Belisario* and *Gemma* in anticipation of their first local performances at the San Carlo. Because of the crisis in the management, both operas had to wait until the following year, 1837, to be given on that stage.

71 On 31 May 1836 Donizetti informed Lanari that 'Barbaja is finally the impresario (*S.d.*1, no. 44, p. 37). To judge by the not always reliable F. de Filippis and R. Arnese, *Cronache del Teatro di San Carlo*, (2 vols., Naples, 1961), vol. 1, p. 72, Barbaja had managed to open the San Carlo on 19 May with *Il furioso*, sung by Adelaide Toldi and Ronconi. This was not the Neapolitan *prima* of *Il furioso*, for it had been given earlier at the Nuovo.

72 Cottrau, *Lettres d'un mélomane*, p. 44.

73 Adolphe Adam, *Derniers souvenirs d'un musicien* (Paris, 1859), p. 307.

74 On 4 June 1836, three days after the *prima* of *Il campanello*, Cottrau sent his brother in Paris two printed sections of the score (see *Lettres d'un mélomane*, p. 44).

75 The *prima* of *Il campanello* took place on 1 June, not 7 June 1836 as many reference works have it.

76 For Ronconi, Donizetti transposed the Gondolier's barcarolle from Act 2 of *Marin Faliero* (which the tenor Ivanoff had sung with widely acknowledged finesse in Paris and London the year before), inserting it into the episode in which Enrico appears disguised as a singer. Donizetti was thus able to make use of an effective item from a score that the Neapolitan censors would not pass in the foreseeable future. Indeed, *Marin Faliero* was not given in Naples until 8 April 1848, the day of Donizetti's death.

77 Z. no. 216, undated (see note 87 below) p. 414.

78 Z. no. 218, p. 416.

79. Adam's *Le chalet*, first performed at the Opéra-Comique on 25 September 1834, proved that composer's first great success, having 1400 performances at that theater during the nineteenth century. The French libretto is, in turn, an adaptation of Goethe's Singspiel text, *Jery und Bätely*. Donizetti's appropriation of Adam's subject would

count against him with Parisian critics at the time of *La fille du régiment.*

80 The following year Donizetti expanded the single act of *Betly* into two by adding a finale to Act 1 and an *introduzione* to Act 2, a matter of some twenty-two pages added to the piano-vocal score. Up to now it has been stated everywhere that the two-act *Betly* was first performed at the Teatro Carolino, Palermo, on 29 October 1837, but this seems open to serious question as is shown by statements in letters written by Cottrau and by Donizetti himself. On 26 August 1837 Cottrau informed his brother in Paris: 'Shortly they will give *Betly* in two acts; soon I shall send you the new pieces.' (*Lettres d'un mélomane*, p. 52.) On 23 September 1837 Gaetano wrote to Toto (Z. no. 264, p. 450): 'I am rehearsing *Betly*'; and indeed *Betly* was revived at the Teatro del Fondo on 29 September. If the expansion of the score was far enough advanced in late August for Cottrau to promise to send his brother the printed music 'soon', there is every likelihood that the new version was available for the Naples performance; moreover, in view of Donizetti's working habits, it seems more plausible that he would rehearse and adjust his new music to *Betly* himself rather than send it off to Palermo for someone else to supervise.

81 Corrected date supplied by John Black (letter to the author, 1 February 1981).

82 See Cottrau, *Lettres d'un mélomane*, p. 47.

83 Z. no. 219, undated, p. 417.

84 Nineteenth-century treatments of this subject mostly stem originally from de Belloy's *Le siège de Calais* (Paris, 1765). An important intermediary between this and Cammarano's libretto for *L'assedio di Calais* was another French play, by M. Hubert (pseudonym of Philippe-Jacques Laroche), entitled *Eustache de St Pierre, ou Le siège de Calais,* a spectacular historical melodrama in three acts, first performed at the Ambigu-Comique, Paris, on 11 April 1822. Hubert's play was almost certainly the source for Luigi Marchionni's *L'assedio di Calais* (also performed as *Edoardo III*); which from the mid-1820s was a prominent feature in his repertory at the Teatro dei Fiorentini at Naples, and which was the means of transmitting the subject to Luigi Henry who used it for his ballet of the same title (Naples, 1828).

85 The scenario and the draft are both at the Conservatorio di San Pietro a Majella, Naples. The draft runs to twenty-nine pages and ends with Cammarano's note: 'End of the drama that is not yet finished.'

86 Z. no. 225, dated 22 November 1836, p. 421, to Ricordi.

87 Z. no. 216, undated, p. 414. Zavadini suggests July 1836 as a plausible date, basing his conjecture upon the reference to Coppola's *La festa della rosa*, with text by Ferretti, which Donizetti had heard 'has made a furore' in Vienna. *La festa della rosa* was first given at the Kärntnertortheater on 29 June 1836.

88 Paul-Bernard Barroilhet (1805–71) was an important French baritone, who sang in Italy, most notably at Naples, during the late 1830s before returning to Paris and making his debut at the Opéra in the premiere of *La favorite*. After his retirement in the 1850s he taught at the Conservatoire until his death. See Jean-Louis Tamvaco, 'Paul-Bernard Barroilhet', *Donizetti Society Journal* 2 (1975), 131–42.

89 Almerinda Manzocchi (?1804–69) was a mezzo-soprano. Before she took the *musico* role of Aurelio in *L'assedio di Calais* she had sung in the first casts of *Elvida* and *Il borgomastro*. For her Bellini wrote his song *Guarda che bianca luna*. Handsome, and an appealing actress, she was one of the candidates proposed as a second wife for Donizetti. Her career lasted from about 1825 to 1843, when she married and settled in Palermo; she died there of cholera. Her sister Eloisa had a brief career as a *comprimaria* in the Neapolitan theaters.

90 In January 1833 Marianna Franceschini had sung the *seconda donna* role of Marcella in the Roman *prima* of *Il furioso*. Her engagement for *L'assedio di Calais* did not materialize, the role intended for her being sung by Caterina Barili-Patti (mother of the famous Adelina).

91 Z. no. 216, p. 414.

92 The divertissement for *L'assedio di Calais* would consist of four dances related to some extent to the action of the opera, and therefore they are described in the original libretto as 'balli analoghi'. Donizetti's use of these dances was exceptional for that period in Italy; it was then customary in the principal theaters to present an opera and one or sometimes even two ballets, each with its own story line. According to the original libretto only two of the four dances were composed by Donizetti. These were the first, the 'Danza dei prigionieri scozzesi', and the fourth, the 'Danza militare'. The music of the second and third dances is by Antonio Vaccari; there is a note in the libretto that the third, a 'Passo d'assieme', was 'expressly' composed by Vaccari, suggesting that the music for the second, a 'Passo a quattro', had originally been used in some other context. The choreography for the first dance was designed by Luigi Henry, for the rest, by Salvatore Taglioni. By 1837 Donizetti had come to feel that the dancing slowed down the action of the opera too much and considered eliminating the ballet.

93 The 1828 ballet of *L'assedio di Calais* was danced to music composed by Cesare Pugni. Earlier, on 15 February 1827, Henry's ballet had begun a run of 27 performances at La Scala, where it was performed as *Edoardo III*. For this La Scala production parts of the score were taken 'from the best productions of Mozart, Rossini, and Mayerbeer [*sic*]'; the balance of it composed by Pugni.

L'assedio di Calais* was not the first of the subjects composed by Donizetti that had previously been treated as a ballet. At the San Carlo in 1824–5 there was danced an *Elisabetta al castello di Kenilworth*; in 1825–6 an *Otto mesi in due ore*; in 1831–2 a *Rosemonda*. A detailed study of the relationship between ballet plots and opera subjects during the first half of the nineteenth century should prove very illuminating.

94 The previous year he had thought of using a *musico* in *Gli illinesi* for Turin, but this was to take what seemed to him the best advantage of the singers available. In the opera that followed *L'assedio*, *Pia de' Tolomei*, Donizetti wrote the role of Pia's warrior brother for a contralto, but only because he was under pressure from both Lanari and the administration of the Fenice to use a second female singer and there was no second important female role in the plot of *Pia*, which from the start had been designed as a vehicle for Fanny Persiani. The only roles Donizetti composed subsequently for contraltos *en travesti* were Pierotto in *Linda di Chamounix*, and Gondì, the gallant in *Maria di Rohan*, but both these

parts belong rather to the adolescent *musichetto* tradition (that of Cherubino, Urbain in *Les Huguenots,* Siébel in *Faust* and Oscar in *Un ballo in maschera*) rather than to the heroic *musico* type. By the time of *L'assedio di Calais,* Donizetti reverted to the *musico* vocal type not from choice, but only when the personnel at hand forced him to.

95 Z. no. 219, undated, p. 417. The italics are Donizetti's. He meant, of course, without a leading tenor; there are several smaller tenor parts in the opera.

96 6 July was the queen-mother's birthday, traditional date for a royal gala.

97 *S.d.*1, no. 47, dated 21 May 1837, p. 40.

98 Umberto Manferrari, *Dizionario delle opere melodrammatiche* (3 vols., Florence, n.d.), vol. 1, pp. 321–5, gives a very unreliable listing of performances of Donizetti's operas. Among them he mentions a *rifacimento* of *L'assedio di Calais* that was performed at the Imperial Theater, St Petersburg, in 1851, but a glance at the list of operas actually performed there that season makes it almost certain that the work in question is not Donizetti's opera, but Rossini's *L'assedio di Corinto.*

99 *S.d.*1, no. 47, p. 40. Donizetti is here implying that Duprez might recreate his role of Edgardo in *Lucia di Lammermoor* at the Opéra.

100 Barbaja's letter contains an understandable slip; it refers to Donizetti's newest opera as *L'assedio di Corinto,* confusing it with the title of Rossini's widely performed work.

101 Z. no. 233, p. 420.

102 Bourbon court etiquette forbade applause at a royal gala.

103 Z. no. 225, p. 421.

104 Barbaja's letter to Prince di Ruffano is to be found in the Archivio di Stato, Naples, under Teatri: Fascio 39. Jeremy Commons drew my attention to these illuminating documents.

105 Much of the Lanari–Donizetti correspondence of the years 1836–8 has been edited by Commons and published in *Studi donizettiani,* 3 (1978), 9–74, which contains forty-five previously unpublished letters. The letters of Lanari, along with many other papers concerning his enterprises, are in the Biblioteca Nazionale Centrale, Florence, and a few are to be found in the Conservatorio di San Pietro a Majella, Naples.

106 *S.d.*1, no. 44, p. 37.

107 The ultimate source of the *Pia* story is a brief passage at the close of Canto V of Dante's *Purgatorio.*

108 Pietro Romani (1791–1877) is dimly remembered today as the composer of an aria, 'Manca un foglio', that up to the days of World War II was customarily substituted for the more difficult aria Rossini composed for Dr Bartolo in Act 1 scene ii of *Il barbiere di Siviglia.*

109 In Marenco's play Pia's brother is not seen, but he is impersonated by a hireling of Ugo (Ghino), who appears only in an interview contrived to arouse the jealousy of Pia's husband. Cammarano's change here is a decided improvement.

110 Z. no. 214, p. 413.

111 Alessandro Luzio, ed., *Carteggi verdiani* (4 vols., Rome, 1935–47), vol. 4, p. 147.

112 As both Salvatori and Ronconi were baritones, this was more helpful news than Lanari's earlier announcement (5 May) that the choice for the role of Nello was between Ignazio Marini, a true bass, or Filippo Coletti,

a baritone. Donizetti could have done little with Nello's music until he knew the range of the singer he was writing for. Donizetti much preferred to change individual notes (*punteggiare*) rather than transpose whole numbers: 'I firmly believe it is a *horror*', and the italics are Donizetti's, 'when the orchestra is transposed down.' (Z. no. 220, undated but assigned to September 1836, p. 418.) His abhorrence of transposition reflects the fact that wind instruments capable of playing a chromatic scale were not yet in use in Italian opera houses.

113 On 21 May 1836 Donizetti had written to Lanari (Z. no. 210, p. 410) expressing his misgivings about *Lucia* with Persiani. He was worried that the public, being quick to assume that she preferred to sing in her husband's operas rather than those by other composers, would interpret any vocal problems she might have as reflecting this preference. Further, he still remembered the row she had caused at Naples at the time of the *prima* because *Lucia* ends with the tenor's tomb scene rather than the heroine's mad scene (an objection that was later shared by Nellie Melba.)

114 These details of *Pia's* reception are condensed from Verzino's transcription of an undated review that had appeared in the *Gazzetta di Venezia* (see Verzino, *Le opere di Donizetti*, p. 198).

115 Z. no. 233, dated 20 February 1837, p. 426.

116 Verzino, *Le opere di Donizetti*, p. 198.

117 Cammarano's new text for the finale to Act 1 of *Pia* is printed in *Studi donizettiani*, 1 (1962), 146–51.

118 In my earlier book on Donizetti I erroneously wrote that for Sinigaglia Donizetti converted Rodrigo into a tenor part. Tom Kaufman has very helpfully supplied me with the correct date and cast for the Sinigaglia *Pia* (letter to the author, 10 July 1978).

119 Eugenia Tadolini, née Savonari (*c.* 1809–?), made her debut as a soprano in Florence in 1828. By 1830 she had married the Bolognese composer and singing-teacher Giovanni Tadolini (?1785–1872) with whom she had settled in Paris; she sang at the Théâtre-Italien but the competition of Pasta and Malibran kept her in the background. By 1833, separated from her husband (whom she divorced in 1834), she had returned to Italy, and she sang that year at the Fenice and La Scala. Before long she was much in demand and in 1840 she opened the Carnival season at La Scala in Mercadante's *Il bravo*. In a letter to Lanari (4 April 1840, quoted in Walker, *The Man Verdi*, p. 73) Strepponi spoke of Tadolini as 'one of the greatest talents we possess'. Throughout the 1840s she was greatly sought after and made the San Carlo, La Scala and the Kärntnertor the chief centers of her activity. In 1848 she sang at Her Majesty's Theatre, making her debut as Donizetti's Linda, but she failed to establish herself with the London public because of the competition of the phenomenally successful Jenny Lind; Chorley (*Thirty Years' Musical Recollections*, p. 215) described her as 'no longer in the bloom of her talent', and as 'ill-dressed' in the role of Linda. After 1851 she drops out of sight, and the circumstances and date of her death are unknown. Besides the role of Linda, in which she won his whole-hearted approval, Donizetti wrote for Tadolini that of Maria di Rohan; her other parts ranged from Rossini's Armida to Verdi's Alzira.

120 Napoleone Moriani (?1808–78) was born in Florence. He made his

debut in Pavia in 1833; by 1838 he was the leading singing-actor among tenors for tragic Romantic roles. Although he sang in only two *prime of* Donizetti operas, *Maria de Rudenz* and *Linda*, his whole career was much taken up with Donizetti's works, for he sang in *Anna Bolena, Belisario, Marin Faliero, Lucia, Pia, Lucrezia Borgia* (in which he was the first tenor to sing the *finale nuovo*) and *Roberto Devereux*. Known as 'the tenor of the beautiful death scenes', Moriani acted in a style that might be regarded as excessive today. In the tomb scene from *Lucia* his 'sighs, laments, contortions, grasping his throat, falling and re-falling, his convulsive and labored effort to get up again' moved Roman audiences to delirium in 1838 (see the article on Moriani in F. d'Amico, ed., *Enciclopedia dello spettacolo* (11 vols., Rome, 1954–62). Yet when Moriani sang at Dresden in 1843, in performances conducted by Wagner, the composer, who had derided Rubini in Paris, would put down his baton and join in the applause.

Moriani sang Ghino in *Pia* at Sinigaglia, and the following year in Rome, with Strepponi as Pia. They sang these roles again in June 1839 at La Scala, but the attractions of the work could lure the Milanese to only three performances. (Frank Walker has suggested that Moriani may have been the father of Strepponi's illegitimate children (*The Man Verdi* (London, 1962), pp. 48–95.)

121 Rosina Mazzarelli could not appear in the Sinigaglia *Pia* because she was then appearing with another of Lanari's troupes at Livorno.
122 Giuseppina Strepponi (1815–97), a soprano, launched her career in 1835 and continued to sing until 1849 though her voice decline was marked as early as 1842; even in 1841 when she created Adelia her voice was not what it had been when she first excited the Romans with her performances of Lucia and Pia in 1838. Her association with Verdi dates from 1839, when she assisted him in getting his first opera, *Oberto*, performed; in 1842 she sang Abigaille in the *prima* of his *Nabucco*. They were finally married in 1859. Her correspondence shows her to have been a woman of remarkable grace and sagacity.
123 The autograph of Donizetti's *sinfonia* for the cantata *In morte di Maria F. Malibran* is in the Ricordi Archives, Milan.
124 Cambiasi, *La Scala 1778–1889*, p. 279, footnote 4.
125 Z. no. 234, undated (arrived Rome 2 May 1837), p. 427.
126 Niccolò Zingarelli (1752–1837) composed at least thirty-two operas, from *I quattro pazzi* (Naples, 1771), written while he was still a student, to *Berenice* (Rome, 1811). His greatest success was an opera seria, *Romeo e Giulietta* (Milan, 1796). Before his tenure at the Naples Conservatory, Zingarelli had served as *maestro di cappella* first at Loreto and later at the Sistine Chapel. A composer of considerable reputation at the turn of the century, he had had the embittering experience of having outlived his fame.
127 *La scuola musicale di Napoli*, vol. 4, p. 46.
128 The Neapolitan school, principally associated with opera, both seria and buffa, exercised a dominant influence on European musical life during the eighteenth century, and among its members were such composers as Alessandro Scarlatti, Porpora, Vinci, Leo, Pergolesi, Jommelli, Traetta, Anfossi, Piccinni, Paisiello, Cimarosa and Spontini; of these

only Scarlatti and Piccinni had not been educated in one of the Neapolitan conservatories.

129 According to Zavadini (*Donizetti: Vita – Musica – Epistolario*, p. 189), the autograph for this Requiem Mass for Zingarelli is lost. Donizetti was prevented from conducting the work by the death of his wife.

130 Cambiasi, *La Scala: 1778–1889*, pp. 276–7.

131 Z. no. 237, p. 429.

132 S.d.3, p. 48.

133 Jeremy Commons informs me (letter to the author, 14 July 1976) that *Eleonora di Gujenna* was one of the titles on Barbaja's list, dated 27 June 1837, of works submitted for approval to the Neapolitan authorities and censors. Barbaja intended *Eleonora* to serve for the Neapolitan debut of Adelina Spech, singing with her husband Salvi, who had made his local debut in *Betly*. The great cholera epidemic of that year crippled the local theaters, and Spech's debut at the San Carlo was delayed until 10 November 1838 – after Donizetti's departure for Paris; she appeared in Mercadante's *Il giuramento*, singing opposite Adolphe Nourrit, who was making his Italian debut on that occasion.

134 These ten pieces from *Eleonora di Gujenna* were published (undated) by Bernard Latte of Paris. The one new number is an aria–finale for Eleonora, 'Tu spergiuro disumano'.

135 See *S.D.* 1, no. 63, dated 19 September 1838, p. 54.

136 Z. no. 240, p. 431. In a postscript to this letter Donizetti reacts to the news that in Bergamo, for the first time, one of his operas (*Belisario*) was to be produced; it was planned for the 1837 summer season at the Teatro Riccardi (now the Donizetti). He asks in Latin: 'Popule, quid feci tibi?' (People, what did I do to you?)

137 Z. no. 242, dated 28 June 1837, p. 432.

138 Z. no. 243, undated but assigned to end of June 1837, p. 433.

139 Ferdinando II had married Maria Theresa, an Austrian archduchess, on 9 January 1837 (his first wife, Maria Cristina, having died on 31 January 1836, two weeks after giving birth to a son).

140 Writing to Spadaro on 26 August 1837, Donizetti advises: 'Tell Donna Teresina [Spadaro's wife] not to fear for her delivery, but rather to fear taking baths when she might be exposed to measles, for in that fashion I have lost everything.' (Z. no. 252, p. 441.)

141 This discussion of possible causes of Virginia's death is the result of views exchanged with Professor Trethowan, of the Department of Psychiatry at the University of Birmingham.

142 Gaetano's grief-stricken letters to Toto cover the period 5 August – 7 October 1837 and are printed as Z. nos. 246, 248, 250, 251, 253–9, 261–8. Toto's side of the correspondence, dated 10 August – 12 October 1837, appears as Z. nos. A9–19, pp. 869–79. Gaetano's sense of loss is revealed in many allusions in his later correspondence, especially in letters written on the anniversaries of his wife's demise.

143 S.D. 1, no. 48, pp. 41–2.

144 Donizetti had assumed the position of musical director of the royal theaters of Naples in 1829 and he would continue to hold it. At the head of Z. no. 245, (p. 435) Donizetti wrote: 'Copy of the letter written to free myself from duties as director of music, to which there was no answer.'

145 The cantata was *La preghiera d'un popolo*. It should be remembered that this cantata was performed on 31 July 1837, the day following Virginia Donizetti's death. The cantata was sung by Adelaide Toldi and the contralto Eloisa Buccini; the main work of that evening was Mercadante's *Caritea, regina di Spagna*.
146 Z. no. 245, p. 435.
147 Z. no. 256, p. 444.
148 Z. no. 258, p. 445.
149 Z. no. 264, p. 450.
150 Corrected date supplied by John Black (letter to the author, 1 February 1981).
151 Z. no. 270, p. 454. Tito Ricordi (1811–88) was the son of Giovanni and had been associated with the firm from the age of fourteen. He took over the directorship when Giovanni died in 1853 and in turn handed it on, apparently some time before his death, to his son Giulio. It is not known why Donizetti addressed this letter to Tito and not to Giovanni Ricordi.
152 *S.D.* 1, no. 50, dated 19 January 1838, p. 43.
153 Chorley, *Thirty Years' Musical Recollections*, p. 90.
154 *S.d.* 3, dated 30 August 1837, p. 57, from Lanari to Donizetti.
155 Z. no. 262, p. 448. Besides the unidentifiable subject referred to here by Donizetti, which Toto had suggested (in a letter now lost), Toto had also sent him an Italian translation of Bulwer-Lytton's *Rienzi*; Donizetti read it straight through, but decided against it, not least because he wanted a subject tailored for Ungher, Moriani and Ronconi. Yet it is an intriguing thought that Donizetti considered this novel, which five years later provided Wagner with the plot of his first operatic success.
156 In a letter dated 21 November 1834 Bellini cites *Un duel* as a subject he would like to compose for Naples the following year, as it is 'dramatic and would make a great effect' (*Bellini, epistolario*, no. CC, p. 478). Donizetti or Cammarano could easily have heard of Bellini's intention from Florimo or another of his circle. Oddly enough, in the same letter Bellini admits to being drawn to the plot of Auber's *Gustave III* (Paris, 1833) (Verdi used the same subject for *Un ballo in maschera*), but to conform with the Neapolitan censorship he would be willing to omit the detail of the royal assassination!
157 Z. no. 265, dated 26 September 1837, p. 450.
158 Although Donizetti here gives no clue about the difficulties Cammarano encountered with *Un duel*, one cannot help wondering if it did not have something to do with the mixture of 'comic and tragic aspects' Donizetti had mentioned to Toto on 19 September. Cammarano and Donizetti finally collaborated on this subject some six years later, and the resulting work, *Maria di Rohan*, is heavily tragic; the only comic relief, provided by the courtier Gondì, has sinister overtones.
159 Z. no. 266, p. 451.
160 *La nonne sanglante*, by Anicet Bourgeois, Cuvelier and Mallian, was first acted at the Théâtre Porte-Saint-Martin, Paris, on 17 February 1835, their play being derived at several removes from M. G. Lewis's novel, *The Monk* (1795). *La nonne sanglante* was later reworked by Scribe and Delavigne to serve as a libretto for Gounod's opera of the same name (Paris, 1854).

161 Z. no. 268, dated 7 October 1837, p. 452.
162 *S.d.* 3, p. 62, from Lanari to Donizetti.
163 *S.d.* 3, dated 16 October 1837, p. 64, from Berti to Lanari.
164 *S.d.* 3, dated 31 October 1837, p. 65, from Lanari to Donizetti.
165 Z. no. 268, p. 453.
166 Z. no. 282, p. 463.
167 For Donizetti's reaction to the fiasco of *Maria de Rudenz* at Venice see
    Z. no. 286, dated 7 March 1838, p. 466, where he tells Toto: 'The letter
    from Bologna was an (anonymous) satire directed against me for the
    fiasco at Venice. Observe in what times we live!'
168 Z. no. 287, dated 9 March 1838, p. 467.
169 Outside Italy *Maria de Rudenz* was staged at Barcelona, Lisbon,
    Alexandria, Rio de Janeiro and Buenos Aires.
170 Luzio, ed., *Carteggi verdiani*, vol. 4, p. 150.
171 Since the whereabouts of the autograph of *Maria de Rudenz* are un-
    known, the Opera Rara edition was based on copyists' manuscripts at
    the Fenice and the Milan Conservatory. It includes a tenor aria (inserted
    in Act 1) that Donizetti intended to give Moriani at Venice in February
    1838, but the first run was terminated before Moriani could sing it on
    stage. This London performance also added a chorus in Act 2 that
    Donizetti composed for the La Scala production of 10 October 1842.
172 Z. no. 247, p. 436.
173 Z. no. 250a, p. 438.
174 Z. no. 252, p. 441.
175 Z. no. 261, p. 447.
176 Z. no. 275, dated 14 November 1837, p. 457.
177 Z. no. 286, dated 7 March 1838, p. 466.
178 Z. no. 289, p. 468.
179 Z. no. 290, pp. 468–9. This letter was written on the first anniversary of
    Zingarelli's death, a date that prompted Donizetti to add a typically
    cryptic and ironical postscript: '5 May. Today. He is dead . . . We are
    alive – better or worse, for him or for us?'
180 Z. no. 298, p. 477.
181 Florimo, *La scuola musicale di Napoli e i suoi conservatorii*, vol. 2, p.
    46.
182 Mercadante was born at Altamura, near Bari, within the borders of the
    Kingdom of the Two Sicilies.
183 Z. no. 300, dated 27 June 1838, p. 478.
184 Cicconetti, *Vita di Gaetano Donizetti*, (Rome, 1864), p. 121.
185 I am grateful to John Allitt for calling this letter to my attention as it
    affords a more accurate clue than any of Donizetti's own corre-
    spondence as to the date on which he began work on *Poliuto* (undated
    letter to the author, 1977).
186 White, 'Donizetti and the Three Gabriellas'.
187 Z. no. 303, p. 480, to Vasselli.
188 Significantly, the first five numbers of the 1838 *Gabriella* are, with the
    exception of the prelude borrowed from *Maria de Rudenz*, all newly
    composed. Of the remaining ten numbers, most are borrowed from such
    sources as *Maria de Rudenz* and *Ugo* and the 1826 *Gabriella*; only two
    of them are new, a sign that the last two-thirds of the score was assem-

bled in considerable haste. In the booklet accompanying the Opera Rara recording of the 1838 *Gabriella* Don White has pointed out in detail the provenance of this music. See also White, 'Donizetti and the Three Gabriellas'.

189 Z. no. 291, pp. 469–70.

190 Donizetti does not mean that Goethe wrote the ballet, rather he is indicating the source of the subject. The ballet was choreographed by Salvatore Taglioni, the music supplied by Roberto Gallenberg and Mario Aspa, and it starred Fanny Cerrito. Donizetti is here repeating a rumor about the dismissals of the superintendents and the censors, and even though they were not in fact carried out, the rumor proves there was a great uproar over the ballet, which was prohibited from further performance. After such a disturbance the censors were likely to be more scrupulous than ever.

191 Z. no. 296, undated but certainly from June 1838, p. 474.

192 Z. no. 310, p. 485.

193 *S.d.* 1, no. 62, dated 7 September 1838, pp. 53–4.

194 Basadonna was the only one of these three who had not formed part of the intended cast for *Poliuto*. Nourrit made his San Carlo debut six weeks later as Viscardo in Mercadante's *Il giuramento* (14 November 1838) and later sang Pollione in *Norma* there. In a mood of acute depression Nourrit committed suicide at Naples on 8 March 1839 by throwing himself out a fourth-floor window of Barbaja's *palazzo* into the courtyard below.

195 This memorandum is published as Z. no. 311, pp. 486–7; appended to it is Benevento's professional opinion.

196 Z. no. 311, p. 486.

197 The opening of this memorandum states that before *Pia* was accepted as a substitute for *Poliuto*, Donizetti had suggested *Elisa Fosco* to take its place. *Elisa Fosco* is an unfamiliar title in the Donizetti canon, but it is that of a substitute libretto attached to the score of *Lucrezia Borgia*, which had not yet been given in Naples. But he discarded this suggestion, perhaps even before it had been forwarded, as he foresaw the possibility that it too might fall foul of the censorship. *Lucrezia Borgia* was not given at the San Carlo until 23 February 1848, and then with its original plot. The enactment of the constitution on 10 February 1848 had greatly eased the censorial strictness in Naples, and for that reason many works hitherto banned, such as *Lucrezia Borgia* and *Poliuto*, were performed that year.

5. 1838–1843: *Les martyrs* to *Dom Sébastien*

1 Charles Duponchel (?1795–1868) had become co-director of the Opéra with Léon Pillet in 1835, both of them serving as front men for the very wealthy Marquis Aguado, friend of Rossini and inveterate pursuer of ballerinas. According to Alphonse Royer: 'Duponchel was not a literary man, neither was he a composer or a man of the theater. He was an artist, an inventor of scenic effects.' (*Histoire de l'Opéra* (Paris, 1875), p. 184). Duponchel was the more influential partner in the early years of their co-directorship; later Pillet's influence came to dominate, until

Duponchel ceded his place in May 1842 for 105,000 francs. When Pillet retired in 1847, Duponchel returned with Nestor Roqueplan as co-director, but he was eased out of his position the following year.

Duponchel was a man of varied interests. He had been a goldsmith. Once he proposed portable wooden houses for factory workers. He wrote pamphlets in the public interest, among them one entitled *Nouveau système de latrines pour les grands établissements publics* (1858).

2 *S.d.* 1, no. 47, dated 21 May 1837, pp. 40–1.

3 François Castil-Blaze (1784–1857), that irrepressible meddler in other composers' music, based one of his many *pastiches* on *Anna Bolena*, but the resulting *Anne de Boulen* (Le Havre, 1835) was, of course, no evidence that Donizetti himself understood the nuances of setting French texts.

4 The vogue for *Lucia* at the Théâtre-Italien survived undiminished by the hiatus that followed the destruction by fire of the Salle Favart on 15 December 1837; the conflagration caused the death of Severini, one of the directors, and seriously injured Robert, his partner, as well as burning up all the costumes and sets belonging to the company. When the company recommenced activity in the Salle Ventadour on 30 January 1838, *Lucia* was back in the repertory as soon as new costumes and scenery could be prepared, and it continued with unabated success after the company moved again in July of that year, this time to the more convenient Odéon. (Whichever theater the company performed in was known as the 'Théâtre-Italien'.)

When the troupe moved on to London a few months after it had introduced *Lucia* to Paris, its success with that opera was repeated. Chorley says: 'A new singer had been added to the company, by whose agency a new composer was set in the place he has since maintained. The singer was Madame Persiani, the composer was Donizetti.' (*Thirty Years' Musical Recollections*, p. 97.)

5 See *S.d.* 1, no. 52, dated 24 February 1838, pp. 44–5.

6 The first act of Romani's libretto on the same subject as Scribe's *Le comte Julien* was rejected by Donizetti in 1835. Later on in this letter to Duprez, he explains why he has not yet read Scribe's text: '[It] arrived four days ago and is still on the mail steamer and cannot be obtained (damn! 26 francs duty from Marseilles to Naples).'

7 *S.d.* 1, no. 56, pp. 48–9.

8 Mario (Giovanni Marchese di Candia) (1810–83) first appeared on stage at the Opéra as Robert in Meyerbeer's *Robert le diable* on 30 November 1838. In 1840 he transferred to the Théâtre-Italien and in time came to be regarded as Rubini's replacement. In 1844 he married Giulia Grisi, after their previous marriages had been annulled. A great popular favorite, especially in England, Mario retired from the stage in 1867.

9 Nicholas-Prosper Levasseur (1791–1871) made his debut at the Opéra in 1813; then after a stint with the Théâtre-Italien (1819–27) he returned to the Opéra where he remained until 1853, creating Bertram (*Robert le diable*), Cardinal Brogni (*La juive*), Marcel (*Les Huguenots*), and Balthasar (*La favorite*). Notwithstanding the lapses of memory that plagued

his final years on the stage, he went on to teach at the Paris Conservatoire until 1870.

10 Cornélie Falcon (1812–97) was the first Rachel (*La juive*) and Valentine (*Les Huguenots*), but vocal difficulties caused her early retirement, in 1838. Her voice was a soprano with a restricted top range, and her name has been given to this sort of voice in France. Her efforts to extend her range upward led to her early vocal disintegration.

11 Z. no. 293, p. 471. The length of rehearsal time then customary at the Opéra must have sounded like leisurely heaven to Donizetti, who had long been inured to the two or three weeks usual in Italy at this period.

12 For the next two months during the summer of 1838 Donizetti was worried that his refusal of Scribe's first libretto had somehow compromised his contract with Duponchel. Accursi kept up a constant flow of inconclusive correspondence on the subject. Eventually, Donizetti was relieved to learn that the choice of libretto could be settled after his arrival in Paris.

13 Z. no. 316, dated 13 November 1838, p. 492. The italics are Donizetti's.

14 Z. no. 317, dated 10 January 1839, p. 493.

15 Z. no. 318, p. 494. Auber's opera was first given at the Opéra on 1 April 1839, and Halévy's on 6 January 1840; in between, three other works entered the repertory: Casimir Gide's ballet, *La tarentule* (24 June 1839), Henri de Ruolz's *La vendetta* (11 September 1839), and Mario Aurelio Marliani's *Xacarilla* (28 October 1839). Thus it would seem that Halévy had also postponed his turn. *Les martyrs* was the next new opera introduced at the Opéra after *Le drapier*.

16 Donizetti's triple repetition of 'felicità' directly imitates the thrice-repeated cadence conventional in Italian scores of the period.

fe - li - ci - tà, fe - li - ci - tà, fe - li - ci - tà.

17 In April 1839, Donizetti expected that his second opera at the chief theater of Paris would be *Le duc d'Albe;* but he left the opera not quite half complete at his death, having done little work on it since 1839. For a discussion of this incomplete work and its posthumous history see pp. 434–6.

18 Donizetti composed no new opera for the Théâtre-Italien in 1839, perhaps because when Louis Viardot resigned the directorship that fall the contracts he had in force were voided. The opera Donizetti had intended for this assignment might have been *Adelaide*, which he might have begun in 1834 and laid aside. It is known that Donizetti had the incomplete score of *Adelaide* with him in Paris, because he used parts of it in *L'ange de Nisida*, which he completed for the Théâtre de la Renaissance in the late fall of 1839.

19 Z. no. 319, dated 8 April 1839, pp. 494–5.

20 I use the term 'grand opera' to mean a work written for the Opéra in which ballet and spectacle play an important part; the most typical example is Meyerbeer's *Robert le diable*.

21 Z. no. 320, p. 495.
22 Z. no. 320, p. 496. Donizetti often teased Dolci about his rotundity.
23 At this period there were four state-supported theaters in Paris: the Opéra (or l'Académie Royale de Musique), the Théâtre-Français, the Opéra-Comique, and the Théâtre-Italien. The Théâtre de la Renaissance had, of course, to have a government license to operate.
24 *Dictionnaire de biographie française,* ed. Roman d'Amat (Paris, 1933–).
25 Albéric Second pays Royer and Vaëz an extravagant compliment in *Les petits mystères de l'Opéra* (Paris, 1844), pp. 54–5: 'One can no longer speak of Castor . . . of Pollux. Pollux and Castor have had their day. They are outdistanced, dethroned, overthrown and replaced by the translators of *Lucie* . . . they are perhaps the only two writers whose friendship has survived a continuing collaboration.'
26 Z. no. 326, pp. 500–1.
27 Flaubert refers to *Lucie* in *Madame Bovary,* Part II (1857), chapter 15, where Emma sees a performance at Rouen, in which the tenor, whom Flaubert calls Lagardy, is, to some extent, modeled upon Duprez.
28 *S.d.* 1, no. 69, p. 58.
29 Cambiasi, *La Scala: 1778–1889,* pp. 280–1.
30 Gossip had linked Juliette Bourgeois's name romantically with Donizetti's in late 1837, when she was appearing at the San Carlo as Giulietta Borghese. Donizetti denied the rumor that he was planning to marry her, or any of a number of other women, including the singers Eloisa Buccini and Almerinda Granchi, in a letter to Toto (Z. no. 276, dated 16 November 1837, p. 458).
31 Leopoldo was Tommaso Persico's brother.
32 Z. no. 328, pp. 502–3.
33 Z. no. 330, dated 6 December 1839, p. 505.
34 The new double aria for Duprez occurs in Act 3 scene i of *Les martyrs,* replacing the comparable arias composed for Nourrit in *Poliuto.* Nourrit could sing only up to A in his chest voice, and Donizetti had limited the tessitura of his music accordingly; Duprez was famous for his high C *de poitrine.*
35 François-Antoine Habeneck (1781–1849) had been made solo violinist at the Opéra in 1815; in 1821–4 he had been director of the theater, and after that he remained as *chef d'orchestre* until 1846. When Donizetti went to Paris in 1838, he carried with him a letter of introduction to Habeneck, written by Nourrit. In spite of criticism of him in certain feuilletons, especially and understandably those by Berlioz, Habeneck seems to have been a rigorous musician and an able conductor.

Contrary to the Italian custom of the day, whereby a composer conducted the first three performances of his new operas, or was at least present at the *cembalo,* at the Opéra a composer was not allowed to conduct the premieres of his works.
36 The plan to alternate rehearsals of *Le drapier* with those of *Les martyrs* was potentially feasible since only one of the principal singers was cast in both operas. *Le drapier* was first sung by Maria Dolores Nau, Annette Lebrun, Mario, Levasseur, Adolphe-Louis-Joseph Alizard and Jean-Étienne Massol. Only Massol also appeared in *Les martyrs,* along with Julie Dorus-Gras, Duprez and Prosper Dérivis.

37 Scribe had written the libretto to *Le drapier*.
38 The contract is in the Bibliothèque de l'Opéra, Paris. It contains some interesting provisions; for example: the first twenty performances were to form an uninterrupted run, unless three performances brought in less than 3000 francs; and Joly agreed not to perform any other new opera until the receipts of five consecutive performances fell below 10,000 francs total. Most curious of all, the contract does not specify how much Donizetti was to receive for the score, suggesting that this was a second agreement intended primarily to ensure the conditions under which *L'ange de Nisida* would be performed.
39 Although Donizetti here speaks of *L'ange* as being 'in three acts', it is perfectly clear both from the autograph libretto and from Donizetti's contract with Joly for the opera, dated 5 January 1840, that it was 'en quatre parties'. That Donizetti should here refer to it as having three acts (which has caused all writers on this subject to follow that description) means that he was probably thinking of the first two acts as two scenes of a single long act.
40 Z. no. 337, p. 513.
41 Another of Joly's operations, though its influence cannot be exactly assessed, must have contributed considerably to the fate of *L'ange de Nisida*. On 27 December 1839 Joly brought out at the Renaissance, evidently with success, a four-act opera entitled *La chaste Suzanne*, composed by Hippolyte Monpou. Charles Duponchel, director of the Opéra, was so angered by Joly's poaching on the area traditionally reserved for his state-subvented theater that about the middle of January 1840 he sought legal action against him; he demanded that *La chaste Suzanne* should be performed only at the Opéra, that 50,000 francs should be paid as damages for infringement of his repertory, and that, in addition, a fine of 2000 francs should be levied for each performance of the work given at the Renaissance in defiance of an order of restraint. The tribunal convoked by the Opéra declared itself incompetent to render judgment, and *La chaste Suzanne* continued its run at the Renaissance. (See L.-Henry Lecomte, *Histoire des Théâtres de Paris: La Renaissance (1838–41, 1868, 1873–1904)* (Paris, 1905), p. 80.) Duponchel's suit against Joly occurred just at the time when rehearsals for *Les martyrs* were beginning in Duponchel's theater, the one above all others in which Donizetti wanted to achieve a success; this may well have encouraged him to persuade Joly to delay *L'ange de Nisida* until after the premiere of *Les martyrs* on 10 April 1840, but by then Joly's affairs were in such a desperate condition that he ceased operations five days later.
42 *La fille du régiment* was one of the last premieres to be given by the company of the Opéra-Comique at the Salle des Nouveautés in the place de la Bourse, which had been its home since 1832. On 16 May 1840 the forces of the Opéra-Comique took possession of the rebuilt 'second' Salle Favart, where it continued its activities until 25 May 1887, when it burned to the ground during a performance of *Mignon*, the fire taking hundreds of lives. (Ironically, the second act of *Mignon* closes with Lothario setting fire to the theater in which Philine has just played Titania.)

43 Mécène Marié de l'Isle was the father of Célestine Galli-Marié, the first
    Mignon and Carmen. Later in the year of 1840, Marié de l'Isle moved
    over to the Opéra, where he sang first as a tenor and then later filled
    baritone roles.

44 Marie-Julie Boulanger, née Hallinger (1786–1850), sang at the Opéra-
    Comique from 1812 to 1845. She was the grandmother of Lilli and
    Nadia Boulanger.

45 Duprez, *Souvenirs d'un chanteur*, p. 95. The lack of success of *La fille
    du régiment* was partly the result of the tenor's frequent lapses of pitch.

46 Hector Berlioz, *Les musiciens et la musique* (Paris, 1903), pp. 149–55.
    Writing of this same performance Théophile Gautier, perhaps because
    he was not a rival composer, takes the opposite position: 'M. Donizetti
    is capable of paying with music that is beautiful and worthy for the
    cordial hospitality which France offers him in all her theaters, sub-
    sidized or not.' (Gautier, *L'art dramatique en France depuis vingt-cinq
    ans* (Paris, n.d.), pp. 29ff.) Reading Berlioz and Gautier side by side it is
    not difficult to imagine the tenor of some of the conversation at the
    Opéra-Comique that contested night of 11 February 1840.

47 Z. no. 332, p. 507.

48 *S.d.* 1, no. 70, p. 59.

49 'I am adjusting, cutting, etc. *La fille du régiment* for La Scala.' (Z. no.
    342, dated 15 August 1840, p. 518, to Dolci.) These adjustments in-
    volved dropping some numbers in characteristic French forms, borrow-
    ing a tenor aria from *Gianni di Calais*, and replacing the spoken dia-
    logue with Italian recitatives.

50 This first *La figlia* at La Scala, with Luigia Abbadia (Maria), Salvi (To-
    nio) and Raffaele Scalese (Sulpizio) was judged 'worthless' and sur-
    vived for only six performances (Cambiasi, *La Scala: 1778–1889*, pp.
    282–3). At La Scala *La figlia* had to wait until 1928 (when Toti dal
    Monte sang Maria) to be given a second chance.

51 Sembrich sang it at the Metropolitan in 1901 in French, Tetrazzini at
    Hammerstein's Manhattan Opera House in Italian, but in the latter re-
    vival John McCormack sang in Italian Tonio's Act 2 aria from the
    French version, which had been dropped from *La figlia*. Hempel sang it
    at the Metropolitan in Italian in 1917, but she fleshed out her part by
    adding Adam's variations from *Le toréador* and *Keep the home fires
    burning*, while Lily Pons at the same theater in 1940 sang in French and
    included, with more relevance, part of the cabaletta from Act 1 of *Lucie*
    (itself borrowed from *Rosmonda*) and *La Marseillaise*.

52 Donizetti wished to have *Les martyrs* performed after Easter because
    during Lent a certain portion of the public, for religious reasons, would
    not attend the theater. In 1840 Easter fell on 19 April; apparently
    Donizetti was insufficiently obstinate for the premiere of *Les martyrs*
    was given on the 10th.

53 Z. no. 334, p. 508.

54 Z. no. 333, p. 507.

55 Julie Dorus-Gras, née Steenkiste (1805–96), of Belgian extraction, was a
    high soprano of noteworthy agility. She made her debut at Brussels in
    1825, and at the Paris Opéra she first appeared in Rossini's *Le comte
    Ory* in 1830, later participating in the premieres of *Robert le diable* (as

Alice), *Les Huguenots* (as Marguerite de Valois) and *La juive* (as Eudoxie), in the last of which Donizetti first heard her. After the retirements of Laure Cinthie-Damoreau in 1835 and Cornélie Falcon in 1838, Dorus-Gras became the reigning prima donna at the Opéra, and in that capacity she sang the role of Pauline in the premiere of *Les martyrs.* Writing of her appearance as Pauline, Gautier said: 'Mme. Dorus-Gras used . . . her aptitude for vocalization, but one could have asked more passion and expression from her, though neither her words nor her music demanded it. She was ravishing in her antique costume.' (*L'art dramatique en France depuis vingt-cinq ans*, p. 49.) In the early 1840s, as Rosine Stolz came to dominate the foreground at the Opéra, she was overshadowed and she withdrew in 1845. After successful appearances in London in 1847–9 she retired from the stage altogether. Writing of her in this final stage of her career, Chorley, after making some reservations about her want of energy as an actress, said: '[she] was nevertheless an excellent artist with a combined firmness and volubility of execution which have not been exceeded' (*Thirty Years' Musical Recollections*, p. 257).

56 Jean-Étienne Massol (1802–87) was a tenor and then a baritone. After studying at the Paris Conservatoire with Plantade and Bordogni, Massol took first prize in singing in 1825 and shortly afterward made his debut at the Opéra as a tenor. After an interruption of several years he returned as a principal baritone, remaining an ornament of that stage until 1858. He was associated with two Donizetti premieres: *Les martyrs* and *Dom Sébastien.* After his retirement he served for some years as director of the Théâtre de la Monnaie in Brussels.

57 Prosper Dérivis (1808–80), a bass, was the son of Louis Dérivis (1780–1856), also a bass, who preceded his son at the Opéra. Prosper Dérivis made his debut there in 1831, as Pharaon in Rossini's *Moïse*; so extensive was his range that he was able to encompass baritone roles like Pharaon and Tell, as well as low-lying parts like Bertram in *Robert le diable.* Soon after the premiere of *Les martyrs* he betook himself to Italy, where he remained until at least 1847. For Verdi he created the role of Zaccaria in *Nabucco*; two months later he was the Prefect in the *prima* of *Linda di Chamounix* in Vienna.

58 In *Les martyrs* 'the sextet, which is a masterpiece . . . always had the reward of a *bis*'. (Félix Clément and Pierre Larousse, *Dictionnaire des opéras* (Paris, n.d.), p. 440.)

59 Gautier, *L'art dramatique en France depuis vingt-cinq ans*, pp. 46ff.

60 Gautier, *loc. cit.*

61 Rosine Stolz (sometimes Stoltz; 1815–1903) was born Victorine Noeb in Paris. She made her debut at the Opéra as Rachel in Halévy's *La juive* in 1837. She created Ascanio in Berlioz's ill-fated *Benvenuto Cellini*, but her palmy days began with her assumption of Léonor in the premiere of *La favorite* (1840). The leading female roles in Halévy's *La reine de Chypre* and *Charles VI* and in Donizetti's *Dom Sébastien* were expressly designed for her mezzo-soprano range. In time she so thoroughly antagonized her colleagues and a segment of the public with her domineering ways that there was a demonstration against her at the first performance of *Robert Bruce* (a pastiche of Rossini's music

assembled by Louis Niedermeyer) at the Opéra on 30 December 1846; in her anger she tore at her handkerchief with her teeth, and her exclamation of 'Merde!' was overheard by the shocked audience. Somehow she completed the performance, but her career was compromised and she left the Opéra in 1847. Returning there briefly in 1854, her reappearance as Léonor left the public cold. After being the mistress of the Emperor of Brazil for a while, she married in succession a baron, a count and a prince.

62 In the French provinces *Les martyrs* fared somewhat better than at Paris, lasting at least until 1845.

63 The *prima* of the original version of *Poliuto* was given at the San Carlo on 30 November 1848, with Eugenia Tadolini (Paolina), Carlo Baucardé (Poliuto), Filippo Colini (Severo) and Marco Arati (Callistene).

64 Francesco Tamagno (1850–1905) began his career in 1870 as a chorister, but when in 1873 he made his solo debut in the secondary role of Nearco in *Poliuto*, the size and metal of his voice won such immediate recognition that he graduated overnight to principal roles. He is chiefly remembered for having created Verdi's Otello.

65 Z. no. 338, dated 29 May 1840, p. 514.

66 Sgregli was the editor of the Neapolitan weekly *Omnibus*, the journal that seven years earlier had omitted reference to the Milanese *prima* of *Lucrezia Borgia*.

67 By 'sell everything' Donizetti is referring to the contents of his apartment on Strada Nardones, no. 14.

68 Donizetti here means that it was not ambition for the directorship of the Conservatory that prompted him to send the articles to Naples to be reprinted.

69 Z. no. 338, pp. 514–15.

70 Two considerations help to explain, if not excuse, the attitude of Florimo and his circle at this time. First, the negotiations for the directorship were, in May 1840, at their final point; dilatory King Ferdinando would announce Mercadante's appointment on 18 June 1840. Second, Florimo's championship of Bellini did not cease with the composer's death. It must have galled Florimo, who believed all the unkind things Bellini had ever written about Donizetti to him and his other friends over the years, that Bellini had died before being offered a contract to write for the Opéra; that this honor had now come to Donizetti was a sore point indeed with the *belliniani*.

71 Cicconetti (*Vita di Gaetano Donizetti*, pp. 126–7) claims that Donizetti composed the one-act *opéra comique Rita* during this visit to Switzerland, and later writers on Donizetti have repeated this assertion as fact. It is not true. The autograph of *Rita* is dated 1841.

72 Marco Bonesi conducted at the Teatro Riccardi each year between 1840 and 1847.

73 Bergamo was making belated amends with a vengeance that summer of 1840, as this was the fifty-year-old Donzelli's first appearance in his native town in a leading role. His association with Donizetti extended back to the crucial *Zoraida di Granata* of eighteen years before.

74 This production of *L'esule* at Bergamo marked the first time that Donizetti worked with Tadolini, who would before long take the title

roles in *Linda di Chamounix* and *Maria di Rohan* at their first performances.

75 Z. no. 342, dated 15 August 1840, p. 517.

76 Z. no. 342, p. 518.

77 Duprez, *Souvenirs d'un chanteur*, pp. 159–60.

78 I refer to this opera throughout by its French title because what Donizetti composed was a French grand opera; he was not involved in making the various Italian versions, which, although they may be more familiar today, are far from faithful to the composer's original score. There is a great need for a modern critical edition of *La favorite*.

79 The autograph of *La favorite* is a patchwork containing large chunks of *L'ange de Nisida* (including some pieces from *Adelaide*), as well as original music. It is evident that the autograph of *L'ange* was literally cut up and interleaved with the new music when Donizetti came to put together *La favorite*: the old text and characters' names are crossed out and new text and names written in, and the music of the role of Sylvia (*L'ange*), a high soprano, is altered downward for the mezzo Léonor (*La favorite*). The sections from *Adelaide* have been altered twice, since that music went first into *L'ange* and from there into *La favorite*. The composite score ends with the date 27 December 1839, which represents the date of completion of *L'ange*, the last page of that score happening also to constitute the last of *La favorite*. A microfilm of this autograph is in the Library of the Performing Arts, New York (the autograph itself was formerly in private hands), and the discarded portions of *L'ange* (about eight or ten numbers or parts of numbers) are in the Bibliothèque Nationale, Paris. There is also a considerable amount of material, which has no antecedents in *L'ange*, that was apparently discarded from *La favorite* during the rehearsal period in October and November 1840; this is partly autograph and is in the Bibliothèque de l'Opéra, Paris. (For a number-by-number analysis of *La favorite*'s sources see Chapter 12, note 14.)

80 In *L'ange* Don Gaspar is a principal character, having an aria and a duet with the King; the corresponding role in *La favorite* is a *comprimario* part.

81 From the opening of *L'ange* Donizetti took Leone's aubade 'Douce ange, une fée inconnue', and inserted it, with slightly modified text and substantially altered music, into the first scene of *La favorite*.

82 Donizetti's musical additions to the final act of *L'ange* in transforming it into *La favorite* were a tenor *romance*, taken from *Le duc d'Albe*, and a prayer for Léonor, which was inserted during rehearsals.

83 Changes of location were a commonplace in sanitizing operas for certain Italian cities; *Lucrezia Borgia* is a case in point. In Italy until 1859 *La favorite* was frequently disguised under other titles, such as *Leonora*, *Elda* and *Daila*, and the action transferred to some non-Christian country. But even with such a change, *La favorite* still contained elements that were to upset the Italian censors for more than a decade.

84 Baculard d'Arnaud's play dramatizes and expands the last few pages of his earlier prose narrative. *Mémoires du comte de Comminge* (1764).

85 Gautier mentions the resemblance between the Comminge story and Act 4 of *La favorite* in his review of the first performance (*La Presse*, 7

December 1840): 'The fourth act . . . recalls a little the tale of the Comte de Comminge.' The final scene of *L'ange de Nisida*, which opens with the monks digging their own graves and exclaiming 'Frères, il faut mourir!' is closer to Baculard than the corresponding moment in *La favorite*. The odd detail that the character who is called 'Un moine' in the first three parts of *L'ange* is renamed 'Le supérieur' in the last part might indicate that the conclusion of the Royer and Vaëz text had originally been intended for a different context.

86 Besides the ballet, the most important new music is that of the arias of Alphonse and Léonor. Some of the music of *L'ange* had originally formed part of *Adelaide* (perhaps begun in 1834) and some of this found its way into *La favorite*. One chorus stems from *Pia de' Tolomei*, and the following female chorus, whose provenance goes back to *Adelaide*, is also included in an early printed score of *Maria Stuarda*.

87 Z. no. 349, p. 524.

88 For this performance Donizetti wrote a new aria and duet for Mario in the role of Gennaro; he also included a compromise version of the so-called *finale nuovo* (first performed at La Scala on 11 January 1840), the compromise consisting of using both Gennaro's arioso as he dies (new) and a shortened version of Lucrezia's final cabaletta (old).

89 Gautier has left a vivid picture of Grisi as an actress in the role of Lucrezia: 'Mlle Grisi, whose great dramatic instinct responds quickly, was sublime in her pantomime at the moment Maffio snatches off her mask. It is impossible to see anything more beautiful than this pale face of marble, terrible in spite of its beauty, like the head of Medusa, whose viper gaze launches venomous and flaming glances . . . one is sure of her vengeance, men looked at thus are dead.' (*L'art dramatique en France depuis vingt-cinq ans*, p. 66.)

90 *Lucrezia* did not return to the stage of the Théâtre-Italien until 16 January 1845, and then disguised as *La rinnegata*.

91 At the Opéra *La favorite* was given more than 600 times; its popularity in the French provinces matched that in Paris.

92 Gautier, *L'art dramatique en France depuis vingt-cinq ans*, p. 83.

93 This Romantic escapism was keenly felt in such lines as: 'J'abandonne mon coeur à la voix qui me crie: Ah, va! dans une autre patrie, va, cacher ton bonheur!' (I abandon my heart to the voice that cries to me: Ah, go, into another country, go, there conceal your happiness!)

94 The modern emergence of *La favorite* in the United States really began in 1944 and 1945, when Bruna Castagna sang her unforgettable Leonora in the Italian production in Philadelphia.

95 Z. no. 339, p. 515.

96 Although Giuseppina Strepponi, whose operatic career began in 1835, had scored much of her success in his operas, Donizetti had never worked directly with her before the time of *Adelia*. In May 1838, when he heard that she would be singing *Pia* in Rome, he had written to Toto: 'I don't know anything at all about la Strepponi.' (Z. no. 291, dated 8 May 1838, p. 470.)

97 Ignazio Marini (1811–73), a bass, was born in Bergamo. Before *Adelia* he had appeared in the first casts of two works by Donizetti, *Gemma di Vergy* and *Gianni di Parigi*. At the time of *Adelia* he was accused of

intentionally singing out of tune, because, as Cametti explains (*Donizetti a Roma*, p. 59), he wished to 'avenge himself for wrongs that the Maestro seemed to have dealt him with his excessive attention to Marini's wife' (the mezzo-soprano Antonietta Rainieri-Marini). Marini's career, which took him as far afield as England and the United States, ended in 1865. He was a true basso profondo. Donizetti seems to have mistrusted his high notes because the role of Arnoldo in *Adelia* scarcely goes above D; four years later Verdi had more confidence in his upper range, for his role in *Attila* exploited that part of his voice up to F.

98 Donizetti had briefly considered this subject (derived from *Un duel sous le Cardinal de Richelieu* by Lockroy and Badon) in 1837; in 1843 he would convert it into *Maria di Rohan*.

99 Carafa's *Adele di Lusignano* was first performed at La Scala on 27 September 1817. Romani's text was later set by several other composers, sometimes with the title *La figlia dell'arciere*.

100 The last act of Coccia's *La figlia dell'arciere* was written to a text by Marchese Domenico Andreotti. Coccia's opera, given at the San Carlo on 19 January 1834, failed even though the cast included Malibran and Lablache.

101 Girolamo Marini (1801–67) was a journalist who wrote for the *Rivista teatrale* of Rome. Late in 1839 he had written the libretto for Otto Nicolai's successful *Il templario*, based on Scott's *Ivanhoe*.

102 Z. no. 343, dated 18 August 1840, p. 519.

103 Z. no. 347, dated 26 September 1840, pp. 522–3.

104 Z. no. 349, dated 1 October 1840, p. 524.

105 Z. no. 350, p. 525.

106 In September 1840 Dolci had written to Donizetti urging him to use his fellow Bergamasc Colleoni-Corti rather than Strepponi in *Adelia*, and Donizetti replied in this fashion (Z. no. 346, dated 25 September 1840, p. 521):

> As to la Colleoni, I am afraid that it is too late. I have already written half the opera, which is for one principal female singer, and besides there was the uncertainty whether I was coming or not and about the libretto I was asked to set by the impresario, who told me it was to be for Strepponi. I had not refused her when I thought for certain Signora Colleoni was going to Bologna. Now I absolutely cannot refuse her, and there only remains to us the hope that Strepponi will be found inferior to la Colleoni. Then without making a sad face I can in the common interest advise the impresario to change the subject for my opera. Pray heaven that it will be so and that it will be possible for me to satisfy her.

When Strepponi took over from Colleoni in *Marin Faliero*, Colleoni moved over to the Valle, where she did not have much success in *L'ajo nell'imbarazzo*, even though Donizetti wrote her a new rondò (see Z. no. 355, dated 4 February 1841, p. 530, to Colleoni-Corti).

107 A first possible step toward the re-emergence of *Adelia* was Montserrat Caballé's inclusion of the heroine's Act 3 aria, 'Chi le nostr'anime', in the program of her 1972 recital at Carnegie Hall.

108 Z. no. 356, dated 18 February 1841, p. 530.

109 Alejandro Maria Aguado, Marquis de las Marismas (1784–1842), a Spaniard by birth, who became a naturalized Frenchman. He was a

banker of vast resources and exercised great influence in theatrical circles, taking effective control of the Opéra over Duponchel and Pillet who were the official co-directors.

110 Z. no. 364, dated 23 May 1841, pp. 540–1.

111 Z. no. 365, dated 8 June 1841, p. 544.

112 François-Louis Crosnier (1792–1867) directed the Opéra-Comique from May 1835 to May 1845. Crosnier's mother was the redoubtable concierge of the stage door at the Opéra, and of all the people who were employed there only Rosine Stolz had the aplomb to address her as 'tu'.

113 The original singers of the roles in *Rita* were: Caroline Lefebvre (Rita), Warot (Peppe) and Barielle (Gaspar). Lefebvre was the wife of the famous baritone Faure.

114 Since 1955 *Rita* has had more than seventy professional productions, and an even greater number of workshop stagings.

115 Merelli managed La Scala until 1850, and then returned briefly to resume that post between 1861 and 1863.

116 Although, technically, one Donizetti *prima* took place during 1836–41 at La Scala, that of *Gianni di Parigi*, I omit it from consideration as it was put on without the composer's permission while he was out of the country.

117 The five composers who had two new operas given at La Scala during this period are: Mercadante, Placido Mandanici, Carlo Coccia, Federico Ricci and Verdi. Verdi's two *prime* during this period were *Oberto* and the solitary performance of *Un giorno di regno*; Verdi could not be considered a serious challenger to Donizetti's position until after the first performance of *Nabucco* in March 1842.

118 Z. no. 58, dated 24 June 1830, p. 277.

119 Z. no. 249, dated 13 August 1837, p. 438.

120 Z. no. 299, dated 26 June 1838, p. 478.

121 Z. no. 336, p. 511.

122 S.d. 1, no. 72, dated 14 June 1840, p. 61.

123 Paolo Branca would shortly become the father-in-law of the librettist Romani, and his house was a gathering-place for musicians and others associated with the arts and letters.

124 Z. no. 348, dated 26 September 1840, p. 523.

125 Z. no. 364, dated 23 May 1841, pp. 540–1. In this letter Donizetti resumes writing to Ricordi, communication between them having been broken off by the suit over *Gianni di Parigi*, and now he addresses him by the formal 'voi', instead of the familiar 'tu' he had used in earlier years.

126 Gaetano Rossi (1774–1855) had begun his career as a librettist with a text for a one-act farsa, *Che originali!*, set by Mayr in 1798. Of the more than 100 librettos Rossi turned out, the best-known are those for Rossini's *Tancredi* and *Semiramide* and for Donizetti's *Linda di Chamounix*.

127 Z. no. 311, dated 25 August 1838, pp. 486–7.

128 Z. no. 372, pp. 552–3.

129 Z. no. 373, dated 29 September 1841, p. 554.

130 Sofia Löwe (1816–66), a soprano, came of a distinguished musical and theatrical family. She made her debut in Vienna in a German produc-

tion of *Otto mesi in due ore*. After successes in Berlin, beginning in 1836, she moved on to London in 1841, where she failed to make headway against Grisi, when she appeared in *La straniera*, *Don Giovanni* (Donna Elvira), and *Marin Faliero*. At the end of that year she created Maria Padilla at La Scala. She is principally remembered as the first Elvira in Verdi's *Ernani*. She retired in 1849 on her marriage to Prince Lichtenstein.

131   Luigia Abbadia (1821–96), a soprano, was the daughter of a Genovese composer, Natale Abbadia (1792–1875). In 1840 she made her La Scala debut as Rovena in Nicolai's *Il templario*, based on Scott's *Ivanhoe*; she appeared next in the ill-fated *prima* of Verdi's *Un giorno di regno*, and then in the Italian *prima* of *La figlia del reggimento*. The following year she sang Ines in the *prima* of *Maria Padilla*. She retired from the stage in 1870 and became a successful singing-teacher in Milan.

132   Z. no. 389, p. 569. The same censors had countenanced Edgardo's suicide in *Lucia* at La Scala two years earlier, but in the case of *Maria Padilla* their objections may have been based on the heroine's compounding suicide with lèse majesté, for she snatches the crown from Blanche de Bourbon's head and claims it as her own.

133   Z. no. 388, dated 18 December 1841, p. 569.

134   The first night of *Maria Padilla* may well have been compromised in part by the two ballets that were performed with it, *L'ultimo imperatore di Messico* and *Un sogno nella China*, both of which were fiascos.

135   *La fama* was a theatrical journal published in Milan.

136   *S.d.* 1, no. 85, pp. 73–4.

137   Accursi performed this function with enthusiasm, as Gaetano informed Toto on 11 January 1842: 'Michele has been driven crazy by the success; he runs here and there, he narrates, embellishes, publishes ... you know him and that is enough.) (Z. no. 392, p. 574.)

138   The italics are Donizetti's. Z. no. 390, dated 28 December 1841, p. 572.

139   The happy ending after this became traditional in *Maria Padilla*. It does not too much distort history: Maria Padilla was the mistress of Pedro, King of Castille (1350–69), before and after his marriage to Blanche de Bourbon, whom he treated outrageously and of whom he soon rid himself; she was the only one of his many lovers to whom Pedro showed even a modicum of constancy.

140   By 'back to the beginning' Donizetti means that he would have to rewrite the soprano role of Hélène (probably designed for Dorus-Gras) for Stolz's dramatic mezzo-soprano. His uncertainty about the vocal range required for the leading female role was an important factor in Donizetti's postponing the completion of *Le duc d'Albe* and in his ultimate failure to finish it.

141   Z. no. 391, pp. 572–3.

142   In mid-January 1842 Donizetti went to Bergamo for three days to see Mayr and to attend the *prima* of an opera, *Lutaldo di Vicolungo*, written by his old schoolmate Gerolamo Forini at the Teatro della Società. Back in Milan he reported to Toto that Forini 'does not lack talent', but 'the libretto written at Bergamo is a botch' (Z. no. 394, p. 575). He returned to Bergamo again in February to see Mayr, who was making a poor recovery from a cataract operation.

143 *La grâce de Dieu* differs from the libretto of *Linda* at several points. In the play, the heroine is seduced by the disguised nobleman who promises to marry her, but Rossi omitted the seduction from the libretto so as not to ruffle Viennese sensibilities; this makes Linda's subsequent loss of reason and other details, such as her being maintained in style at Paris, much less credible. In the play, the heroine's name is Marie, but with four Marias (Stuarda, de Rudenz, the heroine of *La fille du régiment,* and most recently, Padilla) to his credit, Donizetti wanted a less overworked name. It is not clear when the title *Linda di Chamounix* became attached to the opera, but the first time Donizetti mentions it in his letters is on 30 March 1842, three days after his arrival in Vienna. Earlier he always referred to it as either *La grâce de Dieu* or as 'the opera for Vienna'.

144 *S.d.* 1, no. 86, dated 9 January 1842, p. 75.

145 Z. no. 399, p. 579.

146 Benjamin Lumley (born Levy) (1811–75) was originally a barrister, and then, in 1842, he succeeded Pierre-François Laporte as manager of the company at Her Majesty's Theatre in the Haymarket. Before opening his season he had come to Italy to engage singers and to line up new works. In 1847 Lumley would introduce Verdi's *I masnadieri* at Her Majesty's.

147 The principal opera season at Covent Garden or Her Majesty's Theatre ran from April to June, coinciding with the social season; opera-goers frequently had social engagements after the performance and it required an exceptional singer or musical event to keep the audience in the theater until the end of a work. London and St Petersburg audiences were notorious among performers for disappearing before the opera was over; in Italy and France the audience would often arrive late but would stay until the end, while in Vienna performances started early so as to finish in time to allow patrons to fulfill social engagements afterward.

148 Z. no. 382, dated 19 November 1841, pp. 563–4.

149 Z. no. A31, p. 890.

150 Romani would be fifty-four on 31 January 1842. His bride was Emilia Branca, whose biography of her husband, published seventeen years after Romani's death, is as inaccurate as it is worshiping.

151 Significantly, Donizetti uses the indicative rather than the subjunctive in this clause, writing 'ma se era uomo d'onore', thereby implying that there is no doubt that Romani has no sense of honor.

152 The italics are Donizetti's. Z. no. 397, p. 577.

153 The exception was the occasion when Romani failed to make the requested changes in the libretto for *Gli illinesi* in time for Donizetti to compose the opera for the Carnival season of 1835–6 in Turin. By getting out of his agreement with Consul at Turin, Donizetti had freed himself to stage *Maria Stuarda* with Malibran at La Scala.

154 Even if the London opera had been written, Donizetti, as it turned out, would not have been able to go to England in May 1842, because the delayed *prima* of *Linda* did not take place until 19 May, and after that there was the matter of his court appointment in Vienna.

155 Although Rossini had composed parts of the *Stabat mater* in 1832, he did not complete that work until 1841. Its first complete public perfor-

mance was held at the Salle Ventadour, Paris, 7 January 1842, with Giulia Grisi, Emma Albertazzi, Mario and Tamburini as the solo quartet.

156 Donizetti had planned to remain in Milan until Tuesday, 8 March 1842, in order to attend the *prima* of Verdi's *Nabucco* on the 7th; but when the performance was postponed until the 9th, he put off his departure until the 10th.

157 Z. no. 399, dated 4 March 1842, p. 579. Elsewhere in this letter Donizetti describes the unfortunate vocal condition of Strepponi, who in five days would sing the difficult role of Abigaille in *Nabucco*. He is ironical. 'She made such a furore in *Belisario* at La Scala [22 February 1842] that she is the only one who never received any applause and her Verdi did not want her in his opera, but the impresario has obliged him to use her. She was to have gone to Vienna, but the governor has decided he does not want her, and la Marini is going in her place.' For Donizetti this was bad news followed by equally bad because his opinion of la Marini was consistently low.

158 At Bologna the solo quartet for the *Stabat mater* consisted of the English soprano Clara Novello and the Russian tenor Ivanoff, and two *dilettanti*, the mezzo-soprano Clementina degli Antonj and the bass Count Pompeo Belgioioso. Singing in the chorus was one of Rossini's prize vocal students, the nineteen-year-old Marietta Alboni, who the following year was to sing at La Scala the leading role in *La favorite* (disguised by the censorship as *Elda*), and was to have an illustrious international career.

159 Rossini 'with his retention of urine, certainly could never have conducted; he was sternly forbidden to get overheated'. That is Gaetano's explanation to Toto on 4 April 1842 (Z. no. 404, p. 586).

160 Z. no. 401, dated 20 March 1842, p. 581, to Persico.

161 Antonietta Rainieri-Marini, who had come to Vienna in place of Strepponi, was so put out by her reception at the Kärntnertor that she appeared in only three performances. The wife of the bass Ignazio Marini, she was really a mezzo-soprano (her La Scala debut had been as Isabella in Rossini's *L'italiana*), and she did not appear to advantage in soprano roles adapted (*puntati*) for her. According to Donizetti, she was a large, ungainly woman. She is best remembered today for having been in the first casts of Verdi's *Oberto* and *Un giorno di regno*.

162 'Today is the fourth day of rehearsals . . . Everyone is asking me for an overture – very well – I will have to provide one . . . I believe that my *Linda* will appear before the 15th of this month of May.' (*S.d.* 1, no. 90, dated 30 April 1842, p. 82, to Accursi.) This letter indicates within quite narrow limits the date of the conversion of the first movement of the 1836 string quartet into the overture for *Linda*.

163 In Vienna that spring Moriani was not in good vocal condition. Donizetti reported to Accursi that the tenor had to miss the third rehearsal of *Linda* because 'he's at the end of his rope, every time he sings two consecutive performances he remains in bed the following day' (*S.d.* 1, no. 90, p. 82). Chorley describes his appearances in London in 1844: 'He came too late in his . . . career . . . He must have had one of the most superb and richly-strong tenor voices ever heard, with tones full

of expression as well as of force. But either the reign of false taste had set in, encouraging him to drawl and to bawl, or his voice had never been trained. Ere it came here, his command over it was gone.' (*Thirty Years' Musical Recollections*, p. 152.) When Moriani sang at the Théâtre-Italien in Paris in 1849–50 his vocal decline was very marked. He made his last stage appearances at Rouen in 1851.

164 Felice Varesi, born Varèse (1813–89) was a baritone; born in Calais, he pursued his career chiefly in Italy, making his debut, appropriately enough, at Varese. His only creation of a Donizetti role was Antonio in *Linda*. He is best remembered as one of the quintessential early Verdian baritones, having created the roles of Macbeth, Rigoletto and Germont. By 1853 he was experiencing vocal difficulties, but he continued to sing in public until 1864.

165 Agostino Rovere (1804–65) had launched his career as a basso buffo by 1838, and he continued to sing until 1865. Besides singing in the unauthorized *prima* of *Gianni di Parigi*, he created the role of the Marchese in *Linda*, and he sang the title role in *Don Pasquale* when it was introduced to Vienna at the Kärntnertortheater. In the seasons of 1847 and 1848 he appeared successfully in London. He was respected by Donizetti as a superior singer, if not quite in the same class as Lablache.

166 Z. no. 418, dated 24 May 1842, p. 605.

167 Heinrich Proch (1809–78) conducted at the Hoftheater in Vienna from 1840 to 1870. Best remembered today for his coloratura variations, 'Deh torna, mio bene' op. 164, he made German singing-versions of many Italian librettos, including *Linda* and *Il trovatore*. He was also a singing-teacher and counted Therese Tietjens among his pupils.

168 *Allgemeine Theaterzeitung*, 21 May 1842, p. 535, quoted by Rudolph Angermüller in his paper, 'Gli anni viennesi di Donizetti', at the 1⁰ convegno internazionale di studi donizettiani, Bergamo, 1975.

169 Notable among these Lindas were Henriette Sontag, Clara Louise Kellogg, Minnie Hauk, Etelka Gerster, Adelina Patti, and Amelita Galli-Curci. The last professional performance of *Linda* in the United States was at the Metropolitan on 25 March 1935, sung by Lily Pons, Gladys Swarthout, Nino Martini, de Luca and Virgilio Lazzari; in that revival it had been given seven times in New York and once in Brooklyn.

170 Eduard von Lannoy (1787–1853), born in Styria, was a gifted amateur composer, who wrote operas, Singspiele and melodramas, and a number of lieder, orchestral and chamber works which were publicly performed. From 1818 he participated in the concert life of Vienna, and he eventually became the organizer and director of the Viennese Concerts Spirituels. He became genuinely fond of Donizetti, entertaining him and arranging for him to meet key figures in the musical life of Vienna. In the latter part of 1846 and early 1847 Lannoy traveled widely in Germany and France, and was, at that time, able to bring his personal and official influence to bear on Donizetti's family and the Paris authorities in the matter of the composer's confinement in the sanatorium at Ivry. For a helpful account of Lannoy's life and productivity see Wolfgang Suppan, *Heinrich Eduard Josef von Lannoy (1787–1853): Leben und Werke*, Steierischer Tonkünstlerbund: Musik aus der Steiermark, series 4, vol. 2 (Graz, 1960).

171 Rossini had given Donizetti a letter of introduction to Metternich. His friends in Bergamo were eager that Donizetti should urge the building of a railroad to Bergamo (which the authorities had lately decided against), and Donizetti made a point of bringing the matter up with the prime minister.

172 Countess Rossi was better known as Henriette Sontag. After her marriage she abandoned her career until 1849, when the disorders of the preceding year had wiped out her Sardinian husband's fortune. The role in which she made her return to the stage was Linda, and her choice evokes echoes of Vienna and May 1842.

173 Peppina Appiani was a cultured widow who, having a number of dependent children, supplemented her income by boarding 'houseguests'. That there is little or no foundation to the rumors concerning a romance between her and Donizetti is explained by Frank Walker in the chapter 'Donizetti, Verdi, Appiani' in The Man Verdi (London, 1962), pp. 96–166.

174 Since, a few lines above, Donizetti had been citing Rossini's Il barbiere, it seems entirely probable that here, presenting Vienna in detached syllables, he is alluding to the episode where Rosina spells out her name to Figaro in the recitative just preceding their duet, 'Dunque io son'.

175 Z. no. 424, p. 611.

176 After Mozart's death Leopold Koželuch (?1754–1818) succeeded to the position of Hofkapellmeister. At his death Koželuch was followed by Fritz Krommer (1759–1831), who held it for the rest of his life. The post had been vacant for eleven years when it was offered to Donizetti.

177 Z. no. 428, dated 16 June 1842, p. 616.

178 Z. no. 437, p. 624.

179 Donizetti was summoned by the police to appear before the audience at a performance of Maria Padilla, which had entered the repertory of the San Carlo on 28 July 1842, sung by Tadolini, Basadonna and Filippo Coletti. Later, when he had seen one of the performances of the work, he informed Ricordi that the opera had been 'massacred unrecognizably by the censors' and 'in a horrible fashion' (S.d. 1, no. 94, dated 28 August 1842, p. 88).

180 Z. no. 441, dated August 1842, pp. 626–7.

181 'P.S. Do you know that perhaps I will give Le duc d'Albe? Meyerbeer and Halévy are not ready.' (Z. no. 439, postmarked 27 August 1842, p. 625, to Ricordi.)

182 S.d. 1, no. 88, pp. 79–89. At this time Donizetti briefly considered a French version of Belisario for Stolz, which would entail either adjusting the soprano role of Antonina for her or expanding the sympathetic mezzo role of Irene. Nothing came of this project for the Opéra, but Belisario was given (in its original form) at the Théâtre-Italien in October 1843.

183 Z. no. 443, dated 15 September 1842, p. 628.

184 Besides a new number, 'O luce di quest'anima', for this version of Linda, Donizetti added strophes for Marietta Brambilla, sung off stage at Pierotto's first entrance, a new cabaletta for Lablache, and a new section to the tenor–bass duet in Act 3 (see Z. no. 449, dated 22 October 1842, p. 634, to Ricordi).

185 Franz Lachner's *Catarina Cornaro*, revised after its first performance at Munich on 3 December 1841, came out at the Kärntnertor on 19 November 1842 and survived for only five performances. Lachner (1803–90) had been on the musical staff of the Kärntnertor from 1826 to 1834, and was later in Mannheim and Munich. A copious composer in many forms, the only music of his that has much currency today is found in the recitatives he supplied for Cherubini's *Médée* to take the place of the original spoken dialogue.

186 Besides two and a half full-length operas, Donizetti concurrently composed a *Miserere* to be performed at the Concerts Spirituels in Vienna, dedicating it to the Empress Anna.

187 Anelli's libretto to *Ser Marc'Antonio* was first set by Stefano Pavesi and given at La Scala on 26 September 1810. Pavesi's opera buffa managed to hold the stage with some pertinacity for more than thirty years, even against the formidable competition of Rossini's comic works. Significantly, Pavesi's work was staged at the Kärntnertor in German translation on 28 August 1842. Although Donizetti had left Vienna not quite two months before this revival, he was very likely aware that it was to take place, and this could well have suggested his using Anelli's libretto as a point of departure for his own opera buffa.

188 In his letters Donizetti often voices his concern that the period and costumes of his operas should not resemble those of other works being given in close conjunction with them. By using modern dress he had nothing to fear in this regard.

189 Among the pieces borrowed from elsewhere are Don Pasquale's 'Un fuoco insolito' in Act 1, taken from *Gianni di Calais*. Norina's 'Via, caro sposino' had its origins in a cabaletta Donizetti had written for Tadolini for a production of *L'elisir* in Naples in 1841; he had had the foresight to restrict Tadolini's use of this addition to Naples alone. It is invariably said of *Don Pasquale* that Ernesto's serenade, 'Com'è gentil', was an afterthought, added during the rehearsals. Apparently this anecdote goes back to Madame Pearse, Mario's daughter. The aria was, in fact, written well before *Don Pasquale* went into rehearsal, for, on 20 November 1842, more than a week before preparations began, Gaetano informed Toto: 'The setting is Rome; as it contains a serenade, I have sought to imitate the Roman ritornelli with guitars and tambourines.' (*S.d.* 1, no. 96, p. 90.)

190 See Z. no. 456, dated 27 November 1842, p. 640, to Vasselli.

191 Donizetti's autograph scores show that he would write in the vocal line with hasty indications of accompaniment and harmony, only later filling in the rest of the parts on the same pages. That he customarily worked this way is revealed by measures deleted during this first phase of composition; also sometimes the color of the ink used in the first sketch is decidedly different from that of the instrumentation filled in later.

192 Z. no. 452, p. 636.

193 See Piero Rattolino, 'Il processo compositivo nel *Don Pasquale* di Donizetti', *Nuova rivista musicale italiana*, 1 (1970), 51–68, 2 (1970), 263–80.

194 Z. no. 463, dated 4 January 1843, p. 646, to his student Matteo Salvi.

195 Z. no. 465, dated 5 January 1843, p. 648.

196 Gautier, *L'art dramatique en France depuis vingt-cinq ans*, p. 322.

197 Chorley, *Thirty Years' Musical Recollections*, p. 144.

198 *Don Pasquale* reached New Orleans two years and four days after its *prima* at the Théâtre-Italien. No other opera by Donizetti was introduced to the United States so speedily after its first performance.

199 Donizetti remained a corresponding member of the Académie Française. When it was suggested that he become a full member, he refused because he did not want to lose his own sense of himself as an Italian by becoming a French citizen.

200 Z. no. 470, pp. 652–3.

201 Once again Donizetti had returned to Cammarano's libretto based on Lockroy's and Badon's play, on which they had first worked together in 1837. The libretto was completed for Lillo, whose *Il conte di Chalais* was given in Naples in 1839. Three months before the *prima* of Lillo's opera, Federico Ricci's *Un duello sotto Richelieu* (with a libretto credited to three poets: Francesco dall'Ongaro, Antonio Somma and Antonio Gazzoletti) was given at La Scala (on 17 August 1839).

202 *Maria di Rohan* was the second score he worked on for this commitment to the Kärntnertor, for which he had signed the contract on 5 June 1842. The first, *Caterina Cornaro*, he put aside when he heard about Lachner's opera on the same subject; it was later completed for Naples.

203 The connection of this scenario with *Ruy Blas* is not immediately apparent, for to accommodate the censors Hugo's plot had been 'disguised' under the title *Folco Melian* and 'its setting transposed'. The scenario, originally intended for a libretto for Donizetti, was later expanded for Nicola de Giosa (1820–85) and given the new title *Folco d'Arles*; de Giosa's setting of the text was first performed at the San Carlo in 1851. (See John N. Black, 'The Making of an Italian Romantic Opera Libretto – Salvadore Cammarano's *Folco d'Arles*', *Italian Studies*, 35 (1980), 68–80.)

204 Z. no. 471, dated 4 February 1843, pp. 653–4. Before 1838 it would never have occurred to Donizetti to make such a suggestion, because a regular stipulation of Italian operatic contracts in those days was that the composer prepare his score *in piazza* and conduct the first three performances; this was intended to guarantee that a composer be unable to pass off as new a work that had been written previously: if the audience recognized parts of the music he would be on hand to alter it. Indeed, when *Caterina* was first given at the San Carlo in January 1844, Donizetti's absence was so exceptional that some people, particularly his detractors, were quick to assume that he was foisting off a second-hand score on the Neapolitans.

205 If this Flemish subject was, in fact, *Ne m'oubliez pas*, then it is clear that he composed it some time after February 1843, but as yet there is no evidence that permits a more precise dating of these excerpts. Zavadini seems to be wrong when he says it was worked on during 'the second half of 1842' (*Donizetti: Vita – Musiche – Epistolario*, p. 178). There is a letter to Accursi dated 13 February 1843 (*S.d.* 1, no. 98, pp. 92–3) in which Donizetti urges that Saint-Georges's completed libretto be in his hands, 'and that means in my hands', by 1 May, and in a typically practical way he says that it would have to be consigned to the

courier in Paris ten days earlier to reach him in Vienna on the stipulated date. A good conjectural date for *Ne m'oubliez pas* would seem to be the summer of 1843, perhaps after the completion of *Caterina*.

206 The seven numbers of *Ne m'oubliez pas* are not consecutive. The principal characters are Henriette, André and Franz, names which makes the identification of this work with the 'Flemish subject' seem plausible. Opera Rara recorded all seven numbers of *Ne m'oubliez pas* in 1979.

207 Z. no. 470, p. 653.

208 A characteristic instance occurs in his letter to Persico of 4 February 1843. Pleading his unreliable health as a sufficient reason to break his contract with Guillaume, he says: 'If my fevers should be disbelieved, I have Drs Fossati and Maroncelli at Paris, and a doctor here [in Vienna] too, ready to make a thousand certificates for me, that hot weather now produces a nervous fever and that my head often suffers from that complaint.' (Z. no. 471, p. 654.) In those days fevers were a little more subjective than they are today, as it was before the invention of the clinical thermometer.

209 In this context these sentences from a letter from Professor Trethowan shed some light on the inevitable question: if Donizetti suffered from this disease in advanced form, how could he continue to compose, and to compose some of his most memorable music, in 1842–3? Professor Trethowan writes: 'While this is, of course, conjectural it may be noted that the manifestations of chronic and untreated syphilis were, at the time, so widespread it is justified in the absence of any other clear reason to assume that almost any kind of ill-health could have been due to this cause. However, although there may have been some involvement of the nervous system quite early on this was probably confined largely to the brain membranes until 1844 when the personality changes which began to occur suggest a further extension of the disease process with a more massive invasion of the brain substance and spinal cord. This relative latency of his condition would also explain why he was able to compose successfully until about then.' (Letter to the author, dated 6 October 1976.)

210 Z. no. 483, dated 30 March 1843, p. 664, to Dolci.

211 'I have sent the second and third acts of *Caterina* [to Persico] and in a few days the first act will be on its way.' (Z. no. 485, dated 25 May 1843, p. 666, to Giacomo Pedroni of Ricordi). As he had done previously, Donizetti refers to this work as though it were in three acts, but the libretto clearly describes it as having a prologue and two acts.

212 Tadolini sang 'O luce di quest'anima' transposed down a half-tone; the aria had been written for Persiani.

213 *Nabucco* made its Viennese debut on 4 April 1843, with Teresa de Giuli-Borsi as Abigaille and Ronconi, returning to Vienna after a three years' absence, as Nabucco, which he had sung at Milan in the *prima*.

214 Viardot sang Rosina fourteen times that season in Vienna, interpolating the *rondò* from *La Cenerentola* into the lesson scene. In 1843 she also appeared at the Kärntnertor as Delizia in Federico Ricci's *Corrado d'Altamura* and as Alina in Donizetti's *Alina, regina di Golconda*. She was less successful with these parts and less happy in them because she was coping with soprano roles that had only been adapted to her mezzo-

soprano range and not transposed. Later in the year Donizetti wrote to Louis Viardot to tell him that Norina (in *Don Pasquale*) was too high for his wife's voice and that she should not even consider it.

215 Donizetti deserves a good deal of credit for this successful season of 1843 at the Kärntnertor. Seven of the twelve operas given were his, and they accounted for forty-three of the total of seventy performances. Near the end of his stay that year in Vienna, he told his Neapolitan friend Teodoro Ghezzi: 'here I am well regarded, well treated, respected, honored' (Z. no. 490, p. 672).

216 Z. no. 486, dated 6 June 1843, p. 667.

217 *Allgemeine Wiener Musikzeitung*, 5 June 1843, quoted by Angermüller in 'Gli anni viennesi di Donizetti'.

218 Donizetti's habit of adding new music to his scores when he put them on at the Théâtre-Italien was a shrewd business move. Not only did this give his works a special cachet for Paris audiences, but he received separate publishing contracts for his new arias, which would be associated with the names of popular singers like Persiani and Marietta Brambilla.

This was not Brambilla's first encounter with the character of Gondì; in 1839 she had sung the corresponding role in Ricci's *Un duello sotto Richelieu* at La Scala.

219 'I read la *Cornaro* in your library, it is true, and various things that still excite me.' (Z. no. 483, dated 30 March 1843, p. 664, to Vasselli.) Since Donizetti had last been in Toto's library in Rome at the time of *Adelia* (February 1841), it cannot have been Saint-Georges's libretto for Halévy's *La reine de Chypre*, given at the Opéra on 22 December 1841, that he read there.

220 Halévy's opera was performed by Stolz (Caterina), Duprez (Gerard) and Barroilhet (Lusignan). That it was a success Donizetti knew from painful experience; his income from *La favorite* at the Opéra stopped for a period when Stolz ceased to sing Léonor in order to concentrate on frequent performances of Halévy's *La reine de Chypre*.

221 The original of the contract for Donizetti's *Caterina Cornaro* is in the Vienna Stadtbibliothek, and it stipulates that the composer was to receive 12,000 francs for his score.

222 Z. no. 426, dated 6 June 1842, p. 614.

223 The most successful of Sacchèro's librettos was that for Federico Ricci's *Corrado d'Altamura*. He also wrote the texts for Nini's *Odalisa*, Ricci's *Vallombra*, and Pacini's *L'ebrea*, the last an adaptation of Scribe's poem for Halévy's *La juive*.

224 When Donizetti speaks here of Acts 1 and 2 of *Caterina*, he is referring to what are, in fact, the prologue and Act 1.

225 Z. no. 451, dated 8 November 1842, p. 635. To date *Caterina* has never been produced at La Scala.

226 S.d. 1, no. 99, p. 94.

227 Anna Bishop (1814–84) abandoned the composer Sir Henry Bishop, whom she had married in 1831, to elope with the harpist Robert Bochsa. With his encouragement she pursued a career as a prima donna in Vienna, Naples, America and Australia. Having survived shipwreck in the mid-Pacific, she died of apoplexy in New York.

228 Z. no. 489, p. 670. In the light of the fiasco of *Caterina's prima*, one may well wonder how scrupulous was the musical preparation accorded it in Donizetti's absence.

229 Z. no. 490, undated, late June 1843, p. 672. Elsewhere in this letter Donizetti makes what must be an allusion to the banning of *Maria Stuarda* in Naples (when King Ferdinando II forbade it because Mary Stuart was one of his ancestors): 'And then the King [James II of Cyprus] does not belong to the family tree of anyone at all, thus no one can get angry.'

230 I have been unable to discover why *Caterina* was postponed. From the flurry of letters Donizetti addressed to his Neapolitan friends in June 1843 it is clear he believed the *prima* to be imminent (it had originally been scheduled for July 1843). But then on 9 July he writes to Dolci: 'At Naples, I lose 2500 francs and I am not going.' (Z. no. 495, p. 678.) This remark probably alludes to the cut in fee he had had to take for being absent from the *prima*, but he says nothing about a forthcoming performance which he would probably have mentioned had he not heard that it had been postponed.

Some light is shed by his letter of 18 November to Ghezzi. 'I hear of the continual quarreling of the management [of the San Carlo], and I grieve for the public that is always badly served.' (Z. no. 523, pp. 705–6.) Whatever was the nature of these quarrels, all the indications are that once again the San Carlo was in financial difficulties. That this may well have been so is suggested by the *Cronache del Teatro di San Carlo* (vol. 1, p. 77), which shows that there were no new productions between 26 September 1843 and 5 January 1844. Normally several new operas would have been mounted during such a stretch, especially in November when royal galas were traditional.

231 Vincenzo Flauto was then the right-hand man to Guillaume, who was officially the lessee of the royal theaters until 1848. In 1842 Donizetti had dealt with Guillaume, from 1843 on all his dealings over the San Carlo would be with Flauto.

232 The Italian word, translated here as 'harsh treatment', is 'griffe,' literally 'hobnails'.

233 Z. no. 523, p. 706.

234 It has previously always been stated that the *prima* of *Caterina* was given on 12 January 1844. The true date was established by Jeremy Commons, and revealed in his article 'Unknown Donizetti Items in the Neapolitan Journal "Il Sibilo"', *Donizetti Society Journal*, 2 (1975), pp. 145–9.

235 Filippo Coletti (1811–94), a baritone, made his debut at the Teatro del Fondo in 1834, and was soon hailed as a legitimate successor to Tamburini. He continued his career until 1869, when even his loyal Neapolitan public could no longer tolerate his lamentable vocal state and forced him to retire. He sang in the *prima* of *Caterina Cornaro*, but he is better remembered for singing baritone parts in early Verdi operas, having participated in the first casts of *Alzira* and *I masnadieri*. Chorley recalled his first appearance in London in 1840 – where he was greeted by a public protest precipitating the so-called 'Tamburini riot' – as revealing 'an expressive, manly artist, with a fine baritone voice less

flexible and versatile than Signor Tamburini' (*Thirty Years' Musical Recollections*, p. 124).

236 Antonio Farelli was the principal conductor at the San Carlo from 1839 until 1860.

237 *S.d.* 1, no. 111, p. 106 (also published in less complete form as *Z.* no. 538, p. 724). The reference to Anna Bishop and Bochsa in the letter refers to the latter's florid account of Bishop's success in *Linda* at Naples, where, from other reports, Donizetti learned that she had been inadequate.

238 *Z.* no. 542, dated 6 February 1844, p. 728.

239 At Parma in 1845 the role of Caterina was sung by Marianna Barbieri-Nini, who two years later would be Verdi's first Lady Macbeth, Ivanoff sang Gerardo and Felice Varesi was Lusignano; the conductor was Nicola de Giovanni. Put on almost at the close of the Carnival season at Parma, *Caterina* was given five times before it ended.

240 Felice Varesi, who sang the altered part of Lusignano at Parma, was much influenced by Giorgio Ronconi. During the 1840s when Ronconi was elsewhere, Varesi was the most important exponent of the 'new' baritone vocal type active in Italy. Although this type of voice is particularly connected with Verdi, from the time of *Il furioso* Donizetti did much to reveal its dramatic possibilities.

241 His earlier two operas for the Opéra had been *Les martyrs* (derived from *Poliuto*, composed for the San Carlo) and *La favorite* (adapted from *L'ange de Nisida*, intended for the Renaissance).

242 The aesthetic vision of musical drama as it was presented at the Opéra – great drama harnessed to brilliant singing, massive scenery, lavish ballet, great crowd scenes, all sustained by expressive music – was not really supplanted until the opening of Bayreuth in 1876. That the most representative works of the French school of grand opera are generally unperformed today is largely an economic problem. They require larger numbers of first-rank singers than are usually found in a single cast today, and to stage them as they were intended to be staged is enormously expensive. It is the peculiar liability of these works that they do not fare well when performed against unit sets or when sung by singers of less than exceptional vocal accomplishment.

243 *S.d.* 1, no. 99, dated 9 March 1843, p. 94, to Giacomo Sacchèro.

244 *Z.* no. 457, p. 640. This letter lacks an address, most likely because it was sent by hand.

245 Donizetti customarily communicated with Scribe via Accursi. There were probably two motives for this: he could explain himself in Italian to Accursi, saving time; and while Scribe might delay answering letters, he would have to deal with Accursi in person – another way of expediting progress.

246 *S.d.* 1, no. 98, p. 92. Barroilhet would sing the role of the poet, Camoëns; Massol that of Abayaldos, the Moorish chief.

247 *S.d.* 1, no. 100, p. 95.

248 *S.d.* 1, no. 105, p. 100.

249 Donizetti was well aware that Duprez's vocal method, with his famous high Cs from the chest, had compromised his facility in the upper

register. As early as the time of *Les martyrs* in 1840, Donizetti had found his vocal powers diminished. Near the end of March 1843 Donizetti had heard a rumor that the tenor Gustave Roger, who was then engaged at the Opéra-Comique, was to move to the Opéra, and he writes to Accursi: 'If Roger should be engaged, I notify you that my music would go well with him because I have thought of Duprez as quite limited.' (*S.d.* 1, no. 101, dated 26 March 1843, p. 95.) Roger did not, in fact, make his debut at the Opéra until 1849 in the premiere of *Le prophète*.

250 *S.d.* 1, no. 106, dated 23 June 1843, p. 103.
251 What Donizetti really means here is that he has sketched four acts at this point. He did most of the work on the brief Act 5 in early October 1843.
252 Z. no. 496, pp. 678–9.
253 Z. no. 498, p. 682.
254 Z. no. 501, p. 684.
255 Z. no. 505, p. 688. Donizetti does not mention to Scribe his other reasons for feeling the pressure of time. He was committed to prepare *Belisario* at the Théâtre-Italien (introduced on 24 October 1843), and to supervise *Maria Padilla* there, which was to be performed for the first time the night after the *prima* of *Dom Sébastien*!
256 Z. no. 507, p. 690.
257 Z. no. 510, p. 694.
258 Z. no. 516, pp. 698–9.
259 The anecdote about Meyerbeer's dinner is found in Second's *Les petits mystères de l'Opéra*, p. 278.
260 *Dom Sébastien* was sung by Stolz (Zaïda), Duprez (the title role), Barroilhet (Camoëns), Levasseur (Dom Juan de Silva), Massol (Abayaldos), Octave (Dom Antonio), Brémont (Ben-Selim) and Prévost (Dom Henrique). It was conducted by Habeneck.
261 The problem with *Dom Sébastien* from the French point of view is neatly summarized by Clément and Larousse in their *Dictionnaire des opéras* (p. 232): 'This score, full of life, warmth and grace, has been buried by Scribe beneath a text that is lugubrious, absurd, monotonous. Let us feel regret for this new victim of Scribe.'
262 *Dom Sébastien* in German was introduced at the Kärntnertor by Clara (Stöckl-)Heinefetter (Zaïda), Josef Erl (Sebastian), Eduard Leithner (Camoëns), Josef Draxler (Don Juan de Sylva), Franz Wild, *als Gast* (not a permanent member of the company) (Abayaldos), Karl Wolf (Don Antonio) and Gustav Hölzel (Ben-Selim). The German translation was by Donizetti's friend Leo Herz.
263 Donizetti had been worried about how Italian censors would treat the funeral and the trial by the Inquisition in *Dom Sébastien*. The problems were resolved more easily than he could have anticipated: the funeral was treated as a state rather than a religious procession, and the court before which Sébastien and Zaïda are tried was called a 'tribunale', the 'Inquisitori' becoming 'Giudici'.
264 At Florence Fedora Barbieri sang Zaïda, Gianni Poggi was Sebastiano and Enzo Mascherini sang Camoëns.

6. 1843–1848: The last years

1 Léon Escudier, *Mes souvenirs* (Paris, 1863).

2 Z. no. 640, dated 18 June 1845, p. 815.

3 See Z. no. 638, p. 812.

4 Scribe's libretto, dealing with the unhappy life of the daughter of Ferdinand and Isabella, was accepted by Louis Clapisson (1808–66), whose *Jeanne la folle* was first given at the Opéra on 6 November 1848. Menotti's recent opera *La loca* (San Diego, 1979) deals with the same historical figure.

5 Z. no. 646, dated 11 August 1845, p. 820.

6 Z. no. 648, p. 823.

7 Z. no. 654, dated 18 October 1845, pp. 826–7.

8 Alborghetti and Galli, *Gaetano Donizetti e G. Simone Mayr*, Appendix: 'Consultation pour le 28 janvier 1846'.

9 Donizetti's letters from Ivry are printed as Z. nos. 661–9, pp. 831–7; the first seven have dates between 5 and 8 or 9 February 1846, the last two are undated. Four later letters that are practically indecipherable are reprinted in facsimile as Z. nos. 670–3, pp. 837–9; the first two were written in May, the third in September, and the fourth is undated. These thirteen letters were eventually sold by Andrea's sons to a Milanese collector.

10 Z. no. 663, dated 6 February 1846, p. 833.

11 Z. no. 666, dated 7 February 1846, pp. 834–5. The italics are Donizetti's.

12 Delessert (1786–1853) may have had a number of reasons for his antagonism toward Donizetti. A man of rigid moral principles, whose wife was for years the *amie* of Prosper Merimée, he could understandably have become prejudiced against artists as a class, and against those who were the subject of scandal in particular. The author of rigid statutes to enforce standards of dress and demeanor in public places, Delessert might well have been prejudiced against Donizetti because of complaints made to the police during those hectic, tragic months before he was confined at Ivry. The content of the dossier on Donizetti, if such is still preserved in the police archives, might answer many questions about this period of his life.

13 Alborghetti and Galli, *Gaetano Donizetti e G. Simone Mayr*, Appendix: 'Consultation pour le 30 aout 1846'.

14 Z. no. 672, p. 839, in facsimile. I believe this to have been the last letter Donizetti wrote; Zavadini places the undated no. 673 last, but this might have been written at any time from late February 1846 onward.

15 Royer, *Histoire de l'Opéra*, p. 156. Royer says it was he who introduced Dr Ricord to Donizetti after he had become alarmed by the poor state of the composer's health (p. 155).

16 Zavadini, *Donizetti: Vita – Musiche – Epistolario*, dated 22 January 1847, pp. 152–3.

17 Entry dated 24 April 1847. Andrea's daybook is in the Museo Donizettiano, Bergamo.

18 Andrea's daybook, entry dated 10 May 1847.

19 Andrea's daybook, entry dated 23 June 1847.

20 Alborghetti and Galli, *Gaetano Donizetti e G. Simone Mayr*, Appendix: 'Istanza, Constantinopoli, il 16 agosto 1847'.

21 Francesco, the simple-minded brother who had succeeded his father at the Monte di Pietà in Bergamo, had arrived in Paris on 12 August 1847, a token figure to make a public show of family solidarity.

22 Today this portrait hangs in the Museo Donizettiano in Bergamo. Also on display is the armchair fitted with a prop for Gaetano's head, the bed he died in, even the jacket he was buried in (it was removed when his body was transferred to Santa Maria Maggiore in 1875). Of all the memorabilia in the museum, the most poignant is the piano from his Naples apartment which he had presented to Toto's daughter, another Virginia. The brass plaque on it bears the words in which Gaetano had described this instrument to Toto (Z. no. 494, postmarked 3 July 1843, p. 676):

> Do not sell the pianoforte for any price, for contained in it is my whole artistic life. From 1822 I have had the sound of it in my ears; there murmured the *Annas*, the *Marias*, the *Fausta*, the *Lucias*, the *Robertos*, the *Belisarii*, the *Marinos*, the *Martyrs*, the *Olivos*, *Ajo*, *Furioso*, *Paria*, *Castello di Kenilworth*, *Ugo*, *Pazzi*, *Pia*, *Rudenz*. Oh, let it live as long as I live. With that piano I lived my time of hope, my married life, my solitary time. It heard my joys, my tears, my deluded hopes, my honors, it shared with me my sweating and my labor, my talent lived there, in that piano lives every period of my career, of yours . . . Your father, your brother, all have seen it, been familiar with it, all have tormented it. It was everyone's companion and may it be one forever to your daughter as a dowry of a thousand thoughts, sad and gay.

23 Zavadini, *Donizetti: Vita – Musiche – Epistolario*, p. 160.
24 *Ibid.*, p. 161.
25 Alborghetti and Galli, *Gaetano Donizetti e G. Simone Mayr*, Appendix: 'Autopsia', the autopsy confirmed the suspected diagnosis: deep and extensive lesions were found in the pia mater and on the dura mater, the latter extending from the fifth dorsal to the second lumbar vertebra. One of the saddest aspects of Donizetti's disease is that today it could have been easily cured.
26 Not interred with the rest was the top half of the skull. This memento was carried off by a Dr Gerolamo Carchen. When in 1875, at the time that Donizetti's body was transferred to Santa Maria Maggiore, this portion was found to be missing, a search was instituted, and it was discovered being used as a receptacle for change in a store near Bergamo. Retrieved too late to be buried with the rest of his remains, it was placed in a special urn in the Museo Donizettiano where it remained until 1951, when Donizetti's body was moved once more, to another part of Santa Maria Maggiore; on that occasion Guido Zavadini, for fifty years the curator of the Museo, reverently restored it to its fitting resting-place.
27 Unpublished letter in the Museo Donizettiano, Bergamo.

7. Donizetti's operatic world

1 Second (*Les petits mystères de l'Opéra*, pp. 303–4) gives a representative view of Donizetti in 1844:

> M. Donizetti, who is still in his hardy prime, had already composed a formidable number of operas. He is the Alexandre Dumas of music, just as the author of

Antony is the Donizetti of literature. He writes like a steam-engine and passes half his life in a coach; at Paris today, in two weeks at Vienna, and the following month at Naples, at Turin, at Rome, at Venice, at Milan or at Florence, everywhere in short where there is an impresario, a theater, an orchestra and some singers ... M. Donizetti is not only the Alexandre Dumas of music, he is also the Jupiter. If ever his coach should happen to overturn – God forbid that it should – and if he should split his head on a stone in the road, I am quite sure that there would issue from his brain sixty acts all armed like Minerva, that is to say, orchestrated and all ready to go into rehearsal.

A lithograph published in *Panthéon charivarique* (1840), which is reproduced in Zavadini (*Donizetti: Vita – Musiche – Epistolario*, p. 512), shows Donizetti simultaneously writing a serious opera with his left hand and a comic one with his right, alluding to the first performances that spring of *La fille* at the Opéra-Comique and *Les martyrs* at the Opéra. Appended to the picture is a quatrain:

> Donizetti dont le brillant génie
> Nous a donné cent chefs d'oeuvres divers,
> N'aura bientôt qu'une patrie
> Et sera tout l'univers.

(Donizetti, whose brilliant genius has given us a hundred different masterpieces, will soon have only one native country and it will be the whole universe.)

2 The repertory concept that now exists in Europe and the United States – in most of the world's opera houses in fact – reflects more closely the practise of the Théâtre-Italien during the early nineteenth century than it does that of La Scala or the San Carlo.

3 Gatti, *Il Teatro alla Scala*, vol. 2, pp. 11–27. The performance history of La Scala illustrates these points conveniently as it is representative of the activities of an Italian opera house giving year-round performances at that period. The smaller Italian theaters, giving opera only in one month or two of the year, generally staged fewer *prime* and rarely repeated an opera after its initial production, although there are some exceptions. After 1850 repetitions of operas became increasingly frequent in all Italian theaters.

4 Of Bellini's eight operas performed at La Scala during these years, only one (*Bianca e Fernando*) was given in a single season, while *Norma* returned most frequently, appearing in six.

5 Several of Donizetti's operas that had only one production at La Scala during his lifetime went on to enjoy extensive careers there, for instance, *La fille du régiment* and *La favorite*.

6 Patric Schmid and Don White are preparing for publication a detailed survey of this large and complex subject.

7 See White, 'The Three Gabriellas'. For the 1838 version of *Gabriella* Donizetti took from *Maria de Rudenz* the prelude and the basic construction of two duets and of the final cabaletta.

8 Donizetti's libretto to *Le convenienze* reveals that the opera seria being rehearsed is entitled *Romolo ed Ersilia*, the latter a name close enough to *Elvida* to strengthen the allusion to that score. When Donizetti expanded *Le convenienze* into two acts, he dropped the scene from *Elvida*, replacing it with 'È puoi goder, tiranno!' with its cabaletta, 'Or

vicino è il bel momento'. Since the allusion to *Elvida* was at best a local Neapolitan joke (*Elvida* was apparently never given anywhere else), Donizetti decided to substitute another scena that more broadly parodied the tone of opera seria.

9 A scena consists of a *tempo d'attacco*, a first aria or duet, a *tempo di mezzo*, and a cabaletta or stretta to conclude.

10 It is surprising that Tosi should have taken over Amelia's scena from *Il castello di Kenilworth*, because she had sung the role of Elisabetta in the *prima* of that opera.

11 I use the term 'cantabile' in roman type to mean the slow part (or first aria) of a double aria. Such a section may follow a number of patterns – strophic and two-period cantabiles are encountered with some frequency.

12 A cabaletta is the second section of a double aria, usually in a major key and duple meter, consisting of two identical statements. While Verdi's cabalettas (e.g. Violetta's 'Sempre libera') are usually *allegro*, Donizetti's are often *moderato* and sometimes at a slower tempo than the preceding aria. Cabalettas of duets may consist of three statements (one for each participant and a third in which the voices are either in unison or harmony), but particularly in the later scores the voices may have contrasting melodies (as in the Sara–Nottingham duet in *Roberto Devereux*) or share two statements (as in the Caterina–Gerardo duet at the end of the prologue of *Caterina Cornaro*). The statements of a cabaletta may be separated by intermediary material, or may follow each other directly.

13 'Rondò' is the term applied to a particular aria type often used as the second movement of an aria–finale, consisting of a symmetrical melody followed by three variations, each one set off by a short instrumental passage. A conventional two-statement cabaletta could also occupy this position, and Donizetti in fact used 'rondò' indiscriminately to denote the second aria of an aria–finale regardless of its form.

14 In his letter Donizetti makes the curious mistake of referring to this opera as *Bianca di Castiglia*. Could this have been the original title of the work, or perhaps he confused it with *Bianca d'Aquitania*, the first title of *Ugo, conte di Parigi*?

15 Z. no. 389, dated 24–5 December ('midnight') 1841, pp. 569–70.

16 Although Fanny Maray had exasperated Donizetti with her request for a new *rondò* to use in *Lucia*, she was well enough liked in the part by the Romans to be engaged to repeat it the following year.

17 Z. no. 485, dated 30 May 1843, p. 666.

18 Luigi Savi was the composer of a *Caterina di Cleves*, which Merelli had put on at La Scala, 22 September 1841.

19 Z. no. 514, dated 31 October 1843, p. 696.

20 Nor should it be overlooked that Mayr's influence extended to sharing his library of opera scores, some of which he had copied himself, with Donizetti and his other pupils. Among the works he had copies of were: *Médée* and *Demofoonte* by Cherubini; *Gli Orazi ed i Curiazi* by Cimarosa; *Armide, Iphigénie en Aulide, Alceste* and *Orfeo* by Gluck; Haydn's *Armida*; Jommelli's *Attilio Regolo*; Méhul's *Joseph*; Spontini's *La vestale*; and Traetta's *Ippolito*.

21 'In *opera buffa*.. Mayr reveals all the clumsy, elephantine gaiety of a good, dull-witted burgher.' (Stendhal, *Life of Rossini*, ed. and trans. R. N. Coe (Seattle, 1970), p. 23.)

22 *Che originali!*, because its plot invited the interpolation of music, was more often performed as a pasticcio than with Mayr's complete score. As a pasticcio it was frequently retitled, most often as *Il trionfo della musica* or *Il fanatico per la musica*. When the high-handed Angelica Catalani put it on at the Théâtre-Italien in 1817, she retained only one number of Mayr's original score. *Che originali!* indeed!

23 Some earlier examples of operas satirizing musicians are: Haydn's *La cantarina* (1767), Deller's *Il maestro di cappella* (1771), Champein's *La mélomanie* (1781), Mozart's *Der Schauspieldirektor* (1786) and Cimarosa's *L'impresario in angustie* (1786).

24 An example of Mayr's elaborate obbligato writing is to be found in the flute, clarinet and horn parts to Ariodante's monologue in Act 2 of *Ginevra di Scozia* (Trieste, 1801).

25 Ludwig Schiedermair's exhaustive work on Mayr, *Beiträge zur Geschichte der Oper* (2 vols., Leipzig 1907) contains (vol. 1, note 31) a list of the appointments Mayr refused. These include the directorship of Italian seasons in Vienna (1803), St Petersburg (1806), Paris (1806), and Lisbon and London (1807), an invitation to direct the new Milan Conservatory (1808), and one to succeed Paër at Dresden (1808), the position of *maestro di cappella* at the Sistine Chapel, Rome (1816), and the succession to Padre Mattei's post at Bologna, following his death in 1825.

26 Verzino, *Le opere di Donizetti*, p. 185.

27 Bonesi, 'Note biografiche'.

28 I am grateful to Patric Schmid and Don White for pointing out the resemblance between Enrico's cabaletta and Anna's 'Al dolce guidami'.

29 Although Pasta was five months younger than Donizetti and had made her debut as early as 1815 at Brescia, she did not emerge as a major star until her Paris debut in 1821.

30 According to Alberto Cametti (*Un poeta melodrammatico romano* (Milan, 1898), p. 112), Pacini's contributions to *Matilde di Shabran* were the Act 2 trio, 'Deh! serena il mesto ciglio', and the first section of the Act 2 duet, 'No, Matilde, non morrai'. Herbert Weinstock (*Rossini* (New York, 1968), p. 105) quotes Francesco Regli's *Dizionario biografico* (Turin, 1860) as claiming that Rossini asked Pacini to write three pieces for the score.

31 At the San Carlo, at least, *Saffo* proved the most durable of Pacini's scores, returning in thirteen seasons, until 1870.

32 Mercadante's name was absent even longer from the San Carlo billboards than from those of La Scala. No work of his seems to have been performed there between 1825 and 1831, though his operas may have been given at other Neapolitan theaters.

33 Malibran and her emulators traditionally substituted the last act of Vaccai's *Giulietta e Romeo* for the final scene of Bellini's *I Capuleti*. In Vaccai's final scene, Romeo's 'Ah, se tu dormi' was long regarded as a touchstone of the mezzo-soprano repertory.

34 *Stendhal, correspondance inédite*, p. 257.

35 Verzino, *Le opere di Donizetti*, p. 24.
36 Rossini customarily used either 4/4 or 2/4 rhythms in the *allegro* sections of his first finales, but not invariably, as the triple rhythms used at this point in *Zelmira* and *Semiramide* demonstrate. In the finales to Rossini's comic operas the pattern tends to build up to an outburst of loquacity, and dance rhythms are therefore uncommon.
37 The aria–finale is a double aria at the end of an opera for the prima donna, with other voices ('pertichini') added, usually in the *tempo di mezzo*; the second movement is usually either a strict *rondò* or a conventional two-statement cabaletta.
38 Florimo, *Bellini: memorie e lettere*, p. 130.
39 Distinct from the finales are the large-scale ensembles, frequently sextets, often found in the second acts of Rossini's operas. For these ensembles two positions are common: at the outset of the act, as in *Ricciardo e Zoraide*, in the penultimate scene, as in *La Cenerentola*. The septet in *La zingara* is situated like the latter, being the tenth in a score of twelve numbers.
40 The ultimate source of this tale was the fourteenth-century *roman* of more than 8000 lines, *Le chastelain de Couci*. Here the hero is named Renault, not Raoul, and, after many adventures he dies crusading and sends to his lady a final song, a letter of farewell, along with his embalmed heart. The casket containing these mementoes is intercepted by the lady's husband, the Sieur de Fayel, who has the heart cooked up and served to his wife, and she upon learning the source of this ragout renounces earthly food and shortly dies. (See Maurice Delbouille, *Le roman du chastelain de Couci et de la dame de Fayel* (Paris, 1936).)
41 Carafa's *Gabriella* and Rossini's *Otello* had their *prime* at the Fondo because the San Carlo had burned down on the night of 12 February 1816 after a ballet rehearsal; the entire theater was rebuilt with such dispatch that it reopened exactly eleven months later, 12 January 1817 being the king's birthday, with an apposite cantata by Mayr entitled *Il sogno di Partenope*. Perhaps the improvised situation at the Fondo, combined with vestiges of French influence still remaining after the recent restoration of Ferdinando I, were responsible for the censors' ignoring, at least temporarily, the absence of the *lieto fine*. Clearly there was greater pressure in favor of happy endings when Donizetti arrived in Naples in 1822, but the survival of *Gabriella* (annually until 1827) and *Otello* (performed regularly in Naples until about 1880) shows that a degree of success with the public conferred some sort of immunity from the prevailing official taste of the 1820s.
42 Z. no. 27, dated 15 June 1826, p. 247.
43 See Andrew Porter's essay accompanying the Angel/EMI recording of *Il pirata* with Montserrat Caballé.
44 Not at the beginning of the *allegro vivace*, but forty-six measures into it, at the words 'Non casa, non spiaggia raccolga i fugenti'.
45 From *Anna Bolena*, Anna's outburst, 'Ah! segnata è la mia sorte'; from *Il furioso*, Eleonora's 'Nel mio sguardo mezzo spento'; from *Maria Stuarda*, Elisabetta's 'Va, preparati furente a soffrir l'estremo fato'; and from *Roberto Devereux*, Elisabetta's 'Va, la morte sul capo ti pende'.
46 In the cabaletta of the soprano–tenor duet at the end of the prologue to

Caterina Cornaro, 'Va, crudel; maladetto quel giorno', the regular
rhythmic pattern is set to an impetuous scalar melody (A minor) which
increases in tension in its second period (A major) with insistently
repeated sequences; this tension is further heightened in the second
statement when both voices double the major melody.

47 Z. no. 49, dated 24 July 1829, p. 268.

48 Donizetti used the term 'cavatina' quite loosely to apply to a single aria
without cabaletta (such as Nemorino's 'Quanto è bella', which forms
part of the *introduzione* to *L'elisir d'amore*); or to a slow aria with a
cabaletta (such as Belcore's entrance aria, where the second statement
of the cabaletta develops into a concertato), or to a buffo aria (such as
Dulcamara's 'Udite, udite, o rustici'). It is difficult to use the word with
any precision since it obviously did not connote to Donizetti any set
pattern, but rather a wide range of aria types.

49 Both *Le siège de Corinthe* and *Moïse* had been introduced to Italy in
concert form in Rome before their first staged productions.

50 Romani's libretto for *Zaïra* had already been set by Bellini, but that
opera, put on to open the Teatro Regio in Parma (16 May 1829), had
proved a monumental fiasco.

51 *Il giuramento* began a run of ten performances at La Scala on 10 January
1872; the last Mercadante score previously given had been *Il bravo*,
given twelve times from December 1862.

52 According to de Filippis and Arnese (*Cronache del Teatro di San Carlo
(1737–1960)*, vol. 1, pp. 27–93, 209–12), the last nineteenth-century
performance of a Mercadante opera at the San Carlo was *Orazi e
Curiazi* in 1882. The last production of one of his works before that had
been *La vestale* in 1873. Of the twenty-eight works by Mercadante
performed at the San Carlo, only nine returned for a second season or
more. His three most popular works were *Gabriella di Vergy*, given in
four seasons; *La vestale* in seven; and *Il giuramento* in eight, most
recently in 1954–5, when it constituted the first twentieth-century revival of a work by Mercadante at that theater. It is only fair to emphasize
that these figures do not include performances at either the Fondo or
the Nuovo, for which seasonal figures are not readily available.

53 This La Scala survey is based on Carlo Gatti's two-volume work already
cited, and it excludes such non-operatic works as Verdi's *Inno delle
nazioni* and Rossini's *Stabat mater*. Of the other composers whose
works were performed between December 1862 and January 1872, only
Gounod had four productions, and only Halévy had three (all of *La
juive* in Italian). Composers who received two productions include
Antonio Cagnoni, Franco Faccio, Errico Petrella and Antonio Carlos
Gomes; those with one include Mozart, Auber, Flotow, Boito, Filippo
Marchetti, Antonio Bazzini, Giulio Beer, Giuseppe Rota, Hippolyte-
André Chelard, Angelo Villanis, Bartolomeo Pisani, Nicolai, Achille
Montuoro, Prince Józef Poniatowski and Giuseppe Strigelli.

8. Donizetti's use of operatic conventions

1 In its original form for Naples in 1834 *Maria Stuarda* had just a prelude; when he converted the score into *Buondelmonte* Donizetti

adopted an existing overture from an opera not yet produced in Naples (this is suggested by his letter to Ricordi, Z. no. 174, dated 5 September 1835, p. 383). Since that overture would have been recognized in Milan, Donizetti offered to write a new one for the La Scala production of *Maria Stuarda*, for which incidentally he collected an additional fee. The prelude is used in the complete recording of *Maria Stuarda* with Joan Sutherland, the overture in that with Beverly Sills.

2 An example of a later prelude replacing an earlier overture can be found in Verdi's *Aida*.

3 *S.d.* 1, no. 90, dated 30 April 1842, p. 82, to Accursi.

4 Considering the haste with which Donizetti composed *L'elisir*, I have always suspected that he lifted this *larghetto* theme and variations from one of his earlier, non-operatic works, but so far I have been unable to locate a source.

5 The *preludio–introduzione* complex from *Il castello di Kenilworth* became, after considerable amplification and modification, the *sinfonia–introduzione* complex in *Alina*.

6 The overture to *L'ajo* contains material that recurs in the course of the opera: the first theme (in dotted rhythm) is used again in Gregorio's Act 2 aria 'Zitta, zitta, non piangete'.

7 The word 'asymmetrical' is used here and elsewhere to mean 'having sections of unequal or unbalanced length'.

8 In *Ermione* the choral participation in the overture, a lament for the fall of Troy, occurs during the slow introduction.

9 I use the term 'sonatina pattern' to indicate first-movement form without development, but with a modulating bridge passage to make the transition from the end of the exposition to the recapitulation.

10 The first number of *Linda* is headed: 'Introduzione, Scena e Romanza', and here the brief opening offstage chorus is followed by recitative.

11 The third type of *introduzione* – the most advanced and dramatically coherent – is not found in Mercadante's 'reform' operas such as *Il giuramento*, *Il bravo* and *La vestale*; in all these cases Mercadante chose instead an opening chorus followed by recitative.

12 *Le siège de Corinthe* begins with a male chorus; *Moïse* and *Tell* with a mixed chorus. The comic *Le comte Ory* begins with a brief ensemble for solo voices and a mixed chorus.

13 See Gossett, 'Anna Bolena e la maturità di Donizetti', 1⁰ convegno internazionale di studi donizettiani, Bergamo, 1975.

14 Even at the end of his career Donizetti wrote asymmetrical choruses. *Dom Sébastien* opens with the chorus 'Nautoniers, mettez à la voile'; as it was first performed in Paris it contained a full choral statement, followed by a recitative for Dom Antonio and Dom Juan de Silva and balanced by an abridged statement of the chorus. Even though this repetition was subsequently cut by Donizetti for the Vienna production of 1845, it is germane to the discussion here, for he abridged the original precisely by removing everything but the main thematic period (thirty-two measures), which he attached to the coda and cadential figures (thirty measures), leaving the same general pattern already observed in *Belisario* and *Anna Bolena*.

15 See Z. no. 319, p. 494, in which Donizetti informs Mayr of how Parisian

taste is shaping his transformation of *Poliuto* into *Les martyrs*: 'banished are the usual cadences, *felicità, felicità, felicità*'. Professor Gossett pointed out to me how the thrice-repeated 'felicità' imitates the characteristic rhythm of conventional cadential sequences (see Chapter 5, note 16).

16 Very probably there originally was a recitative to Folco's aria which explained his part in the death of Luigi's father, King Lotario; it seems likely that its removal was enforced by the censors since this vital point of motivation is not explained elsewhere in the libretto. Instead of rewording the offending passages, Romani simply suppressed them; Romani was, in fact, so offended by the censors' tampering with his text for *Ugo* that he refused to let his name appear on the printed libretto.

17 Don White and Patric Schmid point out, from their experience with the Opera Rara performance of *Rosmonda d'Inghilterra*, that this score provides an excellent example of forward momentum through the *introduzione* into the next numbers: 'Each piece flows into the next. The audience cannot applaud until the tenor has left, and then not again until the end of Act 1.' (Letter to the author, 10 January 1981.)

18 I use the phrase 'materia di mezzo' to indicate the presence of more than one tempo between the first and second parts of a double aria or ensemble, retaining the more familiar 'tempo di mezzo' when they are separated by a single tempo marking.

19 In *L'italiana* Isabella's *rondò* is followed by an ensemble–finale, while in *Cenerentola* the moralizing ensemble is combined with but dominated by Angiolina's *rondò*.

20 The one-act farsa *La romanziera* ends with a number analogous to that which concludes *Elvida*.

21 Z. no. 38, dated 2 February 1828, p. 257.

22 Among Donizetti's later scores *Maria de Rudenz* approaches and possibly surpasses *Il castello di Kenilworth* in brevity.

23 It is not clear how Donizetti intended *Maria Padilla* to end before the censors insisted that Maria 'die of joy'; but since the title role was written for Sofia Löwe I suspect that the present cabaletta–finale either restores or replaces one originally intended for this point in the score. Donizetti did write a pair of arias for Maria Padilla's entrance, but Ricordi's printed score (probably published not long after the *prima* on 26 December 1841; plate number H 13554 H) includes only her cabaletta, 'Ah, non sai qual prestigio'. The Opera Rara performance of this score in 1974 preceded it with the cavatina.

24 'In *Lucia* I was the victim, because she was certainly not the brightest star, and I myself heard her many times say: "The curtain will fall after the aria of la Persiani!"' (Z. no. 210, dated 21 May 1836, p. 410.) Donizetti's comments clearly indicate that Duprez aroused more enthusiasm than his prima donna.

25 S.d. 1, no. 47, p. 40.

26 There is a powerful confrontation in *Rosmonda* between the King's mistress, Rosmonda, and his wife, Eleonora, which prefigures the dramatic intensity of the encounter in *Maria Stuarda*.

27 On 8 November 1842 Donizetti wrote to Ricordi (Z. no. 451, p. 635) that he had finished Act 1 of *Caterina Cornaro* all except for one chorus

when he put it aside because of Lachner's opera on the same subject. If he had completed so much of Act 1, it seems justifiable to assume that he had completed the prologue as well. In the same month – November 1842 – he began composing *Don Pasquale*.

28 Yet Scribe in his libretto for *Les martyrs* did not everywhere follow Corneille. He omitted Polyeucte's suggestion that, after his death, Pauline should marry Sévère. Further, he dispensed with the conversion of Félix and with Sévère's gesture of sparing the martyrs as well as his promise to end the persecution of the Christians.

29 The original French score contains only two solo statements of the big tune of the duet, but by the end of the nineteenth century, French singers had a tradition of doubling the last part of the second (Léonor's) statement, as may be heard in the recordings by Marie Delna–Albert Alvarez and by Suzanne Brohly–Léon Beyle. The Italian tradition of three statements, two solo and the last in unison, is perpetuated in the current Ricordi score of *La favorita* (plate number 46268).

30 The rhythmic pattern of the accompaniment and the shape of the vocal line of the *Favorite* duet were imitated exactly by Ponchielli in the opening phrases of the duet 'L'amo come il fulgor' in Act 2 of *La gioconda*.

31 A striking affirmation of the indestructible effectiveness of this sextet occurred in Berlin in September 1955, when Karajan allowed his cast, headed by Callas, to encore it.

32 In the *tempo di mezzo* of the *L'esule* trio four confidants of Publio (four basses) appear briefly to order Settimio to return to prison without delay. Otherwise, the trio–finale is exclusively for the three solo characters. Bellini adds a chorus to the trio–finale of Act 1 of *Norma*.

33 *Bellini, epistolario*, no. CXVI, dated 26 December 1831, pp. 290–2.

34 I have always felt that Verdi had a subconscious memory of the *Maria Stuarda* sextet when he composed the quintet, 'S'appressan gl'istanti' (*Nabucco*, Act 2); the second statement at a^1 in the Donizetti ensemble hints at just the sort of canonic exploitation that Verdi masterfully employs in his monothematic quintet.

9. The operas: 1816–1830

1 'Scena lirica' is the designation used by Antonio Sografi in his libretto for Giambattista Cimadoro's *Pimmaglione* (Venice, 1790); it is a direct equivalent of 'scène-lyrique', J.-J. Rousseau's description of his play *Pygmalion* (Lyons, 1770) of which Sografi's libretto is a translation. (Cimadoro's *Pimmaglione* may first have been performed in 1788, see Alfred Lowenthal, *Annals of Opera*, 2nd edn (2 vols., Geneva, 1955), cols. 474–5.)

2 In his letter of agreement with Zancla, Merelli refers to his source, as nearly as his handwriting can be deciphered, as *Giovanna di Monfalcor* (i.e. August von Kotzebue's *Johanna von Montfaucon*). Later, at someone's suggestion (perhaps his own, Mayr's, Donizetti's or Zancla's) the subject for what was to be *Enrico di Borgogna* was derived from another play by Kotzebue – *Der Graf von Burgund*.

3 Z. no. 7, dated 13 October 1818, p. 228.

4 Merelli's opening chorus of shepherds contains this enterprising but scarcely poetical sentiment: 'Il sudor/È grato ognor' (Sweat is always agreeable)!

5 The scenes in Donizetti's librettos are divided off by the entrances and exists of characters; but I use the word 'scene' throughout to mean that part of the action which is played before a single stage set, in the sense of the Italian word 'quadro'. In the libretto of Enrico, the trio under discussion is found at the end of Act 1 scene vi (in the libretto).

6 I learned too late to be able to consult it for this book that there is a copy of the sinfonia to Una follia in the library of the Bologna Conservatory.

7 When Il falegname was put on at the Teatro Comunale, Bologna, in 1823, the libretto described the opera as a melodramma burlesco.

8 'Ah, quel colpo' are the first words of the famous trio for Rosina, Almaviva and Figaro in Act 2 of Rossini's Il barbiere.

9 Zavadini (Donizetti: Vita – Musiche – Epistolario, p. 170) lists La zingara as an opera seria, but since it is a work with a buffo role and the musical numbers are separated by spoken dialogue, it is more properly classified as belonging to the mixed semiseria genre.

10 Stendhal, Life of Rossini, p. 422.

11 'Casacciello' was the nickname given by the Neapolitans to Carlo Casaccia, who had inherited it from his father Antonio, to whom it had first been given. Antonio Casaccia retired from the stage in 1800.

12 Stendhal, Life of Rossini, pp. 456–7.

13 In Alfredo, at the end of the march that concludes the introduzione, Donizetti added this note to the autograph: 'Here it should fade away, but as these things are almost always lost in the theater, I leave it to the listener to imagine it.'

14 The cabaletta, 'No, no, del cielo altrui mercè', to Alfredo's aria di sortita bears a strong family resemblance to the cabaletta, 'Oggetto amabile', of Zoraida's first aria.

15 'Bequadro' is the Italian word for the natural sign in music.

16 The imitation of sounds for comic effect in opera goes well back into the seventeenth century. A representative example is the imitation of animal cries in Buini's Il podestà di Colognole (Bologna, 1730); Mayr employed the same effect in Il piccolo compositore di musica (Bergamo, 1811) to underplay the vocal shortcomings of the thirteen-year-old Donizetti. Cimarosa's intermezzo for buffo solo, Il maestro di cappella (composed between 1786 and 1793) contains a celebrated instance of a singer's imitating musical instruments.

17 'Aria di sorbetto' is a traditional pejorative for vocal music that sounds as though it were written in no more time than it takes for a sherbert to congeal or for one to be consumed.

18 The semiseria tradition survived at least until the middle of the century. Donizetti's most enduring work in that genre, Linda di Chamounix, integrates the buffo character (the Marchese) into the main conflict of the action (he is a buffo counterpart of Rodolfo in La sonnambula), and gives him two fine arias of irresistible gaiety and roguishness.

19 L'opera di Donizetti nell'età romantica, p. 26.

20 See Don White, 'Donizetti and the Three Gabriellas', and see also the

booklet that accompanies the Opera Rara recording (1978) of the 1838 version of *Gabriella*.

21 The other roles in the *prima* of Carafa's *Gabriella* (Teatro del Fondo, Naples, 3 July 1816) were sung by Colbran (Gabriella), the tenor Nozzari (Fayel), Michele Benedetti (King Filippo), Adelaide Carpano (Almeide) and Gaetano Chizzola (Armando).

22 *Olivo e Pasquale* has six other male parts besides that of Camillo, taxing the resources of the small troupe engaged that season at the Valle. Since one of these roles had to be performed *en travesti*, that of the youthful lover was the obvious choice.

23 This circumstantial account of Tamburini's exploit is derived from H. Sutherland Edwards, *History of the Opera from Monteverdi to Donizetti* (2 vols., London, 1862), vol. 2, p. 272, as quoted in W. G. Armstrong, *Record of the Opera in Philadelphia* (Philadelphia, 1884), pp. 182–5. Although the events are ascribed to the year 1822, *Elisa e Claudio* was not given in Palermo until 1825, when both Tamburini and Caterina Lipparini were members of the company at the Carolino.

24 The revisions of *Le convenienze* may be deduced from the following evidence:

(i). The score of the one-act version, *Le convenienze teatrali*, printed by Schoenenberger (Paris, c. 1855); this stands closest to the opera as it was originally performed in 1827.

(ii). The autograph score of a one-act revised version of *Le convenienze teatrali*, in the Bibliothèque Nationale, Paris.

(iii). A non-autograph score of the two-act version, *Le convenienze ed inconvenienze teatrali*, in the Bibliothèque Nationale, containing further revisions and varying considerably from (i) and (ii). The score bears the stamp of the Théâtre Impérial Italien, but there is no record that *Le convenienze* was performed by that company. (Since the Théâtre-Italien could scarcely have been referred to as 'Impérial' before 2 December 1852, there is a serious possibility that this revision was the work of hands other than Donizetti's.)

(iv). A copyist's score in the library of the Milan Conservatory, presumably of the version of the two-act *Le convenienze ed in inconvenienze teatrali* used at the Teatro Canobbiana in 1831.

Modern printed scores are a mixture of parts of the above, along with additional material from others of Donizetti's scores, none of the latter having any connection with *Le convenienze* in any of Donizetti's revisions of it.

A comparison of these versions reveals the differences between them:

(i). The Schoenenberger score consists of eight numbers: (1) *introduzione*; (2) cavatina for Mamm'Agata; (3) aria for Proclo; (4) duet for Prima Donna and Composer; (5) duet for Prima Donna and Mamm'Agata; (6) romanza for Mamm'Agata (with cabaletta); (7) chorus – the rehearsal; (8) *finaletto*.

(ii). The autograph contains only five numbers: (1) *introduzione*, but with the aria 'È puoi goder, tiranno!' for Prima Donna in the middle of it (while in the corresponding place in the Schoenenberger score she sings Elvida's *aria di sortita*, 'Ah, che mi vuoi? che brami?'); (2) cavatina for Mamm'Agata; (3) duet for Prima Donna and Mamm'Agata;

(4) terzetto for Guglielmo (a new character, a German tenor named Guglielmo Kol, perhaps a satire on Berardo Winter), Mamm'Agata and Composer; (5) new finale. As an annex to the autograph there is a 'sestetto nuovo', the number that stands as the finale to Act 1 in (iii) below. The autograph represents a revision of an earlier version, as can be seen on the first page of no. 3, the duet for the Prima Donna and Mamm'Agata; this was originally marked 'no. 5' (the place it occupies in the Schoenenberger score), but the number has been crossed out and altered. In both (i) and (ii) the Prima Donna's name is Corilla; later it was changed to Daria.

(iii). The non-autograph score is divided into two acts and contains all the numbers in the first two versions except nos. 4 and 8 of the Schoenenberger score. The disposition has now become:
Act 1: (1) *introduzione*; (2) cavatina for Mamm'Agata; (3) aria for Proclo; (4) duet for Prima Donna and Mamm'Agata; (5) terzetto for Guglielmo, Mamm'Agata and Composer; (6) first finale: sextet.
Act 2: (7) romanza for Mamm'Agata, but now without cabaletta; (8) aria for Prima Donna; (9) new finale.

(iv). I have not had the occasion to examine this version, but, judging from the performance based upon it that was given in Milan during September 1962, it stands closest to (iii).

Further, the Schoenenberger score contains no recitatives, as the original version used spoken dialogue. All the others contain recitatives, but they vary considerably.

25 I am grateful to Patric Schmid and Don White for pointing this out to me.

26 Cametti (*Donizetti a Roma*, p. 71) describes the revisions the composer made for *Alina* when he supervised its introduction to Rome at the Teatro Valle in 1829:

He retouched it, modifying several pieces and adding new ones, written expressly. We cannot designate them all exactly, but from a comparison of the libretto of the original production with that of the first Roman production, the following changes appear. The first of the added pieces – certainly written in Rome for Pietro Gentili – is the tenor aria, 'Dunque invan mi lusingai', from scene ix of Act 1, inserted just after the recitative for Seide and Hassan. The cabaletta of this aria had a word changed in the oath scene [probably the work of the Roman censors] and has a new quatrain so that it could be repeated a second time. The other change is the *rondò*–finale, for Annetta Fischer, 'Su l'ali dei sospiri', and to make room for it a passage for Alina and Chorus was cut from the last scene. Furthermore, at the beginning of Act 2 came a new scene between Seide and Hassan. Several other excerpts were cut. The Act 2 duet between the tenor and Alina was changed and amplified.

The autograph at Naples shows that Seide's Act 1 aria was originally 'Se valor, rispetto, e fede' (*maestoso*, 4/4, B flat major) and that Alina's original final arias were 'Ciel secondi i difensori' (*maestoso*, 3/4, F major) and 'Ah, lasciate ch'io respiro' (*moderato*, 4/4, F major). Both the substitute arias for these original numbers are also included in the materials of the autograph score.

27 The autograph of Tamburini's aria for *Il giovedì grasso* is in the collection of the Bibliothèque Nationale.

28 Z. no. 49, dated 24 July 1829, p. 268.
29 The Schoenenberger score (Paris, c. 1855) of Il diluvio reflects this revision for Genoa, and corresponds to the autograph in the Ricordi Archives, Milan. Another autograph, in the Conservatorio di San Pietro a Majella, Naples, is of the 1830 original version. When Il diluvio was first given at Genoa it was followed by a ballet with the surprising title of La morte di Macbet, sultano di Persia!
30 Z. no. B6, dated 1 April 1830, p. 913.
31 I am indebted to Tom Kaufman for this information about the performance history of Imelda (letter to the author, 15 August 1978). At Sinigaglia in 1856 the role of Bonifacio was taken by the prominent baritone Leone Giraldoni, while the tenor part of Lamberto was sung by Antonio Giuglini, one year before his successful London debut.
32 Z. no. 38, dated 2 February 1828, p. 257.
33 The 'Argomento' by Tottola that prefaces the 1830 libretto of Imelda refers to the historical facts behind the story. It appears from this that Bonifacio was stabbed by a poisoned blade wielded by Lamberto (at which point Tottola throws in the information that poisoned swords came into fashion from the Saracens). The historic Imelda, instead of being stabbed by Lamberto, hoped to save Bonifacio's life by sucking out the poison from his wound, but she only succeeded in poisoning herself as well, afterward dying in Bonifacio's arms. Apparently Tottola made no effort to get this remarkable episode approved by the Neapolitan censors.
34 Of the twenty-three scores that followed Zoraida only five (Chiara, L'ajo, Alahor, Olivo and Alina) were not first performed in Naples.

10. The operas: 1830–1835

1 The autograph shows that Donizetti originally intended to give this arpeggio to the harp, but he later changed his mind in favor of the strings.
2 One of the few blemishes in Romani's otherwise fine libretto relates to the question of Anna's marriage to Percy, how it was dissolved, and the extent of Enrico's knowledge of it, none of which is clearly explained.
3 In La straniera Alaide's final cabaletta, 'Or sei pago', begins in B flat minor and ends in the relative major. Donizetti wrote final cabalettas that begin in the minor on occasion, as at the end of Lucrezia Borgia and Maria Stuarda (the first statement).
4 One rather elusive example of this irony occurs during Anna's rambling recitative: again delirious, she invites Smeton to tune his harp. At this point the music modulates to B flat major, which is the dominant of the key of Smeton's 'Deh, non voler costringere' in Act 1, the song that Anna had cut off at its mention of 'primo amore', taking this phrase to refer to Percy. That this B flat is a logical step on the way to her upcoming G minor arioso does not affect its fleeting allusiveness.
5 The three stages of the composition of the Seymour–Enrico duet have been illuminatingly examined by Philip Gossett, in his 'Anna Bolena e la maturità di Donizetti'.
6 The work is structurally an opera buffa; 'opera comica' is presumably

Romani's direct translation of 'opéra comique', the designation of Boieldieu's work on which Romani based his libretto.

7 There are changes in the text of the page Oliviero's canzone, 'Mira, o bella, il trovatore', for instance. Opera Rara presented this canzone on the other side of their recording of excerpts from *Ne m'oubliez pas*, and the accompanying booklet sheds some light on the question of the changes to the libretto.

8 There is a copy of *Gianni di Parigi* in the Ricordi Archives, Milan, with important autograph additions supplying pieces not in the autograph at Naples.

9 This other context cannot now be identified, but the autograph of *Francesca di Foix* reveals that the text to which the music of this aria was originally set began 'Questo la vaga intorno'. A further suggestion that this is a self-borrowing also appears in the autograph: the aria, which is there written out in E flat, is marked 'now to be sung in D'.

10 The words of the Gondolier's song are Francesca da Rimini's: 'Nessun maggior dolore/Che ricordarsi del tempo felice/Nella miseria'. (Dante, *Inferno*, Canto V, lines 121–3).

11 Cottrau, *Lettres d'un mélomane*, p. 16.

12 Donizetti's self-borrowing to and from *Ugo* has been extensively and helpfully discussed by Jeremy Commons in the booklet that accompanies the Opera Rara recording of this opera.

13 Verzino, *Le opere di Donizetti*, p. 103.

14 A detailed study of the variety of ways in which Donizetti employed self-borrowings would be most helpful, for while sometimes material is moved intact, other instances show considerable modification.

15 See Commons's discussion of the work in the booklet that accompanies the Opera Rara recording.

16 While the 'history' of Sancia is chiefly another example of period *spagnuolismo*, there actually was a King Garcia of Leon; he reigned between 910 and 914, and was such an inveterate builder of castles that he was responsible for the name of a whole region: Castille.

17 One of the recurrent themes in evaluations of the performances of Lablache and Tamburini was their unusual aptitude for both serious and comic roles. The consistency of such comment shows just how exceptional such versatility was in those days, when most companies employed separate troupes for seria and buffa works.

18 Other examples of a character's entering from a height, but as the initiation of a pantomime episode, are to be found in Act 2 of *Otto mesi* (where Elisabetta totters down a mountain), *L'assedio di Calais* (where Aurelio clambers down a rope from the walls of Calais in the *introduzione*) and *Linda di Chamounix* (where in Act 3, the deranged Linda is led homeward by Pierotto playing his hurdy-gurdy).

19 Another bit of self-borrowing in this score is alluded to by Donizetti in a letter to Ricordi of 13 June 1833: 'In *Il furioso* you will find the cadences of Noè.' (Z. no. 99, p. 314.)

20 Guglielmo Barblan, *L'opera di Donizetti nell'età romantica* (Bergamo, 1948), p. 90.

21 Earlier, Donizetti had written for Ungher the buffa role of Marietta in *Il borgomastro di Saardam* (1827), but that was shortly after Barbaja had introduced her to Italy and before she had realized her full potential.

22 Chorley, *Thirty Years' Musical Recollections*, p. 79.
23 In this chorus, 'Aura soave spira' (Act 1 scene ii), Imelda, the confidante, has an individual line. This can be seen as a middle stage between earlier choruses, where the seconda donna sang in unison with one of the chorus parts, and later arrangements such as that at the beginning of the second scene of *La favorite*, where in 'Rayons dorés', Inès is an independent soloist and the chorus is subordinated to her. This episode from *La favorite* borrows an episode from Act 1 of *Pia*, but there the seconda donna's participation, though separate, is much less prominent than in its French reworking.
24 That Parisina is Ugo's stepmother is not revealed until the penultimate scene of the opera.
25 The dedication of *Tasso* to these three cities reads: 'To the city where he was conceived, to that where he first saw light of day and to that which preserves his remains.' Donizetti described it to Ricordi as 'a bizarre dedication, but I like it (Z. no. 111, dated 6 August 1833, p. 326).
26 Z. no. 185, dated 12 November 1835, p. 391, to Ferretti.
27 Although isolated instances of strained accentuation can be found in Donizetti's work, he frequently shows deep sensitivity in his word-setting. 'Una furtiva lagrima' (*L'elisir d'amore*) is a touchstone in this regard.
28 This reading by Tasso is an interesting variation of an episode in the Francesca da Rimini story, but there the reading leads to the consummation of love, here it prompts only a declaration of love. Paolo reads the tale of Galeotto; here Tasso reads his own verses.
29 Idamore's melody had earlier been grafted into the score of *La romanziera e l'uomo nero*.
30 In a letter from Vienna to Count Melzi of Milan (Z. no. 641, dated June 1845, pp. 816–17) Donizetti complains of Merelli's sending inadequate singers, whom he overpraises, to perform at the Kärntnertor, and of his interfering in the assignment of parts, without regard to range or vocal capacity: Donizetti's concern for good and expressive singing echoes in every line.
31 Chorley, *Thirty Years' Musical Recollections*, p. 115.
32 There is no better model for embellishments to Donizetti's melodies than the composer's own practise in the second strophes of certain arias: Smeton's 'Deh, non voler costringere' (*Anna Bolena*, Act 1), Lucrezia's 'Com'è bello', and Corrado's 'Ah, non avea più lagrime' (*Maria de Rudenz*, Act 1).
33 This Paris version of *Lucrezia* was printed by Bernard Latte (*c.* 1840, plate no. 1921).
34 In 1837 Donizetti revised *Rosmonda* (as *Eleonora di Gujenna*) by rewriting an aria for Eleonora, the new title character, and by altering the finale.
35 The music of *Maria Stuarda* was first performed in a *rifacimento*, with a different plot, called *Buondelmonte* (Naples, Teatro San Carlo, 18 October 1834). Patric Schmid ('Maria Stuarda and Buondelmonte', p. 1063) outlines the changes Donizetti made for this performance as follows: 'The major changes are the loss of the Elisabeth/Leicester Act 1 duet, the opening chorus, and the transformation of Maria's prayer into an ensemble for male voices ... *Buondelmonte* gives us new re-

citatives... and two new choruses.' Four new roles were added (Giovanna, Mosca Lamberti, Oderigo Fifanti and Stiatta Uberti). The order of the numbers in *Maria Stuarda* was retained in *Buondelmonte* except that the Maria–Leicester duet from Act 2 became the Act 1 duet for Irene and Buondelmonte, and Maria's prayer was moved forward to precede what was originally the 'confession' duet (Maria–Talbot). *Buondelmonte* is in two acts, its first act consisting of the material of Acts 1 and 2 of *Maria Stuarda*.

36 The performance history of *Maria Stuarda* during the nineteenth century – more than a dozen performances between 1837 and 1865, most of them occurring between 1843 and 1845 – is documented in an article by Jeremy Commons, Patric Schmid and Don White in *Donizetti Journal*, 3 (1977), 217–42. This whole issue of the *Donizetti Journal* is devoted to *Maria Stuarda*.

37 Julian Budden (*The Operas of Verdi* (3 vols., New York, 1973–81), vol. 2, pp. 97–8) has this to say about the connection between Donizetti's and Verdi's arias: 'But the final working out in 3/4 [of "Di quella pira"] shows the operation of what is surely unconscious memory. For the Milan premiere of *Maria Stuarda* in 1835 Donizetti altered the opening of Leicester's cabaletta "Se fida tanto" (following the significant words "Vo' liberla")... Verdi, who was studying in Milan at the time, is unlikely to have missed a performance; and the echo is unmistakable, though it would not necessarily have struck Verdi's contemporaries since the definitive version of Leicester's cabaletta begins quite differently.'

38 See Z. no. 235, dated 13 May 1837, pp. 427–8, to Raffaele Mazzetti.

39 The word 'supplizio' also conveys the idea of suffering and torture.

40 This is not strictly true, since *Gemma* was performed at Empoli in 1901; but that production was really the last gasp of the opera's nineteenth-century vogue.

41 Chorley, *Thirty Years' Musical Recollections*, p. 65. Nor was Chorley the only one to feel that the prima donna's role was belittled in *Marin Faliero*. At Ferrara in the spring of 1839 Elena was given an aria beginning 'Solo per lui quest'anima' to serve as a *sortita*, preceding Fernando's Act 1 aria; at La Scala in 1840 a prima donna named d'Alberti interpolated Rosmonda's *aria di sortita* at the same point in the score.

42 The Ricordi score I am referring to (published after May 1836) is a concatenation of numbers performed in Paris and Florence, as one can tell from the singers mentioned in the various headings (the two productions involved different casts). This score contains the following plate numbers: 9341, 9342, 8677, 8691, 8678, 8690, 9350 (also 8679 renumbered 9350), 9343, 9344, 9345, 9346, 8681, 8692, 8683, 9347, 9348, 8693, 8697, 8695, 8686–8687, 9349, 8685, 8688, 8689. One should not jump to the conclusion that the plates with numbers in the 8000s contain all the material from Paris, and those in the 9000s all that from Florence, because names of members of the Paris cast also appear on plates in the 9000 series. However, no member of the Florence cast is named on plates in the 8000 series, but then there are plates of choruses, recitatives, and the first finale that have no singers' names.

43 See Alfonso Lazzari, 'Giovanni Ruffini, Gaetano Donizetti e il *Don Pasquale*', *Rassegna nazionale*, 1 and 16 October 1915, reprinted as a separate pamphlet (Florence, 1915).

44 Z. no. 164, dated 3 May 1835, p. 371.

45 Z. no. 180, dated 20 October 1835, p. 387.

46 Z. no. A7, dated 19 May 1836, pp. 867–8.

47 In the Ricordi score, the duet (plate no. 8678) bears the note 'as sung in Paris by Grisi and Rubini'.

48 Chorley, *Thirty Years' Musical Recollections*, p. 65.

49 The Ricordi score (plate no. 8677) makes the absurd mistake of giving the tenor's vocal part a signature of five flats, while presenting the accompaniment with the correct four flats!

50 These are the words that begin Edgardo's famous tomb scene in *Lucia*, but here they are set quite differently.

51 The cabaletta of the Israele–Faliero duet was originally 'Tremar tu sembri e fremere' (*vivace*, 4/4, A flat major). It is not known exactly when Donizetti substituted 'Sì! Trema o Steno', but this new cabaletta was performed in the first Italian production of the opera, in Florence in April 1836. When Mazzini heard it he praised it for its dramatic truth (*Filosofia della musica*, pp. 183ff).

   A suggestion that Donizetti authorized further alterations to the score in 1841 is misleading; it stems from the 'Avvertenza' prefacing a libretto that purports to have been used in Ferrara in 1839. The 'Avvertenza' states: 'Scene v of Act 1 is cut as per a modification made to the score in 1841 by Maestro Donizetti himself, who removed the said scene definitely; added for the same reason are the following words, with which Scene vi of Act 3 should terminate', and the notice goes on to quote Israele's text from 'Odo il suon' down to 'Vil Beltrame'. Tamburini had sung this section of Act 3 at Paris in the first production, but it had been eliminated from Lanari's Florentine production with Paolo Ferretti as Israele; it seems therefore that the management of the company that at some point (1841 or perhaps later) issued this libretto wanted to cite Donizetti's authority and to suggest that what was in reality original material was a recent addition to the score.

52 This passage from *Il paria* could well form the centerpiece of an analysis of Donizetti's self-borrowings.

11. The operas: 1835–1838

1 Phillips LP 9500 183/85, conducted by Jesus Lopez-Cobos, with Caballé as Lucia.

2 Lily Pons, for instance, customarily sang the mad scene in its original key, but this was because she had learned the role in France from a French score, where the correct keys were observed. But at the Metropolitan she sang Lucia's *aria di sortita* and the duet with Enrico in the traditional lower keys.

3 In the booklet that accompanies the Phillips recording of *Lucia* Lopez-Cobos indicates some of his restorations; a full account must await the appearance of the new edition of *Lucia* he is preparing for Ricordi.

4 Chorley, *Thirty Years' Musical Recollections*, p. 100.

5 This note of the flattened sixth (D flat in the key of F) is significant because it recurs prominently in the cabaletta, at the words 'Al giunger tuo soltanto', which stresses its association with Edgardo.

6 See Barblan, *L'opera di Donizetti nell'età romantica*, p. 125.

7 I do not agree with Lopez-Cobos's assumption that this is a clarinet phrase mistakenly written on the wrong stave. I believe Donizetti deliberately changes from oboe to clarinet before Enrico's words 'Mi guardi e taci?' to indicate Lucia's efforts to assume a composure she does not really feel, as she gathers herself to utter her first words, 'Il pallor funesto', four measures later. An examination of the copyist's parts used at the San Carlo in 1835 would help to settle this matter, as Donizetti was in charge of that production.

8 Barblan, *L'opera di Donizetti nell'età romantica*, pp. 131–2.

9 *Belisario*, with Strepponi as Antonina and Ronconi as Belisario, was being staged at La Scala just at the time *Nabucco* was in rehearsal there for its *prima*. Verdi's objection was not only to the accentuation, but to the *contrasenso* that resulted from associating 'sterminatrice', feminine (modifying the noun 'guerra'), with the masculine proper noun 'Bisanzio' in the same musical phrase.

10 This 'quartet' was inserted by Giulini into the concluding scene of *Dom Sébastien* when that opera was revived at the Florentine Maggio Musicale on 2 May 1955.

11 Z. no. 205, dated 19 April 1836, p. 407.

12 This brindisi was first conceived by Donizetti as no. 12 of his collection of songs *Notti d'estate a Posilippo*; the words are by Leopoldo Tarantini.

13 *Couplets* are a French aria form consisting of two strophes that end in an identical refrain. Familiar examples of *couplets* are 'Le veau d'or' from *Faust* and the 'Toreador Song' from *Carmen*.

14 Obviously there was never any question of expanding *Il campanello* into two acts; the night-long action must be continuous or the whole point of the farsa is lost.

15 Donizetti wrote Aurelio as a *musico* role only because there was, in his view, no suitable tenor available at the San Carlo in October and November 1836 (see Z. no. 219, undated, p. 417, to Dolci). He intended to revise the role for Duprez.

16 Of these four dances, only two were by Donizetti (see Chapter 4, note 92).

17 Z. no. 225, dated 22 November 1836, p. 421, to Ricordi.

18 Marchionni's play was *L'assedio di Calais*, also known as *Edoardo III*; besides Cammarano's libretto it further sired Luigi Henry's ballet, danced at the San Carlo in 1828.

19 Besides Eustachio, Donizetti composed for Barroilhet the following roles: Nottingham (*Roberto Devereux*); Severo (*Poliuto*), although he never performed it; Alphonse (*La favorite*), the role of his debut at the Opéra; and Camoëns (*Dom Sébastien*). As a *bariton-noble*, Barroilhet had a usable range from B in the bass clef to high F; his music has an appreciably lower tessitura than that found in the roles written for Ronconi, whose practicable range extended up from C to high G flat (frequently) and to high G (very occasionally).

20 'Pertichini' is the traditional designation for subordinate voice parts that participate in an aria. The word is also applied to understudies.

21 Z. no. 225, p. 421.

22 Hopefully the emotion here generated is sufficient to cover the dubious taste of assigning the line 'son uomo alfine' (I am a man at last) to a *musico*.

23 Surely it is no coincidence that Pia appears, although more briefly, at the corresponding point in the *Purgatorio* to Francesca in the *Inferno*: at one time Donizetti toyed briefly with the idea of an opera about Francesca.

24 *S.d.* 1, no. 44, p. 37.

25 See Black, 'The Making of an Italian Romantic Opera Libretto.'

26 Marenco's *Pia* was later a favored vehicle of Adelaide Ristori, who appeared in it during her tour of the United States in 1866.

27 Rigacci omitted the Act 2 scena for Rodrigo both for his production at Siena and for his RAI broadcast of 1976.

28 See Winton Dean, 'Donizetti's Serious Operas', *Proceedings of the Royal Musical Association*, 100 (1973–4), 123–41.

29 A coincidence that shows a different direction is Rodrigo's Act 2 cabaletta, 'A me stesso', which bears a strong family resemblance to Amina's 'Ah, non giunge' (*La sonnambula*, 1831) (see the musical quotation in my *Donizetti*, p. 403).

30 Although Paolina in *Poliuto* was first written for Ronzi, the royal ban prevented her from appearing in that part. Ronzi also appeared at the San Carlo in Donizetti roles that had first been sung elsewhere – Anna Bolena, Parisina, Antonina and Pia.

31 Mercadante's *Il conte d'Essex* had its *prima* at La Scala on 10 March 1833 and survived for only five performances. Mercadante had the ineffective notion of casting both the title role (sung by Pedrazzi) and that of Nottingham (sung by Reina) as tenor parts, although there was a baritone, the successful Carlo Zucchelli, on the roster at La Scala that season. Mercadante's *Il conte d'Essex* seems never to have been performed at the San Carlo.

32 The prominence of Elisabetta in *Maria Stuarda* would have been greater and her internal conflict clearer had Donizetti found it possible, without destroying the dramatic impetus of the plot, to have set to music the monologue Bardari had provided for her to conclude Act 3 scene i.

33 Verdi could not help but be familiar with *Roberto Devereux*, for this opera was having a run of thirty-eight performances at La Scala just at the time that *Oberto* was in rehearsal for its *prima* there.

34 Winton Dean ('Donizetti's Serious Operas' p. 137) has pointed out the resemblance between Elisabetta's 'Un lampo, un lampo' and the phrase for Leonora in the trio that concludes Act 1 of *Il trovatore*.

35 These symbols had occurred separately in earlier works by Donizetti. A ring is important in the scene between Lucia and Edgardo at the end of Act 1 of *Lucia di Lammermoor*, and a scarf figures poignantly in the action of *Marin Faliero*.

36 Donizetti could not then have been familiar with *Fidelio* from performance, for Beethoven's opera was not given in Italy until 1886, nearly forty years after Donizetti's death.

37 Dean, 'Donizetti's Serious Operas', p. 138.

38 Z. no. 171, dated 21 July [1835], p. 379, to Giuseppe Consul.

39 Not all operas were equally 'safe' in different Italian cities. While Donizetti had particularly recommended the plot of *Pia* to the management of the Fenice as trouble-free, the following year he would have to make a number of changes, including a happy ending (with Nello arriving in time to save Pia), for Naples.

40 Quoted in Commons's 'Donizetti e la censura napoletana'.

41 To precede the finale to Act 1 of *Maria de Rudenz* Donizetti had composed a double aria for Moriani (the first Enrico), but the opera was taken off at Venice after the second performance and before Moriani could sing it on stage. This aria was inserted in the Opera Rara performance of the work in London in 1974; although it is effectively written for the tenor, it reveals nothing that is not already known and it upsets the momentum of this well-timed first act.

42 The movement is less effective dramatically in *Maria de Rudenz* because the big tenor melody is sung by Enrico, an almost peripheral character, while in *Poliuto* it is sung by the hero who dominates the entire scene in the temple of Jupiter. Also the doubling of the tenor's line by the soprano has greater significance in the later context, as Paolina is Poliuto's wife; there is practically no dramatic connection between Maria and Enrico.

43 In *Poliuto* and *Les martyrs*, this quintet becomes a sextet by means of the addition of another bass line.

44 The jaunty tune in *Lucia* that accompanies Enrico's and Arturo's dialogue before the sextet and then recurs after the ensemble has, at both points, the same dramatic significance – to keep up appearances that everything is well, in spite of rumors and embarrassing interruptions. The tune in *Maria de Rudenz*, however, shifts dramatic emphasis when it returns after the *larghetto* of the finale: at its first occurrence it is connected with Corrado and Matilde, but later it is taken over by the opposing party, Maria and her vassals. The more consistent use in *Lucia* produces greater dramatic emphasis.

45 See Barblan, *L'opera di Donizetti nell'età romantica*, p. 152.

12. The operas: 1838–1841

1 Z. no. 300, dated 27 June 1838, p. 478.

2 The score of *Les martyrs* includes only the closing *largo* modulation of the *preludio* to connect the overture to the opening chorus; this arrangement is probably the one Donizetti preferred.

3 In the score these solo voices are identified as those of Nearco, Felice and Callistene, but Donizetti does not mean to indicate that the last two – Paolina's father and the high priest of Jupiter – participated as characters, rather that he wants voices of solo quality to sing this music.

4 The quickening of the tempo indicated by Donizetti in this cabaletta prefigures the similar effect in the 'Sì, vendetta' duet in *Rigoletto*.

5 Z. no. 23, dated 18 August 1824, p. 242.

6 In the libretto for the production of *Poliuto* at La Scala in Carnival 1852–3 (its second there), Callistene's aria has a different text, 'Del proconsole i passi esplorate'; but since the metrical pattern is the same

as that of the original text, it is quite probable that the original music was used. With this single exception, the libretto of the La Scala production conforms to the Cammarano text.

7 These words recur in Chevreuse's aria in Act 3 of *Maria di Rohan*. As Cammarano explained in his preface to the libretto printed for the San Carlo production of *Poliuto* in 1848: 'certain lines of this melodrama, that seemed condemned to oblivion, were incorporated into later works'.

8 For a further discussion of this point, see Franca Cella, 'Il libretto e sue vicende', La Fenice program for *Les martyrs*, 1977–8 season (Venice, 1978). Other articles in this program, by Guglielmo Barblan, Claudio Casini and Rodolfo Celletti, discuss different aspects of *Les martyrs*.

9 In one Ricordi score of *Poliuto* I have seen (plate no. 53483 but with unnumbered variants added) this trio, translated as 'Oggetto de miei voti' and transposed down a half-tone, has been inserted as a *tempo di mezzo* between Paolina's Act 1 cavatina and cabaletta. This arrangement was employed in the La Scala revival of *Poliuto* with Callas and Corelli in 1960.

10 It is difficult to believe that 'Il faut partir' was not somewhere in the back of Verdi's mind when he wrote a very similar minor/major modulation in Violetta's 'Ah, fors'è lui'.

11 I am grateful to Julian Budden for pointing out this instance of Donizetti's self-borrowing (letter to the author, 15 April 1980).

12 When Lily Pons sang Marie at the Metropolitan during World War II, the finale was expanded by the addition of *La Marseillaise*, which she sang flourishing a flag bearing De Gaulle's Croix de Lorraine. *La fille* has an almost unparalleled record for having topical interpolations inserted into it.

13 The Italian version of this aria recorded by John McCormack, 'Ah, per viver vicino a Maria', was used by him when he performed the opera with Tetrazzini in New York in 1909–10 for Hammerstein. Reputedly this was McCormack's own Italian text for the aria, which he had selected himself from the French score as its lyrical suavity was well adapted to his vocal style.

14 The source of each number of *La favorite* is shown in the chart on p. 692 (the description of the numbers – 'Romance', 'Air et choeur' etc. – are those Donizetti used in the French score). Unless otherwise stated, numbers taken from *L'ange de Nisida* occurred in the same act in that opera as in *La favorite* and had the same incipits. The recitatives in the opening scene are all new; from the next scene through Léonor's aria they are a mixture of new material and material from *L'ange de Nisida*; from there to the end they come almost entirely from *L'ange de Nisida*.

15 In my earlier book on Donizetti I quoted a scenario on the subject of Leonora de Guzman that is preserved among the Cammarano papers in the Biblioteca Lucchesi-Palli, Naples, and posed the question of its connection with the conversion of *L'ange de Nisida* into *La favorite*. I am now convinced that this scenario relates not to 1840 or before, but to late 1849, the time of the preparation of *La favorite* for its Neapolitan *prima* (San Carlo, 20 January 1850). The scenario is not, as I had assumed, in Cammarano's hand. (See Black, 'The Making of an Italian Romantic Opera Libretto'.)

La favorite	Source
Overture	new
Act 1:	
Introduction, choeur et récit: 'Pieux monastère'	new
Romance (Fernand): 'Une ange, une femme inconnue'	Freely adapted from *L'ange de Nisida*, Act 1, Leone's aubade 'Ange d'amour, fée inconnue' (musical resemblance slighter than textual).
Duo (Fernand, Balthasar): 'Sais-tu'	new
Air et choeur (Inès): 'Rayons dorés'	Substantially from *L'ange de Nisida*, but ultimately from *Pia de' Tolomei*, Act 1, with expanded use of soloist.
Air et choeur (Inès): 'Doux zéphir sois lui fidèle'	From *L'ange de Nisida* and, in part, *Adelaide*.
Duo (Léonor, Fernand): 'Mon idole'	From *L'ange de Nisida*, but ultimately from *Adelaide*.
Air (Fernand): 'Oui, ta voix m'inspire'	new
Act 2:	
Récit et air (Alphonse): 'Jardins de l'Alcazar' . . . 'Léonor viens' . . . 'Léonor, mon amour brave'	New, but the cabaletta is closely related to *L'assedio di Calais*, Act 1, Eustachio's cabaletta 'Un istante i mali obblio'.
Duo (Léonor, Alphonse): 'Quand j'ai quitté'	From *L'ange de Nisida* (where it was a half-tone higher), but the *larghetto*, 'Ô mon amour' is new.
Airs de danse	new
Finale	Expanded from a trio in *L'ange de Nisida*, but ultimately from *Adelaide*.
Act 3:	
Prélude et trio (Alphonse): 'Pour tant d'amour'	new
Récit et air (Léonor): 'L'ai-je bien entendu?' . . . 'Ô mon Fernand' . . . 'Mon arrêt descend du ciel'	new
Choeur: 'Déjà dans la chappelle'	From *L'ange de Nisida*.
Finale	Chorus and recitative almost entirely from *L'ange de Nisida*; *largo* and stretta from *L'ange de Nisida* but ultimately from *Adelaide*.
Act 4:	
Prélude et choeur (contains Balthasar's 'Les cieux s'emplissent d'étincelles')	From *L'ange de Nisida*, but the *maestoso* (E major, 3/4) derives from an idea in *Pia de' Tolomei*, Act 2 (hermitage scene).
Romance (Fernand): 'Ange si pur'	From *Le duc d'Albe*, but the recitative is from *L'ange de Nisida*.
Récit et choeur: 'Que de très-haut'	From *L'ange de Nisida*.
Duo (Léonor, Fernand): 'Va-t-en d'ici' . . . 'Viens, viens, je cède éperdu'	From *L'ange de Nisida*, but without one section; Léonor's prayer 'Fernand, imite la clémence' was added for Stolz during rehearsals and is new.

16 Pauline Gueymard-Lauters, the first Eboli (Paris, 1867) had the year before sung Léonor in *La favorite* in a successful revival at the Opéra.

17 Dean, 'Donizetti's Serious Operas', p. 139.

18 The clear rhythmic impulse of the French text is lost in the standard Italian translation used for the phrases quoted in Example 71.

19 The erotic note in Alphonse's music has its first faint pre-echo in Donizetti's music for Idamore in *Il paria* (see Example 31).

20 A comparison between the French and Italian versions of this aria shows how its former elegance becomes blunted.

21 Quoted in Cametti, *Donizetti a Roma*, p. 189.

22 Although as late as *La Traviata* Verdi retained the convention that letters read aloud should be spoken rather than sung, Donizetti sets them to recitative here and later in *Maria Padilla*. He keeps to the older convention in his opere buffe, using it in *Don Pasquale*.

23 There is one other character in *Rita*, a servant, who participates, briefly, only in the spoken dialogue.

24 Leo Balk kindly informed me that there is an alternate finale with a French text in the Bibliothèque Nationale, Paris.

25 See Z. no. 370, dated 10 August 1841, p. 550, to Toto Vasselli. Erminia Frezzolini had recently married the tenor Poggi.

26 The autograph of *Maria Padilla* is in the Ricordi Archives, Milan.

27 Since they require very different vocal types for their leading female roles, *La favorite* and *Maria Padilla* do not recommend themselves to joint production such as that of the so-called 'Tudor Ring' for Beverly Sills at the New York City Opera.

28 The duet for the Padilla sisters as sung in concert by Persiani and Jeanne Castellan was one of the sensations of Paris during the 1840s.

29 Although Pedro did in fact marry Blanche, he almost immediately abandoned her, and thus in the long view the 'happy ending' of *Maria Padilla* is at least quasi-historical.

30 A direction in the score instructs Don Ruiz to begin this cabaletta *soffocato*.

13. The operas: 1842–1843

1 The finale of Act 1 of *Linda* depicts a scene that was familiar to Donizetti from his boyhood – the departure of many rural *bergamaschi* for France in work parties to avoid the rigors and poverty of winter at home.

2 It would be interesting to discover if there is any link between the prelude to Act 1 of *Caterina Cornaro* and music that Giuseppe Donizetti might have sent his brother from Constantinople.

3 Regarding the introduction of *Home, sweet home* into *Anna Bolena*, the following anecdote is reported by Armstrong in *Record of the Opera in Philadelphia*, p. 50:

Lord Houghton, writing to the London *Athenaeum*, says: 'I was residing at Milan with my family at the time of the production of "Anna Bolena" (1830). We were very intimate with Madame Pasta. I well remember her calling one day and telling us she was very much discontented with her share in the partition of the last scene of the opera, and added: "You English have so many beautiful airs which you sing among yourselves, that I am sure you could help me." My mother, who was a fine musician, mentioned "Home, Sweet Home". She sang it, and Madame Pasta, sitting down to the piano, said: "It will do! I am sure it will do!" Donizetti adopted it accordingly, and thanked us for having got him out of the difficulty.'

It would be interesting to have this story checked out, if it should prove possible to do so.

4   For a discussion of the *finale nuovo* to *Caterina Cornaro*, see Natale Gallini, 'Inediti donizettiani', *Rivista musicale italiana*, 55 (1953), 257–75.

5   See Lazzari, 'Giovanni Ruffini, Gaetano Donizetti e il *Don Pasquale*'.

6   These initials resulted in the coincidental attribution of the libretto to Michele Accursi, Donizetti's factotum in Paris, but Accursi's only participation in it (see Lazzari, cited above) had been to secure Ruffini's services in the first place. To judge by Accursi's rambling and sometimes barely coherent letters, a libretto by his hand would be unthinkable.

7   Some of Pavesi's music was incorporated by Mayr into his pasticcio, *Il piccolo compositore di musica*, in which Donizetti played the title role.

8   That the tenor part of this duet functions satisfactorily as a solo can be heard in a recording by Tito Schipa (Victor 1282) made in 1925. Other tenors such as Anselmi and de Lucia recorded it as a solo during the era of acoustic recording.

9   This descriptive melody begins at measure 14 of the *introduzione*. In the autograph (in the Ricordi Archives) Donizetti's corrections at measures 20–1 and 24–5 are plainly legible, making it clear how he eliminated exact repetitions and pointed up the chromatic tendencies.

10   The principal opera house of Bologna, the Teatro Comunale, which opened in 1763, did not get around to performing any Mozart opera until 1940!

11   This information is taken from that unreliable source, de Filippis and Arnese, *Cronache del Teatro di San Carlo*, vol. 1, p. 219.

12   There is an interesting discussion of this trumpet solo in Alberto Zedda, 'Caratteristiche della strumentazione nell'opera teatrale di Gaetano Donizetti', 1° convegno internazionale di studi donizettiani, Bergamo, 1975.

13   For the care that went into the composition of 'Cercherò lontana terra', see the study of the sketches by Rattolino, 'Il processo compositivo nel *Don Pasquale* di Donizetti'.

14   The opening outburst of Don Pasquale has a distinctly Mozartean flavor – it would not sound out of place coming from Leporello – and is probably more responsible than any other passage in the score for the frequently drawn parallel between the two composers in relation to *Don Pasquale*.

15   This passage was in part borrowed by Donizetti from one of the discarded numbers of *L'ange de Nisida* – Don Gaspar's *aria di sortita* in Act 1 'Ma puissance n'est pas mince'.

16   Chorley, *Thirty Years' Musical Recollections*, p. 210.

17   Gaetano Cesari and Alessandro Luzio, eds., *Giuseppe Verdi, i copialettere* (Milan, 1913), p. 62.

18 Z. no. 418, dated 24 May 1842, p. 605, to Ricordi.

19 See Dean, 'Donizetti's Serious Operas', and, particularly, Budden, *The Operas of Verdi*, vol. 2, pp. 102–3.

20 A facsimile of autograph materials for *Dom Sébastien* was published by Garland Publishing in New York in 1981.

21 See Friedrich Lippmann, 'Autographe Briefe Rossinis und Donizettis in der Bibliothek Massimo, Rom', *Analecta musicologica*, no. 19 (1980), pp. 330–5. Lippmann reprints a letter from Donizetti to Scribe in French, dated 20 September 1843, proposing the addition of a barcarolle to Act 5.

22 Palianti (*Mise en scène de Dom Sébastien* (Paris, n.d. [1843]), p. 61) includes a description of the opera as it was acted at the premiere, which contains this passage:

> On the final note [of their duet], Zayda, near the table, falls to her knees at the King's feet, when suddenly the voice of Camoëns is heard from *croisée 3* [the window on the set, previously identified as number 3]. Tableau, Zayda and Sébastien listen in silence during the barcarolle. At the moment the chorus takes up its melody again [i.e. at the end of the first verse of the barcarolle], Dom Sébastien advances slowly towards the casement where Zayda, who has resumed an upright posture at the first measures sung by Camoëns, follows him.

I am grateful to Leo Balk who pointed out this passage to me (letter to the author, 15 March 1981).

23 Z. no. 516, p. 699.

24 Z. no. 516, p. 699.

25 In Camoëns's first aria, 'Soldat, j'ai rêvé', both the Viennese and the Ricordi scores contain an emendation of two measures (the fifth and fourth from the end); the melodic line is changed and a Neapolitan sixth chord is introduced to emphasize the accented syllable of 'malheur'.

26 The Mechetti score of the 1845 Viennese production of *Dom Sébastien*, unlike most French and Italian scores of this period, contains metronome markings. Since Donizetti himself prepared and conducted the production, these metronomic indications have some claim to authority. This *vivace*, for instance is marked $\quad \boldsymbol{\downarrow}$ = 144, while the revised *piu allegro* of the coda, in which the original 6/8 is changed to 4/4 and entirely new material is supplied, is marked $\boldsymbol{\downarrow}$ = 100.

27 Liszt made a piano transcription of this funeral march, and it prompted Donizetti to write to Toto Vaselli (Z. no. 624, dated 5 March 1845, p. 802): 'Buy the march as arranged by Liszt; it will scare you.' It was probably in this Liszt transcription that Mahler encountered the march and it stuck in his subconscious to surface in the middle, C major, section of 'Die zwei blauen Augen', last of the *Lieder eines fahrenden Gesellen*. I am grateful to Richard Woitach for pointing out the apparent connection to me.

28 Dom Juan's aria apparently did not form a part of Ricordi's first plates for *Don Sebastiano*, as it was assigned the number 15896½; further, it appears in their listing of the 'numbers' of the score as no. 28½.

29 Z. no. 516, p. 699.

30 Clément and Larousse, *Dictionnaire des opéras*, p. 232.

Appendix I

1 Here and throughout Appendix I descriptions appearing in quotation marks and in parentheses are those used on the score or libretto of the work. Such descriptions are included only where they illuminate the genre titles.

2 *Enrico di Borgogna* is an uncommon mixture of genres. A warrior role for a *musico* is traditionally found in opera seria or *eroica*; yet this plot also contains the buffo part of Gilberto, a characteristic of the semiseria. *Enrico* is, therefore, a *semi-eroica!*

3 Marco Venier (dates unknown), a tenor, sang in only two *prime* of operas by Donizetti – *La zingara* and *Il fortunato inganno*. He married an adopted daughter of the Mozart bass Ludwig Fischer, and with his wife conducted a singing-school in Vienna.

4 Savino Monelli (dates unknown) was described by Radiciotti (*Rossini*, vol. 1, p. 313) as a 'tenor with a sweet, but delicate voice'. He made his debut at La Scala in 1816 as Tamino. The following year he sang in the *prima* of Rossini's *La gazza ladra*. For Donizetti he appeared in the first casts of *Chiara* and *L'ajo nell'imbarazzo*. His elder brother, Raffaele, with whom he is sometimes confused, sang in the *prime* of Rossini's *L'inganno felice* and *La scala di seta*.

5 Nicola de Grecis (dates unknown), a basso buffo, was active at La Scala from 1805 to 1824. He also sang at Venice, appearing in the *prime* of Rossini's *Il cambiale di matrimonio* (his first opera to be staged), *La scala di seta* and *Il signor Bruschino*. For Donizetti he sang only in the *prima* of *Chiara*. Although de Grecis was never in the front rank of buffo singers, he was a representative figure in this golden age of opera buffa: a resourceful improviser of comic business with a voice that was little more than serviceable.

6 Giraud's comedy *L'ajo nell'imbarrazzo* had earlier served as a source for operas by E. Guarnaccia, Giuseppe Pilotti, Filippo Celli and Giuseppe Mosca. Ferretti's libretto was a new one, however, written for Donizetti.

7 The identification of Scatizzi's source as Kotzebue's *Emilia* is the work of Franca Cella ('Il donizettismo nei libretti di Donizetti'). She knows the play only in Italian translation and its German title is not known.

8 There has been much conjecture about how to interpret the initials 'M.A.' given for the librettist of *Alahor in Granata*. That they are not the initials of a name, but stand for a poet who for one reason or another chose to suppress his identity, is suggested by the use of 'M.A.' for the librettist of *Don Pasquale* when Giovanni Ruffini elected to suppress his name.

9 The mock suicide episode in the final scene of *Olivo e Pasquale* was drawn by Ferretti from another play by Sografi, entitled *Il più bel giorno della Westfalia*.

10 Florimo (*La scuola musicale di Napoli*), Zavadini (*Donizetti: Vita – Musiche – Epistolario*, p. 171) and my *Donizetti* (p. 96) all incorrectly list Rubini as the singer of the role of Settimio. The *Giornale del Regno delle Due Sicile*, 7 January 1828, proves that the role was sung by

Berardo Winter; Rubini did not take it over until the second run of performances later in 1828, at which time Donizetti added a new aria for him in Act 2, 'Se finor, bell'idol mio'. For further information on this matter see Benedict Sarnaker, 'Chi cantò *L'esule di Roma*', *Il melodramma italiano dell'ottocento*, ed. Giorgio Pestelli (Turin, 1977), pp. 413–24.

11   It is not clear what intermediate stages (if any) separate Romani's libretto for *Alina* from Sedaine's *Aline*. There had been at least one opéra comique that used this plot – Berton's *Aline* (libretto by Jean-Baptiste-Charles Vial and Edmond-Guillaume-François de Favières), given in Paris in 1803 – and two ballets – one given in Naples (1811) and the other in Paris (1823).

12   Adelaide Comelli-Rubini, née Chaumel (?1798–?1865), a soprano, was of French origin. She married the famous tenor Giovanni Battista Rubini in 1820. After studying at the Paris Conservatoire she went to Naples, where she made her debut in Morlacchi's *Gianni di Parigi*, and later she sang in the *prima* of Rossini's *Maometto II* (Parma, 1828). Naples remained her principal center of activity until 1829, in which year she sang not only in *Gianni di Calais* but also in the first cast of *Il giovedì grasso*. In October 1830 she appeared at Bologna with her husband in Bellini's *Il pirata*, a sort of revenge since Bellini had refused to consider her for the La Scala *prima* of that opera. After Rubini, in 1831, confined his appearances largely to Paris and London, his wife went into semi-retirement. She was regarded as her husband's inferior as a vocalist, but her voice was extensive – two and a half octaves in her prime – and almost always in tune, though not well balanced throughout its compass.

13   Gilardoni is traditionally cited as the librettist of *Il giovedì grasso*. Florimo, without any explanation, names Donizetti himself (*La scuola musicale di Napoli*, vol. 4, pp. 376–7). There is a manuscript libretto at the Accademia Chigiana, Siena, that bears Tottola's name on the frontispiece. A search should be made for contemporary corroboration of the librettist's name.

14   In the autograph score these feuding factions in *Imelda* are identified as Guelphs and Ghibellines, but the printed libretto suppresses this identification. This discrepancy proves that Donizetti started to set the text before it had been approved by the censors, even though by law a libretto was to be submitted for licensing a full year in advance of its performance.

15   Romani's libretto for *Gianni di Parigi* was not originally written for Donizetti, but for Morlacchi in 1818. Boieldieu's *Jean de Paris* had been performed in Naples in 1816.

16   Zavadini, *Donizetti: Vita – Musiche – Epistolario*, p. 42.

17   Donizetti in 1841 made the curious error of referring to *Sancia di Castiglia* as *Bianca di Castiglia* (Z. no. 389, dated 24–5 December ('midnight') 1841, p. 569). This slip may be a reference to the original name of the work, which was perhaps changed for some reason while the opera was under projection; it provides a clue as to one possible source for the libretto. At La Scala on 26 December 1835 a ballet *Bianca di*

Castiglia, choreographed by Livio Morosini, was danced; although this was more than three years after *Sancia*, it is possible that there exists a common source for the opera and the ballet.

18 According to Cametti (*Donizetti a Roma*, p. 85), this play was acted at the Teatro Valle in 1820 by the Vestris company. I have been unable to discover either the name of the dramatist or whether this play had been acted elsewhere previously.

19 Where Byron speaks of Ugo as Az(z)o's bastard and of Parisina as his wife, Romani avoids offense by making Ugo legitimate and pointedly referring to Parisina as Azzo's second wife.

20 During its first two decades *Lucrezia Borgia*, because of what for its time was a sensational subject, was frequently performed under alternate titles: *Alfonso, duca di Ferrara*, *Eustorgia da Romano*, *Giovanna I di Napoli*, *Elisa da Fosco*, *Nizza di Granata* and *Dalinda*. In these versions little more would be changed than the names of the characters, the locale, and a few offensive phrases. When for Paris in 1845 *Lucrezia* became *La rinnegata* the alterations were more than usually extensive; this version was arranged to meet the special circumstances of Victor Hugo's charge of plagiarism.

21 It is possible that this revision was made earlier, for the performance at Her Majesty's Theatre, London, on 6 June 1839, in which Grisi, Mario (making his London debut) and Tamburini took part. It is not unlikely that Donizetti composed Gennaro's new aria ('Anch'io provai le tenere smanie', *larghetto cantabile*, 6/8, C major) for Mario to sing on that occasion.

22 Romani's contribution to Donizetti's *Rosmonda* consisted of making some modifications in the libretto he had written originally for Coccia. This seems to have been the last time they worked together; there was plenty of later talk about projects, but no concrete results.

23 The ballet *Rosemonda* was danced 36 times at La Scala during Carnival 1828–9. The roles of the dancers are listed as: Giuseppe Bocci (Lord Clifford), Maria Bocci (Eleonora di Gujenna), Giovanni Casati (Walter), Maria Conti (Rosemonda), Antonio Ramacini (Enrico II) and Pietro Trigambi (Morton). As this ballet was in performance at about the time that Romani was preparing the libretto of *La straniera* for Bellini at La Scala, he could scarcely have been unaware of it.

24 There is a puzzle about the name of the singer of the role of Arturo at the *prima* of *Lucia*. The name 'Balestrieri' appears in Donizetti's letter to Innocenzo Giampieri, written on the day of the *prima*, 26 September 1835 (*S.d.* 1, no. 37, undated). The name 'Gioacchini' appears in Florimo's *La scuola musicale di Napoli* (vol. 4, p. 302) and it has been widely followed, but Florimo took his information from a printed libretto, probably set in type before 26 September, and Donizetti's 'Balestrieri' may reflect a last-minute change of cast. Weinstock (*Donizetti and the World of Opera in Italy, Paris and Vienna in the First Half of the Nineteenth Century* (New York, 1963), p. 348, note) suggests that since the name 'Balestrieri' does not appear elsewhere in the records of the San Carlo, Donizetti's letter may have been mistranscribed and the singer concerned may have been Achille Balestracci. I have not seen the

autograph of *S.d.* 1, no. 37, and therefore have no concrete evidence either to corroborate or refute Weinstock's hypothesis.

25 In the original scheme of *L'assedio di Calais*, Edoardo appeared after the *introduzione*, but at some point his role was confined to Act 3. I suspect the reason for this alteration was the vocal inadequacy of Federico Lablache, the son of the great Luigi.

26 The first page of the autograph of *Poliuto* bears in Donizetti's hand the words 'Donato a Teodoro [Ghezzi] 1844 Donizetti'. This gift was probably made in recognition of Ghezzi's handling of Donizetti's affairs in Naples during his absence, among them supervising the building of the mausoleum for Virginia.

27 For details of the completion of *Le duc d'albe* see pp. 434–6.

28 Romani apparently made no modifications in the text he had originally written for Carafa when Donizetti used it in 1840.

29 The revised version with the *lieto fine* may have been performed during the first, La Scala production of the opera. Unlike other revisions made by Donizetti to his scores, which may be regarded as alternatives, this version is definitive: he suppressed the original ending in which Maria 'dies of joy', and it is not preserved with the autograph of the work.

30 In *La grâce de Dieu* Marie (i.e. Linda) is in fact the mistress of Charles.

31 Clara (Stöckl-)Heinefetter (1813–57), a dramatic soprano, studied with her sister Sabine and with Giuseppe Ciccimarra, making her debut at the Kärntnertortheater in Vienna in a performance of *Der Freischütz*. Vienna remained the center of her opera activities and in 1845 at the Kärntnertor she sang Zaïda in the German production of *Dom Sébastien* conducted by Donizetti; she continued to sing that role through 1848. When she appeared in London in 1840–2 Chorley described her voice as 'the best soprano voice of this half-century' (*Thirty Years' Musical Recollections*, p. 122).

Appendix III

1 Z. no. 80, dated 18 August 1832, pp. 294–5; Z. no. 82, undated (early September), pp. 296–7; Z. no. 84, dated 16 September 1832, p. 298.

2 *S.d.* 1, no. 98, dated 13 February 1843, pp. 92–3; *S.d.* 1, no. 105, dated 18 June 1843, pp. 99–101.

3 Jeremy Commons, 'Giuseppe Bardari', *Donizetti Society Journal*, 3 (1977), 85–96.

4 Z. no. 402, dated 20 March 1842, pp. 582–3.

5 Black, 'Cammarano's Libretti for Donizetti'.

6 From 1838 on Cammarano worked with a number of composers, particularly with Mercadante, but most notably with Verdi, for whom he wrote *Alzira*, *La battaglia di Legnano*, *Luisa Miller* and *Il trovatore*.

7 Checcherini's wife, Francesca, and daughter, Marianna, sang in the 1828 *Emilia*, making it a family affair.

8 Z. no. 86 bis, p. 301, to Jacopo Ferretti.

9 *Gazzetta ufficiale piemontese*, 25 August 1835. At this date Romani had held the editorship of the *Gazzetta* for about a year and had almost

completely renounced writing librettos. For an informative biography of Ferretti, see Cametti, *Un poeta melodrammatico romano.*

10 Federico Bursotti, *Domenico Gilardoni, autore di dramma per musica* (Naples, n.d. [?1883]). A copy of this rare pamphlet is in the Conservatorio di San Pietro a Majella, Naples.

11 *Bellini, epistolario,* no. X, dated 12 January 1828, p. 41.

12 An account of Marini's activities as a critic for the Roman periodical *Rivista teatrale* and as archivist of the Accademia di Santa Cecilia, may be found in Giuseppe Radiciotti, *Teatro, musica e musicisti in Recanati* (Recanati, 1904), p. 15, note.

13 *Bellini, epistolario,* no. X, p. 41. This letter clearly indicates that Merelli was the agent for the management during the Genoese season that saw the *prima* of Donizetti's *Alina, regina di Golconda.*

14 Emilia Branca-Romani, *Felice Romani e i più ripetuti maestri di musica del suo tempo* (Turin, 1882).

15 Z. no. 456, p. 640.

16 Z. no. 169, p. 377.

17 Pacini, *Le mie memorie artistiche,* p. 33.

Bibliography

Acton, H., *The Last Bourbons of Naples* (New York, 1961)

Adam, A., *Derniers souvenirs d'un musicien* (Paris, (1859)

Alborghetti, F., and Galli, M., *Gaetano Donizetti e G. Simone Mayr: notizie e documenti* (Bergamo, 1875)

Allitt, J. S., *Donizetti and the Tradition of Romantic Love: a Collection of Essays on a Theme* (London, 1975)

'L'importanza di Simone Mayr nella formazione culturale di Donizetti', 1° convegno internazionale di studi donizettiani, Bergamo, 1975

Angermüller, R., 'Gli anni viennesi di Donizetti', 1° convegno internazionale di studi donizettiani, Bergamo, 1975

Antonini, D. G., 'Un episodio emotivo di Gaetano Donizetti', *Rivista musicale italiana*, 7 (1900), 518–35

Armstrong, W. G., *Record of the Opera in Philadelphia* (Philadelphia, 1884)

Arruga, F. L., 'La drammaturgia donizettiana', 1° convegno internazionale di studi donizettiani, Bergamo, 1975

Ashbrook, W., *Donizetti* (London, 1965)

'La composizione de "La favorita'", *Studi donizettiani*, 2 (1972), 13–27

'La struttura drammatica nella produzione di Donizetti dopo il 1838', 1° convegno internazionale di studi donizettiani, Bergamo, 1975

'*Maria Stuarda*: the Vindication of a Queen', *About the House*, 5/iv (1977), 16–21

Baldacci, L., 'Donizetti e la storia', 1° convegno internazionale di studi donizettiani, Bergamo, 1975

Ballini, M., 'Ritorno dell'*Anna Bolena*', La Scala, 89 (1957), 17–22

Barbiera, R., *Il salotto della Contessa Maffei* (Milan, 1895)

Barblan, G., *L'opera di Donizetti nell'età romantica* (Bergamo, 1948)

'Donizetti in Naples', *Donizetti Society Journal*, 1 (1974), 105–19

Barblan, G., and Walker, F., 'Introduzione alla lettura delle centotrentatrè nuove lettere de Donizetti', *Studi donizettiani*, 1 (1962), 1–20

Bellotti, A., *Donizetti e suoi contemporanei* (Bergamo, 1866)

Berlioz, H., *Memoirs*, ed. E. Newman (New York, 1932)

Les musiciens et la musique (Paris, 1903)

Bettoli, P., ed., *Gaetano Donizetti: numero unico nel primo centennario della sua nascità: 1797–1897* (Bergamo, 1897)

Bezzola, G., 'Aspetti del clima culturale italiano nel periodo donizettiano', 1° convegno internazionale di studi donizettiani, Bergamo, 1975

Black, J. N., 'Cammarano's Libretti for Donizetti', *Studi donizettiani*, 3 (1978), 115–29

'The Making of an Italian Romantic Opera Libretto – Salvadore Cammarano's *Folco d'Arles*', *Italian Studies*, 35 (1980), 68–80

'Cammarano's Notes for the Staging of *Lucia di Lammermoor*', *Donizetti Society Journal*, 4 (1980), 29–44

'Cammarano's Self-Borrowings: the Libretto of *Poliuto*', *Donizetti Society Journal*, 4 (1980), 89–101

Bonesi, M., 'Note biografiche su Donizetti', (letter dated 16 July 1861, Biblioteca Civica, Bergamo Alta); ed. G. Zavadini, *Bergomum: bollettino della Biblioteca Civica*, 40/iii (1946), 81–9

Bonetti, G., *G. Donizetti* (Naples, 1926)

Bossi, L., *Donizetti* (Brescia, 1956)

Branca-Romani, E., *Felice Romani e i più ripetuti maestri di musica del suo tempo* (Turin, 1882)

Brown, J. D., and Stratton, S., *British Musical Biography* (London, 1897)

Budden, J., *The Operas of Verdi* (3 vols., New York, 1973–81)

'Donizetti e Verdi', 1° convegno internazionale di studi donizettiani, Bergamo, 1975

Bursotti, F., *Domenico Gilardoni, autore di dramma per musica* (Naples, n.d. [?1883])

Calvi, G., *Gio. Simone Mayr* (Milan, 1847)

Calzado, A., *Donizetti e l'opera italiana in Spagna* (Paris, 1897)

Cambi, L., ed., *Vincenzo Bellini, epistolario* (n.p. [Milan], 1943)

Cambiasi, P., *La Scala: 1778–1889* (Milan, 1889)

Cametti, A., *Un poeta melodrammatico romano: appunti e notizie in gran parte inedite sopra Jacopo Ferretti e i musicisti del suo tempo* (Milan, 1898)

Donizetti a Roma (Turin, 1907)

Il Teatro di Tordinona, poi di Apollo (2 vols., Rome, 1938)

Casini, C., 'Il decennio della fortuna critica di Donizetti a Parigi', 1° convegno internazionale di studi donizettiani, Bergamo, 1975

Caversazzi, C., *Gaetano Donizetti: la casa dove nacque, la famiglia, l'inizio della malattia* (Bergamo, 1924)

Cella, F., 'Indagini sulle fonti francesi dei libretti di Gaetano Donizetti', *Contributi dell'Istituto di Filologia Moderna*, 4 (1966), 343–584

'Il donizettismo nei libretti di Donizetti', 1° convegno internazionale di studi donizettiani, Bergamo, 1975

'Il libretto e sue vicende', La Fenice program for *Les martyrs*, 1977–8 season (Venice, 1978)

Celletti, R., 'La vocalità di Donizetti', 1° convegno internazionale di studi donizettiani, Bergamo, 1975

Cesari, G., and Luzio, A., eds., *Giuseppe Verdi, i copialettere* (Milan, 1913)

Chorley, H. F., *Thirty Years' Musical Recollections* (New York, 1926)

Cicconetti, F., *Vita di Gaetano Donizetti* (Rome, 1864)

Clément, F., and Larousse, P., *Dictionnaire des opéras* (Paris, n.d.)

Codignola, A., *I fratelli Ruffini: lettere di G. e A. Ruffini alla madre dall'esilio francese e svizzero* (Genoa, 1925)

Cominazzi, P., 'Sorsa attraverso le opere musicali di Gaetano Donizetti: Reminiscenze', *La fama*, no. 35 (31 August 1875), 137–8; no. 36 (7 September 1875), 141–3; no. 37 (14 September 1875), 149–51; no. 38 (21 September 1875), 149–51; no. 39 (28 September 1875), 153–4; no. 40 (5 October 1875), 157–9

Commons, J., 'An Introduction to *Il duca d'Alba*', *Opera*, 10 (1959), 421–6

'Emilia di Liverpool', *Music and Letters*, 40 (1959), 207–28

'Donizetti e la censura napoletana', 1ᵒ convegno internazionale di studi donizettiani, Bergamo, 1975

'The Authorship of *I piccioli virtuosi ambulanti*', *Donizetti Society Journal*, 2 (1975), 199–207

'Unknown Donizetti Items in the Neapolitan Journal "Il Sibilo" ', *Donizetti Society Journal*, 2 (1975), 145–9

'Giuseppe Bardari', *Donizetti Society Journal*, 3 (1977), 85–96

'*Maria Stuarda* and the Neapolitan Censorship', *Donizetti Society Journal*, 3 (1977), 151–67

'Una corrispondenza tra Alessandro Lanari e Donizetti (45 lettere inedite)', *Studi donizettiani*, 3 (1978), 9–74

Commons, J., Schmid, P., and White, D., '19th Century Performances of *Maria Stuarda*', *Donizetti Society Journal*, 3 (1977), 217–42

'Maria Padilla', booklet accompanying Opera Rara recording of *Maria Padilla*, (London, 1980)

Cottrau, G., *Lettres d'un mélomane* (Naples, 1885)

d'Amico, F., ed., *Enciclopedia dello spettacolo* (11 vols., Rome, 1954–62)

Dean, W., 'Some Echoes of Donizetti in Verdi's Operas', *3ᵒ congresso internazionale di studi verdiani: Milano 1972* (Milan, 1974), p. 122

'Donizetti's Serious Operas', *Proceedings of the Royal Musical Association*, 100 (1973–4), 123–41

de Boigne, C., *Petits mémoires de l'Opéra* (Paris, 1857)

de Filippis, F., and Arnese, R., *Cronache del Teatro di San Carlo: 1737–1960* (2 vols., Naples, 1961)

Degrada, F., *Il palazzo incantato: studi sulla tradizione del melodramma dal Barocco al Romanticismo* (2 vols., Fiesole, 1979)

de Lajarte, T., *Bibliothèque musicale du théâtre de l'Opéra* (2 vols., Paris, 1878)

Dent, E., 'Donizetti: an Italian Romantic', *Fanfare for Ernest Newman*, ed. H. van Thal (London, 1955), pp. 86–107

Desarbres, N., *Deux siècles à l'Opéra: 1669–1868* (Paris, 1868)

Döhring, S., 'La forma dell'aria in Gaetano Donizetti', 1ᵒ convegno internazionale di studi donizettiani, Bergamo, 1975

Donati-Pettèni, G., *L'Istituto Musicale Gaetano Donizetti* (Bergamo, 1928)

Donizetti (Milan, 1930)

Donizetti, G., letters, see Barblan and Walker (*Studi donizettiani*, 1), Commons (*Studi donizettiani*, 3), Eisner-Eisenhof, Zavadini

Donizetti Society Journal, 1 (1974); 2 (1975); 3 (1977); 4 (1980) [published in London]

Duprez, G., *Souvenirs d'un chanteur* (Paris, 1880)

Edwards, H. S., *History of the Opera from Monteverdi to Donizetti* (2 vols., London, 1862)

Eisner-Eisenhof, A., ed., *Lettere di Gaetano Donizetti* (Bergamo, 1897)

Escudier, L., *Mes souvenirs* (Paris, 1863)

Ferris, G. T., *The Great Italian and French Composers* (New York, 1878)

Florimo, F., *La scuola musicale di Napoli e i suoi conservatori* (4 vols., Naples, 1880–4)
Bellini: memorie e lettere (Florence, 1882)
Fraccaroli, A., *Donizetti* (Milan, 1945)
Freeman, J., 'Donizetti in Palermo and *Alahor in Granata*', *Journal of the American Musicological Society*, 25 (1972), 240–50
Gabriele, A., *Gaetano Donizetti* (Rome, 1904)
Gallini, N., 'Inediti donizettiani', *Rivista musicale italiana*, 55 (1953), 257–75
Gatti, C., *Il Teatro alla Scala* (2 vols., Milan, 1964)
Gautier, T., *L'art dramatique en France depuis vingt-cinq ans* (Paris, n.d.)
Les beautés de l'opéra (Paris, 1845)
Gavazzeni, G., *Gaetano Donizetti* (Milan, 1937)
Gazzaniga, A., 'La produzione musicale donizettiana nel periodo napoletano', 1º convegno internazionale di studi donizettiani, Bergamo, 1975
Geddo, A., *Donizetti, l'uomo, le musiche* (Bergamo, 1956)
Bergamo e la musica (Bergamo, 1958)
Genest, E., *L'Opéra connu et inconnu* (Paris, 1920)
L'Opéra-Comique connu et inconnu (Paris, 1925)
Ghezzi, T., 'Ricordi su Donizetti', *Omnibus*, 7 March 1860
Giorgi, F., *Gaetano Donizetti studente al Liceo Musicale di Bologna* (Bologna, 1928)
Giulini, M. F., *Giuditta Pasta e i suoi tempi* (Milan, 1935)
Gossett, P., 'Anna Bolena e la maturità di Donizetti', 1º convegno internazionale di studi donizettiani, Bergamo, 1975
Gualerzi, G., 'Aspetti della rinascita di Donizetti nella vita musicale del dopoguerra', 1º convegno internazionale di studi donizettiani, Bergamo, 1975
Iarro (pseudonym of G. Piccini), *Memorie d'un impresario fiorentino* (Florence, 1892)
Kaufman, T. G., '*L'esule di Roma*: a Performance History', *Donizetti Society Journal*, 4 (1980), 104–9
'Italian Performances in Vienna 1835–1859', *Donizetti Society Journal*, 4 (1980), 53–71
Kleefeld, W. J., *Don Pasquale von Gaetano Donizetti* (Leipzig, 1901)
Lazzari, A., 'Giovanni Ruffini, Gaetano Donizetti e il *Don Pasquale*', *Rassegna nazionale*, 1 and 16 October 1915, reprinted as a separate pamphlet (Florence, 1915)
Lecomte, L.-H., *Histoire des théâtres de Paris: La Renaissance (1838–1841, 1868, 1873–1904)* (Paris, 1905)
Lespes, L., *Les mystères du grand-opéra* (Paris, 1843)
Lippmann, F.,'Der italienische Vers und der musikalische Rhythmus: zum Verhältnis von Vers und Musik in der italienischen Oper des 19. Jahrhunderts', *Analecta musicologica*, no. 12 (1973), 253–369; no. 14 (1974), 324–410; no. 15 (1975), 298–333
'Die Melodien Donizettis', *Analecta musicologica*, no. 12 (1973), 80–113
'Donizetti e Bellini contributo all'interpretazione dello stile donizettiano', 1º convegno internazionale di studi donizettiani, Bergamo, 1975

'Autographe Briefe Rossinis und Donizettis in der Bibliothek Massimo, Rom', *Analecta musicologica*, no. 19 (1980) 330–5

Lo Presti, F., 'La fortuna di Donizetti oggi in Inghilterra', *Donizetti Society Journal*, 4 (1980), 231–8

Lowenthal, A., *Annals of Opera*, 2nd edn (2 vols., Geneva, 1955)

Lumley, B., *Reminiscences of the Opera* (London, 1864)

Luzio, A., ed., *Carteggi verdiani* (4 vols., Rome, 1935–47)

Malherbe, C., *Centenaire de Gaetano Donizetti: catalogue biographique de la section française à l'exposition de Bergamo* (Paris, 1897)

Manferrari, U., *Dizionario delle opere melodrammatiche* (3 vols., Florence, n.d.) ('Donizetti, Gaetano', vol. 1, pp. 321–55)

Mazzini, G., *Filosofia della musica*, ed. A. Lualdi, 2nd edn (Rome, 1954)

[Merelli, B.], *Cenni biografici di Donizetti e Mayr raccolti dalle memorie di un vecchio ottagenario dilettante di musica* (Bergamo, 1875)

Mikoletzky, L., 'Gaetano Donizetti und der Kaiserhof zu Wien: neue Dokumente', *Analecta musicologica*, no. 13 (1974), 411

Mitchell, J., *The Walter Scott Operas* (Tuscaloosa, 1977)

Monaldi, G., *Gaetano Donizetti* (Turin, 1938)

Olario, T., 'La malattia ed i medici di Gaetano Donizetti', *Minerva medica*, 19 (1938)

Pacini, G., *Le mie memorie artistiche* (Florence, 1875)

Paganelli, S., *Due secoli di vita musicale: storia del Teatro Comunale di Bologna: 1763–1966* (2 vols., Bologna, 1966)

Palianti, L., *Mise en scène de Dom Sébastien* (Paris, n.d. [1843])

Pastura, F., *Bellini secondo la storia* (Parma, 1959)

Piccini, G., see Iarro

Pillon, G., 'I diarii della follia di Gaetano Donizetti', *Il borghese*, 31 July 1977, 1073–6, 1085–8

Pilon, L., 'Gli esordi operistici di Donizetti', 1° convegno internazionale di studi donizettiani, Bergamo, 1975

Radiciotti, G., *Teatro, musica e musicisti in Recanati* (Recanati, 1904)
  Teatro e musica in Roma: 1825–1850 (Rome, 1905)
  Rossini (3 vols., Tivoli, 1927–9)

Rattolino, P., 'Il processo compositivo nel *Don Pasquale* di Donizetti', *Nuova rivista musicale italiana*, 1 (1970), 51–68; 2 (1970), 263–280
  'Unità drammatica della "Linda di Chamounix"', *Studi donizettiani*, 2 (1972), 29–40

Regli, F., *Gaetano Donizetti e le sue opere* (Turin, 1850)
  Dizionario biografico (Turin, 1860)

Ricci, C., 'Donizetti a Bologna: appunti e documenti', *Gaetano Donizetti: numero unico nel primo centennario della sua nascità: 1797–1897*, ed. P. Bettoli (Bergamo, 1897)

Rovani, G., 'Gaetano Donizetti', *Storie delle lettere e delle arti in Italia* (Milan, 1858), vol. 4, p. 619

Royer, A., *Histoire de l'Opéra* (Paris, 1875)

Sacchiero, V., and others, *Il Museo Donizettiano di Bergamo* (Bergamo, 1970) [catalogue]

Sarnaker, B., 'Chi cantò *L'esule di Roma*', *Il melodramma italiano dell'ottocento*, ed. G. Pestelli (Turin, 1977), pp. 413–24

Schiedermair, L., *Beiträge zur Geschichte der Oper: Simon Mayr* (2 vols., Leipzig, 1907)

Schlitzer, F., *L'ultima pagina della vita di Gaetano Donizetti da un carteggio inedito dell'Accademia Chigiana*, Quaderni dell'Accademia Chigiana, vol. 28 (Siena, 1953)

 Donizetti, G.: episodi e testimonianze F. Fiorentino (Naples, 1954)

 L'eredità di Donizetti: da carteggi e documenti dell'archivio dell'Accademia Chigiana, Quaderni dell'Accademia Chigiana, vol. 30 (Siena, 1954)

 Mondo teatrale dell'ottocento (Naples, 1954)

Schmid, P., 'Maria Stuarda and Buondelmonte', *Opera*, 24 (1973), 1060–6

Scudo, P., 'Donizetti et l'école italienne depuis Rossini', *Critique et littérature musicales* (Paris, 1850), pp. 75–100

Second, A., *Les petits mystères de l'Opéra* (Paris, 1844)

Smith, P. J., *The Tenth Muse: a Historical Study of the Opera Libretto* (New York, 1970)

Soubies, A., *Le Théâtre-Italien de 1801 à 1913* (Paris, 1913)

Stendhal, correspondance inédite (Paris, 1855)

Stendhal, *Life of Rossini*, ed. and trans. R. N. Coe (Seattle, 1970)

Stierlin, L., *Biographie von Gaetano Donizetti* (Zürich, 1852)

Studi donizettiani, 1 (1962); 2 (1972); 3 (1978) [published in Bergamo] (references in the notes to letters of Donizetti edited in this journal use the abbreviation 'S.d. 1' etc.)

Suppan, W. *Heinrich Eduard Josef von Lannoy (1787–1853): Leben und Werke*, Steierischer Tonkünstlerbund: Musik aus der Steiermark, series 4, vol. 2 (Graz, 1960)

Tamvaco, J.-L., 'Paul-Bernard Barroilhet', *Donizetti Society Journal*, 2 (1975), 131–42

Tiby, O., *Una stagione lirica di 125 anni fa: Gaetano Donizetti a Palermo* (Rome, 1951)

 Il Real Teatro Carolino e l'ottocento musicale palermitano (Florence, 1957)

Trethowan, W. H., 'Music and Mental Disorder', *The Brain and Music*, ed. M. Critchley and R. A. Henson (London, 1977), pp. 398–432

Vallebona, G. B., *Il Teatro Carlo Felice: cronisteria di un secolo (1828–1928)* (Genoa, 1928)

Verdi, G., letters, see Cesari and Luzio, Luzio

Verzino, E. C., *Contributo ad una biografia di Gaetano Donizetti* (Bergamo, 1896)

 Le opere di Gaetano Donizetti (Bergamo, 1897)

Walker, F., 'The Librettist of *Don Pasquale*', *Monthly Musical Record*, 88 (1958), 219–23

 The Man Verdi (London, 1962)

Weatherson, A., 'Donizetti in Revival', *Donizetti Society Journal*, 4 (1980), 13–26

Weinstock, H., *Donizetti and the World of Opera in Italy, Paris and Vienna in the First Half of the Nineteenth Century* (New York, 1963)

 Rossini (New York, 1968)

 Vincenzo Bellini: his Life and his Operas (New York, 1971)

 'Chi era Marianna Donizetti?', *Studi donizettiani*, 2 (1972) 41–6

White, D., 'Donizetti and the Three Gabriellas', *Opera*, 29 (1978), 962–70

Zanolini, B., 'L'armonia come espressione drammaturgica in Donizetti', 1ᵘ convegno internazionale di studi donizettiani, Bergamo, 1975

Zavadini, G., ed., *Catalogo generale: Museo Donizettiano di Bergamo* (Bergamo, 1936)

    Donizetti: Vita – Musiche – Epistolario (Bergamo, 1948) (references to letters of Donizetti edited in this book use the abbreviation 'Z.. no. 1' etc.)

    G. Simone Mayr (Bergamo, 1957)

    Donizetti l'uomo (Bergamo, 1958)

Zedda, A., 'Caratteristiche della strumentazione nell'opera teatrale di Gaetano Donizetti', 1ᵘ convegno internazionale di studi donizettiani, Bergamo, 1975

Index

Musical works are indexed under their composers; literary works by title; ballets under the general heading 'ballets'. Bold-face type indicates a principal entry.